IDENTITY AND NATIONALISM IN MODERN ARGENTINA

# IDENTITY AND NATIONALISM IN MODERN ARGENTINA

## DEFENDING THE TRUE NATION

JEANE DeLANEY

University of Notre Dame Press
Notre Dame, Indiana

University of Notre Dame Press
Notre Dame, Indiana 46556
undpress.nd.edu

Library of Congress Control Number: 2020937069

ISBN: 978-0-268-10789-5 (Hardback)
ISBN: 978-0-268-10790-1 (Paperback)
ISBN: 978-0-268-10792-5 (WebPDF)
ISBN: 978-0-268-10791-8 (Epub)

# CONTENTS

# ACKNOWLEDGMENTS

This project has been picked up and laid aside more times than I care to admit, and its journey has been a long one. In the course of research, writing, and conceptualizing (and reconceptualizing) its central arguments, I have incurred many debts, both professional and personal. Several scholars read and provided useful feedback on portions of the manuscript, including Michael Goebel, Sandra McGee Deutsch, Nicola Foote, and David Rock. Diego Armus, who generously read the entire manuscript, offered many suggestions that helped me navigate the tricky issue of early twentieth-century racial discourses. While I've not been able to follow all of their advice, this work is immeasurably better for their feedback. I also owe a debt of gratitude to Douglas Klusmeyer, who introduced me to the vast literature on European nationalism and helped me make connections between Argentine and European thought that I would otherwise have missed. Finally, I would like to mention Charles A. Hale and Oscár Terán, both now deceased, who gave generous guidance and encouragement at crucial moments.

Segments of this work have been presented at many conferences, where audience comments helped me clarify and expand my arguments. Of particular importance was the National Endowment for the Humanities conference on New World nationalism organized by Don Doyle and Marco Antonio Pamplona, where a range of scholars focusing on different aspects of nationalism in the Americas came together for fruitful discussion and debate. This work has also benefited from feedback from friends and colleagues at St. Olaf, who read and responded to portions of the manuscript. Worthy of special mention are Gwen Barnes-Karol, Dolores Peters, and Eric Fure-Slocum, whose advice and friendship helped me bring this project to fruition. Research for this project took place over a number of years, and was aided by a number of individuals, who offered ongoing assistance. In Argentina, I wish to thank in particular Lucía Gadano, Magdalena La Porta, and Guillermo Salvías. Closer to home is the dedicated interlibrary loan staff of the St. Olaf library, who tenaciously chased down all sorts of hard-to-access materials.

I feel fortunate that this manuscript found a home at the University of Notre Dame Press. Early on, Stephen Little played an invaluable role in bringing this manuscript to the press's attention. Eli Bortz did more than anyone else to usher it through the review process, and graciously offered editorial advice on several chapters. Working with copy editor Ann Donahue has been a pleasure, as she has sought to improve my prose, correct my punctuation (especially misplaced commas!), and iron out the complexities of citing some of my more obscure Spanish-language sources.

Last, but certainly not least, comes my family. I have been blessed to be part of a large extended family that is both far-flung and tight-knit, and whose support has always sustained me. But it is to my immediate family, my husband, Jeff, and daughter, Mariah, that most thanks are due. They have lived with this project for much too long, and I deeply appreciate their love, support, and infinite patience. It is to them that this book is dedicated.

# Introduction

Nationalism has played an exceptionally powerful role in Argentina's turbulent history and continues to be a potent political force. Even the most casual student of Argentine politics during the last decade could not help but be struck by the nationalist stance of former president Cristina Fernández de Kirchner, who frequently insisted that "Las Malvinas son argentinas" and characterized Argentina's foreign creditors as "vultures" and "extortionists."[1] Many of Kirchner's stances and policies lived up to her rhetoric, including her close ties to the late Hugo Chávez, the expropriation of Spanish-owned shares of the national oil company YPF, and her decree establishing a new Secretariat of National Thought. A Peronist, Kirchner drew from a tradition within Argentine nationalism that was first articulated by the nationalist group FORJA (Fuerza de Orientación Radical de la Joven Argentina) in the 1930s.[2] Founded by Arturo Jauretche (whom Kirchner revered as one of Argentina's most important intellectuals), FORJA promoted a strand of nationalism that celebrated the masses as the embodiment of the "real" Argentina and attacked the country's traditional liberal elite as cosmopolitan *vendepatrias* (sellers of the fatherland). Left-wing and socially inclusive, this strand of nationalism played a key role in shaping the political ideas of Juan Perón in the 1940s and continues to resonate in Argentina today.

Yet as Argentines are well aware, another form of nationalism has played an arguably even greater role in their country's political life. First emerging in the late 1920s, this right-wing strand of nationalism had as its core mission the defense of Argentina's supposedly authentic Hispanic and Catholic character. During the 1930s, this nationalism became increasingly antiliberal, as it drew inspiration from European fascism and found support from the most reactionary elements of the Argentine Catholic Church. Argentina's right-wing nationalists successfully sought to extend their influence within the armed forces and enthusiastically supported the military coups of 1930, 1943, 1955, 1966, and 1976. The latest transition to civilian rule in 1983 failed to extinguish right-wing nationalist sentiment entirely. Although successive civilian governments have largely purged the officer corps of right-wing nationalists, these ideas have been kept alive by an array of civilian groups such as La Juventud Nacional del Partido Popular de Reconstrucción, Movimiento Bastión, and Movimiento por la Identidad Nacional, as well as by scores of personal websites and blogs.

The continued survival of both right- and left-wing forms of antiliberal nationalism raises questions about the long-term prospects for democracy and political pluralism in Argentina. To be sure, many factors have contributed to the weakness of the country's democratic institutions. Among the most important has been the country's economic dependency. Although Argentina has long led Latin America in per capita income, its dependent position within the global economy has produced deep income inequality and stubbornly high rates of poverty, creating conditions that have made it difficult for democracy to thrive. Liberal leadership failures and an interventionist military have also played a role. While long espousing faith in democratic rule, the traditional political class has at crucial moments in the country's history rigged elections and supported military coups to regain power. More broadly, as historian Jorge Nállim has argued, this elite has failed to link political liberalism with the popular ideals of equality, democracy, and social justice.[3]

But any attempt to understand the weakness of Argentina's democratic institutions must also take into account the impact of nationalism and, more specifically, the country's unique experience with its two forms of nationalism. In contrast to other Latin American cases, in which nationalism was either more uniformly right wing (e.g., early twentieth-century Chile and Brazil) or left-wing (e.g. present-day Venezuela, Ecuador, and Bolivia), or where state-promoted nationalism served as a unifying force (Mexico after 1920 and Cuba after 1959), Argentina produced two very different strands of nationalism, whose leaders had long and active careers, and whose ideas had an impact far beyond nationalist circles. This fact has been a key reason why nationalism in Argentina has proved to be uniquely destabilizing, as ideologues from both strands have attacked Argentina's liberal political institutions and, at times, each other.

At no point was the clash between Argentina's two nationalisms more dramatic than in the late 1960s and the 1970s. During these years, Argentina witnessed the emergence of a variety of Peronist guerrilla organizations, which sought to mesh Marxism with a left-wing, socially inclusive form of nationalism. One of the most violent, and by far the most influential, was the Montoneros, a group that captured the imagination of a generation of young middle-class Argentines. The Montoneros took their name from the rural militias of the nineteenth century, and its founders cast themselves as the latest protagonists, or heirs, of a historical struggle to defend the "real" Argentina of the masses against exploitation by foreign capitalists and their domestic allies.[4] But what the Montonero leadership saw as patriotism, others viewed as treason. Right-wing factions within Peronism itself denounced the guerrillas as Marxist-inspired infiltrators, who were seeking to hijack the movement. Similarly, nationalist military officers believed the guerrillas to be under the influence of exotic ideologies that posed a threat not simply to the established order but to the nation itself. The reign of terror these military men unleashed was unprecedented in twentieth-century Argentine history and led to the kidnapping, torture, and killing of more than twenty-five thousand citizens, many of whom had no connection to the guerrillas. The purpose of this "Dirty War," as it came to be called, went far beyond containing the guerrilla threat. Rather, as the regime repeatedly proclaimed, its mission was to wipe out all "antinational" ideas and influences in order to defend the true Argentina.

The intense violence of these years—and the simultaneous claims made by all sides that they represented the "true" nation—obscures the fact that, beginning in the 1930s, left- and right-wing nationalists openly admired each other's books, occasionally published in each other's journals, and even enjoyed cordial personal relations. While these interactions and collaborations never solidified into any kind of alliance, the fact remains that Argentina's two types of nationalists were in many ways kindred spirits, who shared many of the same assumptions about why the country had failed to flourish. In the aftermath of the 1955 coup that ousted Juan Perón, these similarities produced a complex political landscape, in which individuals who began their political careers identifying with one strand of nationalism often swerved toward the other. Indeed, such were the enduring affinities between these nationalist strands that most of the founders of the Montoneros actually began as activists in right-wing nationalist groups, such as Círculo de Plata and Tacuara. For these individuals, as Argentine scholar Hugo Vezzetti has argued, the transition from the right to the left entailed neither a "rupture" nor a "conversion" but is best understood as a kind of leftward slippage that left core beliefs and values intact. According to Vezzetti, even as they transitioned to left-wing radicalism, the Montonero leaders retained a "firm nucleus of convictions" based on the original "nationalist, antiliberal mold."[5] Also striking, as historian Sandra McGee Deutsch has reported, even in the midst of the violence, young guerrillas continued to read the works of prominent right-wing nationalists.[6]

Why did the line between Argentina's two nationalisms prove so permeable? What kind of bridge could exist between two ideological movements, whose leaders had, by the late 1960s, become such bitter enemies? Just as important, how did these two nationalist strands work in tandem to undermine Argentina's liberal traditions? The similarities and shared roots of Argentina's two nationalisms, as well as their broader impact on Argentine political life, form the subject of this book. To tackle these issues, this study shifts the focus away from nationalism per se—understood here to be a set of political ideas articulated by ideologues concerned with the defense of their country's cultural, economic, and political sovereignty—to examine instead how nationalist leaders from the 1930s onward conceptualized or imagined Argentina and the discursive constructions they used to describe the nation and its problems. I take as my starting point the premise that to fully understand any nationalist movement requires understanding the vision of nationhood that animates it.[7] Nations, as numerous scholars have noted, can be imagined in very different ways, and how individuals or specific groups define their nation largely determines what they see as worth defending.[8] In addition, how an individual imagines, writes, or talks about his or her nation is inextricably intertwined with a whole range of beliefs that are central to any nationalist program. Questions pertaining to who can belong to the nation (and especially whether immigrants or minority groups can be accepted as full-fledged members of the national community), whether foreign cultural influences are perceived as threatening or benign, and whether domestic ethnic or religious diversity is viewed as a threat to national unity are inseparable from how individuals conceptualize their nation and what they see as the basis of their collective identity.

This work argues that, despite their very different political programs, Argentina's right- and left-wing nationalists shared a vision of the Argentine nation that had roots in, and thus bore the lasting imprint of, ethno-cultural forms of national identity associated with the Romantic nationalism of nineteenth-century Europe.[9] This is not to argue that Argentine nationalists should be considered Romantic thinkers or, even less, should be identified as such. Rather, my claim is that these nationalists operated within a conceptual matrix rooted in understandings of nationality and history that were inspired by the ideas of Romantic nationalism, ideas that had gained currency in early twentieth-century Argentina during an era of mass immigration. While historically contingent and ideologically plurivocal, the assumptions central to this conceptual framework proved remarkably persistent and structured how post-1930 nationalist intellectuals from across the political spectrum imagined *argentinidad*.

Within the Romantic vision, nations are understood to be organic ethno-cultural communities, whose existence predates the creation of the state and whose members possess intrinsic mental and emotional traits that distinguish them from other nationalities. The supposedly homogenous collective character of the people, rather than their shared political values or loyalties, forms the basis of the nation's identity and serves to bind members together. Moreover, because the nation's identity is believed to be based on the intrinsic qualities of the people that endure across the generations, nationality is understood to be an inherent state of being that can neither be acquired nor shed. Argentina's nationalists embraced an essentialist vision of national identity that strongly echoed the Romantic understanding of nations, although with variations and modifications over time.[10] While disagreeing vehemently about the qualities that defined true Argentines, both right- and left-wing nationalists saw the nation as a bounded, homogenous community that existed independently of the state, whose members shared a set of distinctive traits that marked them as Argentines. According to nationalists, it was Argentines' intrinsic collective character or essence—rather than their conscious embrace of, or loyalty to, the nation's political values and institutions—that defined the "true" Argentina.

The nationalists' vision of the nation as an enduring homogenous community rooted in history contrasted sharply with how the country's founding generation had understood the nation they sought to create. The liberal leaders of Argentina's independence movement had defined their nation primarily in "civic" terms[11]—that is, they understood their nation to be a man-made association of citizens that had broken with Spain, not in the name of a preformed ethno-cultural community, but for the purpose of establishing a new nation on the basis of a new political project.[12] In contrast to twentieth-century nationalists, who drew a sharp distinction between the nation (defined in ethno-cultural terms) and the institutions of the state, nineteenth-century liberals believed that the creation of the state and the nation were inseparable processes. In other words, they believed that, in organizing the state and establishing its institutions, they were creating the nation.

This is not to say that in imagining this new nation, these elites discounted the importance of forming a common culture and a racially homogenous population. Indeed, central to the nineteenth-century liberal vision of the Argentine nation were the intertwined notions of "racial whiteness and cultural Europeanness," qualities that elites sought to bolster by encouraging European immigration.[13] At first glance, this emphasis on white identity suggests an ethnic vision of *argentinidad* that reserved membership in the national community for individuals of European ancestry, and whose primary ties were those of blood. Yet as multiple scholars have noted, while Argentine elites continued to prize whiteness as a marker of civilization and refinement, in practice the category of "whiteness" proved to be extremely elastic.[14] Moreover, this elasticity worked in tandem with the two other beliefs central to early nineteenth-century understandings of the Argentine nation: that membership in the national community was first and foremost a matter of political loyalty, and that the desired cultural traits associated with white Europeans were acquirable rather than innate. This voluntarist understanding of national belonging meant that all native-born individuals who were loyal to the state were understood to be Argentines, regardless of their race. Similarly, while European immigrants were certainly preferred, all newcomers—again regardless of ancestry or race—were seen as potential Argentines.[15]

## *EL SER NACIONAL* AND THE MYTH OF THE TWO ARGENTINAS

In exploring the ethno-cultural vision of Argentine identity at the core of twentieth-century nationalist thought, I focus on two related tropes that were central to the discourses of both right and left nationalists and that continue to have currency in present-day Argentina. The first is the notion of *el ser nacional*, a term that appeared repeatedly in the speeches and writings of the leaders of both strands. Variously translated as "the national being" or "the national soul," nationalists understood *el ser nacional* to be an enduring cultural essence that made Argentines unique and served as the basis of their collective national character. Although a few mentions of *el ser nacional* can be found in Argentine political writings before the 1930s, it was in this decade that the term gained widespread currency and indeed became ubiquitous in nationalist discourses. The second trope, related to the notion of *el ser nacional*, is that of the "two Argentinas." According to both right- and left-wing nationalists, there existed two very different Argentinas: one true and authentic, the other false and artificial. The true Argentina, of course, was an organic community, whose members possessed a unitary collective character rooted in *el ser nacional*. The false Argentina, nationalists argued, was that constructed by liberals. According to both right- and left-wing nationalists, Argentine liberals had always ignored the realities of the authentic Argentina and sought instead to create a new nation on the basis of borrowed values and institutions from liberal Europe. The result, nationalists argued, was an artificial liberal state that had nothing to do with the true Argentina and that indeed threatened its very essence. Like the concept of *el ser nacional*, the trope of the two Argentinas proved to be extraordinarily enduring, and by the 1960s had become a common sense way of understanding the nation and its problems.[16] Indeed, so seductive was this notion that variations of it have been adopted by some non-Argentines as well.[17]

This belief in the existence of the two Argentinas and the conviction that the true nation possessed a unitary *ser* or essence that defined its collective character were enduring elements of both right- and left-wing nationalist thought. Both tropes, of course, were inventions or intellectual constructs. Clearly, there is no such thing as a unitary *ser nacional* to which all true members of the national community are psychologically or spiritually connected. Similarly fantastical is the notion that the country's liberals somehow created a false Argentina at odds with the supposedly "true" Argentina (as is the related claim that anyone who embraces liberal values could not be a "real" Argentine). Emphasizing the invented or imagined nature of these constructs does not, of course, detract from their significance, for, as anthropologist Allan Hanson has noted in another context, "Inventions are precisely the stuff that cultural reality is made of."[18] Unquestionably for Argentina's right- and left-wing nationalists, *el ser nacional* and the two Argentinas were tangible realities. Accordingly, these "facts" helped structure how they understood their country's history, perceived its problems, and imagined solutions. These constructs also provided ideologues of both nationalist strands with a set of guiding myths and historical narratives that were remarkably similar.

Yet what served to unify these two strands of nationalism also acted as a wedge to drive them apart. My focus on the nationalists' shared embrace of an essentialist vision of Argentine identity can also provide insight into the profound differences that divided them. Although both right- and left-wing nationalists believed in an enduring *ser nacional* and in the existence of a "real" Argentina at odds with the "false" liberal state, *how* they imagined the content of this supposed *ser nacional* and the true Argentina differed dramatically. It is in these differences that we can find some of the sources of their often mutual hostility and the reasons behind their failure to unite against the liberal state and the imperialist powers they believed this state served.

This nationalist right's vision of the true Argentina was straight-forward enough. Although they became highly factionalized as the twentieth century wore on, right-wing nationalists shared the assumption that Argentines were by definition Hispanic (or Latin, in some versions) and above all Catholic. For these nationalists, the real or authentic Argentina possessed an ethnic core that was Catholic and Spanish, or Latin, and any individuals or influences that threatened to dilute its purity were causes for concern. The nationalist left, in contrast, had a less tidy understanding of *el ser nacional*, one that was more socially inclusive in that it made room for non-Catholics and non-Hispanics/Latins.[19] First promoted in the 1930s by FORJA, this vision of the true Argentina held that while *el ser nacional* contained elements of the Spanish legacy, it had incorporated other influences and other peoples. As a result, these nationalists understood Argentina's *ser nacional* to be something newer, more original, and distinctively Argentine. Just as importantly, the nationalist left insisted that the true *ser nacional* was most evident in the life and culture of "el pueblo" or the common people. In its view, the Argentine masses—even those born of recent immigrants—formed a unitary, culturally homogeneous folk community that most purely embodied Argentina's supposedly authentic national qualities.

## INTELLECTUAL ROOTS

From where did the essentialist notion of *el ser nacional* and the related (and equally) essentialist belief in a "true," enduring Argentina come? Any attempt to understand the power and resonance these constructs held for Argentine nationalists inevitably leads to the problem of how, why, and when—in a country with a long-standing liberal tradition—such a way of conceptualizing Argentine identity came to enjoy such currency. Clearly, the right- and left-wing nationalists' shared obsession with *el ser nacional* and their belief in the existence of a true Argentine nation at odds with the liberal state did not suddenly materialize from thin air in the 1930s. Accordingly, I seek to understand how and why this occurred by asking the following: Why did so many twentieth-century intellectuals and opinion makers come to accept as "fact" the existence of an Argentine *ser nacional*? Why, in a country "born liberal," did such an influential group of political actors come to believe in the existence of a real or true Argentina that existed apart from (and indeed was threatened by) the liberal state?[20] What events, both in terms of concrete occurrences and new intellectual formations, sparked this new way of thinking and talking about Argentine identity? These questions, of course, lie at the very heart of larger problems in intellectual history—that is, why broad intellectual shifts occur, how new conceptual paradigms and orientations emerge, and what circumstances make it possible for certain ideas to be "thinkable" at particular historical moments.[21]

The answers to these questions, as suggested above, can be found in the tumultuous decades of the early twentieth century. During these years, massive immigration and new intellectual currents from Europe led many Argentines to question traditional notions of Argentine identity. Between 1880 and 1930, the country's robust export economy made it a favored destination for Europeans seeking opportunity, and within the span of a few decades millions of immigrants poured onto Argentine shores. Although the Argentine state had long encouraged immigration, the sheer number of newcomers sparked fears that Argentine society was in danger of being overwhelmed, leading many native intellectuals to call for the defense of the nation's culture and traditions against the incoming tide. At the epicenter of this movement was a new generation of intellectuals, who have since become known as the cultural nationalists. This group of thinkers, I argue, played a central role in undermining the traditional civic vision of the Argentine nation, and helped spark a paradigmatic shift in how significant numbers of Argentines began to understand their nation's identity.

Early twentieth-century Argentina was ripe for such a shift. As British historian Eric Hobsbawm has noted, the experience of rapid immigration and the crowding of cities with new social groups were key factors that led to the rise of ethno-cultural nationalism in late nineteenth-century Europe.[22] Facing similar circumstances, and drawing from Romantic nationalist intellectual currents from Europe (especially Spain), the cultural nationalists began to promote the notion that Argentines formed—or should form—a unitary *raza*, or race, whose distinctive qualities must be defended and nurtured. According to Ricardo Rojas, one of the movement's key intellectuals, the peoples of each nation formed—or at least should form—a homogenous race that possessed its own collective "soul" and a "racial memory."[23] In Argentina's case, he believed that the national race had largely solidified during the nineteenth century, when mystical forces emanating from the Argentine soil had fused together the indigenous and European races to create a unique racial type.[24] Thus for Rojas, Argentina already possessed a distinctive racial profile—a kind of ethnic sponge that could absorb the millions of immigrants arriving on the nation's shores without losing its basic form. Fellow cultural nationalist Manuel Gálvez concurred with Rojas's assessment that Argentines formed a distinctive race, but he disagreed about its content. In his view, the Argentine nation was defined by its Catholic faith and Hispanic heritage, and thus its race was at root Spanish. Declaring Spain to be the "crucible of the race,"[25] he lauded the mother country for its deep Catholic spirituality and indifference to the lure of materialism and urged his countrymen to return to their Spanish origins.[26]

In writing about this presumed Argentine race, the cultural nationalists used the term to denote the shared qualities of an enduring ethno-cultural community rather than to describe people of a particular phenotype. Rojas made this explicit when he insisted that he employed the word *race* not as a scientist would but in the "old, romantic sense [having to do with] collective personality, historical group, cultural consciousness."[27] It is important to note, however, that the line between Rojas's and Gálvez's historical cultural definition of race and biological understandings of race was often fuzzy, an ambiguity fueled by the simultaneous circulation of other notions of race that reflected the emerging discipline of genetics, social Darwinism, neo-Lamarckian notions of the inheritability of acquired characteristics, eugenics, and Italian theories of criminology.[28] And, as Sandra McGee Deutsch has observed, although early twentieth-century Argentines typically spoke about race in cultural terms, the cultural traits that defined this supposed race were seen as innate rather than acquirable.[29] Thus despite their disavowal of biological notions of race, the "Argentine race" envisioned by Rojas and his fellow cultural nationalists was understood to be a bounded ethnic community, whose members shared fixed psychological traits that were transmittable from one generation to the other.[30]

While the cultural nationalists were among the most prominent champions of the idea of an Argentine race, theirs were not lone voices

launched into a void. Rather, as will be developed in chapter 2, these individuals employed language, ideas, and images that resonated with, just
as they helped shape, contemporary understandings of Argentine nationality.[31] Indeed, by the early 1920s, the idea that Argentines formed,
or should form, a distinctive national race, which in turn belonged to a
larger racial family, became widely accepted among those Argentines
who wrestled with the myriad consequences of mass immigration.

What was the connection between the early twentieth-century idea
of "the Argentine race" (however it was understood) and the later notion
of *el ser nacional* that figured so prominently in post-1930 nationalist discourses? I argue that the growing belief that Argentines formed (or
would form) a bounded ethnic community and that a unified "national
type" was developing fundamentally reset the conceptual parameters
within which future debates over Argentine identity would unfold. In
proclaiming the existence (or emergence) of a distinctive, unitary "Argentine race," the cultural nationalists and like-minded intellectuals
undermined the traditional nineteenth-century view that being an Argentine was first and foremost a question of allegiance to the Argentine
state, its constitution, and the political values this document enshrined.
And although the break with Argentina's liberal past was never complete, the spread of the essentialist notion of an Argentine race among
early twentieth-century intellectuals and opinion makers made possible
or "thinkable" the later (and equally essentialist) notion of *el ser nacional*.
Indeed, I believe there is a direct continuity between the two terms in
that during the 1930s this phrase came to replace the term *race*, when the
latter came to have a more strictly biological or genetic meaning.[32] In
other words, after 1930 or so the concept of *el ser nacional* provided a way
of talking and writing about the supposedly intrinsic, collective, and unitary character of the Argentine people, without straying into increasingly
messy questions of bloodlines and phenotypes.

The concept of "path dependence" is useful here in thinking about
intellectual continuities between the pre- and post-1930 periods. First
developed by economic historians to understand the persistence of seemingly obsolete technologies, path dependence holds that in certain instances, contingent historical circumstances, such as random events and
decisions made by key historical actors, have produced technological innovations that eventually become "locked-in," and thus foreclose the

development of other, more efficient technologies.[33] More recently, historical sociologists and historians have adopted the concept of path dependence to explore the persistence of institutions, practices, and ideas that emerge during so-called critical junctures, defined as moments of crisis or change during which traditional practices and understandings are in flux.[34] These critical junctures serve as "genetic moments" that produce new ways of thinking or new forms of social organization that respond to the crisis at hand.[35] Once they take hold, these ideas, practices and institutions persist and continue to drive ways of thinking and behaving long after the disappearance of the conditions that prevailed when they emerged.

Applying this concept to the case of Argentina, I see the early twentieth century as a critical juncture, during which mass immigration and rapid modernization shook the foundations of the traditional social, cultural, and political order. As Argentine intellectuals grappled with these challenges, and more specifically with the problem of how to incorporate immigrants into the nation while at the same time protecting a national culture they believed to be under siege, they seized on a set of ideas that happened to be available at that particular moment and that made sense to them: varieties of the ethno-cultural nationalism then circulating in Europe, and especially Spain. Once the idea of an Argentine race came to be embraced by a substantial segment of the nation's intellectual elite, it achieved a certain "stickiness" and served to channel subsequent discussions about Argentine identity along similarly unitary and essentialist lines, even after the initial triggers (mass immigration and rapid modernization) came to an end in the late 1920s. In other words, during the early decades of the twentieth century, the growing acceptance of the idea that Argentines formed a distinct race or ethno-cultural community produced new ways of thinking and talking about *argentinidad*; this sent subsequent discussions of the nation and its problems along conceptual pathways that reinforced certain understandings of Argentine identity while at the same time closing off—or at least making less likely—alternative ways of imagining the nation.[36]

Just as the concept of path dependence can help explain continuities between the early twentieth-century embrace of the idea of the Argentine race and the later notion of *el ser nacional*, it can also shed light on connections between different formulations of this imagined race and later versions of the (equally) imagined Argentine *ser.* As noted, cultural nationalists Gálvez and Rojas promoted different interpretations of the supposed Argentine race, but both agreed that Argentina already possessed a well-developed ethnic profile that would remain unaltered by mass immigration. Other intellectuals of the period, however, adopted a much more dynamic and inclusive vision of the supposed Argentine race. While still embracing the cultural nationalists' essentialist concept of a unitary national race, such figures as the politician Horacio Oyhanarte and elite writer Francisco Soto y Calvo argued that the national race was still in its infancy. Accordingly, they believed that Argentine ethnicity would be fundamentally reshaped by the millions of immigrants that continued to flood Argentine shores. The ultimate result, in their view, would be a completely different "racial type" that would be both new and completely Argentine. Thus as Argentines struggled with the challenges of mass immigration, the idea of an Argentine race served as an empty screen on which a number of images could be projected. In the starkly different visions of this supposed race that were articulated during this period, I argue, we can see the outlines of the competing versions of *el ser nacional*—one Catholic and elitist, the other popular and inclusive—that were so central to the thought of Argentina's later nationalists.

## HISTORIOGRAPHICAL CONTEXTS

This work seeks to contribute to current scholarship in a number of areas. First, my emphasis on the importance of massive immigration in helping to produce a broad shift in understandings of Argentine identity takes inspiration from Lilia Ana Bertoni's 2001 *Patriotas, cosmopolitas y nacionalistas: la construcción de la nacionalidad argentina a fines del siglo XIX* (Patriots, cosmopolitans and nationalists: the construction of Argentine nationality at the end of the nineteenth century). This work examines Argentine reactions to immigration during the 1870–1900 period, arguing that the arrival of millions of immigrants during these years undermined the traditional understanding of Argentina as a civic community and helped spark the spread of an essentialized notion of *argentinidad* as an inherent state of being or feeling. My work, which clearly owes much to Bertoni's, seeks to build on her insights by extending the story into the twentieth century. In doing so, I accomplish three things. First, I offer new insight into the intellectual influences that shaped early twentieth-century ideas about the nation, a topic that lies beyond Bertoni's chronological coverage. Second, my focus on the early twentieth-century debates over the nature of the imagined Argentine race challenges Bertoni's conclusion that the emerging ethno-cultural vision of *argentinidad* was inevitably xenophobic and elitist. Instead, I demonstrate that, although the increasing numbers of Argentines did indeed embrace essentialized, ethno-cultural understandings of their nation's identity, at least some variants of this vision were inclusive in that immigrants were seen as important contributors to an emerging Argentine race. Finally, because my study includes the post-1930 period, I am able to explore the long-term political consequences of the process that Bertoni first identified.

Another area of scholarship to which this study contributes is early twentieth-century cultural nationalism. Sometimes referred to as Argentina's "first nationalism," this intellectual movement has attracted substantial scholarly attention. The predominant interpretation of cultural nationalism, promoted most forcefully by Enrique Zuleta Álvarez and David Rock, characterizes this phenomenon as a reactionary response to the political and social challenges posed by mass immigration.[37] Because of what they see as cultural nationalism's inherent antipopular, xenophobic thrust, these scholars have portrayed this movement as the direct precursor to the later right-wing variant of Argentine nationalism. My aim here is not to reject this argument entirely; certainly, most cultural nationalists *were* indeed anxious about the impact of immigration, and it is noteworthy that novelist Manuel Gálvez, one of the movement's cofounders, briefly embraced fascism in the 1930s. Yet the fact that fellow cultural nationalist Ricardo Rojas became a vociferous critic of right-wing nationalism indicates that the relationship between this movement and later forms of nationalism was more complex than current scholarship suggests.

In reassessing cultural nationalism, my work argues that its most important legacy stemmed not from the reactionary politics of a few of its proponents but from the fact that collectively these intellectuals promoted ideas about *argentinidad* that encouraged their compatriots to see their nation in ethno-cultural terms.[38] During this critical juncture in Argentine intellectual history, the growing acceptance of these ideas by a broad segment of the cultural and political elite fundamentally reoriented subsequent discussions of Argentine identity along essentialist lines and laid the conceptual groundwork for the later notion of *el ser nacional.* Just as importantly, the above-noted fact that the early twentieth-century Argentines imagined *content* of the supposed Argentine race in dramatically different ways—ranging from the narrow vision of this race as Catholic and Hispanic promoted by Gálvez to the more socially inclusive vision promoted by Oyhanarte and Soto y Calvo—meant that later notions of *el ser nacional* would be similarly divergent, and would be embraced by individuals from across the political spectrum. Thus, I argue, the early twentieth-century cultural nationalists should be seen as helping to create a reservoir of concepts, constructs, and images from which *both* right- and left-wing nationalists of the post-1930 period drew.

My work also seeks to further our understanding of the broader phenomenon of Argentine nationalism by addressing what I see as a glaring gap in the scholarly literature,—that is, the very limited attention paid to the interconnections between right- and left-wing forms of Argentine nationalism. Because of its importance in shaping Argentina's political history, post-1930 nationalism is a much studied topic. To date, the majority of this literature has focused on the right-wing variant of Argentine nationalism. This emphasis was established early on by Marysa Navarro Gerassi, whose foundational *Los nacionalistas* (1968) devoted only two pages to left-wing nationalism.[39] Enrique Zuleta Álvarez's multivolume treatment *El nacionalismo argentino* followed suit,[40] and more recent scholarship, such as works by María Inés Barbero and Fernando Devoto, Cristián Buchrucker, David Rock, Sandra McGee Deutsch, Daniel Lvovich, Luis Fernando Beraza, and Federico Finchelstein, have continued this trend.[41]

Compared to the literature on the nationalist right, scholarship on Argentina's nationalist left is less abundant, although recent decades have witnessed growing interest in the topic as Argentines have tried to make sense of the turbulent 1960s and '70s.[42] Given this impulse, it is understandable that most scholars have been concerned with the post-1955 period. The resulting scholarship has two focal points. The first is the rise of the so-called New Left, a movement that emerged after the ouster of Juan Perón in 1955, when key members of the traditional left (i.e., the different factions associated with the Socialist and Communist Parties) came to reassess their traditional antipathy toward Perón and to advocate for a new, radicalized form of Peronism that sought to blend nationalism with Marxism.[43] The second emphasis has been the Peronist guerrilla movements of the 1960s and '70s, with particular attention paid to the Montoneros.[44]

Despite this rich and ever-growing literature, and the fact that numerous scholars have noted the affinities between Argentina's two nationalist strands, there are remarkably few works that have examined both right- and left-wing nationalism with the aim of illuminating their underlying similarities and points of contact.[45] A partial exception is David Rock's *Authoritarian Argentina*. Although centrally concerned with right-wing nationalism, Rock argues that, during the 1930s, the leaders of Argentina's two forms of nationalism competed with each other for "leadership of the Nationalist movement at large," and in doing so began to "coopt each other's slogans, approaches, and ideas."[46] Writing of the 1960s and 1970s, he notes that the radicalized segments of the Argentine Catholic Church provided an ideological bridge between the two strands of nationalism, leading some young right-wing nationalists to cross over to the left.[47] More generally, Rock has argued that, during these years, right-wing nationalist ideas became "suddenly all-pervasive [as they became] soaked up by groups that were mortal enemies ostensibly occupying the opposition ends of the political spectrum."[48] Indeed, so powerful was the impact of the nationalist right on the left, he believes, that the latter took from the right "its myths and icons, its ideological outlook and its propaganda techniques."[49]

Another important scholar who has sought to draw connections between Argentina's two strands of nationalism is political scientist Alberto Spektorowski. Spektorowski has gone beyond Rock's rather vague notion of "ideological cross fertilization" to provide a more systematic exploration of the similarities between Argentina's right- and left-wing forms of nationalism during the 1930s.[50] Focusing on the first half of the twentieth century, Spektorowski's work examines the rise of the nationalist right and left, and argues that leaders of both strands challenged the traditional liberal elite by promoting a kind of antiliberal "integral nationalism" aimed at changing "the very definition of democracy."[51] In highlighting their similarities, Spektorowski—rightly, I believe—rejects the standard view of right-wing nationalists as backward-looking reactionaries, arguing instead that by the end of the 1930s significant elements of this tendency had come to embrace the nationalist left's goals of "social justice, cultural authenticity and industrial development."[52] In doing so, he argues, Argentina's nationalist right created a new type of nationalism that was both authoritarian and popular, which laid the ideological groundwork for the rise of Juan Perón in the 1940s.[53]

Like Spektorowski and Rock, I am interested in both the striking similarities between Argentina's right- and left-wing nationalists and the ways in which their ideas, writings, and rhetoric helped undermine support for liberal democracy. While building on their insights, my work takes a different approach by placing nationalists' conceptions of Argentine identity at the center of the analysis. By focusing on nationalists' shared obsession with an imagined *ser nacional* and the trope of the supposedly "true Argentina," my work illuminates the ideas and assumptions that provided the conceptual underpinnings of their thought. It argues, moreover, that this shared conceptual substrate framed how right- and left-wing nationalists understood the threats facing Argentina, and thus served as a kind of intellectual bridge that helps explain their enduring affinities. In other words, Argentina's right- and left-wing nationalists "got" each other at a fundamental conceptual level. At the same time, however, because they defined the character of the true Argentina in such radically different ways, these nationalists—despite their shared anti-imperialism and hatred of liberalism—were unable to unite behind a common program.

This focus on how Argentine nationalists imagined, wrote, and talked about national identity aligns with the most recent effort to tackle the complex relationship between the country's two forms of nationalism. Michael Goebel's *Argentina's Partisan Past: Nationalism and the Politics of History* (2011) examines right- and left-wing nationalists' shared hostility toward the official version of Argentine history that celebrated the liberal leaders of the nineteenth century. Using historical revisionism as his guiding thread, Goebel explores the evolving relationship between Argentina's two strands of nationalism, from the Peronist period through the 1990s. In doing so, he links the nationalists' historical revisionism to their promotion of essentialized understandings of Argentine identity, and notes that both right- and left-wing nationalist thinkers justified their claims about the past by appealing to "the supposed essence" of the Argentine nation.[54] He suggests, as well, that the traditional "liberal-nationalist dichotomy [within Argentine political and intellectual history] should be recharted as an opposition between civic and ethno cultural modes of defining a community of co-nationals."[55]

My approach has much in common with Goebel's, and our analyses draw from some of the same theoretical literature on civic versus ethnic forms of national identity. Our studies differ, however, in focus and scope. While certainly agreeing with Goebel about the importance of essentialized notions of Argentine identity to the project of historical revisionism, my work is chiefly concerned with the former. Thus, although the theme of historical revisionism enters into the analysis (especially in the final chapters), my primary interest is in how the related tropes of *el ser nacional* and the "two Argentinas" structured nationalist thought, not simply about the past, but about a wide range of issues that preoccupied both right- and left-wing nationalist ideologues. My work also contrasts with Goebel's in its emphasis on the origins of essentialist understandings of Argentine identity, and in the way in which it links early twentieth-century debates over *argentinidad* to later nationalist thought.

Finally, and on the most general level, this work contributes to the broader field of nationalism studies by examining a country from a region that has received scant attention from European and US specialists.[56] In doing so, I note the ways in which Argentina's early twentieth-century version of ethno-cultural nationalism resembled European varieties, while at the same time highlighting its unique aspects.[57] In particular, I focus on the central dilemma facing Argentina's early twentieth-century promoters of ethno-cultural nationalism: namely, the enduring conviction that Argentina remained a vastly underpopulated country that needed immigrants both as laborers and as permanent settlers. Given this reality, those who believed in the existence of a unique Argentine race were forced to define it in such a way as to *include* rather than *exclude* the immigrant. They often did so by arguing that the Argentine ethnicity was still forming, and that immigrants, or at least their children, would become part of this new national race. I believe this effort to square an ethnic notion of national identity with the need to integrate the foreign born makes the Argentine case unique. Moreover, the capaciousness of this notion of the Argentine race, and the fact that the debates over its content produced wildly different interpretations about what role the immigrant would play, meant that this construct could accommodate radically different political viewpoints. Indeed it was perhaps the very inclusiveness of this construct that was the source of its broad appeal, and allowed it to gain acceptance among individuals who might otherwise have championed the competing vision of Argentina as a civic nation.[58]

## BROADER SIGNIFICANCE FOR ARGENTINE POLITICS

By focusing on the essentialist understandings of identity at the heart of Argentina's two nationalisms, this study seeks to shed new light on their underlying similarities and shared origins. Certainly, the fact that the leading intellectuals of Argentina's two nationalist strains were hostile to both political and economic liberalism is well known. What has *not* been sufficiently explored, however, are the strikingly similar ways in which these individuals framed their attacks on liberalism, and how these conceptual framings provided the rationale for delegitimizing liberal values and the Argentines who promoted them. Armed with an essentialist belief in the existence of an enduring community rooted in *el ser nacional* (however they defined its content), Argentine nationalists saw liberalism not simply as a flawed ideology but as an alien philosophy at odds with the supposed authentic character of the true Argentina. Worse still, they believed, liberalism had been imposed on the nation by a deracinated elite acting on behalf of foreigner capitalists. These elites, nationalists believed, had sold out their country after being mentally colonized by their imperial masters, thereby becoming *"descastados"* (stripped of their ethnicity). They were, in other words, no longer Argentines. Hostile to liberalism in all its forms, both right- and left-wing nationalists believed that the country could prosper economically only by jettisoning liberal democracy and by developing political institutions that were consonant with the supposed authentic character of the Argentine people.

But what influence did these essentialist understandings of national identity have on the political attitudes of the broader public? Did the writings and utterances of a relatively small group of intellectuals shape the ways in which ordinary Argentines understood their nation and affect their view of democracy? Any attempt to provide a definitive answer to these questions would require an altogether different kind of study, one with a much narrower temporal focus that employed different kinds of sources. Given my goal of charting connections between early twentieth-century debates over immigration, the shift from civil to ethno-cultural under-standings of the nation, and Argentina's two nationalisms, such depth is impossible. This broad chronological scope means that any claims about the impact of nationalist thought on public opinion must be suggestive rather than conclusive.

This having been said, there are grounds for some tentative obser-vations. To begin, when considering the effect of nationalist discourses on public ideas and attitudes, it is useful to keep in mind the peculiar status of those individuals within any given society who write or speak about national identity and who promote nationalist ideas. In most areas of scholarly inquiry, there exists a wide gulf between intellectuals and the general public, and it is the norm for a handful of specialists to be con-sumed by matters in which the rest of society has absolutely no interest. But for those engaged with issues of national identity and nationalism (and here I include intellectuals, journalists, activists, and political lead-ers), the relationship between "experts" and the public entails a different dynamic. Here, the connection between what emerges from the pen/mouth of the individual thinker and what enters the cultural mainstream is greater than might be supposed. As scholars of nationalism have long noted, intellectuals have played a central role in shaping national iden-tities and mobilizing the public behind nationalist programs.[59] Indeed, as Ronald Grigor Suny and Michael Kennedy have persuasively argued, nationalist intellectuals are not simply experts in a particular branch of knowledge but are actually "constitutive of the nation itself."[60] Because nations are themselves imagined communities that must be produced and continually reproduced over time, intellectuals "do the imaginative ideo-logical labor that brings together disparate cultural elements, selected historical memories and interpretations of experiences" that provide the content of collective identities.[61] In other words, the very existence of a nation (and indeed the existence of the nation as a *category* within which humanity organizes itself) requires intellectuals and intellectual work.

Moreover, because in the modern world personal identities are almost always linked at some level to national identities, individuals pay attention to the ideas, arguments, and images produced by nationalist intellectuals, making it more likely that they will gain a broad circulation.

Returning to Argentina, one indication of the connections between the Argentine nationalists' ideas and public understandings of national identity (connections that undoubtedly went both ways) was the appearance of the related tropes of the "two Argentinas" and *el ser nacional* in best-selling books, especially those that have enjoyed enduring popularity. As will be discussed in the concluding chapter, the 1930s witnessed the publication of three seminal works that together have become known as the "essays of identity." Raúl Scalabrini Ortiz's 1931 *El hombre que está solo y espera* (The man who is alone and waits/hopes), Ezequiel Martínez Estrada's 1933 *Radiografía de la Pampa* (X-ray of the Pampa), and Eduardo Mallea's 1937 *Historia de una pasión argentina* (History of an Argentine passion) all took as their subject the "true or hidden Argentina" (as opposed to the visible Argentina), and all understood the nation in deeply essentialist terms.[62] Each of these books became an immediate bestseller, and each has been continually reprinted, read, and discussed as an indispensable touchstone of Argentine identity.[63] Taken together, these works have played a key role in naturalizing the concept a unitary, authentic *ser nacional* as an unproblematic "thing" rather than as a construct to be interrogated.[64]

Evidence beyond the naturalization of the notions of *el ser nacional* and the "two Argentinas" suggests that essentialist understandings of national identity became woven into the broader fabric of Argentine political thought. Perhaps the most salient examples are the ideas and rhetoric of the leaders of Argentina's two most important political parties, Hipólito Yrigoyen of the Unión Cívica Radicals (UCR or Radicals) and Juan Perón of the Justicialista or Peronist Party. As subsequent chapters will develop, both Yrigoyen and Perón understood the Argentine nation to be an organic community with a unitary collective character, a perception that shaped their conception of politics in two interrelated ways. First, they shared the conviction that there was a disconnect between the true Argentina and liberal democracy. Accordingly, both believed that nations should develop *sui generis* institutions that were consonant with the supposed *ser nacional*. Essentialist understandings of Argentine identity also shaped how they understood the purpose of political activity. As is well known, both Yrigoyen and Perón were hostile to pluralistic democracy, and rejected the view of politics as a process by which individuals pursued their interests through political parties in the electoral arena. Rather, they believed the point of political activity was to work for the "reintegration of the nationality" and to "organize" the national community in order to pursue the common good.[65] In keeping with this vision, both political leaders eschewed the label "party" to describe the organizations they led, instead insisting that Radicalism and Peronism (respectively) were "movements" that had arisen from the nation as a whole, and thus were consubstantial with the nation itself.[66]

Yrigoyen's and Perón's essentialist vision of Argentina as a unitary organic community, and their insistence that they led national movements rather than political parties, inevitably raised the stakes in any political contest. If one believes that a movement represents the nation as a whole, and indeed is consubstantial with it, then those who belong to an opposing political party or simply choose not to join are seen as enemies of the nation or even as non-Argentines. There are, of course, clear parallels between such views and the nationalists' belief that Argentines who embraced liberalism had lost their nationality. This tendency to define political opponents as no longer "true" Argentines is symptomatic of what Michael Goebel has called the nationalists' "totalizing narratives," which rejected political pluralism and divided the world into starkly different factions.[67] Argentine historian Luis Alberto Romero has echoed this observation and related these tendencies to the nationalists' essentialist understandings of the nation. In his view, the twentieth-century "imperative" to define Argentine identity in terms of "race, language, territory or . . . a mystical historical past," rather than according to the ideals of its citizens, "poisoned" the nation's democratic culture. It is just this climate, he argued, that led to the long-time habit of characterizing one's political enemies as enemies of the nation.[68]

There are also clear parallels between the nationalists' essentialist vision of a unitary *ser nacional* and the generalized climate of intolerance toward ethnic and religious pluralism that characterized twentieth-century Argentina. To be sure, as mentioned above, the creation of a racially homogenous (i.e., white) population preoccupied elites from the very beginnings of the republic. At the same time, the enormous interest in attracting

European immigrants led to an open door policy that, at least in theory, welcomed all nationalities, races, and ethnicities. Moreover, once they arrived, immigrants enjoyed complete freedom to practice their own religions, form their own ethnic associations, and establish their own schools in order to educate their children in their native tongues. What was asked of the newcomers, in other words, was that they embrace the principles central to Argentina's political institutions and that they be loyal to their adoptive country. As the essentialist understandings of Argentine identity rose in the twentieth century (whether in the form of a homogenous Argentine "race" or the later notion of a unitary *ser nacional*), this tolerance for internal diversity dissipated. The nationalist right, of course, believed non-Catholic, non-Spanish immigrants and internal minorities could never be true Argentines, and considered their very presence diluted or contaminated *el ser nacional.* The nationalist left drew the boundaries of belonging differently. As noted, these nationalists believed the true Argentina to be rooted in the culture of the masses, which by the 1930s meant a culture that was at least partially created by working-class immigrants and their descendants. Yet while embracing the immigrant, left-wing nationalists expected the newcomers to assimilate fully and become part of a unitary, undifferentiated pueblo. As FORJA leader Arturo Jauretche insisted, Argentina could not tolerate religious and ethnic minorities who were "inadaptable." Rather, all immigrants were expected to become "amalgamated" into "*lo argentino.*"[69]

As the essentialist tropes of *el ser nacional* and the "two Argentinas" spread through the broader culture, so too did the belief that true Argentines should not have hyphenated identities; thus, immigrants and ethnic minorities should become subsumed within an undifferentiated single people, who were in some way shaped by, and bound to, *el ser nacional.* Historian Hilda Sábato has directly tied such essentialist understandings of Argentine identity to the difficulty of defending the ideal of a pluralistic Argentina. Working against such a vision of the nation, she argues, has been the "persistent attraction" of ideologies that insist on the unitary nature of *argentinidad,* and the insistence that other identities such as class, gender, religion, and ethnicity would—or should—be "dissolved in the supposed essences of national identities."[70] Indeed, as multiple commentators have noted, only in recent years have large numbers of Argentines come to embrace the ideal of a pluricultural nation.[71]

Finally, and most broadly, is the matter of the political consequences of defining a nation in terms of the supposed ethno-cultural traits of its people. Certainly, the nationalists' essentialist vision of Argentina was not *inevitably* authoritarian. At the same time, by detaching Argentine identity from constitutional moorings and thus from the liberal political ideals, rights, and institutions outlined in the 1853 Constitution, the violation of these ideals, rights, and institutions is more easily justified. This seems especially true in the Argentine case, in which both right- and left-wing nationalists—in their insistence that liberalism in all its forms was alien to *el ser nacional*—consistently failed to distinguish between the liberal *political* values of the constitution with its liberal or laissez-fare economic provisions. In (rightly) criticizing free-market capitalism as a system that made the country vulnerable to economic exploitation and dependency, nationalists simultaneously portrayed the democratic values and institutions outlined in the document as similarly harmful, and as having been imposed by an elite working at the behest of foreign powers seeking to weaken the nation. And while it is difficult to make precise claims about how deeply the nationalists' anticonstitutionalism penetrated Argentine political culture, it is surely significant that these ideas came from both right- and left-wing nationalist ideologues. In other words, this anticonstitutional, antiliberal democracy message was broadcast in a kind of political stereo.

## ORGANIZATION AND CHAPTER CONTENTS

This book is organized into two main sections. Part 1, on the pre-1930 period, examines the emergence and spread of new essentialist notions of Argentine identity during the age of mass immigration, a moment that I see as a critical juncture in the nation's intellectual history. Chapter 1 serves as a background to this discussion by providing an overview of how the country's nineteenth-century political elites imagined Argentine nationality. It looks first at the "civic" or "pacted" vision of the nation embraced by the independence leaders, and then examines how this vision became complicated with the emergence of a new generation of thinkers who placed more emphasis on the cultural basis of nationality. Despite this new emphasis, however, the idea that the *primary* source of Argentine identity was shared political values and loyalties continued to predominate. Chapter 2 examines changing notions of national identity during the age of mass immigration. Focusing primarily on the cultural nationalists, it documents the increasing influence of ideas associated with Romantic nationalism on early twentieth-century Argentine thought and, in particular, the emergence of the belief that Argentines were forming a distinctive national race or ethnicity. This chapter also examines the continued survival of the more traditional understanding of Argentine identity, looking especially at the civic-based vision of the Socialist Party.

Chapter 3 explores the sources of these new ideas about nationality by focusing on three different themes. First, it traces how changes in the publishing industry and the emergence of a new youth culture set the stage for the rise of the cultural nationalists. Second, it examines the relationship between late nineteenth-century positivism and the idea of the Argentine race promoted by the cultural nationalists and like-minded individuals. Finally, this chapter explores in greater detail the impact of the ideas associated with Romantic nationalism on early twentieth-century Argentine thought. To do so, it takes a detour to Spain and examines the importance of the philosophy known as Krausism, looking especially at its impact on the Spanish Generation of 1898. Chapter 4 examines the ideology of the UCR or Argentine Radical Party. Here the primary focus is on Radical leader Hipólito Yrigoyen and the influence of Krausist ideas on his political thought. It considers as well the underlying similarities between Yrigoyen's thought and that of the cultural nationalists. Chapter 5 continues to focus on the pre-1930 period, examining how essentialist visions of nationality came to dominate broader discussions of Argentine identity. To highlight both the growing acceptance of ideas associated with Romantic nationalism *and* the ways these ideas sparked strong disagreements about the nature of Argentine nationality, I look at debates over the content of the supposed Argentine race and the question of whether Argentina would, or should, develop its own language.

Part 2 examines the nationalist movements of the post-1930 period. In contrast to the previous chapters, which chart the spread of ideas associated with Romantic nationalism, and how they shaped how Argentina's cultural and political elite understood their national identity, part 2 focuses more narrowly on individuals who self-identified as nationalists. This section begins with chapter 6, which traces the rise of right-wing nationalism between the late 1920s and early 1940s and examines the emergence of the related tropes of *el ser nacional* and the two Argentinas. A central focus is on the intellectuals affiliated with the periodical *La Nueva República,* who defined the true Argentina as Catholic and Hispanic and who worked closely with the military faction that overthrew President Yrigoyen in 1930. It then looks at the rise of a number of right-wing nationalist groups that appeared on the political scene during the prewar period. Chapter 7 also treats the 1930–45 period but focuses on the rise of a left-wing, socially inclusive form of nationalism and the founding of FORJA, an offshoot of the Radical Party. Here I examine the ideas of FORJA leaders Arturo Jauretche, Raúl Scalabrini Ortiz, Atilio García Mellid, and Gabriel del Mazo, all of whom adopted the late president's mystical notion of Radicalism as a movement that reflected the true essence, or "soul," of the Argentine people. This chapter also highlights some of the key differences between left- and right-wing nationalists, as well as moments of collaboration and mutual influence.

Chapter 8 examines the 1940s and the rise of Juan Perón to the Argentine presidency. A military officer with populist inclinations, Perón articulated a new, *sui generis* version of *el ser nacional* that reflected the influences of both the pro-Catholic, pro-Spanish nationalists and the more socially inclusive left-wing strand. Chapter 9 considers the ongoing importance of nationalism and essentialist ideas of Argentine identity after Perón's 1955 ouster and exile, as nationalists from across the political spectrum joined the "Peronist Resistance"—the heterogeneous movement that sought to force the military to allow Perón to return. It was at this moment that the line between Argentina's two forms of nationalism was its blurriest, as many individuals and groups allied with the nationalist right moved leftward; at the same time, although it happened less frequently, some on the left moved to the right. Here I also look at the growing importance of historical revisionism as a vector for the nationalist tropes of *el ser nacional* and the two Argentinas, thereby providing a conceptual bridge between Argentina's two forms of nationalism. Finally, chapter 10 looks at how the growing radicalization of the nationalist left helped drive Argentina's two strains of nationalism further apart, and sparked violent conflicts within the Peronist movement. The chapter also focuses on the hypernationalist tendencies within the Argentine military, and on how the right-wing nationalist vision of Argentina as a Catholic nation helped fuel some of the worst excesses of the regime.

This work concludes by revisiting the question of why essentialist notions of identity—present throughout Latin America—proved so powerful in Argentina. This chapter also examines the continuing importance of the trope of *el ser nacional* after the return to democracy in 1983, and considers whether Argentines have finally gotten over the notion, decried by historian José Luis Romero, that their culture is "something objectified outside [themselves], eternal and immutable."[72] And, now that over three decades have passed since the military last ruled, have Argentines come to see democratic institutions, the rule of law, and the protection of individual rights—rather than an imagined *ser national*—as intrinsic to their collective identity?

PART ONE

# Debating the Nation

Part I traces the rise and spread of new essentialist understandings of Argentine national identity during the early twentieth century, understandings that served as cornerstones of nationalist thought after 1930. It begins with a look back at the nineteenth century, with an examination of the ideas that animated Argentina's independence leaders. These leaders broke with Spain, not in the name of a preexisting ethno-cultural community, but in order to establish a new nation formed on the basis of shared political ideas and loyalties. Despite the influence of Romantic-nationalist currents in later decades, this civic vision of the Argentine nation predominated until the century's end.

Subsequent chapters focus on the 1900–1930 period, when the rapid influx of millions of Europeans sparked concerns that Argentine traditions and culture were in danger of being erased by the immigrant masses. Inspired by a new wave of Romantic ideas that saw nations as distinctive ethno-cultural communities, rather than as human-created political projects, prominent Argentines began to write and speak about the need to consolidate the Argentine "race" or ethnicity in order to protect it from the tide of newcomers. This idea of a national race, most forcefully articulated by a new generation of intellectuals known as the cultural nationalists, gained greater currency over time, as a growing number of cultural elites embraced the notion that Argentines formed, or were forming, a unitary national ethnicity.

Part 1 also explores the intellectual sources of this new way of imagining the Argentine nation, highlighting in particular the impact of the Romantic philosophy known as Krausism. Based on the ideas of

German philosopher Karl Christian Krause, this philosophy dominated Spanish thought during the latter half of the nineteenth century and entered Argentina through two different paths. The first was through the influence of the Spanish Generation of 1898, whose essentialist claim that nations—and families of nations—were organic ethno-cultural communities with distinctive personalities had an enormous impact on the Argentine cultural nationalists. The second route was more direct, as Argentines themselves read Krausist-based Spanish texts. Key here is the figure of Hipólito Yrigoyen, leader of the Unión Cívica Radical party, and the president of the Republic from 1916 and 1922, and again from 1928 to 1930. Owing to Yrigoyen's overwhelming influence, the Radical Party reinforced the notion—already embraced by the cultural nationalists—that nations were homogenous, organic entities possessing unitary personalities and having unique historical missions they were destined to fulfill. In promoting this essentialist vision of the nation, Yrigoyen helped undermine the long-standing, voluntarist vision of Argentina as a civic community and in doing so served to delegitimize liberal democratic values.

This section ends with an exploration of the very different ways in which Argentines defined the nature of the supposed Argentine ethnicity or race. At stake was the question of immigrants' role in shaping Argentine identity. Did the nation, as some prominent Argentines believed, already possess a well-defined ethnic profile that the newcomers threatened to deform or contaminate? Or, as others suggested, could the newcomers be successfully absorbed without altering the qualities of the preexisting Argentine race? Alternatively, as some intellectuals argued, would the growing immigrant population play a central role in the consolidation of a new national race that was still emerging? These radically different interpretations of the imagined Argentine race, I argue, established the conceptual groundwork for later nationalist debates over the nature of the (equally) imagined *ser nacional*.

# ONE

# Nation and Nationality in the Nineteenth Century

As early twentieth-century Argentine elites confronted the challenges of mass immigration, they struggled mightily with the question of how to incorporate the millions of Europeans arriving on the nation's shores. What role should the immigrant play in the country's political life? What would become of Argentina's culture and traditions? Could the country assimilate these immigrants, or would so many newcomers irrevocably change—or even erase—the existing population? One of the central arguments of this book is that this experience of mass immigration represented a critical juncture in Argentine history and produced a radical shift in the way in which large numbers of intellectuals and cultural elites conceptualized the meaning of Argentine nationality. In grappling with how to preserve what they understood to be their nation's identity and to create a unified national community from a newly diverse population, these individuals drew inspiration from European strains of Romantic nationalism, an intellectual movement that envisioned nations as distinctive, homogeneous ethno-cultural communities, whose members were bound by a shared language, religion, and ancestry. The result was a new conceptual framework for imagining what it meant to be an

Argentine. Increasingly during this period, key segments of the Argentine elite came to believe that they and their countrymen formed a unique ethnicity or "race" into which the immigrants would somehow be absorbed.

The notion that Argentines formed a distinctive race would have struck the country's independence leaders as profoundly strange, for in ethnic terms they clearly differed little from their colonial masters. Thus when they broke free from Spain in the early nineteenth century, these men did so not to defend the rights of a distinctive people or ethnocultural community but to establish a brand new nation, whose founding would require the creation of political institutions to be ratified by the newly empowered citizenry. What would join these citizens together, independence leaders believed, was not a common ethnicity but shared political ideals and loyalties to the new state. This contractual or civic-based view of nationhood would be broadly accepted during Argentina's chaotic postindependence years, and, despite the strong impact of European Romanticism on midcentury thought, it would remain the predominant matrix for understanding Argentine identity.

This chapter traces the intellectual shifts of the nineteenth century, with special focus on what might be called Argentina's first Romantic moment. Although rife with contradictions, European Romanticism's assumptions about nationality and history exerted a powerful influence on the so-called liberal Generation of 1837, a group of thinkers that would play an extraordinarily important role in the nation's political life.[1] Indeed, two key members of this generation, Domingo F. Sarmiento and Bartolomé Mitre, served as president of the republic, while a third (Juan Bautista Alberdi) wrote a treatise that served as the basis of the 1853 Constitution.[2] In examining the influence of Romantic understandings of nationality and history on the Generation of 1837, I am not arguing for continuities between these thinkers and early twentieth-century cultural nationalists. Simply put, there were none: the members of this latter group operated in an entirely different context than that faced by the Generation of 1837, and they were drawn to Romanticism's conceptions of nationality and history for entirely different reasons. What's more, they imbibed these understandings from different sources.

Despite this lack of continuity, exploring nineteenth-century understandings of Argentine identity is important for two reasons. First, providing a sense of the shifting ways in which Argentina's nineteenth-century intellectuals and political leaders imagined their nation will make readers better able to judge the significance of the early twentieth-century changes. The second reason has to do with this book's other major aim—that is, exploring the long-term political implications of the ethno-cultural understandings of national identity that gained traction during the era of mass immigration. As explained in the introduction, central to both right- and left-wing nationalist discourses was the claim that Argentines possessed an enduring, unitary collective character (often expressed as *el ser nacional*) that was threatened by liberalism, an ideology these nationalists identified with the Generation of 1837.[3] According to post-1930 nationalists, this group of individuals had led Argentina astray by imposing an ideology on the nation that was both alien to the national character and opened up its economy to foreign exploitation. Given the outsized role the Generation of 1837 has played in the nationalist imagination, it is important to clarify how these nineteenth-century individuals actually thought, wrote, and spoke about Argentine nationality. While it is undeniable that the members of this generation both embraced liberal economic policies and sought to transform Argentines in order to make them more like the peoples of the United States and non-Spanish Europe, later nationalist claims that these individuals wanted merely to copy these societies—or worse, were traitors who sought to hand the country over to foreign capitalists—oversimplifies a more complex story. Instead, under the influence of Romantic ideas about nationality, the members of the Generation of 1837 continually wrestled with the problem of how to construct a new national culture that would be both distinctly Argentine *and* would provide the conditions they believed necessary for economic prosperity and democratic institutions. Our analysis of these issues begins with a look at the independence period, as well as the ideas and political traditions that guided those leaders who called for a break with Spain.

## INDEPENDENCE AND THE IDEA OF THE NATION

Argentina's independence from Spain in 1816 was neither inevitable nor universally desired by the inhabitants of what was then known as the

Rio de la Plata region.[4] Long a backwater of the Spanish American empire, this area achieved importance only in the late eighteenth century, when Bourbon reformers established the new viceroyalty of the Rio de la Plata with the port city of Buenos Aires as its administrative center. Perhaps even more important was the 1777 decision to route Andean silver through Buenos Aires, a move that transformed the city into one of the most dynamic centers of the Spanish empire. Had these reforms occurred a century earlier, local creoles might have judged them a resounding success. But by the close of the eighteenth century, the Atlantic world had changed, and imperial Spain found itself battling new economic ideas that called into question colonial trade restrictions.

This was particularly true in Buenos Aires, where the economic theories of Adam Smith, French physiocrats, and Neapolitan political economists had gained a wide readership among the educated elite.[5] Political ideas were also in flux, as sectors of the educated elite began to rethink traditional notions of governance. One source of these new tendencies came from the colonial center itself, where growing numbers of Spaniards began to reject the view, promoted since the time of Philip II, that monarchal absolutism was part of the natural order.[6] During the late eighteenth century, opponents of absolutism took a new look at Spain's medieval political traditions, highlighting those that emphasized the popular, contractual origins of the sovereign's right to rule.[7] Political currents from the United States and especially France also had an impact. Despite Spain's efforts to isolate its overseas possessions from revolutionary contagion, literate colonials were well aware of events in those countries and the works of Voltaire, Condorcet, Rousseau, and Montesquieu circulated widely.[8]

By themselves, these new ideas and the tensions over trade posed little threat to Spain's hold on its American possessions.[9] In 1808, however, Napoleon's invasion of the Iberian Peninsula and his imprisonment of Spanish monarch Fernando VII suddenly destabilized the colonial pact. Although a junta claiming to rule Spain and its overseas possessions quickly formed in Seville, news of these events prompted leaders in some colonial cities to declare a limited independence. In May 1810, the Buenos Aires cabildo, or municipal council, appointed its own ruling junta and proclaimed it to be the legitimate political authority of the viceroyalty. It also called on cabildos throughout the viceroyalty to elect delegates to a general assembly for the purpose of establishing "the form of government they consider most convenient."[10] Many of these councils joined with the Buenos Aires junta, while others resisted. In some cases, local elites remained loyal to Spain; in others, regional leaders established their own provisional juntas but refused to follow the dictates of Buenos Aires. Thus from the beginning, Argentina's long fight for independence was characterized by a simultaneous effort to cast off Spanish rule and a struggle between regional factions over how much power to grant Buenos Aires.[11]

For our purposes, the central point of interest is how the revolutionary leaders justified their actions and what kind of entity they sought to form. As noted, creole political thought during this period was nourished by two intellectual streams: one from reformist Spain, and the other from revolutionary France.[12] In the months after Napoleon's seizure of the Spanish throne, it was the former that held sway. Particularly useful for would-be revolutionaries was the newly revived medieval theory of *pactum subjectionis*, which held that the "pueblos," or medieval cities, were originally independent entities that had freely entered into a pact with the king, thereby transferring to him their sovereignty.[13] Invoking this notion, creoles throughout the Americas, including Buenos Aires, argued that Fernando's imprisonment meant that the pact between sovereign and subjects was at least temporarily suspended, and that power should "revert" to his overseas subjects.[14] But if the theory of *pactum subjectionis* initially offered a legal justification for declaring self-rule, it quickly became clear that for many revolutionaries, the rights they sought to defend were more in keeping with more modern understandings. This was particularly true for the revolutionaries based in Buenos Aires, many of whom openly embraced the rhetoric of revolutionary France. During this period, the terms *liberty, equality*, and *fraternity* appeared repeatedly in the pages of the pro-Revolutionary *Gaceta de Buenos Aires*.[15] Also significant was the national coat of arms created by the United Provinces Assembly of 1813, which featured the Phrygian cap of the French Revolution in its center.

While these often competing rationales for independence complicated the task of organizing the new state, most noteworthy is what is missing from the discourses of the time. As José Carlos Chiaramonte has argued, in no case did rebellious creoles justify their actions by claiming that the peoples of the viceroyalty had formed a preexisting "historical cultural nation" that, because of its distinctiveness from Spain, required its own state.[16] Accordingly, the creole patriots understood themselves to be in the process of creating a *new* nation, in which the writing of a constitution and the establishment of the state were an integral part.

This conception of nationhood was reflected in the close identification of the terms *nation* and *state* during this period and in the tendency to use them as synonyms. Although *nation* had shifting meanings during this period, it is clear that early nineteenth-century leaders believed that creating the state and creating the nation were the same process. A debate in the Constitutional Assembly of 1824–27 over whether to form a national army is illustrative. Opposing the measure, delegate Juan Ignacio Gorriti argued that it was impossible to establish a national army without first creating the nation. Acknowledging that the term *nation* could be understood in various ways, he argued that the only definition relevant to the constitutional assembly was the political one—a group of people who "rule themselves (*se rige*) by the same law, that have the same government."[17] This meant, he maintained, that a nation had not yet formed in the Rio de la Plata region, since the very purpose of the assembly was to create the political institutions necessary for self-rule and thus "to organize the nation."[18] Fellow delegate Valentín Gómez countered by rejecting Gorriti's argument but not his premise. Accepting the latter's view of nations as pacted, or contractual, entities, he argued that even though the provinces had yet to ratify a constitution, the assembly had in recent months "taken many important resolutions" that had a "national character." The nation, he continued, was "more than a project; there are more than ideas: [we have taken] the steps necessary [to begin the process of organizing] the states."[19] The quarrel, then, revolved not around the question of whether or not the nation was a man-made entity created by individuals but over just how far the process had gone in the Rio de la Plata region.

The vision of Argentina as a new, contractually based nation created by human agency was evident in prevailing ideas about who could, or should, acquire citizenship. From the very beginning of the revolutionary process, leaders throughout the Rio de la Plata region embraced the concept of volitional allegiance. While adopting the policy of *jus soli*, the 1810 junta also insisted that membership in the national community was open to the non-native born, and very quickly acted to define who was, and who was not, a citizen. It also established the means by which the foreign born could become naturalized. Individuals born in Europe could receive citizenship papers by presenting proof of their loyalty to the new authorities, length of time in the territory, and personal fortune. Noticeably absent was any requirement that the applicant be a Roman Catholic, a qualification necessary for naturalization under the colonial regime.[20] Three years later, the Constituent Assembly of 1813 also addressed the naturalization process, providing further evidence of the volitional nature of *argentinidad*. According to the new guidelines, foreigners wishing to become naturalized were to present proof that they had been loyal to the "sacred cause of American freedom" in the years since 1810.[21] Spaniards, not surprisingly, came under special scrutiny, and those perceived to be lacking in revolutionary enthusiasm were often persecuted. But despite anti-Spanish attitudes, what counted was not birth but loyalty to the ideals of the revolution. Indeed, independence leader Bernardino Rivadavia, whose role as head of the Unitarian faction will be discussed below, eagerly sought out liberal Spaniards with useful expertise and granted them speedy naturalization.[22] Immigration policy provided further evidence of this early vision of nationality as a matter of choice rather than as an immutable condition. In a bid to increase the population, in 1812 the new government issued a decree inviting individuals from "all nations" to come to the newly established nation.[23] Indeed, after independence was finally secured, attracting immigrants became one of the government's most urgent tasks.[24]

Finally, the nascent state's stance toward indigenous peoples and people of African descent also reflected the generalized belief that membership in the national community was a question of political loyalties rather than ancestry, cultural traits, or ethnicity. In 1813, the Constituent Assembly granted citizenship to native peoples living within the boundaries of colonial control and declared these Indians to be "perfectly free men, and equal in all the rights of the rest of the citizenry."[25] The subsequent electoral law of 1821 confirmed that all male citizens, including Indians, enjoyed the right of suffrage. Men of African descent faced a stiffer barrier, since slavery was not definitively abolished in Argentina until 1853. Still, the 1821 law explicitly extended voting rights to emancipated black males.[26]

To be sure, this vision of the Argentine nation as a political community open to humanity, whose members were bound primarily by shared loyalties to the new state, contained a glaring contradiction. Despite the apparent universalism and inclusiveness implicit in these early policies, the idea that some peoples were inherently more desirable than others formed a central part of early discourses about nation building.[27] Very early on, independence ideologues assumed that the democratic system they hoped to establish required citizens who shared common aspirations, customs, and habits of mind, and that these qualities were more likely to be possessed by white, non-Spanish Europeans. Such peoples, they believed, would help both to expunge the negative cultural legacy of Spanish colonialism and lessen the taint of Indian and African blood by whitening the population. European immigration, as Rivadavia famously stated, provided the "most efficient, and perhaps the only, means of destroying the degrading Spanish habits and the fatal gradation of castes."[28] The most desirable immigrant, he and his fellow revolutionaries argued, came from Protestant Europe, and the nation they sought to create would be ethnically white and culturally linked to Europe rather than to the rest of Latin America. Still, despite the ideal of Argentina as a white nation (an ideal that has remained unquestioned until very recently), the members of the 1813 Constitutional Assembly clearly saw nonwhites living within national borders and who accepted the authority of the state as legitimate members of the national community.

## UNITARIANS VERSUS FEDERALISTS

Argentina's independence generation's plans to build a prosperous, democratic society within the territorial framework of the old viceroyalty were soon dashed, and the region quickly plunged into turmoil. Indeed, it would take until 1862 for the country to be united under a single constitutional government.[29] Argentina's long and chaotic struggle for independence produced two opposing political movements with deeply conflicting ideas about how power and resources should be apportioned between Buenos Aires and the provinces. The Unitarians, based in the city of Buenos Aires, were energetic reformers, who believed in the need for a strong, centralized state that could bring enlightenment and progress to the creole masses. Federalists, in contrast, championed the cause of local control and favored a loose confederation of provinces rather than a unitary state. Deeply resentful of porteños (inhabitants of the port city of Buenos Aires), the Federalists were led by provincial caudillos (local strongmen) whose ability to mobilize local cowboys or gauchos made them formidable military opponents.

The Unitarians' guiding light was the previously mentioned Bernardino Rivadavia, an avid admirer of French culture and British political thought, who served as president of Argentina from 1826 to 1827.[30] Between the years 1820 and 1829, he oversaw a series of rapid reforms that helped to define Argentine liberalism in all its contradictions. In addition to establishing a university, Rivadavia continued to promote European immigration and actively sought free trade and closer commercial ties with Britain. To achieve this last goal, the government granted generous concessions to British merchants and oversaw the signing of a treaty, by which each country granted the other most favored nation status.[31] More controversially, Rivadavia aimed his sights at the church, curtailing some of its traditional privileges and lowering tithes. Although he was initially intrigued by the idea of establishing a constitutional monarchy, during the 1820s he helped implement a new electoral law, which extended suffrage, and oversaw the writing of the 1826 Constitution, which declared the nation to be a republic.[32] The Unitarian experiment collapsed after Federalist resistance to the new constitution forced Rivadavia to resign. Civil war erupted again, and when the dust settled, Buenos Aires came under the control of Juan Manuel de Rosas, a wealthy rancher and Federalist caudillo. Weary of conflict, the local assembly elected Rosas governor of Buenos Aires Province and granted him dictatorial powers he used to bring stability to what became known as the Confederation of the Rio de la Plata.

Rosas's long and bloody reign, which lasted—with a brief interruption—until his military defeat in 1852, would alter but not fundamentally transform the prevailing understanding of the nation as first and foremost a political community.[33] Evident to most was the fact that the bitter divisions between Federalists and Unitarians were ideological and political rather than ethnic. And while there might exist, broadly speaking, some cultural differences between Unitarian and Federalist leaders (with respect to degrees of religiosity, reading habits, and entertainment preferences, etc.), these were understood to be acquirable, rather than inherent and fixed.[34] Thus the leaders of both factions agreed that national unity was possible and could be achieved, not by some sort of ethnic homogenization, but by forging a lasting political pact between the provinces that could be ratified in a written constitution. Rosas shared the belief that the solution to Argentine instability lay in the political realm, but his view of how to achieve political unity differed from that of both the Unitarians and of his fellow Federalists. Despite pressure from members of his own faction and his earlier pledge to produce a constitution informed by Federalist principles, Rosas resolutely refused to organize a constitutional assembly.[35] Instead, he sought to unify the nation by increasing his personal power and demanding that all citizens embrace a single political faith—that of the Federalist cause.[36]

To achieve this goal, Rosas employed both force and pageantry. Besides ruthlessly persecuting his opponents, he imposed a series of rules requiring citizens to display their loyalty to Federalism by wearing red items. (Red was the signature color of Federalism.) All civil employees and members of the military, for example, had to wear a red badge bearing the inscription "Federation or Death." Over time, the dictator progressively outfitted his troops in increasing amounts of red apparel to include red ponchos, caps, jackets, and hatbands. The expanding vermillion sea soon engulfed the general population and the city itself. New regulations required that housefronts be painted red, and individuals were well advised to wear red whenever in public and to festoon the bridles of their horses with bits of red cloth.[37] To enforce these decrees, Rosas assumed control of all public and private institutions, including the press, courts, and legislature. He also enlisted the aid of the church, which, because of Rivadavia's anticlerical measures, eagerly lent its support to the Federalist cause.

What impact, then, did the Rosas regime have on conceptions of Argentine identity? Although in many ways Rosas represented the antithesis of the progressive Rivadavia and identified his regime with Catholicism, the system he envisioned was one that was fundamentally secular and contractual.[38] As Jorge Myers has convincingly argued, the political discourse of *rosismo* was more than anything else rooted in the tradition of classical republicanism, with its emphasis on civic virtue, political unanimity, and subordination to authority.[39] That having been said, however, Rosas's long rule *did* help to reshape ideas about Argentine identity by introducing more culturalist notions of nationality that competed with, but never displaced, earlier political and state-based understandings.

This occurred in two ways. First, again following Myers's analysis, was the introduction of an "'Americanist' strand" into the nationalist rhetoric of the Rosas period, a strand that stressed the distinctiveness of the recently formed American nations. One aspect of this new Americanist identity put forth by Rosas and his key supporters was the insistence that the new American republics faced very different conditions than those of Europe, and thus required a *sui generis* form of republicanism, the most perfect expression of which could be found in *rosismo*.[40] Also contributing to this new Americanist sensibility were civic rituals, such as the forced wearing of red and the shouting of anti-Unitarian slogans. Although these were imposed from above, they undoubtedly helped forge a shared sense of identity that was as much cultural as political.[41] A final element helping to consolidate this new Americanism was the wave of patriotic fervor aroused by the French and later the French/British blockade of the Rio de la Plata (1838–39 and 1845–48, respectively). Although Rosas himself rarely engaged in outright xenophobia, the general public perceived the blockades as threats to national sovereignty. This emerging Americanist identity, Myers has argued, served to strengthen a sense—already evident during the revolutionary years—that the new nations possessed a distinctive, uniquely New World culture characterized by a love of freedom and independence.[42]

A second, and very different way in which Rosas contributed to the rise of new culturalist understandings of Argentine identity was the dictator's impact on the young intellectuals who came of age during his regime, the above-mentioned Generation of 1837. As heirs to the Unitarian tradition and admirers of the United States and Protestant Europe, these young thinkers were forced to grapple with the fact that Rosas was adored by the popular classes. In an attempt to understand the dictator's appeal, the members of this generation drew on currents of Romantic thought then circulating in Europe. Particularly important were the writings of Edgard Quinet, Jules Michelet, and Victor Cousin, all French interpreters of German Romanticism. Also significant were the ideas of Italian theorist Giambattista Vico, whose writings appeared in the Rio de la Plata region through Michelet's translations.[43] Thus in many ways,

Argentine intellectual trends mirrored nineteenth-century thought in Europe, as Enlightenment universalism gave way to an appreciation of the particular. But in the case of Argentina, what made these ideas attractive was the need to make sense of Rosas's widespread appeal.

In considering why the Unitarian project had collapsed, the members of the Generation of 1837 argued that the independence leaders had erred by failing to recognize the enduring cultural legacies of Spanish colonialism. Drawing from the Romantic notion that the peoples of each nation possess a unitary collective character forged by a common history, language, and religion, these thinkers criticized their predecessors for having thought it possible to create a nation on the basis of liberal principles, simply by establishing the proper institutional framework and without grasping the supposed nature of the Argentine people. In the words of Esteban Echeverría, a key member of the new generation, the Unitarians' great eagerness to establish a democracy had led them to believe that "they could implant representative institutions in one blow."[44] Such an approach had failed, he argued, because Spanish colonial rule had taught the Argentine population to be "vassals and colonists" rather than free men, and thus had produced a people that were ill-prepared for self-government.[45]

Because of this diagnosis, the members of the Generation of 1837 believed that the task at hand was to discover the occult factors and legacies that had formed (or rather deformed) the Argentine people. Undoubtedly the most famous effort to discern the hidden forces, which had supposedly produced a people ill-suited for democracy (and thus led to the rise of Rosas), was Domingo F. Sarmiento's 1845 work *Facundo*. Sarmiento, who became a pariah to post-1930 nationalists, attributed Argentina's contemporary woes to the barbarism of the Argentine countryside. In his view, the vast expanses of the pampas had created a brutish way of life that made civilized society impossible. Also at fault was the process of miscegenation, by which the Spanish, Indian, and Negro "races" that inhabited the countryside had mixed to create a new human type characterized by its "love of idleness and lack of industry."[46] According to Sarmiento, this combination of environmental, ethnic, and biological factors had produced a society prone to fanaticism and barbarism and thus made possible the rise of Rosas.

Such a pessimistic diagnosis of the supposed Argentine national character was leavened by the conviction, rooted in the Romantic view, that all nations inevitably progress as human history unfolds. Moreover, although this process occurred according to hidden universal laws, nations were understood to contain within themselves a unique set of immanent principles that propelled them forward toward their own, pre-ordained future. Within this evolutionary, pluralistic conception of history, the Rosas dictatorship came to be seen not as a catastrophic break down of civilized norms that had doomed the nation but as a moment in Argentina's historical development that was destined to pass.[47] Similarly, the belief that nations evolve along distinctive paths also reassured these thinkers that, although Argentina would not follow the exact historical trajectory of the United States or the more "civilized" countries of Europe, it could still achieve greatness. Embracing this historicist vision, Alberdi affirmed that each pueblo "develops according to its own mode," in a way that obeys "constant laws" but also in response to the specific conditions of a particular time and place. Thus, he concluded, "each pueblo . . . has and should have its own [form of] civilization."[48] This vision of history also provided a basis for celebrating some of the distinctive qualities of Argentine culture. Accordingly, thinkers such as Alberdi and Juan María Gutiérrez called for the production of a literature, philosophy, history, and way of thinking that was uniquely Argentine.[49]

But while European Romanticism provided the Generation of 1837 with both a conceptual framework for making sense of Rosas and a reason to be optimistic about the nation's future, its vision of the nation and history posed inescapable conundrums. One of the most pressing problems inherent within the Romantic vision was the question of whether or not human efforts could shape the course of a nation's historical development. If, as Romanticism held, nations develop inexorably along paths according to internal, immanent principles, what role could these men play in guiding Argentina toward a better future? Historian Elias Palti succinctly captures the dilemma when he notes that the members of the Generation of 1837 found themselves caught between their criticisms of Unitarians for believing that the Argentine people could be changed through an "act of will" and their own "vocation" of eradicating the social vestiges of the colonial period.[50] In that they were self-confident aspirants to political power, it is unsurprising that the members of the

Generation of 1837 believed themselves to be destined to play a central role in leading Argentina forward. Thus, although these individuals wrestled in different ways with the question of human agency in historical evolution, they reached a similar conclusion: men like themselves, who were capable of grasping the occult forces of history, could devise policies and institutions that would speed the nation along its preordained path.[51]

In terms of concrete policies, the Generation of 1837 agreed on the need to continue the Unitarian project of transforming the Argentine people by making them more culturally and ethnically European. These goals could be accomplished, they believed, by fostering industry and commerce, promoting education, establishing appropriate laws, and—most importantly—encouraging European immigration. Following Rivadavia, these intellectuals saw immigration as a means to populate the vast expanses of the national territory and to jumpstart the cultural transformation they envisioned. Alberdi was one of the period's most vocal advocates of European immigration. Famously proclaiming that "to populate is to govern," he argued that the example of immigrants, rather than education, would be the key to improving the Argentine masses. Europeans, he insisted, represented "living pieces" of the qualities of order, self-discipline, and industriousness. Once they were in Argentina, the immigrants' values would prove "contagious," thereby infecting the creole population with new habits of work, thrift, and entrepreneurship.[52]

The understandings of nationality and history associated with European Romanticism also influenced ideas about how best to organize the state. While continually affirming their belief in the principles of equality and democracy, the members of this generation believed that achieving these goals would be a gradual process.[53] What was needed, they argued, were not perfect political institutions imported from other countries but ones tailored to the Argentine people at their particular historical moment. Thus as Alberdi insisted, it was essential to "govern ourselves, think, write and proceed in all things, not through imitation of any other people on earth . . . but exclusively according to the demands of the general laws of the human spirit and the individual laws of our national condition."[54] Similarly, Echeverría proclaimed that it was useless "to work in opposition to the peculiar conditions of [a pueblo's] *ser*."[55]

Instead, he believed, political leaders had to work *with*, rather than *against*, a people's supposed underlying character and situation. For Alberdi and his contemporaries, this meant retreating from the immediate goal of full democracy in favor of an evolutionary model. What was needed at this point, they believed, was the establishment of the "possible republic"—that is, a set of institutions that would limit the voices of the masses. Only once the people were sufficiently "elevated" could these limits be removed and Argentina become a "true republic."[56]

The dual project of developing appropriate political institutions and transforming the Argentine people was evident in the Argentine Constitution of 1853, the blueprint for which was Alberdi's 1852 *Bases y puntos de partida para la organización política de la República Argentina*. Although in many ways advocating for a system similar to that of the United States, Alberdi insisted that his prescription for the new constitution was no mere copy but was rather firmly rooted in Argentine realities and its present stage of development.[57] On the political side, the document followed the US constitution in granting universal suffrage and establishing three branches of government. But in contrast to the US model, Alberdi gave heightened power to the president, a move that reflected his admiration of the Chilean system and his belief that in general Hispanic Americans were not sufficiently "saxonized" for a truly representative system to work.[58] In addition to laying out the institutional framework for the Argentine state, this document also includes classical liberal economic provisions aimed at promoting economic growth, such as a clear defense of individual property rights, prohibition of internal trade barriers between the provinces, and the opening of rivers to foreign commercial vessels. Also key was the explicit requirement that the federal government promote European immigration.

Stepping back, what did the nineteenth-century turn toward Romanticism mean for the Generation of 1837's understanding of Argentine identity? Did Romantic influences provoke a complete reconceptualization of the Argentine nation that rejected the contractualist vision of the early postindependence period? And how did these notions shape how these individuals understood the *bases* of Argentine identity? Were Argentines defined by their supposed shared ethno-cultural traits, or by their loyalty to the Argentine state and the political values it enshrined? Related to this question, of course, was the problem of who could *become* an Argentine and on what terms, a particularly significant issue in light of the Generation of 1837's emphasis on fomenting immigration.

The contradictory nature of mid-nineteenth-century Argentine Romantic thought means that the answers to these questions are themselves contradictory. As noted, while Romantic ideas about nationality and history helped the Generation of 1837 make sense of its circumstances, they also proved an awkward fit with its members' hopes for constructing a nation that would fulfill the liberal promise of the revolution against Spain. In addition to the above-mentioned problem of whether human actions could shape the course of a nation's evolution was the more basic question of the nation's origins.[59] With the exception of Bartolomé Mitre, who argued that the Argentine nation had formed over the course of the colonial period, most members of his generation insisted that the country was a new nation, whose existence dated back only to the break with Spain. Thus while agreeing that the colonial past had marked the Argentine people, they believed the nation itself had been created by the conscious actions of its independence leaders. Echeverría, for example, affirmed that it was through the May Revolution of 1810 that the Argentine pueblo "began to exist as a pueblo."[60] In a similar vein, Alberdi proclaimed that "the popular hymns of our revolution of 1810 announced the appearance on the face of the earth of *a new and glorious nation*."[61] Writing more generally about how nations came to exist, Sarmiento very clearly embraced the contractualist view when he described nations as entities "constituted by deliberate acts by the people represented in assemblies" rather than products of the blind forces of history.[62]

Undoubtedly one reason the members of this generation rejected the idea that the Argentine nation had existed before the break with Spain was their negative assessment of Spanish colonialism, both in terms of the culture it had supposedly formed and the population it had supposedly produced. Thus when members of the Generation of 1837 urged artists, writers, and historians to produce works that were uniquely Argentine, their aim was *not* to celebrate a culture inherited from the colonial past but rather to create a new national culture *against* the past.[63] Moreover, the fact that this generation hoped European immigrants would help transform the habits and values of the native creoles, it is clear they also expected that this new national culture would reflect immigrant contributions.

The conviction that creoles, together with immigrants from liberal Europe, would create a new national culture raises the question of the role these individuals believed cultural traits (or ethnicity) should play in the nation's future identity. In other words, to what extent did the Romantic vision of nations as ethno-cultural entities come to eclipse the older, more traditional notion of Argentina as a fundamentally civic entity, whose members were bound together not by a common language, religion, or ancestry, but by their shared political values and loyalties? Despite the new emphasis on the construction of a distinctive national culture, it seems clear that members of the Generation of 1837 continued to emphasize the political as the basis of national identity and unity. Writing in 1879, for example, Alberdi argued that a solid constitution reflecting the realities of the country represented the "living union" of the people, and "the only real and permanent [source of unity] of each country."[64] In a similar vein, Sarmiento insisted that nations were formed by individuals linked by their "intelligence and will . . . not the land or blood (*sangre*)," reflecting his belief that nations were first and foremost manmade entities, defined by the values and decisions of their creators.[65] Thus Jorge Myers's view that, despite the impact of Romantic influences, political definitions of the nation continued to predominate seems apt. As he has observed for the latter half of the century, during this period, "discourse on the nature of [Argentine] national identity would tend to oscillate between emphasis on cultural and political definitions, but even when it was the cultural attributes which were stressed, these were almost always encompassed within or subordinated to the language of republicanism."[66]

The duel visions of the nation that Myers has observed can also be applied to the Generation of 1837's contradictory views on immigration and the question of who would be welcomed into the national community. European immigrants, of course, were to be embraced with open arms, and these thinkers advocated continuing the Unitarians' generous immigration policies, which would allow the foreign-born to decide the degree to which they retained their prior identities. Accordingly, tolerance for domestic diversity—of a certain sort—was explicitly provided for in the 1853 Constitution. For example, although the constitution called on the state to foment *European* immigration, it also made it illegal to prevent immigration from other regions, as long as the individuals in question came to Argentina to "work the land, improve industries, and introduce or teach the sciences and arts."[67] Once in Argentina, immigrants would enjoy full religious freedom, as well as "all the civil rights" of native-born citizens.[68] Naturalization remained easy to acquire, requiring only two years' residence.[69] In addition, although not spelled out in the constitution, immigrants were allowed to establish their own schools and to educate their children in their native tongues rather than in Spanish. Thus when envisioning the nation, this generation hewed closely to Unitarian understandings of Argentina as first and foremost a political entity, where people of diverse faiths, languages, and nationalities could participate fully in the economic and social life of the nation, and where the foreign born could easily become full-fledged citizens via a simple legal process.

But as was the case with the Unitarians, the Generation of 1837's volitional ideal of *argentinidad* contained contradictory elements, most notably in attitudes toward non-Europeans. Indeed, if anything, the conviction that Argentina was, or should be, a purely white nation intensified. Whereas earlier liberal leaders had at least acknowledged the multiethnic nature of their society by extending citizenship rights to indigenous males and free males of African descent, the men of the new generation held a more negative view of both nonwhites and miscegenation. In Sarmiento's 1845 *Facundo*, it will be recalled, the future president had lamented that the mixture of the Spanish, indigenous, and African "races" in the countryside had produced a people incapable of industry. His views on race and racial mixture would become even more extreme toward the end of his life, as scientific notions of race gained ground in Argentina.[70] For his part, Alberdi imagined an Argentina (and a Spanish America) completely free of nonwhites.[71] Alberdi's vision of an ethnically white nation would also come to inform his views on immigration. While remaining firm in his conviction that Argentina's borders should remain open to all, he insisted that "chinos" (Asians), Indians from Asia, and blacks from Africa were highly undesirable, and would "poison" the country rather than civilize it.[72]

## THE FADING OF ARGENTINA'S FIRST ROMANTICISM

The Romantic understandings of nationality and history that so powerfully shaped the worldview of the Generation of 1837 fell out of favor at the century's end, as political elites increasingly turned toward the new social science of positivism as an explanatory framework for understanding the nation's challenges.[73] Positivism, I will argue in a later chapter, would play a significant role in shaping ideas about Argentine nationality, but for now the important point is how this philosophical movement contributed to the ideal of "scientific politics." Notably eclectic, Argentine positivists stressed the need to develop an empirical or "scientific" approach to the study of politics and society. Through observation and analysis of social phenomena, they believed, it was possible to devise effective policies and modes of governance.[74] In Argentina and elsewhere in Latin America, late nineteenth-century positivism lent a scientific aura to the ruling elite's claim that their societies were best served by strong, highly centralized states that discouraged open electoral contests.

In Argentina, positivism was closely associated with the Partido Autónomo Nacional (PAN), a party that dominated the nation's political life from 1880 to 1914. Founded by Julio Roca, who served as president from 1880 to 1886, the PAN became a highly centralized political machine that used fraud and voter manipulation to retain power. Proclaiming his party's goals to be those of "peace and administration," Roca placed a premium on economic progress and on controlling what he saw as the destructive political passions of the previous decades.[75] Ardently liberal in many respects—his administration included several members of the highly anticlerical *Club Liberal*—Roca embraced the economic liberalism of the Generation of 1837. In the political realm, he also emphasized his debt to previous generations. Embracing their view of the nation as first and foremost a political community, but with an accompanying cultural component, he praised the writers of the 1853 Constitution as having produced a "magnificent cupola" that lay atop the "building of the nationality."[76] PAN's founder seemed particularly attuned to the ideas of Alberdi, especially in his belief that Argentines were still unready for a fully participatory democracy.[77]

The PAN's control was not absolute, and in 1890 a faction of democracy-minded elites staged an armed rebellion that forced a presidential shake up.[78] But for the most part, the party's system of political controls functioned remarkably well. Its success was undoubtedly in part the result of Roca's formidable political skills, but even more important was Argentina's booming export economy. Despite the economy's occasional downturn, the value of Argentina's exports rose spectacularly, soaring in value from 30.2 million gold pesos in 1870 to 483.5 million gold pesos in 1913.[79] Steady demand in Europe for cereals and chilled beef, technological advances in transportation, the expansion of wheat farming, and the eagerness of foreign capitalists to fund the building of railroads, slaughter/packing houses, granaries, and port facilities all came together to catapult Argentina into the ranks of the world's top exporters of foodstuffs. Personal wealth increased accordingly, and by 1913 Argentina's per capita income had topped that of several European countries and was on par with Germany's.[80] Such palpable material progress did much to calm intraelite conflict and provided the PAN with the means and legitimacy to extend its rule until well into the twentieth century.

This economic boom also brought European immigration. Beginning around 1870, what had been a small trickle of immigrants swelled into a veritable human tide. Between 1871 and 1914, almost six million Europeans, primarily from Italy and Spain, arrived on Argentine shores. Of these, approximately 3,200,000 settled there permanently.[81] But these figures tell only part of the story: perhaps more revealing is how the immigrants' numbers measured up against the size of the native population. By 1914, almost a third of Argentina's population of 7,885,237 was foreign born.[82] More striking still were the percentages of foreign born in the city of Buenos Aires, where immigrants tended to settle. According to the 1914 census, just under half of the city's population of 1.57 million was foreign born, and foreign-born males substantially outnumbered native-born males.[83]

It is difficult to overstate the economic, political, and cultural impact of such massive numbers of immigrants on Argentine society. Although the nation's elites remained convinced that any lessening of this human current would prove fatal to the republic's progress, how to incorporate the immigrants, and on what terms, became *the* pressing question of the day. Inextricably bound to this challenge, of course, was the nature of the nation into which the immigrants were to be integrated. Was Argentina understood to be first and foremost a civic entity, into which immigrants were integrated politically, or was the Argentine nation defined primarily by the collective cultural traits of the existing population? If the latter, were these supposed cultural traits acquirable by the newcomers, or were these qualities seen to be rooted in birth or ancestry? Clearly, the debate in Argentina over immigration, like that of *any* society, was also a debate over national identity.

This was the context of Argentina's "second" Romantic moment, one that would cast a long shadow over the nation's intellectual and political life. The fact that Romanticism' vision of the nation as an ethnocultural community proved attractive in early twentieth-century Argentina is not surprising, for it is precisely in societies experiencing mass immigration that ethnic-nationalist movements tend to arise. What puzzles, at first blush, is that the cultural nationalists who promoted this vision of the nation recognized no similarities between themselves and the Generation of 1837. While generally respectful of this venerated group of national leaders, the cultural nationalists found little of use in their ideas. Rather than seeing these men as thinkers who embraced similar Romantic-inspired ideas about nationality and history, and who faced some of the same conundrums inherent in this vision, the early twentieth-century intellectuals tended to focus only on the proimmigration elements of their predecessors' thought. Upon further consideration, however, this one-sided, blinkered view of the Generation of 1837 makes sense, for the two groups of thinkers faced radically different circumstances and drew on Romanticism for radically different purposes. Whereas the Generation of 1837 saw in Romanticism a way to understand the rise of a dictator, the cultural nationalists faced a world whose very contours seemed in flux, and where many native Argentines felt themselves to be drowning in a sea of foreigners and foreignness.

Given the enormous impact of immigration, it is worth pondering how the country would have fared without such a massive influx, and to consider an alternative, hypothetical past in which turn-of-the-century Argentina enjoyed the benefits of foreign demand for its products and received a much more modest number of immigrants.[84] If this had occurred, it seems likely that fifty years of prosperity, along with more rapid long distance transportation and new forms of communication, would have done much to unify the country and create the culturally homogeneous population that nineteenth-century liberals had envisioned. Within this scenario, it is also likely that pride in the country's success and the demands of national unity would have led artists, intellectuals, and state bureaucrats to promote the notion of a common and distinctive

Argentine culture. At the same time, however, it is highly doubtful that these cultural attributes—whether real or imagined—would have come to be seen as the main sources of Argentine identity. Rather, as democratic institutions also evolved and became more representative (a process that culminated in the electoral reforms of 1912), culturalist understandings of Argentine identity would have remained subordinate to the ideal of Argentina as a nation defined first and foremost by its constitution and the political principles it enshrined. This did not happen, of course, and the disruptive arrival of massive numbers of Europeans produced new debates over the very nature of Argentine nationality. It is to these debates that we now turn.

# TWO

# National Identity in the Age of Mass Immigration

*The Romantic Turn and the Ideal of the Argentine Race*

The arrival of millions of European immigrants between 1870 and 1930 transformed the social and cultural terrain on which discussions of Argentine identity took place, and posed inescapable dilemmas for Argentina's intellectual and political elite. While few native elites questioned the continued need for immigrants, the massive influx of foreigners raised fears on a number of fronts. One source of concern was the nature of the immigrants themselves. Whereas nineteenth-century liberals had hoped to attract yeoman farmers from liberal Europe, the immigrants who arrived during the closing decades of the nineteenth century were of a different sort. Predominately from the poorest sectors of Italy and Spain, these often uneducated newcomers formed the basis of the nascent urban working class and were at the forefront of the labor militancy that swept Argentina during the opening decades of the new century. According to many native elites, this unrest stemmed not from low wages and poor conditions but from the "exotic" left-wing ideologies brought by ungrateful foreigners.[1]

Another source of anti-immigrant sentiment stemmed from concern that the newcomers were contributing to racial degeneration, with *racial* here understood in biological or genetic terms. In Argentina, as in the rest of Latin America, the final decades of the nineteenth century witnessed a growing interest in scientific racism as a way of understanding the continent's backwardness vis-à-vis Europe. Racial theories had special poignancy in such countries as Mexico and Brazil, which had large indigenous and African-American populations, but Argentine intellectuals and leaders from across the political spectrum also embraced the goal of social reform through racial/biological improvement. Influenced by the ideas of Britain's Herbert Spencer, French positivist Gustav Le Bon, and Italian criminologists, and fearful that Argentina was receiving "inferior stock" from Europe, adherents to scientific racism often pointed to social unrest, crime, disease, and delinquency as evidence of racial degeneration.[2] This rising xenophobia, however, was tempered by the broadly held consensus that the country continued to need immigrant labor and that these newcomers should settle permanently on Argentine soil.[3] Yet challenges remained. Whereas during much of the nineteenth century, liberal political leaders had seen immigration as a means of establishing a national culture free from Spanish influence, in the era of mass immigration the problem became how to incorporate the newcomers and forge a nation from a heterogeneous people. At this critical juncture in Argentine history, the answers to these challenges were in no way straightforward and inevitably hinged on how Argentines understood what their nation was, as well as on the nature of the bonds that held them together as a people.

## INTEGRATING THE IMMIGRANT INTO THE CIVIC NATION

Given the traditional understanding of Argentina as first and foremost a political community, it is not surprising that many members of the political elite stressed the need to transform the immigrants into participating citizens. As noted, becoming a naturalized Argentine citizen was not difficult, requiring only that the applicant be at least eighteen years of age and have two years residency.[4] But despite this easy path to citizenship, naturalization rates remained extremely low, and averaged about 5 percent for immigrants arriving between 1850 and 1930.[5] One important barrier to naturalization was the reluctance of immigrants to relinquish their native citizenship. Although Argentina allowed for dual citizenship, Italy and Spain—which supplied most of the immigrants—did not. In truth, however, Argentine citizenship offered few benefits beyond the privilege of voting in national elections. Thus although immigrants engaged in informal types of political activity through mutual aid societies and immigrant associations, they—like their native-born counterparts—saw national elections as largely irrelevant to their lives.[6]

For some nineteenth-century elites, these low naturalization rates posed a grave danger to the republic. In the final years of his life, for example, a disillusioned Sarmiento expressed dismay over the immigrants' reluctance to naturalize, seeing this as an impediment to the nation's political and social integrity.[7] Joining Sarmiento was prominent jurist Estanislao Zeballos, who warned that, unless immigrants could be persuaded to naturalize, Argentina would be bereft of the citizens necessary to "use, defend, and perfect" the nation's political institutions.[8] In 1887, both Sarmiento and Zeballos joined other prominent members of Argentine society to form the Comité Patriótico, whose aim it was to promote naturalization. Mainstream newspapers such as *La Prensa* supported these efforts, calling the naturalization of immigrants "a supreme necessity of the nationality."[9] Elite interest in the naturalization question heightened in 1887–90, as various proposals were put forth to deal with the problem.[10] Even the PAN, whose leaders were not noted for their democratic fervor, briefly seized on the issue after the 1890 rebellion by the reformist Unión Cívica. Fearful that the Unión Cívica would win support among the immigrant population, PAN legislators sought to undercut its rival by proposing that all immigrants who had resided in the country for seven consecutive years be granted automatic citizenship. This plan fell apart in large part owing to fears such legislation would discourage potential immigrants.[11]

The great flurry of concern over naturalization died as quickly as it had blossomed. With the exception of the leadership of the newly formed Socialist Party, the country's political elite would never again take up the issue in a serious fashion.[12] At the same time, the question of how best to bind the newcomers to the nation remained, as politicians and educators alike continued to express concern over the country's lack of cohesion. As interest in converting adult immigrants into Argentine citizens waned, attention shifted to their offspring. The result was a heightened emphasis on patriot education aimed at instilling in immigrant children a love of the fatherland or patria. And while certainly different than the Rosas-style nationalism that demanded loyalty to a single political faction, like the propaganda of this period, the new patriotic education placed a premium on blind loyalty to the state while de-emphasizing the rights and obligations of citizenship.

Interest in patriotic education surfaced as early as the mid-1880s, when reformers pushed through curricular changes that placed increased emphasis on Argentine history and geography.[13] In 1884, Congress passed Law 1420 (Ley Nacional de Educación) that—besides banning religious instruction in public schools—called for a greater focus on nationalist themes. The organization most responsive to this new charge was the Consejo Nacional de Educación, whose influential journal *Monitor de la educación común* referred frequently to the issue of patriotic education.[14] In its view, education was the most effective way to build the "cement of nationality"[15] and to give "cohesion to the constitutive elements" of the nation.[16] New regulations requiring that schools display the national flag and observe Argentina's two independence days soon followed, and by the end of the decade a wide-scale effort to infuse the curriculum with a new nationalist content was underway.[17]

These efforts intensified in the new century. Of particular importance was the leadership of José María Ramos Mejía, a prominent positivist intellectual. As president of the Consejo Nacional de Educación from 1908 to 1912, Ramos Mejía urged schools to discard foreign-authored texts and encouraged teachers to organize civic festivals that would instill in their pupils a love for the patria. These festivals often featured military marches and patriotic programs, during which students were encouraged to scream out, in "tortured verses," their love for the fatherland and their "promise to defend the national flag with their last drop of blood."[18] It was through the nationalizing efforts of the schools, Ramos Mejía noted approvingly, that the children of Argentina's varied immigrant population were beginning to be "the depository of the future sentiment of the nationality."[19] Another prominent intellectual, sociologist Carlos Octavio Bunge, was also a key supporter of patriotic education and made clear his acceptance of Argentina's internal diversity, at least for the foreseeable future. Bunge, who famously described Latin America's complex racial make-up as an "indigestible stew," insisted that,

at least for the moment, contemporary societies were unavoidably pluralistic.[20] Given this reality, he argued, it was necessary "to seek social
unity in something distinctive and superior to ethnic, linguistic, religious
or geographic unity." This something, he continued, was the "unity of
sentiment and the idea of the *patria*."[21]

## THE ROMANTIC TURN

The belief that Argentine unity could rest solely on the civic religion of
state patriotism, however, was not universally shared. Concurrent with
efforts to promote a unified patriotic sentiment that would transcend the
pluralism of Argentine society and cement it together was the rise of a
countervailing set of ideas based on the conviction that Argentina's survival required a deeper unity than that imagined by nineteenth-century
liberals. Inspired by the ideas of Romantic nationalism then sweeping
Europe, these individuals embraced the notion that nations, by definition, were ethno-cultural communities, whose members were bound together by language, religion, shared history, and common mental and
emotional traits.

This vision of nationhood came through clearly in late nineteenth-
century parliamentary debates over immigrant-run private schools.
Alarmed by the growing number of such schools, in 1894, Deputy Indalecio Gómez introduced a bill to require that instruction in both public
and private institutions be carried out in Spanish. According to the bill's
supporters, all children living on Argentine soil should learn a single, officially sanctioned language. To be sure, the argument that nations should
be monolingual does not necessarily reflect the influence of ideas associated with Romantic nationalism: individuals who imagine the nation in
primarily political terms can, with some justification, claim that exercising the rights and obligations of citizenship require that citizens share a
common language.[22] But in the case of late nineteenth-century Argentina, it was clear that the call for Spanish instruction was not attributable
to pragmatic grounds. Rather, it stemmed from the conviction that a
single language was essential to maintaining the nation's cultural and
ethnic homogeneity. In defending his proposal, for example, Gómez
argued that preserving Spanish as the national language was important

because language "casts its indissoluble bonds into the depths of the (individual) soul, where sentiment, ideas and character come into being."[23] Deputy Marco Avellaneda also employed reasoning seemingly inspired by Romantic ideas about the links between language and nationality when explaining his support for the bill. Language, he proclaimed was "the basis of national unity" and was "that which is most essentially peculiar to the people, and the most exact manifestation of its character." Continuing, Avellaneda argued that the national language "always conserves the consciousness of the nationality."[24]

Opponents of the bill were unconvinced and very clearly understood that the debate over requiring instruction in Spanish was in many ways a proxy debate over the meaning of nationality. In refuting his colleagues' arguments, Deputy Emilio Gouchón bluntly rejected the link between nationality and language. Pointing to the cases of Switzerland and Belgium, he noted that these were countries where a plurality of languages coexisted with "a profound sense of nationhood."[25] Similarly, Córdoba deputy Ponciano Vivanco argued that, while education itself was supremely important, the language in which it was carried out wasn't. Language, he insisted, was "not an essential element" of nationality. Instead, Vivanco affirmed, "the nation is a collection (*agrupación*) of individuals that have common laws that regulate their relations, occupy an extension of territory, and have their own sovereign government."[26] Francisco Barroetaveña responded more harshly. The bill, he argued, represented an "obscurantist, reactionary" tendency with nefarious consequences. "After the unity of language," he complained, supporters of the bill will ask for "unity of faith, and unity of race." Casting his lot with those who identified *argentinidad* with citizenship, Barroetaveña proclaimed that, if the goal was to fuse together the "Argentine family," this was best accomplished through "the naturalization of foreigners," "wise laws," and the "guarantee of liberties to all inhabitants."[27]

As is clear from this parliamentary dust-up over language, during this period no single vision of nationhood enjoyed hegemony among Argentina's political elite. But despite the clarity apparent in this particular debate, it is important to note that the battle lines between these competing understandings of nationhood were not always so starkly drawn. Overall, the situation could best be described as one of flux and confusion, as different and often conflicting ideas about nationhood and the meaning of nationality circulated freely.[28]

Nowhere is this more evident than in the rhetoric of Argentina's first significant nationalist organization: the Argentine Patriotic League (LPA).[29] The LPA was established in 1919 during the presidency of Hipólito Yrigoyen and in the wake of a general strike in early January.[30] Angered by the government's conciliatory posture toward labor, armed vigilante groups accompanied police in attacking working-class neighborhoods during what became known at the *Semana Trágica*, or "Tragic Week." Jewish immigrants, who the vigilantes believed were Bolsheviks bent on spreading revolutionary ideas, became special targets. Soon afterward, civilian leaders, with the support of the police and the military, organized the LPA.[31] Under the leadership of Manuel Carlés, the league grew quickly, and by the 1920s it had established 550 male and 41 female brigades throughout the country.[32] The league's purpose, according to Carlés, was to defend Argentina against the "human dregs" who had washed up on the nation's shores and who brought with them a "European animosity" that was at odds with the "optimist spirit" of Argentina.[33] Such foreigners, Carlés complained elsewhere, were attempting to "deform Argentine civilization."[34]

What is of interest here is how Carlés understood the nature of this supposed deformation, and how he and his fellow league members understood the nation they pledged to defend. Did league members see *argentinidad* as rooted in a unified bundle of ethno-cultural traits that were intrinsic rather than acquirable? Or did they, like liberals, see shared political values and loyalties as the primary sources of national identity, and thus embrace a vision of nationality that welcomed foreigners who were willing to embrace the constitution and accept local values, norms, and behaviors? There is no single answer to these questions. Rather, what emerges from the speeches and essays of league members is an array of often conflicting notions about the nature of Argentine nationality. These notions, moreover, mirrored a broader ambivalence among native Argentines about their collective identity and the role immigrants would play in shaping it.

Much of LPA rhetoric suggests that league members did indeed embrace the traditional liberal view of Argentina as a civic community, whose members were bound together by their shared political values and loyalties. Besides celebrating historical events, such as the defeat of Rosas, that were central to liberalism's triumph, Carlés insisted that the initial impulse for organizing the LPA was the desire to defend Argentina from foreigners who "threatened to alter the Constitution."[35] The LPA also took great pains to make clear its belief that Argentina should remain open to "good" immigrants, and should reject only those who threatened the established order.[36] Immigrants who respected the country's laws, found productive work, and acquiesced to the status quo, according to the LPA, would continue to be welcomed with open arms. Indeed, so pro-immigration was the LPA that in 1926 it published, as part of the proceedings of its seventh Congress, two reports that expressed concern over the *decrease* in the number of immigrants entering the country.[37]

Further evidence of the LPA's inclusive, civic notion of nationality was the LPA's support for patriotic education, suggesting that it considered loyalty and patriotic sentiment the most important attributes of *argentinidad*. Indeed, the league saw one of its main tasks as that of promoting patriotic sentiment in both immigrants and natives, organizing patriotic festivals that frequently drew larger crowds than those sponsored by the state.[38] Moreover, the focus of this patriotic fervor, according to LPA member José León Suárez, should be on the future and not the past. Argentina, Suárez argued, was a "new society" with a "nationality [still] in formation." Also suggesting an inclusive, civic vision of Argentina was his insistence that league brigades include both natives *and* immigrants.[39] In fact, immigrants, including Jewish ones, did indeed join the league. Despite the generalized anti-Semitism of the Argentine upper class and the common identification of Jews with subversive ideologies, the LPA voted to allow Jewish members. And while exact numbers are impossible to determine, historian Sandra McGee Deutsch has found that Jews often served as officers of brigades, especially in the province of Entre Rios where Jewish colonies were often established.[40]

Taken together, these actions and rhetoric suggest that the league's concept of Argentine nationality differed little from that of traditional liberals: Argentina was first and foremost a civic community, whose identity and unity were rooted in shared political values and loyalties. Yet there is also evidence of a more exclusivist vision of *argentinidad* that was far less tolerant of internal diversity and that hints at the influence of the Romantic vision of nations as homogeneous ethno-cultural communities. The league's views on religion are illustrative. Although league members generally refrained from insisting on the Catholic nature of Argentine society, they were very clear that only Christians could be true Argentines.[41] The importance of Argentina's Spanish (or Castilian) heritage also appeared with some frequency in LPA literature. Writing in 1920, for example, Carlés lauded the "brave and hardy Castilians of the eighteenth century," who had bequeathed to present-day Argentines their democratic instincts, sentimental spirit, and "sense of honor." He affirmed as well that Argentines' innate sense of equality reflected "the pulsation of the Castilian conscience."[42] Carlés would bring these two themes together in 1928, when he criticized the secularism of the Argentine schools. By ignoring God and spiritual matters, he complained, "it seems as though the national education system exists for the purpose of erasing from the Argentine soul all that is noble from its original Castilian race . . . and to replace the congenital generosity of our race with the materialism of a decadent Europe."[43]

We also see, particularly toward the end of the 1920s, an increasing concern with ethnicity and the state of an imagined national "soul," themes that were especially prevalent at the league's 1928 National Congress. In his opening address, for example, Carlés (who remained the LPA's president) lamented that immigration had altered Argentines' "ethnic unity" by introducing into the country so many "races." Because immigrants brought with them diverse ideologies and religions, he opined, it was essential to forge from all these disparate peoples "a single national personality." The central problem with immigration, he concluded, is that "we either reform the strangers or they will deform the Argentine soul."[44] Fellow LPA member Gastón Lestard expressed similar concerns when he warned that care must be taken to prevent immigrants from "subverting" the "Argentine soul." Indeed, Lestard believed it was time to reconsider the country's traditional open door policy.[45] Also included in the published proceedings of the Ninth Congress, somewhat curiously, was a 1906 essay by A. Garlarce. It was unclear if Garlarce participated in the 1928 Congress, or even if he was alive at this point, but the fact that Congress organizers included his essay in the published proceedings suggests that they found its themes relevant. Like Lestard, Garlarce cautioned his fellow Argentines to think carefully about whether to continue welcoming large numbers of immigrants. "We receive from Europe," he complained, people who are mostly poor and who bring to Argentina "the blood of various nations." Because of this heteroge-neity, Garlarce continued, and because this immigration will "continue to change our national characteristic," it was impossible to predict the nature of "our future race."[46]

As is clear from the LPA's contradictory discourse, during this period ideas about the basis and nature of Argentine nationality were very much in flux. But it is also evident that, as the century progressed, the notion that nations were—or should be—homogeneous ethno-cultural communities and that their people should be of a single "race" gained broader acceptance. In other words, the isolated, late nineteenth-century portrayals of Argentina as an organic ethno-cultural community threatened by immigration had, by the late 1920s, become an increas-ingly common framework for discussing the nation's identity.

## CULTURAL NATIONALISM AND THE ROMANTIC TURN

Central to this transition was the deepening influence of a generation of thinkers who came of age in the midst of Argentina's great wave of mass immigration, and who responded to this challenge by turning toward Romantic ideas about nationality. Known later in Argentine historiog-raphy as the cultural nationalists, most members of this group were young men raised in the provinces, who had come to Buenos Aires in their late teens to attend the university. Many, such as Manuel Gálvez, Ricardo Rojas, Emilio Becher, and Juan Pablo Echagüe, were from prominent families, whose social and political connections allowed them an easy entry into Argentina's burgeoning world of letters.[47] A notable feature of the cultural nationalists' thought was their obsession with the supposed cosmopolitanism of Buenos Aires, and the loss of what they saw as Ar-gentina's authentic national traditions. One source of this cosmopoli-tanism, according to these young intellectuals, was the traditional liberal elite, who had long taken their cultural cues from Europe.[48] The cultural nationalists also took aim at immigrants and questioned the wisdom of Argentina's traditional open-door policy. Writing in the Buenos Aires newspaper La Nación, for example, Emilio Becher lamented the ill effects of this "imprudent adventure" that had led to an "anarchy of races" and to the weakening of Argentina's authentic culture.[49]

Given the dramatic changes of the period, such laments about the loss of traditional values and the belief that immigrants were responsible for eroding Argentine culture are not surprising. They have led many scholars to portray the cultural nationalists as xenophobic, backward-looking reactionaries, who paved the way for the right-wing nationalism of the 1930s and beyond.[50] To be sure, an element of nostalgia for a supposedly purer past does indeed run through much of their writings, but what is important for our purposes is the fact that accompanying this call to defend Argentine culture from the corrosive forces of foreign influences was a vision of nationality that bore a strong resemblance to that associated with Romantic nationalism. As discussed above, the idea of Argentina as a unique ethno-cultural community had appeared in the late nineteenth century. But it was during the first three decades of the twentieth century, in large part owing to the influence of the cultural nationalists, that this vision of nationhood gained widespread currency.

The best introduction to the ideas of this generation is the work of Ricardo Rojas, whose 1909 *La restauración nacionalista* (the nationalist restoration) is considered one of cultural nationalism's foundational texts. In this and subsequent works, Rojas promoted a deeply mystical vision of Argentine nationhood that proved surprisingly influential. Although few today take his ideas seriously, he wielded remarkable influence during the early decades of the century. Extraordinarily prolific, Rojas published countless essays and more than twenty books over his lifetime, including a multivolume study of Argentine literature. Indeed, from the appearance of *La restauración* until well into the late 1920s, Rojas was perhaps Argentina's most acclaimed intellectual, and it was he, more than any other figure, who was responsible for injecting ideas central to Romantic nationalism into discussions about Argentine nationality.

Born in 1882 in San Miguel de Tucumán to a socially prominent family, Rojas moved to Buenos Aires to pursue a university degree.[51] Bored with academics, he abandoned the university to pursue a career in letters, quickly securing a position at the prestigious newspaper *La Nación* and rising to the coveted status of columnist by 1905. Despite his lack of experience, Rojas came to the attention of Joaquín V. González, a prominent politician, who in 1907 commissioned Rojas to conduct a study of European teaching methods, a task that entailed a publicly financed tour of Europe.[52] After visiting France, Great Britain, and Germany, Rojas ended his travels in Spain, where he began what was to be a long friendship with Spanish intellectual Miguel de Unamuno.[53] Upon his return to Argentina in 1908, he accepted a position as head of the newly formed Catedra of Argentine literature at the University of La Plata.[54]

Rojas's travels to Europe profoundly shaped his understanding of nationality and apparently helped lead him toward the Romantic view of nations as homogeneous ethno-cultural communities.[55] As he would later recall, it was in Europe that he first witnessed nations where "the soil, the race, language and literature are forged into a single unity." So unified were these nations, he continued, "it is as if each of these is born of the other, and all complement and explain one another in a harmonious cycle."[56] Such nations, he argued, had "pre-existed spiritually" before being formally constituted as political entities. This meant that they enjoyed an ethnic, cultural, and spiritual unity that came from having a coherent "spiritual nucleus," formed as a "consequence of a homogeneous race," whose origins were rooted in the remote past.[57] The experience of seeing European nations also highlighted for Rojas the challenges facing his own country. Argentines, Rojas lamented, had obtained independence from Spain *before* they had formed a spiritually united population.[58] Compounding this problem, Rojas claimed, was the heterogeneous nature of Argentine society. Partially challenging (at least on the symbolic level) the traditional insistence that Argentina was a fully white nation, Rojas argued that Argentina was a mixture of two distinct traditions: the indigenous or autochthonous and the European, which included both Spain and other European nationalities.[59] Adding to this heterogeneity was the impact of the current wave of European immigrants, which had delayed the consolidation of Argentina as a unified "race." Despite these difficulties, Rojas repeatedly expressed confidence that this race, which he explicitly defined as a "psychological" rather than a biological entity, was well on its way to forming.[60]

But just how would its spiritual and psychological unity come about? One avenue for speeding up the formation of the new national race, Rojas argued, was through the public schools. Calling for a "nationalist restoration within education," he urged the government to "imprint the educational system with a national character" by emphasizing Argentine

history and literature.[61] Here, of course, Rojas's call for patriotic education seems to put him in the company of reformers such as Ramos
Mejía and Bunge.[62] Yet the Romantic tendencies evident in his comparisons between Argentina and the older European nations of England and
Germany were much more central to his thought. Although Rojas supported curricular reform, he insisted that patriotic education alone was
insufficient to create a unified nation or a homogenous race. Much more
important, in his view, were the spiritual forces that supposedly ema-
nated from the national soil.[63] According to Rojas, the earth was suffused
with "invisible forces" that were "molders of civilizations." Sometimes
referring to these telluric forces as "place spirits,"[64] as "*genius loci*,"[65] or
simply as the "animating spirit" of "*argentinidad*,"[66] he believed that these
spiritual forces worked to form the inhabitant "according to the environment, until it created a race."[67] This process, he believed, was well underway, and indeed by the nineteenth century had already produced a degree
of racial unity in the form of the Argentine gaucho. The gaucho, he proclaimed, was the "human prototype of the nationality,"[68] a race formed
by the mixture of Spanish and Indian blood,[69] which was fused together
in the "crucible" of the national territory.[70]

Also central to Rojas's vision of Argentina was the essentialist belief
that there are inherent differences between the peoples of different nations. While, as noted in chapter 1, previous generations had acknowledged the distinctive character of Argentine society, most had assumed
(or at least hoped) that Argentina would eventually come to resemble
wealthier, democratic nations, such as England, France, and the United
States. Rojas, in contrast, followed Romantic understandings of nationality and history in insisting that the proper working out of human
history *required* that nations cultivate and defend their supposedly
unique characters. Each nation or race, he believed, had its own predestined role to play in humanity's destiny, which in Argentina's case was to
serve as the "crucible of the Universal and the American."[71] According
to Rojas, humanity's future lay in the Americas, particularly in Latin
America. It was in this region of the world, he believed, that the blending of the European and the autochthonous spirits had initiated a new
stage in world history that "would be transcendent for humanity."[72]

Related to this belief that Argentina had a unique mission to fulfill
was the insistence that Argentines eschew foreign models in order to

cultivate their own distinctive qualities. According to Rojas, only those nations that were true to their authentic characters could thrive and fulfill their distinctive roles in world history. In his view, staying true to Argentina's true character and tradition was so important that the alternative was to disappear as a people. In his words, "If the Argentine pueblo prefers its present suicidal course, if it abdicates its personality and interrupts its tradition, and stops being that which it has . . . been, it will bequeath to history a new example of a pueblo, that, like others, did not deserve to survive."[73] Thus collective self-knowledge and adherence to the nation's supposedly authentic (and immutable) character were essential for its survival.

This conviction that all nations possessed distinctive personalities to which they must remain true was extended to include the essentialist (and Romantic) idea that within the broader realm of humanity, there existed certain families of nations, whose peoples shared common mental and emotional qualities. This notion provided the conceptual underpinnings of *hispanismo*, a movement that swept Latin America during the early decades of the century. Based on the belief that people of Latin or Hispanic descent were inherently different from people of Anglo descent, *hispanismo* was part of a wave of pro-Spanish sentiment that emerged after Spain's humiliating military defeat by the United States in 1898. Although Rojas was not an unqualified *hispanista*—he insisted Spain provided only one component of Argentine identity and criticized the overweening influence of the Catholic Church on Spanish thought[74]—he accepted as a given the claim that the peoples of Spain and Hispanic America shared deep-rooted similarities.[75] Spain, he believed, provided "a third dimension of our *ser americano*," and he described his 1908 visit to that country as an attempt to grasp the "essential sense of *lo español*, that which was perennial of the race."[76] Such were the similarities between peoples of the same "race," he believed, that people of non-Hispanic descent, even Latins, such as the French, were "too rational" to grasp Spain's "hidden and profound" spiritual currents.[77]

This mention of Spain's supposedly hidden spiritual currents highlights another aspect of Rojas's vision that reflects Romantic influences: his belief that intuition, rather than empirical observation, provided the best guide to understanding a nation and its history. Although not entirely hostile to the scientific method (indeed he sometimes claimed his theories to be empirically based), Rojas believed that observable facts constituted only one facet of reality.[78] Of central importance here was his concept of "intrahistory," that he opposed to "external history."[79] According to Rojas, external history concerned observable actions and events, such as the Spanish conquest of America's native population or the wars of independence. Intrahistory, in contrast, concerned the "subterranean currents" that supposedly flowed beneath these surface events. The latter, he believed, was "more essential" than the former and constituted the "real history of our nation."[80] Access to this real history, he argued, could be gained only through intuition, not observation or archival research.[81] This emphasis on intuition as a means of knowing and of discerning underlying historical processes led Rojas, not surprisingly, to tout the importance of individuals who supposedly possessed the heightened sensitivity necessary to grasp so-called hidden truths. For these select individuals, among whom he clearly counted himself, art and literature offered the most important window into the true nature of a people and their past. The artistic creations of a people, he proclaimed, "had a serious historical function," and it was through literature that "the intimate life of the Argentine soul is revealed."[82] Artists themselves were like "demigods," who lived in close contact with the spiritual forces of the land.[83]

Although Rojas was easily the most influential intellectual associated with Argentine cultural nationalism, his core ideas about nationality and history were widely shared by others who identified with the movement. Manuel Gálvez, who along with Rojas is considered one of cultural nationalism's founders, provides a useful example of someone who embraced Rojas's vision of nations as unique, organic ethno-cultural communities charged with a world historical mission, but who had a very different view of the *nature* of this community and its supposed destiny. The scion of a prominent political family, Gálvez spent most of his youth in the city of Santa Fe, capital of Entre Rios, and like Rojas, moved to Buenos Aires to enter the university. While still a student, he co-founded a literary magazine and convinced some of the most prominent writers of the older generation to contribute to its pages.[84] Favored with a government sinecure that left him time to write, Gálvez published twenty novels and almost a dozen biographies during his lengthy life. Despite this output, however, Gálvez is best remembered not for his writing but for his role in promoting the most conservative strain of cultural nationalism in the 1910s and 20s, his deep Catholicism, his love of Spain, and his flirtation with fascism in the 1930s.

Although Gálvez and Rojas would take opposing political paths in the early 1930s (Rojas would become a staunch defender of democracy at exactly the moment that Gálvez swung to the right), during the 1910s and '20s their differences appeared to be relatively unimportant. Much like Rojas, Gálvez saw nations as unique entities possessing distinct personalities and destinies, whose members formed distinct races. In contrast to his fellow cultural nationalist, however, Gálvez placed particular importance on Catholicism and Argentina's Spanish heritage. Devoutly Catholic, he believed that religion formed the defining feature of any particular national community or race.[85] Central to Gálvez's worldview was the essentialist conviction that people of Latin, and especially Spanish, descent differed profoundly from Northern Europeans and that these differences were inextricably intertwined with the two versions of Christianity these two peoples embraced. Latin Americans, he maintained, had been molded by the spirit of Catholicism "that had impressed its character on all expressions of [Latin] American life."[86] While Protestantism might be appropriate for such countries as England and Switzerland, Gálvez believed that its "hard, dry and intolerant spirit" was completely incompatible with the Latin temperament. The young writer was particularly critical of those Latin Americans who believed encouraging Protestant immigration would help introduce modern values that would benefit the region's economic development. Such a change, he argued, would transform "our habits and character for the worst, making us intolerant and cold, stripping us of our notorious generosity and magnanimity."[87] In short, any attempt to spread Protestantism would entail a struggle against Latin American "racial characteristics";[88] if successful, it would result in a complete "denationalization" of Latin American republics.[89]

Given his belief that Catholicism was central to the Argentine national character, it is not surprising that Gálvez became his generation's most ardent proponent of *hispanismo*. According to Gálvez, Argentina's sole hope for salvation in an era of cosmopolitanism and mass immigration was to return to its Latin, and especially to its Spanish, roots. "We are," he proclaimed, "of the Latin race" and "[our] spirit and culture are

Latin." "But within [the greater category of] *latinidad*," he continued, "we are, and will eternally be, ethnically Spanish." This was true despite all the waves of immigrants and "all of the mixtures." These newcomers, Gálvez affirmed, were engaged in an "unconscious labor of erasing our character (*descaracterización*)." However, they had proved incapable of "tearing from us our familial physiognomy." "Castile," he concluded, "created us in its image and likeness. It is the matrix of our people."[90]

Like fellow cultural nationalist Ricardo Rojas, Gálvez believed that all nations were destined to fulfill historical missions.[91] Argentina's mission, he believed, was to carry the virtues of *latinidad* (Latinness) to the New World. Central to this belief was the conviction that the Latin race in Europe was now exhausted, and Argentina's historical mission was to provide this race with a new beginning by infusing it with American energy. This "secret energy," as he called it, was not the "barbaric energy" of North America but one tempered by "Latin elegance."[92] In an early poem entitled "Hymns to the New Energy," Gálvez assured Argentines that "our race, which is expiring in Europe senses that here, for the race, begins a new day." In Argentina, "the beautiful qualities of Italy, France, and above all Spain," would be "reborn as in the old lands, but in new forms."[93] In fulfilling this destiny, Argentines "should use the spiritual lessons taken from Spain simply as a point of departure, as a seed that, transplanted to the moral climate of our fatherland, where it will vigorously take root [and develop] its own form."[94]

Finally, Gálvez also shared Rojas's celebration of artists, of writers, and of those with artistic sensibilities. Only artists, he affirmed, were capable of looking below the surface realities in order to comprehend the true Spain.[95] Moreover, artists and writers had a special role in consolidating the national consciousness of a people. This was especially true in Argentina, where "materialism and skepticism" brought on by mass immigration and excessive cosmopolitanism had replaced the country's traditional spirituality.[96] "We must," he affirmed, "maniacally preach love of the fatherland, of our landscapes and our great men," and make clear the "idealism and originality of our past."[97]

Although the cultural nationalists were instrumental in promoting the idea of nations as organic, ethno-cultural communities, their vision of nationality gained traction largely because it both reflected and reinforced contemporary understandings. Indeed, key elements of their thought can be seen in both the political and cultural spheres. One important example of the former is the rhetoric and policies of Radical leader Hipólito Yrigoyen, who in 1917 (during his first presidency) announced that October 12, the day of Columbus's landfall in the Americas, would henceforth be celebrated as the "Day of the Race." This day, Yrigoyen proclaimed in his brief decree, should be used to honor the *genio* (genius) of Spain and the legacy it bequeathed to the Hispanic American nations. "Spain," he declared, was the "progenitor of nations, nations that had received from the former colonial power, with the leavening of blood and the harmony of its language, an immortal inheritance."[98] Applauding this measure, an editorial in the literary magazine *Ideas* explained that peoples "who possess the same customs, beliefs, aspirations, and above all language . . . are morally of the same race."[99] Moreover, the editorial noted, although Rome was the "common trunk of the Latin race," it was Spain, with its "beliefs, language, and customs" that was "our spiritual mother."[100] Prominent historian Ernesto Quesada also praised the measure. Writing in the literary review *Verbum*, Quesada described Spain as the "common mother" of the Hispanic American republics, all of which contained "the sediment of the common Hispanic race." The ties that bound Spain to its former colonies, he continued, were both "tight" and "invisible" and "represented the common ligatures of the racial atavism, of the unity of language, the sediment of the mentality, customs, beliefs and criteria."[101] In another article in the same issue of *Verbum*, contributor Gaspar Martín also lauded the Day of the Race as an opportunity for Argentines to celebrate "the characteristics of our ethnic personality."[102]

In the cultural realm, the Romantic notion that art, literature, and even architecture provided both an expression of a people's racial qualities and a window into their collective soul also began to gain widespread acceptance. Noted architect Martín Noel, for example, sought to develop a uniquely Hispanic American architectural style that would promote the "racial values" of Hispanic Americans.[103] Legal scholar and essayist Adolfo Casaba expressed similar sentiments. Argentine writers and dramatists, he believed, should "write about Argentine themes" that emerged from the national *índole* (character). These works, he affirmed, should try to "reflect the national soul."[104] Emilio Becher, a long-time associate of both Rojas and Gálvez, echoed these ideas when he warned that Argentines should avoid imitating Spanish literary forms. Writing in *La*

*Nación*, he proclaimed that writers' efforts "should be directed toward developing the genuine elements of nationality, whose roots should reach down to the very entrails of the race."[105] Writer Alberto Gerchunoff expressed much the same thing in a highly favorable review of a work by prominent novelist Roberto Payró. A Russian-born Jew, who became close friends with both Rojas and Gálvez, Gerchunoff praised Payró for his ability to evoke the realities of Argentine life and for his overall concern with tracing the "development of the Argentine soul."[106]

The idea that the only worthwhile art was that produced by artists in touch with the unique qualities of the national race also gained widespread acceptance. For example, Juan Más y Pi, a Catalan critic residing in Argentina, who will be discussed more fully in chapter 5, argued that for most types of art, it was "indispensable that there be a "melding (*consubstancia*) of the artist and the environment." If this were lacking, he believed, the work of art would "lack vigor" and energy and would seem "manufactured," rather than authentic. The most noble art, then, was that which manifested the "sentiment of the race and the place," and the true artist was someone who was best able to "concentrate the sense of the race" in his work.[107] According to some commentators, this relationship between the artist and the national race could be facilitated by decreased contact with the outside world. A contributor to the magazine *Cuaderno Colegio Novecentista*, for example, opined that World War I had benefited Argentine art, because the conflict had isolated Argentina from European influences. As a result, Francisco de Aparicio argued, Argentines were forced to "reconcentrate in our own selves" and thus were producing art that was "more *ours*."[108]

The cultural nationalists' belief that Argentina should reject foreign models in order to cultivate its distinctive personality also resonated with a new questioning of the traditional view that Argentines and other Latin Americans needed to "catch up" with Protestant Europe. One contributor to the literary review *Sagitario*, for example, noted that Argentines no longer accepted the assumption that European civilization was synonymous with the term *civilization* itself. The breakdown of this "cultural monism," Carlos Astrada opined, had led to "a new way of thinking about the historical universe," one that "comprehends and accepts . . . that in all epochs there is a plurality of civilizations, independent worlds with distinctive spiritual modalities and vital propensities."[109]

Juan Propst, the foreign-born editor of the review *Verbum* (who declared himself an "Argentine at heart"), argued that Argentines could define their nationality by affirming "its membership in the circle of Hispanic culture." This was important for both Argentina and the world, he continued, since human progress required a "heterogeneity" that would come from "defined and coherent components" such as the Hispanic-American world.[110] The grouping of nations into distinctive components or cultural circles, Propst believed, enriched all of humanity and helped move mankind toward its true destiny. Writing in much the same vein, Jorge Max Rohde, a founding member of the antipositivist group Colegio Novecentista, decried Argentines' tendency to follow European dictates, lamenting that Argentines "quiver like an errant leaf in the gusts of European wind." It was time, he proclaimed, for the "latent forces of the race" to awaken. Once this occurred, Rohde believed, the "great Hispanic family, united by its language and soul," would cease to imitate other races and would instead offer "new worlds" to the rest of humanity.[111]

## COUNTERCURRENTS

With the passage of time, the idea that Argentines formed a unique race or ethno-cultural community became increasingly pervasive. Indeed, by the 1920s, this essentialist vision of nationality, along with the related belief that nations must be true to their supposed inner essences, had become perhaps *the* dominant paradigm for understanding the challenges facing Argentina's efforts to define itself as a nation. As such, it inevitably shaped views about the immigrant.

There were, however, those who *did* challenge this vision of Argentine identity, and who sought to reclaim the nineteenth-century understanding of the nation as a civic community. For example, a contributor to the prestigious *Revista de la Universidad de Buenos Aires* rejected the notion that the new countries of the Americas could base their nationality on the race, religion, or historical roots of their people. According to A. Calandrelli, this was possible only in the old nations of Europe. In countries of immigration such as Argentina, he believed, these primordial qualities had almost completely disappeared. Seeming to echo the above-mentioned Carlos Octavio Bunge, Calandrelli argued that, for

Argentina, the only real basis of the nation was "the ideal that stimulates men to [construct] a permanent [collective] life," on the basis of similar social and moral values.[112] Juan Álvarez, a prominent jurist and the son of a Spanish immigrant, expressed a similar sentiment. Making it clear that he opposed both the ethno-cultural vision of the nation espoused by the cultural nationalists *and* the hyperpatriotic education advocated by Ramos Mejía, Álvarez believed that attempts to search through the past for the source of Argentine nationality were misguided. Such efforts, he argued, were the work of individuals who believed immigrants were marginal to the nation, and who viewed the newcomers as "simply accessories to a something that preexisted and was superior to them."[113] Álvarez instead believed that immigrants were integral elements of an evolving society, who should be welcomed and integrated into the body politic. The best way to consolidate Argentine nationality and to build loyalty among immigrants, he insisted, was to provide opportunities for them to prosper.[114] The schools, too, had a role to play in consolidating a sense of national identity among immigrant children, but this should be done in an open and honest way, without all the nationalist cant consisting of "vague concepts" and "phrases of doubtful sense."[115] Instead, the public schools should strive to give immigrant children a "realistic picture of Argentina's strengths and weaknesses vis-à-vis other nations."[116] This, he concluded, is "how we make democrats and citizens."[117]

But by far the most consistent defenders of the traditional liberal idea of the nation as a civic community during these years were the leaders of the Argentine Socialist Party. Founded in 1894 by medical doctor Juan B. Justo, Argentina's Socialist Party embraced gradual change and believed that the transition to socialism in Argentina could be achieved through the electoral process and piecemeal legislative reform. Accordingly, the party put its energies into building a political base and fielding candidates for office.[118] With a few notable exceptions, Argentine socialists viewed the new nationalist currents with hostility.[119] Justo, for example, took direct aim at these ideas when he rejected as "mystical" the very idea that nations were "rigorously delimited entities," with distinctive personalities and destinies.[120] While acknowledging that national differences did indeed exist, he stressed that these were due to their different levels of development rather than to the intrinsic ethnic or racial

qualities of their people.[121] Fellow socialist Augusto Bunge agreed with
Justo and believed the new nationalist currents were part of a more
generalized conservative reaction. Attacking the motives of the cultural
nationalists, Bunge ridiculed the notion of ethnic differences as a "soph-
istry dreamed up by poets and politicians." In an obvious reference to
Rojas, he argued that those who sought a "national restoration" were
members of the conservative class, who simply wished to perpetuate the
status quo.[122]

Argentine socialists clearly hewed closely to early nineteenth-
century understandings of nationality. For these individuals, the nation
was above all a political association: membership into the national community had nothing to do with an individual's ethnic characteristics,
language, or even length of residence in Argentina but rather with one's
willingness to participate in the political system and contribute to the
general welfare of the nation. This identification of citizenship and
*argentinidad*, and the belief in the volitional nature of nationality, comes
through clearly in Justo's claim that "the Italian mother, who among us
nurtures future mothers of future Argentine citizens, is more Argentine
than the creole lady who thinks only of wasting her husband's profits in
Europe."[123] In a similar vein, Bunge declared that even the immigrant
who "speaks not a word of Spanish" but who is "honest and loyal to the
country" and "who works with his hands or his brain for the greatness of
the nation" is more completely Argentine than are corrupt politicians
who steal from the people.[124]

Perhaps the most impassioned statement of the idea that *argentinidad* was based on a common political creed rather than on descent or
ethnicity came from socialist leader Enrique Dickmann, a Russian-born
Jew, who became one of the first members of the party to be elected to
Congress. In a somewhat melodramatic speech to that body, Dickmann
related his reactions to a festival he had attended at his children's primary
school in Buenos Aires. Viewing the scores of youngsters assembled for
the ceremony, Dickmann said, he was struck by the diversity of the student body. Before him stood "blondes, brunettes, whites, a few blacks,
one or two mulattos, children of all races . . . and all nations." His initial
reaction, he told his fellow members of Congress, was one of concern
over the excessive cosmopolitanism of Argentine society and the difficulty of creating a unified nation from such disparate elements. These

fears, however, were dispelled when the children rose together to sing the national anthem. So moved was he, Dickmann confessed to his colleagues, that "My eyes filled with tears, my heart compressed with happiness [as I] reflected that up to now the cry of liberty contained in our anthem has been but a vague aspiration, a far-off ideal, that now is being realized by the new political forces and the new Argentine democracy."[125]

Clearly, despite the growing acceptance of Romantic conceptions of Argentine identity among the nation's intellectuals and opinion makers, the competing vision of Argentina as a civic nation continued to have its defenders. As occurred during the previous century, ideas about just what the nation was, the nature of the bonds between its members, and how or if the foreign born could become true Argentines, remained unsettled. The continuing debate over these matters, as Oscár Terán has observed, had as its "terminal points" the traditional liberal vision of Argentina as a civic nation that stressed political and universal values, or the "essentialist" and "culturalist" vision of *argentinidad* that would stress the supposedly inherent ethno-cultural qualities of the Argentine people.[126] But even as the latter vision of Argentina as a distinctive ethnic or racial community gained ground, the question over the nature of this imagined race and the role that immigrants would play in its shaping was hotly contested. These debates will be examined in chapter 5. But before treating this issue, two additional topics will be explored. First, what were the key intellectual influences that shaped early twentieth-century Argentine thought? Second, what impact did these new essentialist ideas about the nation have in the political realm?

# THREE

# Sources of Romantic Nationalism in Early Twentieth-Century Argentina

What lay behind the new interest in the ideas associated with Romantic nationalism during this period in Argentine history? Why did the essentialist vision of Argentine nationality that appeared in embryonic form during the closing decades of nineteenth century become so pervasive, especially among members of the younger generation? Answering this question requires a look at the changing conditions of urban society, the legacy of late nineteenth-century positivism, and above all the impact of new intellectual currents from abroad.

On the most general level, the rise of ethno-cultural nationalism has historically been linked to three interrelated processes: rapid modernization, the massive influx of immigrants, and the explosive growth of urban centers, where these ideas most often take hold.[1] All of these, of course, were occurring simultaneously in early twentieth-century Argentina. It is easy to see why native-born inhabitants would come to fear that the world they had known was fast disappearing, as Argentina—and especially Buenos Aires—rushed full tilt toward modernity and became crowded with foreigners.[2] Besides these general changes, Buenos Aires also was experiencing certain specific social transformations that proved propitious to the growing appeal of ideas associated with Romantic nationalism. The Romantic tendency to exalt creativity and to see writers and artists as privileged individuals, for example, was aided by the rapid expansion of the reading public and the corresponding growth of the Argentine publishing industry.[3] The new opportunities this growth afforded meant that writers could actually make a living by the pen, resulting in a sense of professionalism and corporate identity. This new identity in turn gave rise to what Beatriz Sarlo and Carlos Altamirano have called the "ideology of the artist"—that is, the belief that writers and artists were a privileged class, untainted by the crass materialism that supposedly afflicted the rest of society.[4]

Another aspect of cultural nationalist thought, similarly reinforced by underlying social change, was the more generalized celebration of youth's special purity and the belief in a generational split. As noted in the previous chapter, the cultural nationalists identified themselves as a new generation, whose mission it was to correct the mistakes of their predecessors. Although the theme of youthful purity and the idea of a generational mission were not entirely new in Argentina, these took on a special force during the opening decades of the twentieth century as increasing numbers of middle- and even working-class youth found their way into the universities.[5] Free from the constraints of childhood, and segregated from the adult world, these students very often developed an exalted sense of their own importance and vanguard status. As a result, these young intellectuals often ignored the fact that many of their laments about the materialism of Argentine life had been anticipated by the previous generation.[6]

In addition to these social and demographic developments, the growing circulation of essentialized understandings of race and nationality promoted by early twentieth-century adherents of positivism and the new "science" of eugenics also helped normalize, and thus served to reinforce, cultural nationalism's ethno-cultural understanding of *argentinidad*.[7] As noted in the introduction, "race" was an extraordinarily ill-defined concept in early twentieth-century Argentina and could take on very different meanings depending on the context.[8] Indeed, it was not unusual for Argentine positivists to employ the term in both a biological and a historical cultural sense in the same essay.[9] This conceptual fuzziness about race was not simply an Argentine phenomenon but reflected confusions and slippages within positivism itself.

One understanding of race, employed by Argentine positivists, that bore strong similarities to that of the cultural nationalists stemmed from the influence of French intellectual Hippolyte Taine, the most widely read European positivist in Argentina. Taine, who drew on both English positivism and German idealism, promoted the idea of the nation as an organic community that possessed an intrinsic "elemental moral state," or collective psychology, that sprang from the interaction of "race, milieu and moment."[10] Taine's influence is clearly seen in the writings of Argentine positivist Carlos Octavio Bunge, who attempted to explain the environmental forces that gave rise to the collective psychology of the Hispanic American peoples.[11] According to Bunge, each nation or community of nations possessed a clearly identifiable set of historically and geographically rooted psychological traits that both distinguished them from other nations and determined its future possibilities. Here we can see clear affinities between the cultural nationalists' and Bunge's use of race. While Rojas's mystical belief that telluric forces had somehow produced a unified national character certainly went beyond Bunge's positivist-inspired environmental determinism, the similarities between the two approaches were in many ways more profound than their differences.[12]

The spreading influence of eugenics also reinforced cultural nationalism's linking of race and nationality. As noted in chapter 2, the flood of immigrants—most of them Italian or Spanish and from working-class backgrounds—prompted some elites to fear that Argentina was receiving the dregs of Europe. Inspired by the pseudoscience of eugenics, which sought to improve the human species by limiting the fertility of supposedly inferior peoples, intellectuals from across the political spectrum discussed ways to ensure that immigrants would improve, rather than degrade, the "national race."[13] The result was an ongoing debate among Argentina's political and intellectual elite about whether to limit the influx of supposedly inferior stock, although here again historico-cultural understandings of race often supplanted biological ones. For example, as historian Diego Armus has noted, some Argentine immigration experts saw the Basque "race" as more vigorous and energetic than the "Galician" race. In particular, they believed the latter to be apt to contract tuberculosis.[14] Others promoted the notion that the mixing of dissimilar "races" should be avoided, and advised encouraging the immigration of

Latin peoples who could better meld with the existing population.[15] Although efforts to develop a more selective immigration policy invariably failed, what is important for our purposes is the fact that eugenicists saw race and racial mixture as "crucial elements of the nation-building project" and believed that a new "national type" would eventually form.[16] Such reasoning, while supposedly predicated on scientific grounds and thus ostensibly in conflict with Romantic understandings, served to weaken the traditional vision of the nation as a civic community by insisting on a racial definition of *argentinidad*.

The cultural nationalists' conviction that peoples who belonged to the same racial community shared inherent mental and emotional qualities was also shaped, and reinforced by, the wave of essentialist thinking that followed the Cuban-Spanish-American War of 1895–98. As is well known, the 1898 entry of the United States into the Cuban war of independence against Spain provoked a continent-wide backlash against "Anglo-Saxon" aggression. Although most Latin Americans were sympathetic to the Cuban cause, they increasingly came to view the conflict between Spain and the United States as a clash between two distinct races.[17] Spain's rapid defeat, coupled with the US's annexation of Puerto Rico and occupation of Cuba, fueled fears of further US aggression in the region. The consequence was a wave of anti-imperialism focused on the United States, an increased sympathy for Spain, and a "sharpening of Hispanic American ethno-cultural consciousness."[18]

No work of the period more fully captured and reinforced this intellectual trend than José Enrique Rodó's book-length essay *Ariel*. A Uruguayan, Rodó was fully integrated into the Buenos Aires intellectual community and enjoyed close relations with both the Spanish Generation of 1898 and the Argentine cultural nationalists.[19] His most famous work, *Ariel*, quickly became a bestseller throughout Latin America and gave rise to the intellectual movement known as *arielismo*. Published in 1900, the book featured characters from Shakespeare's *The Tempest* but inverted them in order to convey what Rodó viewed as the inherent differences between Latin and Anglo-Americans.[20] The Anglo-Saxon United States, according to Rodó, was a nation of Calibans: rough and crude people who had produced technological progress and wealth, but whose society lacked art, idealism, and spirituality. Latin Americans, in contrast, were temperamentally similar to the more spiritually refined

Ariel, who symbolized the higher values of creativity and idealism. The book's central message was that the youth of the continent must forge a new path forward that would celebrate the unique qualities of Latin American peoples. Rather than mindlessly emulating the United States, Rodó argued, Latin Americans should reject "artificial and improvised imitation" and take care to avoid "denaturalizing the character—the *personality*—of the nation."[21] This, Rodó insisted, was important both for Latin Americans' self-respect and because of their duty to the rest of humanity. "We Latin Americans," he affirmed, "have a heritage of race, a great ethnic tradition, to maintain, a sacred place in the pages of history that depends upon us for its continuation."[22]

Another important intellectual whose writings circulated during this period, and whose essentialist ideas about nationality were at least partially shaped by US intervention in the Spanish-Cuban conflict, was Argentine writer Manuel Ugarte (1875–1951). Born into a wealthy family from the province of Buenos Aires, Ugarte spent much of his life in Europe; in the wake of the Cuban-Spanish-American War, he traveled to the United States, to Mexico, and to Cuba. A strong supporter of Spain, he developed a lasting correspondence with Spanish intellectual Miguel de Unamuno, whose deep impact on the cultural nationalists will be discussed below.[23] Ugarte returned to Argentina in 1903, and in 1911 he published *El porvenir de la América Latina*, a work that provoked widespread commentary throughout the Spanish-speaking world.[24] Following Rodó's vision of the "two Americas," Ugarte argued that the "Latin" Americans and "Anglo-Saxon" Americans formed two distinct races, and that the differences between the two were innate and permanent. The United States, in his view, had been formed by "cold-natured and analytical peoples," who abhorred racial mixture and who poured their energies into industrialization.[25] Latin Americans, in contrast, were by nature a "warm" people, who were free of racial prejudices and who had produced a more "liquid" society.[26] As a result of this lack of prejudice, the Latin American race was one of mixture. While retaining the "essential nucleus" provided by the original Spanish (or, in the case of Brazil, the Portuguese) conquerors, this race had absorbed the native Indians and Africans, and was still in the process of absorbing the most recent waves of immigrants.[27] These additions meant that the Americans of the South, while fundamentally Latin, formed their own distinctive human group or race, which constituted "an indispensable fragment of the universal soul."[28]

Rodó, Ugarte, and the passions aroused by US involvement in Cuba's war of independence against Spain all had undeniable impacts on the cultural nationalists. Rojas, in particular, enjoyed a warm relationship with Rodó. For his part, Manuel Gálvez developed a close friendship with Ugarte, both in Buenos Aires and on a lengthy 1905 visit to Paris, where he dined with Ugarte almost daily. There were other important influences on this young generation of thinkers. From France came the ideas of Ernest Renan, Maurice Barrés, Charles Maurras, and León Daudet; less frequently mentioned, but still significant, were the ideas of German philosophers, such as J. G. Fichte, Friedrich Schiller, J. W. Goethe, and Friedrich Nietzsche.[29]

But by far the cultural nationalists' most important source of intellectual inspiration came from the so-called Spanish Generation of 1898, especially the ideas of Ángel Ganivet and Miguel de Unamuno.[30] Rojas's long personal and professional relationship with Unamuno is well known, dating back to 1903, when the young Argentine sent a copy of his first book to the famous Spanish writer. Although the two met only once (in 1908, when Rojas visited Salamanca), their friendship was sustained by an extensive correspondence that spanned decades. Unamuno's intellectual impact on the younger writer proved enormous, and it is clear from Rojas's letters that he considered the Spaniard a mentor. Particularly notable was Rojas's deep admiration for Unamuno's seminal *En torno al casticismo*, which undoubtedly influenced his own *La restauración nacionalista*.[31] Rojas was also an enthusiastic admirer of Ángel Ganivet, whom he considered "one of the rarest and strongest talents in contemporary Spain"[32] and whose *Idearium español* he cited as one of the bases of his theory about the impact of the national territory on the spirit of the people.[33] Gálvez also knew and read these intellectuals. In *El solar de la raza*, for example, he explicitly notes the impact of Ganivet, Unamuno, Macías Picavea, and Joaquín Costa, proclaiming that "the small group we (in Argentina) formed exercised the same mission," as did the Spanish generation: to help their nation "observe itself and to know itself profoundly."[34] Elsewhere he indicates his keen admiration for Azorín, Pio Baroja, and Valle-Inclán, the last of whom he had met in Spain.[35]

The similarities between the ideas of these two generations of thinkers were clearly profound, as the Argentines themselves readily acknowledged. Yet there is another link in this chain of European intellectual influences I wish to explore, and that I believe helps illuminate two aspects of early twentieth-century Argentine nationalist thought that have long remained murky. The first aspect is the strong affinities between Argentine cultural nationalism and German Romantic thought, especially the striking similarities between the ideas of Rojas and the German Romantic philosopher Johann Gottfried von Herder (1744–1803). Indeed, so strong are these similarities that scholars have repeatedly claimed that Rojas was a devotee of Herder.[36] There is, however, no evidence to support a direct link between them. The second aspect involves the striking similarities between the ideas of the cultural nationalists and those of the leadership of the Argentine Radical Party, especially Hipólito Yrigoyen. Although the affinities between the ideas of the Radicals and the cultural nationalists have provoked almost no scholarly comment, when viewed through the optic of Romantic conceptions of nationality, they are clear indeed.[37]

In what follows I wish to consider these questions: (1) Why did the Argentine cultural nationalists sound so much like German Romantic thinkers? (2) Why were the ideas and rhetoric of the cultural nationalists and the UCR's leadership so similar? Answering these questions requires a backward glance at the Spanish philosophical movement known as Krausism. Based on the ideas of German Romantic thinker Karl Christian Friedrich Krause (1781–1832), Krausism dominated Spanish thought through much of the nineteenth century and provided the Romantic underpinnings of the Generation of 1898's understanding of history and nationality. Tracing the intellectual continuities between Spanish Krausism, the Generation of 1898, and the Argentine cultural nationalists finally establishes a line of continuity between this last group and German Romanticism. Krausism, through its impact on Yrigoyen, also played a more direct role in early twentieth-century Argentina. As will be elaborated on in chapter 4, as a young man Yrigoyen developed a deep fascination with Krause's thought, and many of his ideas and policies make sense only when keeping this Krausist influence in mind. Thus it was the Romantic philosophy of Krausism, I argue, that provides the link between the Radicals and the cultural nationalists. To begin our analysis, we turn first to the phenomenon of Spanish Krausism.

## SPANISH KRAUSISM

The history of Krausist thought in Spain represents the unusual case of a philosopher who gained his most loyal following posthumously, and in a country he never visited. Born in Germany in 1781, Karl Christian Friedrich Krause studied under the well-known Romantic philosophers Fichte and Schelling. Although promising and ambitious, he remained in the shadow of his contemporary G. W. F. Hegel, enjoying success only outside his native land. Championed by Heinrich Ahrens, a German legal scholar who taught in Brussels and Paris, Krause's philosophy gained a modest foothold in France and Belgium. But it was in Spain, and later in Spanish America, where Krausism would have the greatest impact. From 1850 to about 1875, Krausism, or "harmonic rationalism," as it was also called, enjoyed enormous prestige in Spain and occupied the center of academic life. Although its strength as a coherent philosophical movement waned after 1875, Krausism continued to influence Spanish thought well into the twentieth century.[38]

Krausism's enormous impact in Spain can be traced largely to the efforts of Spanish philosopher Julián Sanz del Río and to succeeding generations of his students. Sanz del Río first came into contact with Krausist ideas as a law student through Ahrens's writings, especially his *Curso completo de derecho natural de filosofía del derecho*, a standard text in Spanish law schools after 1839. In 1843, after having completed his degree, Sanz del Río was sent by the Ministry of the Interior to Germany for the purpose of studying the major philosophical schools. But having already developed an intense enthusiasm for Krause's ideas, he focused exclusively on Krausist philosophy. After more than a year of instruction in Heidelberg, he returned to Madrid in late 1844 and spent the next several years reading and reworking Krause's ideas.[39] The ultimate fruit of these efforts was his most important work, *Ideal de la humanidad para la vida*, a loose adaptation of Krause's 1811 *Urbild der Menschheit*.[40] Finally published in 1860, *Ideal* became the foundational text of Spanish Krausism.

Once he began to publicize his ideas, Sanz del Río quickly developed a cult-like following among university students.[41] Imitating the master, young Krausists "dressed soberly, usually in black," and cultivated a taciturn, preoccupied manner. Such a somber style had nothing to do with Krause and his ideas but instead reflected Sanz del Río's own personal tastes.[42] Still, a Spanish Krausist style was born, one that the famously austere Hipólito Yrigoyen would later adopt. After Sanz del Río's death in 1869, his ideas were carried forward by his students, who were almost as influential and who acquired followings of their own.[43] One of the most prominent members of this second generation was Francisco Giner de los Ríos, who, like Sanz del Río, continued to modify Krausist ideas through his reading of other German Romantics, such as Herder. In an attempt to spread Krausism's influence further, Giner and other Krausists founded in 1876 the Institución Libre de Enseñanza, which had as its goal the training of an elite capable of guiding the country according to Krausist principles.[44]

What were the principal ideas of Spanish Krausism? As it was understood by its Spanish interpreters, Krausism is best described as a hybrid philosophy combining elements of German Romanticism and Enlightenment liberalism. On the liberal side, Krausism stressed the importance of reason and complete intellectual freedom.[45] This insistence on the right of each individual to exercise his or her powers of reason meant that Spanish Krausists were also strong advocates of religious tolerance. While seeing themselves as Christian, they believed all religions were manifestations of a single religious spirit. In the context of nineteenth-century Spain, such views placed the Krausists squarely in the liberal camp, and indeed many followers of Krausism supported the liberal Revolution of 1868. This did not mean, however, that Krausists were advocates of radical egalitarianism and universal suffrage. Indeed, Spanish Krausists rejected what they viewed as the "doctrinaire liberalism" of the French Revolution and the supposedly inorganic democracy it promoted.[46] Instead, theirs was a liberalism deeply shaped by the Romantic milieu from which it had originally emerged.

Among Krausism's many Romantic elements, one of the most central was the view of the nation as a natural, organic entity with its own personality or character, much like a human being.[47] According to Krausists, nations were "moral persons," possessing a unique personality, a soul, and inalienable rights.[48] The idea that the people of each nation share similar emotional and mental traits was also central to Spanish Krausism. Drawing from Krause and Herder, Giner argued that all nations possess a specific collective psychology, or *genio nacional*.[49] Historian Rafael Altamira, a Giner disciple, who sought to renovate Krausism within a positivist framework, expressed a similar view. Devoting himself to the study of the putative Spanish character, he affirmed that "transcending all the local differences there are common interests, ideas, affinities, aptitudes and defects . . . that make the Spaniard a characteristic type in the psychology of the world, and [make of Spain] a real and substantive entity."[50]

Krausists also embraced the Romantic notion that the physical landscape played a large role in shaping the national character by anchoring and maintaining the purity of a supposedly eternal tradition or essence. According to Sanz de Río's reading of Krause, the natural qualities of a nation's territory, combined with climatic factors, played a significant role in giving form to the character and culture of its people.[51] Krause's Spanish followers enthusiastically embraced this view of the natural environment. Giner in particular enjoyed the countryside and believed the study of nature and the Spanish landscape to be an essential part of students' education.[52] Revealing both Romantic influences and the impact of nineteenth-century theories of environmental determinism, Giner expressed his conviction that the collective "tastes, habits, arts, work and entire mode of life" of human groups were shaped by the land they inhabited.[53]

A teleological vision of history was also integral to Krausism. Like all Romantics, Spanish Krausists understood humanity's future to be predetermined, with history developing according to a hidden, divine plan.[54] The endpoint of history, they believed, was the formation of a single, supranational organism that would encompass all of humanity. This eventual union would not, however, entail a process of homogenization. Rather, just as the constituent organisms within each nation worked in harmonious, complementary fashion to realize the well being of the whole, so too would each nation contribute in a unique way to this all-encompassing organism. Thus for Krausists, this "opposition of national characters" was essential for human progress; indeed to suppress these differences would be to "dry the source of the inner and fecund life of humanity itself."[55]

The working out of humanity's destiny, according to Krausists, was a gradual process that would occur as individuals, groups, and nations gradually became conscious of their roles in the universal scheme. The first step toward unification, they believed, was the joining together of peoples who shared common origins, as well as a common language and religion, among other cultural qualities, and who would then form families of nations. These families would in turn unite with other similar groups until the entire world formed a single organism. Not surprisingly, then, Spanish Krausists were enthusiastic advocates of *hispanismo*.[56] Among the most energetic Hispanicists was Rafael Altamira, who assisted Giner with the founding of the Institución Libre de Enseñanza. Proclaiming the need to preserve Spanish spiritual values in the New World, Altamira joined with other Krausists to organize a cultural mission to Spanish America in 1909–10.[57] Altamira's stay in Argentina proved particularly successful. During his time there, he accepted an invitation from the University of La Plata—where, it will be recalled, Ricardo Rojas held the chair in Argentine Literature—to teach a three-month course.[58]

Another important Spanish Krausist involved in promoting hispanismo was Joaquín Costa, an intellectual who had particularly strong links with the Generation of 1898 and whom Manuel Gálvez would later cite as an influence. Echoing a theme that both Argentine cultural nationalists and the Radicals embraced, Costa affirmed the need for a powerful Spanish race in both Europe and America. Humanity's full development, he declared, required that this race serve as a counterweight to the "Saxon race," so that "the moral equilibrium in the infinite game of history" would be maintained. Alongside the "British Sancho," Costa proclaimed, these must also be the "pure and luminous Spanish Quixote," who . . . [with his] passion and faith make the world something more than a factory and a market where things are bought and sold." In making these claims, Costa insisted that he did so "not for reasons of vanity, but because the greater cause of humanity demanded it."[59] Thus, according to Costa, the preordained mission of the Hispanic nations was to promote idealism within an increasingly materialistic world, or—as Rodó would have it—to play the Latin Ariel to the Anglo-Saxon Caliban.[60]

Given their belief that human history developed according to a divine plan, how did Spanish Krausists understand the role of human agency? This was a question, it will be recalled, that Argentina's Generation of 1837, also influenced by the ideas associated with European

Romanticism, also faced. When taken to an extreme, of course, the view that nations are natural organisms that develop along predetermined paths can lead to fatalism. Such, however, was not the case for Kraus-ists, who insisted that "Humanity, in its historical organism" was the "author of its works."[61] Accordingly, while Krausists believed that hu-manity's march toward progress could not be permanently thwarted, they also saw this march as a "costly process, full of struggles, mistakes and meanders," which could be favored or retarded by human actions.[62] Those who could favor or help this process, Krausists believed, were exceptional individuals, who "excelled in perception, spirit, energy and strength of character." Under the leadership of such individuals, nations could in a sense shorten history, by speeding up their march along their preordained path.[63]

What caused "mistakes and meanders" in a nation's progress, and what could the exceptional person do to move history along? According to Krausists, nations were unable to fulfill their unique historical mis-sions when they were blocked by impediments, which in Spain took two forms.[64] The first was physical misery. Extreme poverty, Krausists argued, prevented individuals from using their powers of reason to comprehend their roles in the collective's destiny, thus frustrating both their own in-dividual development and that of the larger community. Accordingly, Krause and his followers embraced the concept of social rights, asserting that the state should guarantee food, shelter, and education to all citi-zens.[65] But the obstacle that preoccupied Spanish Krausists more was or-thodox Catholicism, which they saw as a perversion of true Christianity. In the eyes of the Krausists, the Spanish church's sins were twofold. First, by imposing censorship and cutting Spain off from the rest of Europe, the church had prevented the circulation of ideas necessary for Spaniards to freely realize their individual and collective destinies. As Krause put it, in order for history to unfold as it should, the "idea and end" of each nation must be "clearly known and freely realized by the people." At that point only "each one could recognize and fulfill her or his part . . . in the realization of the great historical tasks and the definitive union" of the entire world into a single family.[66] The church's second sin, according to Spanish Krausists, was its rigid, joyless brand of religion, which had caused Spaniards to lose touch with their true, authentic selves. The real Spain, Giner believed, was deeply mystical, and the Spanish people possessed an inherent, intuitive sense of the divine.[67] Orthodox Catholicism, which he traced back to the rule of Philip II (1556–98), had suppressed this inherent spirituality and mysticism. The result, according to Giner, was a pueblo that for the past three centuries had been "amputated" from the part of its past that was the "most spiritual and profound."[68] Fellow Krausist Francisco de Paul Canalejas concurred, arguing that Spain's original religious tradition, which had stressed the individual's free and mystical communion with God, had been distorted by orthodox Catholicism.[69]

Losing touch with their true essence or character, according to Krausists, had left Spaniards weak and confused. In the words of Giner, Spain was among those nations that had "ignore[d] the [interior] voice that incessantly calls them to their historical task." Accordingly it had often wandered without direction, and its external life had become a "hieroglyphic, that is at times indecipherable."[70] The only remedy was to reconnect the nation with its true mystical essence and thereby regain the path that had been lost in the sixteenth century. And here, according to Krausists, was how exceptional individuals could help in the proper unfolding of history. By understanding the true national essence and by defending and nurturing their nation's unique qualities, such individuals could help their nation fulfill its divine mission and thus carry out its responsibility to the rest of humanity.

Critical to this task of grasping a pueblo's true essence or nature, Krausists believed, was the study of history, but in a particular way. Krausists, as Spanish scholar Dolores Gómez Molleda has argued, "understood and valued the past subhistorically," meaning that what mattered was knowledge not of long ago political events, wars, dynasties, and individual statesmen but of the hidden, interior life of the Spanish people.[71] Accordingly, historians such as Giner urged his disciples to study "the deepest levels of the nation's [collective] psychology."[72] Access to these levels, Krausists believed, could come only through the study of the art and literature of a given epoch. Like all Romantics, Krausists saw artists and writers as individuals who were particularly in tune with the true spirit of the people. Accordingly, historians should study literature as a means of gaining a "profound understanding of the character and way of being" (*modo de ser*) of nations.[73] The plastic arts also provided an indispensable window into the national being or soul. Accordingly, art historian Manuel Bartolomé Cossío, who was closely associated with the Institución Libre, believed that it was through paintings that the character of a particular time and place could be grasped. Writing in 1885, he insisted that Spanish art included "all those works that carry the imprint of the national seal, that shows the distinctive and peculiar traits of the *genio* of the country and the time and place in which it was produced; in sum, that which has *character*."[74]

These, then, were the central concepts of Spanish Krausism. Primarily a Romantic philosophy, it combined an organic understanding of society and a teleological view of history with an insistence that all individuals should be free to exercise their powers of reason. In doing so, it offered mid-nineteenth-century Spanish reformers the philosophical tools to claim a middle ground between the radical individualism of liberalism and the oppressive hand of the church. While preserving—albeit in a different guise—Catholicism's view of society as a corpus mysticism, Krausism's hostility toward unfettered capitalism and its belief that history is divinely preordained allowed its Spanish adherents to work for reforms that would tame the power of the church and open Spain to intellectual currents from the rest of Europe.[75] The resulting intellectual freedom, they believed, would allow Spaniards to throw off the impediment of orthodox Catholicism and regain their true historical trajectory.

## THE GENERATION OF 1898 AS KRAUSIST CONDUIT

In tracing the connections between the Spanish Krausists and the Generation of 1898, it is first important to note that there was no clear temporal divide between the two groups. Because Spanish Krausism lived on beyond the death of Sanz del Río through various waves of disciples, many important Krausist intellectuals were contemporaries of the Generation of 1898.[76] Not surprisingly, these groups had a great deal of contact, both directly through personal dealings and indirectly through shared friendships and readings. For example, novelist and literary critic Leopoldo Alas (aka Clarín), who is considered a direct precursor and the most important literary influence on the Generation of 1898, had deep personal and intellectual ties with Krausists in Madrid and dedicated his 1878 university thesis to Giner.[77] Joaquín Costa, who is sometimes counted among the members of the Generation of 1898, was a student and close associate of Giner and was also considered a third generation Krausist.[78] Azorín was an open admirer of Giner, and indeed is counted among the "third wave of his disciples."[79] Miguel de Unamuno, perhaps the most influential member of the *noventayocho* group, also came under Krausism's sway in his early years and directly displayed Krausist tendencies in his most important writings.[80] Many members of the Generation of 1898 also shared institutional ties with Krausist intellectuals. The Centro de Estudios Históricos, established in 1910 under the liberal government of José Canalejas, brought together older Krausists, such as Rafael Altamira, and younger intellectuals, such as Menéndez Pidal and Ortega y Gasset.[81]

What were the most important intellectual continuities between Krausism and the Generation of 1898? At the most general level were their shared insistence on religious tolerance, respect for individual liberty, and general support for the liberal cause.[82] Both groups, however, rejected classical liberalism that reduced the role of the state to that of safeguarding individual liberty and the free working of the marketplace.[83] This embrace of liberalism was also tempered by a rejection of the contractual notion of the nation in favor of the Romantic belief that nations were living, organic entities that emerged naturally from the depths of history, with the help of a guiding force or collective soul. As *novecentista* Ganivet argued, society was best understood as an organism of interdependent parts that, over time, become more integrated and unitary as they come to be governed by a "dominant and central force," in which "the ideal of the race is lodged."[84] Unamuno echoed this view, referring to the existence of a "collective spirit of the people," which—using the German term—he called the *"Volkgeist."* According to Unamuno, this spirit had a transcendent, collective quality and contained within it "all the sentiments, desires and aspirations" of the people.[85] Similarly, Azorín wrote of the "genius of the [Spanish] race," which he believed to be rooted in an underlying, eternal sense of spiritual mysticism.[86]

As for the source of this common soul and its distinctive character, the Generation of 1898—like the Krausists—placed enormous emphasis on the national territory, and saw it as the primary shaper of the national *ser* or way of being.[87] Indeed, the preoccupation with the Spanish landscape was one of the defining aspects of the Generation of 1898, producing, as Ramsden has noted, a "generation of excursionists," whose "underlying determinist quest for eternal tradition" led them to the countryside. [88] For Unamuno, "to know a *patria*, a pueblo, it is not enough to know its soul . . . [it is] necessary to know also its body, its soil, its land." Contact with the Spanish countryside, he maintained, allowed one to "feel a sense of brotherhood with the trees, rocks and rivers; one feels that these are also of our race, are also Spanish."[89] In much the same vein, Azorín believed in the "supreme and inexpressible union" of the landscape with the Spanish "race, history, art and literature."[90] For Ganivet, the central force in the formation of Spain's "psychological structure" or its "irreducible nucleus" was the national territory. Indeed, he insisted, the country's development could be understood not by the "external events of its history" but through the grasping of the "permanent, invariable spirit created by the land that creates, infuses and maintains" the Spanish people.[91]

Another key idea associated with the Generation of 1898 with Krausist roots, which reappeared in the thought of the cultural nationalists, was that the nation must stay true to its authentic character or being. Both Unamuno and Ganivet followed Giner's dictum that a nation that "struggles against" or in some way acts against this underlying character becomes disoriented and loses its way. Conversely, a nation that "lives as one" with its authentic nature enjoyed strength and prosperity.[92] Moreover, many—although not all—individuals associated with the Generation of 1898 agreed with the Krausists that Spain's problems could be traced to conservative Catholicism, which had led the people to lose touch with their true essence.[93] According to Unamuno, Spanish decline began in the seventeenth century, when the Inquisition shut Spain off from the rest of the world. When this occurred, Spaniards lost touch with the part of their tradition that was "eternal," thus stifling their development.[94] Azorín expressed similar sentiments, arguing that the "Castilian and Catholic austerity" had closed the national spirit off from "all sensations of aesthetic intimacy."[95] The path toward regeneration, both Krausists and members of the Generation of 1898 agreed, lay in opening up their country to foreign currents. Like the Krausists, they believed that, rather than denationalizing Spain, this contact with outside influences would invigorate the nation, fortifying the best and most authentic elements of Spanish culture and cleansing it of the fanaticism and intolerance that had deformed the national character.

For both the Krausists and the members of the Generation of 1898 (as was the case with the cultural nationalists), one of the first steps toward national regeneration lay in understanding the true Spain and grasping the essence of the Spanish people. Given this conviction, it is not surprising that both groups of intellectuals believed in the importance of collective self-knowledge.[96] Moreover, the Generation of 1898's understanding of how to gain this self-knowledge reflected strong Krausist/Romantic influences. As noted, both Krausists and members of the Generation of 1898 believed contact with the countryside was essential to the understanding of the national character, or *ser*. Just as important was an understanding of the nation's "intrahistory." Like the Spanish Krausists, the *noventayocho* intellectuals expressed a marked distaste for the study of traditional history. What *was* important, they believed, was the search for the supposedly hidden history of those permanent phenomena that lay beneath the visible history of events. For Unamuno, "This intrahistorical life [that is] as silent and fecund as the very depths of the sea, is the substance of progress, the true tradition, the eternal tradition."[97] Ganivet also embraced the concept of intrahistory, arguing that to grasp the true nature of a country, it was necessary to go beyond describing its external institutions and ideologies. Rather, he insisted, one must "go more deeply and search for the very reality of the irreducible nucleus" of a people by looking at the only element that is truly permanent: its territory or the "territorial spirit."[98]

Access to the authentic, hidden Spain could be obtained, members of the *noventayocho* group believed, through art and literature. Like the Krausists (and the cultural nationalists), the Generation of 1898 believed art offered a window into the Spanish essence, and that its value lay not in the creativity of the individual artist but in its capacity to reflect the character of a particular people. For Ganivet, an artistic masterpiece was by definition in harmony with the spirit of the nation; moreover, the "closer the concordance [between a work and this spirit], the greater the merit of the work."[99] Azorín shared this belief. Like Ganivet, he insisted that the merit of a particular work of art often had nothing to do with the artist's technical talents but rather with his ability to comprehend the "true and deep characteristics that lay beneath the superficial characteristics and differences." An artist without such intuitive abilities would never be able to produce works that reflected "the true and authentic Spain."[100]

A final continuity between the Krausists and the Generation of 1898, which reappeared in the thought of the cultural nationalists, was the shared belief in hispanismo and the idea that the family of Hispanic peoples, like all nations or peoples, had a crucial historical mission to fulfill. As noted above, such ideas reflected the Romantic conception of history that saw humanity as moving toward a single, organically united whole, where each branch or "race" would play a distinctive and complementary role. Accordingly, like the Spanish Krausists, the members of the Generation of 1898 group were energetic Hispanicists, who believed Spaniards and Hispanic Americans formed a single spiritual and cultural group. Ganivet, for example, proclaimed that Spain's "past and present ties us to Hispanic America," and that Spaniards must always take into account that "their words and actions were not only for the peninsula alone . . . but also for the great territory in which our spirit and language rule."[101] Elsewhere he noted that it was Spain's "great historical mission" to "reconstitute the familial union of all the Hispanic pueblos, and to infuse them with the cult of the same ideals, of our ideals."[102]

CLEARLY THEN, many factors converged during the early twentieth century to give rise to what might be called Argentina's second Romantic moment. Material factors, such as rapid modernization and mass immigration, delivered an understandable shock to native-born Argentines, producing a critical juncture, during which traditional ideas and understandings came into question. At the same time, changes in the publishing industry and student life helped give rise to a new youth culture and the so-called ideology of the artist. Intellectual influences also played an indispensable role. Positivism's and eugenics' emphasis on social organicism, racial categories, and collective psychology, as well as the essentialist thinking of Rodó and Ugarte, nudged notions of Argentine national identity away from their traditional contractual or civic bases; in doing so, they established the conceptual groundwork for Romantic understandings of nationality. Finally, I have emphasized the importance of Spanish Krausism, tracing its emergence in nineteenth-century Spain and its subsequent impact on the Generation of 1898, and thus on the Argentine cultural nationalists.

As noted above, the Spanish Generation of 1898 was only one avenue by which Krausist ideas came to penetrate early twentieth-century Argentina. Another, more direct route, was through Argentines' own readings of Krausist texts. Such was the case with the leaders of the Radical Party, especially Hipólito Yrigoyen, who as a young man developed a keen and enduring interest in Krausist thought. Yrigoyen's outsized role within the party, and the fact that he was twice elected president of the republic meant that his Krausist-inspired ideas about nationality and history would have a direct impact on the fate of Argentine democracy. It is to the Krausist-Radical connection that we now turn.

# FOUR

# Romantic Influences and the Argentine Radicals

Up to this point, much of our discussion has focused on the early twentieth-century cultural nationalists, emphasizing how the ideas associated with Romantic nationalism inspired their notions of nationhood and served as a conceptual filter through which they perceived and made sense of the changes transforming their society. As argued in the previous chapter, a key source of these ideas was the Spanish philosophical movement known as Krausism, whose Romantic concepts made their way to Argentina via the influential Generation of 1898. But to appreciate the extent to which Krausist assumptions shaped early twentieth-century Argentine thought, we must broaden our analysis to include another group that also came to embrace such notions: the Unión Cívica Radical (UCR) or Radical Party.

As noted, the individual most responsible for the Krausist-Radical connection was Hipólito Yrigoyen, who led the main faction of the Radicals from 1896 to 1930. Largely as a result of Yrigoyen's outsized influence on the party, Radical discourse became infused with an oddly mystical language strongly resembling that of the cultural nationalists. Just as striking, and even more fateful for the fortunes of Argentine democracy, was Yrigoyen's understanding of nationality and history. Following Krause, the Radical leader saw nations as natural, organic entities imbued with their own souls and destinies, whose members shared an enduring racial and spiritual unity. Accordingly, he viewed competitive party politics as divisive. In contrast to the founders of the UCR, who sought to create a modern political party that would articulate a clear platform and compete with other parties in the electoral arena, Yrigoyen rejected the very term *party*. Instead, he insisted on calling the UCR a *movement* or *cause*, and proclaimed it to be consubstantial with the nation itself. To highlight this illiberal aspect of Radical thought, we begin our analysis with a look at the early years of the UCR, before Yrigoyen assumed control.

## THE UCR OF LEANDRO ALEM

The origins of the UCR date to 1890, when a dissident faction of the political elite challenged the fraudulent rule of the Partido Autónomo Nacional (PAN). During the early 1880s, the PAN had encountered only limited opposition, successfully using voter fraud to ensure a steady string of electoral victories. Its troubles began in 1886 with the election of Miguel Juárez Celman, a maladroit politician, who quickly alienated many PAN members. On September 1, 1889, some of the country's leading political figures, university students, and members of the public gathered in an open meeting to voice their opposition. The goal of the meeting, in the words of organizer Emilio Gouchón, was to push for clean elections, allow Argentines to "exercise their political rights as citizens," and to "provoke the awakening of the national civic life."[1] Also addressing the crowd was Leandro Alem, a former activist in the Republican Party and the uncle of future president and Radical leader Hipólito Yrigoyen. Alem's speech electrified the crowd, and he immediately emerged as the spokesperson of the movement. The outcome of this public rally was the establishment of a formal opposition group named the Unión Cívica (UC), with Alem elected as its head. The plan was for the UC to seize power and establish a provisional government that would oversee new elections free of fraud.

Fortunately for the conspirators, elements of the army were also dissatisfied with Juárez Celman and helped organize an armed insurrection that began on July 26, 1890. Although government forces squashed the rebels, Juárez Celman was forced to cede power to his vice president. For some members of the UC coalition, this victory was sufficient, and they agreed to cooperate with the new government. Others, led by Alem, opposed the deal and announced the establishment of a new political party called the Unión Cívica Radical (UCR) or Radical Party.[2] Under Alem's leadership, the UCR became a modern-style political party, holding nominating conventions (a novel practice in Argentina) and fielding candidates in local and national elections. At the heart of the Radicals' objection to the PAN was their conviction that it had subverted the political values enshrined in the 1853 Constitution. Radicals believed that by reducing politics to a question of mere administration, the PAN had hollowed out the very core of the Argentine political life. Rejecting the PAN's view of political parties as a source of instability, the UCR saw "open rivalry and the competition of political parties as the main guarantee of a healthy political life" and the expression of a young, vigorous democracy.[3] Thus interspersed with the UCR's attacks on the PAN were similarly loud calls to the Argentine people to exercise their political rights and to support the UCR in its efforts to "inspire in citizens a just desire ( *justo celo*)" for their political rights and civic duties.[4]

Accompanying Alem from the beginning of his rise to prominence was his nephew, Hipólito Yrigoyen. The son of Alem's older sister, Yrigoyen had moved into his uncle's household in Buenos Aires as an adolescent. After entering the university to study law, he ran for political office and won a seat in the provincial assembly. In 1882, with his first legislative term over, Yrigoyen faced the possibility of completing the final requirements for his law degree or continuing his political career. He chose neither, and for reasons that are not entirely clear withdrew from public life. From 1882 to 1890, he dedicated himself to two activities: teaching at the Escuela Normal de Maestras in Buenos Aires (a teaching-training academy) and ranching, an activity that took him to the countryside for days at a time. His ranching operations prospered, but he continued to live in Buenos Aires in Alem's household until 1889. Yrigoyen reentered political life during the crisis of 1889–90 and followed his uncle when he established the UCR.

Yrigoyen clearly benefited from his ties to Alem, and he quickly rose to prominence within the UCR. Although taciturn and somewhat reclusive, he proved to be an exceptional organizer. Shunning public speeches, he preferred one-on-one interactions, through which he built a network of intensely loyal followers. Yrigoyen concentrated his efforts in the province of Buenos Aires and soon established his own independent power base. This ambition came at a cost, however, and his relationship with Alem began to sour as early as 1891. Matters worsened in 1894, when a rebellion organized by Alem was quickly shut down by the authorities, and Alem blamed his nephew for the defeat. Then, in July 1896, Alem stunned his followers by committing suicide with a gunshot to the head. No clear motive has ever been established, and whether his troubled relationship with his nephew played any role is, of course, unknowable.

Alem's sudden and dramatic death left behind a party in disarray, and with no clear successor in place. As events unfolded, the struggle for control pitted the UCR of the federal capital against Yrigoyen and his provincial allies. One of the issues dividing the two groups was whether or not the UCR should make deals with other political groups, a strategy the future president bitterly opposed. In 1897, he and his followers declared their independence from the national organization. This split greatly weakened the party, and by 1898 the UCR was a shell of its former self. The party remained largely dormant for the next several years, finally resurfacing in 1903, when Yrigoyen organized a civic procession in the streets of Buenos Aires.[5] A year later, the newly resurrected UCR held its first party convention since 1897. Yrigoyen's next move was to organize yet another attempt to unseat the government by force. In 1905, the UCR launched a series of revolts that were easily crushed. Still, the rebellions galvanized opposition to the PAN, brought new attention to Radicalism, and allowed Yrigoyen to expand the newly rebuilt UCR into a national political force. When the 1910 election of Roque Sáenz Peña as president brought a new direction to Argentina, Yrigoyen and the UCR were well prepared. Once in office, Sáenz Peña pushed through a reform bill that brought sweeping changes to the electoral system and soon transformed the Argentine political landscape. In the provincial elections of 1912, the UCR lifted its policy of abstentionism and scored decisive victories in the federal district and the provinces of Santa Fe, Jujuy, and La Rioja. By 1914, it had gained a few more governorships.

Finally, riding the swell of unprecedented voter mobilization, Yrigoyen won the 1916 presidential elections by a wide margin.

The party that muscled its way into the center of Argentine politics after the 1912 reforms was one that differed dramatically from that of Alem.[6] When rebuilding the party, Yrigoyen had been careful to represent the new UCR as a direct continuation of the old, with himself as Alem's heir. Besides using its original name, Yrigoyen employed many of the themes central to the original UCR, including its insistence on its own purity, continual blasts against the PAN for its betrayal of the 1853 Constitution, and a call for moral and civic regeneration.[7] But despite this recycled rhetoric, the UCR under Yrigoyen was a very different organization, one that was powerfully shaped by a vision of Argentine history and nationality that had strong Krausist roots. The result was a hybrid political ideology that can perhaps best be compared to a palimpsest, with the original language of Alem's UCR often seeping through a newer, quite different layer of ideas and understandings.[8]

## KRAUSISM AND THE UCR

Just what was the impact of Krausism on Yrigoyen's thought and, more generally, on the ideas that guided the newly reconstituted UCR? Krausism's influence on Yrigoyen himself has been well documented. Although the Radical leader spoke very little about Krause, there is overwhelming agreement among both contemporaries and, later, historians that Krausist ideas profoundly shaped his political ideas.[9] Yrigoyen's first contact with the philosophy probably came during his years studying law at the University of Buenos Aires, where, as had occurred in Spain, Krausist texts, such as Ahrens's *Curso completo de derecho natural* (Complete course in natural law) were widely known.[10] Perhaps more important, however, were his many years spent teaching philosophy, civics, and Argentine history at the Normal School for Teachers. According to Manuel Gálvez, who published a biography of Yrigoyen in 1939, the future Radical leader became enamored of Krausist philosophy around 1880–81, when he was searching for appropriate teaching materials for his classes at the Normal School. Horacio Oyhanarte and Adolfo Korn Villafañe, both close associates of the Radical leader, also noted the importance of the writings of Belgian philosopher Guillaume Tiber-ghien as a source for Yrigoyen's understanding of Krausist ideas.[11]

The problem of determining the impact of Krausism on the UCR as a whole, however, is more complicated. Is it reasonable to claim, as historian Hugo Biagini has suggested, that because of Yrigoyen's attraction to the ideas of a long dead, obscure German philosopher, the "origins of Argentine democracy" had a "Krausist backdrop"?[12] Caution is clearly in order, and in the end the question of just how Krausist-style Romantic thought shaped the guiding ideas of the post-1903 UCR is an omelet that can only be partially unscrambled. Still, what we *do* know is that Krausism exerted a powerful influence on Yrigoyen, who in turn placed an indelible stamp on the Argentine Radical Party after its twentieth-century rebirth. Moreover, it is clear that many other important figures in the UCR, both friends and foes of Yrigoyen, also expressed ideas that appear to have Romantic roots.[13] Whether these ideas came from the Radical leader, from their own reading of Krausist texts, or from the general intellectual climate of the time is impossible to determine with any precision. Ultimately, what is most important for the argument here is that Romantic notions of nationality and history became central to Radical ideology once Yrigoyen took control of the party.

One of the most important Krausist assumptions embraced by Yrigoyen and his fellow Radicals, and one shared by the cultural nationalists, was the mystical vision of the nation as a natural, organic entity imbued with its own personality, rights, and soul. Although members of the newly reconstituted UCR often referred to the 1853 Constitution as the touchstone of Argentina's political traditions and the independence years as the moment of the country's birth, the idea of the nation as solely the product of human agency ran counter to Radicalism's new, Krausist-inspired vision. Yrigoyen, for example, spoke of Argentina's independence period as a moment when democratic principles and the republican system of government had been "adopted" by the "Argentine nationality."[14] The use of the term *Argentine nationality* rather than *Argentine people* implies that somehow this nationality possessed its own form of agency, and suggests a belief in the existence of sentient essence or entity that predated the break with Spain. Radical politician Horacio Oyhanarte, who belonged to Yrigoyen's innermost circle, employed the term *nationality* in much the same fashion. For example, in his 1916 paean to the Radical leader, Oyhanarte wrote of the period in Argentine history when caudillos ruled the country. During this period of disorganization, he argued, "the spirit of the nationality floated in the chaos." At the same time, however, this national spirit "worked in silence . . . without being conscious of its own consciousness" as it sought its own "unity" and "consolidation."[15]

This notion of nationality as an active, living force was reinforced by the Radicals' repeated use of language that stressed the natural, almost human qualities of the nation. The manifesto of February 4, 1905, for example, justified the UCR's recent uprising by accusing the PAN of having reduced Argentina's "moral personality."[16] Elsewhere Yrigoyen described Radicalism's struggle as that of defending the nation's inalienable *fueros*, a term that is best translated as collective or corporate rights.[17] Here, the choice of the term *fueros*, rather than the more common *derechos*, is significant and underscores the Radical belief that they were defending the rights of a corporatist entity, rather than the rights of individual citizens. The idea of the nation as a living being also comes through in Yrigoyen's 1909 statement that the goal of the UCR was to "restore the *patria* in all the supremacy of its being" and to work for the "full reestablishment of its organism."[18]

The Romantic belief that Argentina, and nations in general, possessed a spirit (*genio*) or soul (*alma*) surfaced repeatedly in Radical discourse. In some cases, the terms seemed interchangeable, signifying a mystical spirit or inner force that propelled societies or individuals forward. This was the sense in which Yrigoyen used the term *spirit* in his explanation of how individual societies or nations fulfill their destinies. According to Yrigoyen, there were laws that determined the predestined "harmonious and orderly" advance of societies, although at times the way forward was blocked. But, he maintained, it was precisely at these moments, in the struggle to regain their rightful trajectory, that "pueblos reveal the *spirit* with which they had been granted or imbued." This, he continued, was the work of God, who had "put in the soul of humanity" a spirit that propelled it forward though history.[19] Radical politician José Bianco, whose 1927 work *La doctrina radical* was one of a spate of books published to help secure Yrigoyen's reelection the following year, employed the term *soul* in a similar fashion.[20] In his words, "The national soul floats as an indivisible one, above all the divergences, in order to point the path of the historical trajectory in the eternal tomorrow."[21]

At other times, *soul* denoted the supposed collective consciousness of the Argentine people. Writing of the 1853 Constitution, for example, Radical polemicist Alberto Etkin proclaimed that the document had failed, because it had "constantly clashed with our cultural soul."[22] This meaning of the term *soul* also came through in Radical descriptions of Yrigoyen's relationship to the masses. A 1926 newspaper account of a recent public appearance by Yrigoyen, for example, enthused that the "soul of the pueblo vibrated in an intimate and magnetic correspondence" between the people and the Radical leader.[23] In a similar vein, but without using the actual term *soul*, an anonymous contributor to the Radical daily *El Periódico* proclaimed that Yrigoyen came from "the very spirit of *argentinidad*,"[24] while another party member insisted that the Radical leader came from the "depths of the national consciousness (*conciencia*)."[25] Yrigoyen too believed himself to be in touch with the Argentine soul. In *Mi vida*, for example, the Radical leader wrote of the "intimate identification of my spirit with the *soul* of the nationality," claiming that he "embodied, in its most pure and genuine essences, the very spirit of *argentinidad*."[26]

Also central to Radical ideology was Romantic nationalism's teleological notion of history, a belief evident in Yrigoyen's claim that human history was predetermined by laws set by Providence and that the proper working out of providential design required that all peoples and nations remain true to their distinctive characters.[27] The above-mentioned Joaquín Castellanos, for example, maintained that nations are "differentiated organs of humanity," whose peoples have different aptitudes and who contribute different elements to world civilization.[28] Yrigoyenist Antonio Herrero held similar views, proclaiming that "in the concert of the world, each race has a mission" that corresponds with its particular strengths or inherent qualities.[29] Yrigoyen himself clearly embraced this vision, arguing that Argentina must remain faithful to "its cause, tradition, and the mission which Providence has set for it in the universal schema."[30] According to the Radical leader, Argentina's contribution to world civilization was to provide humanity with an example of a new type of democracy, a democracy that would respect individual liberties, refrain from aggression, and dedicate itself to social harmony. Yrigoyen was convinced that Argentina's destiny was, in the words of biographer Félix Luna, to serve as the "renovating seed (*germen renovador*) of Western Civilization," a theme he returned to repeatedly.[31] At the time, this conviction did not seem entirely farfetched. Many Argentines of the period were convinced that Europe's moment had passed. With the "Old World" plagued by class conflict, inherited hierarchies, and the horrors of mechanized warfare, it appeared to some that the locus of civilization had shifted toward the Americas, and more specifically to Argentina. Argentina, Yrigoyen proudly proclaimed, was a young country possessing rich natural resources, and blessed with inhabitants who possessed "qualities of spirit and generous daring of heart," who were in the process of building an advanced type of democracy.[32]

No doubt it was this belief that Argentina had a predestined role to play in world history that led Yrigoyen to maintain a policy of strict neutrality in WWI, despite intense pressure from the United States and an impassioned domestic political movement that pressed for support for the Allied cause. This conviction also led him to insist that the Argentine delegation to the 1920 assembly of the League of Nations held in Geneva take the bold step of demanding changes to the organization's charter. When the assembly refused, Yrigoyen ordered the Argentine delegates to withdraw.[33] He explained his position to Marcelo T. Alvear, his vice president and head of the delegation, in a long and mystical telegram. This was the moment, Yrigoyen insisted, that Argentines "have to tell the world what we are, and what we want." Humanity, he continued, had arrived at a "universal hour, a supremely historical hour that belongs to us, we Argentines." Accordingly, it was up to Argentina to "rise up" and lead humanity toward its "collective salvation." As Argentines march toward the future, he assured Alvear, "the world will follow us."[34]

Other Radicals shared Yrigoyen's belief that Argentina was destined to lead the West and likewise saw the war as a pivotal moment in world history. Alberto Etkin, for example, described Europe's "soul" as "old and spent" and "at the end of its cosmic cycle." In its place, he affirmed, a "new cosmic concept" was "stirring minds and souls" and was signaling the "birth of a new soul and a new culture." If Argentina were led by the Radical Party, Etkin believed, it would play a key role in this new stage in world history and bring to humanity "unknown forms with infinite radiances."[35] The above-mentioned Antonio Herrero sounded a similar theme. According to Herrero, the Great War had signified the end of a world culture dominated by objectivity and quantitative thinking. In the new era, in which Argentina would play a key role, the guiding values would be "universality, holism (*totalismo*), an ethic, and a mystical sense of life."[36] Fully embracing Romantic nationalism's identification of nationality with race and the essentialist belief in the opposition between the supposedly pragmatic "German-Saxon race" and the more spiritual and idealistic Latin race, Herrero proudly identified with the latter.[37] Argentines, he proclaimed, belonged "psychologically" to the Latin race, whose "values and qualities are very distinct, almost the opposite of those of the German-Saxon race."[38] It was up to the Latins, he believed, to lead humanity in this next phase of history. "Now," he insisted, "it falls to us the Latins, because the vital axis of the future evolution [of humanity] will be that of intuition, which is our fundamental quality."[39] Not surprisingly, Herrero also believed that Argentines were destined to serve as the vanguard of the Latin race, proclaiming that Argentina had the responsibility of carrying out the "most transcendent task of human evolution: that of liberating the soul of humans from instrumentalism."[40]

As Herrero's analysis of humanity's future suggests, the essentialist belief that peoples of Hispanic or Latin descent shared an underlying spiritual and racial unity was also part of Radical thought, and one that reflected both Krausist inspiration and the (by then) generalized view that Latins and Anglos-Saxons were intrinsically different. This sense of commonality and unity based on the Hispanic past undoubtedly lay behind Yrigoyen's decision, mentioned in chapter 2, to declare October 12 the "Day of the Race." October 12 became an important date for Yrigoyen's followers. From the early 1920s on, the Yrigoyenist newspaper *La Época* devoted increasing coverage to celebrations of the holiday, taking every opportunity to praise Yrigoyen for his "Immortal Decree." To ensure that readers continued to associate Yrigoyen with the Day of the Race, each year *La Época* reprinted a facsimile of the decree with the president's signature. In addition, it carried notices of different festivals organized to commemorate the date, dedicating whole sections to reprinting telegrams sent to Yrigoyen by celebrants. Typical of these was a message from the *Club Social Político "Hipólito Yrigoyen"* (Social Political Club "Hipólito Yrigoyen") of Tucumán that lauded Yrigoyen for his "clear vision" in establishing the holiday. The president's 1917 decision, the message proclaimed, had "shaped forever the true concept of Argentine nationality" by channeling its development toward the unity of the "great and glorious bloodline (*estirpe*)" of Spain and its former colonies.[41] In much the same vein, a group called the Comisión de la Juventud Hispano Argentino (Commission of Hispanic Argentine Youth) praised Yrigoyen's characterization of Spain as the "progenitor of nations" and called for the "spiritual unification of the Spanish-speaking nations of America and the mother country (*madre patria*)."[42]

In addition to their acceptance of the Krausist belief in the existence of racial families, Radicals also embraced the Krausist/Romantic notion that, although human history was preordained, the destinies of individual nations could be blocked by man-made obstacles. The consequences of such an interruption in Argentina's development, Radicals believed, would be disastrous for Argentina and for humanity in general. Thus, Yrigoyen warned, the Republic "should not consent to any proposition that causes it to deviate from its historical trajectory." To do so, he insisted, would result in "new and more dramatic misfortunes."[43] In the same vein, the Radical leader proclaimed that those individuals who "subjugate or detain societies in their progressive march carry the seal of eternal sin."[44] This idea of a lost march or deviation from a preordained historical trajectory was also central to the Radical notion of *reparación* (reparation), a term Yrigoyen used repeatedly when explaining the mission of the UCR. In Yrigoyen's words, "Reparación" was the "great crusade undertaken by the Argentine essence (*la argentinidad*) to regain or retake (*retomar*) the lost march of its historical tradition."[45]

But what sort of obstacles had impeded Argentina's development and caused it to deviate from its (supposed) historical mission? Spanish Krausists, it will be recalled, saw orthodox Catholicism as their nation's primary impediment. For the Argentine Radicals, in contrast, the issue was not so straightforward. Indeed, it is in the shifting and sometimes confused answers to this question that we glimpse the ambiguities inherent in the Radicals' attempt to graft Romantic concepts onto the UCR's original liberal stalk. As noted earlier, during the first years of the UCR, Argentina's problems were seen in fairly clear-cut terms. According to the party's founders, the crisis had been caused by the PAN's subversion of the democratic institutions outlined by the liberal Constitution of 1853 and its deliberate weakening of the Argentine peoples' civic spirit.

Thus the 1892 manifesto accused the PAN of violating "the fundamental laws of the Republic," resulting in the "profound alteration of the institutional regime." The remedy accordingly was the "repair of Constitutional mechanisms" and the moral regeneration of the citizenry.[46]

After Yrigoyen assumed leadership of the party, these diatribes against the PAN continued but were couched increasingly in terms that reflect the influence of Romantic nationalism, and it is here we see the Krausist theme of impediments or constraints emerge. In one of his public letters to Radical dissident Pedro Molina, for example, Yrigoyen decried the regime's refusal to hold "free and guaranteed elections." Significantly, in describing the damage inflicted by this refusal, Yrigoyen stressed its effects on the nation, rather than on the citizens. Anthropomorphizing the nation as a living person fighting for air, he argued that if such elections were held, the result would be transformative, since Argentines could see the "transcendental difference there is between a nation strangled (*ahogada*) by all the pressures that encircle it, and one breathing in the full plenitude of its being."[47] This image of the strangled nation gasping for air was apparently central to Yrigoyen's understanding of what ailed Argentina, for he used the exact same language six years later in a message to the Juventud del Partido Nacionalista del Uruguay.[48]

Yrigoyen also employed imagery that seemed to reflect Romantic influences when attempting to explain to his critics the nature of the UCR's program. Describing the Radicals' mission, Yrigoyen declared that the UCR was in "absolute rebellion" against those who harmed the republic by detaining it "on its road to regeneration and new life."[49] Besides couching the party's democratic demands in Romantic terms, Yrigoyen and his followers also expanded their list of complaints against the PAN to include its supposed cosmopolitanism and materialism, which they—like the cultural nationalists—saw as a threat to the Argentine national character. As Paula Alonzo has noted, the belief that luxury and materialism had in the past deleterious effects on the Argentine people had also been one of Alem's favorite themes. In Alem's case, however, the fear had been not about the loss of an imagined national personality but about the impact of easy wealth and luxury on Argentines' civic spirit.[50] Yrigoyen's Radical Party, in contrast, adopted language that was strikingly similar to that of Gálvez and Rojas, reflecting its own Krausist-inspired beliefs about the need for each nation to cultivate its unique qualities. Radicals, for example, accused the PAN of "betraying national traditions"[51] and of seeking to impose "modalities contrary to the national character."[52] Such policies, they believed, had the effect of "psychologically 'deargentinizing' various generations of Argentines."[53] Radicals also identified the PAN with positivism, which they (again like the cultural nationalists) identified with materialism, greed, and excessive individualism. Accusing the regime of promoting "positivistic materialism,"[54] Radicals believed that decades of PAN rule had deformed Argentine values, creating a new culture created on the basis of "sensual and egoistic materialism."[55] Thus in ways similar to the cultural nationalists, the Radicals believed that cosmopolitanism and its associated values had caused the nation to lose touch with its true essence and to deviate from its historical mission.

With this expanded diagnosis of the nation's ills, Yrigoyen and his fellow Radical leaders saw their task as a struggle for more than mere democracy: it included as well the defense of Argentines' authentic culture and traditions. In Yrigoyen's words, one of the UCR's most important aims was to "form and accentuate [the nation's] character."[56] Radical activist Adolfo Korn Villafañe agreed, proclaiming that true governance consisted in "developing the ethical and esthetic personality of the inhabitants of a nation." In Argentina, Korn Villafañe believed, this meant "awakening" the native (and supposedly authentic) spirit based in the provinces so that it could do battle with the "intrusive cosmopolitan soul" of Buenos Aires.[57] According to the Radicals, such a nationalist, anticosmopolitan stance was not selfish or narrow-minded but rather reflected the imperative that each nation had a duty to fulfill its role in the adoption of a grand scheme of human destiny. As Radical leader Joaquín Castellanos expressed it, "The most rational way for man to love humanity . . . is not to negate or suppress the nation in homage to the universal, but to consolidate and make our nationality greater."[58] Contrasting their program with the supposed antinationalism of the ruling political elite, the Radicals—again like the cultural nationalists—argued that only they could protect the nation from the pernicious effects of excessive cosmopolitanism. Radicalism, according to party militant Claudio Pozuelo, offered a uniquely Argentine solution to the nation's problems, which could not be solved with "universal doctrines."[59] In a similar vein,

Castellanos argued that the UCR served as a "jetty" protecting Argentina from the "anti-nationalist tide."[60]

At times, the Radicals' idea of defending *argentinidad* seemed to slide into a full-blown acceptance of ethnicity as the basis of nationhood. Going beyond the desire to promote and conserve the nation's authentic culture and traditions, they sometimes saw their task as that of defending the "race" itself. Writing in 1923, for example, Yrigoyen explained that the term *reparación* was a "revolutionary action" that would allow the nation to regain its "lost march," and by doing so would "conserve the essential virtues of the race."[61] Castellanos used similar language when he proclaimed that the Radicals sought the "evolution of the race and of the customs of the country [that were based] in the Argentine soul."[62]

A final similarity between the Radicals and the cultural nationalists that seems to have Krausist roots was a belief in the existence of unique individuals, who appear at certain moments in order to help their nation develop along its preordained path. According to Radical leaders, in times of crisis, were the nation to flounder and lose its way, special individuals or groups would inevitably emerge to set it back on course. Such was the role of Yrigoyen and the UCR, Radical stalwarts believed. Horacio Oyhanarte, for example, described Yrigoyen as the "pre-destined one."[63] Antonio Herrero went further, proclaiming that "Argentina was the bow [as in a ship] of Latinism, and its current helmsman is Yrigoyen." Shifting metaphors, he described the Radical leader as someone who was "plowing a new row," which would cause the "torrent of human energy to crystallize in new forms."[64] In another instance, Radical politician Enrique Pérez Colman deliberately borrowed ideas and terms from Ricardo Rojas to describe Yrigoyen, suggesting some crossover between cultural nationalism and Radicalism. In a speech given in 1922, Pérez Colman proclaimed that in a given historical moment "exceptional men" appear who are meant to lead the nation toward its true destiny. Quoting Rojas, he proclaimed that such men are those in whom "'the forces of the [national] soul are personified.'" Still quoting Rojas, he continued, "'The destiny of such souls consists in realizing a decisive and exclusive need of the national soul to which they belong.'"[65] Yrigoyen himself referred openly to the importance of his own mission, proclaiming in a 1921 message to Congress, "I well know that I have come to fulfill a destiny . . . the reintegration of the nationality upon its fundamental bases."[66]

Indeed, Radicals as a whole also saw themselves as having been chosen or elected (in the providential sense) to lead the country. Following Yrigoyen's insistence that the UCR's "historical mission" was to save the nation,[67] a 1910 manifesto proclaimed that only through the Radicals' efforts could Argentina "proceed to the useful and fecund life that Providence itself has fixed for it."[68]

In portraying themselves as Argentina's sole rescuers, Radicals—like the cultural nationalists—identified their cause with that of the nation itself. Yrigoyen, for example, insisted that the movement had a "national character, because it represents that which is authentically Argentine . . . and is rooted in the very spirit of the race."[69] Using similar terms, a 1923 campaign pamphlet for Radical politician Arturo Goyeneche described the movement as consonant with "all the lofty, good and noble qualities of the native soul" and the "very force of the nationality."[70] For Oyhanarte, Radicalism was "the pueblo of the Republic searching for its definitive organization."[71] In a similar vein, Joaquín Castellanos proclaimed that the Radicals "sought to fulfill the complementary labors of the nationality, [that were] directed from the depths of history by the clairvoyant (*vidente*) instinct of the race."[72] This identification of Radicalism with a supposed Argentine essence very clearly represented a reimagining of the UCR, one that had little to do with the earlier vision of the UCR as a political party organized to compete in the electoral process. Indeed, as mentioned above, when referring to Radicalism, Yrigoyen rejected the term *party*, calling it instead a *cause* or a "conjunction of forces emerging from national opinion."[73] This "political cause," he insisted, is "a movement that has a national character, in that it represents that which is authentically Argentine." Because it was rooted in "the very spirit of the race," he continued, its strength stemmed from having "gestated over a long period of time, during which its essences were nourished and purified (*decantando*) by adversity and pain." Thus, he affirmed, the UCR was "the fatherland (*patria*) itself."[74]

Such an understanding of the UCR, of course, eventually proved problematic. By identifying their party with the nation itself, Radicals tended to view their opponents not as citizens exercising their right to endorse alternative political programs but as enemies of Argentina, an unfortunate tendency that proved to be enduring. It is thus not surprising that Radical stalwart Alberto Etkin described "Anti-Radicalism" as "a sickness for the motherland [and is] something that threatens its very existence."[75] Horacio Oyhanarte expressed much the same view when, in his biography of Yrigoyen, he described Radicalism as a national movement consisting of virtually the entire population. In words that seemed to anticipate those of Juan Domingo Perón a few decades later, Oyhanarte assured his readers that "within the UCR, as in the first hour of [Argentine] independence, there is room for the entire Argentine pueblo in all its diversity of opinions, interests and doctrines." At the same time however, he affirmed that the UCR and the Argentine pueblo were "correlative terms." "All those who are not within [the UCR's] ranks, even those who are indifferent, are the opposite force: they are the regime, whose existence is based on illegality."[76]

THIS CHAPTER'S PRIMARY GOAL was to trace Krausism's second point of entry into early twentieth-century Argentina, and in doing so to make clear just how pervasive Romantic ideas about nationality and history had become during this period. As is evident, when Romanticism enters the political arena, the results can be hostile to democratic practices. By adopting a homogenous, essentialist vision of *argentinidad*, in whose name they claimed to speak, the Radicals defined as illegitimate, and thus as anti-Argentine, all those who opposed them. Indeed, it is one of the great ironies of Argentine history that the political party most closely associated with democracy would come to reject the label "political party." As a consequence, it would challenge the very notion that a healthy democracy is defined by electoral contests between political parties that allow citizens to choose between well-defined programs.

As should also be clear, in nations where notions of identity inspired by Romanic nationalism prevail, pluralism of almost any kind can be seen as a threat to the nation itself. When national communities are understood to be homogenous organic communities, those individuals who, by virtue of their race, ethnicity, religion, place of birth, and so on, are considered permanent outsiders are often systematically "othered" and thus dehumanized. It is not surprising, therefore, that anti-Semitism has had a long and at times virulent presence in modern Argentina. But without minimizing this legacy of intolerance in Argentina, it is also true that the vision of nationality inspired by Romantic nationalism fit uncomfortably with realities on the ground, and in particular with the fact that Argentina was unavoidably a nation of immigrants. As often occurs when there is a disconnect between abstract models and concrete realities, efforts to reconcile the irreconcilable can give rise to unexpected and creative ways of imagining the social world. Such was the case for the early twentieth-century Argentines who embraced the vision of the nation as an ethno-cultural community but who also agreed that the nation still needed immigrants. In the next chapter, we return to the theme of the Argentine race in order to explore how the growing acceptance of this construct produced controversy rather than consensus, as the nature and content of this imagined race became a topic of intense debate.

FIVE

# Defining the Essence of *Argentinidad*

*Debating Ethnicity and Language, 1900–1930*

As the century progressed and increasing numbers of Argentines began to embrace the essentialist notion of a national race, the idea of Argentina as a civic community continued to weaken and the burden of identity shifted toward ethno-cultural criteria. Certainly, the tendency to conflate nationality with ethno-cultural traits was not unique to Argentina, but in the Argentine context, the "nation-as-race" construct posed particular challenges. Given the consensus that the country's prosperity depended on the continued influx of immigrants, closing the country's doors to preserve the population's imagined ethnic unity was never a serious option. Rather, those who adopted this essentialist vision of nationality had to decide what role the immigrants would play in this supposed Argentine race. Did Argentina already possess a well-defined racial type capable of absorbing millions of immigrants without altering its supposedly essential traits? And, if so, just what *were* these traits? Alternatively, was this race still in the early stages of an evolutionary process, the outcome of which would be at least partially shaped by immigrant influences? These questions were hotly contested during this period, making it clear that the spreading acceptance of the notion of the "Argentine race" produced not consensus but controversy. At no point,

112

however, did the ideal of Argentina as a white nation come under question. Indeed, if anything, the debates over the future of the supposed Argentine race—because they centered on the role of the European immigrant in the development of the national ethnicity—served to further erase nonwhite Argentines from elite understandings of *argentinidad*.[1]

This chapter explores the controversy over the nature of the imagined Argentine race by examining two related debates that dominated early twentieth-century intellectual life. The first directly concerned the nature and content of the supposed Argentine ethnicity, focusing specifically on what role immigrants would (or should) play in its formation. The second debate was over what language Argentines should speak, and how—or if—Argentine Spanish should evolve. As noted in chapter 2's discussion of the late nineteenth-century parliamentary debates over whether or not immigrants should be educated in Spanish, one of Romantic nationalism's central tenets was that language, ethnicity, and nationality are inextricably intertwined, and that a nation's language should reflect its underlying racial personality or soul. Within this understanding of nationality, only peoples that speak a single and distinctive language can form true nations. Accordingly, the defense of the national language from contamination was seen as crucial to the protection of the organic community.[2] Such a view posed significant problems for the many Argentines who had come under Romanticism's sway but had resisted the idea that Argentina should develop its own form of Spanish. It also forced those engaged in identity debates to grapple with the question of whether foreign words and immigrant dialects should be incorporated into the national language, and if these changes represented an enrichment or a corruption of Argentine Spanish. Thus, in many ways the language controversy served as a proxy for the ongoing debate over the role of immigrants in shaping the Argentine race.

Exploring these interrelated debates is important for three reasons. First, these often-heated controversies provide further evidence of the spread of Romanticism's ethno-cultural notion of national identity during this period. Second, the wide-ranging nature of these debates provides clues about why this particular way of imagining Argentine nationality came to exercise such widespread appeal. In most countries, ethno-cultural understandings of national identity are by definition hostile to non-natives and to ethnic minorities. In Argentina, in contrast, the "nation-as-racial-entity" construct was not necessarily xenophobic or even exclusive; it could be stretched to accommodate radically different interpretations of *argentinidad.* These different interpretations, in turn, reflected very different attitudes toward the immigrant, ranging from a defensive elitism that saw the immigrants as contaminants to a more inclusive vision that celebrated the new wave of European immigrants as essential ingredients of an evolving national race. Finally, an exploration of these early twentieth-century debates sets the stage for our examination of the two different strands of post-1930s nationalism. The divergent interpretations of Argentine identity articulated during the critical juncture of the early twentieth century would serve as touchstones for both right-wing Catholic nationalists and their left-wing counterparts. Thus in many ways, these early debates over the nature of the Argentine race prefigured, and indeed set the terms for, subsequent debates over the nature of the imagined *ser nacional.*

## IMAGINING A PREEXISTING ETHNIC CORE

Most of the intellectuals considered thus far agreed that an Argentine ethnicity had largely formed *before* the era of mass immigration, and that Argentina would somehow absorb the millions of newcomers while retaining the essence of *argentinidad.* They remained divided, however, on the nature of this supposed ethnic core and its characteristics. Manuel Gálvez, it will be recalled, saw the Argentine race as essentially Latin and, within the greater family of *latinidad*, Spanish. But just as important to the country's racial identity was Catholicism, which Gálvez insisted was "one of the essential fundamentals in which nationality resides."[3] Gálvez's highly restrictive vision of *argentinidad* would gain greater acceptance as the century wore on and, indeed, formed the cornerstone of later right-wing nationalism. But during the early decades of the century, this position was considered extreme and attracted few adherents.

A more common view among those who believed in the existence of an already-formed Argentine race was that expressed by cultural nationalist Ricardo Rojas. Rojas downplayed the importance of Spain and Catholicism and proclaimed the Argentine race to be a blend of indigenous and European elements, with Spain being only one among the latter. This mixture, he maintained, had produced the Argentine creole, which was best embodied in the nineteenth-century gaucho. The now-vanished gaucho, Rojas believed, had constituted the archetype of the Argentine race and as a result had bequeathed to the nation an enduring ethnic core that could absorb the newcomers without losing its basic texture and shape. The interpretation of Argentina as a mixture, and the elevation of the once-despised gaucho as the very prototype of Argentine ethnicity, became increasingly widespread during these years and, indeed, endures in some sectors today.[4]

Another key promoter of the gaucho as Argentina's authentic racial type was Leopoldo Lugones, who later became an outspoken right-wing nationalist. Lugones's political thought and trajectory will be considered in more detail in chapter 6, but because of his importance in promoting the gaucho as Argentina's racial prototype, he is worth mentioning here. A celebrated poet, Lugones expounded his ideas about the gaucho in a highly publicized series of 1913 lectures, which were attended by such luminaries as Argentine president Roque Sáenz Peña. The lectures were published in the newspaper *La Nación* and later appeared in book form under the title *El Payador, Hijo de la pampa* (The gaucho balladeer, son of the pampa). Like Rojas, Lugones affirmed that the herdsman had been produced by the mixing of Spanish and Indian blood and represented the "prototype of the present-day Argentine." Present at the very birth of the nation, the gaucho was the "most genuine agent" of Argentine nationality, whose qualities of familial love, pride, bravery, and extravagance continued to form the basis of the Argentine personality.[5] Yet Lugones's interpretation of the gaucho's legacy differed from that of Rojas in two key ways. First, through a convoluted analysis of traditional gaucho ballads, Lugones—who was personally hostile to Catholicism—came to the conclusion that the European element of the gaucho was more Greco-Roman than Spanish.[6] He also affirmed that the physical disappearance of the gaucho had extinguished all traces of indigenous blood from the present-day Argentine race.[7] The result, according to Lugones, was an Argentine race that had emerged from the ethnic template of the nineteenth-century gaucho but was more Latin than Spanish, and completely devoid of indigenous influence.

As these examples make clear, even those who believed that the Argentine race had formed *before* the onset of mass immigration disagreed about its content. But there was an even greater gulf between those in the "preformed" camp and those who argued that an entirely new race was in the process of emerging. In contrast to intellectuals who believed in a preexisting ethnic core that would absorb millions of immigrants, others insisted that the Argentine race was still in its embryonic stages and its character remained in flux. Accordingly, they believed, immigrants would play a key role in its formation.

Not surprisingly, this notion of Argentine identity was often expressed by individuals who were themselves immigrants or first generation Argentines.[8] For example, Dr. Salvador Debenedetti, a prominent archeologist, who was the son of an Italian immigrant of Jewish extraction, insisted on the dynamic character of the Argentine race. Writing in the prestigious *Revista de Filosofía*, Debenedetti proclaimed that "What we are now seeing . . . is the soul of the future race, characterized by common aspirations and forming itself slowly and locally under the influence of the social medium and the environment."[9] Juan Más y Pi, a well-known literary critic from Catalonia, who spent much of his adult life in Argentina, espoused a similar view. Seeming to exult in Argentina's current heterogeneity, he described the country as one of "great ethnic confusion, [an] enormous conglomerate of all the races and castes." And from this "confused conglomeration," he optimistically affirmed, "a great race . . . would inevitably emerge."[10]

Argentines with deeper roots in the country sometimes took a similar stance. Wenceslao Tello, a physician born in the northwest province of Jujuy, also embraced the notion of a new Argentine race. In two related articles that combined biological and Romantic ideas about race,[11] Tello declared approvingly that Argentines were in the process of forming a new human race[12] that would be neither "Saxon nor Latin."[13] Races, Tello believed, were produced by the interactions of climate, geography, and moral education and once formed were impossible to alter. Thus, he maintained, "from a Frenchman you can never make an Englishman or a North American from a Spaniard."[14] In the case of Argentina, however, Tello believed that the race's essential traits remained in flux. Accordingly, he insisted that the country's most pressing task was "to give a soul" to the Argentine race that was still forming. Making no reference to a preexisting national character or ethnic core, he argued instead that the new Argentine race would be forged from the "abundant immigration that comes to us from all parts of the world."[15]

Eduardo F. Maglione, a prominent jurist with liberal tendencies, took a similar stance.[16] In a two-part article published in the respected magazine *Renacimiento*,[17] Maglione argued that the country's current "motley cosmopolitanism" was only a stage, and that a new, "true Argentine race and nationality" would eventually emerge from the incoming waves of Europeans.[18] Moreover, he affirmed, as it formed, the new emerging ethnic type would completely erase Argentina's traditional creole race. This "denationalization,"[19] Maglione assured his readers, was a positive development, one that would naturally occur through the "contact, juxtaposition and fusion" of immigrants and creoles currently taking place in Argentina. In this process, those with the "most energy" and "greater vitality" would inevitably triumph, resulting in a new, superior race that would have little or nothing in common with the old.[20]

Occupying a middle ground between those who embraced the notion of a preexisting core and those who believed Argentina was forming an entirely new race were the Argentine Radicals. Although the Radicals clearly embraced the idea of a national race, they had surprisingly little to say about its content or about immigration in general. This was certainly true of Yrigoyen, and we are left to infer his views from scattered statements. Given the Radical leader's decree declaring October 17 the Day of the Race, and his description of Spain as the "progenitor of [Hispanic American] nations," it is evident that he believed the Spanish heritage to be an important component of Argentine ethnicity.[21] At the same time, however, Yrigoyen's willingness to side with the largely immigrant working class in labor disputes suggests an inclusive vision of Argentine identity that accepted the newly arrived Europeans and their offspring as legitimate members of the national community. Also significant is the fact that Yrigoyen, perhaps in keeping with Krausism's ecumenicalism, never spoke publicly about Catholicism or made claims about the religious basis of Argentine nationality. Thus, while seeing *some* elements of the Spanish legacy as central to Argentine identity, he was by no means in Gálvez's camp. Finally, his insistence—noted in the previous chapter—that Argentina was a young country with its own historical mission, which had produced a "racial type" capable of building a new kind of democracy, makes clear that he viewed the Argentine race as fundamentally different from that of its former colonizer—that is, one that presumably included the immigrants and their offspring.[22]

Other Radical leaders of the period stressed similarly inclusive notions of Argentine nationality. As historian Matthew Karush has argued, Radical politician Ricardo Caballero espoused a criollista-style nationalism that glorified the gaucho while also seeking to identify *argentinidad* with the country's multiethnic working class. Caballero, whose base of operations was the city of Rosario, believed Argentina's authentic culture was rooted in the values of nineteenth-century caudillo leaders and their gaucho followers. In his view, these values—which included the willingness to fight for an ideal, for manliness, and for austerity, as well as a lack of interest in material wealth—had been undermined by economic prosperity.[23] But while celebrating the supposedly pure, authentically national creole of the pre-1880 period, Caballero also courted Rosario's working-class voters, a large number of whom were first generation Argentines. As Karush notes, he did so by crafting a new brand of popular nationalism that identified the authentic Argentina with the working class and portrayed *all* workers as creoles, who had been oppressed by wealthy foreigners or the domestic elites who had sold out to foreign interests.[24] Thus, regardless of their ethnicity or ancestry, workers were encouraged to see themselves as part of Argentina's original creole ethnic core or as the "true descendants of yesterday's manly caudillos."[25]

A final variation of Argentine identity emerging from the Radical leadership during these years, and one that was even more welcoming toward immigrants, came from politician Horacio Oyhanarte. Oyhanarte, who belonged to Yrigoyen's inner circle, espoused a vision of Argentine identity that closely resembled that of Tello and Más y Pi. In his view, the Argentine race was still evolving and would contain the best elements or "essence" of all the races that had come—and were still coming—to Argentina. Explicitly rejecting the claim that Argentina's racial prototype could be found in the figure of the mixed-race gaucho, the Radical leader asserted that, during the colonial period, there had in fact been very little miscegenation between natives and Spaniards. Thus, he affirmed, the "rich vein of our pure [Spanish] blood" had been only slightly diluted. Moreover, any indigenous or African blood that had survived into the nineteenth century had been completely washed out by the great wave of "civilized races," which had continued to crash onto Argentine shores. From this "enormous alloy" of Spaniards, Italians, French, and English, Oyhanarte proclaimed, a new and more perfect racial prototype would form.[26] In the meantime, he insisted, these European immigrants should consider themselves to be Argentine. In his words, only those who were unable "to feel the . . . solidarity of the race, of this prodigious race in gestation" were foreigners.[27]

## RACE AND THE LANGUAGE QUESTION

Different perspectives on the content of the emerging national race were also reflected in the continuing preoccupation over language. As discussed in chapter 2, during the 1890s some Argentine politicians became concerned about the proliferation of immigrant-run schools, especially those where children were taught in a language other than Spanish. Fearful that Argentina was on its way to becoming a multilingual society, individuals such as Indalecio Gómez and Marco Avellanedo had sought to require that Spanish be the language of instruction in all schools, both public and private. By 1900, however, the focus of the language controversy shifted away from fears that Argentina was becoming a multilingual nation to anxiety over whether Argentine Spanish was being corrupted by the new words, phrases, and inflections introduced by immigrants. Now the question became whether Argentine Spanish itself was changing, and, if so, was this a positive or negative development?

The individual most responsible for casting the twentieth-century language debate in Romantic terms, and indeed for sparking the debate itself, was neither an Argentine nor a native Spanish speaker. The French linguist Luciano Abeille had lived and worked in Argentina for several years before publishing his 1900 book *Idioma nacional de los argentinos* (The national language of the Argentines).[28] Clearly steeped in the ethno-cultural nationalism sweeping Europe, Abeille embraced both the concept of national races and the assumption that a nation's language was the expression of its unique racial soul.[29] Accordingly, he opined, a "nation that lacks its own language is an incomplete nation. It is as necessary to have its own language . . . as it is to have its own flag."[30] Fortunately, Abeille assured his readers, Argentina was well on its way to solving its linguistic problem. Just as the new Argentine race was evolving, he insisted, so too was the language Argentines spoke. Indeed, he affirmed, Argentine Spanish was being transformed into an entirely new language that would reflect the unique character of the emerging Argentine race.[31] In his view, to think otherwise was pure folly and even unpatriotic, for "to deny that the Argentine language is not evolving is to declare that the Argentine race will not reach its full development."[32] The emergence of this new language, Abeille believed, was inevitable, but he worried that this process was being stymied by educators who insisted that their students speak only pure Spanish.[33] By deforming and falsifying the emerging Argentine language, he warned, this practice was running the risk of "perturb[ing] the national soul that is reflected in this language."[34] A much more sensible approach, Abeille assured his readers, was for schools to teach the national language in a way that mirrored its natural evolution.

Abeille's book hit a sensitive nerve among those Argentines who were already concerned about what they saw as the corruption of Argentine Spanish by immigrant influences. The focal point of this anxiety was the growing popularity of two distinct jargons, both associated with the working-class immigrant population. *Lunfardo* was a street slang associated with the figure of the *compadrito*, a lower-class, dandified tough guy; *cocoliche* was a kind of Spanish-Italian hybrid or pidgin spoken by Italian immigrants that became associated with criollismo, a form of popular theater and literature. It featured dramatic comedies about rural life that were very much in vogue among the immigrant working class.[35] The appeal of criollista theater and literature was not limited to the popular classes, and, indeed, some of the most famous criollista writers and playwrights came from the upper ranks of society. For many such individuals, criollismo represented an authentically Argentine cultural movement that was part of a new national identity, which included, and indeed celebrated, the immigrants' contributions. For its detractors, in contrast, criollismo represented a bizarre parody of Argentine rural life that falsely emphasized the antisocial tendencies of the gaucho, and thereby promoted immorality among the immigrant working sectors. Worse still, because of its heavy use of cocoliche, criollista literature and theater served as key sources of linguistic corruption that needed to be combated at all costs.

One of the first responses to Abeille's work came from Miguel Cané, a distinguished political figure and prominent member of Argentina's late nineteenth-century liberal political class. In an article published in the prestigious newspaper *La Nación* shortly after the appearance of Abeille's book, Cané condemned the Frenchman's ideas as not only foolish but even as dangerous for a country, such as Argentina, that had such a large immigrant population. Cané also rejected the Frenchman's overall argument that all true nations should have their own languages. Argentines, he insisted, should speak Spanish—the purer, the better. Thus, he believed, "only those countries where the spoken language is correct (*de buen habla*) have good literature, and good literature signifies culture, progress and civilization."[36]

Cané, of course, was still working with traditional nineteenth-century notions of what it meant to be civilized, but most participants in the polemic over Abeille's book showed themselves to be more in step with the new ideas linking language to nationality. Significantly, even the Frenchman's harshest critics accepted his assumption that language and nationality were inextricably intertwined. One of the most outspoken was historian Ernesto Quesada, who had previously published his own work outlining his views on the language issue. Written in 1900 in the immediate aftermath of the Cuban-Spanish-American War of 1898, *El problema del idioma nacional* (The problem of the national language) reflected the rising *hispanismo* and anti-US sentiment of the era. In this work, Quesada strongly opposed the formation of distinctive dialects or national languages within Spanish America. Such a development, he reasoned, would weaken the linguistic unity of the region, thus leaving Spanish America vulnerable to cultural penetration from the north.[37]

Two years later, Quesada picked up his pen again, this time to enter into the debate unleashed by Abeille. His direct target, however, was not Abeille but the work of fellow Argentine Francisco Soto y Calvo, an upper-class Argentine living in Paris, who in 1901 had published a book-length poem titled *Nostalgias* (Nostalgias). The poem had nothing to do with the language question per se but was written in criollista style. In a two-hundred-page essay in the pages of the journal *Estudios*, Quesada used Soto y Calvo's poem as a springboard for a scathing critique of criollismo, which he described as low-class literature and theater that gratified "all the lowest passions of the uncultured masses."[38] The idea that the jargons associated with criollismo should be considered the beginnings of a new national language was similarly repugnant to Quesada. Certainly, Quesada admitted, it was at times appropriate for writers to employ words from cocoliche, lunfardo, and gaucho speech in order to give their work local flavor, but—and here he took direct aim at Abeille— "to go from this [type of usage] to converting these jargons into a national language—or into the 'language of the Argentines' as a certain French professor seeks to do . . . there is an immense distance, a distance as large as that which exists between what is, and is not, reasonable."[39] Concluding his long essay, Quesada affirmed his acceptance of the Romantic vision of race and language, insisting that language was "the depository of the spirit of the race, of its very *genio*." It was for this very reason, he continued, that men of letters were duty bound to protect Argentine Spanish from "contamination." Given the cosmopolitanism of contemporary society, it was essential that the "national tradition be maintained unscathed" and that Argentines honor their forefathers and "the genuine Argentine imprint" by defending "the purity and gallantry of our language."[40]

Quesada's call for the defense of pure Spanish prompted his supporters to publish congratulatory letters in the capital's major newspapers. Writing in *La Nación*, for example, Miguel Cané lauded Quesada's erudite analysis and reiterated his own belief that vulgar speech reflected moral depravity. Accordingly, he opined, the teaching of pure Spanish must be a top priority for the nation's schools.[41] In a similar letter published in *El Tiempo*, contributor Carlos Astrada lauded both Quesada and Cané for their efforts to discredit Abeille's thesis, adding his own voice to the chorus. Cocoliche-infused literature, he proclaimed, was the *"flor de sapo"* (toad flower) of Argentine letters, which had grown like a noxious weed.[42] Paul Groussac, one of the most prominent intellectuals of the 1880–1900 period, concurred. Writing in the prestigious *Anales* of the National Library, he insisted that Argentines should "conserve with religious respect" the Spanish language, which was the "living tradition of the race."[43]

But not all prominent Argentines disagreed with Abeille. One example was journalist Carlos Olivera, who praised the Frenchman's study and noted that recent advances in the field of psychology had incontrovertibly established the link between language and the "way of being (*modo de ser*) of each pueblo."[44] Thus it was clear, he insisted, that Abeille had been right to claim that "each pueblo should have its own language" and that efforts to confine the development of the Argentine language would lead to distortions in the national character.[45] In Olivera's words, "each pueblo molds its own soul" and it was essential that this occur as freely as possible by allowing the national language to develop along with it. Paying excessive homage to "old rules and modes of speech," he continued, would retard the "florescence of our national spirit."[46]

Another prominent Argentine sympathetic to Abeille was Carlos Pellegrini, president of Argentina from 1890 to 1892, to whom the Frenchman had dedicated his book. Reacting to the torrent of criticism, Abeille sought Pellegrini's support and asked the former president to organize a conference that would allow him to confront his detractors. Pellegrini demurred, but in a public letter to Abeille he made clear his support for the Frenchman's ideas. Organizing a conference, he argued, would be unnecessary since Abeille's theories were clearly correct.[47] Reiterating his support for Abeille's central argument, he expressed his own belief that while Argentina's new language was still in its infancy, its transformation from a "stammering, a cocoliche" into a real language was inevitable. It would be best, Pellegrini publicly counseled his friend, to ignore the "purists," who "entertained themselves with examining [this new language] with a microscope" and who found it deformed and offensive. Their "mania," he continued, was inconsequential, for regardless of such fears, a new Argentine language would inevitably emerge. To pretend otherwise was to ask that a pueblo that is "transforming [itself into] a race" and was transforming its "institutions, ideas, usages and customs" would somehow not transform its language as well.[48]

Francisco Soto y Calvo, whose book *Nostalgias* had been the spark that had set off Quesada's early attack on criollista literature, also entered the fray. In 1903 he published a rejoinder, in which he criticized scholars such as Quesada for their "precious aesthetic sensibility."[49] Under the pretext of developing a literature with universal significance, Soto y Calvo complained, Argentine writers had produced a "colorless" national literature that "could have as easily been written in Paris as in Buenos Aires."[50] Only by liberating themselves from academic Spanish and incorporating the language as it was spoken by the masses, he maintained, could Argentine writers produce a truly authentic national literature. It was the "cocoliche dialect" and "gauchesque norms" of speech that "are most genuinely Argentine, and for this reason brings us more honor than those things we bring from abroad and learn like parrots."[51]

The intense controversy over Abeille's book waned somewhat after a few years, but the question of whether or not Argentines would—or should—develop a distinctive language remained an issue of active concern. With few exceptions, cultural elites continued to embrace uncritically the Romantic identification of language, race, and nationality. At the same time, however, they remained divided over whether Argentines should defend their Spanish from foreign "corruptions," or whether these were salutary changes that represented the early steps toward developing a truly national language. Among those who continued to argue that Argentine Spanish should be kept as pure as possible was the Spanish-born linguist Miguel de Toro y Gómez. Writing in the above-mentioned 1918 volume of *Verbum* devoted to celebrating the "Day of the Race," Toro y Gómez argued that languages gave peoples their underlying unity by imprinting on them "the same soul, the same law and the same spiritual orientation."[52] Accordingly, Toro y Gómez deemed it essential that all Spanish speakers, regardless of their nationality, maintain the "integrity and purity" of the language.[53]

Not surprisingly, cultural nationalist Manuel Gálvez also weighed in on behalf of the purists. Perhaps because he was still relatively unknown in 1900, when Abeille's bombshell exploded, Gálvez had contributed nothing to the debate.[54] Still, his predilections were clear in his 1913 *El solar de la raza* (The crucible of the race), when he declared that one of the book's aims was to propagate "the love of the [Spanish] language; the most beautiful, most sonorous, richest and virile of all the modern languages."[55] Years later he commented explicitly on the language question in his response to an *encuesta*, or survey, sponsored by the progressive newspaper *Crítica* in 1927. In this survey, the newspaper asked prominent individuals to respond to the question, "Will we come to have our own language?" In his contribution, Gálvez impatiently dismissed the very notion as ridiculous. "The enmity against pure Spanish," he contended, "is something which is more a defensive attitude that stems from youthful ignorance rather than being a true sentiment."[56]

Joining Gálvez and Toro y Gómez in the purist camp was nativist José P. Barros, who in a 1926 address to the Liga Patriotica Argentina, lamented the "intoxication" of Argentine Spanish by foreign influences.[57] Quoting German linguist Friedrich Max Müller—whose theory about the links between language, thought, and ethnicity, or race, had also influenced Abeille—Barros proclaimed language to be the "sacred soil" formed by the "deposit" of a people's thought. Accordingly, it served as a "psychological document" that provided an invaluable window into the national mentality.[58] Language, in Barros's view, was the "Herculean column that sustains the unity of nationality," which was as central to a people's identity as their racial heritage.[59] A staunch supporter of pure Spanish, he insisted that any change to Argentine Spanish, whether introduced by immigrants or the native born, represented a linguistic corruption that threatened the very nationality itself.[60]

But the defenders of pure Spanish did not entirely win the day, and the idea that Argentines should develop their own language also continued to gain adherents as the century wore on. This was especially true among those who embraced criollista literature and theater. Playwright José Antonio Saldías, for example, argued that such a language was becoming increasingly necessary as Argentines adopted new expressions, words, and phrases into their everyday speech. Driving this phenomenon, he argued, was the "composition of the new Argentine race," which had already emerged and was continuing to develop. Significantly, Saldías insisted that this new language would come from the people themselves, who needed "to express [their thought] spontaneously and fully." Chiding those excessively "prim and proper" Argentines who fought this development, Saldías argued that resistance was futile and whether elites or the Argentine government accepted or rejected this new language was immaterial. Once the new words, phrases, and expressions have become generally diffused among the people, he insisted, the people themselves "have made it law."[61]

Also supporting this position was another respondent to the *Crítica* survey, writing under the English pseudonym Last Reason and identified only as a master of creole theater. Fully embracing ethno-linguistic nationalism, Last Reason maintained that the formation of a distinctive language was central to the nation's emerging identity. Without this new language, the writer contended, "Buenos Aires would be merely a cosmopolitan, European city that lacked its own personality." What now seemed a crude slang, he believed, would form the basis of a new and ultimately rich national language. Attacking the elitism of "doctors," who worried about the vulgarity of this new language (here Last Reason specifically mentions Rojas), he proclaimed, writing in language laced with *lunfardo*,

> [So you think] the language we use is barbaric and phonetically incorrect? I agree. . . . The kid is so ugly it's difficult to kiss him. Nonetheless, the baby is ours. . . . But take note: one day the kid will grow and be beautiful, he will be a man. . . . One day he will enter into the history of nations through the front door, speaking in a loud voice a language which is beautiful, graphic, musical and vibrant. . . . This language will be the product of that rude and bastard dialect which today burns the lips of the doctors. . . . Tomorrow it will be the powerful clarion that shouts to the decrepit and worm-eaten nations, the coming of a great and glorious nation.[62]

The new evolving Argentine language, in other words, would become ever-more melodious as it reflected the country's increasing greatness.

Finally, an intermediate stance on the language question was taken by those who agreed that language and nationality were intimately interwoven, and who also accepted that Argentine Spanish would inevitably evolve over time. But in contrast to those who believed this linguistic evolution would come up from below, these individuals insisted that any changes in Argentine Spanish would (and should) be tightly controlled by the educated elite. This was the position of Leopoldo Lugones, who treated the language issue extensively in his 1910 *Didática* (Didactic). While decrying the "pernicious additions" to Argentine Spanish made by the "inferior" European immigrants who were currently arriving on the nation's shores,[63] he nonetheless rejected the rigidity of what he called academic Spanish. Languages, he stressed, are "living organisms" that are inevitably influenced by the environment or society.[64]

Joining Lugones in this middle position was Ricardo Rojas, who addressed the language issue in several works. Rojas was very much aware of Abeille's theories, and a heavily underlined copy of the Frenchman's 1900 work can be found in his private library.[65] According to Rojas, Abeille's theories were "unscientific" and had provided fodder for "the most barbaric and vain inclinations of a vulgar creole patriotism" (*patrio-*

*terismo criollo*).[66] He did, however, acknowledge the problem Argentines faced in speaking a language that was not uniquely their own, which made the development of an authentic national literary tradition more difficult.[67] In such situations, Rojas affirmed, it was essential to "search for the characteristics of the nationality in the spirit (*genio*) of the pueblo itself," which surfaces in the "new content" of our literature, in its regional tone, and in the linguistic changes that inevitably occur.[68] This recognition of regional variations of Spanish meant that, in Rojas's view, it was perfectly acceptable (and natural) for Argentine Spanish to evolve to include words and sounds unknown on the peninsula.[69]

But like Lugones, Rojas believed that any changes to Argentine Spanish must be the work of the educated, rather than the popular, classes. In a 1928 speech to the students of the Colegio Nacional de Buenos Aires, for example, he affirmed that Spanish would always be the "synthesis of our national personality and race [and was part of] the collective memory of tradition and culture."[70] It was, therefore, important for educated individuals to combat corrupting influences such as lunfardo. "At the bottom of this complex problem," he maintained, "is nothing other than the age-old antagonism between culture and lack of culture (*incultura*)." Describing his audience as Argentina's "future cultural workers," he urged them "not to vacillate" but to enter into the struggle to protect Argentine Spanish from contamination from below.[71]

THE WIDE RANGE OF VIEWS on the nature of the evolving Argentine race, and the language it would ultimately speak, make it abundantly clear that the spread of Romantic ideas about nationhood did not produce anything close to a homogeneous vision of *argentinidad*. While those who participated in these debates shared a common vision of Argentina as an organic ethno-cultural community, they differed radically in how they understood the content and characteristics of this community. Thus instead of agreement about what it meant to be Argentine, what emerged was a broad spectrum of views, ranging from the exclusivist (and usually elitist) vision of the Argentine race as essentially Spanish or creole to the more inclusive (and usually more egalitarian) argument that this race would inevitably be a new ethnicity, of which immigrants would be an essential ingredient. The language debate reflected similar divergences. Between those who sought to defend Argentine Spanish from the linguistic changes bubbling up from the immigrant working class and those who celebrated these new changes, there was a vast chasm.

The notion that Argentines formed a distinctive ethno-cultural community that existed independently of the Argentine state cast a long shadow. Although mass immigration largely halted in the late 1920s, the vision of Argentine identity it helped trigger did not suddenly evaporate. Rather, the identity discourses produced during this critical juncture, along with the vision of nationality that informed them, continued to shape discussions of *argentinidad* and to channel them along essentialist lines. But while the ideas and assumptions survived, some of the language changed in response to new circumstances. As I argued in the introduction, during the 1930s, the term *race* began to take on a more strictly biological meaning, and the phrase "Argentine race" began to drop from general usage. Instead, those engaged in debates about the nation's identity began to speak and write about *el ser nacional* (the national being, the soul, or the intrinsic character of the Argentine people). Similarly essentialist, those who used this term believed that Argentines formed a distinctive people and possessed a unitary, enduring collective character. The strikingly different versions of the Argentine race articulated by early twentieth-century intellectuals, political figures, and opinion makers also survived and helped shape conflicting interpretations of *el ser nacional*. Thus, the chasm between those who defined this imagined race as Catholic and Spanish and those who embraced a more inclusive vision would continue to reverberate for decades to come.

# PART TWO

# Identity and Nationalism
# in the Post-1930 Era

Argentina would approach the 1930s with a political and cultural elite that was deeply divided over what it meant to be Argentine. During this critical period of mass immigration, the question of how to incorporate the newcomers sparked a series of debates that was powerfully shaped by new ways of imagining Argentine nationality. To be sure, the nineteenth-century vision of the nation as a civic community, whose members were joined primarily by their shared political ideals and loyalties, never disappeared entirely, and many Argentines remained convinced that liberal democratic values were central to their collective identity. But as we have seen, these years also witnessed the growing acceptance of a competing vision of what it meant to be Argentine. Influenced by ideas associated with Romantic nationalism, a substantial segment of the country's intellectuals, politicians, and opinion makers began to embrace the essentialist idea that Argentines formed (or were in the process of forming) a distinctive ethnicity or "race." For these individuals, becoming Argentine had nothing to do with changing one's legal status but instead entailed becoming subsumed—in some fashion—into a culturally and ethnically homogenous community, whose unitary character would strengthen and endure over time.

Certainly, as previous chapters have made clear, not all early twentieth-century Argentines who embraced the ideal of the Argentine race were reactionary xenophobes. In contrast to other areas of the world,

where the rise in ethno-cultural understandings of nationhood has produced hostility toward ethnic minorities and even ethnic cleansing, in
Argentina the belief in the existence of a national race could also provide
a conceptual framework for envisioning how to *incorporate* rather than
exclude the immigrant. But inclusiveness, of course, is not the same as
pluralism. The weakening of the traditional liberal vision of Argentina
as a civic community, and the notion that becoming Argentine meant
becoming part of a unitary national race, inevitably narrowed the possibilities for immigrants to hold on to their former national or ethnic
identities. In other words, when the burden of nationality shifted from
political to ethno-cultural criteria, it became more difficult for newcomers and their children to maintain hyphenated identities. It is also clear
that the growing acceptance of ethno-cultural understandings of Argentine identity was far from politically neutral. Although not all early
twentieth-century Argentines who adopted these notions of nationality
were hostile to democracy, by promoting the notion that *argentinidad*
was, or should be, rooted in the presumed ethno-cultural traits of its
people, proponents of this vision helped detach Argentine identity from
its constitutional bases. During the first three decades of the twentieth
century, this weakened link between Argentine identity and the 1853
Constitution did little to undermine the belief that Argentina should be
democratic.[1] At the same time, as is evident from the ideas of Yrigoyen
and his followers, the belief that the nation formed a homogenous ethno-
cultural community led to new definitions of democracy. Rejecting the
notion that a thriving democracy required vigorous competition between
political parties, with well-defined platforms and representing diverse interests, Yrigoyen believed the Unión Cívica Radical to be a movement—
consubstantial with Argentina itself and tasked with helping the nation
realize its true destiny. In the post-1930 period, the antiliberal political
implications of essentialist conceptions of nationality would become ever
more pronounced.

Part II explores the legacies of the early twentieth-century shift in
understandings of Argentine identity by examining the role that essentialist notions of national identity played in post-1930s nationalist
thought. The decade of the 1930s witnessed two interrelated phenomena
that shaped both Argentine political life and attitudes toward internal

diversity. First was the rise of two distinctive yet related variants of nationalism: one right wing and elitist, the other left wing and socially inclusive. Second was the growing acceptance of the notion of *el ser nacional*, or national essence. As noted in the introduction, during the 1930s and '40s, the notion of an Argentine "race" gradually lost currency as the term *race* came to be used more consistently to denote a biological category. In its place came the equally essentialist notion of *el ser nacional*: a supposedly enduring national essence that made Argentines a distinct and unitary people. Despite the shift in terminology, the idea of Argentina as a unique, homogenous community, whose members shared common mental and emotional traits (that were somehow connected to an enduring *ser nacional*), came to dominate discussions of Argentine identity and became a cornerstone of post-1930 nationalist thought.

Central to both right- and left-wing nationalists' diagnoses of Argentina's ills was the conviction that liberalism in all its forms was alien to *el ser nacional*, or the true Argentina. Writing in a time of economic crisis, when it had become clear that the country's longstanding adherence to laissez-faire economic principles had led to disaster, nationalists across the spectrum from right to left cast blame on the nation's traditional liberal elite.[2] This elite, nationalists argued, had been mentally colonized by Great Britain, whose agents had promoted liberalism as a means of gaining political and economic control of the country. By internalizing the ideas of their imperial masters, nationalists charged, the Argentine upper class had turned its back on the "real" Argentina and had sought to impose ideas, policies, and institutions that ran counter to Argentina's authentic *ser nacional*. In doing so, this elite had created a political and economic system (i.e., the "false" Argentina) that was completely out of touch with the "true" Argentina. The disconnect between the two Argentinas, nationalists insisted, had left the country weak and confused, and thus vulnerable to foreign exploitation. What Argentines needed to thrive, they believed, was to rid themselves of the false Argentina and to develop institutions and policies that were consonant with the nation's true character.

The nationalists' belief in the existence of a unitary *ser nacional* and their hostility toward liberalism had obvious implications for how they viewed both liberal democracy and cultural pluralism. Significantly, in portraying liberalism as an exotic import, neither right- nor left-wing nationalists distinguished between economic liberalism and liberal democracy. Rather, they saw liberalism in all its forms as a tool of imperialism. And while laissez-faire policies had indeed locked the Argentine economy in a position of dependency, rejecting this economic model did not necessarily require jettisoning liberal political ideals. Nor, of course, did it require making the essentialist argument that Argentines were somehow intrinsically unsuited for democracy. But by conflating liberal democracy with economic dependency, and by casting liberalism in all its forms as alien to the true Argentina, nationalists effectively demonized democracy as anti-Argentine and those who sought to defend the nation's democratic traditions as agents of the antipatria. The nationalists' essentialist ideal of a unitary *ser nacional* also had implications for how they viewed internal diversity. Although left-wing nationalists proved to be less preoccupied than their right-wing counterparts with defending the distinctive qualities of the supposed *ser nacional* from the influx of foreigners and foreign influences, their belief that the roots of the "true Argentina" could be traced to rural masses of the nineteenth century worked against any attempt to recognize Argentina for what it was: a modern society with a dynamic, pluralistic culture.

Previous chapters have been broad in scope, as I have sought to capture the ways that the new intellectual currents associated with Romantic nationalism circulated in different spheres of Argentine cultural and political life. In examining this critical juncture in Argentine history, I cast a wide net, looking at the different pathways through which new concepts of nationhood filtered into Argentina, the key individuals who embraced and promoted them, the ways in which these ideas reshaped the ideology of the Radical Party, and the impact of these ideas on the wider debates over national identity, immigration, and language. In the chapters that follow, the discussion will narrow in order to focus on how essentialist, unitary notions of Argentine identity became central elements of both right- and left-wing nationalist thought and sometimes bridged these two strands. We begin with the rise of the nationalist right.

SIX

# The Rise of the Nationalist Right and the Ideal of the Catholic Nation

The vision of Argentina as a homogenous ethno-cultural community defined by its Catholic, Hispanic heritage was just one of several understandings of *argentinidad* that circulated during the early twentieth century, when widely different (although equally essentialist) versions of the imagined Argentine race competed for primacy. During the 1930s, this highly restrictive understanding of national identity would gain a lasting foothold within key sectors of Argentine society. Although this view of *argentinidad* was never embraced by the majority—Argentina's population was too diverse and too secular for this to occur—the notion that there existed a "true" nation that was both Catholic and Spanish found a receptive audience among the most conservative members of the national elite, the military, and the clergy. It was due to their efforts, both as individuals and through the nationalist organizations they formed, that this essentialist belief in a unitary, enduring national character, or *ser nacional*, spread. Their success in propagating the notion of a Catholic, Hispanic Argentina eventually altered the course of the country's intellectual and political history. Beginning in the 1930s and gaining strength in subsequent decades, the conviction that all patriotic Argentines must

133

defend the true (i.e., Catholic and Hispanic) *ser nacional* from the corrosive forces of "exotic" ideologies such as liberalism and communism would play a powerful role in the most violent and repressive moments in the twentieth century.

This chapter charts the growing strength of this vision of Argentine identity by examining the key civilian players who promoted it, along with the intellectual, political, and economic circumstances that shaped their thought. As previous chapters have made clear, the precursor of this narrow, ethno-cultural vision of *argentinidad* was the earlier ideal of an Argentine race defined by its Catholic, Hispanic heritage, an ideal that thinkers such as Manuel Gálvez and Ernesto Quesada had vigorously promoted during the period of mass immigration. With the sharp decline of transatlantic immigration by the late 1920s, the challenges (and, for some, the threat) posed by the arrival of so many foreigners had vanished. Yet the disappearance of the initial factors that had helped trigger the rise of the new, ethno-cultural understandings of Argentine identity did not mean the disappearance of these understandings. Once they were articulated in the public sphere, they reset the conceptual parameters of subsequent thinking about Argentine identity, and thus became available for (or "thinkable" by) subsequent generations. This is not to argue that the survival of these understandings of Argentine identity was inevitable. As this chapter makes clear, the essentialist claim that Argentina's true identity was rooted in its Catholic, Hispanic heritage gained increasing currency as a result of efforts by individuals who had a personal, professional, or political stake in this vision. These individuals, moreover, drew inspiration from a new set of intellectual influences and operated in a changed national and international context that made such a narrow, essentialist vision of *argentinidad* both plausible and compelling to themselves and others.

Scholars have rightly attributed the rise of right-wing, antiliberal nationalism in Argentina to a group of young activists who became politically active in the late 1920s. This group, whose core consisted of the brothers Rodolfo and Julio Irazusta, Juan E. Carulla, and Ernesto Palacio, were drawn together by their Catholic faith, fear of communism, and hostility toward democracy. In addition to launching the weekly newspaper *La Nueva República* (The new republic or *LNR*) in 1927, these young nationalists actively reached out to like-minded members of the military. One of their most important military contacts was General José F. Uriburu, the retired general who in 1930 would oust President Yrigoyen. Although not directly involved in the military action itself, the LNR circle played a central role in preparing public opinion for the coup.

The guiding forces behind the LNR group were Rodolfo and Julio Irazusta, who anchored the publication throughout its various incarnations. Sons of a landowning family from the province of Entre Rios, the Irazusta brothers maintained a close intellectual partnership throughout their lives. The Irazustas were joined by two other nationalist thinkers who would become core members of the LNR circle. The oldest of the four, Juan E. Carulla, came from a well-connected family from Entre Rios. Carulla had spent much of World War I in France, where he worked as a medic for the Red Cross. He returned to Argentina and in 1925 founded the short-lived nationalist publication *La Voz Nacional* (The national voice). Described by one of his contemporaries as Argentina's first critic of *demoliberalismo* (i.e., liberal democracy), Carulla was an early proponent of the key ideas that would define right-wing nationalism in Argentina.[1] The final core member of the LNR group was Ernesto Palacio. Like the rest of *LNR*'s editorial staff, Palacio came from a socially prominent family. Born and raised in Buenos Aires, he studied law at the university and was widely recognized as the publication's most talented polemicist.

Linking together these four men, besides their upper-class backgrounds, their deep belief in "rule by the capable,"[2] and their hostility toward Yrigoyen, was their unshakeable belief that *argentinidad* and Catholicism were consubstantial. For these thinkers, the Catholic faith and Hispanic heritage were the twin wellsprings of an underlying cultural and spiritual tradition that shaped the collective personality of the Argentine people and defined the nation. Spain, in Carulla's words, had provided Argentina and the rest of the Hispanic world with their "blood, culture and religion,"[3] which were "component elements" of these nations.[4] Within this vision of Argentine identity, of course, only Catholics could be true Argentines: Protestants, Jews, communists, and other nonbelievers were regarded as alien elements, whose presence weakened the spiritual unity of the Argentine people and who were thus a threat to its Catholic nature. What Argentina needed, according to the LNR's opening manifesto, was a patriotic campaign to "purge" from the nation "all those elements that are contrary to its spiritual unity." Central to this campaign, they believed, was reestablishment of Catholic education in the public schools, a practice that had been abolished by the secular educational reforms of the late nineteenth century.[5]

Among the key intellectual influences on this group of thinkers were conservative Spanish thinkers such as Juan Donoso Cortés, Jaime Balmes, and Marcelino Menéndez y Pelayo.[6] Of particular importance were the writings of Menéndez y Pelayo, who insisted that Spain's "true self" was Catholic and who, accordingly, believed the church to be the historical guardian of Spanish nationality.[7] Also notable was the impact of Spanish political theorist and sometime diplomat Ramiro de Maeztu. Himself a follower of Menéndez y Pelayo (and often considered a member of the Generation of 1898), Maeztu had published regularly in the Argentine press since 1905 and was well known to the reading public. Between 1928 and 1930, he served as Spain's ambassador to Argentina, during which time he established a firm friendship with the LNR group. Maeztu also developed a close relationship with Zacarías de Vizcarra, a right-wing Spanish priest, who served the Spanish immigrant community in Buenos Aires and who would play a central role in the revitalization of the Argentine church. During his years as ambassador, Maeztu became a vocal proponent within Argentina of *hispanidad*, giving frequent lectures on the spiritual links between Spain and its former American colonies. These lectures formed the nucleus of his 1934 *Defensa de la hispanidad* (Defense of *hispanidad*), which strongly condemned liberalism and called on Hispanic peoples to return to their supposedly authentic selves. This book, along with Maeztu's other writings, would serve as a central referent for generations of Argentina's right-wing nationalists.[8]

Another important influence on the LNR group was French nationalist thinker Charles Maurras. A staunch monarchist, Maurras was obsessed with combating the ideas that had inspired the 1789 Revolution. Carulla had become acquainted with Maurras's ideas years earlier during his time in France, where he developed close ties with several key figures associated with the Maurrasian movement.[9] The Irazusta brothers, particularly Rodolfo, also came under Maurras's sway when they traveled to France in 1923. Palacio eventually developed an appreciation for Maurras's ideas, which he absorbed through his association with the Irazustas. Several of Maurras's key ideas proved highly compatible with the views of the Argentine nationalists and in some measure influenced them.[10] One commonality was the notion that national groups formed distinct "races," a notion with Romantic roots but one that Maurras had absorbed from Comtian positivism.[11] Thus for Maurras, Frenchness was an inherent state of being rather than a status that could be acquired. In his view, foreigners who had settled in France, whom he dubbed *les métèques* (the Greek term for "outside the household"), were permanent outsiders.[12] A committed classicist, Maurras also celebrated the Latin "race," which he believed to be humanity's most advanced. Not surprisingly, he saw Paris as the epicenter of the contemporary Latin world and believed France's glory would be restored only if it returned to its Latin roots.

Of the members of the LNR group, Carulla proved to be the most enthusiastic proponent of *latinidad*. Like fellow nationalist Leopoldo Lugones, Carulla stressed that Argentina and the rest of Latin America were heirs to the Greco-Roman tradition that provided the basis of Western civilization.[13] Moreover, in his view, the Latin world was on the verge of a renaissance, in which the nations of Latin America would play a key role. In a manner reminiscent of Manuel Gálvez, Carulla proclaimed that it was the "mission" of Spain's former colonies to "complete and give nuance to" Western civilization.[14] Other members of the LNR circle were less enthralled with the concept of *latinidad*, which they saw as a rhetorical device dreamed up by France in order to expand its influence in the Americas. Instead, they preferred the term *Iberoamérica*, which "united cousins in both [Iberian] Europe and America."[15] Regardless of their specific terminology, all members of the LNR circle embraced the assumption that humanity was divided into distinctive ethnic or racial groups, believing that all countries of Iberoamerica formed a "community of origin, language, religion and culture."[16]

Another Maurrasian stance shared by the LNR group was an intense hostility toward Protestantism and individualism, two phenomena that the French ideologue believed had led to the 1789 Revolution.[17] As staunch Catholics, who believed their version of Christianity formed the very basis of *argentinidad*, the members of the LNR circle echoed these sentiments but with an anti-imperialist twist. Decrying the spread of Protestantism in Latin America by US missionaries, Julio Irazusta called for a coordinated plan "to block the enormous power of Washington."[18] The Argentine nationalists also shared Maurras's hatred for Jean-Jacques

Rousseau, whom the French thinker blamed for having introduced the nefarious idea of the social contract, and the idea that society was a man-made rather than natural entity.[19] Following Maurras, Palacio referred to Rousseau as the "psychopath of Geneva" and scorned the very notion of a social contract.[20] According to Palacio, a fundamental divide existed between those political thinkers, "who consider society as a natural phenomenon, and those that believe it to be a more or less artificial creation of individuals." In his view, only the former could be nationalists, because these individuals "accepted society as a fact that was anterior and superior [to the individual]; they could submit themselves to it."[21]

A final element of Maurras's thought that reappeared in the ideas of the LNR group was the Frenchman's distinction between the *pays légal* and the *pays réel*, or the "legal country" versus the "real country." In Maurras's view, the "real" France was Catholic and monarchical, while the "legal" country consisted of the republican institutions that were layered over the true France like a "grotesque mask."[22] The LNR group echoed Maurras's dichotomy, soon to be recast as the notion of the "two Argentinas." "The *país real* and the *país oficial* had arrived at such a complete divorce," according to Rodolfo Irazusta, that the current political institutions reflected none of the people's interests or aspirations.[23] Indeed, in the view of the members of the LNR circle, it was the elite's failure to understand the deeply Catholic, Hispanic character of the Argentine nation that lay at the very heart of Argentina's ills. In the inaugural manifesto of the magazine, for example, the Irazusta brothers proclaimed that the country suffered from a profound spiritual malaise, caused by the ruling elite's inability to articulate an "organic idea" that would "square with our spiritual nature."[24] In other words, instead of developing institutions that were consonant with a supposed Argentine temperament, Argentina's leaders had attempted to rule the country using abstract political principles.

The strong similarities between the ideas of Maurras and those of his Argentine admirers led some contemporary critics to complain that these nationalists had come under the spell of foreign doctrines and were following the country's long-standing tradition of blindly following European intellectual cues. What such critics overlooked, however, was the fact that—aside from his deep hostility toward democracy and hatred of Rousseau—there was very little in Maurras's thought that was new to

Argentines. The essentialist identification of race with nationality (a notion with both positivist and Romantic roots) had of course gained widespread currency in Argentina enduring the opening decades of the century. Similarly, the belief in the inherent differences between Latins and Anglo-Saxons had earlier champions. Even Maurras's distinction between the *pays réel* and the *pays légal* had an Argentine analog in Ricardo Rojas's concept of *intrahistoria* (intrahistory), which had posited the notion of a hidden reality that could be apprehended only through intuition.[25] Finally, Maurras's belief that France could regain its former glory only when it returned to its true Catholic self was strikingly similar to the idea, articulated by cultural nationalist Manuel Gálvez decades earlier, that in order to thrive Argentina must reattach itself to its Catholic, Hispanic roots.[26]

## THE LNR GROUP AND THE CONSTITUTION

Although the members of the LNR circle were united in their disdain for democracy and a desire for hierarchy, their initial prescriptions for change were timid at best. Indeed, as historian Fernando Devoto has rightly noted, during the first few years of the publication's existence, its editors demonstrated a marked reluctance to break with Argentina's liberal tradition.[27] Rather, they argued that the country's political problems could be solved simply by reforming the existing constitution in order to bring it back in line with what they believed to be the original intent of its framers.[28] At the heart of this claim was their conviction that the original 1853 Constitution had outlined a *republican* rather than a democratic form of government.[29] Drawing from classical political theory, the LNR collaborators described the republic as a type of state that respected and preserved the natural hierarchies of society and privileged the public good over private interests.[30] In such a system, suffrage was restricted to the most capable, and elections served to delegate power to an individual or body, whose task it was to defend the rights of the collective society. Democracies, in contrast, insisted on the "primacy of the individual," a principle that inevitably led to a system where "all the excesses of personal dignity, capriciousness, and of [private] interests" resulted in votes against the state.[31] To remedy this problem and to restore the constitution to its original intent, the LNR group called for the immediate roll back of the 1912 electoral reforms.[32]

The LNR group also affirmed that the 1853 Constitution had established a Catholic state. To be sure, the constitution did indeed express that the Argentine state "sustained" the Catholic faith. Equally true, however, was the fact that it also guaranteed complete religious freedom.[33] Discounting this latter provision, Rodolfo Irazusta insisted that Argentina's state and constitution were by necessity Catholic because *Argentina* was Catholic.[34] A "true Argentine," he affirmed, "is born, lives and dies with the sacrament of the Church. The entire society is formed in accordance with the laws of Catholicism. The Constitution does not say otherwise, and the State cannot be anything but Catholic."[35] This was tortured logic indeed, and it is thus not surprising that within just a few years the intellectuals associated with the LNR would jettison their constitutional scruples entirely. For the moment, however, these individuals continued to assert that restoring the nation's political health would require little more than a series of relatively minor constitutional reforms, which would supposedly restore the original intent of its framers.[36]

Yrigoyen's return to the presidency in 1928 spurred the LNR group toward greater activism. Carulla's friendship with General José Uriburu, a man with corporatist tendencies and an admirer of Primo de Rivera and Mussolini, provided the group with just the military contact they sought.[37] A member of a prominent landholding family, Uriburu had been educated at the prestigious Colegio Militar and had risen quickly within the ranks.[38] Despite owing much of his meteoric rise to his political connections, Uriburu professed disdain for politicians and began to seek allies, both in and outside the military, who shared his antiliberal sympathies. Within the military, he was aided by rising anti-Yrigoyenist sentiment among the officer corps, which resented the president's interference in the military's internal affairs.

Dislike for Yrigoyen, however, did not automatically translate into a rejection of Argentina's liberal tradition, and Uriburu's corporatist program found little support among the higher ranks. Given this narrow base, it is not surprising that he welcomed connections with the young collaborators of LNR. For their part, Uriburu's young admirers saw him as a man of action, who "knew, like few others, the soul of the country."[39] In late 1928, Uriburu met frequently with Carulla and Rodolfo Irazusta and favored the entire LNR circle with his presence at the magazine's first anniversary banquet.[40] During this period, the LNR members also began recruiting other would-be rebels, joining with fellow journalists from the ferociously anti-Yrigoyen newspaper *La Fronda* to create the group called *Liga Republicana*. Of the three individuals who made up the Liga Republicana's core leadership, two—Rodolfo Irazusta and Juan E. Carulla—were associated with the *LNR*. The third, Roberto de Laferrère, would figure prominently in right-wing circles during the 1930s. Palacio was also active in the Liga, as was Federico Ibarguren, the son of noted nationalist Carlos Ibarguren, Sr.

The goal of the Liga Republicana was straightforward: to prepare public opinion for a military coup.[41] Accordingly, much of the Liga's energies were spent papering the city with anti-Yrigoyen posters and organizing street protests. Civil disturbances intensified in the early months of 1930, as the Liga joined with other anti-Yrigoyen groups, such as the Liga Patriótica Argentina, to promote an atmosphere of crisis. But even at this late hour, the young nationalists who placed their hopes in a military coup continued to express fealty to the Argentine constitution. The group's manifesto, pronounced at a public meeting on November 7, 1929, proclaimed the goal of defending the values contained in the country's constitution against the corrupt Yrigoyen administration.[42]

## THE CATHOLIC CHURCH AND THE RISE OF RIGHT-WING NATIONALISM

Another crucial actor in Argentine society that helped foment the ideal of Argentina as a Catholic nation, and which also continued to express fealty to the 1853 Constitution, was the Catholic Church.[43] During the 1930s and '40s, the church played an especially important role in converting key segments of the military to Catholic nationalism and would become a powerful force in Argentine politics. This had not always been the case. Throughout much of the nineteenth century, the Argentine Catholic Church had been among the weakest in Latin America. Cut off from Rome after 1810, and continually strapped for resources, it developed a mutually supportive relationship with the Argentine state, while always remaining in a dependent position. This relationship was exemplified by the provisions of the 1853 Constitution, which established the principle of religious tolerance. Although the political position of the church strengthened after the renewal of diplomatic ties between Argentina and the Vatican in 1858, Catholicism among the population lost ground. Overall, between the fall of Rosas in 1852 and the end of the century, the political elite pursued a cautious policy of gradual secularization aimed at drawing a sharper line between church and state, while avoiding a clerical backlash.

This delicate balancing act sometimes fell apart. As noted, during his first presidency (1880–86), Julio Roca included within his administration several members of the highly anticlerical Club Liberal, pushing strongly for congressional approval of Law 1420. This law, passed in 1884, made primary school obligatory and secular and stipulated that any religious instruction take place outside of normal school hours and be conducted by a member of the clergy, not a public employee.[44] The resulting protest on the part of the Catholic hierarchy led Roca to break with the Vatican. Four years later, under the administration of Juárez Celman, liberals won another victory when marriage became a civil, rather than religious, institution.

These assaults on the church's traditional areas of control deepened the Catholic hierarchy's hostility toward liberalism and led it to support the Unión Cívica's 1890 rebellion against Juárez Celman. It also sought new ways to become relevant to a largely indifferent population. Inspired by Leo XIII's papal encyclical *Rerum Novarum* (of revolutionary change), which decried the ill effects of unfettered capitalism on the working class, in 1892 the church established "workers circles" aimed at ameliorating the conditions that made the poor vulnerable to socialism's siren call. Modeled on a similar movement in Europe, the workers circles preached a type of reformism that recognized the rights of both labor and capital, emphasized class harmony, and called for a middle path between capitalism and socialism. The efforts soon bore fruit, and by the early twentieth century, Argentine Catholicism began to experience something of a revival. Helping too was the fact that many new recruits into the priesthood were the children of immigrants. Such individuals, historian Loris Zanatta has argued, were particularly drawn to "the new mysticism of a national identity that was tied to Catholicism."[45] The monthly review *Estudios*, published in the opening years of the century by prominent lay Catholics, provided a new venue for Catholic writers. In 1911, another Catholic journal, also named *Estudios*, saw the light. Funded by the Jesuit order, it took a more explicitly conservative stance than the earlier journal and attracted such writers as the prominent anti-Semitic novelist Gustavo Martínez Zuviría. Also noteworthy was the appearance in 1917 of the Catholic group Ateneo Social de la Juventud, founded by lay Catholics Tomás Casares and Atilio Dell' Oro Maini.[46]

But by far the most important development in the church's road to revitalization, and the one most closely tied to the new nationalist tendencies, was the founding of the Cursos de Cultura Católica (Courses of Catholic culture). Organized in 1922 by lay Catholics Tomás Casares, Atilio Dell'Oro Maini, and César E. Pico, the Cursos was conceived as a Catholic alternative to the supposedly atheistic public universities. Initially independent of the church, by the late 1920s it had been brought under its control. The Cursos sponsored a variety of academic and social activities and opened its doors to the public free of charge. The core academic offerings, taught by members of the religious orders, consisted of a multiyear curriculum featuring courses in philosophy, ecclesiastical history, scripture, and Latin.[47] Cursos leaders also organized a wide variety of lectures, sometimes featuring distinguished foreign visitors, such as Jacques Maritain and Reginald Garrigou-LaGrange.[48] One of the key invited lecturers of the late 1920s was Spanish cleric Zacarías de Vizcarro. An energetic Hispanicist, who would play a prominent role in the Franco regime, Vizcarro was instrumental in guiding the Argentine church toward Catholic nationalism.[49] In large part as a result of his influence, the Cursos would become, in the words of Loris Zanatta, "a laboratory of Catholic revanchism and a study group for young nationalists."[50]

The resurgence of Catholicism was evident in other areas as well. In 1931, the Argentine church established its own branch of Catholic Action. Following the Italian model, its purpose was to form a new group of lay activists, who would be under the authority of the hierarchy. The organization was immediately successful, attracting over twenty-five thousand by 1934 and over a hundred thousand by 1943.[51] Another effort to broaden Catholicism's reach was through the founding in 1928 of the weekly Catholic journal *Criterio*. Like the Cursos, *Criterio* would play a central role, both in cementing the relationship between Catholicism and nationalism and in disseminating these ideas to a broader public.[52] Although the magazine initially published authors from a variety of backgrounds, by its second year this eclecticism vanished,[53] and it came to rely on an array of noted Catholic nationalists, including Manuel Gálvez, César Pico, the Irazustas, Ernesto Palacio, and Juan Carulla.[54] Another important contributor was the above-mentioned Ramiro de Maeztu, whose arrival in 1928 as Spain's ambassador to Argentina was much celebrated by *Criterio*'s editors.[55]

All these endeavors were part of a broader project to combat liberal, secularist tendencies and to bring about, for the first time in Argentine history, the identification between Catholicism and *argentinidad*. A necessary part of this enterprise, the Catholic hierarchy believed, was the transformation of the church's overall role. Rejecting the traditional liberal view of the church as merely one actor out of many in a pluralistic society, the hierarchy sought to convert the church into the "common matrix" of the entire social body by driving home the message that Catholicism formed the bedrock of Argentine nationality and provided the "immutable principle" that gave shape to the nation's identity.[56] One of the champions of this message was the activist priest and philosopher Father Gustavo Juan Franceschi, who took a leading role in the Catholic revival of the 1930s. An adamant opponent of both communism and liberalism, Franceschi fully embraced the ideal of the Catholic nation, arguing that religious faith and traditions formed the basis of Argentine identity. Directly challenging the nineteenth-century vision of Argentina as a civic nation, he strongly rejected the claim that "democratic principles are the very essence of our nationality." If these institutions disappeared, Franceschi insisted, the nation would still remain.[57]

Other nationalist priests, such as Gabriel Riesco, concurred with Franceschi's vision of the nation. In an article in the Catholic daily *El Pueblo*, Riesco described Argentina's Spanish heritage and Catholic religion as "the diamond axis of our *ser*" and Catholic and Hispanic values as the "great seedbed (*vivero*) of *argentinidad*." Accordingly, Riesco continued, "We cannot renounce these traditions of religion and race without destroying the basis of our nationality. . . . Anything that doesn't come from the Hispanic sentiment and the Catholic conception is a threat to our *ser*."[58] In a similar vein, Luis Barrantes Molina, a prominent lay Catholic and editorialist for *El Pueblo*, argued that Argentine "civilization is Catholic and of Spanish origins," and Catholicism constituted "our principal national bond." Those who attack Catholicism, he affirmed, "are enemies of the fatherland."[59]

The identification of an imagined Argentine *ser* with Catholicism was greatly strengthened by activist clerics, who worked closely with lay Catholic nationalists and who contributed to the many nationalist publications of the 1930s, 1940s, and 1950s. Three deserve special mention: Fathers Juan Sepich, Leonardo Castellani, and Julio Meinvielle. All were closely associated with the Cursos and were prolific writers, who remained exceptionally active well into the 1970s. Sepich, a trained philosopher and specialist in the work of Martin Heidegger, became a valued contributor in the late-1930s to the ultra-Catholic nationalist review *Sol y Luna*, directed by Mario Amadeo and Máximo Etchecopar. During the military regime of 1943–46 and the early Peronist years, he served in various capacities in the educational bureaucracy. Castellani, a member of the Jesuit order, was similarly active, and in the 1950s he published extensively in the nationalist publications *Cabildo* and *Azul y Blanco*. He also enjoyed close ties with the military. Meinvielle, probably the most influential of the three, was particularly noted for his criticism of capitalism. His 1932 *Concepción católica de la economía* (Catholic conception of the economy), which glorified the Middle Ages as the apex of human existence, served as a dispensable guide for generations of Catholic nationalists.[60] Meinvielle also contributed frequently to nationalist magazines, such as *LNR*, *Baluarte*, *Crisol*, and *Cabildo*, and founded two of his own (*Nuestro Tiempo* and *Balcón*). During the latter half of the 1950s, he would serve as a spiritual advisor to the extremist Catholic youth organization *Tacuara*, known for its violence..

It should be stressed, however, that the Argentine church's position toward the new nationalist tendencies was far from uniform, especially during the late 1920s and early 1930s. Notwithstanding the institution's new activism, many members of the ecclesiastical hierarchy continued to believe in the need to coexist with the liberal state. This position, most prominently espoused by the highly respected Monsignor De Andrea, held that democracy was compatible with a Catholic society and indeed should be valued.[61] Also indicative of the church's ambivalence toward the new nationalism was a series of conflicts between *Criterio*'s permanent staff and the members of the LNR group, which resulted in the latter's leaving the publication altogether in 1929.[62]

## LEOPOLDO LUGONES AND CONSTITUTIONALISM

As is clear, breaking with Argentina's liberal political tradition was not done lightly, and during the late 1920s and early '30s, even individuals with strong nationalist tendencies remained ambivalent about discarding the 1853 Constitution. There was, however, one highly visible nationalist who harbored no such qualms: poet Leopoldo Lugones. Lugones, discussed earlier in connection with the gaucho, was a man of ideological extremes. A socialist in his younger years, he had by the early 1920s swung sharply to the right and had come to see all acts of labor militancy as dangerous "harbingers of Bolshevism."[63] In July 1923, he outlined his new worldview in a series of lectures delivered in the Teatro Coliseo, at the behest of the Liga Patriótica Argentina. In a lecture laced with xenophobia, Lugones warned of the dangers posed by mass immigration and urged his audience to remember that "We (i.e., native Argentines) are the owners of the country."[64] In subsequent presentations, the poet darkly proclaimed that the Great War had clearly demonstrated the weaknesses of the liberal order, leaving contemporary societies with the choice between Bolshevism and fascism.[65]

Lugones's positive comments about fascism raised more than a few eyebrows in the audience, and LPA president Manuel Carlés took pains to distance the organization from the poet's more extreme comments.[66] More inflammatory still was the speech Lugones gave the following year in Peru, excerpts of which were published in the pages of *La Nación*. In this now infamous speech, Lugones glorified the violence of the wars of independence and provocatively proclaimed that "for the good of the world, the hour of the sword has arrived again."[67] It was the sword, Lugones argued, that had won Latin America its independence from Spain, and the military struggles of that period had provided Latin American societies with a sense of discipline and order. These qualities, Lugones lamented, had unfortunately been lost in subsequent decades, when misguided elites attempted to impose democracy on the newly established nations. The constitutional system of the nineteenth century, he proclaimed, was now "outdated" and it was time for the military to rule the region.[68]

Lugones's words proved prescient. Although his early attacks on constitutional democracy provoked an outcry among his countrymen, just a few years later such rhetoric would be standard fare among Argentine nationalists and would find a receptive audience among the most extreme elements of the military. But more important for our purposes is how the celebrated poet framed his critique of democracy. For Lugones, the problem with Argentina's democratic institutions, and with the constitution itself, was not simply that they did not provide protection against communist infiltration; he also complained that the 1853 Constitution was at odds with Argentina's underlying *índole*.[69] This nuance is important, and represents a way of framing the country's political problems that would serve as a standard trope in virtually all subsequent nationalist discourses of both the right and left. In Lugones's analysis of Argentina's ills, we see publicly articulated for the first time not simply a vision of national identity unmoored from constitutional foundations but the claim that the constitution itself was an alien document at odds with the supposedly inherent nature of the Argentine people. In other words, the constitution and the liberal tradition that produced it were actually harmful to *el ser nacional.*

Following his analysis, set out earlier in his Martín Fierro lectures (and like José Enrique Rodó and others), Lugones insisted that Argentines were a Latin people formed by the Greco-Roman tradition. Accordingly, the system of government that best suited them was a republic, though one organized along very different lines than that of the United States or other Anglo-Saxon peoples. In Lugones's view, Anglo-Saxons were by nature orderly and deliberative, and thus were best governed by a parliamentary democracy.[70] Peoples of Latin descent, in contrast, were intrinsically artistic in their outlook and interests. Unlike Anglo-Saxons, who sought material success, Lugones maintained, Latins lived lives conditioned by "esthetic" norms and the desire for glory rather than material success.[71] Accordingly, they required different forms of political representation that were consonant with their supposed "*índole.*" In his view, parliamentary forms of government, such as the one outlined by the 1853 Constitution, were entirely unworkable for Latins, and were even "repugnant" to them.[72] Worse still, Lugones argued, Argentina's 1853 Constitution had set in motion forces that had begun to erode its true character.[73]

Lugones's belief that the Argentine national character was based on its Latin heritage, rather than on its Spanish roots and Catholic faith, made him an outlier among right-wing nationalists.[74] Still, the poet's critique of liberalism, along with his authoritarianism and celebration of the military, won him an admiring audience among many young nationalists of the right. It was not until the early 1930s, however, that they would come to share his rejection of the constitution.

## SEPTEMBER 6 AND THE LNR GROUP'S ANTICONSTITUTIONAL JOURNEY

By mid-1930, Lugones, the Irazustas, Laferrère, and others had helped set the stage for the coup that ended Argentina's experiment with popular democracy and brought to power, albeit briefly, a nationalist military government with corporatist aspirations. For the young members of the Liga Republicana, who had devoted themselves to the cause, these were heady times. Having thrown in their lot with Uriburu, they saw themselves as valued advisors of the new president. Moreover, they were convinced that the Argentine public was hungry for the changes they envisioned. The swiftness with which Yrigoyen was ousted seemed to confirm this assumption. Carried out by a small contingent of cadets from the Colegio Militar, the coup met with little resistance from either the civilian population or the rest of the military. But the generalized support within the military for Yrigoyen's overthrow masked deep divisions about the coup's purpose. In one camp were Uriburu and his nationalist supporters, who envisioned significant—although still ill-defined—constitutional reforms that would institute some kind of corporatist-style state. In the other were those officers who remained firmly allied with the traditional conservative political class, and who saw the coup as a means only of getting rid of Yrigoyen. Once this was accomplished, they believed, the country should return as quickly as possible to normalcy—that is, to a system of representative democracy.[75]

This second group, which included most of the officers, coalesced around Uriburu's principal rival, General Agustín P. Justo. The former minister of war under Radical president Marcelo T. de Alvear, Justo was a favorite of the conservative political elite.[76] Followers of Uriburu and Justo began planning Yrigoyen's ouster in January 1930, but their deep ideological differences made cooperation difficult.[77] Realizing the weakness of his position, Uriburu was forced to tone down the original revolutionary manifesto that Lugones had penned. The resulting document contained little that might trouble Argentina's traditional conservatives, either civilian or military. In addition to announcing the military's desire to defend the constitution, it promised that the coup leaders would play no role in the government once the situation was normalized.[78]

Whether or not Uriburu's moderate, precoup rhetoric was part of a calculated strategy to hide a more extreme agenda is unclear.[79] What *is* unquestionable, however, is that regardless of Uriburu's true sentiments, the traditional elite had little appetite for such fundamental change or even for rolling back the 1912 electoral reforms.[80] Almost immediately after the coup, civilians and the Justista sector of the military began to press for a return to "normalcy," or to the electoral process codified in the constitution and the Sáenz Peña reforms. Finding his support eroding, Uriburu was forced, in the words of historian Tulio Halperin Donghi, to make a "less than spontaneous conversion to the cause of constitutionalism and democracy."[81] While still reluctant to relinquish his hopes for radical reform, Uriburu announced that any changes to the constitution must be carried out using constitutional means, a process that required the permission of Congress. He also agreed to new provincial elections, with those in the province of Buenos Aires coming first, on April 5, 1931.

Catholics were divided on the issue of elections. The Catholic daily *El Pueblo* joined the chorus of those calling for a rapid return to constitutional normalcy, while *Criterio* suggested that more fundamental change was necessary.[82] Also revealing was Franceschi's October 11 sermon, in which he praised Argentina's armed forces as the "guarantor of the [Argentine] nationality."[83] The choice of words is significant. As Loris Zanatta has pointed out, Franceschi did not describe the military as the protector of the constitution or even the nation. Rather, the monsignor saw the military as embodying, and thus defending, the immutable values of *"el ser nacional."*[84] And just a year later, Franceschi made clear his belief that Argentines' adherence to their liberal traditions had made them culturally, economically, and politically vulnerable. Writing in *Criterio*, he lamented that "neither parliamentarianism nor the general liberalism of our institutions permits an efficient defense against communism, the Jewish spirit, Marxist disorganization and the general ruin of the economy."[85]

But if the church was ambivalent about the return to electoral normalcy, those who had hoped for more fundamental change were uniformly disappointed. One of the earliest to express concern over the general's loss of nerve was Rodolfo Irazusta. Hoping to make the case for fundamental change, he published an article arguing that Argentina's political institutions must be altered to reflect the needs of the country, a task that liberalism was incapable of achieving. Under liberalism, Rodolfo complained, the Argentine state had become completely ineffective and unable "to channel the activities of the pueblo."[86] A few days later, and in the wake of Uriburu's announcement that any constitutional reforms would require congressional approval, Rodolfo wrote a private letter to his brother Julio, expressing his frustration and complaining that the coup's real beneficiaries were the moderate conservatives, who continued to embrace the despised "demo-socialist liberalism."[87] Publicly, however, Rodolfo tempered his criticism of Uriburu and praised the new regime as the best and most authentically Argentine government of the past two decades. The aim of Argentina's new leader, he proclaimed, was not simply to promote efficient administration, a goal that would be suitable for lesser nations such as Switzerland or Uruguay. For a great nation such as Argentina, which was destined to "leave a profound mark in history," it was necessary to develop "very original institutions, which were born of its [specific] political and economic conditions."[88]

After finding himself pushed to the fringes of Uriburu's circle, Rodolfo Irazusta made a final attempt to influence the general. In February 1931, he proposed to the president a new system of corporatist representation at the municipal level. But having repositioned himself as a defender of constitutionalism, Uriburu rejected the plan on the grounds that it would be impossible to implement within the present legal system.[89] It was at this point that the Irazusta brothers, along with Palacio (who also had become disillusioned with Uriburu), finally openly denounced the Argentine constitution. In mid-1931, they joined with Lugones and other prominent nationalists to form a new group called Acción Republicana. In a manifesto dated July 9, 1931, the group sharply criticized the traditional political class's call to return to electoral normalcy, proclaiming that there was "nowhere to return to" and that the Argentine constitution "no longer exists." It was, instead, a "foreign instrument" that had served the interests of international capital and the conservative oligarchy rather than the nation. What Argentines needed, the manifesto continued, was a constitution that was "ours," and thus truly Argentine.[90] In the following months, the Irazustas and Palacio continued their attacks on the constitution and the conservative elite. Writing in the pages of the *LNR*, they repeatedly asserted the essentialist claim that there existed a fundamental disconnect between the true nature of the Argentine people and the political institutions inscribed in the constitution. Rodolfo Irazusta, for example, repeatedly stressed its supposed imported character, proclaiming that the document had been produced by a generation seeking to erase the supposedly true "*índole* of the country."[91] The only resolution to the "secular tragedy of our public life," he continued, would be to develop new institutions that would "reconcile the national temperament with the norms of the State."[92]

Given the LNR group's long-standing hostility toward popular democracy, and the peculiar logic of its earlier defense of the 1853 Constitution, it is unsurprising that its members ultimately came around to Lugones's point of view. But what does surprise is that, in their disillusionment with Uriburu, several members developed a new, more positive appraisal of both the Argentine masses and the Radical Party.[93] Whereas once the nationalists of the LNR circle had viewed the Radicals as dangerous demagogues, in the aftermath of the Uriburu debacle, they began to promote a new, more positive image of Radicalism.

Surely one reason for this about-face was the dawning realization that any successful nationalist program would require some degree of popular support, something the Unión Cívica Radical continued to enjoy. But another factor driving this reappraisal of Yrigoyen was the nationalists' adoption of a new interpretation of the Radical experience, one based on essentialist assumptions about the nature of the Argentine masses. According to Rodolfo Irazusta, the masses harbored an innate (and Catholic) preference for caudillo rule and an intrinsic desire to return to "natural" social hierarchies.[94] According to this interpretation, Radicalism had triumphed because it "naturally tended to be personalistic" and "because its character is completely national." In other words, "caudillismo," in Rodolfo Irazusta's words, was "the institution par excellence of Argentine politics."[95] What the pueblo wanted, he insisted—and what he believed suited its collective personality—was not "parties and their programs," or "ideas and discourses," but "a strongman to which it could offer the unanimity of its collective will."[96]

LNR stalwart Ernesto Palacio seconded this new interpretation of Radicalism, arguing that the movement represented "the only nationalist force with popular roots." He went on to praise the "anonymous mass of Radicalism" for its "nationalist sense" (*sentido nacionalista*), noting that, although the people had erred in their support for Yrigoyen, they would never make the mistake of following "exotic (i.e., foreign) adventurers."[97] These nationalists also praised Radicalism's supposedly warm support of Catholicism. Radicalism, Rodolfo Irazusta affirmed, had "always been closer to God" and had always "respected and venerated the traditional religion of the Nation."[98] While remaining critical of the Yrigoyen regime for its corruption and bloated bureaucracy, the LNR group now lauded the Unión Cívica Radical as the only political party that was in sync with the true values of *el ser nacional*.[99]

## CATHOLIC NATIONALISM UNDER JUSTO

The provincial elections of April 1931, in which the Radicals were allowed to participate, provided a critical test for the Uriburu regime. The easy triumph of Radical candidates forced Uriburu to hold presidential elections the following November. This contest pitted a progressive slate led by the Partido Demócrata Progresista or PDP (Democratic Progressive Party) founder Lisandro de la Torre against General Agustín Justo, Uriburu's old rival whose coalition included the Conservatives and a faction of the anti-Yrigoyenist Radicals.[100] Justo handily won the contest, and his victory signaled the reassertion of Argentina's traditional political class's control and the return to nominal constitutional rule. With the Socialists and PDP winning a respectable number of seats in Congress, Argentine conservatives could again boast of having a competitive democracy. Undermining the appearance of normalcy, however, was the fact that Argentina's most popular political party, the UCR, had refused to participate in the elections. This policy of abstentionism, taken in protest against Uriburu's refusal to allow former Radical president Marcelo T. de Alvear to run for president, lasted until 1935. Thus began the period known in Argentine history as the "infamous decade," during which the political class systematically employed fraud to remain in power, while at the same time claiming to rule by popular consent.[101]

For right-wing nationalists, these were paradoxical times. Certainly, the failure of Uriburu's corporatist agenda and the political elite's insistence that the country return to constitutional rule reflected just how tenaciously the Argentine upper class held on to its long-standing belief that democracy was a hallmark of civilization and modernity.[102] This remained true even as the new ruling coalition, known as the *Concordancia*, was forced to use fraud to remain in power.[103] Among the general public, support for democracy also remained high, as demonstrated by the massive turnout for the April elections. At the same time, however, the 1930s also witnessed the heyday of right-wing nationalist activism in Argentina.

Several factors converged to provide a propitious environment for the nationalist right. One of the most important was the impact of the Spanish Civil War, a conflict that Argentines avidly followed. Although the Argentine public in general supported the Republican cause, the church, right-wing nationalists, and even some conservatives rallied behind the Falangists.[104] Priest and prominent nationalist scholar Julio Meinvielle expressed the sentiment of many when he declared the conflict to be a "holy war" pitting Catholicism against godless communism.[105] For right-wing nationalists, the civil war provided the opportunity to affirm their belief in the inherent uniqueness of Spain and, more generally, to air ideas about the nations and nationality. Nationalist Federico Ibarguren, for example, described the rise of the Spanish Falange as "the heroic reaction of the Race" against the republican cause.[106] In true Romantic fashion, he proclaimed that the Falange would prevail because "every pueblo, like every individual, has a historical destiny, charge or mission." Spain's destiny, Ibarguren affirmed, was to defend and preserve the purity of the Catholic faith. Despite its current struggles, "today, as in the past, Spain would without a doubt fulfill the mission that history has outlined for it."[107]

Another factor influencing and encouraging the Argentine right was the rise of fascism in Europe, especially the Italian and Spanish varieties. Scholars have long debated whether Argentina's right-wing nationalists should be considered fascists.[108] Federico Finchelstein, who has strongly argued for the existence of an Argentine fascism, insists that fascism is best understood not as a single ideology or formula but as a "matrix" containing a shifting "set of tropes and ideas" about "violence, war, nation, the sacred and the abject."[109] Thus, while acknowledging that a full-fledged fascist regime never developed in Argentina, he argues that Argentina's right-wing nationalists "shared a strong enthusiasm for fascism," and selectively appropriated elements of European fascism, rejected others, and reformulated the ideology to produce a domestic variety that was distinctively Argentine.[110] The most important distinguishing feature of Argentine fascism, in Finchelstein's view, was its insistence on the centrality of Catholicism in Argentine society. The result was a new "Christianized fascism" that embraced European fascism's emphasis on violence, hostility toward liberalism, anti-Semitism, and the mythic cult of the personality, while at the same time insisting that the state should be subordinated to the will of God.[111]

Parsing the question of whether or not Argentine right-wing nationalism merits the designation "fascism" is not of interest here: there are persuasive arguments to support either position. A more relevant question for our purposes is whether we should see right-wing Argentine nationalism as a simple outgrowth of European fascism. I think not, and like scholars on both sides of the fascism debate, see Argentine right-wing nationalism as emerging primarily from domestic concerns, while at the same time being shaped by European ideas and movements. To be sure, some Argentine nationalists had direct contact with European (and especially Italian) fascists, and identified themselves as part of international fascism.[112] Many more were clearly influenced by fascist movements and shared with their European counterparts a similar diagnosis of society's basic problems and a prescription for how to address them.[113] Yet what made these ideas "thinkable" in the Argentine context was the fact that the key assumption that made fascist ideology "thinkable" in Europe in the first place (i.e., the notion that nations are organic, homogenous spiritual or racial communities) had already gained currency in Argentina well before fascism's rise in Europe. Thus when Mussolini saw Italy as defined by its ethnic and linguistic unity, Argentines who had come under Romantic nationalism's sway found nothing odd about such a claim, for they already imagined their own nation in similar terms.

This did not mean, of course, that *all* those who came to define the Argentine nation in ethno-cultural terms were attracted to fascism. As argued in chapter 5, this way of imagining Argentine identity had many variations, appealing to individuals from across the political spectrum. Rather, what occurred in the Argentine case is that those intellectuals who defined *argentinidad* in the narrowest terms—that is, those who saw Catholicism and the Spanish heritage as its two most essential traits— were the most likely to move toward fascism the 1930s. The most well-known example is that of cultural nationalist Manuel Gálvez, who was this generation's most ardent Hispanicist and the only one to embrace fascism.[114] For individuals such as Gálvez, defending the Catholic basis of Argentine identity should be the primary goal of any patriot. Accordingly, these nationalists found in European fascism a useful alternative to the liberal, secular state: one that promised to protect what they believed was most essential to *argentinidad*. Fascist ideas and practices, then, were not desirable in and of themselves. Rather, they should be understood more as a means to an end. In his comparison of European and Latin American fascism, Spanish Falangist José María Pemán captured the dynamic:

> It is the case that the Latin American processes of reaction followed an inverse path to that of Europeans. Here [in Europe] it is the nacionalista and imperialistic consciousness that initiates the processes, and [European fascists] look for a way to accommodate Catholic principles and the church. There [in Latin America] the Catholic groups initiate the process and they start looking for collaboration with fascist instruments and styles. Here is force and violence that, with a decorative intention, later call upon Catholic principles. There, these Catholic principles call upon force in order to defend themselves.[115]

In other words, Argentina's fascists were first and foremost nationalists seeking to defend the ideal of the Catholic nation. What European fascism offered were the institutions and practices to do so.

The intensification of right-wing sentiment during the 1930s led to the emergence of over a dozen right-wing nationalist groups, resulting in an ever-expanding alphabet soup of acronyms and initials. Among the most important were the paramilitary group Legión Cívica Argentina (LCA; Argentine civic league), formed in late 1930 by military and civilian supporters of the Uriburu regime; the group Acción Nacionalista Argentina-Afirmación de una Nueva Argentina (ANA-ADUNA; Nationalist action of Argentine affirmation of a new Argentina), active 1932–36; Amigos de Crisol (AdC; Friends of the publication *Crisol*), active 1936–43, and publisher of the profascist newspapers *Crisol* and *El Pampero*; and the Unión Nacionalista de Estudiantes Secundario-Alianza de la Juventud Nacionalistas (UNES-AJN; nationalist union of secondary students-alliance of nationalist youth), active 1936–43, which later became the pro-Peronist group Alianza Libertadora Nacionalista (liberating nationalist alliance).[116]

The leaders of these groups made several attempts to unify their forces.[117] Ultimately, however, these efforts came to naught, and nationalists were unable to mount a serious challenge to the Justo regime. Many of their conflicts stemmed from purely personal rivalries or differences over strategy, while others revolved around the question of whether some nationalist groups, particularly those most openly sympathetic to fascism, were guilty of embracing exotic, top-down, elitist ideologies that aided and abetted the traditional oligarchy. This was especially true in the latter half of the 1930s, with the emergence of new groups that openly sympathized with the Axis powers.[118] Mainstream elements of the church also continued to criticize the "exaggerated nationalism" of such groups, warning against any ideology that was excessively totalitarian and that sought to invade the "middle" spheres of society.[119]

One important obstacle to right-wing nationalist unity was President Justo himself, who proved a difficult target against which to rally. A consummate politician, Justo sought to defuse the nationalists' hostility by publicly lauding Uriburu and allowing the deceased president's paramilitary organization, the Legión Cívica Argentina, to keep its legal status.[120] Also helping to placate at least some of the nationalist right was Justo's willingness to crack down on Radicals who organized a series of armed rebellions, as well as his strategic appointment of nationalists to minor government posts.[121] The nationalist right was also stymied by Justo's assiduous cultivation of the church, most visibly during the 1934 International Eucharist Congress held in Argentina. In the months leading up to the Congress, Justo threw the government's full support behind the project and personally participated in the event itself.[122]

Justo did, however, provide one important target for nationalists that helped solidify opposition to his administration and—more importantly for our purposes—added a new dimension to the nationalist right's critique of liberalism. During the late 1920s, the focus of the nationalist right had been the reassertion of rule by the "capable" elite and the need for a cultural defense of Argentina's Catholic *ser nacional*. What changed in the early 1930s was the addition of an *economic* component to this critique. According to this expanded indictment of liberalism, the Argentine elite's embrace of liberal economic principles had allowed foreign capitalists to gain control of the economy. Furthermore, nationalists believed, the elite had not become infatuated with liberalism by accident. Rather, they argued, British diplomats and bankers had carefully cultivated Argentina's upper class as part of a broader strategy to infiltrate the country and exploit it economically. This new emphasis on liberalism's role in Argentina's economic woes and the need to defend Argentina against imperialism did not, however, displace earlier essentialist concerns about defending Argentina's real or authentic national character. Instead, these new grievances were folded into the old, and, as the country contended with the collapse of the agro-export economy, nationalists from across the political spectrum came to believe that the anti-imperial struggle to protect Argentina's economic sovereignty went hand in hand with defending the country's authentic *ser nacional*.

A key event that led to the rise of economic nationalism was the 1933 signing of a new trade agreement with Great Britain known as the Roca-Runciman pact.[123] The treaty, energetically pursued by the Justo government, guaranteed Argentina continued access to British markets for its beef at a moment when Great Britain was turning inward.[124] In exchange, however, Argentina was required to use the proceeds of these sales to purchase British manufactures. Although the pact provoked little initial public reaction, nationalists were outraged. In their view, the treaty was a humiliating concession to British demands that underscored both the inherent folly of the agro-export model and the complicity of the traditional liberal elite in selling out the country to foreign capitalists.

To be sure, elements of economic nationalism had surfaced before,[125] but it was only in the 1930s that economic nationalism, antiliberalism, and anti-imperialism would become inextricably intertwined with essentialist notions of Argentine identity. Clearly, economic nationalism is not necessarily tied to authoritarian political tendencies, or even to cultural nationalism. It is possible, and indeed it is often the case, for these phenomena to exist alone or in some combination. Yet in post-1930 Argentina, the conviction that achieving economic sovereignty and defending the true nation were both inextricably intertwined *and* required the rejection of liberal democracy became central to nationalist thought. Here, the argument against democracy had nothing to do with the fear that democratic states were too weak to defend the nation's culture or wealth. Rather, nationalists argued that liberalism itself was an instrument of imperialism: an alien political philosophy at odds with the true nation that threatened to corrode the very essence of the Argentine people. Worse still was the "fact" that liberalism had been imposed on Argentina by foreign actors, with the aid of their domestic lackeys, for the hidden purpose of weakening the nation in order to more easily exploit its resources.

Here again, the Irazusta brothers took the lead in making these connections. As was the case in their halting journey toward a full rejection of the 1853 Constitution, the Irazustas' enmity toward foreign capital took time to ripen. Writing in 1975, Julio Irazusta remembered that, during the late 1920s, his and Rodolfo's ideas about the evils of international capitalism were still "incipient."[126] Indeed, in a 1931 article they continued to be convinced that, in younger countries such as Argentina, foreign capital was still necessary as long as its excessive profits were curbed.[127] The turning point for the Irazustas (or what, in Julio's words, "opened our eyes") was the Roca-Runciman pact.[128] Just a year after the treaty was negotiated, the brothers published what would be a watershed book, *La Argentina y el imperialismo británico: Los eslabones de una cadena. 1806–1933* (Argentina and British imperialism: the links of a chain), in the history of Argentine nationalism. Its title left no doubt about their position. According to the Irazustas, by acquiescing to the treaty, the Justo government had sold out the Argentine people with a trade agreement that sealed Argentina's fate as a mere producer of primary products. Worse still, it had been forced on them by the very country that had kept the Argentine people in "chains" since the very beginning of the republic.

The Irazustas devoted much of their book to the trade mission itself and to an analysis of what they saw as the treaty's damaging impact. The most caustic sections, however, sought to explain why the trade mission, led by former vice president Julio Roca (Jr.), had accepted the pact. According to the Irazustas, Roca's actions were so misguided that it was impossible to attribute them to his personal failings. Rather, this upper-class scion was acting merely according to the values and attitudes of his social class, the Argentine oligarchy, which had long been mentally colonized by the British.[129] The origins of this process, the Irazustas argued, could be traced to the nefarious actions and attitudes of Unitarian leader Bernardino Rivadavia. Blinkered by a misplaced faith in liberalism and an implacable hatred of Catholic Spain, the Unitarian leader had sought to transform a "Catholic nation" into a "liberal country."[130] Ready to assist in this forced march toward "enlightenment" (and in the denationalization of the Argentine people) were British capitalists. Once allowed in by Argentina's misguided leaders, these imperialists had quickly seized control over the most productive areas of the economy, promoting the ideology of liberalism as a means to further their dominance. Rather than resisting the takeover of their country, the Irazustas argued, the Argentine oligarchy had obediently embraced liberalism and eagerly abetted their new British masters' efforts to turn the country into a "factory" for the benefit of foreign interests.[131]

For the Irazustas, the decades-long regime of Federalist dictator Juan Manuel de Rosas was the only hiatus in this long history of imperialist penetration. Calling Rosas the "Restorer," they saw the former dictator as the champion of the true Argentina—that is, the Argentina based on the traditional values of Catholicism and social order.[132] Moreover, the Irazustas believed, the Rosas years represented a missed opportunity in Argentina's history, during which the nation's heart (i.e., Rosas and the values he stood for) could have corrected the "missteps" (*desviaciones*) of the head (i.e., the hyper-rationalism of Rivadavia and his intellectual heirs). The failure to reconcile these two opposing ideologies or political factions, in their view, had been a national tragedy that had led to an enduring schism between two very different Argentinas.[133] The blame for this rupture, the Irazustas insisted, lay squarely on the shoulders of the Argentine Generation of 1837, whose members had fled the country during the Rosas years and who had rebuffed his invitation to work for a "political and cultural restoration."[134] Refusing all compromise, these arrogant youths had dreamed instead of establishing in Argentina "a nucleus of European life" that was "very liberal, that is to say, very Protestant, very civilized, that is to say, very foreign."[135] Domingo F. Sarmiento was especially censured for having done the most to erase all that was authentically Argentine. In order to carry out his misguided project of converting Argentina into a modern country, Sarmiento had insisted that it was necessary to "totally change the country, its *índole*, its customs, its ideas, its religion, its character."[136]

As is clear, the Irazustas' analysis of British imperialism, like their rejection of the 1853 Constitution, was an exercise in historical revisionism. By casting the liberal political leaders of the nineteenth century as sellouts who had betrayed their country, and by portraying Rosas as the heroic defender of the true Argentina, the Irazustas were calling into question the long established official version of Argentine history that had glorified the Generation of 1837 as the founders of modern Argentina. Certainly, as noted earlier, there had been previous efforts to achieve a more balanced view of the Rosas period.[137] None of these earlier revisionist efforts, however, could match the impact of the Irazustas' work, on both subsequent nationalist discourse and on the public imagination.

Although largely ignored by the country's mainstream press, *Argentina y el imperialismo británico* met with immediate commercial success, selling out its two initial printings of two thousand each within the first few months.[138] It quickly became a touchstone for nationalists from across the political spectrum and helped lead to the founding of the right-wing Instituto de Investigaciones Históricas Juan Manuel de Rosas (Rosas Institute for Historical Research; hereafter Rosas Institute) in 1938.[139] It also garnered praise from a wide variety of intellectuals, including individuals as diverse as Radical historian Emilio Ravignani, liberal writer Eduardo Mallea, cultural nationalist Manuel Gálvez, and LPA president Manuel Carlés.[140] Some of the most lavish (and, for the Irazustas, unexpected) praise came from literary critic Ramón Doll, whose review of the Irazustas' work highlighted the essentialist aspect of their analysis and, in doing so, undoubtedly helped shape the book's reception. The son of Basque immigrants, Doll in his early years had embraced socialism, but later he became aligned with some of the most extreme elements of the nationalist right. At the time he reviewed the Irazustas' book, however, Doll still identified with the left, prompting a surprised Julio Irazusta to seek him out. Although the two would continue to operate in different spheres, they enjoyed a long, friendly relationship.[141]

Doll's review, published in the left-wing journal *Claridad*, praised the originality and *argentinidad* of the work, and proclaimed it to have exposed the "profound reality" of the country.[142] The Irazustas, in Doll's view, had correctly criticized the Argentine oligarchy and intellectual class as having sold out the nation's interests to the foreign capitalists. This "intellectual class" (*clase pensante*), he affirmed, had from the very moment of the May Revolution "deserted *el ser nacional*" and had as its goal that of replacing its "Hispanic American personality" with that of a British colony.[143] These "diluters of the nationality,"[144] Doll believed, had attempted to introduce a "spirit that was contrary to popular customs" and one that was profoundly disdainful of "all that was genuinely creole."[145] Opposing this Europeanizing elite was Argentina's "more popular" Federalist tradition, which was personified by the figure of Juan Manuel de Rosas.[146] In words that echoed those of the earlier cultural nationalists, Doll proclaimed that Federalism was the expression of the "spirit of the race and the land," and was thus "conservative, localist and democratic."[147]

Doll's hyperbolic prose provides important clues as to why the Irazustas' work proved so influential. Certainly, part of the book's appeal was that it resonated with the economic hardships of the day and offered to its readers an explanation for Argentina's dramatic reversal of fortune. More importantly for our purposes is that it brought together two interrelated themes that were instantly familiar to anyone conversant with the earlier debates over Argentine identity. One was the essentialist claim that there existed a "real" or authentic *ser nacional* that was rooted in the land, an assertion that had been prefigured by Ricardo Rojas's belief in the existence of an Argentine race shaped by the telluric forces of the national territory. The other was the similarly well-worn trope of the hidden or submerged historical reality that lay beneath superficial, observable phenomena. Related both to Ricardo Rojas's idea of "intrahistory"[148] and to the Maurrasian dichotomy of the *pays réal* versus the *pays légal*, this trope was the basis for the notion of the two Argentinas: one visible and false, the other hidden and true.

The idea of Rosas as the defender of Argentina's economic sovereignty and of the true Argentine nationality very quickly became one of the bedrock assumptions shared by all right-wing nationalists. By the mid-1930s, two principal strains of revisionist historiography had emerged among the right wing.[149] One, championed by such individuals as the Irazustas, Doll, and Palacio, saw Rosas as the early embodiment of a popular form of Argentine democracy, whose later incarnation was Hipólito Yrigoyen. The other, more reactionary strain of revisionism found its key promoters in such individuals as Federico Ibarguren, Alberto Escurra Medrano, Ricardo Font Escurra, Héctor Llambías, and H. Sáenz y Quesada.[150] For these individuals, the Rosas regime represented the "magnificent flowering of the old Hispanic American imperial tradition" and, like all of Argentina's authentic caudillo leaders, was a "genuine echo of the colonial past."[151] They remained, however, hostile to Yrigoyen, whom they saw as a symbol of the corruption of modern politics.

The differences between these two strains of right-wing nationalism, however, should not be exaggerated, for both recognized that they shared common goals: exposing what they saw as the falsity of the official version of Argentine history propagated by the liberal oligarchy, and lauding Rosas for his defense of the true nation. In his celebrated 1939 work *La historia falsificada* (The falsified history), for example, pro-Yrigoyenist Ernesto Palacio continued to excoriate nineteenth-century liberals for attempting to "strip Argentines of their ethnicity,"[152] and he praised Rosas's efforts to defend Argentines against the "doctrines that sought to rob them of their ethnic qualities" (*doctrinas de descastamiento*).[153] These efforts had been successful, Palacio proclaimed, because foreign ideas and influences could never "denaturalize the invariable substance" of our Spanishness.[154] Right-wing nationalist Federico Ibarguren, who belonged to the anti-Yrigoyen camp, reiterated these same themes in a 1940 conference delivered at the Rosas Institute. During the nineteenth century, he proclaimed, the common people—that is, those who had followed Rosas—"had conserved, almost intact, their original Hispano-Catholic character (*forma*)." This underlying character had endured, he assured his audience, despite the exoticism of the urban governing class.[155] Similarly, revisionist historian Alberto Escurra Medrano, who also rejected any attempts to compare Yrigoyen to Rosas, proclaimed that the Unitarians' attempt to weaken the church, and open the way for religious tolerance, had provoked a popular reaction centered around the personality of Juan Manuel de Rosas. Rosas's movement, he affirmed, was aimed at restoring "that which is ours" (*lo nuestro*). And that which is ours, he continued "could not be anything except Catholic."[156]

BY THE MID-1930s, the cornerstones of right-wing nationalist thought were firmly in place. Although nationalist groups would continue to form and fissure throughout the decade, their members shared a core set of assumptions about Argentine nationality that proved more important than any of the doctrinal, personal, or strategic rifts that divided them.[157] The most important for our purposes here, of course, were the notion of the two Argentinas and the essentialist belief in the existence of an underlying, immutable Hispano-Catholic tradition that formed the basis of the true Argentina or *el ser nacional*. Rejecting the nineteenth-century liberal vision of the Argentine nation as a civic community that could tolerate at least some degree of religious, of ethnic, and even of linguistic diversity, the nationalist right insisted that the Argentine nation was first and foremost a homogeneous ethno-cultural community defined by Catholicism and its Hispanic or Latin heritage.

With the crystallization of this vision of Argentina as a Hispano-Catholic nation came a new appraisal of the 1853 Constitution and the political values it enshrined. Whereas during the early decades of the century, those who embraced the notion of an Argentine race had seen no real contradictions between an ethno-cultural vision of Argentine nationality and the country's liberal political traditions, for the nationalists of the 1930s, this incompatibility was self-evident. As they confronted the political crises of the late 1920s and early 1930s, they came to see the source of Argentina's problems as being a fundamental disconnect between the supposed *índole* of the Argentine people and the institutions that had governed them. The economic disruptions of the early 1930s provided these nationalists another line of attack against the country's liberal institutions. Eager to unmask the "real" reasons behind the country's economic ills, a new generation of historical revisionists followed the Irazusta brothers' lead, both in blaming the liberal elite and in lauding Rosas as the defender of the true Argentina. For these revisionists, the defense of the supposedly true Argentina or authentic *ser nacional* was part and parcel of the same struggle against economic exploitation by foreign imperialists and their domestic allies.

# SEVEN

# Anti-imperialism, FORJA, and the Defense of the True Argentina

Scorn for the traditional elite, hostility toward British capital, a belief in the existence of a true or "real" Argentina rooted in an immutable *ser nacional*, and the conviction that the liberal 1853 Constitution was at odds with the true Argentina: such were the main tenets of Argentine right-wing nationalist thought of the 1930s. The nationalist right, however, was not the only political entity to embrace these notions. Just as the early twentieth-century idea of an Argentine race appealed to individuals with a wide range of attitudes toward immigrants, so too did the post-1930 notion of *el ser nacional* attract adherents from across the political spectrum. And just as individuals imagined the Argentine race in very different ways, the nationalist right and left of the 1930s also differed in their understandings of the imagined *ser nacional*. This chapter examines the rise of the nationalist left during this decade and the founding of the political group known as FORJA. A splinter group of the Radical Party, whose formal existence lasted only a decade (1935–45), FORJA defined what it meant to be a left-wing nationalist and served as a kind of intellectual doppelgänger of the nationalist right. In doing so, the organization provided a more politically progressive and socially inclusive counterpart to the right's elitist and exclusionary understanding of Argentine nationality. Although its core membership never exceeded more than three hundred, like the Catholic nationalists, the group's leaders were well-known public figures, whose ideas had an outsized impact on public opinion.[1] Indeed, long after the organization had disbanded, its leaders and ideas would continue to shape public opinion, achieving their greatest influence during the turbulent years of the 1960s.

Founded in 1935, FORJA emerged from a deep schism within the Radical Party. As noted in chapter 3, from its very inception Radicalism had been riven by internal tensions, tensions that only increased after Yrigoyen won the Argentine presidency. The Radical leader's penchant for viewing the party as his personal political instrument and for bypassing normal party procedures incensed many of the older Radicals who had followed Alem.[2] In 1919, the so-called Blue Group of dissidents emerged within the party, strongly criticizing Yrigoyen's "personalism" and the lack of democratic practices within the party.[3] The following year, yet another schism appeared when the Radical governor of Salta, Joaquín Castellanos, joined with Benjamín Villafañe, a Radical deputy from Jujuy, to form the Principista faction. Angered by Yrigoyen's practice of meddling in local affairs, the group sought to preserve provincial autonomy and defend provincial economic interests.

Conflicts over the direction of the party only increased after 1922, which marked the end of Yrigoyen's six-year presidential term. Prohibited by law from running for a second consecutive term, he selected fellow Radical Marcelo T. Alvear as the party's presidential candidate. Alvear won easily, and, once in power, began to chart his own course. Ideologically closer to the anti-Yrigoyen faction of the party, now known as the antipersonalists, Alvear appeared immune to the mystical elements of Yrigoyenism. He also began to dismantle Yrigoyen's political machine and to reboot Argentina's democratization process along more traditionally liberal lines. These actions, along with his decision to include in his cabinet a number of individuals known to be hostile to Yrigoyen, endeared him to the antipersonalist faction, as well as to many members of the conservative elite.[4]

Yrigoyen's 1928 announcement that he would run again for the presidency incensed the antipersonalists, who ran their own slate of candidates.[5] Despite their efforts, Yrigoyen won overwhelmingly.[6] The 1930 military coup that deposed the Radical leader pushed the party even further into disarray and complicated the personalist/antipersonalist cleavage. Some antipersonalists blamed Yrigoyen for the disaster, and sought to reconstitute the UCR by inviting conservatives into the fold.[7] Others, however, believed that Radicalism's survival required that the two branches reconcile.[8] Alvear's return to Argentina in April 1931 added yet another twist. Alvear, who had been living in France, was greeted by both the Radical masses and much of the UCR leadership as the one person who could mend the party. Yrigoyen agreed, and despite their ideological differences he urged his followers to unite behind his former protégé. The national elections scheduled for November 1931 represented Alvear's best chance to regain the presidential sash and restore the party's fortunes. These plans, however, were soon thwarted by an uprising in Corrientes by a group of military officers loyal to Yrigoyen. Although Alvear was not involved in the affair, it gave Uriburu a pretext to send him into exile.[9]

Alvear's efforts to consolidate his control over the UCR faced internal obstacles as well. While many Radicals heeded Yrigoyen's call to rally around Alvear, some remained implacably opposed. Among those who refused to fall in line were two prominent personalists, Manuel Ortiz Pereyra and Julio Barcos. During the 1920s, journalist and politician Ortiz Pereyra had distinguished himself as one of the few Radicals to voice concerns about Argentina's extreme dependence on foreign capital and markets. His 1926 book, *La tercera emancipación*, proclaimed the need for a "third emancipation" that would "complete [Argentine] nationality" by giving the nation economic independence from foreign domination.[10] In this work, and more explicitly in his 1928 *Por nuestra redención cultural y económica* (for our cultural and economic redemption), Ortiz Pereyra linked Argentina's lack of economic independence with the elite's long tradition of taking its cultural and intellectual cues from abroad. In his view, his countrymen's lack of faith in *lo nuestro* (that which is ours) had led Argentines to "practice the mimeticism of orangutans." As a result, the nation's leaders had failed to address local needs and develop solutions that were as "singular as our country."[11] Soon after the 1930 coup, Ortiz Pereyra went into exile in Montevideo. During that time, he established ties with fellow exile Julio Barcos, a recent convert to Radicalism.[12] Upon their return to Buenos Aires, both men joined the tendency known as the *Radicales Fuertes* (strong Radicals), whose members included Juan B. Fleitas, Félix Ramírez García and Homero Manzione (who later became known as popular poet Manzi), Arturo Jauretche, Ricardo Rojas, Gabriel del Mazo, Luis Dellepiane, and Atilio García Mellid. All staunch Yrigoyenists, this group adamantly opposed Alvear.[13] Several of the younger members of the *Radicales Fuertes* would go on to form FORJA in 1935.

Although Barcos ultimately did not join FORJA, his early writings—like those of Ortiz Pereyra—are of interest because they capture the ideas of this strand of Radicalism, and anticipated by a few years the Forjistas' meshing of anti-imperialism with essentialist understandings of Argentine nationality. In his 1933 work *Por el pan del pueblo* (for the bread of the people), which he published before the appearance of the Irazustas' 1934 diatribe against British capitalists, Barcos railed against the "economic dictatorship that foreign monopoly capital exercised over [Argentina's] primary industries."[14] The coming struggle against these foreign exploiters, he maintained, must also take aim at the imperialists' allies, who aided this process of exploitation.[15] Most interesting for our purpose is Barcos's interweaving of anti-imperialism and understandings of nationality associated with Romantic nationalism, understandings that echoed those of Yrigoyen and the cultural nationalists of previous decades. Barcos proclaimed, for example, that Argentines had a "great historical destiny" and that the world was at the cusp of a new era, during which the "Argentine Nation and all the pueblos of the race" would experience an "economic, social and spiritual rebirth."[16] According to Barcos, the global economic crisis had proven that the era of unfettered capitalism, with its belief in absolute property rights, was over.[17] During this era, he argued, Anglo-Saxon peoples had prospered, because their attachment to private property was "profoundly rooted in [their] soul," and indeed was the most salient "psychological trait of the race."[18] Latins, in contrast, had been formed by "the humanistic Greco-Latin traditions of the Renaissance," and thus valued human beings over material things.[19] Accordingly, he argued, "the peoples of our race are better suited to finding a humane solution to the problem of property than are the Anglo-Saxons."[20]

Barcos, like his right-wing counterparts and the Forjistas, who would soon follow, also saw the 1853 Constitution as harmful to the nation. The democratic institutions it outlined, he maintained, were both at odds with the country's underlying essence and had provided foreign capitalists with tools to gain control over its economy.[21] The result was a political system that was not a real democracy at all but an empty façade behind which powerful interests operated.[22] Accordingly, Barcos urged Argentines to embrace a new "defensive" nationalism by creating political institutions that would protect the country's economic sovereignty.[23] These institutions, he believed, would be the basis of a new type of democracy that would allow Argentines to develop a national culture rooted in the country's native "spirituality."[24] The task of building this new type of democracy, Barcos believed, would inevitably fall to the Radical Party. As the only party with "deep psychological roots" in the country,[25] only the Radicals could develop institutions that were authentically creole and grounded in Argentina's "autochthonous culture."[26]

## THE FOUNDING OF FORJA

For Radicales Fuertes, such as Barcos and Ortiz Pereyra, the years after the 1930 coup were filled with debates over how best to carry on Yrigoyen's legacy. Despite the former president's call to avoid violence, dissidents participated in a series of antigovernment rebellions between 1930 and 1933. The most important was the so-called Paso de los Libres rebellion of December 1933, in which three key future members of FORJA participated: Arturo Jauretche, Raúl Scalabrini Ortiz, and Luis Dellepiane.[27] Besides bringing together many of FORJA's future leaders, the rebellion served to exacerbate tensions within the Radical Party, whose more traditional leadership harshly criticized the action. Another point of contention between the future Forjistas and the UCR leadership was the growing debate over whether the party should continue to abstain from the electoral process, a policy begun after the barring of Alvear's candidacy in the 1931 presidential elections. After the country returned to a nominal democracy under Justo, factions within the UCR urged the party to rejoin the political process. The young Radicals, who would ultimately form the core of FORJA, however, remained firmly opposed to participating in an electoral process they saw as corrupt.[28] In a 1934 manifesto probably penned by Arturo Jauretche, the dissidents accused those who wished to participate in elections of being *vendepatrias*, or sellers of the fatherland.[29] Those Radicals who "spoke of a national peace," it continued, were in truth seeking to "sell themselves—and sell us out—to the [foreign] monopolies."[30]

Matters came to a head in mid-1935, when on a chilly June afternoon in the midst of the austral winter, approximately forty young men gathered in a basement office in central Buenos Aires to formally constitute FORJA.[31] The name of the organization, like the endeavor itself, was Jauretche's brainchild. *Forja* in English translates to "forge," and like its English cognate can be used as either a noun or a verb. It was taken from the phrase, widely attributed to Yrigoyen, "Todo taller de forja parece un mundo que se derrumba" (every forge seems like a world crashing down).[32]

At the time of FORJA's founding, Jauretche, who would play a key role in the radicalization of Argentine politics in the 1960s, was a relative newcomer to the UCR. Born into a small town in the province of Buenos Aires, the future FORJA leader came from a family of middling means, whose fortunes were closely tied to the PAN. Known both for his sense of humor and appetite for a good fight, Jauretche as a teenager became deeply involved in politics during secondary school and was expelled after organizing a violent protest against Yrigoyen-sponsored school reforms. In 1920, he left for Buenos Aires, where he worked odd jobs and struggled to continue his studies. After finally finishing high school in 1925, he entered the University of Buenos Aires to study law. Even before he officially enrolled in the university, Jauretche had become involved in student politics. Deeply influenced by the Mexican Revolution, he began to rethink his previous opposition to the university reform movement of 1917 and to gravitate toward Radicalism. Ultimately, he became one of Yrigoyen's most ardent supporters, and worked actively in the 1928 presidential campaign. After the 1930 coup, he immediately joined with other Yrigoyenists to oppose both the military regime and the efforts of Alvear and the antipersonalists to gain control of the UCR.[33] His activism within the party continued until the mid-1930s, until the founding of FORJA.

Although Jauretche was the key figure behind the establishment of FORJA, he refused to serve as its president, preferring instead to focus on political activism. Elected in his place was Luis Dellepiane, who, like

Jauretche, had participated in the failed Paso de los Libres revolt. The son of a prominent army general, who had served as secretary of war under Yrigoyen, Dellepiane was an ardent anti-Catholic who had been an active participant in the university reform movement. During the late 1920s, he became increasingly involved in the UCR, and after the 1930 coup, he aligned with the Yrigoyenist branch of the party. As FORJA's president, Dellepiane championed three of its most important goals: the need to reform UCR from within, the struggle against foreign imperialists and their oligarchic lackeys, and, in the late 1930s, the defense of Argentina's neutrality in the Second World War. But despite his role as the organization's president, Dellepiane always remained in the shadow of the more flamboyant Jauretche, who along with Scalabrini Ortiz continually sought to push the organization in a more radical direction. Indeed, as will be discussed below, it was because of his differences with these two men that Dellepiane resigned his post and broke entirely with FORJA in 1940.

Joining Jauretche, Dellepiane, and García Mellid at this initial meeting were the above-mentioned Ortiz Pereyra, who had served as a kind of mentor to Jauretche; Gabriel del Mazo, a fervent Yrigoyenist who had been a key student leader of the Reform; and Homero Manzione. Both Del Mazo and Manzione had become friends with Jauretche during their years as university students. Missing from the list of FORJA's early adherents was Julio Barcos, who, despite sympathizing with the goals of the organization, opted not to join. Instead, he remained active within the regular party structure of the UCR, working with other members of the Yrigoyenist branch to push for a more nationalist agenda.[34] Some members who tended toward this approach, such as Honorio Pueyrredón, Adolfo Güemes, and Ricardo Rojas, subscribed to Forjista publications and occasionally contributed funds to keep the group afloat.[35]

Also missing from the official membership list of FORJA was Raúl Scalabrini Ortiz, who, despite his oversized role in shaping the group's ideology, refused to become a formal member. The sticking point for Scalabrini Ortiz was FORJA's insistence that it represented the authentic core of the Radical Party and, therefore, required that all its members must first become members of the UCR. Although he would eventually develop a deep respect for Yrigoyen, Scalabrini Ortiz resisted this vision of FORJA, believing that it was necessary to create an entirely new movement outside Argentina's traditional political system.[36] But despite his lack of official standing within FORJA, Scalabrini Ortiz proved to be one of its most prolific propagandists and its key ideologue. Working closely with Jauretche, he gave countless public lectures on FORJA and supplied its many publications with lengthy articles focused on the evils of British imperialism.[37] Indeed, so central was he to FORJA that Jauretche would later claim that the group's primary accomplishment was to make Scalabrini Ortiz's ideas part of the "popular consciousness" and "the thought of the majority of Argentines."[38]

Nothing in Scalabrini Ortiz's background suggested that he would become one of the most important voices of Argentina's nationalist left.[39] Born in 1898 to an Argentine mother and an Italian-immigrant father, who became a famous naturalist, Scalabrini found early critical success as a fiction writer and essayist. But it was his 1931 book-length essay *El hombre que está solo y espera* (The man who is alone and waits/hopes), that made him famous.[40] A deeply mystical attempt to "inquire into [the nature] of the soul of the porteño (inhabitant of the port city of Buenos Aires),"[41] *El hombre* was an instant bestseller that went through four printings in the first five months.[42] The work also enjoyed instant critical acclaim and was named Best Book of the Month by the prestigious PEN club of Buenos Aires. The content of *El hombre* and its vision of *argentinidad* provide important insight into Scalabrini Ortiz's and thus FORJA's understanding of the true Argentina, which will be explored in depth below. For now, however, we need to note only that this 1931 work provided no hint of Scalabrini Ortiz's future role as one of Argentina's most vocal anti-imperialists.

Just why this transformation took place is not completely clear. What is known, however, is that by 1933 Scalabrini Ortiz seems to have experienced a sort of epiphany that induced a deep antipathy toward foreign intervention in Argentina. His participation in the ill-fated Paso de los Libres revolt, for example, was more about anti-imperialism than about defending the Radical Party.[43] After the revolt (and a brief stint in jail), Scalabrini Ortiz's hostility toward foreign capitalists, especially those from Great Britain, seems to have intensified. Shortly after his release, he left for Europe with his new wife. Included in the couple's travels was a visit to Germany, where the Nazis had already seized power. While in Germany, Scalabrini Ortiz was invited to contribute articles concerning contemporary Argentina to the prestigious daily *Frankfurter Zeitung*.[44] Using the opportunity to air his views on what he saw as the great divide in Argentine society, he argued that there were two very different Argentinas: that of the "whole nation, the whole people, without distinction as to rank or class" and of those who exploited them—that is, British and US capitalists and their well-paid Argentine accomplices.[45] Scalabrini Ortiz's stay in Germany and his contact with the German press would later help fuel suspicion that he was a Nazi sympathizer.[46]

After his return to Argentina in 1935, Scalabrini Ortiz threw his energies into exposing what he believed to be the pernicious impact of Great Britain on Argentina's economic and political development, a theme that because of the Irazusta brothers' 1934 text had begun to gain common currency.[47] His articles caught the attention of Jauretche, who was at that time in the midst of launching FORJA. Naturally, Jauretche invited the writer to join. Although Scalabrini Ortiz refused to become a formal member, he readily agreed to lend his pen to the cause. He also asked Jauretche to join him on the staff of the weekly review *Señales*, thus beginning an intellectual and political collaboration that would span three decades. Under their combined leadership, the magazine, and then FORJA itself, would become vocal critics of British imperialism.

## FORJA IDEOLOGY

What, then, was the ideology of FORJA, and in what ways was Forjista nationalism similar to, and different from, right-wing nationalism? The most obvious similarity between these two strands of nationalist thought was their shared conviction that the Argentine people had been victimized by both British imperialists and the native oligarchy, whom they lambasted as *vendepatrias* and *cipayos*.[48] This belief that Argentina had been doubly victimized also led Forjistas to embrace another element of right-wing nationalism—historical revisionism, a project in which Scalabrini Ortiz and Jauretche took the lead.[49] Like Ernesto Palacio, whose revisionist work *Historia falsificada* was "devoured" by Forjistas, Scalabrini Ortiz was convinced that the traditional liberal (or "official") version of Argentine history was fraudulent.[50] This interpretation of the country's history, he affirmed, was "a work of imagination," whose "facts have been consciously and deliberately deformed, falsified and strung together in accordance with a preconceived plan." Directing this plan, Scalabrini Ortiz believed, were British diplomats, whose behind-the-scenes maneuverings were the "subterranean force behind the major events that occur throughout this continent."[51] Jauretche concurred, proclaiming that the falsification of Argentine history had been a deliberate policy promoted by foreign interests and the national oligarchy. By portraying the nation's nineteenth century as a struggle between the enlightened liberals and the barbaric masses, and by representing British loans and investments as necessary for the nation's development, the elite had taught ordinary Argentines to see Great Britain as their ally rather than their enemy.[52]

Beyond these points of ideological convergence were other key similarities between the two strands of nationalism. One of the most important for our purposes was the Forjistas' tendency, inherited from Yrigoyen and the earlier generation of Radicals, to define the Argentine nation in essentialist terms and to see *argentinidad* as based first and foremost on an underlying ethno-cultural tradition rather than on collectively held political ideals. In other words, Argentine nationalists of both the right and left shared the belief that the Argentine nation existed independently of the political values and institutions inscribed in the 1853 Constitution. Indeed, as will be developed below, like their right-wing counterparts, Forjistas would ultimately come to see this constitution and the liberal tradition it sprang from as a threat to the true Argentina or *el ser nacional*.

But how did FORJA define the true Argentina? In understanding FORJA's vision of Argentine nationality, it is first important to recall the value the Forjistas placed on their self-proclaimed status as Yrigoyen's only legitimate heirs and to note the continuities between their ideas and those of the former president. Chief among these was a penchant for mystically infused rhetoric and the embrace of notions of nationality and history reminiscent of Krausist-style Romanticism. The already-cited manifesto published in 1934 by members of the Radicales Fuertes, and later considered one of FORJA's founding documents, provides an example.[53] According to this document, only those who possessed "love, the feeling of unity, and spiritual identification" could comprehend the "mysterious" bond between Radicalism and the Argentine masses. The masses, moreover, were imbued with "their own irradiation" or "invisible force" that served to strengthen and purify the movement.[54] In a similar fashion, a 1935 FORJA manifesto proclaimed that only Forjistas had remained faithful to the ideals of the UCR, whose original aim it was to "define the spiritual unity of the pueblo" and to "repair or make good (*reparar*) its moral and material goods," which had been reduced (*cercenados*) by mercantilism."[55] Its authors expressed confidence as well that the Argentine people would respond to the UCR, because the Argentine pueblo possessed "infinite moral reserves" that "lie and palpitate . . . in the breast of the UCR." These common people, the manifesto continued, would soon "hear our convocation to fulfill their destiny."[56] In much the same vein, García Mellid proclaimed that Radicalism's leaders were influential only insofar as they "showed themselves to be interpreters of that old subterranean current that was national and popular, and that runs through the whole of our history." Radicalism, he continued, "was not a capricious invention of Yrigoyen; rather it was the reencounter of the mysticism of the nationality that unifies the land, man and destiny in a common style of life, of unmistakably American cast."[57]

Forjistas also followed Yrigoyen in insisting that the UCR was a movement, rather than a political party.[58] Radicalism, its members opined, cannot be "contained within the limits of a meeting house, or in a list of names, or in programs written in the stupidity of fallacious conventions."[59] It was, instead, "the Nation marching toward its more perfect social form."[60] An unsigned article in FORJA's *Boletín* sounded similar themes, noting approvingly that Yrigoyen had never allowed his followers to use the term *political party* to describe the UCR. This was because parties, the article argued, were entities that compete in elections "behind the little banner of a little program." The UCR, it insisted, was "much more," and indeed was "the Nation itself, reacting in accordance with the noblest elements of its permanent attributes." In doing so, it would "destroy the arbitrary apparatus" that was preventing Argentina from fulfilling its destiny of "universal liberation."[61] In a similar fashion, Forjista Amable Gutiérrez Diez declared that Radicalism "was the nation itself, struggling from the most intimate [recesses] of its *ser*, to realize its destinies."[62]

Another aspect of Radical (and Romantic) thought to which the Forjistas remained tethered was belief in the existence of exceptional

men, who possessed special sensibilities that allowed them to comprehend the nation and its true path more clearly. Accordingly, they celebrated Yrigoyen as the "mystic and demiurge" of Argentine reality,
who experienced in his "heart" and "lacerated flesh" the reality of the
Argentine multitudes.[63] Elsewhere, Forjistas lauded the former president
as someone who came to "realize, in his individual consciousness, the
profound and vast consciousness of the pueblo." Yrigoyen was, in other
words, the "materialization of the mysterious unity that the pueblo
sensed within the U.C.R."[64] For FORJA stalwart Gabriel del Mazo, Yrigoyen "embodied like no other the authenticity of the pueblo" and was
the "bearer . . . of the soul of the Argentine people."[65] Yrigoyen's embrace
of a teleological vision of history, including the belief that it was the
UCR's mission to restore the nation to its preordained historical trajectory, was also shared by Forjistas. A 1935 Forjista flier, for example, proclaimed that the organization's goal was to "recover the Unión Cívica
Radical in order to fulfill its intransigent, reparative and revolutionary
destiny," and to "retake the historical route of the nationality from which
it had been thrown off by the anti-[Argentine] oligarchies."[66]

The Radical/Romantic notion that the Argentine nation possessed
an authentic underlying essence, spirit, or *índole* was also a central element of Forjista thought. Del Mazo, for example, promoted the well-
worn essentialist view that Argentines, and Latin Americans in general,
were a people that valued spiritual matters over material wealth. Latin
Americans were not, he proclaimed, "businessmen (*comerciantes*), nor do
we possess a passion for money." Rather, they were a people who were
inherently emotional, preferring to approach the world with a stance
that was "spirit[ual]," rather than one based on "calculation." They preferred, he continued, "hospitality to conquest."[67] Elsewhere, in an address
delivered to commemorate October 12, or the Day of the Race, Del
Mazo repeated these themes, adding in a dash of anti-intellectualism. In
his words, what this pueblo, or "race," valued most was not "knowledge,
science or technology, or even less, wealth or power (*poderío*)." Rather, it
valued the whole individual and his conduct in the world. "We belong,"
he concluded, "to an emotional lineage, against which material civilization committed death and distortion, but [in the end] did not triumph."[68]

This essentialist belief in the existence of a unified, continuing national character ran through much of Forjista writing, surfacing in the

organization's response to virtually any situation or problem. For example, when in 1941 the government called on Argentine youth to spurn extremist ideologies, such as fascism, FORJA issued a manifesto expressing its agreement. But the real problem troubling young Argentines, the document's authors argued, lay in the "colonial spirit" of the older generation that had rejected Yrigoyen. Given that these liberal leaders had betrayed the country, it was understandable that a segment of the nation's youth would commit the error of adopting "forms that are alien to our national essence."[69] Similarly, when the United States pressured Latin America to support the Allies in World War II, García Mellid reacted with skepticism borne of an essentialist vision of Argentine (and Latin American) identity. Such an enterprise, he warned, required that Argentines closely scrutinize the "virgin leavening of our *ser americano*" (*levadura virgen de nuestro ser Americano*), in order to ascertain whom this policy truly served. Comparing the United States to colonial Spain, and present-day Latin Americans with the continent's indigenous population, García Mellid argued that for more than four hundred years, "América" has suffered at the hands of self-styled "benefactors," leading to a situation in which "even the most intimate [aspects] of its *ser* . . . have been subjected to deviation (*desviación*) and appropriation."[70]

Clearly, then, Forjistas shared with their right-wing counterparts a view of Argentina as having a homogeneous character or essence that served as the basis of the nation's identity, and one that shared an underlying unity with the rest of Latin America. The critical question for our purposes is how Forjistas understood the *content* of this imagined Argentine essence or *ser* and how it differed from that of the ultraright. For right-wing nationalists of the 1930s, of course, the nature of the Argentine *ser* had always been straight forward: *argentinidad* was inextricably bound to the country's Hispanic roots, and especially to the Catholic faith.[71] Accordingly, any political institutions, values, or policies that failed to recognize this basic truth, and thus failed to defend these supposedly immutable qualities of *el ser nacional*, were, by definition, antinational and anti-Argentine. For Forjistas, in contrast, the essence or nature of Argentine nationality was more complex. While most applauded aspects of the right's revaluation of Argentina's Spanish heritage, their claim to represent the popular masses meant that FORJA's vision of the true Argentine had to include the offspring of the working-class immigrants, many of whom were neither Catholic nor of Latin descent.[72] Also making the Hispanic-Catholic option impossible for Forjistas was Radicalism's tradition of religious tolerance, as well as the fact that key FORJA leaders, such as Jauretche and Scalabrini Ortiz, were indifferent Catholics at best. Indeed some, such as Dellepiane, were actively hostile to the faith.

The problem of how to conceptualize a nation whose basis was a unitary, homogeneous essence that was capacious enough to include both natives and immigrants was of course not new in Argentina. As we have seen, this puzzle dominated debates over national identity during the 1910s and 1920s. Indeed, it could be argued that it was the effort to grapple with this conundrum that gave these debates both their originality and their sometimes contradictory quality. This was also the case with the Forjistas. Consider, for example, a manifesto published in 1941 that defended the cause of Argentine neutrality in World War II. Looking forward to the aftermath of hostilities, the document affirmed that once the conflict ended, Argentines should "establish a national policy that defines the personality of the Republic in consonance with its own *ser* and in consolidation with the American republics of the same *estirpe*."[73] Here the use of the term *estirpe*, meaning bloodline, pedigree, or lineage, suggests a vision of nationality based on descent. Very quickly, however, the manifesto reversed course, and without skipping a beat, affirmed that by acting in concert with the other Latin American nations, Argentines could "fulfill our own nation's ends, which is to announce to the world a new form of human society, without oppressors or oppressed, and without exclusions based upon race or blood."[74]

As discussed in previous chapters, for the early twentieth-century cultural nationalists, the problem of reconciling the vision of the nation as a unique ethno-cultural community with the need to incorporate the immigrant was solved, at least conceptually, by positing the existence of an Argentine race that could absorb immigrants without losing its essential qualities. The Forjistas of the 1930s took another route, but their effort to wrestle with the inherent contradictions of such a project often produced its own logical lapses and flights of fantasy. Central to the FORJA's understanding of the Argentine *ser nacional*, I argue, is Scalabrini Ortiz's above-mentioned work, the wildly successful *El hombre que está solo y espera*. Although published a few years before the founding of

FORJA, this book-length essay contained within it all the elements that would be central to the Forjista vision of the Argentine *ser nacional.* Indeed, in the judgment of literary critic Beatriz Sarlo, Scalabrini Ortiz's 1931 exploration of the putative national soul was a kind of challenge or "wager" that FORJA would "take up" just a few years later.[75] It is to this work that we now turn.

*El hombre* is a profoundly strange book that, in methodological terms, draws from two different intellectual traditions.[76] The first tradition was turn-of-the-century positivist sociology, especially its empiricist strand. Employing a sociological approach, Scalabrini Ortiz used part of his essay to explore the factors behind what he identified as the salient emotional qualities of the archetypical man of Buenos Aires, a figure he called "the man of Esmeralda and Corrientes," in reference to the intersection of Esmeralda Street and Corrientes Avenue in downtown Buenos Aires.[77] According to Scalabrini Ortiz, this man suffered from loneliness, inwardness, and sadness, traits that could be traced to the "sexual tragedy" that afflicted young males in Argentine society.[78] This tragedy, he believed, was the result of the acute gender imbalance caused by the massive influx of predominantly male immigrants. Deprived of normal contact with women, the men of his generation—both immigrants and natives—turned inward, becoming muted and sad. At the same time, however, this shared experience bound these young men together and created a single porteño spirit that encompassed both newcomers and those of "long lineage" in the city.[79]

It was this union between native and immigrant, and the fusion of the two into a single national archetype, that forms the larger theme of the book, and is the issue that concerns us here. In describing this process, Scalabrini Ortiz trades the sociological model for one that echoes the mystical musings of cultural nationalists, such as Ricardo Rojas, whom some scholars see as having strongly influenced Scalabrini Ortiz.[80] Recall that Rojas also promoted the notion of a national archetype. In his case, of course, it was the mixed-race gaucho who served as the spiritual template of a new, emerging Argentine race, into which the immigrant—with the help of the telluric forces of the Argentine soil—would be absorbed. Like Rojas, Scalabrini Ortiz insisted that Argentines formed an emerging race that was neither purely Spanish nor purely autochthonous. In his view, the archetype of that race was the sum of many parts, "a chemical combination of races that nourish its birth" and a "droplet of water" that from the fusion of two disparate elements creates something entirely new.[81] This man, Scalabrini Ortiz proclaimed, descended from "the four distinct races that mutually annul themselves and fuse together."[82]

Scalabrini Ortiz also followed Rojas's lead by positing the existence of a powerful "spirit of the land" that bound the immigrant to his adopted country and transformed him into an Argentine. So "irresistible" was the assimilative power of this telluric force, he believed, that it "broke the continuity of blood" between the immigrants and their children, with the latter becoming completely Argentine.[83] Inviting his reader to imagine this spirit as a "giant man," or "giant archetype," he proclaimed that this being "nourishes itself and grows with the immigrant contribution, devouring and assimilating millions of Spaniards, Italians, Britons, and Frenchmen."[84] In the process, however, this spirit remained unchanged. Just as the individual "who ingests pieces of pork, veal ribs or chicken breasts is changed very little," declared Scalabrini Ortiz, so too did the Argentine spirit retain its original character despite the influx of millions of immigrants.[85] The immigrants themselves who were consumed in this process, like the native Argentines, became part of this gigantic being.[86]

Two more aspects of Scalabrini Ortiz's account of the emergence of the new Argentine archetype reflected his deep affinities with the Romantic milieu of the opening decades of the century. First was a teleological understanding of history. According to Scalabrini Ortiz, the spirit of the land had a mission and destiny, of which it was conscious. For example, in one of his rare pre-1930 mentions of US cultural imperialism, Scalabrini Ortiz notes the fears among some older Argentines that the country's youth was in danger of become "North Americanized." This, he assured his readers, would not happen, because the "spirit of the land would not permit it." This spirit, he continued, has "a destiny, and it must be fulfilled."[87]

A second noteworthy aspect of *El hombre* was its essentialist assumptions about the supposedly distinctive nature of the Argentine man. According to Scalabrini Ortiz, the true Argentine possessed a unique set of traits that distinguished him from other nationalities. Echoing the early twentieth-century writings that celebrated the inherently spiritual nature of Latin Americans, Scalabrini Ortiz insisted that the man of

Corrientes and Esmeralda was indifferent to material accumulation and looked with bemusement at the desperate strivings of the newly arrived immigrant.[88] Similarly, this man was endowed with an almost instinctual power to grasp the hidden truths that lay beneath outward appearances. Scalabrini Ortiz called this ability of the Argentine archetype his *pálpito*, or intuition.[89] It was because of his *pálpito* that the man of Corrientes and Esmeralda would be able to protect his country from excessive exploitation from foreign capital. In Scalabrini Ortiz's words, "The man of Corrientes and Esmeralda, although he knows nothing about finances, intuitively knows that capital represents international energy, and it can never be made to be an organic part of the country. He knows intuitively, if it was in capital's interest to sacrifice the country, it would do so without scruples." It is for this reason, Scalabrini Ortiz continued, that the man of Corrientes and Esmeralda would never allow international capital to infiltrate the government.[90] (Just a few years later, of course, Scalabrini would argue that international capital had indeed taken over the country.)

Despite these very strong similarities between Scalabrini Ortiz and earlier thinkers, such as Rojas, there were important differences. FORJA's future intellectual leader argued, for instance, that the new national type had emerged not in the countryside but in Buenos Aires where—somewhat paradoxically—the spirit of the land had become concentrated. Indeed, according to Scalabrini Ortiz, the intersection of Esmeralda Street and Corrientes Avenue constituted the "hydraulic, commercial, sentimental and spiritual basin" of Argentina.[91] Accordingly, the man who waited there was the "vortex in which the whirlwind of *argentinidad* comes together in its most powerful spiritual frenzy."[92] Moreover, it was through an examination of this man that the spirit of the nation could be discovered.[93]

Another key difference with Rojas's analysis was Scalabrini Ortiz's insistence that the man of Corrientes and Esmeralda was an everyman, a member of the anonymous multitude, who intuitively sensed the "invisible pulsations" of the city.[94] In a somewhat similar fashion, Rojas had argued that Argentina's racial archetype was the lowly gaucho. But by the time the cultural nationalist had proclaimed this figure to embody the national essence, the herdsman had already faded into history. Moreover, Rojas believed that it was up to intellectuals like himself to intuit the gaucho's significance and to resurrect him as a symbol of *argentinidad*. Scalabrini Ortiz's analysis, in contrast, had a strong anti-intellectual, anti-elitist cast. In his view, it was the popular classes, rather than the educated elite, who possessed the powers of intuition necessary to grasp Argentina's authentic reality. Most intellectuals, he maintained, had lost contact with the spiritual forces of the Argentine land. "Encased" in their own literary ambitions, these individuals had cut themselves off from this spirit and the pueblo that it had formed, producing a literature that was "but a vain cloud of words."[95] A truer expression of the real Argentine (i.e., the man of Corrientes and Esmeralda), he maintained, could be found in the tango lyrics and "stuttered scenes of the *sainete*" (popular plays) produced in the working-class neighborhood, where immigrants and creoles had created a new, authentically Argentine form of expression.[96]

Summing up, Scalabrini Ortiz's attempt to define the true Argentina essence or *ser* took him along familiar conceptual pathways, but with some new twists. For him, as for the cultural nationalists, the source of Argentine unity was not shared political values or institutions, or even loyalty to the nation. Rather, this union was understood to be a racial or spiritual one that would be created by the fusion of disparate elements into a single, homogenous people through the supernatural powers of the Argentine soil. Nor was Scalabrini Ortiz's insistence that the popular classes were the real embodiment of the true Argentina a completely novel idea. Recall, for example, that several participants in the debate over whether or not Argentina should develop its own language held similar views, arguing that the developing national language would be largely shaped by the new terms and pronunciations contributed by working-class immigrants. Rather, what would give Scalabrini Ortiz's vision of *argentinidad* its lasting impact was what came later, when he combined this deeply essentialist and even mystical vision of *argentinidad* with a strident anti-imperialist message. Thus for Scalabrini Ortiz and the Forjistas—and, of course, their right-wing counterparts—economic emancipation and the defense of Argentina's authentic *ser* became inextricably linked.

How, then, did Scalabrini Ortiz's *El hombre* shape Forjista understandings of Argentine identity? To be sure, there is little direct evidence that the FORJA members consciously drew inspiration from Scalabrini

Ortiz's 1931 work. Still, given his importance within the organization, and the enormous popularity of *El hombre* among the general public, it can be assumed that almost all Forjistas had read Scalabrini Ortiz's masterwork at least once. Moreover, the fact that the title of one of FORJA's publications, *Una gota de agua* (a drop of water), was a metaphor lifted directly from *El hombre* suggests that the essay formed part of the Forjistas' collective mental furniture. It is clear, too, that the themes of *El hombre* were never far from Scalabrini Ortiz's own thoughts. Even as he focused his energies on writing diatribes against British imperialism, Scalabrini Ortiz continued to republish—and in some instances, rework—various editions of *El hombre* during the 1930s and '40s. Such continued engagement with his celebrated book suggests that Scalabrini Ortiz remained committed to keeping the vision of *argentinidad* it promoted before the public eye.[97] Indeed, in historian Nicola Miller's estimation, Scalabrini Ortiz "sought economic independence not so much in order to gain benefits in terms of national economic progress or improvements in the welfare of the people, but rather on the grounds that, without it, the Argentine spirit would be insubstantial and therefore incapable of sustaining itself."[98]

With only indirect evidence that Forjistas drew inspiration from Scalabrini Ortiz's national archetype, we are left with examining the similarities between his ideal and the socially inclusive vision of *el ser nacional* that surfaced in FORJA publications. There are several. First, it is very clear that Forjistas identified the true Argentina with the common people and believed that the masses formed, in Jauretche's words, the "live instrument" of the nation.[99] That Forjistas also believed the working-class immigrant to be an integral part of Argentine masses (and thus of the true Argentina) is also clear. An editorial appearing in the 1938 inaugural issue of the Forjista publication *Argentinidad* makes the point directly. In words reminiscent of the early twentieth-century cultural nationalists, the editorial urged Argentines "to detoxify [themselves] from all imported doctrines," and to reject the "cosmopolitan materialism" that has left them "stripped of [their] ethnicity (*descastado*) and corrupted." At the same time, however, the editorial hastened to add that these corrupting values had come not from immigrants, but from the native oligarchy that had blindly embraced "transplanted ideas." Thus "the gringo with calloused hands is not the one that has stripped us of our ethnicity (*que nos ha descastado*)." Rather, those that had corrupted Argentina were the members of high society, "the bastard sons of the Nation, the ones who have lost their ethnicity, and who impoverish the soil that nourishes them and that gave them a patria."[100]

Forjistas also followed Scalabrini Ortiz in their insistence that *el ser nacional* was one of mixture or fusion. Accordingly, they rejected out of hand the nationalist right's view that Argentina was defined solely by its Hispanic, Catholic past. A 1943 manifesto by the Organización Universitario de F.O.R.J.A. provides a clear example.[101] This particular manifesto was penned in response to an address given by Jordán Bruno Genta, a right-wing nationalist who had been appointed by the new military government to head the Universidad del Litoral.[102] In his speech, Genta had called on Argentines to protect themselves against colonialism by returning to their Greco-Roman roots. Forjistas reacted strongly. While agreeing that Genta was correct in asserting that the majority of Argentines was indeed of the "Roman and Hispanic *estirpe*," they argued that this did not mean that the "Argentine Nation . . . as a nation, was of the same *estirpe*."[103] Rather, they insisted, Argentina was "rooted in and nourished by all the pueblos of diverse *estirpes* that had contributed to our development." Once separated culturally from the "colonial trunk," Argentina had begun "the formation of a new culture that, while benefitting from the contributions of Spain and Rome, was not limited by them." In contrast to the vision of *argentinidad* offered by Genta, the authors declared, "we aspire to an Argentine culture [with a] a richer destiny than that which reflects only a single part of its past."[104]

In much the same vein, Arturo Jauretche and fellow Forjista Luis Peralta Ramos also promoted the notion of the Argentine *ser* as one of mixture. According to Peralta Ramos, although Argentine nationality was "of Spanish descent," it was distinctively "American." "Our future," he continued, "cannot consist of [imitating] the decadent modalities of an exhausted civilization" but in "the development of our own values."[105] Jauretche expressed similar views. While he at times praised right-wing nationalists for contributing to the "revalorization of the Hispanic American roots of Argentina with their racial and religious values,"[106] it was clear that he viewed the Spanish legacy as only one element in the nation's identity. The real Argentina, he insisted, was the Argentina of the "multitudes."[107] In a speech given in the aftermath of the 1943 military coup, Jauretche noted that, because the country's population was one such mixture, it would be absurd to "even pretend that we could restore *lo argentino* on the basis of blood." But, he continued, "this does not mean that we can avoid [dealing with] the problem of minorities that because of language, blood or religious faith are inadaptable. All [who come to this country] have to amalgamate themselves into *lo argentino* or disappear."[108] Finally, Forjistas embraced Scalabrini Ortiz's notion that Argentine nationality was something new and distinctively American. In making this point, Jauretche employed the familiar nationalist trope of the two Argentinas: one inauthentic and visible, the other "subterranean" and authentic. The inauthentic Argentina, he assured his readers, was coming to an end, while the latter—the authentic Argentina that had been submerged for so long, remained "young" and "vigorous."[109] This subterranean Argentina, of course, was the Argentina of the future, which would reach its potential through the efforts of FORJA. Writing elsewhere, he assured his fellow Forjistas that Argentina was in the process of creating something "authentic and original," which would reflect "the modalities of [the country's] realities."[110] An anonymous contributor to the Forjista publication *Argentinidad* made much the same claim. Contrasting the United States with Latin America, he argued that, while the former was more or less a copy of European society, the latter was entirely new and utterly original. "Our America," the article argued, "is a window open to new forms" that represented for humanity the opportunity to fulfill its true destiny.[111]

It is evident, then, that the Forjista conception of *argentinidad* was closely aligned with the more popular, socially inclusive vision of Argentine identity outlined by Scalabrini Ortiz in 1931. Similarly clear is that, despite the many points of agreement between the Forjistas and the nationalist right, the two strands of nationalism rested on very different conceptions of *el ser nacional*. Indeed, it was this difference that constituted one of the principal obstacles that prevented Forjistas from joining forces with those members of the nationalist right, such as Ernesto Palacio and the Irazusta brothers, with whom they otherwise enjoyed friendly relations. This is especially true for Scalabrini Ortiz, who invited both the Irazusta brothers and Palacio to contribute to his short-lived newspaper, *Reconquista*, and who, after the rise of Perón, would join a pro-Peronist group organized by Palacio called the Unión Revolucionaria.[112]

But despite these sporadic collaborations and agreement on the fundamental issues of British imperialism, the *vendepatria* oligarchy, and historical revisionism, the chasm between Forjistas and even the most socially inclusive strain of right-wing nationalism was just too great. Jauretche in particular was firm on this point. For Jauretche, one of the inescapable problems of the right wing was its top-down political formula, by which the enlightened few were to lead the ignorant masses. Such models, he asserted, were based on imported foreign ideas rather than being "the creation of [Argentina's] own reality."[113] Just as significant for Jauretche was the right's uncritical celebration of Argentina's Hispanic, Catholic roots.[114] FORJA, he insisted, provided Argentines with a better alternative, because its nationalism looked forward rather than backward. In Jauretche's words, the key difference between the two strands was that the nationalism of the right "resembles the love of a son beside the tomb of his father; [while] ours resembles the love of a father beside the cradle of his son."[115]

## FORJA AND DEMOCRACY

What, then, was FORJA's attitude toward democracy and the 1853 Constitution? Given their strident anti-imperialism and their belief that Argentine identity was based on a unitary essence, rather than on shared political principles, it is not surprising that Forjistas ultimately followed their right-wing counterparts in conflating the defense of the country's economic sovereignty with rejection of liberal political institutions. But—as occurred with the LNR group—for many Forjistas, relinquishing the idea that the Constitution of 1853 and the principles it enshrined were integral to Argentine nationality was neither an easy nor an automatic step. Indeed, like the right-wing members of the LNR group, Forjistas launched their organization with a manifesto that proclaimed the goal of defending Argentina's democratic institutions and the constitution.[116] Complicating matters further for many Forjistas was their claim to be the true heirs of UCR, a party whose very origin in the 1890s resulted from its claim to be the champion of Argentine democracy and the only true defender of the 1853 Constitution.[117]

Thus the process by which Forjistas moved into the anticonstitutionalist camp and renounced Argentina's liberal heritage was, in the words of historian Miguel Ángel Scenna, achieved "at the cost of much mental torture and internal struggles."[118] It also required, if an episode recounted by FORJA member Roberto Tamagno is accurate, a certain degree of bullying on the part of Scalabrini Ortiz and Jauretche. In an interview with historian Scenna, Tamagno reminisced—fondly it seems—about his ideological battles with Jauretche. In his words,

> I continued being a liberal and admirer of the [generation that produced the 1853 Constitution]. Jauretche would corner me and the sessions were true dog fights. I drew upon my entire arsenal of knowledge and brought in my friends to help me do battle with him. I martyred myself defending the rubbish I had learned at the university. The liberties guaranteed by the [18]53 Constitution were my resource. Jauretche interrupted me: "What liberties?" "That of [the freedom of international trade on Argentina's] rivers," I haughtily said. "Aha!" he responded. "And before they were free, to whom did the rivers belong?" At this . . . I confessed my ignorance and became angry at those who continued to tout such fraudulent ideas. "The only *free* [i.e., open to international trade] rivers besides ours are those of the Congo," Jauretche added. I folded completely and he put away his knife.[119]

This episode is telling for two reasons. First, although the precise date of this exchange is unknown, it is clear that at some point in the organization's ten-year history, it became an uncomfortable place for people who defended the country's constitution. Second, in relating this account, Tamagno seems to ignore the fact that it is certainly possible to embrace the liberal democratic institutions enshrined in the 1853 Constitution while also rejecting its free market economic provisions.

Jauretche's and Scalabrini Ortiz's efforts to push FORJA toward a more antiliberal position were both helped and hindered by external events. During the Justo years, FORJA's stance on democracy and the 1853 Constitution could remain vague, since its leaders could reasonably claim that any participation in elections served only to legitimize a fraudulent system. The triumph of Roberto M. Ortiz in the 1938 presidential elections, however, muddied the political waters considerably. A former member of the antipersonalist branch of the UCR with a reputation for rectitude, Ortiz had been Justo's handpicked successor. The choice surprised many conservatives, who feared that the new president might take democratic principles too seriously.[120] These fears were realized when, after some wavering, Ortíz renounced fraud and signaled his intention to restore integrity to the electoral process. For Forjistas, such as Scalabrini Ortiz and Jauretche, a return to clean elections posed an obvious threat. If the public regained its faith in the democratic process, the possibilities of pursuing a truly nationalist, antiliberal agenda would be lost.[121] Thus it is not surprising that FORJA's complaints about democracy increased toward the end of the decade.

Also fortifying the antidemocratic elements within FORJA was the fallout from the internal debate over Argentina's neutrality in World War II. In keeping with Yrigoyen's position during the First World War, Forjistas staunchly promoted the cause of neutrality. Even Luis Dellepiane, a noted Francophile who despised Germany, believed Argentina's interests were best served by remaining neutral.[122] But after 1940, when the fall of France made the defeat of Great Britain appear to be a real possibility, Dellepiane reconsidered his position and began to question FORJA's incessant diatribes against British imperialism.[123] Scalabrini Ortiz, in contrast, was unfazed, and his attacks on the besieged nation continued unabated. Adding to the discomfort Dellepiane felt toward Scalabrini Ortiz was concern that the latter was receiving funds from the German embassy to finance his short-lived newspaper, *Reconquista*.[124] Although the German connection to the newspaper was never established, Scalabrini Ortiz's refusal to reveal the sources of his funding, his open hostility toward parliamentary democracy, and his very obvious hatred of the British kept rumors about German involvement alive.[125] Adding to the general climate of suspicion was the sudden emergence of several right-wing, ultranationalist publications, such as *Crisol*, *El Pampero*, and, later, *Cabildo*, all of which were openly enthusiastic about fascism's spread in Europe. In the supercharged political atmosphere of the late 1930s and early 1940s, as many pro-Allied Argentines came to link the defense of democracy in Europe to the defense of democracy at home, it is not surprising that members of FORJA became tarred as

Nazis. Such an association particularly pained Dellepiane, who vigorously disputed the charge.[126]

The breaking point came in mid-1940, when Dellepiane challenged
Scalabrini Ortiz to prove his democratic credentials by joining the UCR,
thus allowing him to become an official member of FORJA. Jauretche
intervened by proposing that the requirement that FORJA members
first join the UCR be lifted, a change the organization's national assembly quickly approved. Dellepiane, who was still serving as FORJA's
president, immediately resigned; Gabriel del Mazo and several other
members followed suit. Although the actual fight was over FORJA's
relationship to the UCR, Dellepiane's subsequent letter to FORJA's
secretary-general Atilio García Mellid suggests that Scalabrini Ortiz's
apparent support for fascist Germany was at the root of the conflict.[127]

With Jauretche and Scalabrini Ortiz taking the lead, antiliberal Forjistas developed a multifaceted critique of the 1853 Constitution. One
main complaint, certainly justifiable under the circumstances, was that
the 1853 document had produced only the illusion of democracy.[128] A
second line of attack against Argentina's liberal tradition, and one already promoted by the Irazusta brothers, was that the country's democratic institutions were actually instruments of British imperialists. On
this point, Scalabrini Ortiz was especially vociferous and early on proclaimed that the "nominal political liberty" guaranteed by the constitution only served to obscure the "invisible chains" that kept the country
enslaved to foreign imperialists. "Since 1853," he asserted, ". . . the pueblo
could vote for whichever of the candidates had been previously selected
by English representatives."[129] An unsigned 1940 editorial in *FORJANDO*
expressed much the same sentiment, when it criticized the "electoralist
politicians," including the mainstream Radicals, who "clamored for political liberties" while at the same time fighting over spoils and public
sinecures. Such "conductors of this process of economic and mental en-
slavement," the writer insisted, were obeying an occult plan to bring
Argentina more and more under the "fraudulent domination of the
speculators of London."[130]

A final complaint about the 1853 Constitution that began to take
shape during the late 1930s, and that is most interesting for our purposes,
was that the document and the values it enshrined were alien to the national personality, or *ser*. Like their right-wing counterparts, Forjistas

came to believe that there existed a fundamental disconnect between the true Argentine nation and its political institutions, and that this disconnect was the source of Argentina's economic, political, and even cultural problems. Jauretche openly embraced this argument, attributing the disconnect to the fact that Argentina's political system had been crafted by an intellectual class that had been "permanently divorced from the country." These individuals, he maintained, had dismissed the need to observe and comprehend the concrete realities of its "*ser*."[131] Scalabrini Ortiz made a similar assessment of Argentina's laws and political institutions. In his words, the nation's laws were "like literary elucubrations," completely detached from Argentine realities that "float about the country like a cloud."[132] García Mellid concurred and argued that the disconnect between Argentina's formal political system and the nation itself was the country's most pressing problem. What was needed, he affirmed, were "institutional forms that safeguard and stimulate the effective experience of our *ser nacional*."[133]

What kind of political system, then, *would* be suited to the supposed underlying character of Argentines? Forjistas gave only vague hints about the system they hoped to construct. While insisting that their values were "profoundly democratic," they also made clear that this would be a new type of democracy having nothing to do with the one outlined in the 1853 Constitution.[134] An unsigned editorial in *FORJANDO*, for example, argued that real democracy was when the government was truly popular and "respected the sovereignty of the people." Making clear its rejection of liberalism, the editorial affirmed that the only times Argentines had lived in a democracy were during the reign of the Federalist caudillos and the presidencies of Yrigoyen.[135] For his part, Jauretche limited himself to defining democracy as the "presence of the pueblo in the State."[136] He stressed as well that democracy and "electoralism" were not the same, and indeed were sometimes completely incompatible.[137] Elsewhere, Jauretche argued that an "authentic" democracy in Argentina would require a powerful state. "The State that we want," Jauretche affirmed, "has to be strong in order to make us free." It must, he continued, have the power to "strangle the power of money so that [man's potential] can be realized." This state should also control the media if a true democracy were to flourish. According to Jauretche, there was no such thing as freedom of expression if the media were in the hands of the capitalist oligarchy. The truly "democratic solution" was to substitute "the liberty of the press or radio [enjoyed by the oligarchy] . . . with a liberty of the press that is attainable only when it does not depend on [financing by] capitalist interests."[138]

García Mellid provides more evidence of the antiliberal cast of FORJA's version of democracy. The political system that best suited the Argentine temperament, García Mellid argued, was one based on caudillo-style, personalistic rule.[139] In contrast to the "doctors," whose "petulant doctrinarianism" was out of touch with the common man, the caudillos of the past had "*understood* their country" and had reflected the pueblo's ideals and "peculiar virtues."[140] Indeed, he affirmed, caudillo rule had represented "*the Argentine form of liberty*," and the caudillos themselves had laid the foundations for Argentina's own brand of democracy.[141] This distinctive form of democracy, he continued, was social in character and sought to protect the interests of the nation and its people, rather than bothering with abstract formulas.[142] It was also one that relied on the prestige of an individual leader. According to García Mellid, the ideal leader for Argentines was a vigorous man who naturally commanded respect, who could move the multitudes with a "prophetic voice," and who embodied the "myth and mysticism" of the nation.[143] Such a form of democracy would of course have little use for competitive political parties or the protection of individual rights.

FORJA's RISE DURING THE 1930s marked the emergence of a left-wing, socially inclusive strand of Argentine nationalism that in many ways mirrored its right-wing counterpart. Central to both was a preoccupation with economic nationalism and the defense of a supposedly unitary character or *ser nacional.* Although embracing very different understandings of the nature of this imagined *ser*, both strands harbored a deep hostility toward liberalism, considering Argentina's most urgent task to be creating new political and economic forms that would reflect its authentic character and preserve its independence.

FORJA's importance, again like the nationalist right, lay not so much in the number of people who directly participated in its activities, but in the enduring power of its ideas. Critical to FORJA's long-term influence was the rise of a new, and deeply polarizing figure in Argentine politics: Juan Domingo Perón. Although Forjistas' relationship with

Perón would often be rocky, they saw in the ambitious general an individual who shared their key goals and was capable of stirring the masses. Indeed, so enamored of Perón were its leaders that in 1945 they officially disbanded FORJA in order to free members to join the Peronist movement. Not surprisingly, given that they shared many of FORJA's assumptions, many members of the nationalist right also embraced Perón. As will be developed, it is in Perón that we see the fusing together of some of the key elements of Argentina's two strands of nationalist thought. The resulting amalgamation, however, would prove highly unstable and its coming apart explosive.

# EIGHT

# Essentialism in the Era of Perón

As is clear from the two previous chapters, during the 1930s the belief that Argentines formed a natural organic community defined by an underlying, homogeneous national essence, or *ser*, was a key component of both right- and left-wing nationalist thought. In many ways, of course, the nationalists of those years were building on ideas that had gained currency during the first three decades of the century. In some circumstances, such as those of Scalabrini Ortiz and his fellow Forjistas, the lines of influence between the ideas of the earlier period and the 1930s are easily drawn. The same was true for the nationalist right, although we must also note the additional influence of such figures as Spaniards Marcelo Menéndez y Pelayo and Ramiro de Maeztu and French ideologue Charles Maurras. Also key was the impact of the newly invigorated Argentine church, whose insistence on the Hispano-Catholic character of the nation neatly dovetailed with the right's own belief that religion and a set of immutable cultural traits formed the basis of an imagined *ser nacional.*

But while there were strong continuities between the nationalist thought of the 1930s and the identity debates of previous decades, it is also clear that, as these ideas began to operate in a new context, their sig-

nificance became radically transformed. Whereas, during the early decades of the century, most intellectuals who embraced the essentialist
notion of the Argentine "race" saw no conflict between an ethno-cultural
vision of nationality and Argentina's liberal traditions, in the new period
of economic crisis nationalist thinkers came to see the 1853 Constitution
and all it represented as a threat to the true nation. Thus, while cultural
nationalists of earlier decades had criticized the Argentine ruling class
for taking its cultural cues from Europe, the nationalists of the 1930s
upped the ante considerably. What these individuals sought was not
simply an authentic national literature or a public school curriculum that
celebrated *argentinidad*. Rather, both right- and left-wing nationalists
were convinced that liberal political values were alien to Argentines' collective personality, and that these values could not be extricated from the
liberal economic policies. Because they believed these conditions had
made them vulnerable to foreign imperialists, they called for a new set of
political institutions that would reflect the (imagined) *ser nacional* and
help the nation regain economic sovereignty.

Given their shared diagnosis of Argentina's ills and common hostility toward liberalism, these nationalists not surprisingly desired a
strong, authoritarian state that would defend the collective interests of
the nation, rather than protect the rights of individual citizens. Accordingly, nationalists of both tendencies looked favorably on the events of
June 4, 1943, when a group of upper-ranking military officers with nationalist views overthrew the civilian government of Ramón Castillo.
Members of the secretive military organization known as the GOU,
these officers had disapproved of Castillo's selection of Robustiano
Patrón Costas as the official candidate for president.[1]

The reaction of the civilian nationalist right to the coup was enthusiastic. Although the GOU had had little contact with right-wing
groups, it regarded them as allies and praised them as "the purest forces,
those with the greatest spiritualism within the Argentine political pano-
rama."[2] The sentiment was returned by right-wing nationalist Marcelo
Sánchez Sorondo, who greeted the coup as the "revolution that we [the
right-wing nationalists] announced."[3] In a similar fashion, the ultraright
nationalist newspaper *Cabildo* publicly thanked God for having delivered
the nation from "corrupt politicians" and "vendepatrias at the service
of foreign monopolies." The military's action, the newspaper affirmed,

was what "the authentic Argentine country" had anxiously awaited and was "the triumph of the national spirit."[4] The Catholic hierarchy also lauded the new government. Having spent much of the 1930s building ties with the military, the church was particularly influential among the members of the GOU.[5] In a lengthy editorial praising the new regime, Monsignor Franceschi proclaimed that it was the "duty of every conscientious Argentine" to support the government in its efforts to rid the nation of "corrupt, self-centered politicians and functionaries."[6]

The coup itself had been relatively bloodless. Lacking sufficient troops to carry out the plan, the conspirators had enlisted the support of Arturo Rawson, the commanding officer of the cavalry. Rawson agreed to supply the necessary troops but then quickly installed himself in the presidency after deposing Castillo. He lasted less than a week. On June 7, nationalists replaced him with General Pedro Pablo Ramírez, a key member of the GOU. Behind the scenes, the situation was even more fluid, as different groups within the military jockeyed for position. During the early months of the new regime, the struggle pitted nationalists against the liberal faction. Once the nationalists gained the upper hand against the liberals, the contest for power became one between the ultraright Catholic nationalists and the nationalists with a more popular bent.[7]

Ramírez's presidency represented the apogee of this ultraright tendency. Once in office, the general immediately made clear his belief in the Catholic basis of Argentine nationality. In a public letter to Franceschi, the new president explained that the armed forces had "assumed the historic responsibility of restoring the traditional values of Argentine culture," values that had been undermined by "suicidal policies" that had sought to negate "the national identity." It was for this reason, Ramírez proclaimed, that he would organize his government "in accordance with the most authentic and profound [nature of] Argentine reality," a reality that was rooted in the "depths of our history" and in Argentina's Spanish, Catholic heritage.[8] Some days later, the new president sounded similar themes in an address to the armed forces, when he spoke of the military's mission to halt the forces of social disintegration that were "eating away at the very bases of our nationality."[9]

Such statements were in keeping with the generalized xenophobia of the GOU and its belief that Jews and foreign organizations, such as the Rotary Club International and the Freemasons, were threats to the nation.[10] Ramírez's essentialist ideas about nationality were also evident in his radio address of October 12, 1943. In a speech celebrating the Day of the Race, he lauded "mother Spain" for having given birth to a family of nations bound together "by blood and language." The "Day of the Race," he continued, was also "the day of *hispanidad*."[11] To further bolster this pro-Hispanic message, the following day the regime announced a new law that made it illegal for parents to give their children non-Spanish proper names. Decree 11.609 prohibited foreign names, or those that were "contrary to our customs," and required that a child's official name be one that was commonly accepted within the Spanish language.[12]

In that same month, a cabinet purge allowed Ramírez to intensify his efforts to return Argentina to its supposedly true Catholic character. One of his most visible appointments was that of Gustavo Martínez Zuviría to the post of minister of justice and education. A well-known anti-Semite, Martínez Zuviría immediately reinstated compulsory Catholic education in the public schools and appointed several "interveners" (*inventores*), whose task it was to purge universities of liberal and leftist elements. Many of the new interveners were individuals directly linked to the *Cursos de Cultura Católica*, such as Thomist philosopher Tomás D. Casares, R. Etcheverry Boneo, and Novillo Saravia.[13] Another, of course, was the previously mentioned Jordán Bruno Genta, whose pro-Spanish proclamations at the University of the Litoral had so provoked the FORJA-dominated Federation of University Students. Nationalists Federico Ibarguren, Ramón Doll, and Héctor Llambías also received appointments in the public bureaucracy.[14]

Folklore was another of the regime's concerns. Within the Romantic tradition, of course, the rural "folk" are idealized as the unthinking vessels of the true national essence that resist modernity. Thus the study of folklore is understood to be an enterprise of national importance. Martínez Zuviría clearly embraced this notion and persuaded Ramírez to establish the National Institute of Tradition. Charged with collecting and disseminating material elements of Argentina's traditional culture, the institute met with immediate approval from the nationalist right. The publication *Cabildo*, for example, roundly applauded the measure, proclaiming that it fulfilled the "unavoidable duty of good government" to preserve the "noble manifestations . . . of our [national] personality."[15]

Significantly, Martínez Zuviría's choice for the director of the new institute was Juan Alfonzo Carrizo, a folklorist from Catamarca, who was
famous for his claim that Argentina's folkloric traditions were purely
Spanish and contained no trace of indigenous influences.

What was the response of FORJA to these events? Except for the
Forjista students' rebuke of Genta mentioned in the previous chapter,
FORJA members were generally supportive of the new military regime.
Jauretche saw the coup as a salutary interruption of the electoral process
and thus as an opportunity to redirect Argentine politics along more
revolutionary lines. In the weeks before the coup, Jauretche's military
contacts had kept him apprised of developments, and he received advance news of the June 4 coup. By ten o'clock that morning, he had
gathered approximately three hundred Forjistas at the organization's
headquarters.[16] Once assembled, the group made its way through central Buenos Aires, accompanying, but not mingling with, the military
column that was marching toward the Plaza del Congreso.[17] It was there
that FORJA secretary Darío Alessandro gave a speech that was later described as the first oration to greet the new government.[18] FORJA also
issued a manifesto signaling its support for the new regime. Penned by
Jauretche, it lauded the coup as the "first stage in a more encompassing
policy to reconstruct the nationality [and a political system that will be]
the authentic expression of [Argentine] sovereignty."[19] During the first
few months of the Ramírez presidency, Forjistas remained cautiously
optimistic. In a pamphlet published in July, for example, Jauretche expressed his belief that it was possible "to radicalize the revolution and
revolutionize Radicalism."[20] In subsequent months, he and his colleagues
were heartened by several measures designed to rein in foreign capital
and improve the lives of the working class.[21]

At the same time, Forjistas were well aware of the tensions within
the military regime, particularly between the moderate liberals, the ultra-
Catholic nationalist right, and the more popular, socially inclusive strand
of nationalism. Within this last group were the men supporting General
Edelmiro Farrell, who assumed the presidency after Ramírez was forced
out in February 1944. Of particular interest to Jauretche was Farrell's energetic aide, Col. Juan Domingo Perón. One of the key members of the
GOU, Perón served in a number of positions before becoming Farrell's
vice president. His most important post was as head of the National

Office of Labor. Appointed in October 1943, Perón recognized the potential power of the working class and astutely used the newly established Ministry of Labor to build a political base. By urging workers to organize and using his position to arbitrate between labor and capital, Perón quickly gained the loyalty of this previously ignored segment of the population.

Eager to take Perón's measure, Jauretche worked through his military contacts to arrange a personal meeting. Perón, who had been reading FORJA's publications since 1936, readily agreed.[22] Both men deemed the meeting a success, and for months afterward they met almost daily.[23] If Jauretche's account can be trusted, during this period the FORJA leader served as a kind of informal advisor to Perón.[24] They continued to meet throughout the first half of 1944 but had a falling out in June, when Perón reneged on his promise to appoint Forjistas to several political posts. Ultimately, relations were mended when Jauretche swallowed his irritation and opted to support the individual he believed represented Argentina's best hope for a popular nationalist program.[25] Although Jauretche would never again have the access he enjoyed earlier, from that point on, FORJA linked its fortunes to Perón.

The details of Perón's meteoric rise from labor champion to the Argentine presidency in 1946 are well known and need only the briefest retelling here. By early 1944, Argentina's traditional political parties began to pressure the government to hold elections. As civilian opposition to the government increased, much of it came to be directed at Perón, whom liberals believed to have fascist tendencies. Meanwhile, at the opposite end of the political spectrum, the government also ran into difficulties with the nationalists. Faced with the inevitable Allied victory, Farrell finally declared war on the Axis powers in March 1945. Nationalists, particularly those on the right, were outraged and openly attacked the president. Pressure mounted in September, when prodemocracy forces staged a huge rally in Buenos Aires in support of the Argentine constitution. On October 8, bowing to pressure from the traditional liberals and Perón's enemies within the military, Farrell relieved Perón of his official duties.[26] Four days later, he had his former vice president detained. In the days that followed, Perón's partisans within the military and labor worked feverishly to organize a response. When the powerful Confederación General de Trabajadores (General confederation of

Argentine workers, or CGT) announced a general strike for October 17, hundreds of thousands of workers responded by marching through the streets toward the Plaza de Mayo.[27] Facing this massive display of popular anger, Perón's enemies were forced to allow him to address the gathered crowd. Farrell quickly regained control and announced presidential elections for early 1946. In February of that year, with the help of working-class voters, several Catholic groups, and a handful of nationalist factions, Perón won the presidency with 54 percent of the vote.[28]

## THE NATIONALISTS' DILEMMA

Argentina's nationalists were witnesses to, rather than the protagonists of, these extraordinary events. FORJA, of course, was delighted. Eager to show its support for the October strike, the group issued a pro-Perón manifesto on that morning, and many Forjistas, including an ecstatic Jauretche, also joined the demonstration.[29] Scalabrini Ortiz, who two months earlier had finally overcome his earlier doubts about Perón, was also in the crowd and was visibly moved by the spectacle of a mobilized working class.[30] After Perón's release, FORJA found itself at a crossroad. In so many ways, Perón seemed to embody the organization's hopes and ideals, and in the following weeks, individual Forjistas began to participate in newly established pro-Perón entities. As one of Argentina's most tumultuous years drew to a close, Forjista leaders reached a decision and in December announced the group's dissolution. Proclaiming that "the thought and goals that prompted the creation of FORJA are fulfilled" with the emergence of Perón's movement, the organization disbanded.[31] In the years that followed, Jauretche, Scalabrini Ortiz, Homero Manzi, and García Mellid, along with dozens of other former Forjistas, became active supporters of the new regime, working either as independent publicists or within the bureaucracy.

For Forjistas, Peronism represented the kind of popular, nationalist movement that they themselves had failed to spark. But it is also clear that, for many of FORJA's members, Peronism signified something more: the emergence of the hidden, profound Argentina they saw as the true Argentina. In a now-famous 1948 speech, Scalabrini expressed what he had witnessed during the October 17 protest, and what the events of that day had meant for him. Describing the working-class men and women who had taken to the streets, he wrote,

> Before my eyes paraded faces, burly arms, husky torsos, with their matted hair uncovered and their scarce clothing covered with fatty stains, the bits of tar, greases and oils. They arrived singing and proclaiming, united in the impetration of a single name: Perón. It was the most irregular crowd that the imagination could conceive. The traces of their origins shone through their physiognomies. The descendent of Southern Europeans walked with the blonde of Nordic features and the dark-skinned, coarse-haired individual in which the blood of a distant Indian still survived.[32]

"It was," he continued, "the subsoil of the *patria* rising in rebellion," a moment when the "basic cement of the nation" became visible.[33] Marveling at the spectacle, he reached back to his famous 1931 book, *El hombre que está solo y espera*, to convey to his readers the significance of what he believed had happened that day. "That which I had dreamed of and intuited for so many years was there, present, in the flesh, tense and multifaceted, but one in a conjoined spirit. They were the men who were alone and waiting/hoping to begin again their work of vindication. The spirit of the land was present as I never believed I would see it."[34]

Forjista Atilio García Mellid, who would serve in Perón's Department of Culture and later as his ambassador to Canada, used similarly mystical language to praise the populist leader. In his words, Perón's participation in the 1943 coup had represented a blow against the "multiple and insidious" forces that had sought to "frustrate the true intimacy and peculiarity of the Argentine soul." The authors of the coup, he enthused, had sought to restore the "spiritual unity" of the nation, by being faithful to its Greco-Roman, Hispanic past while at the same time embracing the "modalities and tendencies of the native genius."[35] García Mellid also cast Perón in the role of Yrigoyen's spiritual heir. Yrigoyen, he believed, had been an authentic caudillo and a gifted interpreter of the "national and popular subterranean current that ran throughout the whole of Argentine history."[36] After the Radical leader's death in 1933, García Mellid proclaimed, this true or authentic Argentina had been without an interpreter until Perón had taken up the task. In Perón, the nation's "mystical essence" had found its "new caudillo and incarnation."[37]

Scalabrini Ortiz also embraced this comparison between Yrigoyen and Perón, writing of the continuing "historical line" that connected the two leaders. The masses who had filled the Plaza de Mayo on October 17, 1945, he affirmed, were the same Argentines who had celebrated Yrigoyen's inauguration in 1916, and who had gathered en masse to mourn his death in 1933.[38] Supporters of Perón also made comparisons between Radicalism and Peronism. An unsigned editorial in *Hechos e Ideas*, the pro-Peronist monthly review to which Forjistas frequently contributed, noted that Peronism, like Radicalism, was not a political party but a movement that encompassed the nation as a whole. It was, the editorial continued, "the Nation marching forward, a sentiment of nationality. The synthesis of the telluric, moral and spiritual phenomena whose harmony gives us a style that is our own, that is Argentine."[39]

If FORJA's decision to cast its lot with Perón seemed like an obvious choice, the nationalist right found itself deeply divided over how to respond to such an unexpected actor on the Argentine political stage.[40] For members of this strand of Argentine nationalism, Perón was appealing for several reasons, including his military background, nationalist rhetoric, and strong identification with the ideal of Argentina as a Catholic nation. Attractive too was the church's favorable opinion of Perón, at least in the early years.[41] Working against the nationalist right's embrace of Perón, of course, was his willingness to invite the masses into the political arena. While almost all right-wing nationalists had proclaimed the need to improve the lot of the working class, the system they envisioned was authoritarian and paternalistic, with an emphasis on controlling rather than mobilizing the workers. Other members of the extreme right found Perón's nationalistic credentials suspect. A particular sore point for many was the Farrell government's declaration of war against the Axis powers, an unforgiveable sin that tainted Perón as well. Finally, some right-wing nationalists saw Perón as little more than a demagogue, who stirred up class resentment. The Irazusta brothers, for example, accused him of promoting an "unhealthy envy" among the masses and of promoting inflationary economic policies.[42]

Still, some important members of the nationalist right *did* become significant supporters of Perón. Among the most prominent was Ernesto Palacio, whose enthusiasm for the new leader led him to launch the pro-Peronist newspaper *Política*. Other right-wing nationalists who joined the Peronist cause included Ramón Doll, Raúl G. Carrizo, and revisionist historian Vicente Sierra. Nationalists Marcelo Sánchez Sorondo and Héctor Llambías were far less enthusiastic but did accept university posts. Peronist-sponsored cultural publications constituted another realm of right-wing nationalist involvement. Gustavo Martínez Zuviría was tapped to be the editor of *Argentina*, a middle-brow magazine that counted Carlos Ibarguren and Manuel Gálvez among its contributors.[43] More ambitious was the cultural review *Sexto Continente*, which offered additional opportunities for writers. Conceived as a pan–Latin American journal, whose board of directors included (at least on paper) such notable intellectuals as Mexican José Vasconcelos and Peruvian Manuel García Calderón, *Sexto Continente* drew contributions from a number of prominent right-wing nationalists.[44]

Also noteworthy was the support, at least partial, of the right-wing nationalist group Alianza Libertadora Nacionalista (ALN), a quasi-fascist organization that had developed out of the Uriburist Legión Cívica Argentina of the early 1930s.[45] Composed largely of young men, and known for its public demonstrations and Nazi-inspired symbolism, by 1940 it had become the country's largest nationalist organization with an estimated eleven-to-fifty thousand members.[46] The ALN was one of the few right-wing nationalist groups that reached out to workers, and openly applauded Perón's rise to power. Although its leader Juan Queraltó attempted to maintain a degree of independence, the group nonetheless hailed Perón as their symbolic leader and supported his campaign for the presidency.[47]

## PERÓN AND THE TRUE *SER NACIONAL*

Although he enjoyed the support of a wide range of nationalists, once in office Perón admitted none to his inner circle. Instead, nationalists were generally awarded positions in the area of culture and education, positions with some visibility but little real power.[48] Nor did Perón weigh in on the issue of historical revisionism, a topic that continued to preoccupy nationalists from across the political spectrum. Indeed he remained aloof from this project, even as the Rosas Institute became increasingly filled with Peronists.[49] Despite these disappointments, Perón's economic nationalism and his frequent use of essentialist language undoubtedly served to reassure civilian nationalists. Perón and the nationalists, it was clear, shared many of the same key assumptions about the nature of *argentinidad.*

Interestingly, if somewhat ironically, Perón made clear his adherence to these ideas in his June 4, 1946, speech to Congress, in which he assumed the presidency and swore his fealty to the Argentine constitution. In a speech laden with tropes made commonplace by nationalists, Perón spoke of the "hidden forces that have detained the economic progress of the nation" and of the "artificial" nature of Argentine prosperity. Defeating these forces, he affirmed, was possible because of Argentina's working people, who had kept the sentiments of the true Argentina alive. Continuing in mystical language that seemed directly drawn from early twentieth-century cultural nationalism, Perón lauded the fact that Argentines were "returning to that which is ours (*lo nuestro*)" and to "the intimate being of this soul of ours." This soul, he believed, had been damaged by generations of Argentine elites, who had forced it "to assimilate an alien culture." As a result, the nation had lost "its unique characteristics, leaving it without the traits that defined the vigor of its potent individuality."[50]

Perón sounded similar themes in a 1948 essay on cultural policy. Calling on Argentines to remain true to their authentic essence, he proclaimed that "each pueblo possesses inherent modalities, some principles that are consubstantial with its own *ser*, a destiny that is traced by Providence [and that] constitutes its true personality." The preservation of this "national personality," Perón affirmed, required that Argentines renounce their individual projects and to instead worship *"this immaterial, impalpable and prodigious something that constitutes something like the guiding genius of each pueblo."* These sentiments of sacrifice and veneration, Perón continued, were not automatic, and thus it was the highest duty of the state to encourage and cultivate them. Moreover, given the importance of conserving "the national soul in its most pure manifestations," it was essential that "no deviation" of any kind be tolerated. Without taking such precautions, he concluded, a nation's culture "becomes diluted in a sea of random spiritual inquietudes." Once this happens, the "task of recuperation is extremely difficult, because the wrecking of a pueblo's culture means the loss of its own *ser nacional.*"[51] Such a recuperation of *el ser nacional* was, however, possible. Writing elsewhere, Perón noted that a country could overcome the weakness caused by foreign "trivialities and influences" by "reencountering" itself.[52] In keeping with the aim of purifying and fortifying Argentine culture, in 1949 the regime imposed a 50 percent import tax on "foreign cultural goods" and decreed that radio stations devote 50 percent of their musical programming for Argentine music.[53]

Another element of Perón's thought that was a mainstay of 1930s nationalism was his insistence that Argentina must eschew foreign political and economic models in order to follow its own path and develop institutions suited to its needs and supposedly intrinsic character. As he proclaimed in a 1952 essay, "All pueblos that enjoy self-determination possess a style of life, aspirations, purposes and [their] own goals." In such nations, he continued, a "national doctrine" that "conforms to the spirit of the nation arises spontaneously." Not surprisingly, of course, Perón argued that Peronism, or what he called the "Justicialista doctrine," had arisen naturally from the Argentine people. As a "creation of the Argentine people," he affirmed, it was "positive" and "authentically national."[54] This conviction that Argentina should chart its own path lay behind a central element of Peronist ideology: the so-called Third Position—that is, a path of development would chart a course between the extremes of individualism and collectivism, and between capitalism and communism. Both doctrines, Perón believed, were imperialistic, seeking to impose their "crudely materialistic" systems on the rest of the world.[55] Certainly, Perón's idea of the Third Position had strong roots in Catholic social teachings dating back to Leo XIII's 1891 Rerum Novarum, but it also reflected the nationalist belief that the country must pursue its own destiny and stay true to its distinctive *ser*. To do otherwise, Perón believed, was to court disaster. In his words, "Everything that we do that is not in keeping with our *ser nacional*, the historical sentiment of our pueblo and our race, will collapse as noisily as an avalanche."[56]

But while insisting that Argentina's institutions be consonant with *el ser nacional*, Perón avoided directly rejecting the country's liberal past. His speech to Congress on June 24, 1946, illustrates the fine line he walked as he professed respect for the 1853 Constitution, while at the same time he was seeking its reform. After lauding the country's return to "institutional normalcy," Perón proclaimed the beginning of a new era, in which the "will of the people" would shape "the legislative evolution that the country needs." The new government, he continued, intended to "interpret" the constitution in such a way that it corresponded to and fulfilled the "essence *of our own ser.*" "If we . . . embark on new paths that are up to now unknown," he continued, "it will not . . . [be for the purpose of weakening] our Fundamental Charter, but for the imperative of a new resurgence of its wise principles."[57] Three years later, Perón would push through a new constitution that presumably accomplished these goals, by deemphasizing individual rights and freedoms while placing more weight on "corporate rights emanating from the state."[58] This concern with creating institutions that fit an imagined national character remained a cornerstone of Perón's political thought. Indeed, in an essay completed just a few months before his death in July 1974, he insisted that his Peronism was not the "result of a set of ideas and values" that had been grabbed from thin air or merely made up. Rather, these ideas had been "deduced, and obtained, from the *Ser* of our own pueblo."[59]

But how did Perón understand this underlying personality, or *ser*? When he spoke in 1946 of the need to return to the "intimate being" of the Argentine soul, just what did he see as this soul's most salient qualities, and from what sources did it spring? Undoubtedly, Perón's ratification of the 1943 decree making Catholic education obligatory in the public schools, as well as his failure to annul the decree prohibiting the use of non-Spanish names, reassured right-wing nationalists that the new president shared their vision of Argentina as a Catholic, Hispanic nation.[60] His highly publicized speech on October 9, 1947, would have been similarly comforting. Delivered at the Argentine Academy of Letters for the purpose of celebrating the four-hundredth anniversary of Cervantes's birth, the speech was published repeatedly during the next few years.[61] In his address, Perón lauded "Mother Spain" for having given birth to the pueblos of the "Hispanic community," which had all been imprinted with a common "seal" that made them "like Spain in their essence and nature." Echoing the essentialist (and, by now, widely shared) view of Latin peoples as inherently spiritual, Perón argued that Spain had also bequeathed to its American offspring a unique spirituality that had allowed Argentines to oppose the "blind impulse of force" and the "cold impulse of money." This spirit, he continued, had also given shape to the Argentine "race," a race that "constitutes a sum of imponderables that make us who we are and pushes us to be what we should be, according to our origin and destiny." It was these "imponderable" qualities, Perón proclaimed, that prevented Argentines from becoming a "copy of other communities whose essences are alien (*extrañas*) to ours." "For us," he concludes, "race constitutes our personal stamp (*sello*) [that is] indefinable and impossible to confuse."[62]

Perón repeated many of these same points in a 1947 public event, where he praised the cultural legacy received from "Mother Spain," a legacy he described as rooted in the Greco-Roman tradition.[63] In his words, Spain "had known how to liberate the essences of antiquity" in order to create a culture that had been the "seed (*germen*) of the cultures of our continent."[64] Unfortunately, the president lamented, several baneful influences had led Argentines to forget their Spanish cultural heritage. Among these were the "frivolous outsiders" and native elites, who had "wasted their fortunes in the gay and cosmopolitan cities [of non-Spanish Europe]." These elites, he continued, had then mingled with undesirable immigrants, who had introduced into Argentina "an indefinable sentiment of repudiation" toward the Hispanic creole tradition. As a result, the nation's literature, art, science, jurisprudence, and philosophy had "acquired hybrid forms" that were "diffuse and extinguished" (*apagadas*).[65] It was up to the newly reformed universities, Perón believed, to reverse this process and return Argentina to its Spanish and thus Greco-Roman roots.

Also indicative of Perón's vision of the Argentine essence, or *ser*, was his administration's attitudes and policies toward immigration. With the end of the war, Argentina once more became a favored destination for European immigrants. The prospect of new waves of immigrants, combined with declining Argentine birthrates, raised yet again the specter of a nation inundated by newcomers. Of particular concern to many was the fact that these newcomers might be European Jews displaced by war. Anxious to preserve what he saw as Argentina's ethnic unity, Perón adopted policies designed to attract immigrants he believed would blend into, rather than alter, the imagined Argentine essence. For example, the Ley de Bases contained within the Five-Year Plan of 1947–51 called for immigrants that "by virtue of their place of origin, habits, customs and language" would be "most easily assimilated into the ethnic, cultural and spiritual characteristics of Argentina."[66] Accordingly, the Peronist government, through direct recruiting efforts and a series of bilateral agreements with Spain and Italy, worked to ensure that the vast majority of the post–World War II immigrants came from these two countries.[67]

Such policies and rhetoric suggest that Perón shared with the right-wing nationalists the vision of Argentina as a Catholic, Hispanic (or at least Latin) nation, whose very essence was threatened by religious and ethnic pluralism. This was only partially true; in fact, other evidence indicates that Perón's understanding of *el ser nacional* was more complex and inclusive than that promoted by the Catholic right. Although riddled with contradictions, Perón's view of the Argentine *ser nacional* had a stronger affinity with that of the Forjistas.

One element of Perón's more expansive vision of the Argentine *ser nacional* can be seen in his government's official promotion of folklore, and his insistence that Argentina's authentic folk culture was both European and indigenous. In his government's Five-Year Plan of 1947–51, for example, Perón noted the importance of promoting Argentine culture as "*the culture acquired through tradition* whose principles go back to the noblest origins of European culture, transmitted by the conquistadores and influenced by autochthonous elements."[68] Accordingly, the plan called for the promotion and study of "folkloric expressions, music and popular dances [that are] the essence of the feeling of a pueblo."[69] Not surprisingly, a key symbol of the Peronist regime was the mixed-race gaucho. Perón referred frequently in his speeches to the character of Martín Fierro, the gaucho protagonist of José Hernández's famous nineteenth-century poem and in 1948 decreed that the poet's birthday become a nationwide holiday.[70] This identification of Peronism with the gaucho was reinforced by individuals, such as Carlos Astrada, one of the most prominent intellectuals associated with the new regime and a frequent contributor to *Sexto Continente*. A native of the interior province of Córdoba who had studied philosophy in Germany, Astrada saw the gaucho as the archetypical Argentine and the source of the modern-day Argentine's "physiognomic traits" and "psychovital aspects."[71] The gaucho, Astrada maintained, had been formed by the "telluric essences" of the national territory, and thus constituted the "cement of our national life," the "living rock (*roca viva*) upon which the Argentine political community rested."[72]

The Peronist promotion of the mixed-race gaucho directly challenged the deeply held ideal of Argentina as a white nation, an ideal embraced generally in Argentina but especially by the nationalist right, which insisted on the purely Hispanic/Latin Catholic roots of *argen-*

*tinidad.* Although intellectuals such as Ricardo Rojas and Leopoldo Lugones had clearly long-touted the gaucho as the prototype of the Argentine race, and indeed Rojas had proclaimed Argentina to be a blend of indigenous and European influences, their celebrations of the indigenous component of *argentinidad* were based on the assumption that both the gaucho and indigenous people had disappeared long ago, leaving only an ineffable essence rather than any real biological traces. Perón, however, celebrated real people with real indigenous blood. As Oscar Chamusa had noted, the folkloric festivals and performances sponsored by the regime frequently featured dark-skinned, mixed-race performers, who would often share the same stage with either Perón or his wife, Evita. Such practices would provide a powerful visual argument that people of indigenous ancestry were integral members of the national community.[73] Perón also signaled his belief that native peoples were indeed bona fide Argentines in his June 4, 1946, address before Congress cited above. Significantly, in his inaugural speech Perón took pains to pay homage to the contribution of indigenous peoples to the Argentine personality, proclaiming that "we cannot extract from our blood and our spirit the ancestral voice of the aborigines that for millennia populated our lands." He insisted that it was the "fusion of both cultures . . . [that together] have given our pueblo a human sense of life."[74] Also suggestive of his view was a section in his first Five-Year Plan, where Perón called for the study of indigenous languages, "not only as relics of an idiomatic past that still endures, but also as a live element" in many areas of the country.[75]

Perón further distanced himself from the ideal of Argentina as a homogenous white nation in his embrace of the *cabecitas negras.* Literally translated as "little blackheads," *cabecitas negras* was a derogatory term used by the urban middle and upper classes to denote the dark-skinned, mixed-race men and women who had recently arrived from the provinces. During the 1930s and '40s, as import-substitution industrialization took off, hundreds of thousands of people from the countryside flooded into the cities and formed a key element of Perón's political support.[76] Together with the lighter-skinned, working-class descendants of the European immigrants who had arrived at the turn of the century, these mixed-race workers filled the ranks of the urban working class, the so-called *descamisados* or shirtless ones—meaning people who made their living as manual laborers. It was the urban *descamisados*, along with the rural folk, Perón believed, who formed the basis of the Argentine masses and who embodied the real Argentina.

Finally, Perón's dealings with Argentina's Jewish community also suggest a more expansive vision of Argentine nationality than that of the ultra-Catholic right. Despite his efforts to shape the postwar immigrant stream to include mostly Catholic immigrants of Latin descent and his support for mandatory Catholic instruction in the public schools, Perón actively courted Argentina's Jewish leaders, and indeed appointed several Jews to his administration. Many of his public statements also reflected a more open vision of *argentinidad*. In his 1948 speech at the headquarters of the Organización Israelita Argentina, for example, Perón insisted that anti-Semitism and *argentinidad* were incompatible.[77] "How can it be accepted," he asked rhetorically, ". . . that there would be anti-Semitism in Argentina? In Argentina there should be no more than a single class of men: men who work for the national good, without distinctions. [Individuals] are good Argentines, whatever their place of origin, race or religion, when they work daily for the greatness of the nation."[78]

Perón's insistence that practicing Jews could be good Argentines, along with his acknowledgment of Argentina's indigenous peoples and their languages, represents for historian Raanan Rein, "an unprecedented recognition of cultural and ethnic difference" for a country long preoccupied with homogeneity.[79] Indeed, Rein maintains, by the early 1950s, Perón and his movement "had adopted a more inclusive approach whereby respect for all religions became one of its defining features."[80] Rein's analysis is suggestive but should be balanced by Perón's continued preference for Catholic immigrants and his open admiration for Spain's Franciso Franco, whose hospitality he accepted during much of his exile. Also undermining the view that Peronism had shifted toward an ecumenical, inclusive vision of *argentinidad* were the occasional outbursts from the more right-wing elements within the movement, which continued to hold fast to the ideal of the purely Catholic nation.

One such outburst, amusing but still instructive, was a 1949 attack on Santa Claus and Father Christmas that appeared in the Peronist daily *La Época*. Published in early January in the wake of the holiday season, this unsigned article complained that these two "exotic" figures had begun to appear in Argentine homes and shops, despite the fact that they were completely "foreign to our customs and religious traditions." What's more, the article continued, the use of Santa Claus and Father Christmas, even by those without ill intentions, represented "an action that is contrary to the religious spirit of our nationality" and that threatened to "denaturalize the fundamental traditions of our faith." Accordingly, the writer called on Perón to take action to prohibit the dangerous "infiltrations" of foreign symbols.[81]

That this article appeared after Perón's 1948 assurances to the Jewish community suggests less a clear shift toward the embrace of a pluralistic society than an accumulation of increasingly contradictory perspectives. These conflicting messages about what constituted the true Argentina reflect the fact that, on one level, the Peronist movement was actually quite heterogeneous, drawing support from a wide variety of nationalists with sharply different understandings of *el ser nacional*. But it is also probable that Peronism's internal tug-of-war between a highly restrictive Hispanic Catholic vision of *el ser nacional* and a more capacious, inclusive understanding of Argentine nationality reflected its leader's own personal ambivalence. Having made his career in the Argentine military precisely at the moment when the church's influence within that institution reached new heights, Perón had undoubtedly internalized many elements of what Loris Zanatta has called the "myth of the Catholic nation."[82] At the same time, however, the experiences of the Ramírez and Farrell governments had made eminently clear the impossibility of imposing a unified Catholic culture on a society that was both ethnically diverse and still stubbornly secular. Perhaps it was this reality that led Perón to a more inclusive, pluralistic understanding of Argentine identity, suggesting that the abrupt transition Rein notes was likely based more on political opportunism than on a personal change of heart. What seems more likely is that Perón, like his followers, continued to hold conflicting notions about the cultural and ethnic content of *argentinidad*.

But if on a conceptual level Perón's ideas about Argentine identity were a hodgepodge of different tendencies, on a political level they achieved a disturbingly coercive clarity. Simply put, for Perón, *argentinidad* became consubstantial with Peronism, and thus to be anti-Perón was to be anti-Argentine. Like Yrigoyen before him, Perón rejected the idea that Peronism was a mere political party, insisting instead that it was an all encompassing national "movement" representing the interests of the nation rather than those of political parties or factions.[83] Tellingly, Perón also made clear that being a Peronist, and thus being a true Argentine, involved much more than simply agreeing with the tenets of the so-called national doctrine or even joining the Peronist Party. "It was not enough," he explained in a speech to his fellow Peronists, "to have taken part in our movement." Rather, "What is required and indispensable is that everything that is being said is profoundly felt." But having a "feeling" for the Peronist project, he goes on to suggest, was not a matter of conscious choice but rather the result of "spiritual forces" that "guide a man and carry him along, although he may wish to resist them." The individual who lacked this spiritual force, Perón believed, would not be in harmony with his fellow Peronists and, by extension, with the rest of the nation.[84] It was no wonder, then, that Perón defined as non-Argentines all those who rejected Peronism, and believed that "no true Argentine [can disagree] with the basic principles of our doctrine without first reneging on his identity as an Argentine!"[85] The end result was a vision of Argentine nationality that strongly echoed the essentialist, mystical constructs of earlier decades. What was different with Perón, of course, was that he was willing—and able—to use the coercive powers of the state to impose his version of *el ser nacional* on his countrymen and to define as non-Argentines those who failed to embrace the Peronist vision.

It was precisely this effort to transform Peronism into an all encompassing civic religion that caused Perón to lose his greatest ally: the Catholic Church. Beginning in the late 1940s, the church grew increasingly wary of the government's propagandizing and its insertion of Peronism into all facets of Argentine life. A particular flashpoint was the expanding role of Perón's charismatic wife, Eva, whose well-funded personal foundation took over and eclipsed many of the functions of traditional Catholic charities. Even more offensive was the use of the public school texts to glorify the former radio actress and identify her with the Virgin Mary.[86] By 1951, most prominent Catholics, including early supporters, such as Catholic nationalist Ernesto Palacio, had moved into the opposition. Relations became further strained when the church failed to properly acknowledge Eva Perón's death in 1952. Two years later, tensions mounted further when an increasingly beleaguered Perón accused the church of attempting to undermine the government. Taking direct action against his one-time ally, Perón closed down Catholic Action, expelled a number of clerics, and prohibited the church from organizing public religious processions. More scandalous still was his insistence that Congress legalize both prostitution and divorce.[87] Matters came to a head in June 1955, when Peronist followers blamed the Catholics for an abortive coup that resulted in hundreds of civilian deaths. Seeking revenge, angry mobs burned churches and desecrated sacred objects.

Within three months, a military coup would force Perón out of office and into exile. His attacks on the church had eroded public support for the regime and emboldened his traditional enemies within the upper class, the liberal sectors, and the traditional left. Among the military branches, the navy and air force had moved solidly into the opposition, while the army—the most powerful of the three—was deeply divided. Besides the divisions between Peronist and anti-Peronist factions, the army was also split between Catholic nationalists and liberals, who had very different visions of a post-Perón Argentina. Leading the liberals was General Pedro Eugenio Aramburu, while the head of the Catholic nationalists was retired general Eduardo Lonardi, who had long opposed Perón. It was Lonardi who gained the presidency as a result of the so-called "Liberating Revolution" of September 1955.

The overthrow of Perón spelled neither the end of essentialist understandings of *argentinidad* nor of the Manichean mindset it helped engender. Instead, the belief in the existence of an underlying real or authentic Argentina continued to shape ideas about Argentine nationhood and to nourish a persistent pattern of political thought that was hostile to both liberalism and most forms of pluralism. As before, opposing ideas about the nature of the supposedly authentic *ser nacional* continued to divide left- and right-wing nationalists; what still united them was their shared conviction that liberal democracy was alien to the true national character and that free market capitalism had made the country the victim of British and US imperialism. Accordingly, both sought a nationalist program that would guarantee Argentina's economic independence and a set of political institutions that would reflect what they believed to be the authentic character of the organic community.

# NINE

# Resistance and Revisionism

*Argentina's Two Nationalisms after Perón*

The decades after Perón's ouster would be among the most chaotic and violent in Argentine history, as successive regimes—both military and civilian—sought to govern a deeply divided nation. For much of this period, the greatest schism was that between Peronists and anti-Peronists, or between those who saw Perón as Argentina's savior and those who believed him to be a national nightmare. Ultimately, however, Peronism itself would be torn apart, and indeed the violence of this process would help propel Argentina toward the abyss of 1976. The country's two variants of nationalism played a central role in the movement's fracturing. As Peronism both absorbed and was itself changed by nationalists of diverse political leanings, the movement would ultimately become as divided as the nation. In examining Argentine nationalism in the decade or so after the 1955 coup, this chapter explores how the country's two nationalist strands became intertwined with—and in fact helped produce—the internal divisions within Peronism. In doing so, it highlights how long-standing essentialist tropes, through the vector of historical revisionism, continued to undergird nationalist thought and to serve, at least for a time, as a bridge between the two strands.

Making sense of the complex dynamic between right- and left-wing nationalism during this turbulent period requires looking at both the nationalist right that functioned at least partially independently of Peronism, and at the emergence of left- and right-wing variants of nationalism *within* Peronism. This chapter is divided into two main sections. The first examines the reemergence of what might be called "traditional" right-wing nationalists—that is, those nationalists who adhered to the ideal of Argentina as a Catholic nation. These nationalists were, of course, deeply hostile to Argentina's liberal tradition, but after the Cuban Revolution of 1959, they became increasingly concerned about what they saw as the threat of communism. Here the focus of my discussion is the two most influential nuclei during this period: the newly launched weekly *Azul y Blanco*, which brought together the voices of the most important right-wing nationalists from the older generation, and the highly anti-Semitic, ultraright youth organization known as Tacuara, which was founded in 1956–57. The members of both groups were initially hostile to Perón, but subsequent years witnessed the evolution of new, more positive perspectives on the Peronist movement, leading to what Juan L. Besoky has termed the "Peronization of the [nationalist] right."[1]

Section 2 focuses on the Peronist Resistance—meaning those individuals or organizations who actively identified with Peronism and worked for their leader's return. Although all Peronists saw themselves as nationalists seeking to defend the "true Argentina," they hewed to very different strands of nationalism and defined the true Argentina in radically different ways. Some factions within the resistance had direct links to Argentina's right-wing nationalist tradition and embraced the right's long-standing ideal of Argentina's essential Catholic identity. For the individuals within this strand, the return of Perón offered the possibility of defending Argentina's authentic Catholic *ser nacional* from the corrosive forces of political and economic liberalism and, after 1959, from the threat of communism. Others, in contrast, embraced a left-wing, socially inclusive nationalism that in many ways echoed that of FORJA, one that located the true Argentina in the "pueblo." Linking the modern-day masses (and themselves) to the Federalist fighters of the nineteenth century, left-wing Peronists saw the masses as the bearers of Argentina's enduring culture and the source of the nation's authentic identity. For these members of the Peronist Resistance, the Cuban

Revolution pointed to new possibilities, and many sought to mesh Peronism with Marxism.[2] Accordingly, these individuals saw the return of Perón not as part of the struggle to defend Argentina's Catholic identity but rather as an effort to establish a Peronist-led "patria socialista."

That these two forms of nationalism within post-1955 Peronism would ultimately clash now seems obvious. Yet as many scholars have observed, one of the most salient features of post-1955 Peronism, at least until about the late 1960s, was the high degree to which nationalists and nationalist organizations shifted between different ideological poles. Particularly striking was the tendency for right-wing groups and individuals, both inside and outside of Peronism, to move toward the left wing of the Peronist Resistance, although the opposite ideological journey also occurred. Certainly, multiple factors contributed to what one historian has described as the "sometimes baffling political mobility" that characterized this era.[3]

One such factor, of course, was the Cuban Revolution, whose anti-imperialism attracted both right- and left-wing nationalists, but whose turn toward communism repelled the right. Just as important, especially in the Argentine case, was the impact of liberation theology. As historians, such as David Rock, have stressed, the new radicalization of the Argentine church pulled many devout (and previously conservative) Catholics toward the left and especially toward the Peronist left.[4] Key here was the figure of left-wing priest Carlos Mugica, who guided a generation of young Catholics toward armed struggle, and who explicitly identified liberation theology with socialism and Peronism. Also serving to cement the Christianity/Peronism/socialism nexus was the magazine *Cristianismo y Revolución*, published between 1966 and 1971. Directed by ex-seminarian and former right-wing nationalist Juan García Elorrio until his death in 1970, *Cristianismo y Revolución* sided openly with left-wing Peronism and urged the new generation of Peronists to "consolidate the revolutionary tendency [within] Peronism" by following the heroic example of Che Guevara.[5]

But also contributing to the extreme ideological fluidity within the greater field of Argentine nationalism, and the one that concerns us here, was the survival and even enhanced vitality of long-standing essentialist tropes that had long been central to both left- and right-wing nationalism. The notion of an enduring *ser nacional* and the related construct of the two Argentinas, had always provided common conceptual ground for the country's two nationalist strands, sometimes serving as a bridge between them. In the aftermath of Perón's ouster, these essentialist tropes continued to form the conceptual matrix of both right- and left-wing nationalist thought, and indeed were revitalized by a new wave of historical revisionism promoted by key intellectuals within the Peronist Resistance. The enormous success of these revisionists (and the tropes they promoted), I argue, helps explain both the striking ideological mobility between left- and right-wing nationalism in the post-1955 era and why nationalists of both tendencies believed they could find a political home within Peronism.

## THE PARTIAL PERONIZATION OF THE "TRADITIONAL" NATIONALIST RIGHT

The right-wing nationalists, who had applauded the 1955 coup, certainly did not expect that eventually many within their ranks would come to accept Peronism—even less did they suspect that some would join the Peronist Resistance. By the 1950s, it will be recalled, Perón's relationship with the church had soured, and almost all right-wing nationalists had moved into the opposition. Perón himself had always treated the nationalist right warily, and had successfully marginalized those members of the movement he was unable to coopt. As a consequence, right-wing nationalism, the guiding vision of which continued to be the essentialist ideal of Argentina as a Catholic nation, emerged from the Peronist years badly bruised.[6]

Not surprisingly, the members of the nationalist right were greatly cheered by the coup and its initial outcome, which brought General Eduardo Lonardi to the presidency. Lonardi, they believed, was one of their own and would preserve the nationalist gains of the Peronist regime while reining in the totalitarian excesses and the anti-Catholicism of its final years. For a brief period, these hopes were realized. Proclaiming that there should be "neither victors not vanquished," Lonardi surrounded himself with well-known Catholics, called for reconciliation between labor and industrialists, and sought to continue many of Perón's policies. Several of Lonardi's key appointments, such as those of well-known

nationalists Mario Amadeo, Juan Carlos Goyeneche, and Atilio Dell'
Oro Maini, also heartened his right-wing supporters.[7] But Lonardi's attempt to continue many of his predecessor's policies proved his undoing.
For the anti-Peronist or *gorila* faction within the military, nothing short
of a complete de-Peronization of Argentine politics and society would
suffice.[8] On November 13, this faction, urged on by civilian anti-Peronists,
forced Lonardi out and installed General Pedro Aramburu as president.

Under Aramburu, the Argentine state took a sharp turn back toward
the "liberal-conservatism" of the Justo years. Aramburu, who remained
in power until 1958, identified his government with the liberal project of
independence and signaled his intent to return the country to electoral
normalcy by dispensing with the 1949 Constitution via presidential
decree.[9] He also sought to erase all vestiges of Peronism. To this end, the
military regime outlawed the Peronist Party and prohibited the display
of Peronist images and propaganda. Also targeted were Peronist sympathizers within the military, universities, and public bureaucracy. On the
economic front, the new government followed the ideas of noted economist Raúl Prebisch, who advocated a mixture of liberal prescriptions,
along with developmentalist measures, such as state support of industry
and agriculture. Outraged by these supposedly antinationalist economic
policies, right-wing nationalists quickly became some of Aramburu's
harshest critics.[10]

At the forefront of right-wing nationalist dissent was the newly established weekly magazine *Azul y Blanco*. Founded in mid-1956 and directed by long-time nationalist Marcelo Sánchez Sorondo, *Azul y Blanco*,
which served as the "primary agglutinating center" of the nationalist
right, was one of the few nationalist publications to form during these
years.[11] It immediately found an audience and achieved a circulation of
over one hundred thousand within the first five months.[12] Because its
contributors included virtually all of the important nationalist thinkers
active during the late 1950s, the magazine opens an indispensable
window into the perspective of the era's right-wing nationalist politicians and intellectuals.[13]

The editors of *Azul y Blanco* attacked the Aramburu government on
a number of fronts. One complaint, of course, concerned the new president's promise to restore the nation's democratic institutions.[14] Other
criticisms included Aramburu's failure to reinstate religious education in
the schools, as well as his regime's supposedly "antinational, antipopular

and anti-Christian" economic policies, which right-wing nationalists believed were delivering the economy into the hands of international capital.[15] These nationalists also lambasted Aramburu's decision to hold a new constitutional assembly that would officially invalidate Perón's 1949 Constitution and replace it with an updated version of the liberal 1853 Constitution. Writing against reviving the nineteenth-century document, Mario Amadeo insisted that the Peronist constitution contained many reforms, including the affirmation of national sovereignty over subsoil rights and rivers, the nationalization of key public services, and the defense of workers' rights, that were desired by the majority of the people.[16] Another contributor went further, arguing that the plan to reinstate the 1853 Constitution was a ploy to install a "political structure" that would once again allow foreign capital to dominate the Argentine economy.[17]

In attacking the proposed change, *Azul y Blanco*'s contributors frequently couched their criticisms in essentialist terms that strongly echoed the language of previous generations of right-wing nationalists. Amadeo insisted, for example, that the 1949 document "symbolize[d] [Argentine] nationality" and was rooted in the underlying "native tradition." While hastening to add that his defense of the 1949 Constitution was *not* a defense of Perón (whom he still opposed), Amadeo insisted that those who wished to revert to the liberal Constitution of 1853 were a small minority seeking, once again, to impose a political system that was "incompatible with our national style." Such individuals, he charged, wished to alter the nature of Argentines by turning the country into "a type of Switzerland [that is] antiseptic and impersonal."[18] In a similar fashion, a later editorial accused the government of using the constitutional assembly to destroy Argentine traditions and of attempting to "tear out by the roots" the link between the state and the Catholic faith.[19]

In February of 1958, Aramburu made good on his promise to return the country to democracy, resulting in the election of Arturo Frondizi, who resoundingly defeated the government's preferred candidate. *Azul y Blanco*'s editorial board initially lauded Frondizi's triumph. Indeed, much of Frondizi's rhetoric seemed to echo ideas shared by both right- and left-wing nationalists. In his 1957 book *Industria argentina y desarrollo nacional* (Argentine industry and national development) for example, Frondizi proclaimed Argentina to be facing two very different choices. One would return Argentina to the economic model of the past, whereby it would continue to produce agricultural products for the industrialized world. In this schema, the traditional oligarchy, based in Buenos Aires, would again rule on behalf of foreign interests. The other path, Frondizi argued, would lead to a more balanced mode of development, one that would stimulate industry and develop other sources of wealth throughout the entire country. This model, the future president affirmed, would lead to a more prosperous future and provide the material base for the further integration of the Argentine *"ser nacional."*[20]

In the days after the election, *Azul y Blanco*'s editorial board made clear that its approval of Frondizi stemmed from the conviction that the president-elect shared its belief in the need to defend the authentic or true Argentina. One unsigned article, for example, lauded Frondizi for wisely recognizing "the importance of Catholicism in the life of the country," while another enthused that his victory represented the triumph of the "Real Country (*País Real*)."[21] A month later, the tone was still positive, although a hint of skepticism had crept in. While still expressing hope for Frondizi's presidency, the magazine warned that a successful leader must recognize that Argentina's problems were both economic and cultural. As one contributor put it, "every collective entity has an interior style, a *tradition of the soul,*" that must be maintained. This truth, the writer concluded somewhat darkly, is something that Frondizi could not afford to ignore.[22] A similar article warned of the need to define "the profile" of the nation. "If the country is to be what it should be," it insisted, "its culture and its national personality, which is the same thing, cannot [be allowed to] break down." A people that loses its integrity as a "cultural being," it concluded, becomes little more than a factory.[23]

By mid-1958, *Azul y Blanco* had moved squarely into the opposition. Here again, many of its contributors couched their criticisms of Frondizi in essentialist terms. One key complaint concerned the new president's leadership style, which editorialists deemed weak and vacillating, and thus unsuited to the supposed Argentine temperament.[24] Others complained about Frondizi's new efforts to encourage European immigration to Argentina. Calling immigration a "fundamental problem of the nationality," an anonymous author warned against encouraging immigrants who could not easily be assimilated into the existing population. Such immigrants, he argued, could "gravely affect the future ethnicity of the Nation," by potentially altering the "biological, human and cultural basis of the Argentine *ser*." The modern-day creole, the writer affirmed, formed Argentina's "true human archetype" and had always constituted the ethnic core of the community. To ensure the continued viability of this creole core, he concluded, it was necessary to prevent the influx of the "unassimilable foreigner."[25]

Such concerns over immigration were seconded by Francisco P. Olmedo, an occasional contributor to the periodical. Praising *Azul y Blanco* for highlighting a matter that was so vital "to the conservation of our bloodline (*estirpe*)," Olmedo opined that one of Argentina's central conflicts was between those who wished to convert Argentina into a colony and those who were fighting to prevent the "total liquidation of the Argentine *ser*." The struggle, in his view, was not going well for the latter group. Citing the proliferation of foreign names among university faculty members, he proclaimed that "we find ourselves in grave danger of . . . losing our physiognomy as a Hispanic-creole, Latin and Catholic pueblo." Uncontrolled immigration, in his view, posed a direct threat to the very basis of the "national soul" and thus to Argentine nationality itself.[26]

*Azul y Blanco* also began to ratchet up its anticommunism rhetoric, including emphasizing what it believed were the hidden links between liberalism and communism. Echoing the long-held nationalist conviction that liberalism had destroyed the unity of the West by replacing spiritual ties with "the heavy chains of dollars and pounds," contributors argued that the same process had occurred within Argentina itself. With liberalism's triumph, Argentina's traditional religious values had been replaced by "sensualism" and the "idolatry of money."[27] As a result, Argentines had been robbed of their supposedly unique collective sense of being, had been "stripped of their ethnicity (*descastados*)," and were "without a patria."[28] This breakdown of Argentine ethnicity, right-wing nationalists believed, had left the people vulnerable to the materialistic seductions of communism.[29] Behind it all, many argued, were Jews and the British, two groups they believed had long conspired to exploit the country.[30]

Given this fear that Argentina was sliding toward communism, what political solution did the nationalist right envision? In answering this question, it is important to remember the nationalists' continued obsession with the supposed disconnect between the character of the Argentine people and the liberal institutions supposedly imposed on them by the vendepatria elite. In the words of one of *Azul y Blanco*'s editorialists, "Our long . . . political crisis results, above all, from the phenomenon of inadaptation or the lack of fit between the REAL COUNTRY (PAIS REAL) and those organs and groups that . . . govern it."[31] Echoing this analysis, another contributor lauded the insights of British historian Cecil Jane, whose work *Libertad y despotismo en la América Hispana* (Liberty and despotism in Hispanic America) argues that Hispanic America's turmoil stemmed from the unsuitability of its political institutions, which had been "copied from abroad." These institutions, according to Jane, had been ineffective, because they failed to "respect the idiosyncrasies of the region's people."[32] Such an analysis (ironically from a British author), served to validate the nationalists' essentialist view that Argentines were inherently unsuited for democracy, and instead harbored a collective and deeply rooted desire for caudillo rule.[33] In modern times, this meant a state run by a "directing minority" or "aristocracy" made up of a rarified group of both military and civilian men who best reflected the virtues and qualities of the collectivity. This "necessary class," according to Máximo Etchecopar, was composed of those who somehow embodied the "national *genio*," or the "living nucleus," of their particular society.[34]

Aiding this enlightened group of leaders, according to right-wing nationalists, would be the Catholic Church and the popular classes, with the latter of course in a subordinate position. Like the cultural nationalists of the early twentieth century, who had drawn inspiration from the ideas of Romantic ethno-cultural nationalism, the right-wing nationalists of the 1950s professed to have a deep respect for the common people, believing them to be reservoirs of national feeling and *argentinidad*. Writing in 1959, for example, long-time nationalist Rodolfo Irazusta praised the pueblo for having "instinctively repudiated" the liberalism of the sellout elite.[35] In a similar fashion, Ramón Doll also lauded the political instincts of popular classes, noting that mass demonstrations against the Frondizi regime revealed the existence of a new type of democracy that "flowed and ran behind the back of parliamentary and liberal democracy's politicking." This popular democracy, he affirmed, was "vital, personal, and alive (*vivaz*)."[36]

The post-1955 period also witnessed the emergence of a new youth organization dedicated to defending the ideal of the true Catholic nation. Founded in 1956–57 by the remnants of the right-wing student group UNES, the *Movimiento Nacionalista Tacuara* (nationalist tacuara movement or MNT), or *Tacuara*, took its name from the makeshift lance used by the nineteenth-century "gauchos montoneros."[37] Among Tacuara's key influences was the fiercely anti-Semitic nationalist priest Julio Meinvielle, who served as a kind of intellectual mentor to the group. Also important to Tacuarista thought were Spanish Falangist José Antonio Primo de Rivera, and Jaime María de Mahieu, a French sociologist, who promoted a conservative brand of communitarianism and who would ultimately provide an important link to Peronism.[38]

In its initial years, Tacuara's membership came primarily from the middle- and upper-middle class, whose exclusively male adherents were Catholic high school and university students. The group first gained notoriety in 1957 for its often violent participation in the public demonstrations surrounding the so-called lay or free educational reform. The following year the group outlined its larger ambitions in a document titled "Programa Básico Revolucionario" (Basic revolutionary program). Approved under the leadership of the young Alberto Ezcurra Uriburu, who counted among his ancestors both the wife of nineteenth-century dictator Juan Manuel de Rosas and 1930 coup leader General José Félix Uriburu, the document called for a corporatist revolution based on social justice and propelled by organized labor. Following this corporatist, pro-labor vision, Tacuara successfully expanded its base to include working-class youth, some with Peronist backgrounds.[39] Its members also participated in some of the most important labor strikes of 1959, often alongside activists from now-proscribed Peronist groups.[40] Thus, like the traditional nationalists surrounding *Azul y Blanco*, many of the early Tacuarists viewed Peronism with a degree of sympathy, while at the same time believing it to be a flawed vehicle for a truly nationalist program.

Notwithstanding its support for labor militancy, Tacuara's core ideology remained firmly rooted in the essentialist understandings of right-wing nationalism, which in turn harkened back to the ideas of the most conservative early twentieth-century cultural nationalists. Its above-mentioned Programa Básico Revolucionario for example, proclaimed Argentina to be not a mere "conglomeration of individuals" but rather a "community of race, religion, culture and history." This community, moreover, possessed a "unity of destiny" derived from its status as an "heir of Imperial Spain." As such, Argentina had a "historical mission" to fulfill within the larger destiny of humanity. Doing so, of course, meant that Argentines must remain faithful to "Catholic Truth," which was "rooted in an irrevocable form in our historical destiny and in our *ser nacional.*" This required among other things, that Argentina take steps to retain its ethnic unity. Accordingly, Tacuarists believed, immigration should be controlled and selective. In a clear reference to Jews and other non-Christians, the group insisted that individuals from "ethnic and cultural groups that were unassimilable" should not be allowed into the country. The document also insisted that the naturalization of immigrants should be highly restricted. According to Tacuara, only those individuals who had contributed great service and who had demonstrated a "total identification with the national community" would be allowed to become citizens.[41] That this "total identification" meant that non-Catholics should not be allowed to naturalize was clearly implied.[42]

Tacuara, like both right- and left-wing nationalists of the 1930s, was deeply hostile to liberalism in all its forms and believed Argentine politics had long been dominated by liberals who had sold out the country to foreign interests.[43] Indeed, as Ezcurra expressed in a 1962 interview, the root of Argentina's problems could be traced back to the "bourgeoisie liberal regime" that he believed had ruled the country with few interruptions since the defeat of Rosas in 1852. This regime, he argued, had "incarnated materialism [and] negated the permanent and spiritual values of the nationality." It had, moreover, established a system of liberal democracy and capitalism that had acted like a "straight jacket placed on the real country."[44] Writing elsewhere, Ezcurra insisted that the liberal state, with its "political parties and the Rousseauian notion of simple majority rule (*la 'mitad más uno'*), could never be the real interpreter and servant of the National Community."[45] Accordingly, Tacuara urged right-wing youth to join with its effort to "overthrow the idols and myths of democratic liberalism," and "the capitalist monster" it had produced. The goal, Tacuara affirmed, was a "National Revolution" that would eliminate political parties and replace them with syndicalist bodies designated by an executive power.

In the economic realm, this state would eliminate capitalism, which it deemed "parasitic" and "antinational." Rather than leaving the market to allocate resources, the group called for the state to be in charge of developing heavy industry. Private businesses, Tacuarists believed, should be collectively owned by the workers, and production should be oriented around "national necessities." Finally, in the area of education, schools should eschew the "materialism" of both liberalism and Marxism and instead "affirm the spiritual values" of Catholicism.[46]

Like all Argentine nationalists, Tacuarists also embraced historical revisionism and celebrated the nativist traditions of the "true" Argentina that they believed had been suffocated by liberal rule. As part of their revisionist philosophy, Tacuarists saw rural Argentina as the source of authentic national values, and they frequently gathered at Ezcurra's family estate to engage in military training and hold discussions about Argentine folklore.[47] The group also devoted much of its energies to honoring events and individuals from the Federalist past. Following the practices of the by-then defunct UNES, inductees were often asked to swear their fealty at the mausoleum of the nineteenth-century Federalist caudillo Facundo Quiroga.[48] Tacuarists were also highly visible participants in the celebration of the "Day of National Sovereignty," an annual event that honored Rosas's 1845 naval victory over a combined Anglo-French fleet, which had occupied the Paraná River.[49]

There was, of course, nothing new in Tacuara's essentialist ideas about Argentine nationality or in its insistence on the need to celebrate the nation's "true" history: such notions about the existence of a true Catholic nation had underpinned right-wing nationalist thought since the 1930s. There were, however, two elements that distinguished it from what might be called traditional right-wing nationalism. First was Tacuara's interest in promoting the unity of countries of the Global South as a means of combatting imperialism. Noting the anticolonialist "awakening in Asia and Africa," Tacuara called for the establishment of a "new block of National States" that would include all of Latin America and the liberated states of Asia and Africa. By cooperating with each other, Tacuarists believed, these states could defend themselves against the imperialism of both the United States and the Soviet Union.[50] Tacuarists were particularly enthusiastic about Egyptian leader General Gamal Abdel Nasser, whom they admired as a nationalist and as an "authentic Arab who accepted the spirit of his race in its totality." They also praised the fact that, although Nasser was stridently anticommunist, he had the courage to stand up to the United States and Israel.[51] This incipient Third Worldism, as we shall see, was also taken up by the nationalist left.

Tacuara's second novel quality was the group's penchant for violence, a tendency that went beyond that of the notoriously violent ALN.[52] Violence for Tacuarists was both a political weapon and a means of affirming their masculine readiness to shed blood for the greater cause of the nation.[53] The most intense violence was inflicted on Argentina's Jewish population. Like the ALN under Juan Queraltó, Tacuara was deeply anti-Semitic, linking Jews to both international capitalism and communism. Accordingly, its members often targeted Jewish-owned schools, synagogues, and community centers. With the police often turning a blind eye, Tacuarists would bash windows, lob Molotov cocktails into buildings, and paint anti-Semitic slogans on walls. Less frequent, but still relatively common, were verbal or physical attacks on individuals.

Tacuarists also took aim at groups perceived to be liberal or leftist, disrupting meetings and shouting nationalist slogans. In 1959, for example, Tacuarists descended on an event organized by the Socialist Party honoring Sarmiento, reportedly kicking the sixty-year-old Alicia Moreau de Justo, one of Argentine socialism's most revered figures, to the ground.[54] At times these confrontations would turn deadly, as happened in 1962, when a student confrontation led to gunfire, resulting in a death and several injuries. While these actions caused consternation among the general public, Tacuara's "cult of violence" earned it admiration within some sectors within the Peronist Resistance. Andrés Castillo, who began his political career in the Juventud Peronista (JP; Peronist youth) and ultimately became a member of the Montoneros, explained that Peronist activists found Tacuara attractive for its "theme of nationalism, of violence, of the . . . truth of fists and pistols above the rational."[55]

Tacuara's founding in the mid-1950s marked the beginning of the florescence of new organizations, many of them offshoots of Tacuara itself, that promoted nationalist ideas. Driving most of these fractures were disagreements over Peronism and the Cuban Revolution. The first split occurred in 1960. Disturbed by Tacuara's lessening hostility toward Peronism and its initial support for the Cuban Revolution (which many Tacuarists lauded for its nationalism and anti-imperialism), a group headed by Roberto Echenique split to form the ultra-right-wing Guardia Restauradora Nacionalista (GRN).[56] Subsequent ruptures, however, were prompted by individuals seeking to align with Peronism. As will be discussed below, by the early 1960s, many members of Tacuara or its offshoots either directly joined Peronism or collaborated in some way with groups within the Peronist Resistance.

As the examples of both the *Azul y Blanco* group and Tacuara demonstrate, after Aramburu assumed the presidency, right-wing nationalism reemerged virtually unchanged from its pre-Peronist form. At the same time, the government's attempt to turn back the clock and reinstate the liberal/conservative system meant that Peronism exerted a powerful gravitational pull on these nationalists. Thus, although almost all had supported Perón's ouster, Aramburu's attempt to reimpose a liberal political and economic order by purging Argentina of all things Peronist—including the 1949 Constitution—gave right-wing nationalists a new appreciation for both the populist leader and the movement he had created. For the older nationalists of the *Azul y Blanco* group, this appreciation remained tempered by the memory of Perón's assaults on the church, his mobilization of the working class, and his failure to consistently defend the true Catholic nation. Still, in the new political context, in which both liberalism and communism seemed on the rise, many of his former right-wing opponents remembered Perón as having offered at least the possibility of a state that reflected the supposedly authentic character of the Argentine people. Thus, with a few exceptions, most older right-wing nationalists adopted the stance of being "tolerant anti-Peronists,"—that is, unwilling to join the Peronist Resistance but appreciative of its corporatist, nationalist goals.[57] By the early 1960s, however, the growing influence of the Cuban Revolution would prod some of these nationalists further into the Peronist camp. Increasingly fearful that Argentina might follow Cuba, many members of the nationalist right, including most of the *Azul y Blanco* group, came to see Peronism as the only sure bulwark against communism.[58] The case of younger activists of Tacuara, however, was different. For many of these individuals, the move toward Peronism was a move toward the left.

## THE PERONIST RESISTANCE AND ARGENTINA'S TWO NATIONALISMS

The growing connections between individuals and groups within the nationalist right and the Peronist Resistance were made easier by the fact

that, after Perón's ouster, Peronism itself became increasingly heterogeneous. As is well known, in the years after the coup, two major fault
lines developed within the Peronist Resistance that, while still incipient
during the first decade or so, took on greater importance with the passage of time. The first was the division between the so-called *linea blanda*
(soft line) and the *linea dura* (hard line). The "blandas" were those Peronists, principally labor leaders, who adopted a pragmatic position vis-à-
vis the government and used the power of the Peronist unions to influence labor policy.[59] By the early 1960s, this conciliatory stance had
become identified with "bureaucratic syndicalism" and the increasingly
controversial union leader Augusto Vandor.[60] The "duras," in contrast,
adamantly refused to reconcile with the government. Encouraged by
Perón, adherents to this line resisted by engaging in acts of industrial
sabotage, arson, bombings, and boycotts.[61]

The second fault line, and the one that concerns us here, was the
division between what would become known as the Peronist left and
right.[62] That post-1955 Peronism would experience such a right-left
cleavage is not surprising. As discussed in chapter 8, in creating his
movement, Perón had drawn promiscuously from Argentina's two nationalist strands. Moreover, his own views on the nature of the true Argentina and the (imagined) *ser nacional* were contradictory and appear to
have evolved over time. As a military officer, Perón had been steeped in
the tradition of the nationalist right with its vision of Argentina as a
nation defined first and foremost by Catholicism and its Hispanic heritage. In the course of his rise to power, Perón also found inspiration in
FORJA's more inclusive vision of the presumed "true Argentina," which
included the descendants of the working-class immigrants, a vision that
was further broadened by his inclusion of the mixed-race "*cabecitas
negras*" from the interior. And while, as noted earlier, some evidence suggests that Perón had begun to move toward a more pluralistic vision of
Argentina—one unified by the civic religion of Peronism—this transformation was never complete. As events would soon make clear, the two
nationalisms that had originally nourished the movement had survived
Perón's amalgamating efforts.

The heterogeneous nature of what would become known as the
Peronist Resistance was immediately apparent. One of the earliest responses to the coup came from the Alianza Libertadora Nacionalista

(ALN), the right-wing nationalist group that, for most of its existence, had been known for its anti-Semitism, anticommunism, and unwavering defense of the ideal of Argentina as a Catholic nation. The ALN, it will be recalled, had been one of the few right-wing nationalist groups to support Perón. Led by the fiercely anti-Semitic Juan Queraltó, the organization initially attempted to maintain some autonomy vis-à-vis the movement. Soon, however, it became folded into Peronism, albeit in a marginalized role. In 1953, Perón had intervened directly in the ALN, replacing Queraltó with acolyte Guillermo Patricio Kelly, who toned down the group's traditional anti-Semitism while retaining its strong antiliberal, anti-imperialist, and anticommunist stance.[63] Under Kelly, the ALN became a kind of shock force used to harass Perón's enemies. On the day of the 1955 coup, members of the ALN took to the streets, refusing to turn over their weapons. The military responded by leveling the group's headquarters with tanks and arresting Kelly.[64] Despite this blow and despite strong persecution from the new regime, the ALN played an important role in organizing some of the first Peronist Resistance groups.[65]

In addition to the ALN, the Resistance included several key activists who identified with right-wing nationalism, either as Catholics or as pro-Rosas historical revisionists. One of the first to respond to the coup was journalist Alejandro Olmos, a prominent figure within nationalist circles, who in November of 1955 launched the pro-Peronist weekly *Palabra Argentina*. The newspaper quickly gained a wide readership, and Olmos used it to promote revisionist themes and to communicate with the Peronist masses.[66] Other prominent members of the Peronist Resistance with ties to right-wing nationalism were Fermín Chávez and José María Rosa, both of whom moved leftward with time. Chávez, a former seminarian, had come to nationalism in the late 1930s through his reading of works by right-wing nationalists, such as Ernesto Palacio, Ramón Doll, and Enrique Osés, and through his association with the Catholic group "Restauración" (restoration); José María Rosa's ties to the nationalist right were rooted more in anti-imperialism and historical revisionism than in his Catholic faith. In the 1940s, he had joined the ALN and during Perón's second presidency had served as director of the Rosas Institute. Throughout his time in the directorship, Rosa described himself as a Peronist "sympathizer" rather than an activist. After the coup, however, he ran afoul of the Aramburu government and was jailed for months. This experience prompted Rosa to move firmly into the Peronist camp, and he began concentrating his efforts on teaching, writing, and public speaking about revisionist themes as a means of criticizing the government and supporting Perón.[67]

Individuals exhibiting left-wing tendencies were also key figures within the Peronist Resistance. Among the more prominent was the charismatic John William Cooke, who served in Congress as Peronist deputy from 1946 to 1951. Cooke also had a deep interest in historical revisionism and, in 1951, was elected vice president of the Rosas Institute, serving simultaneously with Rosa.[68] After the 1955 coup, Cooke quickly took a leadership role in the emerging Peronist Resistance. Despite being jailed by the regime, he worked through intermediaries to organize the "Comando Nacional Peronista" (national Peronist command) and was so trusted by Perón that in November 1956 the exiled leader designated Cooke as his political successor in case of his (Perón's) death. Cooke also distinguished himself as one of the most left-wing members of the Resistance, a stance that by 1959 would strain his relationship with Perón.[69] In that year he moved to Cuba, where he embraced socialism and developed a Marxist/Gramscian reading of the Peronist movement.[70]

Joining Cooke in his effort to mesh Peronism with Marxism were Juan José Hernández Arregui, Rodolfo Puiggrós, and Jorge Abelardo Ramos. Hernández Arregui, who had studied Marxism during his years at the University of Córdoba, entered politics as a supporter of Amadeo Sabattini, the Radical governor of Córdoba, whose ideas resembled those of FORJA.[71] In 1947, at the urging of his friend Arturo Jauretche, he moved to Buenos Aires and joined Peronism. After the 1955 coup, Hernández Arregui became active in the left wing of the Resistance and emerged as one of the most important intellectuals of the Marxist-oriented "National Left."[72] Also working within this vein were Rodolfo Puiggrós and Jorge Abelardo Ramos, both of whom had participated in groups within the radical left before coming to Peronism. Deeply affected by the events of October 17, 1945, Puiggrós broke with the Communist Party in 1948 to form the pro-Peronist Movimiento Obrero Comunista (Communist worker movement). Abelardo Ramos came from a Trotskyist background, and in 1953 he broke with the Socialist Party to establish the Partido Socialista de la Revolución (Socialist party of the revolution). Like the Movimiento Obrero Comunista, the Partido Socialista de la Revolución allied with Peronism, which it saw as an authentically nationalist movement with transformative potential.[73]

Also joining the left wing of the Peronist Resistance were former leaders of FORJA, although none ended up embracing Marxism. Arturo Jauretche, who had kept a low profile after resigning his post at the Provincial Bank in 1950, reentered public life after 1955 to oppose the military regime. Raúl Scalabrini Ortiz, following a similar path, joined Jauretche in his protests against Aramburu's repression of Peronism. Between 1956 and 1958, the two collaborated on the weekly magazine *Qué*, using its pages to defend the nationalist economic policies of Perón and to attack those of the new government.[74] Another former Forjista who contributed to the resistance was Atilio García Mellid, the most Catholic member of the former Forjistas. García Mellid had served continuously within the Perón administration and maintained a correspondence with the exiled leader throughout the 1960s. In the months after the coup, García Mellid worked with fellow Peronist Juan Atilia Barmuglia to form the first "neo-Peronist" political party; their goal was to unify the working class and salvage the best elements of Peronism in accordance with the country's Western and Catholic heritage.[75]

A final segment of the Peronist Resistance to take shape in the late 1950s was the Juventud Peronista. Established in 1957 by Gustavo Rearte, Envar El Kadri, Susan Valle, and Jorge Rulli, among others, the JP represented a new type of Peronist organization, one that was noted for its militancy and independence. To be sure, young people had always participated in the Peronist movement, either individually or as members of associations; and in 1951, youthful activists in the city of La Plata launched a version of the JP aimed at bringing these disparate actors together. This "original" JP received little direct attention from Perón and remained very much under the control of the party machine. Shut out from decision-making roles, its members served largely as helpmates of the Peronist Party, working to promote candidates in elections, organize demonstrations, and spread propaganda.[76] The second JP, in contrast, emerged during the period when Perón was in exile and the party bureaucracy was in disarray. Although its members pledged loyalty to their exiled leader and expressed admiration for Cooke, the new JP had little use for the Peronist old guard, including those who had formed the first JP. Instead, they saw themselves as the new generation that, in the words of historian Omar Acha, "was inclined to affirm its own power and its right to imprint upon Peronism a new, more combative and revolutionary sensibility."[77] Deeply influenced by revisionists, such as Rosa, Jauretche, and Scalabrini Ortiz, this new JP would push the Peronist Resistance leftward years before the Montoneros appeared on the scene.[78]

The tearing apart of Peronism was a slow-motion process, one that took unexpected twists and was unavoidably influenced by historically contingent forces external to the movement. One factor preventing the immediate fracturing of the Peronist Resistance was, of course, the need for Perón's followers to unify in the face of fierce repression and the common goal of fighting for Perón's return.[79] In such circumstances, the need to marshal all available forces trumped any drive for ideological purity and helped mute tensions between the left and right wings of the resistance. Cooke, for example, quickly urged Perón to recognize the value of Alejandro Olmos's activism, despite the fact that at the time of the coup relations between Olmos and the exiled leader had been tense.[80] Similarly, Cooke's Comando Nacional Peronista welcomed the participation of members of the ultra-right ALN.

Beyond the shared goal of fighting for Perón's return, personal bonds of friendship borne out of these shared nationalist sentiments and personal interactions also helped dampen potential conflicts between individuals adhering to different strands of nationalism. As noted above, the pro-Rosas revisionist José María Rosa was the director of the Rosas Institute at the same time that Cooke served as the organization's vice president. Such was their relationship that, after the coup, Rosa sheltered Cooke in his own home when the latter was on the run from the authorities. (Rosa's generosity was for naught. Once Cooke was apprehended, Rosa himself was arrested and jailed for harboring a fugitive.) Cooke also developed an admiration for Guillermo Patricio Kelly, the leader of the ALN, after the two spent several months imprisoned at the same facility.[81] Tacuarist José Luis Nell's friendship with Envar El Kadri, one of the founders of the JP, provides another prominent example. When El Kadri's activism landed him in jail in 1962, Nell schemed with members of the JP to help him escape. Although the plan was never realized, Nell's willingness to risk his life for El Kadri solidified his relationship with other leaders of the JP.[82]

On a broader scale, as Laura Ehrlich has observed, during these years, nationalists from across the ideological spectrum—both Peronist and non-Peronist—interacted regularly in an array of places, including cafes, bookstores, and, after 1958, the newly reopened Rosas Institute. These specialized "spaces of sociability," she argued, provided opportunities for nationalists of different political stripes to form friendships and exchange opinions.[83] Nationalists from across the political spectrum also joined together regularly for commemorative events. One of the most important was the "March of Silence," organized by right-wing Peronist Alejandro Olmos. This annual event, which commemorated a group of military men executed after a failed coup attempt against Aramburu, became an important unifying ritual for nationalists. Nationalists from across the ideological spectrum also contributed to pro-Peronist publications, such as "Columnas del Nacionalismo Marxista de Liberación Nacional" and "Santo y Seña."[84] Finally, many Peronist political organizations and events attracted a wide array of individuals with diverse political leanings. The Peronist-sponsored Congreso for National Liberation of 1959, for example, brought together Peronists ranging from those on the left (Cooke and Hernández Arregui) to Catholic Peronists (Fermín Chávez and Antonio Cafiero) to former Forjistas (Jorge de Río) and "Rosistas" (José Rosa) and to right-wing, antisocialists (Rodolfo Arce).[85]

But another factor that helped keep the Resistance from fracturing, and one that is of most interest to us here, is the fact that in the first decade or so after Perón's ouster, the lines between left- and right-wing Peronism, and between traditional right-wing nationalism and Peronism, proved to be surprisingly permeable. Simply put, it was difficult for divisions to crystalize when there was so much movement between ideological poles. During the fifteen or so years after Perón's ouster, groups and individuals identified with one ideological position reinvented themselves and shifted course. In other cases, militant nationalist organizations split apart and gave birth to new and very different groups, as clusters of militants hived off in different ideological directions.

The ALN under Kelly provides an important example of a group reinventing itself. In 1964, Kelly changed the name from the "Alianza Libertadora Nacionalista" to the "Alianza de Liberación Nacional" (alliance of national liberation), and in doing so allied the organization with the most left-wing elements of the resistance. Declaring that "Perón marches toward socialism," the group's principal organ published an extensive interview with Cooke, in which he advocated purging Peronism of its Catholic right wing.[86] The experience of Tacuara illustrates how new groups were born of older ones. Indeed, so fracture prone was this organization that historian Juan Manuel Padrón has counted more than a dozen nationalist organizations founded in the 1960s that had their roots in Tacuara.[87] As will be recalled, the organization's first split came in 1960, when a group mentored by the ultra-right-wing priest Julio Meinvielle broke off to form the GRN. A second rupture occurred a year later, when another group from the so-called Sindicalist Brigades wing of Tacuara broke to create the Movimento Nueva Argentina (new Argentine movement, or MNA), an organization that later formed part of what became known as the Peronist right. The year 1963 saw yet another schism, when long-time Tacuara members Joe Baxter, José Luis Nell, and Alfredo Ossorio split to form the Movimiento Nacionalista Revolucionario Tacuara (nationalist revolutionary movement of Tacuara or MNRT).[88] Under Baxter, the MNRT distanced itself from Tacuara's anti-Semitism, and the new organization openly allied with what became known as the Peronist left.[89] Members of the MNRT would later found the left-wing Peronist guerrilla group Fuerzas Armadas Peronistas (FAP) in 1967/68.[90]

This pronounced ideological mobility was also evident on the individual level.[91] According to Michael Goebel, "a significant proportion" of the Cuba-inspired Peronist guerrilla group Uturuncos came from the right-wing ALN. Also striking is the number of individual activists, who, having begun their political careers on the Catholic right or in Tacuara, went on to become important figures in the Montoneros. The Montoneros' founding members, Fernando Abal Medina and Gustavo Ramos, as well as noted Montoneros Rodolfo Galimberti, José Luis Nell, and Horacio Carril, all had their start in the original Tacuara. Although Mario Firmenich, who ultimately assumed the leadership of the Montoneros, had not been affiliated with Tacuara, he had been active in other right-wing Catholic organizations.[92] Another prominent figure who experienced extreme ideological mobility was Juan Manuel Abal Medina, the older brother of Montonero cofounder Fernando Abal Medina. A devout Catholic, Juan Manuel had been a member of the ultra-right-wing Tacuara splinter group GRN and had also worked closely with Catholic nationalist Marcelo Sánchez Sorondo on the staff of *Azul y Blanco*. After the death of his Montonero brother in 1970, however, Juan Manuel moved toward Peronism and was selected by Perón to be general secretary of the movement in 1972.[93]

There were also some instances of individuals and groups that moved from the left to the right, although, as noted, this journey was less common. Luis Alfredo (Freddy) Zarattini, for example, who was a member of the left-wing MNRT in the early 1960s, later moved steadily toward the right wing of the Peronist movement. According to journalist (and ex-Montonero) Miguel Bonasso, in the 1970s Zarattini ended up serving as an operative in the notorious 601 Batallion, a secret intelligence branch of the Argentine army that hunted down leftists.[94] Norma Kennedy's path was similarly extreme. Having first entered politics through the Communist Party in the early 1950s, Kennedy joined the Peronist Resistance after 1955 and traveled to see the exiled Perón during his stay in Panama. Back in Argentina, she joined the Peronist Comando de Organización, which in the early 1970s violently confronted the left-wing Montoneros.[95]

Several scholars have sought to explain the remarkable fluidity between left- and right-wing Peronism (and thus between left- and right-wing nationalism) of these years. Michael Goebel and Juan Luís Besoky, for example, have attributed these shifts to Peronism itself, which served, in the words of Besoky, as a "vaso comunicante" (communicating vessel) between nationalists of diverse political inclinations.[96] Sociologist Huberto Cucchetti, in contrast, has looked beyond Peronism itself to consider the broader political, social, and institutional contexts of these groups and of their members that eased the way for shifts in ideological directions. Associations, such as religious organizations, labor unions, political parties, and even the family unit could serve as a "passageway," through which individuals moved toward new political commitments. Helpful for my purposes is Cucchetti's additional argument that certain "political-cultural representations" served as shared "spaces" or as a common "language" that also functioned as bridges between different groups within the Peronist Resistance. Here he points to nationalism, anticapitalism, and historical revisionism, all of which the young militants of this era—regardless of whether they leaned toward the right or left—embraced with fervor.[97]

Cucchetti's observations do much to explain the ideological fluidity of the post-1955 period. At the same time, his limited temporal focus risks seeing the permeability between the two strands of nationalism within Peronism as peculiar to the hothouse political environment of these years, rather than as a permanent feature of Argentine nationalism. As this work has argued, since the country's two nationalisms emerged in the 1930s, their proponents have been bound together by a shared set of understandings about the very nature of Argentine nationality—often expressed in the essentialist tropes of *el ser nacional* and of the dichotomy of the "two Argentinas." To use Cucchetti's terminology, these tropes served as "shared spaces" or as a common "language" that framed the way Argentine nationalists of all political stripes interpreted their nation's history and the challenges it faced, serving as a bridge between them. Thus, just as the leaders of right- and left-wing nationalism of the 1930s "got" each other at a conceptual level, so too did later nationalists— regardless of their ideological leanings—share a common conceptual matrix based on essentialist understandings of Argentine nationality. This shared and remarkably persistent matrix, I argue, made possible historian Diana Quattrocchi-Woisson's observation that the "differences between the 'left' and 'right' Peronists [of the post-1955 period] could not hide the more essential agreements surrounding their interpretation of the past and the values of *'argentinidad.'*"[98]

To make this argument, of course, requires demonstrating the continued survival and vitality of these nationalist tropes. Intellectual constructs, however deeply rooted in the collective imagination at a particular historical moment, are not eternal things. Rather, to live on and retain their power to shape perceptions and influence behavior, they must be kept alive and transmitted to new generations. This can occur in different ways—for example, through physical vectors of memory, including inherited texts, monuments, art, and established collective rituals, as well as through the ongoing efforts of human actors, who continually work to make past ideas and constructs relevant to the present. In post-1955 Argentina, the survival—and indeed revitalization—of the essentialist tropes of a true Argentina rooted in an enduring *ser nacional* was due to the emergence of a new wave of historical revisionism promoted by prominent intellectuals within the Peronist Resistance. It was through their writings, conferences, and public lectures that the project of historical revisionism, along with the essentialist tropes central to this antiliberal interpretation of the Argentine past, enjoyed a remarkable florescence in the post-1955 era.

## REVISIONISM AND ESSENTIALISM IN POST-1955
## PERONIST DISCOURSES

That historical revisionism would become central to the Peronist Resistance of the late 1950s and beyond was not inevitable. As noted in the previous chapter, during his first two terms in office, Perón had kept historical revisionism, and the nationalists who promoted this line of thinking, at arms length. Refusing to enter into the dispute, he famously (and pragmatically) proclaimed that he "had enough problems with the living to be concerned with the history of the dead."[99] Instead, the populist leader had maintained a somewhat ambiguous position vis-à-vis Argentina's liberal past, neither vilifying historical figures associated with nineteenth-century liberalism nor glorifying Rosas. But by 1957, the exiled Perón had switched course entirely. In his *Los vendepatria*, published that same year, he fully embraced the revisionist line, excoriating Rivadavia as a traitor and lauding Rosas as the heroic defender of Argentina from both its external and internal enemies.[100] This about face, as Mariano Plotkin has argued, can be seen as a strategic move by the exiled Perón, who sought to encourage the support of those nationalists who had allied with the resistance in Argentina.[101]

Perón's rejection of the liberal past and his new enthusiasm for Rosas became all the more necessary as more and more of his followers in Argentina began to tout revisionist ideas. This welling up of revisionist fervor can be explained by two factors. First, despite Perón's dismissive stance toward revisionism, it was clear that it had always mattered to many of his supporters. Now, in the leader's absence, these voices became more audible.[102] A second reason had to do with the Aramburu government's constant linking of Perón to the barbarism of Rosas, and its accompanying claim that the 1955 coup was analogous to the defeat of Rosas in 1852. For many Peronists who suffered under the new military regime, this linking of Rosas and Perón (to which they often added independence leader José de San Martín to form the slogan "San Martín-Rosas-Perón") was embraced as a badge of honor. As Michael Goebel has observed, "Peronist publications reacted to [the identification of Rosas with Perón], accepted it as true, but inverted its values" into something positive.[103] Thus within just a few years, revisionism became, in the words of Mariano Plotkin, "the official historiography of Peronism."[104]

Central to the spread of revisionist narratives—and of the essentialist tropes embedded in them—was a group of intellectuals from varied backgrounds, who became key figures in the Peronist Resistance. One cohort within this larger group consisted of former FORJA members: Arturo Jauretche, Atilio García Mellid, and Raúl Scalabrini Ortiz. Jauretche proved particularly influential and indeed during this era became one of Argentina's most prolific and widely read authors. Between 1960 and 1972, he published scores of articles and six books focusing on nationalist themes; all of the latter underwent numerous printings and some became instant bestsellers.[105] One of Jauretche's most important works, and one that became a foundational text for young militants, was his 1959 *Política nacional y revisionismo histórica* (National politics and historical revisionism). In this book, the former FORJA leader repeated themes that had been central to both right- and left-wing nationalist thought of the 1930s, reiterating for a new generation long-standing tropes that that pitted the vendepatria elite and its foreign masters against the supposedly true Argentina. Employing the essentialist notion of an enduring *ser nacional*, Jauretche insisted that the official version of Argentine history—that is, the one that celebrated liberal leaders such as Rivadavia, Sarmiento, Alberdi, and Mitre, was the work of minorities "unable to appreciate or understand the nature of 'our *ser*.'"[106] Psychologically and culturally divorced from the reality of their own country, the members of this elite had been dazzled by "theoretical conceptions" from abroad and, as a consequence, had "sought to impose [on the country] imported institutions, modes and schemes" that were alien to the country's true character.[107] This falsified, pro-liberal vision of Argentina's past, Jauretche maintained, had been encouraged by Great Britain, which sought to separate Argentines from their past, so they would accept the liberal economic structures that "accommodated" the country to Britain's "imperial schemes."[108] Accordingly, he affirmed, "The politics of [our] falsified history is, and was, the politics of the anti-nation, the negation of *el ser* [nacional] and of our own possibilities."[109]

Another former FORJA member who contributed to the new wave of historical revisionism was García Mellid. His 1957 *Proceso al liberalismo argentino* (Process of Argentine liberalism) employed traditional revisionist themes by lambasting the "official historiography" and its practitioners. According to García Mellid, liberal historians had ignored

what truly mattered—namely, "the preservation of the traditional essences that form the subsoil of the nationality." These "vernacular values,"
he maintained, had always stood in opposition to liberalism, an alien
ideology that had been used by the native oligarchy to "close off the
Catholic and Hispanic sources" of Argentine culture. Like Jauretche,
García Mellid linked this supposed attempt to destroy Argentina's authentic *ser nacional* to the hidden agendas of international capitalists
and their local allies, affirming that the imposition of liberalism was part
of the "implacable war of the oligarchy against the pueblo," and thus part
of a larger strategy to weaken the nation and transform it into a mere
factory.[110]

A final Forjista who contributed to this growing wave of revisionism
was Raúl Scalabrini Ortiz. Although he died in 1959, Scalabrini Ortiz's
revisionist works, which very clearly influenced the Argentines who
came of age in the 1960s, continued to be read and reread during the
1960s and the mid-1970s. Between 1957 and 1973, his *Política británica en
el Río de la Plata* (British policy in the Rio de la Plata) was issued at least
four times and his *Historia de los ferrocarriles argentinos* (History of Argentine railroads) was reprinted at least five times between 1958 and
1971. And although Scalabrini Ortiz's masterwork *El hombre que está solo*
did not directly treat nationalist themes, its essentialist vision of *argentinidad* continued to strike a chord with the reading public, with at least
five editions issued between 1964 and 1975.[111] (The fact that a favorite
gathering spot for young Peronists became the intersection of Esmeralda
Street and Corrientes Avenue—a spot made famous by *El hombre*—
suggests the importance of this work for the resistance.)[112]

Peronists who identified with Marxism also contributed heavily to
post-1955 revisionism and helped promote the essentialist tropes that
were central to this line of analysis. One of the most important intellectuals within this camp was Juan José Hernández Arregui, who, like
Jauretche, enjoyed his high water mark in the 1960s.[113] In his bestselling 1960 *Formación de la conciencia nacional* (The formation of the national conscience), for example, Hernández Arregui echoed the standard
nationalist conviction that the proliberal interpretation of the Argentine past was the product of a conspiracy between the vendepatria elite
and Argentina's imperialist exploiters. Since the nineteenth century, he
insisted, historical writing in Argentina had been "in essence the tool

of [foreign dominators] seeking to break the national spirit by hiding the historical truth."[114] Hernández Arregui was also deeply concerned about defining the national spirit, or *ser nacional*, that the official history had supposedly occluded. In 1963, he published another bestselling book titled *¿Qué es el ser nacional? la conciencia histórica iberoamericana* (What is the national being? The Iberoamerican historical conscience), which uncritically reproduced in its very title the essentialist notion of an enduring *ser nacional*.[115] In describing this (imagined) *ser*, Hernández Arregui signaled his partial agreement with right-wing nationalists by affirming that the "origins of '*el ser nacional*'" were rooted in the Hispanic or colonial period.

He added, however, that Argentine nationality also included a strong indigenous element.[116] In terms reminiscent of early twentieth-century cultural nationalist Ricardo Rojas (whom some revisionists saw as an early, albeit misguided interpreter of the authentic Argentina),[117] Hernández Arregui claimed that the native peoples had exercised a reciprocal influence on their conquerors, producing a new entity that was something new, something distinctively "American."[118] Moreover, the mixture of these two groups had created a people of "dark complexion," who provided the "foundational bloodline (*estirpe*) of the patria," and who continued to serve as the "unrecognized conductors" (*conductores incógnitos*) of the national culture or *ser nacional*.[119] So tough and resilient was this culture, Hernández Arregui believed, that it was impossible to kill. Comparing this enduring culture to a persistent plant, he proclaimed that, despite the efforts of the vendepatria elite, *el ser nacional* remained "coiled up in the pueblo like the yuyo weeds found in the countryside." What's more, he continued, "One can clean and clear the land, one can cover it with bricks, but after a time, coming up between the slabs, will be the dogged, long suffering and humble wild thicket [of Argentina's true essence]."[120]

Another key Peronist who embraced Marxism and joined in this revisionist effort was Jorge Abelardo Ramos. Following the standard revisionist line, Abelardo Ramos was a harsh critic of the nineteenth-century "antinational" liberal oligarchy based in Buenos Aires.[121] This oligarchy, which he referred to as Unitarians of "frac" (referring to the English-styled frock coat) "knew London and Paris, but had never placed a foot in [the interior provinces of ] Córdoba or La Rioja." This ignorance of the realities of the provinces, coupled with its admiration for Great Britain's ideology of "free trade," Abelardo Ramos charged, had led the oligarchy to impose disastrous trade policies that had ruined the productive capacity of the interior. As a result, the inhabitants had been reduced to misery and transformed into "a simple market for English-made ponchos."[122] Like many Peronist revisionists with Marxist inclinations, Abelardo Ramos declined to celebrate Rosas, whom, he believed, had placed the interests of the pro-free trade cattle-ranching class above those of the nation as a whole.[123] In his view, it was only in those interior provinces, which had isolated themselves from international markets and organized their economies around "nationalist" or "protectionist" policies, that the true Argentina was allowed to emerge. Thus for Abelardo Ramos, the country's interior was the "center (*foco*) of genuine [Argentine] nationalism," and the only true nationalists were the Federalist caudillos of the provinces, such as Facundo.[124]

A final subset of Peronists devoted to historical revisionism either came from religious backgrounds or had been associated with the nationalist right, such as José Maria Rosa and Fermín Chávez. In contrast to many of his fellow Peronists from left-wing backgrounds, Rosa lauded Rosas as a nationalist hero, who had defended the country against European imperialism and the antinational liberalism of the Unitarians. Just as important, he insisted, was the fact that Rosas was able to understand and connect with the common people, who, in his view, formed the bedrock of Argentine nationality. Employing a long established nationalist trope, Rosa promoted the notion of the "two conceptions of *argentinidad*." One, of course, was the *argentinidad* of liberal elites, who had sought to impose on Argentines a version of European "civilization" in the form of the 1853 Constitution and free market capitalism. The other was the real or invisible Argentina, that of "the immense majority of Argentines." Echoing essentialist understandings of nationality that could easily have been uttered by the early twentieth-century cultural nationalists, Rosa proclaimed the true Argentina was "something real and alive" that had its "own modalities, manner of feeling and thinking," which gave the nation its own distinctive character. This nationality, he affirmed was not in "legal forms (*digestos*) but rather in the people (los hombres) and the things of the land."[125]

Former seminarian Fermín Chávez was another important contributor to historical revisionism from a right-wing background. His 1955 *Civilización y barbarie en la historia de la cultura argentina*, an obvious play on Sarmiento's famous dichotomy, was one of the first revisionists works to appear after Perón's ouster. In this book, Chávez predictably lambasted Argentina's nineteenth-century liberal intellectuals for having "turned their backs on the real Argentina," and for having introduced a sinister ideology that was "not only alien to *el ser nacional*" but also prejudicial to the spiritual health of the pueblo.[126] Embracing the familiar trope of the two Argentinas, Chávez described Argentina's primary problem as first and foremost one of a disconnect between the "real country" and the "formal" country, that is the codes and constitutions produced by the liberal elite.[127] Quoting the words of Saúl Taborda, a provincial nationalist active during the 1930s, Chávez proclaimed the need to develop political institutions "in accordance with the character or *índole* of the nation, of the preexisting nation from the interior of its ethnos (*en las entrañas de sus ethnos*)."[128]

Chávez was also centrally concerned with defining *el ser nacional*, which he saw as the basis of the Argentine character.[129] Arguing that "nothing is created ex nihilo," he criticized the liberal view that Argentina could be defined by its political institutions and that the state should seek to build a sense of shared nationality through patriotic education.[130] The nation, he affirmed, did not need to be created or even solidified, because Argentina's existence predated the break with Spain. Thus what held Argentines together and made them a people was not their shared political values or allegiances but an underlying tradition that "imprinted us with a seal that was peculiar to our physiognomy."[131] For Chávez, the content of this *ser nacional* was clearly Spanish, which he believed provided the original and enduring matrix of Argentine identity.[132] Significantly, however, he identified Argentina not with the Spain of the Counter-Reformation but with the tradition of humanism that he believed ran through Spanish history like "a golden thread."[133] Accordingly, Chávez affirmed, Argentina's war of independence was neither anti-Spanish nor animated by "recently and only superficially acquired ideas from foreign political thinkers" (i.e., liberalism). Rather, the impulse for independence was "the expression of the essence of the deepest sentiments of the race."[134]

As is evident, the intellectuals who authored the explosion of revisionist texts during the late 1950s and 1960s had come to Peronism through different routes and at different points in their lives. What united them was their intense feelings of nationalism, anti-liberalism, and anti-imperialism, and the belief that Peronism, and Perón himself, offered the best chance for a fundamental reordering of Argentine politics and the economy along nationalist lines. Some, such as Abelardo Ramos and Hernández Arregui, believed Peronism and Marxism to be compatible and hoped that Perón's return meant a socialist revolution. Others, such as Jauretche, García Mellid, Rosa, and Chávez were less enthusiastic about Marxism, although even Chávez—perhaps the most conservative of the revisionists—affirmed that Marxism itself was nothing to fear. The important thing, he believed, was to have a revolution based on popular, nationalist principles.[135]

What also united them, of course, was the way in which their revisionist works recycled long-standing essentialist tropes about the very nature of Argentine nationality, and how they used these tropes to delegitimize liberalism and pluralism in all their forms. While they differed on their views of Rosas, common to all was the uncritical acceptance of the idea of a true, enduring Argentina that was rooted in *el ser nacional* and existed in opposition to the false Argentina of the liberal, vendepatria elite. What's more, the revisionists believed this dichotomy ran through all of Argentine history and explained present-day conflicts. Such reasoning, of course, entailed reducing a complex national history to a simplistic, dichotomous struggle between the patria and the antipatria, leading the revisionists to interpret modern conflicts and problems as mere reiterations of the nineteenth-century conflicts between Unitarians and Federalists. The new Peronist revisionism proved to be much more than an intellectual exercise. As subsequent developments would make clear, the revisionists' interpretation of Argentine history—and the essentialist understandings of national identity they employed—would have an enormous impact on a new generation of activists.

TEN

# From Revisionism to Revolution
# and Repression

In the turbulent decade of the 1960s, the Peronist Resistance gained unexpected strength when it captured the imagination of middle-class
youth, who saw in Perón a route to a more just future. During the 1940s
and '50s, Argentina's educated sectors had largely shunned Peronism,
seeing it as authoritarian, antiliberal, and hostile to their own aspirations.
Although a variety of Peronist youth organizations formed in the 1950s,
the majority of high school and university students strongly opposed the
regime.[1] Those who entered adolescence in the 1960s, however, adopted
a very different stance. Too young to have memories of Perón's years in
power, and caught up in the new currents of nationalism and anti-
imperialism then sweeping Latin America, large numbers of young
people came to see Peronism as the country's best hope in the fight
against imperialism and social injustice.

Because historical revisionism had become integral to the Peronist
Resistance, this antiliberal interpretation of the Argentine past also
gained greater currency. As Juan Alberto Bozza has observed, during the
1960s, "the discourses, language and symbolism" of historical revisionism

came to permeate broad swaths of popular culture, including publishing, mass media, and film.[2] Through the writings and advocacy of the Peronist revisionists, almost all of whom remained active until the 1970s, what had been a set of ideas embraced by a small circle of nationalists now became broadly accepted. Indeed, so hegemonic did this way of thinking about the past become that it achieved the status of common-sense for a generation of Argentines. By the end of the decade, as historian Halperin Donghi noted, "the work of historical revisionism [could be] considered complete; the intellectual movement that it has promoted has achieved an unexpected triumph."[3]

In addition to upending traditional liberal interpretations of the past that celebrated the contributions of such men as Alberdi, Sarmiento, Mitre, and Echeverría, revisionism's growing acceptance also served to spread and naturalize essentialist understandings of Argentine nationality. Revisionists, of course, were not just attacking the statesmen of the nineteenth century for their flawed economic policies. Rather, they were also promoting a set of long-standing tropes about the nature of *argentinidad* that portrayed these men as agents of the antipatria and liberalism as an alien philosophy at odds with Argentina's true, enduring national essence. Such notions, then, came to form central elements of the young Peronists' worldview, and provided them with a common framework for interpreting both the past and the challenges of the present.

This is not to claim, of course, that these constructs in and of themselves radicalized this generation. These were radical times throughout the Western world, and many people throughout Latin America— including in Argentina—decided to risk their lives for a socialist revolution without resorting to essentialist thinking. But what these constructs *did* do was provide these mostly urban youth with a narrative that allowed them to place their actions within an imagined arc of Argentine history: that is, to see themselves as the defenders of the true Argentina and the modern-day torchbearers of a struggle that had begun almost a century and a half earlier. And because revisionist narratives had gained such broad acceptance within the public at large, the militants' story, and the tropes and imagery they employed, rang true to other sectors of Argentine society.

## ESSENTIALISM AND PERONIST GUERRILLAS

It is, of course, difficult to quantify the power of intellectual constructs and to determine with any degree of certainty their role in shaping behavior. At the same time, a comparison of the fortunes of the Peronist Montoneros, which eventually absorbed almost all other Peronist guerrilla groups, and those of non-Peronist guerrilla groups, is suggestive. As is well known, the guerrilla organizations that burst on the national scene during the late 1960s fell into two broad camps: Peronist and non-Peronist. Among the latter, the most important groups to appear during these years were the Revolutionary Army of the People (ERP) and the Fuerzas Armadas de Liberación (FAL), with the latter merging into the ERP in 1972.[4] Formally established in 1970 to serve as the armed branch of the Trotskyite Revolutionary Workers Party, the ERP drew its primary inspiration from the Cuban Revolution.

Belonging to the second camp, and the ones that interest us here, were the various guerrilla groups associated with Peronism. Certainly, there was a degree of overlap between the Peronists and non-Peronists. After 1959, any young person in Latin America who joined a guerrilla organization, whatever its particular orientation, could not escape the influence of the Cuban Revolution. The images of Castro's triumphal march into Havana, strikingly photographed and widely disseminated, inevitably formed part of this generation's shared mental landscape. Potent too, was the example of the Argentine-born Che Guevara, whose theories of guerrilla warfare made him an inspiration for all those who took up arms in the name of socialism. And both Peronists and non-Peronist guerrillas, of course, believed that socialism was the only option for freeing Argentina from the chains of imperialism and for creating a more just society.

But despite their common goals, the differences between these two camps were evident to both the military and the wider public. As Daniel Lutzky has noted, these groups drew from different "representations" and "myths" to explain themselves and to legitimize their use of violence.[5] According to Lutzky, in the discourses of Argentina's non-Peronist guerrillas, "the national theme didn't appear." Instead, "the themes of the social [question] and of armed struggle occupied the center of analysis."[6]

The Peronist left, in contrast, drew inspiration from a different set of images. Claudia Hilb has argued that one of the key characteristics of the new Peronist left was its "authoritarian thought" and their insistence on "the non-division, of the oneness" (*unicidad*) of the nation. In her words, for the nationalist left of these years, "Power [was] the emanation of an essence: the Patria, the Nation, the Pueblo. This essence is one and indivisible; Power identifies with the essence. Social divisions are not thinkable in terms other than exclusion: anti-Pueblo, anti-Patria, anti-Nation."[7] The Argentine military also made a distinction between the two guerrilla camps. Jorge Rafael Videla, leader of the military junta that took power in 1976, related how he and his colleagues viewed the non-Peronist ERP as more threatening because they believed it emerged from foreign influences. According to Videla, "By virtue of its ideological and military preparation, the ERP was more of an enemy than the Montoneros; it was something foreign (*ajeno*)." "It was," he continued, "something else, without a sense of the national." The military, in contrast, saw the Montoneros as homegrown, and therefore less dangerous. For Videla, the group "conserved elements of the nationalism, Catholicism and Peronism from which it had emerged. From the very start, the nationalism of the Montoneros was a given."[8] The Argentine public, especially youth, also seemed to make this distinction. In contrast to the non-Peronist ERP, which continued to be composed of isolated fighting units, it was the Peronist Montoneros (and the Peronist groups it absorbed) that captured the imagination of the younger generation. Claiming to represent a distinctly Argentine path to socialism via Peronism, the Montoneros' broad appeal was made clear by its ability to summon hundreds of thousands of young sympathizers into the streets. Thus, as Tulio Halperin Donghi has observed, it was the Montoneros, not the non-Peronist ERP, that "promised for the first time to naturalize a radical left-wing current in the unpromising soil of Argentine politics."[9]

The Montoneros' unprecedented ability to mobilize such numbers suggests that its leaders were tapping into a widely held set of ideas, sentiments, and understandings that proved more powerful than the non-Peronist guerrillas' more abstract appeals to social justice and anti-imperialism. A useful example of this new Peronist generation's rhetoric is the manifesto *Nacionalismo o guerra civil. Análisis del proceso revolucionary* (Nationalism or civil war, analysis of the revolutionary process), published in pamphlet form by the Centro de Cultura Nacional "José Hernández."[10] To be sure, the document's exact relationship to the Montoneros is unclear. Penned by individuals claiming to represent the "Movimiento Nacional Peronista" (national Peronist movement), *Nacionalismo o guerra civil* is undated, although the curators of the digital archive Ruinas Digitales have established its year of publication as 1967.[11] The curators have also placed it within a digital file labeled "Documentos Montoneros," reflecting their belief that the anonymous authors were part of the group that would later become the Montoneros.

Despite this uncertainty, *Nacionalismo o guerra civil* is useful precisely because of its generic quality, in that it could have been produced by any number of left-leaning Peronist groups of the 1960s. Laden with ideas and images that would have been instantly familiar to both right- and left-wing nationalists of the 1930s and 1940s, and which had by the 1960s become widely accepted by large swaths of the population, the document begins by proclaiming that Argentina's historical development had been defined by the conflict between "national currents" and "anti-national currents." Those who had championed *"lo nacional,"* of course, were San Martín, Rosas, and Perón.[12] The tropes of the "real country" and *"el ser nacional"* also appear. In a section celebrating the revisionist work of Hernández Arregui, Rodolfo Puiggrós, Jauretche, Scalabrini Ortiz, and José María Rosa, for example, the pamphlet's authors laud these men as having understood the "necessities of the real country."[13] The phrase *el ser nacional* is mentioned twice, first in a description of the events of October 17, 1945, when *el Ser Nacional* had made itself evident through the masses that had flooded into Buenos Aires, and again when the author(s) express confidence that *el Ser nacional* would eventually make evident what course of action to take.[14] A final important trope is that of the patria/antipatria. Affirming that "the national doesn't exist outside of Perón," the document warns that those who are "anti-Peron" are "the final residual of the antipatria."[15]

Regardless of whether the document's authors were indeed Montoneros, the admiration it expresses for revisionist thinkers was clearly echoed by the organization's leadership. Montonero leader Roberto Perdía, for example, described how historical revisionism had "inundated" the political discussions of his generation, noting especially the importance of works by Juan José Hernández Arregui, Arturo Jauretche,

Rodolfo Ortega Peña y Eduardo Luis Duhalde, Jorge Abelardo Ramos, José María Rosa, and Rodolfo Puiggrós.[16] Montonero journalist Raúl Cuestas also emphasized the continuities between the Montoneros and earlier left-wing nationalists, citing Raúl Scalabrini Ortiz, John William Cooke, Rodolfo Puiggrós, Juan Hernández Arregui, and Arturo Jauretche as inspirations for the group.[17]

The document's revisionist themes were also clearly central to Montonero ideology and self-legitimization. The group's founders, for example, chose the name Montonero to signal what they believed to be their link to the popular resistance struggles of the past. A now-famous 1970 manifesto published in the left-wing magazine *Cristianismo y Revolución* made this connection clear. From the beginning, the leadership affirmed, they had identified themselves as Peronists and Montoneros, and in doing so were also identifying with a long history of popular struggle. "We do not believe" the manifesto proclaims, that "the popular struggles began with us. Rather, we feel ourselves to be part of the latest synthesis of a historical process that took off 160 years ago, and that with its advances and retreats experienced a definitive leap after October 17, 1945." Continuing, the document affirms that "this national and popular current was expressed as much in 1810 as in 1945, as in all the battles of San Martín's army and of the montonero gauchos of the past century, in the heroic struggles of those immigrants who gave their lives in the early days of our labor movement, and in the Yrigoyenist nationalism. It was in this way, through these struggles, that the Argentine pueblo has been writing in stages its true history."[18] In similar terms, Montonero leader Mario Firmenich drew a direct line between past and present, presenting a century of history as a continual struggle between the patria and the antipatria. "We are," he claimed, "Montoneros, Federalists, Yrigoyenists and Peronists, and for this reason we are the enemies of the Unitarians, the conservatives and the gorilas."[19]

Other individuals and groups within left-wing revolutionary Peronism echoed these revisionist themes. Peronist politician Héctor Cámpora, who occupied the Argentine presidency from May to July of 1973, and who enjoyed close ties with the Montoneros, described Peronism in similar terms. The present struggle, he affirmed, was but a "marvelous stage in the pueblo's fight against colonialism and oppression." It is, he continued, "the historical continuity of the actions of Independence, and the affirmation of the most pure values of this land."[20] An anonymous contributor to *Cristianismo y Revolución* echoed these sentiments, proclaiming that "Peronism is the historical continuation of our independence patriots . . . of the caudillos and gauchos Montoneros from Rosas to el Chacho and Felipe Varela, who defended the integrity of the Nation and fought against the all powerful merchant oligarchy of Buenos Aires."[21]

The Peronist guerrillas also fully embraced the nationalist trope of the two Argentinas: one liberal, official, and false and the other antiliberal, popular, and authentic. According to the Montoneros, throughout Argentine history there were "two great political currents: on one side was the liberal *Oligarquía*, that was clearly anti-national and vendepatria, on the other side was the *Pueblo* identified with the defense of its interests that are the interests of the Nation."[22] Former Montonero Ignacio Vélez Carreras described Argentina's historical conflicts in similar terms, arguing that in those years "Argentina's principal contradiction was defined as the confrontation between the pueblo/anti-pueblo that had been manifested throughout the history of our country."[23] References to the "real" Argentina and its "real" history also occurred. Looking back on his activism in the Peronist left, which included participation in the Movimiento Nacionalista Revolucionaria Tacuara and the Fuerzas Armadas Peronistas, Carlos Arbelos suggested that one gain of those years was the creation of a new consciousness about Argentina's true founding fathers, including Rosas, Facundo Quiroga, and others, who had fought for the nation's sovereignty against foreign exploitation. Such figures, he maintained, were "much more rooted in the real Argentina" than those celebrated in the official history promoted by the imperial powers.[24]

Peronist guerrillas also embraced the view, central to the nationalist left, that the Argentine masses were the bearers of the nation's authentic culture. In keeping with this belief, the magazine *Militancia* proclaimed culture to be an "element of liberation," as long as it was generated by the pueblo. Argentina's true popular culture, it continued, had been marginalized by the liberal economic model imposed after Perón's ouster. To remedy this situation, it called for the establishment of new "Centers of Cultural Mobilization" that would reverse this tendency.[25] Not surprisingly, the Peronist left of the 1960s and '70s often identified this authentic popular culture with the rural, rather than urban, masses. In a review of a new feature film about the nineteenth-century outlaw gaucho Juan Moreira, for example, a contributor to *Militancia* praised the director for helping to launch a new kind of cinema "profoundly rooted in our soil." Just as importantly, the critic enthused, in making a film about Moreira the filmmakers had "given a citizenship card to our true identity." This true identity, he continued, "had remained intact in the bowels (*entrañas*) of the pueblo," despite attempts by hostile interests to "asphyxiate" it.[26] This belief that Argentina's traditional rural culture must be recuperated was also evident in an increasing interest in more "authentic" forms of entertainment. Like the youth of right-wing nationalist groups, the Peronist left organized traditional bonfires, musical gatherings, and festivals featuring guitars and other traditional instruments. In doing so, according to Montonero leader Roberto Perdía, middle-class youth, who had long taken their cultural cues from Europe and the United States, became acquainted with their own national culture and came to revalue what "the official culture had systematically displaced."[27]

Finally, like the nationalist left of the 1930s and '40s, and Perón himself, the Peronist revolutionaries of these years saw themselves and the "people," in whose name they fought, as the only legitimate members of the national community. Within their deeply polarized vision of the world, there was only the "patria" and the "antipatria"—that is, the vendepatria oligarchy and their imperialist masters.[28] Not surprisingly, then, the guerrillas insisted that their movement was consubstantial with the nation itself. Quoting Eva Perón, whom they revered, they proclaimed that "we (Peronists) are the Pueblo . . . and we are invincible because we are the Patria itself."[29] This exclusivity continued, albeit in a somewhat attenuated form, even after the definitive defeat of the guerrilla movement. In a 1982 interview, exiled Montonero leader Mario Firmenich affirmed that "the national unity cannot be with all Argentines, it cannot include the oligarchy."[30]

## THE PERONIST RIGHT

While it was the left-wing Peronist guerrilla groups that seized the Argentine public's imagination during the 1960s, these were also years of

ferment within the Peronist right. Scholars have noted the relative difficulty of studying this segment of the Peronist Resistance. In contrast to
the many survivors of the militant left, who have published memoirs and
have publicly spoken of their experiences, those who were active within
the Peronist right have remained largely silent.[31] The generalized (and
sometimes unfounded) assumption that all those active within the right
participated in the notorious Peronist death squad known as the Triple
A (Argentine Anti-communist Alliance), or helped the military after the
coup, has meant there had been little sympathy for, or interest in, recon-
structing the mental world of this segment of Peronism.[32] And while
there are still many Argentines who look back with on the 1960s with at
least some nostalgia for a time when young men and women on the left
risked their lives to bring about a more just social order, no whiff of the
heroic surrounds the memory of the right.

When examining this segment of Peronism, it is first important to
keep in mind that the men and women who were active in its various
groups and publications did not *see* themselves as right wing. Rather,
they saw themselves as the authentic, or "orthodox," Peronists, who—
like the early Perón—were adamant anti-Communists and identified
with his call for a "Third Way" between unfettered capitalism and godless communism. Accordingly, much of their energy was directed at defending the supposedly true Peronism against what they saw as Marxist
infiltrators.[33] In the words of Pedro Eladio Vásquez, a prominent activist
within the Peronist right (who did indeed participate in the Triple A),
"There is neither a Peronism of the left nor a Peronism of the right.
There is only one Justicialista (that is, Peronist) doctrine that has been
written with the pen of Perón and with the blood of the Argentine
pueblo."[34] This sentiment appeared repeatedly in the right-wing weekly
publication *Retorno*, which frequently proclaimed that "the Peronist
Movement is incompatible with Marxism" and, touting the Third Position, insisted that they (that is, the so-called Peronist right) were "not
Yankees, not Marxists [but] Peronists!"[35]

It is not difficult to understand why members of the non-Marxist
sectors of the Peronist Resistance, who continued to embrace the traditional Peronist idea that Argentina should pursue a "third way" to modernity, came to believe that their movement had been hijacked by
leftists. This was especially true given the Peronist left's great admiration

for the Cuban Revolution, and the fact that many guerrilla leaders had spent time training in Cuba. At the same time, it is undeniable that many the members of the Peronist right were deeply racist. Like the traditional nationalist right from which they drew, activists within this strand of Peronism embraced the essentialist ideal of the true Argentina as a unitary ethno-cultural community, whose identity was rooted in an enduring *ser nacional* and that was by definition Catholic and Hispanic. This meant that individuals from other ethnicities or religious faiths could never belong to the true Argentina but would always be outsiders, who at best were tolerated and, at worst, persecuted. Accordingly, in their view, it was the duty of patriotic Argentines to defend the true nation against the threat of cultural and ideological contamination, a duty that went hand-in-hand with defending the country's economic sovereignty.

The Peronist right's highly exclusionary definition of Argentine identity also meant that the nation it imagined had a long list of enemies, including liberals, Marxists, and all non-Catholics, especially Jews. Anti-Semitism, of course, had always been a feature of right-wing nationalism. But during Perón's years in office, Peronists who adhered to this strand of nationalism had been forced to keep such views largely private or risk running afoul of their leader's more inclusive vision. Recall, for example, that in 1953, Perón had intervened in the Peronist-allied Alianza Libertadora Nacionalista, forcing out the deeply anti-Semitic Juan Queraltó and replacing him with the more ecumenical Patricio Kelly. But with Perón in exile, anti-Semites within the Peronist Resistance gained a new freedom to express their bigotry. Events in 1960 only reinforced this tendency. In May of that year, Israeli special forces entered Argentina and spirited away the notorious Nazi war criminal Adolf Eichmann. Because of the secret nature of the operation and Israel's decision not to ask for official extradition, many within Argentina saw this action as an affront to national sovereignty. The "kidnapping," as it was referred to in the press, unleased a wave of anti-Semitism, which included increased violence against the Jewish community.

This increased anti-Semitism served to embolden the most reactionary elements of the Peronist right. In 1964, for example, Peronist deputy Juan Cornejo Linares asked Congress to establish an "Interparliamentary Commission on Anti-Argentine Activities," with the aim of exposing the existence of a "dangerous Zionist/Communist conspiracy" that supposedly threatened "the real essence of our nationality."[36] Two years later, Cornejo Linares continued his attacks on Jews in his book *El nuevo orden sionista en la Argentina* (The new Zionist order in Argentina; published by Tacuara), which continued to warn against Zionism's nefarious plans for world domination. Raúl Jassén, a former member of the ALN and frequent contributor to the right-wing Peronist publications of the period, also warned against the Zionist threat, suggesting that Jews were especially interested in Argentina because they believed that massive immigration had created a society without a national identity. Criticizing the "Zionist thesis" of Argentine pluralism, he rejected what he believed to be Zionists' claim that Argentines lacked "common bonds of culture, language, morality, religion, traditions and tellurism (*unidad telúrica*)."[37]

In the mid-1960s, anti-Semitism and anti-Zionism became folded into the new preoccupation with *Sinarquía*, a supposed world-wide conspiracy perpetrated by the United States, USSR, Jews, freemasons, liberals, and the post-Concilar Catholic Church. Fundamentally, Sinarquísts were believed to be members of a secret society that sought to achieve world domination by erasing national communities and replacing their states with a single world government. The concept of Sinarquía was introduced in Argentina largely through the efforts of Carlos Alberto Disandro, a philologist and theologian, who as a young man had participated in the Cursos de Cultural Católica. In 1946, Disandro joined the faculty of the University of La Plata, where he was part of a group of young Catholics who openly supported Perón. After the 1955 coup, he was forced out of his university post; in 1958, he founded the right-wing Concentración Nacional Universitaria (national university concentration, or CNU). In the 1960s, the CNU would become integrated into the right wing of the Peronist Resistance. According to historian Juan Ladeuix, Disandro's belief that nations were enduring entities that existed apart from, and were superior to, the political institutions of the state was central to his support for Peronism. Argentina under Peronism, Disandro believed, represented a distinctive case in which the state/nation divide had been overcome. In his view, the Peronist state had grown organically out of Argentina's own traditions, and thus provided a form of political organization that could protect the true nation or *argentinidad* from "the sinister forces of Sinarquía."[38] Once introduced,

Sinarquía became a central part of right-wing Peronist thought, gaining currency among the broader Argentine right during the mid-1960s.

On the political level, during the latter half of the 1960s the Peronist right drew increasingly close to the trade union faction of the movement, the so-called *blandas*. United by their shared hatred of communism and their hostility toward what they saw as the "Marxist infiltrators" of the Peronist movement, together they would claim to be the champions of the real Peronism. The Peronist right also developed a bond with Isabel Perón, who spent nine months in Argentina in 1965 on Perón's behalf. During that time, several figures within the Peronist right served on her security detail. In stark contrast to the Peronist left, who worshipped the memory of Eva Perón and disdained Perón's third wife, most members of the Peronist right defended Isabel and supported placing her name on the vice presidential ballot. They embraced as well the principle of "verticalism," meaning that they believed Perón should rule the party and the country, and their role was to follow orders.

What was Perón's position vis-à-vis his increasingly fractured following? From the beginning of his long exile, Perón had sought to maintain control of the movement and create the conditions for his return by practicing a cynical ecumenicalism. Youth, he hoped, would play a central role in forcing the military to allow his return. To that end, he assiduously courted the new left-leaning Peronist organizations that sprang up in the 1960s, doing nothing to disabuse his youthful followers of their conviction that his return would be the first step toward the construction of the "Patria Socialista." While his own signals on socialism remained ambiguous, as Mariano Plotkin has noted, "Far from discouraging [this pro-socialist] reading of his 'doctrine,' he encouraged it."[39] Perón also emphasized his contribution to the emerging Third World movement, despite the fact that he had not actually played a role in its formation. Still, he reminded his Argentine followers that as early as the 1940s he had proclaimed the need to stake out a third position between capitalism and communism. He encouraged as well the use of violence as a tactic, referring to the guerrilla groups as "special formations" of Peronism.[40] At the same time, Perón also maintained contact with key members of the Peronist right, which he believed would provide a counterweight to the left. In particular, he was careful to maintain a warm correspondence with such figures as Cornejo Linares and Carlos

Disandro, writing both to praise their anti-Semitic books.[41] Confident in his abilities to balance these forces, Perón believed himself to be the consummate puppet master, able to activate and restrain his followers at will. He would turn out to be very wrong.

Perón's long-distance machinations would likely have been for naught if Argentina's military government had not lost control of the country on its own. In 1969, the Onganía regime faced its worst crisis when a labor dispute in the city of Córdoba turned into a multiday riot that came to be known as the "Cordobazo." From that moment on, Córdoba was ungovernable, and the events of 1969 became a turning point for the country as a whole. Elsewhere, escalating violence—including targeted bombings, kidnappings, bank robberies, and attacks on military installations—increased dramatically. In late May 1970, the Montoneros made their presence known with their first public action: the kidnapping of General Pedro Eugenio Aramburu. After subjecting him to a "peoples' trial," the guerrillas executed the former president. This was only the beginning of what would be a spectacular series of actions by the Montoneros and other guerrilla groups, both Peronist and non-Peronist. Unable to control the violence, the military began to search for an electoral exit from power. Shortly after assuming the presidency in March 1971, General Alejandro Lanusse started negotiations with the exiled Perón to find a solution that would restore order. The "Grand Accord" as it was called, stipulated that the 77-year-old Perón would be allowed to return to Argentina, and elections would be scheduled. Under the agreement, Peronists could field candidates, but Perón himself would not be allowed to run.

The prospect of Perón's return electrified the nation, but it also exposed the long-standing fissures within the Peronist Party. Although there had long been tension between the right- and left-wing sectors of the party, the stark conflicts between the Peronists and non-Peronists, and between the intransigent "duras" and the accommodationist "blandas," meant that the left and right had coexisted largely without violence. However, when it became clear that Perón would indeed return, the left-right divide suddenly took on new significance. In January of 1972, this schism was thrown into sharp relief when the Consejo Provisorio de la Juventud Peronista (provisional council of the Peronist Youth) distinguished between what it called the *Tendencia Revolucionaria* (revolutionary tendency), made up of those groups that supported armed struggle, and those that did not.[42]

It would be the run-up to the March 11, 1973, presidential elections, Juan Besoky has convincingly argued, that marked the definitive breakup of Perón's highly divided movement.[43] Against the wishes of the right-wing sectors of the party and the unionist leaders, Perón chose as the party's presidential candidate Héctor Cámpora, a long-time Peronist, whose two sons were active in the Peronist Youth and who had close ties to the Montoneros. Perón also appointed as head of the Peronist Youth the left-wing Rodolfo Galimberti, who interacted closely with the Montoneros and would later become an important figure within the organization. To further seal the deal with the left, Perón appointed as the new general head of the Justicialista Party Juan Abal Medina, who—although he had originally been part of the *Azul y Blanco* group—had moved leftward after the death of his Montonero brother Fernando Abal Medina. Serving to increase tensions further was Perón's insistence that the party present a unified front by offering a single candidate for each office, leading to pitched battles over who would appear on the electoral slate.

Cámpora's electoral victory only intensified divisions between the left-wing Tendencia and what would become known as the *Ortodoxos* (orthodox ones), or right-wing sector of the movement. Having campaigned with the understanding that Perón would soon take his place, Cámpora acquiesced to the exiled leader's insistence that the new government accommodate both sectors of the party. At Perón's direction, the newly elected president placed the Ministry of Labor in the hands of long-time unionist Ricardo Otero and appointed the right-wing José López Rega to lead the powerful Ministry of Social Welfare. López Rega, a secretive man with a long-time interest in the occult, had met Isabel Perón in 1965 and had since wormed his way into Perón's inner circle. After Perón's return to Argentina, he would play a key role in organizing the repression. For its part, the Peronist left gained control of the University of Buenos Aires, when Cámpora appointed Marxist Rodolfo Puiggrós to the rectorship. Puiggrós delivered his address surrounded by Rodolfo Galimberti, Montonero leader Mario Firmenich, and Juan Abal Medina.[44]

As this polarization deepened, Peronism became increasingly structured around the left/right divide. New groups emerged within the

Orthodox sector, including the Juventud Peronista de la República Argentina (Peronist Youth of the Republic of Argentina, or JPRA) and the Juventud Sindicalista Peronista (Sindicalist Peronist Youth), which was directly linked to the trade unions. The ALN even reappeared, once again under the leadership of the wildly anti-Semitic Juan Queraltó. But despite the very clear divide between right and left, it is important to keep in mind, as Juan Besoky reminds us, that the right itself was heterogeneous and included both long-time Peronists who sought to distance themselves from the radical left, and individuals from the ultraright, who were ferociously anticommunist and anti-Semitic.[45] It is from this latter group that the intraparty violence would come.

It would not take long. On June 20, 1973, Perón was scheduled to arrive at Ezeiza International airport, located on the outskirts of Buenos Aires. In an area set up for Perón to address his followers, the Montoneros sought to occupy the section closest to the podium. Perón's "security detail," composed of various groups within the Peronist right—trade unionist gangs, the JPRA, the Comando de Organización, Agrupación Peronista 20 de Noviembre, and the Concentración Nacional Universitaria, the Comando de Orientación Revolucionaria, and the ALN—opened fired on a column of the Montoneros. At least thirteen people died, and hundreds were wounded. The message was clear. In the words of historian Hernán Merele, Ezeiza "marked the beginning of an offensive by the orthodox sectors to recuperate the spaces of power they had lost to the Tendencia."[46] For Perón, it was a shocking return from a long exile. Incensed, the newly arrived former president gave a speech that laid the blame on the party's left wing. Calling for actions to be taken against the "enemies" of Peronism, he warned against those who were seeking to co-opt the movement.[47] In mid-July, Cámpora and his vice president were forced to resign, so that new elections could be called in October. In the months that followed, violence increased dramatically. Then, in a bold and bloody move, the Montoneros assassinated José Ignacio Rucci, the secretary general of the Confederación General del Trabajo, just a few days before Perón won his third term in office.

Rucci's murder outraged both Perón and all of Orthodox Peronism. Subsequent days witnessed a wave of violence targeting the left and the beginnings of a purge or process of "ideological purification" of the movement as a whole.[48] In a document signed by Perón, which was sent

to the provincial party leaders and published in the press, Perón denounced the killing of Rucci and what he described as the Marxist infiltration of the movement. To combat these elements, he called on Peronist
organizations to actively fight the "Marxist enemy" with "all the methods considered efficient, in each place and each opportunity." In addition,
he announced the start of a campaign to clarify the differences between
Peronism and Marxism.[49] It was also after Rucci's murder that Perón
took steps to carry out semi-clandestine operations to murder, in a targeted way, left-wing militants from his own party responsible for the
violence. He looked to López Rega to carry out the task.

### THE TRIPLE A AND THE DEFENSE OF *EL SER NACIONAL*

The Triple A began as a somewhat amorphous security group within
López Rega's Ministry of Social Welfare. According to historian Paul
Lewis, because the ministry was also in charge of combatting the drug
trade, it received US government loans to purchase weapons. It also received generous funding from the ministry itself, along with clandestine
donations of light arms from right-wing nationalist officers within the
military.[50] Over time, the Triple A grew to include retired military officers and policemen, as well as recruits from civilian groups within Peronism's right wing, such as the CNU, the JPRA, the ALN, and the CdO,
Juventud Sindical and the Agrupación 20 de Noviembre (the 20th of
November group).[51] The Triple A's extralegal killings were something
new in Argentina, in terms of both their scale and their brutality. Under
the orders of López Rega, small bands of operatives would kidnap individuals and take them to clandestine detention centers or even to the
Ministry of Social Welfare. There, members of the police would question
and torture their victims before executing them.

The unofficial mouthpiece of the Triple A (and more generally of
the Peronist ultra right) was the weekly publication *El Caudillo de la Tercera Posición* (The caudillo of the third position).[52] Funded by López
Rega, with support from the Metal Worker's Union, the publication first
appeared on November 16, 1973, five days before the Triple A's first public
action. *El Caudillo*'s only known contributor was Felipe Romeo, who had
in earlier years been a member of the ultra-Catholic, ultra right (and

anti-Peronist) Guardia Restauradora Nacionalista. In subsequent years, Romeo had moved toward Peronism, working to consolidate the movement's right wing. Also central to *El Caudillo*'s operations was Alberto Moya, another former member of the GRN, as well as recruits from the CNU and JPRA and various journalists with openly fascist sympathies. As the mouthpiece of the Peronist ultra right, *El Caudillo* used its pages to rail against the militant left and Sinarquía, and (less often) against the liberal oligarchy. The publication would also attack individuals by name, and those who appeared in its pages would often be targeted by the Triple A.

Besides shedding light on the rise of the Triple A, *El Caudillo* provides an invaluable window into the worldview of the most radical elements of the Peronist right. Here, not unexpectedly, we see the continued importance of historical revisionism and the essentialist, totalizing tropes that had long been central to left- and especially right-wing nationalism. Revisionist themes and the glorification of Rosas (a particular issue for the nationalist right) were constant concerns of the magazine. Images of the nineteenth-century dictator appeared repeatedly in *El Caudillo*'s pages, as did the identification of the "Peronist Patria" with the "Federal Patria" of Rosas.[53] In keeping with this belief in the essential continuity between the eras of Rosas and of Perón, *El Caudillo* maintained, for example, that the Peronist masses who flooded the Plaza de Mayo in 1945 were the same as those who had supported Rosas.[54] Throughout, Perón is portrayed as the twentieth-century heir of Rosas, who "fought for God, for the patria, and against the oppressive, cosmopolitan traitors" (*el cipayaje opresor y extranjerizante*).[55]

The idea of Argentina as a unitary ethno-cultural community that had preexisted the establishment of wars of independence was also an important theme. Using extensive quotations from Perón's famous 1947 speech celebrating both Cervantes and the Day of the Race, *El Caudillo* affirmed that Spain was the "original trunk" of Argentina and had created the nation using "the CROSS and the SWORD." Spain, then, was the source of Argentina's unitary "race" (understood in the spiritual sense), which "was the sum of imponderables that make US WHO WE ARE and that drives us TO BE WHAT WE SHOULD BE." Quoting further, *El Caudillo* insisted that it was this "racial" heritage that prevented Argentines from committing the error of "imitating other communities whose ESSENCES ARE FOREIGN to ours."[56] Just as importantly, according to *El Caudillo*, the ethno-cultural legacy that formed the basis of the true Argentina had been preserved and transmitted by the rural masses. Ignoring the contributions of immigrants and urban dwellers, the magazine maintained that it was "the native, the son of the Argentine land," who had fought with nineteenth-century caudillos, that represented the authentic Argentine. In current times, according to *El Caudillo*, it was the "cabecita" [negra], the "pariah son of the gaucho" who carried on this tradition.[57]

*El Caudillo* also affirmed that the nation existed independently of the constitution, and indeed was superior to it. To believe otherwise was to confuse the real nation with the false nation, which, according to one contributor, could have dangerous consequences. An essay appearing in January 1974, for example, lamented that young soldiers were being taught that the military's role was to defend the constitution. This way of thinking was correct, the writer affirmed, *only* "if we understand the constitution to mean the essence of the nation." This, however, was often not the case, since "before the Constitution [existed], the Nation existed." Moreover, the contributor continued, if "the Nation (understood here to be a unitary entity with a single will) considered the Constitution to be a dead letter," it was not worth defending.[58]

The need to defend the true Argentina against the forces of the antipatria also appeared repeatedly in the publication's pages. Among the agents of the "antipatria," of course, were nineteenth-century leaders, such as Sarmiento and Mitre. These men, *El Caudillo* affirmed, had used the educational system to "mentally colonize the upper class," thereby creating a ruling elite that had "solidified the structure of the liberal, antinational and antipopular state."[59] In contemporary times, it believed, the forces of the antipatria had multiplied to include not simply liberal elites allied with the forces of international capitalism but also the "boiches" (Bolsheviks) of the "Tendencia," who had infiltrated the Peronist movement.[60]

Just as troubling for *El Caudillo*, it seems, was the rise of a youth culture in Argentina, which it believed both corrupted Argentina's young people and undermined the nation's authentic values and cultural traditions. Indeed, one way to taunt the Peronist left was to mock its tastes in fashion and entertainment as foreign affectations that were completely at odds with the true nation. One article, for example, chastised these young people for thinking that liberation meant listening to "imported music," reading "Yankee magazines," and wearing "bluyins" (blue jeans). In order to truly become liberated, the magazine admonished, "you have to begin to learn what the Patria is, and what is the *ser argentino*."[61] Those in this camp also "obeyed a foreign, worldly philosophy" with an "origin completely distant from our idiosyncratic nature and national way of thinking."[62] To combat this perceived attack on the true Argentina, *El Caudillo* called for a "national cultural revolution" to rid the nation of foreign influences. Singling out television as an "arm of imperialism," the publication complained that children were being targeted daily by the "North American doctrine of liberty and democracy." It was time, the article affirmed, to "break with the dictatorship" of liberalism and take control of the means of communication to "light the way toward a genuine national culture."[63]

PERONISM'S TWO WINGS agreed on many things. Both imagined the Argentine nation in essentialized terms: as a distinctive, organic community possessing a unitary culture that had formed independently of the state and had deep roots in the past. Both agreed, as well, that this state, and the liberal principles that informed it, were alien to Argentina's authentic character, having been imposed on the national community by an elite serving the interests of foreign masters. They also agreed that the struggle against the liberal state had been at the center of Argentina's nineteenth-century conflicts, when the "real" Argentina had sought to reassert itself by reclaiming the nation's resources and defending its supposedly authentic culture. Finally, both agreed that Peronism was but the latest phase of this long struggle and that Perón and his followers represented the "real" Argentina rising up against the "antipatria."

These shared understandings, however, were insufficient to keep the movement together, and at the heart of the differences were conflicting visions of the true Argentina. For the Peronist right, Argentina was, and should always remain, a Catholic, Hispanic nation that must defend its culture and essence from the contaminating influence of godless communism, as well as from foreign religions, music, ideas, and "bluyins." The left's vision of the true Argentina was different but still bore some resemblances to that of the right. More open to the world—the young Peronists liked their blue jeans and their Che—they nonetheless remained convinced that Argentina's present struggles were between the patria and the antipatria and were a direct continuation of the Unitarian/Federalist conflicts of the nineteenth century. To see themselves as the present-day incarnation of nineteenth-century caudillos, of course, required an act of imagination that radically misinterpreted that moment in their nation's history and completely ignored the profound changes of the past century. The Argentina of the 1970s was no longer a nation of gauchos and caudillos oppressed by liberal Buenos Aires—the "true nation" oppressed by the false one. Rather, the true Argentina was a modern, multiethnic society, that possessed—as do all modern societies—a dynamic culture encompassing a plurality of subcultures. Moreover, this true Argentina faced complex problems that required complex solutions, solutions that themselves required compromise, patience, and nuanced analysis, items that were in very short supply in the Argentina of the 1970s.

THAT THE STORY OF ARGENTINA's two variants of nationalism did not end with the conflict between Argentina's two Peronisms is surely one of the country's greatest tragedies. Yet the Triple A's violence, which begot more violence, was only the first phase of what would be a long and murderous season. To understand the ferocity of the killing and the widespread use of torture, we must turn again to Argentina's nationalist tradition, for those who carried out these horrific acts did so because they—or their superiors—believed themselves to be patriots who were defending the true Argentina. The strand of nationalism that shaped this understanding of what it meant to be a patriot was, of course, part of the larger current of right-wing nationalist thought that had emerged much earlier in the century, which in many respects barely diverged from right-wing Peronism. What distinguished it, however, was its deep hostility to Perón and the movement he created. What these nationalist sought was an ordered, hierarchical society with God—not Perón—at its center—one whose Hispanic, Catholic essence would be defended from the corrosive forces of liberalism, Marxism, and modernity in general.

These nationalists had the vision; what they needed was the muscle. It was no wonder, then, that they sought out like-minded military men who could provide it.

## WOOING THE GENERALS

With Perón in exile and Aramburu in power, right-wing nationalists had faced a dilemma: to support the Peronist resistance or to place their hopes in the military. For those who chose the latter path, finding allies in the armed forces strong enough and committed enough to defend the Catholic nation would be no easy task. Nationalists knew that, while there were many kindred spirits in the military, there were also military men of a more liberal bent, who believed that Argentina should return as quickly as possible to constitutional norms. Finding an entry point would take time. This was the aim of Ciudad Católica, an organization modeled on France's *Cité Catholique*, which had also sought to bring members of the military over to the nationalist cause.[64] Founded in 1959, the organization's initial nucleus included nationalists Juan Carlos Goyeneche, Roberto Pincemin, Col. Juan Francisco Guevara, and Mateo Roberto Gorostiaga, the last of whom directed the group's publication *Verbo*. Aiming to "form the hearts and minds" of military officials, Ciudad Católica favored a quiet, behind-the-scenes approach that relied on personal, face-to-face proselytizing through "courses, private conversations [and] retreats."[65] In doing so, it sought to create small cells of "our men," who represented "the selection of the best, the most *conscientes*, the most self-sacrificing," and who would create other cells that would spread the vision of a Catholic Argentina throughout the country.[66] *Verbo* served as the nerve center of this quietly expanding web, and promoted the works of such well-known nationalist authors as Federico Ibarguren, Jordán Genta, and Julio Meinvielle.

Individual nationalists both inside and outside the Catholic Church also worked to win allies within the officer corps. Two of the most successful were Meinvielle and Genta, who have been described as the most "influential philosophers behind the Military Process" of 1976–83.[67] Father Meinvielle, whose activism in nationalist causes stretched back to the early 1930s, remained one of Argentina's most influential Catholic thinkers and continued to churn out works warning of the threat communism posed to the nation's Catholic identity.[68] During the 1960s, the energetic priest complemented his writings with a new activism. Besides his above-mentioned mentoring of the members of the group Tacuara, Meinvielle continued to seek out "virtuous ones" within the armed forces who were capable of carrying out a nationalist revolution.[69]

Genta similarly courted members of the armed forces. One of Meinvielle's most ardent disciples, Genta had achieved prominence within the nationalist sectors of the military as early as the 1940s, when he was tapped by the ultra right Ramírez regime to reform the University of La Plata along nationalist lines. In the early 1960s, through his friendship with the chaplain of the Aviation School of the Air Force, Genta began giving classes designed to instill nationalist values in pilot trainees.[70] In 1962, he produced an instructional manual for his students that outlined the "doctrine" of counterrevolutionary warfare, and a year later he published a book-length treatise on the same topic.[71] *Guerra contrarrevolucionaria* proclaimed the military's most important mission to be the defense of Western Civilization. Like Argentina's other right-wing nationalists, Genta identified Western Civilization as Catholic and believed the West's road to decline had begun with the Protestant Reformation, a road that led inevitably to Marxism.[72] Not surprisingly, Genta took aim at Argentina's own liberal tradition, accusing nineteenth-century political thinker Juan Bautista Alberdi of having sought to transform *"el ser nacional* by changing the religion and even race of the people."[73] Repeating the standard nationalist belief in a fundamental disconnect between the nation and its political institutions, he described the 1853 Constitution as "essentially liberal, anti-Catholic and anti-Hispanic"—in other words, a document that failed to reflect *"el ser nacional."*[74]

In this spirit Genta argued that, although soldiers should be willing to die for the patria or fatherland, the same sacrifice should *not* be made for the constitution. The 1853 Constitution, he believed, had nothing to do with Argentine identity, and indeed was harmful to the true nation. According to Genta, it was "beautiful" for soldiers to die for "all that is essential and permanent" in the patria, such as "the unity of its *ser*, moral and natural integrity, national sovereignty, the Church of Christ." However, he warned, it was senseless to "die for things that are accidental, transitory or contrary to the *ser* of the Patria." In this latter category, he included "circumstantial laws, popular sovereignty, universal suffrage, laicism [and] pluralism."[75] In other words, only the Catholic *ser nacional* was worth dying for, not something as trivial as the Argentine constitution. Not surprisingly, Genta believed that officer training should be geared toward helping military men understand this distinction. Only with the proper ideological preparation, he believed, could soldiers learn the difference between "*that thing that is the Patria*, its essence and its destiny (*fin*)" and the political institutions that in many cases contradicted "*el ser nacional*."[76]

The impact of Catholic nationalist ideas on key sectors of the military became evident during the dictatorship of General Juan Carlos Onganía (1966–70), who took power after ousting civilian President Arturo Illia. A devout Catholic with ties to Opus Dei and the Cursillos de Cristiandad,[77] Onganía filled his cabinet with individuals known for their strong Catholic faith. Many, including two members of the Ateneo de la República (athenaeum of the republic) and several associated with the Ciudad Católica, also had longtime nationalist credentials.[78] Right-wing nationalism's influence could be seen in a number of areas. First, was Onganía's announced intention to stay in power indefinitely. Whereas the leaders of previous military regimes had promised a rapid return to civilian rule after the restoration of order, Onganía pledged to retain control long enough to effect a fundamental restructuring of the Argentine state.[79] In 1969, he attempted to make good on this pledge by approving a new "Fundamental Charter," drawn up by his minister of the interior, Guillermo Borda, and Mario Díaz Colodrero, both identified with right-wing nationalist tendencies.[80] Intended to supersede the 1853 Constitution, this document replaced the Congress and other elected bodies with a corporatist system.[81] Initially, at least, Onganía also sought to take a more nationalist approach to the economy by tapping businessman Néstor Salimei to head the Ministry of the Economy. A practicing Catholic, who rejected laissez-faire capitalism, Salimei believed the state should play an active role in the economy to harmonize the interests of capital and labor.[82]

Nationalist values also shaped educational and cultural policies during this period. Responding to his fellow Catholic nationalists' complaint that Argentina's educational system had become a breeding ground for communists, Onganía stripped the country's universities of their traditional autonomy and placed nationalists in key faculty and administrative positions. Most dramatically, he authorized the police to seize control of the University of Buenos Aires. In a violent action that was later dubbed "the night of the long sticks," club-wielding police invaded university buildings and severely beat faculty and students. The regime also embarked on a broader effort to inculcate nationalist values within the schools and combat what it saw as the rampant immorality of youth culture. Minister of education José Mariano Astigueta, for example, attempted to reinstate mandatory religious education in the public schools and to reform the high school history curriculum to reflect nationalist views.[83] The government also took aim at sexual conduct, outlawing films that seemed to justify adultery and in some cities harassing young couples and prohibiting women from wearing miniskirts and pants in schools and public offices.[84]

Notwithstanding these policies, it is important to note that Onganía and his nationalist colleagues were never fully free to pursue their own agenda. As suggested earlier, since the mid-1950s, the Argentine military had been deeply divided between nationalists and liberals, two factions that were themselves internally diverse.[85] Both liberals and nationalists were deeply opposed to communism, but the former tended to be stridently anti-Peronist and pro-free market capitalism and saw the military's role as that of restoring stability in order to return the country to constitutional rule.[86] Nationalist officers, in contrast, followed their civilian coreligionists in viewing "secular liberalism [as] an opening wedge" enabling communist ideas to enter.[87] They also favored strong state involvement in the economy and believed their liberal rivals to be antinational cosmopolitans who were in league with imperialists.[88] This division meant that, although the nationalists gained ascendency during the Onganía regime, their liberal opponents pushed back in significant ways. In the area of economic policy, for example, liberals successfully forced Onganía to replace Salimei with economist Adalberto Krieger Vasena. Once in charge, Krieger Vasena drew the ire of nationalists by reversing course and devaluing the peso, cutting domestic subsidies, and lowering tariffs in a bid to make the economy more competitive. Liberals also stymied the proposed constitutional changes, thus thwarting Onganía's attempt to impose a corporatist system. This regime, then, is best understood as an unstable hybrid that reflected the underlying schisms within the armed forces.

THIS LIBERAL-NATIONALIST CONFLICT, so evident during the Onganía regime, would continue to divide the Argentine military, and thus would also shape the policies of the 1976–83 dictatorship. The ruling junta, comprised of army general Jorge Rafael Videla (who also served as Argentina's de facto president from 1976 to 1981), navy admiral Emilio Eduardo Massera, and air force brigadier-general Orlando Ramón Agosti, seized power on March 24, 1976, amid escalating violence waged by both guerrilla groups and right-wing Peronist paramilitary squads.[89] Pledging to restore order, the regime announced the beginning of a new phase in Argentine history, which it termed the *Proceso de Organización Nacional* (Process of national reorganization). What followed was a period of unprecedented repression, during which, in the words of one prominent scholar, the Argentine military "became one gigantic killing machine."[90]

Estimates of those killed or "disappeared" during what has become known as the "Dirty War" vary widely, ranging from a low of six thousand by the Organization of American States Human Rights Commission to a high of forty thousand. Perhaps the most reliable and recent (2003) figures come from Argentina's Secretary of Human Rights, which has put the number at thirteen thousand.[91] Whatever the controversy over numbers, there is no debate over the extraordinarily savage treatment suffered by the victims. Most endured some form of torture, both psychological and physical. Beatings and the application of the cattle prod to the mouth and genitals (often when the victim was tied to a metal bed frame and doused with water) were the most common. Also frequent was suffocation, either by forcing the victim's head into a bucket of feces or by covering it with a plastic bag. In some cases, more elaborate forms of torture were devised. Among the most sadistic was the so-called rectoscope. Usually reserved for Jewish prisoners, this entailed inserting a tube in the anus (or, in the case of women, the vagina) and then placing a rat inside the tube. In an effort to escape, the rat would gnaw the internal organs of the victim.[92]

What role, then, did nationalist myths and ideology have in producing this level of savagery, and in shaping the rest of the regime's policies? For some scholars, the link between right-wing nationalism and the intensity of the repression is clear-cut. Historian David Rock, for example, cites the growing influence during the 1960s of right-wing nationalist ideas on such institutions as the military, the church, and the country's political parties.[93] More recently, James Scorer has affirmed this view by drawing a continuous direct line linking the xenophobic utterances of Leopoldo Lugones during the 1920s with the military junta's practice of "materially excluding" (i.e., murdering) individuals they deemed subversive.[94] Certainly, there is significant rhetorical evidence to support the claim that right-wing nationalist ideas had a deep impact on the 1976 military regime, and even liberal-leaning officers sometimes used nationalist tropes, such as *el ser nacional*. Thus, Rock is correct when he notes that by "the late 1970s, the statements of senior military officers rang constantly with the language and figurative constructions of the Nationalists."[95]

Many military men, it is clear, saw the war against the guerrillas as a struggle to defend the very essence of *argentinidad*. Such was the case with brigadier general Luciano Adolfo Jáuegui, who promised to hunt down and "annihilate without quarter" those who sought to "poison our youth with foreign doctrines . . . and to deform our *ser nacional*."[96] The ruling junta itself used such terms. In their opening proclamation of March 24, 1976, for example, the members of the ruling junta affirmed their commitment to the "unity of Argentines and to the recuperation of *el ser nacional*."[97] Employing similar language, the regime promulgated a new law in June 1976 that dissolved all organizations seeking to disseminate "ideologies [that were] alien (extrañas) to *el ser nacional*." Among those organizations targeted by the law were the Union of Agricultural Producers, the Commission of Relatives of Political Prisoners, and the Movement of the Defense of the National Patrimony.[98] Indeed, so frequently did the military justify its actions in the name of *el ser nacional* that this claim itself became a target of the regime's critics. In a now-famous open letter to the military, appearing on the first anniversary of the 1976 coup, journalist and Montonero member Rodolfo Walsh publicly mocked the regime's repeated invocation of *el ser nacional* in its messages to the public.[99]

It was also clear that key figures within the armed forces continued to embrace the notion of Argentina as a Catholic nation and to see the defense of the patria in terms of a religious crusade. Direct evidence of such beliefs can be found in the actions and rationales of air force officers, who attempted a coup against the government of Isabel Perón in December 1975. According to their manifesto, the aim of the coup was to overthrow the civilian government in order to install a "new order of refoundation (refundación), with a national and Christian character." To drive the point home further, several of the conspirators wore rosaries and painted the planes used in the attempted coup with the inscription "Cristo Vence" (Christ triumphs). Not surprisingly, many of the participants were former students of Genta.[100]

Civilian Catholic nationalists also kept up a steady drumbeat during this period, continuing to exert influence on military men despite the deaths of three key ideologues. In 1973, Meinvielle died of injuries sustained in a car accident. The following year, Genta and another Meinvielle disciple, Thomist scholar Carlos Alberto Sacheri, were both gunned down by the ERP. Enraged by these two murders and by what they saw as the increasing Marxist threat, the nationalist right openly urged the generals to step in. The newly established magazine *Cabildo* became a fount of right-wing Catholic, essentialist thinking. In its first issue of May 1973, for example, the opening editorial declared that the restoration of "Argentine greatness" could be accomplished only by returning to "the ideas of the nation, that which was national (*lo nacional*), that which was nationalist." This meant, it continued, returning to "our classic and Catholic culture" and thereby restoring the "dignity" that Argentina enjoyed during the "zenith" of its history: the dictatorship of Rosas.[101] The magazine also warned of a "conspiracy against the essences of *el ser nacional*" carried out "by a Peronism now infiltrated by Marxism."[102] Constantly reaffirming the Catholic basis of Argentine nationality, the magazine lauded the armed forces as one of the "basic pillars" of the country's moral order.[103] With a nod back to early nationalist Leopoldo Lugones, the cover of one issue was emblazoned with a photograph of soldiers with arms extended in the Roman salute and the slogan "La hora de la espada" (The hour of the sword). Also splashed across the cover was the phrase "They die for the NATION NOT for the CONSTITUTION."[104]

But despite the military's nationalist-inspired rhetoric and the continuing importance of right-wing nationalists within and outside the military, caution is in order when making blanket claims about the impact of Catholic nationalism on the 1976 junta's policies. As occurred during the Onganía regime, Argentina's military remained deeply divided between Catholic nationalists and liberals. In important ways, the liberals held the upper hand, in part because their nationalist opponents had been weakened by the failed coup attempt of December 1975.[105] Videla, who served as the country's de facto president, was a liberal, as was his eventual successor, Roberto Viola. Indeed, of the three members of the original junta, only Massera of the navy had close contacts with nationalists.[106] Interestingly, Videla would later claim that one reason he and his liberal colleagues carried out the coup was because they feared inaction would bring with it a very real risk that "some nationalist colonel" would beat them to it, and thus install a nationalist regime.[107]

Videla's liberalism, then, meant that most of the junta's policies and pronouncements fit comfortably within the parameters of US Cold War ideology, particularly, the National Security Doctrine.[108] Under this doctrine, internal "subversion" within Latin America was understood to be part of an international communist plot to gain a foothold in the hemisphere. Thus, protecting the United States and its economic interests required coordinating with Latin American militaries to eliminate the communist threat. It also required tolerating, and indeed often aiding, regimes that engaged in brutal repression. According to the doctrine, because the enemy was internal and refused to adhere to the classical conventions of warfare, drastic and often unconventional methods were required. In other words, adherents of the National Security Doctrine believed it was sometimes necessary to overlook such measures as torture and extralegal killing in order to attain the greater goal of halting communism's advance, an outcome that cold warriors saw as the ultimate violation of human rights.[109]

Thus while Videla had no qualms about employing draconian measures against the guerrillas, he did so not as part of a nationalist crusade but on pragmatic grounds. Only extreme force, he insisted, would bring a quick end to the violence and thus allow a more rapid return to civilian rule.[110] As Videla would later explain to journalist Ceferino Reato, he saw himself as "a dictator in the Roman sense of the term, as a transitory remedy, for a defined time span, in order to save the institutions of the Republic."[111] Videla and his liberal colleagues also differed from their nationalist counterparts in how they defined *Western Civilization*, a term that both liberals and nationalists within the military used repeatedly while fundamentally disagreeing about its nature.[112] For liberals, such as Videla, "the West" very much included the United States and the liberal ideals and values arising from the Enlightenment and the French Revolution.[113] Such a definition was, of course, in direct contrast to that of the nationalists, who saw liberalism not as the hallmark of Western civilization but as the first step on the road to godless communism. The regime's economic policies also reflected the predominance of liberals. The man tapped to serve as minister of the economy was José A. Martínez de Hoz, a wealthy industrialist from one of the country's oldest families. Much to the ire of nationalists, Martínez de Hoz, who stayed in office for the next five years, prescribed a set of neoliberal shock policies inspired by the free market Chicago school.[114]

The liberal credentials of Videla and Viola, along with the regime's economic policies, have led some scholars to downplay the influence of Catholic nationalism on the 1976 regime.[115] This liberal/nationalist paradox has been resolved, however, by recent research focusing on the internal dynamics within the military during these years. As Mark Osiel and Paula Canelo have convincingly argued, although the nationalist officers were not part of the ruling junta until the early 1980s, they took the leading roles in two key arenas: educational policy and the war against the guerrillas. Economic matters were left to the liberals.[116] Following the example of the Onganía regime, the new government assigned a high priority to educational reform. This made sense, given that in Argentina— as in the rest of Latin America—the protagonists of the revolutionary struggles of the 1960s and '70s were overwhelmingly young, middle-class youths, who had become radicalized during their student years.[117] Convinced that the country's universities and secondary schools had become incubators of subversion, the junta sought to purge the educational system of supposed communist elements and to infuse the curriculum with a nationalistic ethos that would enforce the nationalists' version of the Catholic *ser nacional*. And, as had occurred during the Onganía regime, this task fell to the nationalists, who were given control of the Ministry of Education throughout the period of military rule.

Mass firings of educational professionals occurred immediately after the coup. Within the first four months, approximately three thousand teachers, teaching assistants, and administrators were expelled from secondary schools.[118] By the six-month mark, a similar number of university professors had lost their jobs.[119] Many, both students and professors, met a darker fate. According to the National Teachers' Confederation, over six hundred teachers "disappeared" during the years of the dictatorship, while an estimated 20 percent of the total of the permanently missing were students.[120] In order to identify its targets, the regime developed an elaborate network of spies extending throughout the system and strongly encouraged teachers to participate. To guide their efforts, the Ministry of Education distributed a booklet entitled *Subversión en el ámbito educativo* (*Conozcamos a nuestro enemigo*) (Subversion in the educational sphere [Getting to know our enemy]).[121] Published in 1977, the seventy-five page booklet affirmed that teachers had a central role to play in the battle to protect "the values of Christian morality, of the national tradition and of the dignity of the Argentine *ser*" and urged them to "act with clarity and energy to rip out the subversion by its roots."[122]

The regime also sought to purge supposedly subversive ideas from the curriculum. In an effort to reorient the curriculum toward nationalist ideals, the Ministry of Education asked teachers to engage in "the incessant search for *el ser nacional* and to fight without quarter to consolidate [students'] consciousness of it."[123] As one early resolution declared, the purpose of the Argentine educational system was to form individuals "capable of conducting themselves in accordance with the values of Christian morality, the national tradition and the dignity of *el ser argentino*."[124] In much the same vein, General Ovidio J. A. Solari opened his address to an audience of teachers by invoking "the protection of God" as they seek to "mold within the pure spirits of children the fundamental qualities of *el Ser Nacional*."[125] General Luciano B. Menéndez expressed similar sentiments when he affirmed that educational reforms were a necessary part of the fight against subversion. Through new efforts in the schools and universities, he proclaimed, "the forces of order" must fight the guerrillas by promoting the "spiritual values that reaffirm the essence of *el ser nacional*."[126]

One key element in curricular reform was the prohibition of works by Freud, Piaget, and, of course, Marx in the classroom.[127] In doing so, the Ministry of Education reflected the convictions of junta member Emilio Massera, who believed that much of Argentina's contemporary ills could be traced to certain key thinkers, whose theories about the individual, society, and even the universe had dangerously weakened the religious foundations of the West. In Massera's case, the culprits were Marx, whose *Das Kapital* "questioned the inviolable character of private property"; Freud, whose *Interpretation of Dreams* questioned "the sacred space of (man's) internal being"; and Einstein, whose theory of relativity "put the static condition of the material world in crisis."[128] (The fact that all three were Jews was not mentioned but was something that was self-evident to his audience.)[129] In at least one instance, the regime went further, publicly burning books and pamphlets it believed were "pernicious" and harmful to "the intellect and our Christian way of being." An official communiqué published in several newspapers around the country explained that the burning was necessary to ensure "that our youth is not tricked any longer about the true good that our national symbols, family and church—in short, our most traditional spiritual estate synthesized in God, Fatherland and Home—represent."[130] In other cases, teachers were forbidden to assign group work on the grounds that such pedagogical methods undercut the traditional teacher-student hierarchy and encouraged dialogue between peers.[131] In one province, nationalist officials deemed modern math to be potentially subversive, prohibiting its teaching.[132]

Such ideas seem bizarre to anyone existing outside the Catholic nationalists' mental universe. They make sense, however, in the context of nationalists' understanding of Argentine identity and the nature of the forces that supposedly threatened it. Because of their deep-rooted fear of liberalism and anything else that hinted at modernity, the military's nationalists were fighting enemies that were legion in both number and variety. Historian José Moyano's description of a graph used by instructors of the Air Force Academy during the 1970s starkly illustrates the multitude of forces Catholic nationalists believed were arrayed against them. According to Moyano, the graph featured a tree with roots in three forces: Marxism, Zionism, and Freemasonry. Branching off from the tree itself were a variety of groups and tendencies, including liberal democracy, communism, guerrilla organizations, progressive Catholicism, Protestantism, feminism, and even the Rotary Club.[133] This expansive definition of the enemy, of course, greatly widened the scope of the repression.

The nationalist officers who took charge of the war against the guer-rillas formed a powerful and elite group within the armed forces. These "señores of the war," as they have come to be called,[134] were deeply influ-enced by civilian nationalists. Indeed, even after the return to democracy in 1983, many who participated directly in the repression spoke openly about their attachment to the ideas of Genta and Meinvielle.[135] Among the highest ranking within the nationalist faction were General Carlos Guillermo Suárez Mason, the charismatic commander of the First Army Corps, who oversaw numerous clandestine detention centers; Ramón Génaro Díaz Bessone, commander of the II Army Corps, who was in charge of military zone II;[136] and General Luciano Benjamín Menéndez, commander of the III Army Corps based in Tucumán. General Santiago Omar Riveros headed one of the country's largest secret detention cen-ters, located at the Campo de Mayo army barracks, while General Osvaldo Azpitarte took charge of Army Corps V. Other important na-tionalist figures who played central roles in the repression were the no-torious General Eduardo Acdel Vilas, General Jorge Olivera Róvere, and the infamous General Ramón Camps, who as head of the Buenos Aires police admitted to having "disappeared" five thousand individuals.[137]

The repression was carried out in a highly decentralized fashion. The army had divided the country into four zones, each of which was controlled by a different corps. (A fifth zone was added later.) Each zone was divided into subzones, which were in turn divided yet again, first into areas and then into subareas.[138] Although technically subordinate to the ruling junta, this organizational structure meant that zone com-manders enjoyed almost complete autonomy and operated with vir-tually no oversight.[139] In a recent interview, Videla—who, it must be noted, has never shied away from taking ultimate responsibility for the repression—affirmed that the decision for each case (i.e., the kidnapping and subsequent fate of each individual) was up to the zone commanders. According to Videla, each commander "utilized the method he believed most appropriate . . .[and] had autonomy to find the method that was the most rapid and carried the least risk." "The commanders or chiefs of the zones," he continued, "never asked me permission to proceed: I con-sented by omission."[140]

Why Videla so completely relinquished control to his zone com-manders is not entirely clear, especially since almost all were known nationalists. One reason, undoubtedly, was because he and his fellow liberals shared the nationalists' conviction that mass repression was necessary and should be carried out as quickly as possible (and thus extralegally), before domestic and international opinion could be aroused.[141] Thus, at least initially, liberals found the nationalists' willingness to take charge of the killings to be very useful. It may also be true, as Osiel has argued, that the decision to put the nationalists in charge of the war against the guerrillas was part of a power-sharing agreement between the two factions—one that allowed liberals to control the all-important area of economic policy.[142]

In any event, the decision to turn the guerrilla problem over to the nationalists, and to allow them to do so without judicial restraints, proved fateful. Because of the nationalists' expansive definition of subversion, the number of potential targets came to include people with few or even no ties to the guerrillas. Thus it is not surprising that the nationalists' estimates of the number of people they expected to kill greatly exceeded Videla's estimate of seven-to-eight thousand. General Luciano Benjamín Menéndez, for example, proclaimed that "we are going to have to kill 50,000 people: 25,000 subversives, 20,000 sympathizers, and we will make 5,000 mistakes."[143] General Ibérico Saint-Jean's estimate was more open ended. In his now infamous words, "First we will kill all the subversives; then we will kill all their collaborators, then their sympathizers; then those who remained indifferent; and finally we'll kill the undecided."[144]

Evidence also suggests that the ideal of the Catholic nation helped motivate the lower-level military men, who actually carried out the kidnappings and torture. According to anthropologist Antonius C. G. M. Robben, at the time of the 1976 coup, ultra-Catholic nationalist Major Mohamed Alí Seineldín (leader of the infamous Carapintadas group responsible for several uprisings against the civilian governments of the post-1983 period) was instructed to instill within his underlings a "more conscious awareness of personal faith and a collective religious identity."[145] The above-mentioned General Acdel Vilas also recognized the importance of a religious identity for instilling a fighting spirit in the rank and file. In a 1976 article in the *Revista de la Escuela Superior de Guerra*, for example, he argued that, because the struggle against the guerrillas was a new type of warfare that differed from war against a foreign enemy, it required that troops be adequately prepared to make the necessary sacrifices. Critical to this process, according to Vilas, was the creation of a "winning mystique" that would convince ordinary soldiers they were participating in a "real war." This mystique, he continued, must be "impregnated with national feeling, in defense of Argentinian principles that we inherited from our ancestors."[146] That such efforts proved at least partially effective is evident in the fact that some of those involved in kidnapping operations would begin raids with the battle-cry "For God and Country!" and would leave religious graffiti painted on the walls of victims' homes.[147]

The influence of Catholic nationalism on lower-level troops was also evident in the especially brutal treatment of Jewish prisoners. Despite the deep anti-Semitism of Argentine Catholic nationalism, there is no known case of any individual being targeted solely on the basis of religion. Rather, Jews were kidnapped for the same reasons as non-Jews: political militancy of some type; prominence in fields the Catholic right deemed suspect, such as education, law, or psychology; or just sheer bad luck.[148] Still, what is undeniable is that, once Jews were seized by the security forces, their Jewishness mattered a lot. As noted above, the most heinous forms of torture were generally reserved for Jews. Nazi symbols and propaganda were also evident in the clandestine detention centers. The notorious torturer "Julien the Turk," for example, wore both a swastika and a Christian cross, and some prisoners were forced to yell out "Heil Hitler!" Former prisoners who survived their ordeals reported that guards often painted swastikas on the bodies of their Jewish victims; one young Jewish woman was singled out to repeat five hundred times "Long live Videla, Massera and Agosti, God, Home and Country!" Jews were also intensely questioned about their ties to Israel, and about a supposed Israeli plot to take over Patagonia.[149]

CLEARLY, NATIONALIST CONSTRUCTS, images, and tropes played a key role in fueling the violence that swept Argentina during the 1970s. For Peronist groups such as the Montoneros, the conviction that their struggle was the continuation of a war begun over 160 years earlier by the gaucho militias gave special weight and meaning to their sacrifices. Those who fell, either in battle or in the detention centers, died not simply for the cause of a more just future but to honor past generations of Argentines who had also given their lives for their country. It was, in other words, a patriotic war in which the defense of the true nation—a nation rooted in the culture of the creole masses—was at stake. Right-wing Peronists also, of course, saw themselves as defending the true Argentina (and the true Peronism). Denouncing the Peronist guerrillas as "infiltrators" touting exotic ideologies, they believed their fellow Peronists posed an existential threat to the Argentine *ser nacional*. No longer facing the constraints imposed during Perón's first two terms, the newly unleashed Peronist right clearly displayed its right-wing nationalist roots by embracing the vision of Argentina as a homogenous ethno-cultural nation, rooted in Catholic Spain and threatened by liberalism, Marxism, and Jews. Thus for these Peronists, purging both their movement and Argentina of enemy infiltrators was their patriotic duty.

The military officers who were most directly involved in the repression after 1976 also saw themselves as patriots. Indeed, in significant ways, these military men operated in a conceptual universe that was more similar to that of their Peronist enemies than the one inhabited by their liberal colleagues. In contrast to those military colleagues who defined patriotism as defending the institutions of the republic and the values of a US-dominated West, these nationalist officers saw themselves as defending the nation itself, which they considered independent of—and in conflict with—the liberal state. And like both right- and left-wing Peronists, these nationalist officers believed the nation to be defined by an enduring *ser nacional*, whose defense was as important as defending the country's economic sovereignty. As it was for both strands of Peronism, the struggle for these military men was not a battle between conflicting ideologies but between the patria and the antipatria. And, like their adversaries, they believed themselves to be the true defenders of the true Argentina.

# Conclusion

The story told here has a long arc. In exploring the similarities and points of contact between Argentina's two strands of nationalism, I have argued that Argentine nationalists shared a particular way of imagining their nation's identity. Highly essentialist in nature, it had in turn nourished a powerful set of myths, tropes, and historical narratives that were remarkably similar. Although they interpreted the content of the imagined *ser nacional* in very different ways, both right- and left-wing nationalists firmly believed in its reality. In their eyes, *el ser nacional* formed the basis of the true Argentina and was the source of Argentines' supposedly unitary collective character. Moreover, according to nationalist mythology this "real" Argentina had long been under siege by the creators of the "false Argentina" (i.e., liberals), who—in league with foreign capitalists— had imposed on the nation economic structures, laws, and political institutions that were alien to *el ser nacional*. Indeed, nationalists believed, liberal influences were part of a larger imperialist conspiracy to seduce the local elite and thereby gain control of Argentina's resources and markets. Thus only by rejecting liberalism in all its forms, they argued, could Argentines defend the true nation and secure their country's economic and political sovereignty.

The related notions of *el ser nacional* and the two Argentinas did not, of course, suddenly emerge out of thin air in the 1930s. Accordingly, another aim of this study has been to illuminate the origins of these constructs. In doing so, I have emphasized the importance of the period of mass immigration, when the arrival of millions of foreigners sparked a nationalist backlash. During this critical juncture in the nation's history, as Argentines grappled with the challenges of how to incorporate the newcomers, key members of the intellectual elite came under the influence of ideas associated with Romantic nationalism, especially the vision of nations as homogeneous ethno-cultural communities. For these individuals, Argentines formed—or were in the process of forming—a distinctive race or ethnicity, whose unique character or essence must be defended. This new way of imagining Argentine nationality and the vocabulary with which it was expressed had long-term effects. One of the most important was the weakening of the traditional nineteenth-century vision of Argentina as a civic community, whose members were understood to be bound together first and foremost by common political values and loyalties. Although it was never completed, this at least partial detachment of Argentine identity from political moorings, and its redefinition in essentialist terms, established the conceptual groundwork for later nationalist narratives and served to situate subsequent nationalist thinking about Argentina and its problems within a certain range of meanings.

An exploration of the early twentieth-century notion of an Argentine race also sheds light on the varied nature of later essentialist understandings of Argentine identity and helps explain why the idea of *el ser nacional* proved attractive to nationalists from across the political spectrum. As I have argued, the notion that Argentines were forming a distinctive race gained widespread acceptance among Argentina's intellectual elite precisely because the content of this construct could be defined in very different ways. The result was a series of often-heated debates about the nature of the imagined Argentine race and the role immigrants would play in shaping it. These disputes were never settled, and there remained a world of distance between individuals who argued that the newcomers were to be subsumed into a preexisting ethnic core, defined by Spanish ancestry and Catholicism, and those who insisted that the working-class immigrants would fundamentally reshape the Argentine race. It is in these debates over the content of this imagined race that we can see the outlines of the later controversies over the nature of *el ser nacional*.

In making claims about the early twentieth-century roots of the later notions of *el ser nacional* and the true Argentina, it is important to stress that there was nothing inevitable about the course of Argentine nationalism. Even less am I suggesting that the ethno-cultural understandings of Argentine identity that gained currency during the early twentieth century led inexorably to the violence of the 1970s.[1] Far from it. As was made clear in previous chapters, not all individuals who adopted the essentialist notion of an Argentine race during the opening decades of the twentieth century began to goose-step in the 1930s. Although there were those who certainly did embrace fascism—Leopoldo Lugones and (at least for a time) Manuel Gálvez are obvious examples— other prominent promoters of the idea of the Argentine race, such as Ricardo Rojas, became important defenders of Argentina's democratic tradition. Moreover, as noted in the final chapter, there were many factors—both internal and external to Argentina—that contributed to the 1976 coup and the firestorm that followed. Still, it is undeniable that nationalist ideas and the essentialist notions of Argentine identity that informed them also played a powerful role in the conflict and gave it much of its intensity.

Some questions remain. Why did essentialist understandings of national identity and the related trope of the two Argentinas—one invisible, authentic, and profound, the other visible, false, and superficial— prove to be so powerful in Argentina? And why has the notion of an enduring *ser nacional* under siege figured so prominently in Argentines' efforts to understand their nation's struggles? In answering these questions, we must remember that Argentina is not the only Latin American country where essentialism has been a key element in identity discourses. As noted in chapter 3, claims that Latin Americans are somehow inherently similar—and that there are fundamental psychological differences between Latin and Anglo-Americans—date back to at least the earliest days of the twentieth century, when José Enrique Rodó's 1900 essay *Ariel* swept the region.[2] Argentine socialist Manuel Ugarte, who preached much the same message about the inherent differences between "Latins" and "Anglos," also gained a following throughout Latin America. Less well known, but just as important, was the transnational impact of Krausism. During the early twentieth century, this philosophy, with its insistence on the inherent qualities of nations (or families of nations), came to exercise influence throughout much of Latin America.[3] Such ideas about the nature of the region's identity found expression in the writings of a diverse array of twentieth-century Latin American intellectuals, including such luminaries as José Vasconcelos, Victor Raúl Haya de la Torre, Gilberto Freyre, and Octavio Paz.[4]

Why the essentialist claim that Latin Americans were inherently different from their northern neighbors has found such an enthusiastic reception in the region has never been subjected to sustained analysis, but recent scholarship on the origins of the terms *Latin America* and *Latin American race* is illuminating. As Aims McGuinness and Michel Gobat have both argued, the spread of these terms among Latin Americans during the mid-nineteenth century was directly linked to the growing conviction that the nations of the region must join together to defend themselves against the United States and Europe.[5] Surely another reason, and one complementing the anti-imperialist impulse, has to do with what sociologist Liah Greenfeld has called the "creative power of *ressentiment*."[6] *Ressentiment* here refers to a sense of collective frustration or envy deriving from the realization that one's homeland is inferior to another's, and one can never catch up.[7] As Greenfeld has argued, intellectuals commonly respond to this frustration by denigrating the very qualities, such as a knack for material accumulation, reason, pragmatism, emotional reserve, and so on, that have apparently put their nation's rivals ahead. Instead, these intellectual and cultural elites focus on celebrating the supposedly higher virtues of their own people.[8] In other words, in many instances essentialist thinking is employed to counter a collective sense of inferiority, salvage national pride, and create a positive sense of national or ethnic identity.[9] Some elements of both anti-imperialism and ressentiment were likely at work in early twentieth-century Argentina, particularly among those who were angered by US intervention in the Spanish-Cuban conflict. Although the United States largely refrained from meddling in Argentine affairs until the 1930s, the great popularity of Rodó's celebration of Latin idealism, Manuel Ugarte's anti-US writings, and Manuel Gálvez's *hispanismo* suggests that Argentines were becoming increasingly wary of US power.

Yet as this study makes clear, there were other factors at work in Argentina, at least during the opening decades of the century. Notwithstanding Hispanicists, such as Gálvez, who seemed to feel a sort of empathetic ressentiment on Spain's behalf, Argentines themselves had no reason to feel inferior to the rest of the world or pessimistic about their country's prospects. On the contrary, theirs was an extraordinarily successful nation, whose prosperity had made it a preferred destination for emigrating Europeans. For those who lived through these heady years, it seemed only a matter of time before Argentina would join the ranks of the world's most advanced nations. Thus the rise of Argentina's distinctive form of ethno-cultural nationalism during these years stemmed not from envy or anti-imperialism but from anxiety over mass immigration. For this reason, Argentina's early twentieth-century experience, especially the desire to protect the existing culture from foreigners, seems to have much in common with the rise of anti-immigrant, race-based nativism in the United States during the same period.

This does not mean, however, that feelings of ressentiment or anti-imperialism were irrelevant to the course of Argentina nationalism. When the export economy collapsed, and it became clear that Argentina would never again experience the prosperity of the boom years, frustration and anger were inevitable. Once catching up to Western Europe and the United States was no longer a possibility, Argentine nationalists naturally would take solace in celebrating the supposedly unique, anti-materialist qualities of *el ser nacional*, however they defined it. Thus at least a partial answer to why, among all Latin American peoples, Argentines seemed especially obsessed with essentialist ideas about national identity may lie in their unique, two-staged historical experience: the first mirrors that of societies grappling with the cultural consequences of mass immigration and the second reflects the collective pain of dashed expectations and anger at foreign powers.

Another route to explore in figuring out why essentialist ethno-cultural understandings of *argentinidad* had such an impact on the country's political life is to ask why Argentine liberals were unable to counter nationalists' narratives with a convincing one of their own. Specifically, why were liberals unable to combat these new essentialist discourses—and especially the trope of the disconnect between liberalism and the Argentine *ser nacional*—by defending the claim (hegemonic during much of the nineteenth century) that the Constitution of 1853 and the political values it promoted were the defining elements of *argentinidad*? Although an examination of the weakness of twentieth-century Argentine liberalism falls beyond the purview of this work, some general observations can be made. First, we must reject out of hand any arguments that suggest liberals failed because Argentines were somehow inherently receptive to essentialist discourses. Such an interpretation reproduces nationalists' own essentialist assumptions about Argentines' "natural" preference for caudillo rule. Second, it is important to note that some liberals *did* insist that liberal values were central to *argentinidad*, and that the Constitution of 1853 was integral to the nation's identity. This was especially true during the 1930s and '40s, when thousands of Argentines mobilized to protest European fascism, a struggle they saw as key to preserving democracy at home. Moreover, although liberalism continued to lose ground during the twentieth century, references to democracy and liberal values never disappeared from Argentine political discourse.

Yet the fact remains that the liberal vision of Argentine identity proved a weak counter to the seductions of a notion of an enduring *ser nacional*. One way of understanding this weakness is to consider the relative appeal of what might be called the liberals' "story," or narrative, compared to that of the nationalists. Although he is not interested in narratives per se, Jorge Nállim's work on the 1930–55 period is illuminating. According to Nállim, liberalism weakened in Argentina during these decades because its proponents failed to link the popular ideals of equality, democracy, and social justice with liberalism.[10] My work complements Nállim's analysis by highlighting the relative strength of nationalist narratives vis-à-vis those of liberals. Simply put, nationalists came up with a more convincing story about the nation's difficulties. Drawing from the essentialist visions of national identity that had gained currency during the period of mass immigration, nationalists were able to produce powerful narratives offering a plausible, emotionally satisfying explanation for the country's problems that cast ordinary Argentines as victims of greedy foreigners and domestic oligarchs. That the stories of left- and right-wing nationalists were actually quite similar, and featured many of the same assumptions, heroes, and villains, undoubtedly broadened their appeal. Moreover, it is undeniable that key aspects of these narratives rang true because they *were* true. After all, nineteenth-century liberals *were* disdainful of creole culture, the export economy *did* indeed collapse in 1930, and Britain *had* dictated the terms of the Roca-Runciman trade agreement. As Michael Goebel has put it, to be convincing, "nationalist narratives, however invented, need to fulfill a required minimum of plausibility."[11]

It may also be that Argentine liberals were unable to counter essentialist definitions of Argentine identity because they themselves often subscribed to them, at least partially. As scholars of Argentine literature are well aware, there is a genre within Argentine letters known as the "essays of identity," whose heyday was the 1930s but whose influence has proved enduring. During this period, three books with deeply essentialist understandings of national identity appeared that would have a lasting impact on how Argentines understood themselves. One, Scalabrini Ortiz's *El hombre que está sola y espera*, we have already considered in the context of FORJA, but it should be noted that even people unsympathetic to nationalist currents formed part of *El hombre*'s vast audience. The other two were Ezequiel Martínez Estrada's 1933 *Radiografía de la pampa* and Eduardo Mallea's 1937 *Historia de un pasión argentina*.[12] Although neither identified with nationalism, both Mallea and Martínez Estrada fully embraced the nationalists' essentialist trope of the two Argentinas and the opposition between a supposedly invisible, authentic nation and a false, visible one. Mallea, for example, decried the hollowness and superficiality of the nation's visible culture and referred repeatedly to the "submerged, profound Argentina."[13] Following the tellurism of cultural nationalists Ricardo Rojas and Scalabrini Ortiz, Mallea believed the way to restore the hidden or real Argentina was for the Argentine himself to reconnect with the "spiritual territory of his land" in order to become a "new man, a spiritual son of the land."[14] Martínez Estrada's *Radiografía de la pampa* was also concerned with exploring the hidden Argentina, taking as its central metaphor the medical X-ray capable of penetrating the outer layers of reality. Moreover, like nationalists of both stripes, Martínez Estrada censured the liberal Generation of 1837 for imposing "exotic" ideals and institutions that "had no basis in Argentine tradition or history."[15] The extraordinary commercial success of these books, and their iconic status within Argentine letters, make clear that essentialist notions of national identity have long appealed to liberals as well as nationalists.

A final obstacle liberals faced in constructing a robust counternarrative to the essentialist visions of left- and right-wing nationalists was the problematic nature of the Argentine Radical Party. The Radicals, it will be recalled, were instrumental in pushing forward the cause of democracy in Argentina. Throughout the twentieth century, the party remained one of the country's most important, and indeed it was a Radical president who took power after Argentina returned to democracy in 1983. Given this history, it would make sense that Radical leaders would be champions of the liberal cause. But the party's principal leader, Hipólito Yrigoyen, was an entirely different story. Yrigoyen's embrace of a mystical, Krausist-inspired ethno-cultural vision of nationality led him to reject the principle of political pluralism and to see Radicalism as the one and only legitimate political force of the supposedly unitary national community. Thus it was the supposedly democratic Yrigoyen who had initiated the nation's unfortunate tradition of portraying political enemies as un-Argentine. Although the party evolved throughout the century, and in many instances has indeed championed democracy and individual human rights, its early antiliberalism—magnified by the emergence of the pro-Yrigoyen FORJA in the mid-1930s—meant that Radicalism's political legacy has been ambiguous at best.

What of contemporary Argentina? Are Argentines still obsessed with defending an imagined *ser nacional*? At the core of my analysis is the insistence that national identities are constructs, and thus subject to contestation and change. Just as ideas about nationality inspired by Romanticism largely displaced the traditional political or civic notion of Argentine identity after the turn of the twentieth century, the essentialist belief in a subjacent, enduring Argentine *ser nacional* has been challenged and at least partially supplanted by other, more dynamic understandings of identity and culture. Such fundamental conceptual shifts do not simply happen, of course. Like facts, collective identities can be stubborn things. Still, to survive over time, they must somehow be transmitted from one generation to another, a process that goes smoothly only as long as received wisdom continues to square with lived reality. But shocks to the collective system, such as mass immigration, economic or political collapse, and war, can undercut inherited identities and lead to the formation of new ones.

Evidence suggests that the Dirty War produced just such a shock and led many Argentines to challenge essentialist understandings of *argentinidad*. At the forefront of this effort have been several prominent intellectuals, most notably Carlos Altamirano, Hilda Sábato, and Luis Alberto Romero, who have in different ways sought to highlight and thus to "denaturalize" the notion of an Argentine essence or *ser nacional*.[16] Key political figures, such as the late Radical politician Raúl Alfonsín, who won the presidency in 1983 after campaigning on a platform of human rights and democracy, also took aim at unitary, essentialist notions of Argentine identity. In a speech to Congress in May 1987, Alfonsín lambasted the "diverse tendencies" within Argentine nationalism that had "converted the sense of belonging to the nation into an absolute thing, thereby negating the natural conflicts of a complex society and of political pluralism in the interest of positing an artificial and authoritarian homogeneity." Continuing, he criticized the tendency of Argentina's extremist factions to "convert the nation into a crystalized ideology" as a means of justifying the imposition of their "particular and partial vision of reality" on the rest of society. Such an "abstract" and outdated vision, Alfonsín dismissively proclaimed, ignored the realities of modern nations by "anachronistically fusing relations between [members of the nation] into an absolute supraindividual entity, as would any type of outmoded organicism."[17]

Alfonsín, it was clear, hewed closely to earlier liberal notions of Argentina as a civic community. Indeed, he had used his inaugural address to proclaim the need for Argentina to rebuild its democratic institutions in order to guarantee "a genuine pluralism of a coexistence (*convivencia*) free of discrimination and oppression." Pluralism, Alfonsín affirmed, was "particularly important in a nation such as [Argentina]" that had been formed by men and women of "different ancestral origins" and whose basis for national unity was the citizenry's "common love of the land and the free participation in institutions and modes of government that were equally free."[18] In an attempt to drive home the identification of the Argentine nation with its democratic values and institutions, Alfonsín imposed a new rule requiring the entire officer corps to swear allegiance to the constitution. Up to that point, military men had been asked to swear allegiance only to the country and the national flag, *not* to the constitution.[19]

The way forward, however, was not easy. Once in office, Alfonsín faced a series of revolts from a faction of the military calling themselves the "*carapintadas*" (painted faces). Highly nationalistic, the *carapintadas* were led first by Lieutenant Colonel Aldo Rico and then by Colonel Mohamed Alí Seineldín. Despite his Muslim ancestry, Seineldín was a fanatical Catholic who worshipped Argentina's patron saint, the Virgin of Luján, and proclaimed the need to protect Argentina's Hispanic Catholic character from Anglo-Saxon imperialism. An admirer of Perón, he enjoyed some degree of support from remnants of both the Peronist left and right. In an interview with *Ariel*, an intriguingly named magazine aimed at the students of the Liceo Militar, Seineldín railed against the 1884 Law 1420 that prohibited Catholic instruction in public schools, arguing that it had robbed Argentine education of "the natural essence (*savia*) that sustained our Western culture over the centuries." Argentina, he proclaimed, had "two basic institutions: the Church and the Armed Forces," both of which were under attack. If their enemies succeeded in weakening them, he warned his readers, the "Patria will practically cease to exist."[20]

Elements of the Catholic Church also registered their discontent with the new democratic order. Some prominent Catholics participated in the group *Familiares y Amigos de los Muertos por la Subversión* (Relatives and friends of the victims of subversion), or FAMUS, an organization formed to defend the actions of the military dictatorship. This group, which included military and civilian members, accused Argentine democrats of promoting "leftist ethics, modernist culture, Anglo-Saxon Atlanticism . . . international Jewry [and] Masonry."[21] The Argentine bishops were somewhat more circumspect. In an official document released in April 1984, they affirmed their support for democracy and freedom of conscience but insisted that the "soul of our Patria is Christian" and that it was the duty of all good Argentines to "defend that cultural identity of our pueblo." "The Nation," they proclaimed, "was essentially constituted by its culture." As such, it was part of the greater Latin American culture that "had been established throughout a period of five centuries, and that contained a nucleus of fundamentally evangelical values." Under the present circumstances, the bishops continued, they felt forced to express their "concern" over the introduction of "new currents into our culture that are contrary to our *ser nacional*."[22]

Further evidence of continued resistance to Alfonsín's pluralist vision came in the form of two deadly terrorist attacks, one of which occurred after he left office. The first was the bombing of the Israeli Embassy in Buenos Aires, which killed 29 and wounded 242. An even deadlier attack occurred two years later in July 1994, when a nitrate-filled van exploded outside the Asociación Mutual Israelita Argentina (AMIA, or Argentine Israelite Mutual Association). The bomb leveled the building, killing 85 people and wounding hundreds more. The perpetrators were never brought to justice, but in both cases suspicions fell on Argentine security forces, and especially on the local police, who were thought to have collaborated with foreign agents to carry out the attacks.[23] Although the case remains unsolved, the rumored involvement of the security forces suggests that most Argentines found such a connection plausible, with the implication that most Argentines believed that the police and military still harbored essentialist visions of Argentina as a homogenous Catholic nation in which Jews would be permanent outsiders.

Yet paradoxically, the *carapintadas* mutinies (the last occurring in 1990 under the presidency of Carlos Menem) and the Israeli Embassy and AMIA bombings had the effect of demonstrating the weakness, rather than strength, of right-wing nationalism and the narrow vision of Argentine identity on which it rested. With the return to civilian rule in 1983, and new revelations about the extent of the military regime's human rights abuses, the liberal ideals of individual rights, democracy, and due process became central to Argentine political discourse. This rejection of authoritarianism was made evident by the public's decisive reaction to the first and most serious *carapintadas* revolt that took place during Holy Week of 1987. With the fate of civilian rule hanging in the balance, tens of thousands of citizens poured into the Plaza de Mayo to support the Alfonsín government. As Michael Goebel has noted, the crowd's prodemocracy chants, coupled with the waving of Argentine flags, reflected "the degree to which the value of democracy" had become intertwined with national symbols and thus with Argentine identity.[24]

Public reactions to the Israeli Embassy and AMIA bombings were similarly vigorous. Two days after the embassy attack, a crowd of 90,000 Argentines—both Jews and non-Jews—marched through central Buenos Aires in protest. The AMIA explosion drew an even stronger response, as a crowd of over 150,000 demonstrated in front of the congressional building. Expressing solidarity with the victims, the protesters hung banners across the streets with the slogan *Hoy somos todos judíos* (Today we are all Jews).[25] Also significant was the Jewish reaction to the attacks. After the AMIA bombing, local Jewish Argentines formed a group called "Memoria Activa" (Active memory) that sought to emphasize both their Jewish and Argentine identities. The group held regular public gatherings in the Plaza Lavalle between 1994 and 2004, often combining Old Testament readings and the blowing of the shofar with calls for justice for *all* Argentines who lost their lives in the Dirty

War. As Karen Faulk has argued, through these actions Memoria Activa sought to locate "the Jewish community as an integral part of the nation while simultaneously asserting the right to Jewish specificity and difference." In doing so, it challenged long-time notions of Argentine identity that characterized Jews as outside the national community and instead proposed a "redefinition of the national imaginary as essentially plural, multiethnic, and multicultural."[26]

Such efforts to redefine *argentinidad* in pluralistic, multicultural terms were bolstered by legal changes. One important change came with the constitutional reforms of 1994, which finally dropped the requirement that the Argentine president and vice president be Catholic. These reforms also gave, for the first time, explicit recognition of Argentina's indigenous peoples as preexisting "ethnic and cultural" pueblos. With this recognition came the guarantee of their right to a "bilingual and intercultural education."[27] This new emphasis on pluralism and internal diversity also made its way into the Buenos Aires city charter, the 1996 preamble of which affirmed the goal of promoting "human development in democracy based on liberty, equality, solidarity, justice, and human rights, recognizing identity in plurality."[28] The growing acknowledgment of the heterogeneous nature of Argentine society received an additional boost with changes to the long-standing prohibition against giving children non-Hispanic names. Although the federal law prohibiting most foreign names remains in effect, the provinces and the Federal District of Buenos Aires are now able to make their own list of acceptable names. Thus in the Federal District, it is now legal for parents to name their sons "Peter" and their daughters "Judy." Many foreign unisex names, such as "Taylor," are also acceptable, although these must be accompanied by a second name that makes clear the child's gender.[29] On a more symbolic level, the push to undermine unitary notions of *argentinidad* have also been evident in what Faulk has called "state-sponsored visions of multiculturalism." Two of the examples she cites are the visits of Presidents Carlos Menem (1989–99) and Néstor Kirchner (2003–7) to Jewish synagogues, where both donned kippahs.[30] This more multicultural, multiethnic vision of the nation was also evidenced by the 2010 census, which for the first time in more than a century included categories for peoples of African and indigenous descent.[31]

These trends must be balanced against the partial resurgence of popular nationalist rhetoric under the presidencies of Kirchner (who died in 2010) and of his wife, Cristina Fernández de Kirchner, who succeeded him in 2007 and served as president until 2015. As students, both Kirchners had identified with the left wing of the Peronist movement and indeed began their political careers in the Peronist Youth during the 1970s. Given this history, and the fact that they rose to national power during a period of economic crisis clearly linked to the country's crushing foreign debt and the neoliberal policies of Carlos Menem, it is little wonder that these two figures helped rekindle the flames of anti-imperialism and the accompanying notion of the two Argentinas.[32] Nor is it surprising that the crisis helped renew interest in left-wing nationalist thinkers such as Hernández Arreguí and Jauretche, an interest directly promoted by Cristina Kirchner.[33]

Still, the Argentina of today is very different from the Argentina of the 1970s. In part because of the trauma of the Dirty War, political extremism—driven by Argentina's two nationalisms and the essentialist notions of identity that nourished them—has greatly lessened. Argentina's democratic institutions, while far from perfect, have now functioned for over thirty years, and the idea that the military might once again step in to "save" an imagined Catholic national essence can no longer be seriously entertained by even the most die-hard right-wing nationalists. Likewise, the Argentine left has developed a new appreciation for democratic norms and practices, and the notion that liberal democracy is somehow alien to the true Argentina—or that the nation itself should be understood in such unitary and static terms—has ceased to be a part of leftist discourses. Although the historical legacy of the 1976 coup remains unsettled, and citizens continue to debate the causes of the Dirty War, there exist among most Argentines the twin convictions that democracy forms an integral part of the nation's identity and that Argentine society—like all modern societies—is inescapably heterogeneous. Thus as Argentines work to ensure that the horrors of the last dictatorship will not be repeated, the ghosts of past essentialisms are indeed fading.

# NOTES

## INTRODUCTION

1. *Las Malvinas* is Argentina's name for the British-owned Falkland Islands, which Argentines have long claimed. Kirchner held the Argentine presidency from 2007 to 2015. She succeeded her husband, Néstor Kirchner, who served as president from 2003 to 2007 and held similarly nationalist views.

2. FORJA was an offshoot of the Unión Cívica Radical or Radical Party. The organization's name is sometimes written as F.O.R.J.A.; I have opted to use the more common FORJA, except when reproducing the title of a publication

3. Jorge Nállim, *Transformations and Crisis of Liberalism in Argentina, 1930–1955*, Pitt Latin American series (Pittsburgh: University of Pittsburgh Press, 2012), 189.

4. Miguel Bonasso, *Diario de un clandestino* (Buenos Aires: Planeta, 2000), 38. Bonasso played a key role in the leadership of the Montoneros from 1970 to 1980.

5. Hugo Vezzetti, *Sobre la violencia revolucionaria: Memorias y Olvidos* (Buenos Aires: Siglo Veintiuno, 2009), 186–87. Other prominent scholars have made similar claims about the strong resemblance between the Montoneros and the nationalist right, noting their authoritarianism and penchant for violence. On this point see Juan José Sebreli, *Los deseos imaginarios del peronismo: ensayos críticos* (Buenos Aires: Editorial Legasa, 1983), 168–69; and Federico Finchelstein, *The Ideological Origins of the Dirty War: Fascism, Populism, and Dictatorship in Twentieth Century Argentina* (New York: Oxford University Press, 2014), 96.

6. Sandra McGee Deutsch, *Las Derechas: The Extreme Right in Argentina, Brazil, and Chile, 1890–1939* (Stanford, CA: Stanford University Press, 1999), 327. Unless otherwise noted, all translations from Spanish to English are mine.

7. On the need to connect notions of national identity to different forms of nationalism, see Katherine Verdury, "Whither 'Nation and Nationalism'?," *Daedalus* (Summer 1993): 37–46; and M. Ranier Lepsius, "The Nation and Nationalism in Germany," *Social Research* 52, no. 1 (Summer 1985): 43–64.

8. The notion of nations as "imagined" entities was popularized by British historian Benedict Anderson, whose *Imagined Communities* (1983), his seminal work on the rise of the nation-state, reinvigorated nationalism studies. While Anderson was concerned primarily with the institutional and technological changes that allowed individuals in isolated hamlets to feel part of a larger national community, he also noted the importance of just *how* this community was imagined. Rejecting the notion that there are somehow "authentic" nations that emerge out of preexisting ethnic communities and "inauthentic" nations constructed by elites, he insisted that national "communities are to be distinguished, not by their falsity/genuineness, but in the style in which they are imagined" (*Imagined Communities: Reflections on the Origin and Spread of Nationalism*, rev. ed. [London: Verso, 2006], 6).

9. The intellectual center of European Romantic nationalism was Germany, and it is especially associated with the philosophers Johann Gottfried Herder (1744–1803) and J. G. Fichte (1762–1814). The works of these thinkers were not widely disseminated in Argentina, but, as will be elaborated on later, their ideas would be filtered through the writings of nineteenth-century French and Spanish intellectuals.

10. The term *essentialist* has reached vogue status in some pockets of academic writing, yet the concept of essentialism often remains poorly defined. I use it here to refer to the practice of portraying the culture of any group as a unitary set of fixed, enduring, and intrinsic traits that are necessary to the group's identity. The supposed unitary nature of the group's culture may stem from a variety of sources. Thus essentialism, according to the useful definition of anthropologists Kay Warren and Jean E. Jackson, "refers to discourses of enduring commonalities—common ethnic roots and historical pasts, cultural essences, and experiences that are seen as naturally binding people together. Essences can be defined in terms of a transcendental spirituality, ties to a place, common descent, physical differences, cultural practices, shared language, and common histories of suffering." See their introduction to Warren and Jackson, eds., *Indigenous Movements, Self-Representation, and the State in Latin America* (Austin: University of Texas Press, 2002), 8. For more on how anthropologists understand essentialism, see Michael Hersfeld, "Essentialism," in *The Routledge Encyclopedia of Social and Cultural Anthropology*, ed. Alan Bernard and Jonathan Spencer (London: Routledge, 2010), 288–90. Also of interest are various posts on the Theory in Anthropology website discussing the tension between the

need to make generalized classifications and the danger of falling into essentialist modes of thinking (http://openanthcoop.ning.com/group/theoryin anthropology/forum/topics/what-is-essentialism-and-how).

11. The distinction between ethno-cultural and civic forms of identity, which is central to my overall analysis, draws on a rich theoretical tradition in European nationalism studies. First popularized by Hans Kohn in his seminal work *The Idea of Nationalism* (1944), this framework in recent decades has undergone substantial modification and refinement. Scholars, such as Craig Calhoun, Bernard Yack, and Anthony Smith, have criticized Kohn's broad contrast between "Eastern" (i.e., ethnic) and "Western" (i.e., civic) nationalism by noting that elements of both ethnic and civic ideals of nationhood are present in virtually every society. Ruud Koopmans and Paul Statham ("Ethnic and Civic Conceptions of Nationhood," 227) have concurred, arguing that "competitive tensions between ethnic and civic conceptions of citizenship and nationhood" have been a feature of the nation-state since its original emergence. In a similar vein, Brian Singer ("Cultural versus Contractual Nations," 312) has insisted that the civic/ethnic distinction most often applies to "political tendencies within countries [rather than] national differences between countries." The argument that ethnic and civic ideals of the nation often compete with each other within a given society, and are best understood as elements of opposing political projects, has breathed new life into Kohn's original insights and has been especially useful in illuminating sources of political tension in both established nations and in the "newer" nations of postcommunist Eastern Europe. My own work has been directly informed by this latest wave of scholarship. For an overview of Kohn's original argument and some initial criticisms, see Krzysztof Jaskulowski, "Western (Civic) 'versus' Eastern (Ethnic) Nationalism: The Origins and Critique of the Dichotomy," *Polish Sociological Review*, no. 171 (2010): 289–303, www.jstor.org/stable/41275158. For more in-depth criticisms of Kohn's original framework, see Craig Calhoun, *Nations Matter: Culture, History, and the Cosmopolitan Dream* (London: Routledge, 2007), 145; Bernard Yack, "The Myth of the Civic Nation," in *Theorizing Nationalism*, ed. Ronald Beiner (Albany: State University of New York Press, 1999), 103–18; Anthony Smith, *Nationalism and Modernism* (London: Routledge, 1998), 212; and Brian Singer, "Cultural versus Contractual Nations: Rethinking Their Opposition," *History and Theory* 35, no. 3 (October 1996): 309–37. Recent examples of scholars who have employed the civic/ethnic distinction to illuminate contemporary political debates include Geneviève Zubrzycki, "'We, the Polish Nation': Ethnic and Civic Visions of Nationhood in Post-Communist Constitutional Debates," *Theory and Society* 30, no. 5 (2001): 629–68, www.jstor.org/stable/658104; Stephen Shulman, "The Contours of Civic and Ethnic National Identification

in Ukraine," *Europe-Asia Studies* 56, no. 1 (2004): 35–56, www.jstor.org/
stable/4147437; Yitzhak Conforti, "Between Ethnic and Civic: The Realistic
Utopia of Zionism," *Israel Affairs* 17, no. 4 (2011): 563–82; Ruud Koopmans and
Paul Statham, "Ethnic and Civic Conceptions of Nationhood and the Differ-
ential Success of the Extreme Right in Germany and Italy," in *How Social
Movements Matter: Social Movements, Protest and Contention*, ed. Giugni Marco,
Doug McAdam, and Charles Tilly (Minneapolis: University of Minnesota
Press, 1999), 225–52; Helge Blakkisrud, "Blurring the Boundary between Civic
and Ethnic: The Kremlin's New Approach to National Identity under Putin's
Third Term," in *The New Russian Nationalism: Imperialism, Ethnicity and Authoritarianism 2000–2015*, ed. Helge Blakkisrud and Pål Kolstø (Edinburgh:
Edinburgh University Press, 2016), 249–74, www.jstor.org/stable/10.3366/j
.ctt1bh2kk5.16; and André Lecours's analysis of Québécois nationalism, "Ethnic and Civic Nationalism: Towards a New Dimension," *Space and Polity* 4,
no. 2 (2000): 153–65. Another important work, and one that explores the
ethnic/civic tension within the United States, is Gary Gerstle's *American Crucible: Race and Nation in the Twentieth Century* (Princeton, NJ: Princeton University Press, 2001).

12. Tulio Halperin Donghi, *Tradición política española e ideología revolucionaria de Mayo* (Buenos Aires: Centro Editor de América Latina, 1985),
115–19.

13. Paulina Alberto and Eduardo Elena, "The Shades of the Nation," introduction to *Rethinking Race in Modern Argentina*, ed. Paulina Alberto and
Eduardo Elena (New York: Cambridge University Press, 2016), 2.

14. Indeed, as Oscar Chamosa has argued, since at least the latter half of
the nineteenth century, the drive to preserve the notion of Argentina as a white
nation has led elites to classify their dark-skinned compatriots not as members
of nonwhite races but as representatives of the lower classes or as exotic
"popular types." See "People as Landscape: The Presentation of the *Criollo* Interior in Early Tourist Literature in Argentina, 1920–1930," in Alberto and
Elena, *Rethinking Race*, 54, 64–65.

15. As Paulina Alberto and Eduardo Elena have noted ("Shades of the
Nation," 5), from the earliest years of the republic, the view of citizenship as
"political and voluntaristic" was in theory—and usually in practice—"race-
blind or raceless." Mónica Quijada has argued nineteenth-century notions of
Argentine citizenship were also strongly linked to the national territory. Although liberal elites rejected any notion that the indigenous past formed a part
of the nation's history, or that living Indians contributed in any way to its culture, nonbellicose, native-born Indians, who lived within the territory under
state control, were automatically recognized as Argentine citizens. See Quijada,

"Imaginando la homogeneidad: la alquimía de la tierra," in *Homogeneidad y nación: con un estudio de caso: Argentina, siglos XIX y XX*, ed. Mónica Quijada, Carmen Bertrand, and Arnd Schneider (Madrid: CSIC, 2000), 203.

16. The pervasiveness and persistence of the related notions of *el ser nacional* and the "two Argentinas" in the Argentine imagination will be discussed below.

17. A prominent example is literary scholar Nicolas Shumway's *The Invention of Argentina* (Berkeley: University of California Press, 1991). According to Shumway, the roots of Argentina's late twentieth-century problems can be found in the nineteenth century, and in "the peculiarly divisive mind-set created by the country's nineteenth-century intellectuals." The two opposing visions of Argentina articulated during the early decades of the Republic, he believed, "bequeath[ed] to the modern Argentine nation an ideological divide that in odd ways still thwarts consensus and stability" (80). Shumway's insistence that nineteenth-century liberal elites' anti-Spanish, antipopular attitudes created a permanent, unbridgeable divide between Argentines (a view that Argentine nationalists strongly embraced) assumes that there were direct continuities between the mid-nineteenth century and the twentieth century. Such a claim ignores the enormous changes that transformed Argentine society during the 1880–1930 period, not the least of which was the arrival of millions of European immigrants. Similarly important was the almost half century of relative political peace and consensus that began in the 1880s. During this period, as is well known, many of the conflicts that fueled the civil strife of the nineteenth century were finally put to rest. And while later nationalist thinkers generally dismissed these years as ones during which the "real" or authentic nation languished beneath the cosmopolitan veneer of the "official" Argentina, such an interpretation ignores real historical processes that transformed the country in significant and lasting ways. At the same time, it is important to note that the nationalists' trope of the "two Argentinas" does indeed harken back to a dichotomy made famous by nineteenth-century thinker and former Argentine president Domingo F. Sarmiento. In his 1845 work *Facundo*, Sarmiento proclaimed Argentina to be torn between the "civilization of the Europeanized cities and the "barbarism" of the creole countryside. Twentieth-century nationalists, who loathed Sarmiento, considered *Facundo* the epitome of liberal disdain for the "real" Argentina and argued that liberal efforts to remake Argentina in the image of Europe (and thus to sell out the country to imperialists) had been the source of all of Argentina's ills. The point here is not that nationalists completely invented the notion of the two Argentinas but that they appropriated Sarmiento's dichotomy, inverted it, and used it for their own purposes, all the while proclaiming a false continuity between the mid-

nineteenth century and their own present. It is this notion of continuity over such a long period of time that must be challenged, for such claims are based on an approach to cultural memory that ignores how beliefs and ideas are transmitted transgenerationally. As scholars of collective memory have repeatedly emphasized, ideas and beliefs never remain static over long periods of time, but for them to survive they must to be invoked, affirmed, and re-elaborated by subsequent generations, who themselves confront new realities and come in contact with new intellectual influences.

18. Allan Hanson, "The Making of the Maori: Cultural Invention and Its Logic," *American Anthropologist* 91, no. 4 (1989): 890–902.

19. This notion of two variants of ethno-cultural forms of identity complicates the civic-ethnic dichotomy that has dominated so much of theoretical literature on European nations but syncs with Stephen Shulman's work on Ukraine. According to Shulman ("Contours," 36), there were two versions of ethnic-national identity (one ethnic Ukrainian and the other Eastern Slavic) that currently "compete for supremacy" in present-day Ukraine.

20. The phrase comes from the title of Tulio Halperin Donghi's much-cited essay "Argentina: Liberalism in a Country Born Liberal," in *Guiding the Invisible Hand: Economic Liberalism and the State in Latin American History*, ed. Joseph Love and Nils Jacobsen (New York: Praeger, 1988), 99–116.

21. As practitioners of intellectual history are aware, recent decades have witnessed a shift from the study of ideas or ideologies (–isms) per se to an interest in the study of the shared conceptual premises and linguistic conventions that allow ideas to be "thinkable" and thus to be articulated in particular historical moments and places. As Elías Palti has put it, "What the 'new intellectual history' now looks for is not only *what the author said* (the manifest contents of his or her discourse) but also, and fundamentally, *how it was possible for him or her to say what he or she said*—to trace the categorical soil and the set of assumptions underlying a given order of discourse and to observe how they shifted over time, thus paving the way for the emergence of new intellectual constellations." See "Historicism as an *Idea* and as a *Language*," *History and Theory* 44 (October 2005): 433.

22. According to Hobsbawm, the rise of ethno-cultural nationalism in late nineteenth-century Europe stemmed from three key developments: rapid changes associated with modernity that threatened traditional groups, the emergence of new social classes in the urban areas, and massive migrations that brought different groups in contact with each other for the first time. All, of course, are relevant to the Argentine case. See *Nations and Nationalism since 1780: Programme, Myth, Reality*, The Wiles Lectures (London: Cambridge University Press, 1990), 109.

23. Ricardo Rojas, *Eurindia*, vol. 5, *Obras de Ricardo Rojas*, 2nd ed. (Buenos Aires: Librería "La Facultad," de J. Roldán, 1924), 128, 175.

24. As will be developed in subsequent chapters, Rojas believed that the product of the fusion between the European and the indigenous forces was the lowly Argentine gaucho or cowboy, whom he identified as the prototype of the Argentine race. See *La literatura argentina: Ensayo filosófico sobre la evolución de la cultura en el Plata*, vol. 8, *Obras de Ricardo Rojas*, 2nd ed. (Buenos Aires: Librería "La Facultad," de J. Roldán y [ca. 1924]), 1:144–45. It should be noted that Rojas's belief that the Argentine race also included an indigenous element should not be seen as a call to recognize mestizaje or racial mixture as central to national identity. His focus on the gaucho (a figure who had largely disappeared by the late nineteenth century) as the embodiment of the indigenous element, and the fact that he was writing during the period of massive European immigration, meant that Rojas was free to celebrate the indigenous element of *argentinidad* without challenging Argentina's self-proclaimed status as a purely white nation.

25. *El solar de la raza* (1913; repr. Madrid: Editorial "Saturnino Calleja," s.a., 1920), 59.

26. Gálvez, *El solar*, 57.

27. Ricardo Rojas, *Silabario de la decoración americana* (Buenos Aires: Editorial Losada, 1930), 151.

28. For a discussion of various meanings of the term *raza* in the early twentieth century, see Eduardo Zimmermann, "Racial Ideas and Social Reform: Argentina, 1890–1916," *Hispanic American Historical Review* 72, no. 1 (February 1992): 23–46, esp. 25–28; and Diego Armus, "Desirable and Undesirable Migrants: Disease, Eugenics, and Discourses in Modern Buenos Aires," *Journal of Iberian and Latin American Studies* 25, no. 1 (2019): 57–79, DOI: 10.1080/14701847.2019.1579492. For a discussion related specifically to the thought of Manuel Ugarte, see Eduardo Elena, "Nation, Race and Latin Americanism in Argentina: The Life and Times of Manuel Ugarte, 1900s–1960s," in *Making Citizens in Argentina*, ed. Benjamin Bryce and David Sheinin (Pittsburgh: University of Pittsburg Press, 2017), 62–82, esp. 71.

29. Sandra McGee Deutsch, "Insecure Whiteness: Jews between Civilization and Barbarism, 1880–1940s," in Alberto and Elena, *Rethinking Race*, 28.

30. The ways in which both positivist and biological understandings of race contributed to and served to reinforce the cultural nationalists' notion of an Argentine race will be developed in chapter 3.

31. This equation of race and nationality was not limited to those Argentines who embraced a predominantly historico-cultural understanding of race. Chapter 2 will show that intellectuals who adopted what they saw as a scien-

tific or biological definition of race *also* promoted the idea that Argentines would eventually form a single race, thus reinforcing the cultural nationalists' identification of nationality and race.

32. Eduardo Elena has argued that the reluctance to use the term *race* in Argentine political discourse can be traced to the early years of Peronism, when the Nazi's use of racial theories made such categories unacceptable. See "Argentina in Black and White: Race, Peronism, and the Color of Politics, 1940s to the Present," in Alberto and Elena, *Rethinking Race*, 187. My own reading of the evidence, however, suggests that at least in nationalist writings, *race* faded from general usage earlier.

33. While making sense at the time, these technological decisions, once made, direct subsequent innovations along certain pathways that inhibit the development of superior technologies. The classic example, outlined in a seminal article by economist Paul David, is that of the QWERTY keyboard on early typewriters. As David notes, the QWERTY design was developed to avoid the jamming of the type bar when keys were struck in rapid succession. Once adopted, the QWERTY keyboard became standard on all typewriters, despite the development of other, superior keyboard arrangements (such as the DSK) and the fact that the original typebar mechanism that made QWERTY useful has long since disappeared. See "Clio and the Economics of QWERTY," *American Economic Review* 75, no. 2 (1985): 332–37, www.jstor.org /stable /1805621.

34. Useful introductions to the concept of path dependence in the social sciences are provided in James Mahoney, "Path Dependence in Historical Sociology," *Theory and Society* 29, no. 4 (August 2000): 507–48; and Giovanni Capoccia and R. Daniel Keleman, "The Study of Critical Junctures: Theory, Narrative, and Counterfactuals in Historical Institutionalism," *World Politics* 59, no. 3 (April 2007): 341–69. Path dependence has also become a standard concept for sociologists working in the field of collective memory. On this point and for some useful citations, see Hiro Saito, "Reiterated Commemoration: Hiroshima as National Trauma," *Sociological Theory* 24, no. 4 (December 2009): 353–76, esp. 354–55. For an example of how path dependence has been applied to the study of intellectual history, see Altug Yalcintas, "Historical Small Events and the Eclipse of *Utopia*: Perspectives on Path Dependence in Human Thought," *Culture, Theory, and Critique* 47, no. 1 (2006): 53–70.

35. The term *genetic moments* comes from Capoccia and Keleman, "Study of Critical Junctures," 343.

36. This is not to claim that this early twentieth-century flirtation with ethno-cultural nationalism *inevitably* reshaped subsequent discussions about Argentine identity. To do so would be to fall into the same "continuity trap" of

those who have argued that the country's problematic political life can be traced to the creation of two opposing Argentinas in the nineteenth century (see note 17). Rather, the trick—and the task—is to trace *how* the essentialist notions of Argentine identity that gained currency during the opening decades of the twentieth century were taken up by later nationalist intellectuals. Who were the key actors? What were their intellectual debts, both acknowledged and otherwise? What new events and intellectual influences reinforced the notion that Argentina was first and foremost a unitary ethno-cultural community that existed independently of the state?

37.  Enrique Zuleta Álvarez, *El nacionalismo argentino* (Buenos Aires: Ediciones La Bastilla, 1975), 85; David Rock, "Intellectual Precursors of Conservative Nationalism in Argentina," *Hispanic American Historical Review* 67, no. 2 (1987): 271–300. See also María Inés Barbero and Fernando Devoto, *Los nacionalistas (1910–1932)* (Buenos Aires: Centro Editor de América Latina, 1983), esp. chap. 1; and Aníbal Iturrieta, "El primer nacionalismo argentino," in *El pensamiento político argentino contemporáneo*, ed. A. Iturrieta (Buenos Aires: Grupo Editor Latinoamericano, 1994), 17–43, esp. 27.

38.  This theme is developed more fully in Jeane H. DeLaney, "Imagining *El Ser Argentino*: Cultural Nationalism and Romantic Concepts of Nationhood in Early Twentieth-Century Argentina." *Journal of Latin American Studies* 34, no. 3 (2002): 625–58, www.jstor.org/stable/3875463?seq=1#page_scan_tab _contents.

39.  Marysa Navarro Gerassi, *Los nacionalistas* (Buenos Aires: J. Alvarez, 1968).

40.  Zuleta Álvarez devoted only one of twenty-one chapters in *El nacionalismo argentino* to the left.

41.  María Inés Barbero and Fernando Devoto's *Los nacionalistas (1910–1932)* (Buenos Aires: Centro Editor de América Latina, 1983) devotes a single chapter, titled "El otro nacionalismo," to the nationalist left. Cristián Buchrucker also pays scant attention to the left in his *Nacionalismo y peronismo: la Argentina en la crisis ideológica del mundo (1927–1955)* (Buenos Aires: Editorial Sudamericana, 1987), 258–76. To be sure, Buchrucker goes a bit further than most by including in his treatment of Peronism some information on the influence of FORJA. More recent works have tended to focus on more specialized themes within the broader topic of Argentine nationalism, and here again the primary emphasis has been on the right. Prominent examples include Sandra McGee Deutsch, *Counterrevolution in Argentina, 1900–1932: The Argentine Patriotic League* (Lincoln: University of Nebraska Press, 1986); Deutsch and Ronald H. Dolkart, *The Argentine Right: Its History and Intellectual Origins, 1910 to the Present*, Latin American Silhouettes (Wilmington, DE: Scholarly

Resources, 1993); and Deutsch, *Las Derechas*, as well as Federico Finchelstein, *Transatlantic Fascism: Ideology, Violence, and the Sacred in Argentina and Italy, 1919–1945* (Durham, NC: Duke University Press, 2010); and *Ideological Origins*; Daniel Lvovich, *Nacionalismo y antisemitismo en la Argentina* (Buenos Aires: Javier Vergara, Grupo Zeta, 2003); and Luis Fernando Beraza, *Nacionalistas: la trayectoria política de un grupo polémico, 1927–1983* (Buenos Aires: Cántaro, 2005). Although the overwhelming emphasis on the nationalist right may indeed be due to its violence and more inflammatory language, semantics may also play a role. As Michael Goebel has perceptively argued, the widespread use (by scholars writing in both Spanish and English) of the Spanish term *nacionalismo* to denote Argentina's right-wing strand of nationalism inevitably conveys the impression that this was the only form of nationalism that ever existed in Argentina. See *Argentina's Partisan Past: Nationalism and the Politics of History* (Liverpool: Liverpool University Press, 2011), 7, 231.

42. When arguing that scholarship on left-wing Argentine nationalism has been overshadowed by research on nationalism of the right, I am of course excluding the topic of Peronism, which has generated a vast historiography. Peronism was (and is) a multifaceted phenomenon encompassing much more than nationalism.

43. Among the most notable works focusing on the New Left are Oscár Terán, *Nuestros años sesentas: la formación de la nueva izquierda intelectual argentina, 1956–1966* (Buenos Aires: El Cielo por Asalto, 1993); Carlos Altamirano, *Peronismo y cultura de izquierda* (Buenos Aires: Temas Grupo Editoriales, 2001); Claudia Hilb and Daniel Lutzky, *La nueva izquierda argentina, 1960–1980: política y violencia* (Buenos Aires: Centro Editor de América Latina, 1984); and María Cristina Tortti, Mauricio Chama, Adrián Celentano, and Horacio Robles, *La nueva izquierda argentina (1955–1976): socialismo, peronismo y revolución* (Rosario, Colombia: Colección Universidad, 2014).

44. The literature on the Montoneros is particularly voluminous. In addition to some of the works cited above, which cover the 1970s, there are several scholarly works that focus primarily on the Montoneros. Among the most notable are Richard Gillespie, *Soldiers of Perón: Argentina's Montoneros* (Oxford: Clarendon Press, 1982); María José Moyano, *Argentina's Lost Patrol: Armed Struggle, 1969–1979* (New Haven, CT: Yale University Press, 1995); Beatriz Sarlo, *La pasión y la excepción* (Buenos Aires: Siglo Veintiuno Editores, 2003); Lucas Lanusse, *Montoneros: el mito de sus 12 fundadores* (Buenos Aires: Zeta, 2010); and Hugo Vezzetti, *Sobre la violencia revolucionario*. This latter literature has largely focused on the guerrilla leadership, the generalized climate of extremism, and public attitudes toward political violence. Beyond these two focal points, the early history of the nationalist left has received relatively little

attention. Most of the literature on this topic has rightly focused on FORJA, with the majority of works penned by either FORJA sympathizers or former members. One of the most comprehensive treatments is Miguel Ángel Scenna's sympathetic two-volume *F.O.R.J.A.: una aventura argentina (de Yrigoyen a Perón)* (Buenos Aires: Ediciones La Bastilla, 1972). Also useful is FORJA founder Arturo Jauretche's *FORJA y la década infame: Con un apéndice de manifiestos, declaraciones y textos volantes* (Buenos Aires: Editorial Coyoacán, 1962), which includes some useful primary sources. Left-wing historian Norberto Galasso has produced several works that provide information on FORJA, the most important being biographies of Jauretche, such as *Jauretche y su época* (Buenos Aires: Peña Lillo Editor, 1985), as well as numerous works on FORJA's most important intellectual, Raúl Scalabrini Ortiz. Also informative, as well as the most neutral, is Mark Falcoff, "Argentine Nationalism on the Eve of Perón: The Force of Radical Orientation of Young Argentina and Its Rivals, 1935–45" (PhD diss., Princeton University, 1970). A quite recent but not terribly helpful addition to this literature is Oscár Sbarra Mitre's brief and highly partisan *F.O.R.J.A.: El destino es un camello ciego* (Buenos Aires: Quinqué Editores, 2005).

45. On this point see Diana Quattrocchi-Woisson, *Los males de la memoria: historia y política en la Argentina*, 2nd ed. (Buenos Aires: Emecé Editores, 1998), 107. Quattrocchi-Woisson herself takes a step in this direction by exploring efforts on the part of the right and left to debunk Argentina's liberal historical tradition. For examples of other scholars who have noted the affinities between right- and left-wing nationalism, see note 5.

46. David Rock, *Authoritarian Argentina: The Nationalist Movement, Its History, and Its Impact* (Berkeley: University of California Press, 1993), 123.

47. Rock, *Authoritarian Argentina*, 215–16.

48. Rock, *Authoritarian Argentina*, 231.

49. Rock, *Authoritarian Argentina*, xiv–xv.

50. Rock, *Authoritarian Argentina*, 122.

51. Alberto Spektorowski, *The Origins of Argentina's Revolution of the Right* (Notre Dame, IN: University of Notre Dame Press, 2003).

52. Spektorowski, *Origins*, 10.

53. Spektorowski, *Origins*, 10.

54. Michael Goebel, *Argentina's Partisan Past: Nationalism and the Politics of History*, Liverpool Latin American Studies, new ser. 11 (Liverpool: Liverpool University Press, 2014), 146.

55. Goebel, *Argentina's Partisan Past*, 238.

56. On the omission of Latin America from discussions of nationalism, see Don Doyle and Marco Antonio Pamplona, "Americanizing the Conversa-

tion on Nationalism," in *Nationalism in the New World*, ed. Don Doyle and Marco Antonio Pamplona (Athens: University of Georgia Press, 2006), 1–15. This essay, which argues that *all* of the Americas have been largely overlooked in nationalism studies, serves as the introduction to their edited volume, which aims to redress this issue. A prominent exception to the neglect of Latin America is Benedict Anderson's seminal work *Imagined Communities*, which unexpectedly gave the region a central role in the construction of the modern nation. It should be noted, however, that Anderson's "creole Pioneers" thesis has been roundly rejected by Latin Americanists. For a sampling of criticism, see the essays in *Beyond Imagined Communities: Reading and Writing the Nation in Nineteenth-Century Latin America*, ed. John Chasteen and Sarah Chambers (Baltimore: Johns Hopkins University Press, 2003). Also useful is Eric Van Young, "Revolution and Imagined Communities in Mexico, 1810–1821," in Doyle and Pamplona, *Nationalism in the New World*, 184–207.

57. This neglect has led to misunderstandings. Eric Hobsbawm, for example, concluded that Spanish America "has remained largely immune to the modern ethnic-cultural nationalism to this day." See "Nationalism and Nationality in Latin America," in *Pour une histoire economicque et social internationale: mélanges offerts à Paul Bairoch*, ed. Bouda Etemad, Jean Baton, and Thomas David (Geneva: Editions Passé Présent, 1995), 313.

58. Diana Quattrocchi-Woisson makes a similar point in her excellent study of historical revisionism in Argentina, when she notes that the revisionist impulse that sought to rehabilitate the reputation of nineteenth-century dictator Juan Manuel de Rosas "drew nourishment from two sources of inspiration: one of a popular character, the other elitist." This, in her estimation, was the secret to revisionism's "great vitality." See *Los males*, 27.

59. Ronald Grigor Suny and Michael D. Kennedy, *Intellectuals and the Articulation of the Nation* (Ann Arbor: University of Michigan Press, 2001), 2. This is of course true whether the scholar has a primordialist or constructivist understanding of the nation. In either case, the role of intellectuals in articulating what the nation is and how it is distinctive, along with what binds its citizens together, is understood as crucial.

60. Suny and Kennedy, *Intellectuals*, 3.

61. Suny and Kennedy, *Intellectuals*, 2. See also Peter Lambert's discussion of the role of intellectuals and historians in producing national narratives that become central to individual identity. Peter Lambert, "Myth, Manipulation, and Violence: Relationships between National Identity and Political Violence," in *Political Violence and the Construction of National Identity in Latin America*, ed. Peter Lambert and Will Fowler (New York: Palgrave Macmillan, 2006), 24–25.

62. In the mid-1930s, Scalabrini Ortiz became a key figure within the nationalist left. He and his work *El hombre* will be examined extensively in chapter 7. Ezequiel Martínez Estrada and Eduardo Mallea are usually considered "liberal," despite the fact that the former spent several years in Castro's Cuba. Neither of these men, whose work will be treated in the conclusion, identified with nationalism.

63. Scalabrini's *El hombre* was first published in July 1931; by November 1932, it was in its fifth printing. This work's enduring popularity will be treated in chapter 7. Ezequiel Martínez Estrada's *Radiografía de la pampa* has been reissued at least fifteen times; the last edition appeared in 2017. Eduardo Mallea's *Historia de una pasión argentina* proved to be similarly popular and has been reissued at least twenty times since its first publication in 1937. What appears to be the latest edition was published in 2001. The source of this information is WorldCat, which, because it contains only those editions that made their way into the collections of US libraries and selected European libraries, surely represents an undercount.

64. Among innumerable examples to illustrate the significance of these works in naturalizing the essentialist notion of *el ser nacional* is an essay on the 1930s that appeared in a recent general history of Argentina. Writing in 2001, Sylvia Saítta described the authors of this decade as being engaged in a search for the "interpretive keys into the modes in which '*el ser nacional*' has been constituted, with the intention of defining the identity and authentic nature of the Argentines." To be sure, the author's insertion of quotation marks around *el ser nacional* suggests some unease with the term. Still, the absence of a definition indicates her confidence that it would be familiar to an Argentine audience. See "Entre la cultura y la política: Los escritores de izquierda," in *Nueva historia argentina*, vol. 7, *Crisis económica, avance del estado e incertidumbre política (1930–1943)*, ed. Alejandro Cattaruzza and Juan Suriano (Buenos Aires: Ed. Sudamericana, 2001), 387. It is important to note that, while this broad and uncritical acceptance of essentialized notions of Argentine identity has never been subjected to sustained scholarly analysis, many prominent Argentine intellectuals have noted (and often lamented) this phenomenon. In various publications and at various times, Alberto Ciria, Carlos Altamirano, Hilda Sábato, José Luis Romero, Federico Neiberg, and Luis Alberto Romero—to name just a few— have all commented on the ways in which the constructs of *el ser nacional* or the "two Argentinas" have shaped how Argentines understand their collective identity. On the pervasiveness and persistence of the trope of *el ser nacional*, see José Luis Romero, "Las ideologias de la cultura nacional," in *La ideologías de la cultura nacional y otros ensayos* (Buenos Aires: Centro Editor de América Latina, 1982), 75–85. (This essay first appeared under the same title in *Criterio* 46, no.

1681–82 (December 1973). For similar perspectives on the national obsession with the putative *ser nacional*, see Alberto Ciria, "Elite Culture and Popular Culture in Argentina, 1930–1955," *Interamerican Review of Bibliography* 37, no. 4 (1987): 503; Carlos Altamirano, "Algunas notas sobre nuestra cultura," *Punto de Vista* 6, no. 18 (August 1983): 8; and Rita Laura Segato, "Identidades políticas/ Alteridades históricas: una crítica a las certezas del pluralismo global," in *La nación y sus otros: raza, etnicidad y diversidad religiosa en tiempos de políticas de la identidad* (Ciudad Autónoma de Buenos Aires: Prometeo Libros, 2007), 49. On the pervasiveness and importance of the trope of the two Argentinas among the educated sectors in the late 1950s and early 1960s, see Federico Neiberg, "Ciencias sociales y mitologías nacionales: La constitución de la sociología en la Argentina y la invención del *peronismo*," *Desarrollo Económico* 34, no. 136 (January–March 1995): 533–56; Carlos Altamirano, "Las dos Argentinas," in *Peronismo y cultura de izquierda*, 27–38, Colección Temas sociales 4 (Buenos Aires: Temas Grupo Ed. (2001); and Carlos Altamirano, *Bajo el signo de las masas (1943–1973)*, vol. 6 of *Biblioteca del pensamiento argentino* (Buenos Aires: Ariel Historia, 2001), 31. See also Hugo Vezzetti (*Sobre la violencia revolucionario*, 44), who has argued that the trope of the "two Argentinas"—initially elaborated by the nationalist right in the 1930s, was later "activated and exalted" by Peronist guerrilla groups of the 1960s and '70s. Also telling is an autobiographical comment by eminent anthropologist Néstor García Canclini, a native Argentine, who went into exile in Mexico after the 1976 coup. Now a naturalized Mexican citizen, who considers himself an "Argenmexican," García Canclini has recounted how the years away from his native country provided him with the critical distance necessary to recognize the peculiarity of the Argentine "dream" of a "national being." See *Imagined Globalization* (Durham, NC: Duke University Press, 2014), 189. While not referring explicitly to the trope of the two Argentinas, Tulio Halperin Donghi has argued that the underlying diagnostic, which cast nineteenth-century liberal leaders as having played "the demonic role" in Argentine history, had by 1973 become the predominate interpretation of the past among the general public. See "Argentina's Unmastered Past," *Latin America Research Review* 23, no. 2 (1988): 5. It should be noted as well that the notion of the two Argentinas continues to exercise appeal in some circles. See, for example, Victor Mariano Sonego's recently reprinted *Las dos argentinas: para una lectura crítica de nuestra historia* (Buenos Aires: Edebe Editorial Don Bosco Argentina, 1999). The book was originally published in 1983; the 1999 printing is its fifth.

    65. On "reintegration of the nationality," see Hipólito Yrigoyen, Mensaje al Congreso, October 15, 1921, http://constitucionweb.blogspot.com/2012/06

/mensaje-al-congreso-del-presidente-h.html. "Organizing" the national community was a recurrent theme in Perón's speeches. See Perón's *La comunidad organizada y el estado justicialista*, Cartilla Doctrinaria 2 (Buenos Aires: Presidencia de la Nación, Secretaria de Prensa y Difusión, 1974).

66. In a 1998 study of political participation and citizenship in Argentina and Chile, political scientist Lucy Taylor noted the ongoing sense among adherents of both Radicalism and Peronism that these organizations were more than mere political parties. According to Taylor, both "are based not on ideology, but on a mystical sense of belonging." Moreover, in her view, "party affiliation appears to depend more on identity and emotion than thought and opinion which raises the stakes in terms of passion and to the detriment of reason." See *Citizenship, Participation and Democracy: Changing Dynamics in Chile and Argentina* (New York: St. Martin's Press, 1998), 100.

67. Goebel, *Argentina's Partisan Past*, 146.

68. Luis Alberto Romero, "Apogeo y crisis de la Argentina vital," *Revista de las Américas,* no. 1 (Spring 2003): 99, 100, 101. Worse still in Romero's eyes has been the periodic emergence of individuals and groups proclaiming themselves the "interpreters, spokesmen or custodians of '*lo nacional.*'" These "self-proclaimed saviors of the nation," in his view, played a central role in the disastrous collapse of democracy in 1966 and 1976.

69. Arturo Jauretche, speech delivered in the aftermath of the June 4, 1943, coup, Papers of Darío Alessandro, Biblioteca del Congreso Nacional, Argentina, 11. Jauretche's insistence that all immigrants fully incorporate into a single unified Argentine identity remained central to his thinking and informed his 1964 polemic over Zionism against Jewish activist Daniel Finkelstein. According to Jauretche, although Jews should be accepted in Argentina, they should be fully assimilated—that is, *Argentines, not Jewish Argentines.* Zionism, moreover, was incompatible with this full assimilation and posed a threat to national unity. For Raanan Rein, Jauretche's rejection of a pluralistic Argentina and his belief in the need for cultural homogeneity places the FORJA uncomfortably close to the ideas about nationality espoused by the nationalist right. On this polemic, and Rein's assessment, see Raanan Rein, "Entre el peronismo y el nacionalismo de extrema derecha: Jauretche, los argentinos-judios y la acusación de doble leadtad," in *Pensar a Jauretche*, ed. Gustavo Maragoni (Buenos Aires: UNIPE, 2105), 215–38.

70. Hilda Sábato, "Pluralismo y nación," *Punto de Vista* 7, no. 34 (July–September 1989): 2.

71. This will be discussed in the conclusion.

72. Romero, "Las ideologías," 75.

CHAPTER 1.    Nation and Nationality in the Nineteenth Century

1. As discussed in the introduction, when I speak of the impact of Romanticism in Argentina (during both the nineteenth and twentieth centuries), it is essential to keep in mind that I am *not* referring to a philosophical system or even to a coherent set of ideas that Argentines deliberately borrowed and applied to their own situations. Rather, Romanticism's impact can be understood as the more or less unconscious adoption of a set of understandings about nationality and history, current in Europe during the nineteenth century, that proved attractive to Argentine audiences, because they seemed relevant to the challenges posed by immigration. Thus, those who adopted these understandings did so not in conscious opposition to the civic or political vision of the nation that had prevailed during the earliest years of the republic but rather to make sense of their historical moment.

2. Other key members of this generation include Esteban Echeverría, Juan María Gutiérrez, Vicente Fidel López, José Mármol, and Félix Frías.

3. In the context of nineteenth-century Argentina, *liberal* denotes an individual who favored a republican (i.e., nonmonarchical) form of government grounded in the rule of law and codified in a constitution that guaranteed individual freedom, allowed for some form of representative democracy, and placed checks on arbitrary rule. Nineteenth-century Argentine liberals also embraced free trade, sought closer economic ties with Europe, and promoted European immigration. Culturally, liberals viewed Spain as backward, admired the United States and non-Spanish Europe, and believed the domestic population needed improvement. As will be clear, while the members of the Generation of 1837 embraced these ideas, much of their thought had nothing to do with classical liberalism.

4. This region refers to the great expanse of territory that includes present-day Argentina, as well as to Uruguay, Bolívia, and Paraguay. During the colonial period, this region was part of the same administrative unit.

5. Jeremy Adelman, *Republic of Capital: Buenos Aires and the Legal Transformation of the Atlantic World* (Stanford, CA: Stanford University Press, 1999), 54–55.

6. Tulio Halperin Donghi, *Tradición política e ideología revolucionaria de Mayo* (Buenos Aires: Centro Editor de América Latina, 1985), 93.

7. Halperin Donghi, *Tradición política*, 93.

8. Eduardo Dürnhöfer, "Trascendencia de la filosofía de la revolución francesa en la revolución de Mayo," in *Imagen y recepción de la revolución francesa*

*en la argentina*, ed. Noemí Goldman (Buenos Aires: Grupo Ed. Latinoamericano, 1990), 73.

9. Tulio Halperin Donghi, *Politics, Economics and Society in Argentina in the Revolutionary Period*, trans. Richard Southern (Cambridge: Cambridge University Press, 1975), 111.

10. Cabildo Acts of May 25, 1810, Art. 9, quoted in Adelman, *Republic of Capital*, 80.

11. Independence was not actually declared until July 9, 1816, in the name not of Argentina but of the United Provinces of South America.

12. The term *creole* denoted an individual who was of Spanish ancestry but was born in the Americas.

13. For a history of the notion of a contractual relationship between sovereign and subject from the medieval period to the early nineteenth century, see Halperin Donghi, *Tradición política española*.

14. *Reglamiento de la división de poderes sancionado por la Junta conservadora (30 de septiembre a 29 de octubre, 1811)*, in José Carlos Chiaramonte, ed., *Ciudades, provincias, estados: orígenes de la Nación Argentina, 1800–1846* (Argentina: Compañia Editora Espasa Calpe Argentina/Ariel, 1997), 349.

15. Patricia Vallejos de Llobet, "El léxico de la revolución francesa en el proceso de estandarización lingüistica del español bonarense," in *Imagen y recepción de la revolución francesa en la argentina*, ed. Noemí Goldman (Buenos Aires: Grupo Ed. Latinoamericano, 1990), 79–99.

16. José Carlos Chiaramonte, "Formas de identidad en la región de la Plata luego de 1810," *Boletín del Instituto de Historia Argentina y Americana "Dr. E. Ravignani,"* 3rd ser., sem. 1, no. 1 (1989): 83.

17. Juan Ignacio Gorriti and Valentín Gómez, "Discursos de Juan Ignacio Gorriti y Valentín Gómez en el debate relativo a la creación y organización del Ejército Nacional, iniciado en la sesión del 3 de mayo de 1825," in Chiaramonte, *Ciudades*, 519.

18. Gorriti and Gómez, "Discursos," 520.

19. Gorriti and Gómez, "Discursos," 522–23.

20. Hans Vogel, "New Citizens for a New Nation: Naturalization in Early Independent Argentina," *Hispanic American Historical Review* 71, no. 1 (February 1991): 117.

21. Vogel, "New Citizens," 117.

22. Vogel, "New Citizens," 122–23.

23. *La Gaceta Ministerial*, September 4, 1812. Quoted in Jorge Carlos Mitre, "La inmigración en la Argentina y la identidad nacional," *Historia* 7, no. 26 (June–August, 1987): 43–44.

24. Tulio Halperin Donghi, "¿Para qué la inmigración? Ideología y política inmigratoria y aceleración del proceso modernizador: el caso argentino (1810–1914)," *Jahrbuch für Geschichte von Staat, Wirtschaft und Gesellschaft Lateinamerikas* 13, no. 1 (1976): 443.

25. "El redactor de la Asamblea de 1813," in *Pensamiento político de la Emancipación*, compiled by José Luis Romero and Luis Alberto Romero (Caracas: Biblioteca Ayacucho, 1977), 309. Quoted in Mónica Quijada, "¿'Hijos de los barcos' o diversidad invisibilizada? La articulación de la población indígena en la construcción nacional argentina (Siglo XIX)," *HMex* 53, no. 2 (2003): 478.

26. Quijada, "¿'Hijos de los barcos' o diversidad invisibilizada?" 478. It should be emphasized that extending suffrage to men of color was neither an exercise in multiculturalism nor a recognition of racial equality. Rather, the 1821 extension of citizenship mirrored the generalized practice of Latin American liberals who sought to break down indigenous communities (and identities) by granting citizenship to native peoples. This homogenizing project was central to nineteenth-century liberalism throughout Latin America.

27. This contradiction, of course, was not unique to Argentina. Indeed the conflict between civic and ethno-cultural understandings of the nation is one of the central fault lines running through US history. For a sweeping treatment of this tension in twentieth-century US thought, see Gary Gerstle, *American Crucible: Race and Nation in the Twentieth Century* (Princeton, NJ: Princeton University Press, 2001).

28. Bernardino Rivadavia. Quoted in Halperin Donghi, "¿Para qué?," 443.

29. The resulting Argentine nation would, of course, be minus the territories that now make up modern-day Bolívia, Paraguay, and Uruguay.

30. During that period what is now Argentina was called the United Provinces of La Plata.

31. David Rock, *Argentina, 1516–1982: From Spanish Colonization to the Falklands War* (Berkeley: University of California Press, 1985), 100.

32. Rock, *Argentina, 1516–1982*, 98, 101.

33. Rosas assumed the governorship of the province of Buenos Aires in December 1829, at which point Argentina had no overarching government system. In 1831, he signed a pact with leaders of other provinces, creating the Argentine Confederation. After leaving office at the end of his term in 1832, he returned to power in 1835 and ruled until 1852.

34. Some, such as Alberdi, downplayed the cultural differences between the leadership of the two factions, noting that many of Rosas's most powerful supporters were city educated, while some of the most important Unitarians were men of the countryside. Juan Bautista Alberdi, *Argentina, 1852: Bases y*

*puntos de partida para la organización política de la República Argentina* (Barcelona: Linkgua Ediciones, 2007), 69–70. Hereafter, *Bases y puntos.* This having been said, it should be noted that Sarmiento tended to associate Federalism with the castes or people of mixed race. On this point, see Ariel de la Fuente, *Children of Facundo: Caudillo and Gaucho Insurgency during the Argentine State-Formation Process (La Rioja, 1853–1870)* (Durham, NC: Duke University Press, 2000), 151.

35. Indeed, so vehemently did Rosas reject the writing of a constitution that he threatened those Federalists who dared remind him of his earlier pledge. See Tulio Halperin Donghi, "Argentine Counterpoint: Rise of the Nation, Rise of the State," in *Beyond Imagined Communities: Reading and Writing the Nation in Nineteenth-Century Latin America*, ed. Sara Castro-Klarén and John Charles Chasteen (Washington, DC: Woodrow Wilson Center Press, 2003), 50.

36. Tulio Halperin Donghi, "Un término de comparación: liberalismo y nacionalismo en el Río de la Plata," in *Los intelectuales y el poder en México. Intellectuals and power in Mexico: memorias de la VI Conferencia de Historiadores Mexicanos y Estadounidenses: Papers Presented at the VI Conference of Mexican and United States Historians*, ed. Roderic Ai Camp, Charles Adams Hale, and Josefina Zoraida Vázquez (México: El Colegio de México, 1991), 115.

37. The classic English-language study of Rosas's rule is John Lynch's *Argentine Dictator: Juan Manuel De Rosas, 1829–1852* (Oxford: Clarendon Press, 1981). For details of the requirements on wearing red during this period, see 179–80.

38. It should be noted, however, that although later right-wing nationalists would laud Rosas as a defender of the true Catholic Argentina, the dictator very clearly took an instrumentalist approach to religion. While Rosas valued the church as a tool for social control, he was quick to punish members of the clergy who failed to support the Federalists.

39. Myers develops this theme extensively in his *Orden y virtud: El discurso republicano en el régimen rosista* (Buenos Aires: Universidad Nacional de Quilmes, 1995).

40. Myers, *Orden y virtud*, 60–61.

41. Jorge Myers, "Language, History and Politics in Argentine Identity, 1840–1880," in *Nationalism in the New World*, ed. Don Harrison Doyle and Marco Antonio Villela Pamplona (Athens: University of Georgia Press, 2006), 121–22.

42. Myers, *Orden y virtud*, 58–72.

43. My discussion of the impact of Romanticism on the Generation of 1837 draws substantially from Jorge Myers, "La revolución en las ideas: La ge-

neración romántica de 1837 en la cultura y en la política argentinas," in *Revolución, república, confederación (1806–1853)*, ed. Noemí Goldman (Buenos Aires: Editorial Sudamericana, 1998), 382–443; Jeremy Adelman, *Republic of Capital*, especially chap. 7; and Elías José Palti, *El momento romántico: nación, historia y lenguajes políticos en la Argentina del siglo XIX* (Buenos Aires: Eudeba, 2009).

44. Esteban Echeverría, *Dogma socialista y otras páginas políticas* (Barcelona: Red Ediciones S.L., 2011), 23, e-book. Citations refer to the e-book.

45. Echeverría, *Dogma socialista*, 91.

46. Domingo F. Sarmiento, *Facundo*, 8th ed. (Buenos Aires: Editorial Losada, 1963), 23, 24, 28.

47. As Palti has noted, although the members came to see the Rosas regime as temporary, they differed in their assessment of the dictator's place in Argentine history. While Alberdi ultimately concluded that Rosas was an aberration or obstacle blocking Argentina's march toward its destiny, Sarmiento came to see him as a necessary moment in the nation's historical development. On this point see Palti, *El momento romántico*, 50–51, 65–85.

48. Juan Bautista Alberdi, "Doble harmonía entre el objeto de esta institución" (Discurso de Juan Bautista Alberdi, en la inauguración del Salón Literario, el 23 de Junio de 1837), in Buenos Aires, Concejo Deliberante, Comisión de Biblioteca, *Antecedentes de la Asociación de Mayo, 1837–1937: Homenaje del honorable Consejo Deliberante de la Ciudad de Buenos Aires en su fundación* (Buenos Aires: Los talleres gráficos de Cantiello y cía., res. ltda, 1939), 41.

49. Myers, "Language, History and Politics," 122.

50. Palti, *El momento romántico*, 27.

51. Indeed, as Palti has argued, the Generation of 1837's belief that it could discover the underlying laws that supposedly determined the nation's evolution gave these thinkers their sense of generational identity and provided them (at least in their own eyes) with the "symbolic capital" necessary to justify their claims to be legitimate players on the national political stage. See *El momento romántico*, 35–36.

52. Juan Bautista Alberdi, *Bases y puntos*, 74.

53. In Echeverría's words, "Democracy . . . is the only regime that suits us, and the only one possible for us" (*Dogma socialista*, 72).

54. Juan Bautista Alberdi, *Fragmento preliminar al estudio del derecho* (Buenos Aires: Ciudad Argentina, 1998), 8.

55. Echeverría, *Dogma socialista*, 17.

56. Alberdi, *Bases y puntos*, 61–62.

57. Jeremy Adelman, "Between Order and Liberty: Juan Bautista Alberdi and the Intellectual Origins of Argentine Constitutionalism," *Latin American Research Review* 42, no. 2 (June 2007): 101.

58. On his admiration for Chile's constitution, see Alberdi, *Bases y puntos*, 63. On his belief that the Hispanic American republics were not sufficiently saxonized for representative governments, see *Bases y puntos*, 61.

59. On the importance of this problem in the thought of this generation, see Palti, *El momento romántico*, 28.

60. Echeverría, *Dogma socialista*, 16.

61. Alberdi, *Bases y puntos*, 116.

62. D. F. Sarmiento, "Espíritu y condiciones de la historia en América," Memoria leída el 11 de Octubre de 1858, en el Ateneo del Plata, in *Obras de D. F. Sarmiento T. 21*, by Domingo Faustino Sarmiento and Augusto Belin Sarmiento (Buenos Aires: 1899), 106.

63. Significantly, the above-mentioned Bartolomé Mitre, the sole member of his generation to insist that Argentina had existed as a distinct national entity before the break with Spain, had a positive view of the colonial experience. According to Mitre, the conditions of colonial life in the Rio de la Plata region, along with the predominance of the European race, had produced a distinctive "Argentine sociability" that was democratic in nature. It should be noted that Elías Palti has argued that Mitre developed this notion of a preexisting Argentine sociability only in the third and final version (1879) of his masterwork, *Historia de Belgrano y la independencia argentina*. See Palti, *El momento romántico*, 93. It should be noted as well that Mitre's contemporaries found his argument ridiculous. For a discussion of the reception of Mitre's work over time, see Sergio Mejía, "Las historias de Bartolomé Mitre: operación nacionalista al gusto de los argentinos," *Historia Crítica*, no. 33 (January–June, 2007): 98–121.

64. Alberdi, "Paginas explicativas," preface to *Bases y puntos*, 21.

65. D. F. Sarmiento, "Espíritu y condiciones," 106.

66. Jorge Myers, "Representations of the Nation: Language, History and Politics in the Elaboration of an Argentine Identity," paper delivered at Vanderbilt University, A Conference on Nationalism in the New World, October 9–11, 2003. Elsewhere, Myers has stated that Republican values continued to provide the foundation of Argentina's political culture and served as a sort of intellectual screen through which Romantic ideas were filtered. See "La revolución," 418.

67. Art. 25, Constitution of 1853.

68. Art. 20, Constitution of 1853.

69. Nor were immigrants pressured to naturalize, and those who did take this step were allowed to retain their original citizenship. The path to citizenship was eased further by exempting naturalized male citizens from military service for a period of ten years after the date of naturalization (Art. 21).

70. Drawing from Swiss paleontologist Louis Agassiz, Sarmiento later adopted the view that miscegenation between peoples of different color produced weakened hybrids. See *Conflicto y armonías de las razas en América: Tomo Primero*, 8th ed. (Buenos Aires: Impr. de D. Tuñez, 1883), 37.

71. Ignoring the existence of peoples of African descent altogether, Alberdi declared the indigenous peoples of the region to be irredeemable savages and thus permanent outsiders. See *Bases y puntos*, 68.

72. Alberdi, "Páginas explicativas," in Alberdi, *Bases y puntos*, 24. Alberdi's argument for keeping an open immigration policy was based on pragmatic grounds, since he believed that any measures to keep out undesirables would serve as a barrier to desirables. Also, it should be noted that Alberdi's definition of an undesirable was not based strictly on nonwhiteness: Europeans, he believed, could be "savage," too. Indeed, as would become increasingly common during the age of immigration, Alberdi expressed concern that the immigrants coming to Argentina were the "scum" (*escoria*) of Europe (23).

73. Palti, *El momento romántico*, 151.

74. Argentine positivists drew their primary inspiration from French theorists Auguste Comte, Hippolyte Taine, and Gustav Le Bon, as well as from English social Darwinist Herbert Spencer. The literature on Argentine positivism is extensive; for an excellent introduction, see Oscár Terán, *Vida intelectual en el Buenos Aires fin-de-siglo (1880–1910): Derivas de la "cultura científica"* (Buenos Aires: Fondo de Cultura Económica de Argentina, 2000).

75. Useful introductions in English to the PAN and the so-called Generation of 1880 are Ezequiel Gallo, "Society and Politics," in *Argentina since Independence*, ed. Leslie Bethell (Cambridge: Cambridge University Press, 1993), 79–111; and Paula Alonso, *Between Revolution and the Ballot Box: The Origins of the Argentine Radical Party in the 1890s* (Cambridge: Cambridge University Press, 2000), chaps. 1–3.

76. Julio Roca. Quoted in Oscár Cornblit, Ezequiel Gallo, and Alfredo O'Connell, "La generación del 80 y su proyecto: antecedentes y consequencias," in *Argentina, sociedad de masas*, ed. Torcuato S. Di Tella, Gino Germani, and Jorge Graciarena (Buenos Aires: Editorial Universitaria de Buenos Aires, 1966), 45. Original source: Arturo Carranza, *La cuestión capital de la República*, V (Buenos Aires: Talleres J. L. Rosso, 1932), 678.

77. Alonso, *Between Revolution*, 39–40.

78. The details of this rebellion and its implications will be discussed in chapter 4.

79. Roberto Cortés Conde, "The Growth of the Argentine Economy, c. 1870–1914," in *Argentina since Independence*, ed. Leslie Bethell (Cambridge: Cambridge University Press, 1993), 65.

80. Rock, *Argentina, 1516–1987*, 172.

81. Gallo, "Society and Politics," 83.

82. For comparison's sake, the highest percentage of foreign-born in the United States since the Civil War era was 14.8 percent in 1910.

83. Argentina, *Tercer Censo Nacional, Levantado el 1° de junio de 1914, Etc.* (Buenos Aires: Oficina del Censo, 1916), 202.

84. In considering an alternative past for an Argentina that lacked mass immigration, I draw inspiration from the work of path dependence theorists Giovanni Capoccia and R. Daniel Keleman. Capoccia and Kelemen have argued that recognizing critical junctures that lead societies to follow new, self-reinforcing paths requires us to look closely at the decisions made by key political actors during moments of flux and consider counterfactuals—that is, how other decisions would have led to other trajectories. See "The Study of Critical Junctures: Theory, Narrative, and Counterfactuals in Historical Institutionalism," *World Politics* 59, no. 3 (April 2007): 341–69. Here, however, I am looking at the material factors (also historically contingent) that precipitated Argentina's identity crisis—namely, the onset of mass immigration. There was nothing inevitable about this process or its timing. Rather, it occurred when it did because Northern Europe had a high demand for Argentine products, Southern Europe had a surplus of population disposed to emigrate, and Argentina had an elite willing and able to take advantage of both. In the absence of any one of these factors, Argentine history—and Argentine understandings of national identity—would have been very different.

CHAPTER 2.   National Identity in the Age of Mass Immigration

1. For contemporary perceptions of the connection between immigration and labor unrest, see, for example, Francisco Stach, "La defensa social y la inmigración," *Boletín Mensual del Museo Social Argentino* 5, nos. 55–56 (July–August 1916): 360–89; and Lucas Ayarragaray, "Política inmigratoria," in La Liga Patriótica Argentina, *Noveno Congreso Nacionalista*, Biblioteca de La Liga Patriótica Argentina (Buenos Aires: Imp. P. Ventriglia, 1928), 469–79.

2. Eduardo Zimmermann, "Racial Ideas and Social Reform: Argentina, 1890–1916," *Hispanic American Historical Review* 72, no. 1 (February 1992), 36.

3. The return rate of immigrants to Europe was often quite high, especially during moments of economic crisis. For details, consult Roberto Cortés Conde, "The Growth of the Argentine Economy, c. 1870–1914," in *Argentina*

*since Independence*, ed. Leslie Bethell (Cambridge: Cambridge University Press, 1993), 47–77.

4. Even these requirements could be waived in certain circumstances.

5. David Rock, *Argentina, 1516–1982: From Spanish Colonization to the Falklands War* (Berkeley: University of California Press, 1985), 143. This compares with a naturalization rate of almost 70 percent in the United States during the same period.

6. Why so few immigrants chose to become citizens has been continuously debated. For different perspectives, see Tulio Halperin Donghi, who argues that electoral fraud under the PAN discouraged immigrants from participating, in "¿Para qué la inmigración? Ideología y política inmigratoria y aceleración del proceso modernizador: El caso argentino (1810–1914)," *Jahrbuch für Geschichte von Staat, Wirtschaft und Gesellschaft Lateinamerikas* 13, no. 1 (1976): 437–89; Oscár Cornblit, Ezequiel Gallo, and Afredo O'Connell, "La generación del 80 y su proyecto: antecedentes y consequencias," *Argentina, sociedad de masas*, ed. Torcuato S. Di Tella, Gino Germani, and Jorge Graciarena (Buenos Aires: Editorial Universitaria de Buenos Aires, 1966), 48–51; and Torcuato Di Tella, "El impacto inmigratorio sobre el sistema político argentino," *Estudios Migratorios Latinoamericanos* 4, no. 2 (August 1989): 214. On the issue of the general lack of interest in voting among the native born, see Hilda Sábato, "Citizenship, Political Participation and the Formation of the Public Sphere in Buenos Aires, 1850s–1880s," *Past and Present*, no.136 (August 1992): 139–63.

7. Domingo F. Sarmiento, "La nostálgia en América," first published in *El Nacional*, January 24, 1884. Reprinted in *Obras completas*, by Domingo F. Sarmiento, vol. 36, *La condición del extranjero en América* (Buenos Aires: Librería "La Faculdad" de Juan Roldán, 1900), 73–78. Citations refer to the 1900 edition.

8. Estanislao Zeballos, Congreso Nacional, Cámara de Diputados, *Diario de Sesiones*, October 21, 1887. Quoted in Lilia Ana Bertoni, *Patriotas, cosmopolitas y nacionalistas: la construcción de la nacionalidad argentina a fines del siglo XIX* (Buenos Aires: Fondo de cultura económica, 2001), 124.

9. Editorial, *La Prensa*, October 25, 1887. Quoted in Bertoni, *Patriotas, cosmopolitas y nacionalistas*, 126.

10. Bertoni, *Patriotas, cosmopolitas y nacionalistas*, 127.

11. Romolo Gandolfo, "Inmigrantes y la política en Argentina: La Revolución de 1890 y la campaña en favor de la naturalización automática de residentes extranjeras," *Estudios Migratorios Latinoamericanos* 6, no.17 (1991): 23–55.

12. This is not to claim that the issue died entirely. Sandra McGee Deutsch has noted that the Liga Patriótica Argentina, to be discussed below,

expressed some interest in promoting the naturalization of certain types of immigrants, most notably property owners. See her *Las Derechas: The Extreme Right in Argentina, Brazil, and Chile, 1890–1939* (Stanford, CA: Stanford University Press, 1999), 84.

13. Hobart Spalding, "Education in Argentina, 1890–1914: The Limits of Oligarchical Reform," *Journal of Interdisciplinary History* 3, no. 1 (Summer 1972): 42.

14. The Consejo Nacional de Educación had jurisdiction over the public schools in the federal district.

15. "Nuestra palabra," *El Monitor* 6, no. 111 (1887): 331–34. Quoted in Bertoni, *Patriotas, cosmopolitas y nacionalistas,* 45.

16. *El Monitor* 8, no. 156 (1889): 819. Quoted in Bertoni, *Patriotas, cosmopolitas y nacionalistas,* 115.

17. Bertoni, *Patriotas, cosmopolitas y nacionalistas,* 45.

18. This image comes from Halperin, "¿Para que?," 479.

19. In José María Ramos Mejía, *Las multitudes argentinas,* ed. José María Bolaño, Biblioteca Universal de Sociología (Buenos Aires: Guillermo Kraft, 1952), 312, 310.

20. The "indigestible stew" comment comes from Carlos Octavio Bunge, *Nuestra América* (1903; repr., Buenos Aires: Coni Hermanos, 1905), 97.

21. Carlos Octavio Bunge, "La educación patriótica ante la sociología," *Monitor de la Educación Común,* August 31, 1908, 67–70. Quoted in Carlos Escudé, *El fracaso del proyecto argentino: educación e ideología* (Buenos Aires: Instituto Torcuato Di Tella, 1990), 38. To be sure, positivists, such as Ramos Mejía and Bunge, should not be considered pure adherents to the notion of Argentine as a civic nation, because they also embraced the notion of collective psychology and believed that eventually a new, more homogenous Argentine national character would form. Until that happened, however, they accepted that internal diversity was an unavoidable reality. The positivist vision of nationality will be discussed in chapter 3.

22. Such a view is based on what Rainer Bauböck (following Joseph Carens) has called a "thin theory of language." See Rainer Bauböck, "Cultural Citizenship, Minority Rights and Self-Government," in *Citizenship Today: Global Perspectives and Practices,* ed. T. A. Aleinikoff and Douglas Klusmeyer (Washington, DC: Carnegie Endowment for International Peace, 2001), 328–29.

23. Congreso Nacional, Cámara de Diputados, September 1896. Quoted in Bertoni, *Patriotas, cosmopolitas y nacionalistas,* 200. These discussions took place on September 4, 7, and 9 and were recorded in *Diario de Sesiones,* 751–831.

24. Congreso Nacional, Cámara de Diputados, September 1896. Quoted in Bertoni, *Patriotas, cosmopolitas y nacionalistas*, 194.

25. Quoted in Natalio Botana and Ezequiel Gallo, *De la República posible a la República verdadera (1880–1910)* (Buenos Aires: Espasa Calpe, 1997), 70.

26. Congreso Nacional, Cámara de Diputados, September 1896. Quoted in Bertoni, *Patriotas, cosmopolitas y nacionalistas*, 193.

27. Quoted in Bertoni, *Patriotas cosmopolitas y nacionalistas*, 193. It should be noted that, although the bill failed to pass in the Senate, two years later it was approved by both chambers of Congress. At that point, however, the executive vetoed the measure, arguing that it might be perceived as anti-immigrant. See Spalding, "Education in Argentina, 1890–1914," 42–43.

28. On this point see Bertoni, *Patriotas, cosmopolitas y nacionalistas*, 119.

29. The best treatment of the LPA to date is Sandra McGee Deutsch, *Counterrevolution in Argentina, 1900–1932: The Argentine Patriotic League* (Lincoln: University of Nebraska Press, 1986).

30. Yrigoyen, whose ideas about nationality will be discussed extensively in chapter 4, won the presidency in 1916 as the candidate of the Unión Cívica Radical, or Radical Party. This victory was made possible owing to the electoral reforms of 1912, which placed elections under the supervision of the military and made voting obligatory.

31. On the links between the vigilantes, police, and military, see Deutsch, *Las Derechas*, 82–84.

32. According to Deutsch, this translated into around 11,000 male members and 820 female members. See *Las Derechas*, 86, 88.

33. Manuel Carlés, *Definition of the Argentine Patriotic League (A Guide to Social Welfare)* (Buenos Aires, 1922), 2, 11. This is an English translation of Manuel Carlés, *Definición de la Liga Patriótica (Guía del buen sentido social)*, 24-page pamphlet, 1920.

34. Carlés, *Definition*, 4.

35. On the celebration of the defeat of Rosas, see various speeches reprinted in Liga Patriótica Argentina, *Humanitismo práctico* (Buenos Aires: Comisión de Propaganda, LPA, 1921), esp. "Discurso del Sr. Sixto Vela," 17–18; "Discurso de la señorita Avigliani," 24–26; and "Discurso del Sr. Contrera Ríos," 28–30. On the need to defend the constitution, see Manuel Carlés, "Discurso del Dr. Carlés," in *Humanitismo Práctico*, 18–21; and Carlés, *Definition*, 2. Significantly, the cover of this pamphlet contains the phrase "The Argentine Patriotic League salutes the Argentine people, its Flag and its Constitution."

36. The league's key function, according to Carlés, was to combat those elements that sought "to transform our country into a second Russia." "Interview with Dr. Carlés," *Buenos Aires Herald*, May 2, 1919.

37. Esteban Palacios, "El ambiente migratorio," and Raymundo Ortíz, "La inmigración," both in *Séptimo Congreso Nacionalista de la LPA* (Buenos Aires: Imp. A. Baiocco, 1926), 151–54; 153–57.

38. David Rock, *Politics in Argentina, 1890–1930: The Rise and Fall of Radicalism* (Cambridge: Cambridge University Press, 1975), 195–96.

39. José León Suárez, *La Liga Patriótica*, pamphlet (Buenos Aires, 1919), 3, 4. It should be noted that despite Suárez's upbeat and inclusive language, he made clear that, when labor disputes turned violent, it was the duty of the LPA to enter the fray to fight these "subversive acts" (5). Carlés also advocated using violence, warning that league members would not hesitate to use "creole methods" to fight against those who threaten the established order. "Interview with Dr. Carlés," *Buenos Aires Herald*, May 2, 1919.

40. Sandra McGee Deutsch, "The Argentine Right and the Jews, 1919–1933," *Journal of Latin American Studies* 18, no.1 (1986): 123. According to Deutsch, anti-Semitic statements were rare in LPA propaganda.

41. Carlés, *Definition*, 8.

42. Carlés, *Definition*, 9.

43. Manuel Carlés, Opening address of the 9th Congress of the Liga Patriótica Argentina, May 1928. In La Liga Patriótica Argentina, *Noveno Congreso Nacionalista*, Biblioteca de La Liga Patriótica Argentina (Buenos Aires: Imp. P. Ventriglia, 1928), 93.

44. Carlés, Opening address, 78.

45. Gastón Lestard, "El sentimiento de la nacionalidad y la selección inmigratoria," in La Liga Patriótica Argentina, *Noveno Congreso Nacionalista*, Biblioteca de La Liga Patriótica Argentina (Buenos Aires: Imp. P. Ventriglia, 1928), 467.

46. A. Galarce, "Las escuelas de truantes," in Liga Patriótica Argentina, *Novena Congreso Nacionalista*, Biblioteca De La Liga Patriótica Argentina (Buenos Aires: Imp. P. Ventriglia, 1928), 279.

47. The principal members of this group included Manuel Gálvez, Ricardo Rojas, Ricardo Olivera, Juan Pablo Echagüe, Alberto Gerchunoff, Emilio Becher, Emilio Ortiz Grognet, Mario Bravo, Atilio Chiappori, Alfredo López Prieto, Ernesto Mario Barreda, Luis María Jordán, and Abel Cháneton. Of these, only the last four, as the core members of this group, were native porteños. Manuel Gálvez, *Amigos y maestros de mi juventud*, vol. 1 of *Recuerdos de la vida literaria* (Buenos Aires: Hachette, 1961), 39.

48. This complaint about Buenos Aires's vulgarity and cosmopolitanism was the central theme of Manuel Gálvez's highly successful 1916 work *El mal metafísico* (the metaphysical malaise). The original 1916 edition was followed by ones in 1917, 1920 (in Brazil), 1922, 1930, 1943, 1947, and 1962. Ricardo Rojas also railed against cosmopolitanism and the traditional elite's penchant of aping Europe, rather than defending and developing an authentically Argentine culture. See, for example, "La demonstración a R. Rojas," a reprint of Rojas's speech delivered at a banquet given in his honor, in *Nosotros*, yr. 2, vol. 3, nos. 13–14 (August–September 1908): 124–27.

49. Emilio Becher, "La tradición y el patriotismo," *La Nación*, June 15, 1906. Reprinted in Becher, *Diálogo de las sombras y otras páginas* (Buenos Aires: Facultad de Filosofiá y Letras, Instituto de Literatura Argentina, 1938), 223.

50. For relevant citations, see the introduction.

51. Biographical material comes from Eduardo José Cárdenas and Carlos Manuel Payá, *El primer nacionalismo argentino en Manuel Gálvez y Ricardo Rojas* (Buenos Aires: A. Peña Lillo, 1978); and Graciela Perosio and Nannina Rivarola, "Ricardo Rojas. Primer profesor de literature argentina," in *Historia de la literatura argentina*, vol. 3, *Las primeras décadas del siglo* (Buenos Aires: Centro Ed. de América Latina, 1981), 217–40.

52. Rojas's travels took him first to France, the obligatory beginning of any proper European tour, and then to Great Britain, where he developed an intimate friendship with the Spanish/Vasque journalist Ramiro de Maeztu. He then completed his travels with visits to Germany and Spain. For details, see Cárdenas y Payá, *El primer*, 63–64.

53. For details of their meeting and other important relationships established in Spain, including those with Marcelino Menéndez y Pelayo, Ramón Menéndez Pidál, and Benito Pérez Galdós, see Cárdenas y Payá, *El primer*, 73–75. See also Rojas's *Retablo español* (Buenos Aires: Editorial Losada, 1938), esp. 240–55.

54. This offer came from his mentor Joaquín González, who had founded the university in 1905 while serving as minister of justice and public instruction. After Quintana's death in office, González was appointed president of the university (a position that would be renamed "rector"). He retained that position until 1918.

55. On this point, see Rojas's preface to *Eurindia*, vol. 5 of *Obras de Ricardo Rojas*, 2nd ed. (Buenos Aires: Librería "La Facultad," de J. Roldán, 1924).

56. Rojas, "Dante y la gente latina," *La Nación*, June 15, 1921. This is the text of a speech delivered at the Facultad de Filosofía y Letras.

57. Rojas, *La restauración nacionalista*, 3rd ed. (Buenos Aires: A. Peña Lillo, 1971), 136.

58. Rojas, *La restauración nacionalista*, 136.

59. To be clear, when Rojas argued that the Argentine "race" was the product of the blending of the European and indigenous traditions, he was NOT arguing that Argentines were a mestizo people. Rather, Rojas's tendency to speak about race in spiritual and psychological terms allowed him to see the Indians' contribution to the putative Argentine race as an ill-defined essence that in no way undermined the overall whiteness of the national community. Rojas's discussion of the indigenous contribution to the racial formation of the Argentine people via the gaucho will be discussed below.

60. See, for example, Ricardo Rojas, *La literatura argentina: ensayo filosófico sobre la evolución de la cultura en el Plata*, vol. 8, *Obras de Ricardo Rojas*, 2nd ed. (Buenos Aires: Librería "La Facultad," de J. Roldán [ca. 1924]), 117, 139.

61. Rojas, *La restauración nacionalista*, 145, 108.

62. Rojas's call for these reforms led historian Fernando Devoto to associate Rojas, erroneously in my view, with the "secular-democratic tradition of France's Third Republic." Fernando J. Devoto, *Nacionalismo, fascismo y tradicionalismo en la Argentina moderna, Una historia* (Buenos Aires: Siglo Veintiuno de Argentina, 2002), 63.

63. Even in his 1909 *La restauración nacionalista*, which was ostensibly dedicated to education, Rojas makes clear that these human efforts should be seen only as a complement to the real forces at work that would ultimately forge the Argentine race—that is, the telluric forces of the Argentine soil. In Rojas's words, "Our aim, for now, should be to create a community of national ideas among all Argentines, thereby completing the creation of a national character that is in itself being carried out" by the forces of the national territory. Indeed, he goes on to suggest that the foreign born, because they were not subjected to these telluric forces of the land at birth, could never really belong to the nation. In his words, "The European immigrant of today is like that of the colonial period: he returns to his land or he dies in ours: he is something that passes. But what will endure of him is his child and the descendants of his children." These "creole" offspring, Rojas assured his readers, would be true Argentines, since they would share with other natives the "common distinctive character (*matíz común*) imposed upon them by the American environment" (136–37).

64. See for example, Ricardo Rojas, *Eurindia*, 131.

65. Rojas, *La literatura argentina*, vol. 8 of *Obras*, 114.

66. Rojas, *Eurindia*, 151.

67. Rojas, *La literatura argentina*, vol. 8 of *Obras*, 113–14.

68. Rojas, *La literatura argentina*, vol. 9 of *Obras*, 816.

69. Rojas, *La literatura argentina*, vol. 8 of *Obras*, 137.

70. Rojas, *La literatura argentina*, vol. 8 of *Obras*, 141.

71. Rojas, *Eurindia*, 197.

72. Rojas, *La literatura argentina*, vol. 9 of *Obras*, 837.

73. Rojas, *Restauración nacionalista*, 236.

74. On this point see Ricardo Rojas, "Letras Españoles," *Ideas*, yr. 2, vol. 3, no. 10 (February 1904): 162–80.

75. Rojas, *Eurindia*, 81.

76. Ricardo Rojas, "Retablo español," *La Nación*, July 10, 1938.

77. Rojas, "Retablo español," *La Nación*, July 10, 1938.

78. See, for example, his claim that the utopian concept of Eurindia "is not a caprice of my imagination, but has been suggested to me by our experience" (*Eurindia*, 335).

79. The concept of "intrahistoria" appears first in Rojas's 1909 work, *La restauración nacionalista* (62) but is more fully explained in *Eurindia*.

80. Rojas, *Eurindia*, 177–79. Here he writes of tradition as the subterranean river that flows beneath the surface (177–79). Moreover, tradition is described as the "collective memory" of the pueblo and is thus the source of its unity (139).

81. On Rojas's own use of intuition to grasp historical truth, see *Eurindia*, 7–11.

82. Rojas, *La literatura argentina*, vol. 8 of *Obras*, 21.

83. Rojas, *Eurindia*. On the artist as a demigod, see 364. On artists as being in touch with the land, see 341.

84. For his own account of the founding of *Ideas*, and some of the individuals who contributed to its pages, see chapter 4 of Manuel Gálvez, *Amigos y maestros de mi juventud*, vol. 1 of *Recuerdos de la vida literaria* (Buenos Aires: Librería Hachette, 1961). Among the most prominent contributors were important figures from the previous generation, including Roberto Payró, Pedro B. Palacios (Almafuerte), Ernesto Quesada, Belesario Montero, Eduardo Wilde, Rafael Obligado, José Ingenieros and David Peña, and Manuel Ugarte, who may have been in Europe at that time (*Amigos y maestros*, 58).

85. Manuel Gálvez, *El diario de Gabriel Quiroga: opiniones sobre la vida argentina* (Buenos Aires: Arnoldo Moën, 1910), 67.

86. Gálvez, *El diario*, 66.

87. Gálvez, *El diario*, 69.

88. Gálvez, *El diario*, 69.

89. Gálvez, *El diario*, 67.

90. Manuel Gálvez, *El solar de la raza, obra premiada por el gobierno de la República Argentina* (1913; Madrid: Editorial "Saturnino Calleja," s.a., 1920), 59. Segments of this work had already appeared in the prestigious *La Nación*. When it was published in book form, it was an immediate success, quickly selling out its first edition of four thousand copies.

91. The new Argentine race, he believed, was "predestined" for a "magnificent destiny." See *El solar de la raza*, 38.

92. Gálvez, *El solar de la raza*, 60.

93. Manuel Gálvez, "Los himnos a la nueva energía," *El Monitor de la Educación Común*, yr. 30, vol. 39 (1911): 73.

94. Gálvez, *El solar de la raza*, 16.

95. Gálvez, *El solar de la raza*, 39–40.

96. Gálvez, *El diario*, 51.

97. Gálvez, *El solar de la raza*, 17.

98. I have consulted a copy of the decree reprinted in *La Época*, "El decreto inmortal instituyendo el Día de la Raza," October 11, 1927, 1. The law was originally signed on October 4, 1917.

99. "Día de la raza," *Ideas*, yr. 1, no. 1 (October 1918): 2. (This publication should not be confused with the earlier literary magazine by the same name published by Gálvez.)

100. "Día de la raza," *Ideas*, 2.

101. Ernesto Quesada, "El día de la raza y su significado in Hispano-América," *Verbum* 12, no. 46 (October 1918): 8, 11.

102. Gaspar Martín, "La raza como ideal. Posibilidad y necesidad de su concreción," *Verbum* 12, no. 46 (October 1918): 50.

103. "La nueva dirección," *Síntesis* 1, no. 8 (December 1927): 133–34.

104. Significantly, Casabal defined the Argentine soul as "our own soul, and that of the immigrant." The belief that the immigrant would contribute to this putative national soul or race will be discussed in chapter. 5. See "Algo sobre el carácter nacional," *Estudios* 4, yr. 2 (n.d. ca. 1902): 449.

105. Emilio Becher, "La tradición y el patriotismo," 224. This essay originally appeared in *La Nación*, June 28, 1906.

106. Alberto Gerchunoff, "La obra de Payró," *Nosotros*, yr. 6, vol. 7, no. 36 (January 1912): 23, 21.

107. Juan Más y Pi, "El arte en la Argentina," *Renacimiento*, yr. 2, no. 6 (January 1911): 308–9.

108. Francisco de Aparicio, "El arte nacional en 1918," *Cuaderno Colegio Novecentista*, yr. 3, vol. 3, no. 7 (January 1919): 38.

109. Carlos Astrada, "La deshumanización del occidente," *Sagitario* 1, no. 2 (July–August 1925): 196.

110. Juan Propst, editor's note, *Verbum* 12, no. 45 (October 1918): 5.

111. Jorge Rohde, "Apuntes," *Cuaderno Colegio Novecentista*, yr. 1, vol. 1, no. 3 (December 1917): 133. It should be noted that the editors of this journal strongly identified with the "work and intellectual orientation of Ricardo Rojas." See "Notas," 184, of same issue.

112. A. Calandrelli, "Cultura y nacionalismo," *Revista de la Universidad de Buenos Aires*, 2nd ep., sec. 2, nos. 1–2 (1925): 261. This was originally delivered at the Colegio de Buenos Aires, July 4, 1925.

113. Juan Álvarez, "La escuela argentina y el nacionalismo," *Revista Argentina de Ciencias Políticas* 12 (1916): 337.

114. Juan Álvarez, "La escuela argentina," 340.

115. Juan Álvarez, "La escuela argentina," 341.

116. Juan Álvarez, "La escuela argentina," 341.

117. Juan Álvarez, "La escuela argentina," 341.

118. After the electoral reforms of 1912, the Socialists became Argentina's second strongest party.

119. The most prominent exceptions were Alfredo Palacios, an early member of the party and Argentina's first Socialist Congressman, and Manuel Ugarte, both of whom were ultimately ejected from the party. Ugarte will be discussed in chapter 3.

120. Quoted in Adolfo Dickmann, *Nacionalismo y socialismo: El socialismo y el principio de nacionalidad. Los argentinos naturalizados en la política* (Buenos Aires: Talleres gráficos Porter hnos, 1933), 29.

121. Juan B. Justo, *La Vanguardia*, December 9, 1918.

122. Augusto Bunge, *El ideal argentino y el socialismo* (Buenos Aires: Libreria La Vanguardia, 1918), 41.

123. Juan B. Justo, "1 de Mayo de 1918," in Justo, *Internacionalismo y patria* (Buenos Aires: Vanguardia, 1933), 158. This was a speech given at the Coliseo, Buenos Aires.

124. Bunge, *El ideal argentino*, 53.

125. Quoted in Adolfo Dickmann, *Nacionalismo y socialismo*, 50.

126. Oscár Terán, *Vida intelectual en el Buenos Aires fin-de-siglo (1880–1910): Derivas de la "cultura científica"* (Buenos Aires: Fondo de Cultura Económica de Argentina, 2000), 56–57.

**CHAPTER 3.**  Sources of Romantic Nationalism in Early Twentieth-Century Argentina

1. E. J. Hobsbawm, *Nations and Nationalism since 1780: Programme, Myth, Reality*, The Wiles Lectures (Cambridge: Cambridge University Press,

1990), 109. Cultural nationalism, of course, can also rise as a result of external threats from other states or in colonial situations.

2. Not surprisingly, the sense of disequilibrium was especially keen among the young cultural nationalists, many of whom were raised in smaller provincial cities. See, for example, Ricardo Rojas, "Ricardo Rojas, maestro y discípulo de sí mismo," *Leoplan* (July 4, 1945): 19; and Emilio Becher, "La ciudad," *La Nación*, April 26, 1906.

3. Jorge Rivera, "La forja del escritor professional (1900–1930)," in *Historia de la literatura argentina*, vol. 3, *Las primeras décadas del siglo* (Buenos Aires: Centro Ed. de América Latina, 1986), 349. For a discussion of the publishing industry during this period, see Hector René Lafleur, Sergio D. Provenzano, and Fernando Alonso, *Las revistas literarias argentinas, 1893–1967* (Buenos Aires: Centro Editor de América Latina, 1968).

4. Carlos Altamirano and Beatriz Sarlo, "La Argentina del centenario: Campo intelectual, vida literaria y temas ideológicos," in *Ensayos argentinos: de Sarmiento a la vanguardia*, by Carlos Altamirano and Beatriz Sarlo (Buenos Aires: Centro Editor de América Latina, 1983), 77–78.

5. On the expansion of the student population during these years, see Sergio Bagú, "Estrateficación social y estructura nacional del conocimiento en la Argentina, 1880–1930," *Revista de la Universidad Nacional de Córdoba*, yr. 2, nos. 1–2 (March–June, 1962): 14.

6. On this point, see Carlos Real de Azúa, *Historia visible e historia esotérica: Personajes y claves del debate latinoamericano* (Montevideo: Arca, 1975), 162–63.

7. Such an idea would have been anathema to the cultural nationalists, who rejected biological notions of race and saw positivism's emphasis on science and empiricism as alien to the spiritual values they believed formed the core of the supposed Argentine personality. Thus in championing the defense of this imagined personality, cultural nationalists and their sympathizers saw themselves as antipositivists. For a good synthetic discussion of positivism in Latin America, see Charles Hale, "Political and Social Ideas in Latin America, 1870–1930," in *The Cambridge History of Latin America*, ed. Leslie Bethell, vol. 4 (New York: Cambridge University Press, 1986), esp. 382–96. For Argentine positivism in particular, see various essays in *El movimiento positivista argentino*, ed. Hugo Biagini (Buenos Aires: Editorial de Belgrano, 1985); and Oscár Terán, *Vida intelectual en el Buenos Aires fin-de-siglo (1880–1910): Derivas de la "cultura científica"* (Buenos Aires: Fondo de Cultura Económica de Argentina, 2000).

8. Diego Armus, "Desirable and Undesirable Migrants: Disease, Eugenics, and Discourses in Modern Buenos Aires," *Journal of Iberian and Latin American Studies* 25, no. 1 (2019): 59, doi.org/10.1080/14701847.2019.1579492.

See also Eduardo Zimmermann, "Racial Ideas and Social Reform: Argentina, 1890–1916," *Hispanic American Historical Review* 72, no. 1 (February 1992): 23–46.

9. For an example of a prominent early twentieth-century positivist who toggled between definitions of race in a single article, see José Ingenieros, "La formación de una raza argentina," *Revista de Filosofía* 1, 2nd sem. (1915): 464–83.

10. Hale, "Political and Social Ideas," 398.

11. Carlos O. Bunge, *Nuestra América*, 2nd ed. (Buenos Aires: Coni Hermanos, 1905), 3,7. For Taine's impact on Bunge, see José Vazeilles, "Positivismo, política e ideología: El caso de Carlos Octavio Bunge," *Punto de Vista*, no. 6 (June 1979): 19–27.

12. Interestingly, Rojas initially sought to ground his theory of an emerging Argentine race shaped by telluric forces by appealing to Taine's theory of geographic determinism. See, for example, *La restauración nacionalista*, 3rd ed. (1909; Buenos Aires: A. Peña Lillo, 1971), 68. He later dismissed Taine as too mechanical. See Rojas, interview by "Silvano," *Atlántida*, November 15, 1923.

13. As Eduardo Zimmermann has argued ("Racial Ideas," 23), during the early twentieth century the idea that science could be used to manage and improve a population's racial make up was considered to be progressive and attracted would-be reformers from across the ideological spectrum.

14. Armus, "Desirable and Undesirable Migrants," 64–70.

15. Armus, "Desirable and Undesirable Migrants," 59–60.

16. Armus, "Desirable and Undesirable Migrants," 59, 60. The term *national type* (and the idea that one would emerge) appears in Emilio Frers's response to a 1919 encuesta, or survey, conducted by the *Boletín del Museo Social Argentino* on the question of immigration.

17. Mónica Quijada, "Latinos y anglosajones: el 98 en el fin de siglo sudamericano," *Hispania: Revista Española de Historia* 57, no. 2 (1997): 596.

18. Quijada, "Latinos y Anglosajones," 599. Indeed, recent scholarship has argued that US meddling in the region produced a "sharpening of ethnocultural consciousness" among Latin Americans as early as the mid-nineteenth century. On this point, see Aims McGuinness, "Searching for 'Latin America': Race and Sovereignty in the Americas in the 1850s," in *Race and Nation in Latin America*, ed. Nancy Appelbaum, Anne S. Macpherson, and Karin Alejandra Rosemblatt (Chapel Hill: University of North Carolina Press, 2003), 87–107. Michel Gobat extends this argument by pointing to the impact of the pan-Latin American reaction to US president Franklin Pierce's 1856 recognition of filibusterer William Walker's claims on Nicaragua. See "The Invention of Latin America: A Transnational History of Anti-Imperialism, Democracy and Race," *American Historical Review* 118, no. 5 (December 2013): 1345–75.

This seems particularly true in Central America, where the US presence and active interference were greatest. Argentina's greater distance from the United States and its closer economic and political ties with Great Britain meant that anti-US sentiment remained muted until well into the twentieth century.

19. Rojas, in particular, enjoyed a warm relationship with the Uruguayan writer, who spent a great deal of time in Buenos Aires. See Carlos Real de Azúa, "'Ariel,' libro porteño," in *Historia visible e historia esotérica* (Montevideo: ARCA Editorial, 1975), 170.

20. This borrowing was undoubtedly inspired by Ernest Renan's 1878 philosophical drama *Caliban*.

21. José Enrique Rodó, *Ariel*, trans. Margaret Peden (Austin: University of Texas Press, 1988), 72. Italics in the original.

22. Rodó, *Ariel*, 73.

23. Unamuno wrote the preface to Ugarte's 1901 novel, *Paisajes parisienses*.

24. The complete title of the work is *El porvenir de la América Latina: la raza; la integridad territorial y moral; la organización interior.*

25. Manuel Ugarte, *El porvenir de la América Latina: la raza; la integridad territorial y moral; la organización interior* (Valencia: Sempere, 1911), 84–85, 72.

26. Ugarte, *El porvenir*, 84–85, 23.

27. Ugarte, *El porvenir*, 70.

28. Ugarte, *El porvenir*, 319.

29. On the European roots of Argentine cultural nationalism, see David Rock, "Antecedents of the Argentine Right," in *The Argentine Right: Its History and Intellectual Origins, 1910 to the Present*, ed. Sandra McGee Deutsch and Ronald Dolkart (Wilmington, DE: Scholarly Resources Books, 1993), 1–34. See also Altamirano and Sarlo, "La Argentina del centenario," 74–75.

30. The concept of the Spanish Generation of 1898 and its membership has been long debated. For a useful summary of the controversy up to 1973, see H. Ramsden, "The Spanish 'Generation of 1898': The History of a Concept," *Bulletin of the John Rylands University Library*, issue 56 (1973–74): 463–91.

31. Ricardo Rojas, postcard to Miguel de Unamuno, March 2, 1908, repr. in Manuel García Blanco, "Ricardo Rojas y Unamuno," *Revista de la Universidad de Buenos Aires* 3, no. 3 (July–September 1958): 416.

32. Ricardo Rojas, letter to Miguel de Unamuno, November 17, 1904, repr. in García Blanco, "Ricardo Rojas y Unamuno," 410.

33. Ricardo Rojas, *Restauración nacionalista*, 68.

34. Manuel Gálvez, *El solar de la raza*, 16. Mónica Quijada has also noted that Gálvez, along with the rest of the members of his generation, was deeply influenced by Unamuno, and especially by his concept of intrahistoria. See *Manuel Gálvez: 60 años de pensamiento nacionalista* (Buenos Aires: Centro Editor de America Latina, 1985), 27.

35. Gálvez, *Amigos y maestros de mi juventud*, vol. 1 of *Recuerdos de la vida literaria* (Buenos Aires: Hachette, 1961), 263, 233.

36. Earl Glauert, for example, credits Rojas with introducing Herder's ideas of *Volk, Volkgeist,* and *Kulturauftrag* to his fellow Argentines. See "Ricardo Rojas and the Emergence of Argentine Cultural Nationalism," *Hispanic American Historical Review* 43, no. 3 (August 1963): 2. Likewise, Natalio Botana and Ezequiel Gallo describe Rojas as being influenced by the "first wave of German nationalism," as does Nicola Miller, who argues that he was "strongly influenced by Herder and his concepts of *Volk*." See Botana and Gallo, *De la República posible a la República verdadera (1880–1910)* (Buenos Aires: Espasa Calpe, 1997), 105; and Miller, *In the Shadow of the State: Intellectuals and the Quest for National Identity in Twentieth-Century Spanish America* (London: Verso, 1999), 166. Somewhat more obliquely, María Teresa Gramuglio and Beatriz Sarlo note that Rojas's "aesthetic and philosophical Romanticism" shaped his understanding of the importance of the Argentine gaucho. See "José Hernández," in *Historia de la literatura argentina*, vol. 2 (Buenos Aires: Centro Editor de América Latina, 1980), 18. Mónica Quijada also points to the importance of Herder (or at least his ideas) in shaping the broader intellectual currents of the era, noting that "the Herderian model very clearly underlies the most important manifestations of Hispano-Americanism during the beginning of the twentieth century" ("Latinos y anglosajones," 606).

37. Although some students of the period have noted affinities between the ideas of the Radicals and those of the cultural nationalists, none have posited any connections or mutual influences. For an example, see Beatriz Sarlo and Carlos Altamirano, who briefly acknowledge some similarities but have gone no further ("La Argentina del centenario," 133n55).

38. Arturo Andrés Roig, *Los krausistas argentinos* (Puebla: José M. Cajica Jr, 1969), 35. In the words of Inman Fox, in Spain, Krausism would be "the principal animator of Spanish cultural life until very far into the beginning of the twentieth century." See *La invención de España: nacionalismo liberal e identidad nacional* (Madrid: Cátedra, 1997), 30.

39. This background comes from Juan López-Morillas, *The Krausist Movement and Ideological Change in Spain, 1854–74* (New York: Cambridge University Press, 1981). Originally published as *El krausismo español*, 1956.

40. Sanz del Río's version, however, was much more than a simple translation, representing instead a substantial reworking of Krause's ideas. According to many of his contemporaries, Sanz del Río had so adapted the original text that many sections of *Ideal* belonged more to the Spaniard than to the German original. The dual authorship of the work is recognized in how it is officially cited: Karl Christian Friedrich Krause and Julián Sanz del Río, *Ideal de la humanidad para la vida* (Madrid: M. Galiano, 1860).

41. Sanz del Río's fame among students began before *Ideal* was published and dates back to his opening address of the 1857–58 academic year at the Universidad Central.

42. López-Morillas, *Krausist Movement*, 27.

43. On the many generations of Spanish Krausists, see O. Carlos Stoetzer, *Karl Christian Friedrich Krause and His Influence in the Hispanic World* (Köln: Böhlau, 1998), 106.

44. Giner founded the Institución Libre in response to the 1876 royal decree prohibiting teachings at the university that were contrary to Catholicism or the constitutional monarchy. Its goal, which was at least partially achieved, was to create "nucleos" of individuals imbued with the values of liberalism, tolerance, laicism, democracy, and an appreciation for science. On the Institución, see Fox, *La invención de España*, 31–32.

45. According to Krause, "Free societies are formed . . . when, by natural reasons people who are friendly and similar in culture establish among themselves a free exchange of ideas." See Krause and Sanz del Río, *Ideal*, 138.

46. On this point, see Juan José Gil Cremades, *Krausistas y liberales* (Madrid: Seminarios y Ediciones Castilla, S. A., 1975); and Dolores Gómez Molleda, *Los reformadores de la españa contemporanea* (Madrid: C.S.I.C., 1966), 7.

47. According to Sanz del Río's reading of Krause, this idea was "fundamental." Krause and Sanz del Río, *Ideal*, 5.

48. Krause and Sanz del Río, *Ideal*, 108.

49. On Giner and the concept of *genio nacional*, see Gómez Molleda, *Los reformadores*, 102.

50. Rafael Altamira, "Psicología español," *La España Moderna* 2, no. 123 (March 1899): 5. Quoted in Elena M. de Jongh Rossel, *El krausismo y la generación de 1898*, Albatros Ediciones Hispanófila 38 (Valencia, Spain: Albatros Hispanofila, 1985), 121.

51. Krause and Sanz del Río, *Ideal*, 153, 177.

52. On the importance of the landscape for Spanish Krausists, see Manuel Pedroso, "En el cincuentinario de la Institución Libre de Enseñanza," *Boletín de la Institución Libre de Enseñanza* 51, no. 802 (January 31, 1927): 30, http://prensahistorica.mcu.es/es/publicaciones/numeros_por_mes.cmd?anyo=1927&idPublicacion=1000225.

53. Giner, "Paisaje," *Ensayos y cartas*, 40. Quoted in Jongh Rossell, *El krausismo*, 155.

54. Krause and Sanz del Río, *Ideal*, 35–36.

55. Krause and Sanz del Río, *Ideal*, 108, 110.

56. Thus Frederick Pike has argued, Krausism seemed "naturally destined to encourage interest in *Hispanismo*." See *Hispanismo, 1898–1936: Spanish Con-*

*servatives and Liberals and Their Relations with Spanish America* (Notre Dame, IN: University of Notre Dame Press, 1971), 147.

57. Financed by private contributions, this mission allowed Altamira to visit most of the major Hispanic American nations in 1909 and 1910.

58. The invitation to La Plata was issued by university rector Joaquín González, who had served as a mentor to Ricardo Rojas. Altamira's visit was followed by that of Adolfo González Posada, another prominent Krausist, who also taught a course at the University of La Plata and was also one of Altamira's long-time associates. Pike, *Hispanismo*, 156.

59. Quoted in D. Gumersindo de Azcárate, "Educación y enseñanza según Costa," *Boletín de la Institución Libre de Enseñanza* 44, no. 720 (March 31, 1920): 69, https://babel.hathitrust.org/cgi/pt?id=uc1.b2877074&view=1up &seq=78.

60. Given the similarities between the ideas of Rodó and those of the Spanish Krausists, it is not surprising that the Uruguayan found a warm reception among the latter. Krausist Rafael Altamira, for example, lavishly praised *Ariel*, as did Leopoldo Alas, who had deep ties with the Krausists. These warm feelings were reciprocated by Rodó, who praised the Spanish Krausists' efforts to encourage stronger links between Spain and the former colonies. On these points, see Pike, *Hispanismo*, 67, 156. Whether Rodó was himself influenced by Krausist ideas is unclear. Pike suggests this was the case but provides no concrete evidence (*Hispanismo*, 140).

61. Krause and Sanz del Río, *Ideal*, 125.

62. Gómez Molleda, *Los reformadores*, 94.

63. Stoetzer, *Karl Christian Friedrich Krause*, 34.

64. On the idea of obstacles or impediments, see Guillaume Tiberghien, A. García Moreno, Nicolás Salmerón y Alonso, Urbano González Serrano, and Federico Escámez Centeno, *Ensayo teórico é histórico sobre la generación de los conocimientos humanos* (Madrid: Nueva Biblioteca Universal, 1875), 270.

65. On the Krausist approach to property, see Stoetzer, *Karl Christian Friedrich Krause*, 65.

66. Krause and Sanz del Río, *Ideal*, 109.

67. For a fuller discussion of Spanish Krausists and Catholicism, see Gómez Molleda, *Los reformadores*, 104.

68. Francisco Giner de los Ríos, "Problemas urgentes de nuestra educación nacional," *Boletín de la Institución Libre de Enseñanza*, yr. 26, no. 509 (August 31, 1902): 225, http://prensahistorica.mcu.es/es/publicaciones/numeros _por_mes.cmd?anyo=1902&idPublicacion=1000225.

69. Gómez Molleda, *Los reformadores*, 104.

70. Francisco Giner de los Ríos, *Estudios de literatura y arte* (Madrid: Suarez, 1876), 176–77.

71. Gómez Molleda, *Los reformadores*, 95.

72. Lopez-Morillas, *Krausist Movement*, 68.

73. D. Francisco de Giner, "*Poesía erudita y poesía vulgar*," in *Estudios literarios* (Madrid, 1866), 162. Similarly, Giner believed that paintings could also serve as a window into the collective soul. On this point, see Jongh Rossel, *El krausismo*, 158.

74. Cossio, *Historia de la pintura español.* Quoted in Fox, *La invención de España*, 157. According to Fox, this work was used extensively as a pedagogical text.

75. This apparent ability to reconcile two very different intellectual and political traditions was undoubtedly the source of Krausism's great appeal. On this point see Pike, *Hispanismo*, 110.

76. Jongh Rossel, for example, writes of the "convivencia de las generaciones" (*El krausismo*), 85. See also Gómez Molleda, *Los reformadores*, 359–84.

77. Gómez Molleda, *Los reformadores*, 348.

78. Pike (*Hispanismo*, 64), for example, includes Costa in the list of Spaniards who would call for the "Great Ideal" that unites Spain and Spanish America. Also on the list are Unamuno, Ganivet, and Macías Picavea.

79. Gómez Molleda, *Los reformadores*, 359. For more on Azorín and the Krausists, see Jongh Rossel, *El krausismo*, 169.

80. On Unamuno and the Krausists, see Gómez Molleda, *Los reformadores*, 385–416. For Unamuno on Costa, see Miguel de Unamuno, "Sobre la tumba de Costa," in *Obras completas*, vol. 8, *Ensayos*, by Miguel de Unamuno and Ricardo Senabre (Madrid: Fundación José Antonio de Castro, 2007), 1017–33. More generally, Pike (*Hispanismo*, 110) describes the members of the Generation of 1898 as the "intellectual offsprings" of the Krausists.

81. Fox, *La invención de España*, 98–101. The methods and aims of the center reflected, in the words of Fox, the "mentality of krauso-positivism," in that it incorporated supposedly objective forms of historical research with the Krausist focus on language, literature, art, and history as central to national identity. On this point, see especially 98–99.

82. As mentioned above, Ángel Ganivet represented something of an exception. It should also be noted that some individuals associated with the Generation of 1898 were considered liberals in 1898 but subsequently moved toward the right. Ramiro de Maeztu is perhaps the most prominent case of an individual closely associated with this generation who became a conservative.

83. Indeed, key members of the Generation of 1898, such as Unamuno and Maeztu, called for a kind of "democratic socialism" then on the rise in Germany and England. On this latter point, see Fox, *La invención de España*, 139.

84. Ángel Ganivet, *Idearium español: el porvenir de España*, ed. E. Inman Fox (Madrid: Espasa Calpe, 1999), 98.

85. Miguel de Unamuno, *En torno al casticismo*, ed. Enrique Rull Fernández (Madrid: Alianza Editorial, 2000), 147.

86. J. Martínez Ruíz (Azorín), *El alma castellana: 1600–1800* (Madrid: Librería internacional, 1900), 115, https://babel.hathitrust.org/cgi/pt?id=txu .059173024325649&view=1up&seq=153.

87. The Argentine Radicals, however, seemed not to have appropriated this element of Krausism.

88. H. Ramsden, *The 1898 Movement in Spain: Towards a Reinterpretation with Special Reference to En Torno Al Casticismo and Idearium Español* (Manchester, UK: Manchester University Press, 1974), 141, 155.

89. Miguel de Unamuno, "Excursión," in *Obras completas*, by Miguel de Unamuno and Manuel García Blanco, vol. 1 (Madrid: Escelicer, 1966), 282.

90. J. Martínez Ruíz [Azorín], *Los valores literarios* (Madrid: Rafael Caro Raggio, 1921), 291.

91. Ganivet, *Idearium español*, 66–67.

92. On Unamuno's and Ganivet's belief that nations must stay true to their inner essence, see Ramsden, *1898 Movement in Spain*, 16.

93. Ganivet represents a somewhat different case, and one that is in many ways closer to the Argentine cultural nationalists. As Ramsden has noted (*1898 Movement in Spain*, 33), for Ganivet, Spain's confusion could be traced to "undigested foreign influences."

94. Ramsden, *1898 Movement in Spain*, 31.

95. J. Martínez Ruíz [Azorín], *La voluntad*, ed. Inman Fox (Madrid: Castalia, 1972), 215. Quoted in José Carlos Mainer, "Tres lecturas de los clásicos españoles (Unamuno, Azorín y Machado)," *Mélanges de la Casa de Velázquez* 31–32 (1995): 181, http://www.persee.fr/web/revues/home/prescript/article/ casa_0076–230x_1995_num_31_2_2743.

96. In Unamuno's famous phrase, "If 'know thyself' is the principle for life and regeneration of the individual, it is—with even more reason—true for a people." See "De la enseñanza superior en España," *Revista Nueva* 2 (August–December 1899), 53. Quoted in Jongh Rossel, *El krausismo*, 118.

97. Unamuno, *En torno al casticismo*, 42.

98. Ganivet, *Idearium español*, 66.

99. Ganivet, *Idearium español*, 155.

100. Such were Azorín's criticisms of painter Ignacio Zuloaga. See "La España de un pintor," in *Tiempos y cosas*, by J. Martínez Ruíz [Azorín] and Pedro de Lorenzo (Spain: Salvat; Alianza editorial, 1970), 144.

101. Ganivet, *Idearium español*, 223.

102. Ángel Ganivet, *Cartas finlandesas* (Granada: Impr. de el Defensor de Granada, 1906), 157–58.


CHAPTER 4.  Romantic Influences and the Argentine Radicals

1. Emilio Gouchón, "Declaración de Principios," repr. in Carlos J. Rodríguez, *Irigoyen; su revolución política y social: La Unión Cívica Radical* (Buenos Aires: Editorial "La Facultad," Bernabé y cía, 1943), 62. Yriogen's name is sometimes spelled "Irigoyen."

2. Leandro Alem. Quoted by Claudio Pozuelo, in "El radicalismo argentino: Origen y finalidad," *Revista Argentina de Ciencias Políticas* 10 (July 1915), 378.

3. This paragraph draws largely from Alonso's excellent analysis in *Between Revolution and the Ballot Box: The Origins of the Argentine Radical Party in the 1890s* (Cambridge: Cambridge University Press, 2000), 109.

4. Leandro Alem, "Manifiesto a los pueblos de la República." Quoted in Rodríguez, *Irigoyen*, 85.

5. Alonso, *Between Revolution*, 201.

6. Here I follow Paula Alonso's conclusion that there was very little continuity between the UCR under Alem and the UCR under Yrigoyen. See Alonso, *Between Revolution*, 202–3.

7. Alonso, *Between Revolution*, 201–2.

8. For Ana Virginia Persello, the consolidation of Yrigoyen's leadership of the UCR did not mean the complete erasure of the "liberal matrix" that Alem had earlier impressed on it. Rather, in her words, "Alem and Yrigoyen both continued to live and coexist within radicalism, and this coexistence both strengthened the movement and led to its division." Ana Virginia Persello, *El Partido Radical: gobierno y oposición, 1916–1943* (Buenos Aires: Siglo Veintiuno Editores Argentina, 2004), 19.

9. Among Yrigoyen's contemporaries who stressed the importance of Krausism in shaping Yrigoyen's thought were Horacio Oyhanarte and Manuel Gálvez (both of whom wrote biographies of the Radical leader), as well as Yrigoyen acolyte Adolfo Korn Villafañe. See Horacio B. Oyhanarte, *El hombre: Hipólito Irigoyen, apostol de la democracia* (1916; Buenos Aires: Editorial Claridad, 1945), 21; Manuel Gálvez, *Vida de Hipólito Yrigoyen, El hombre de misterio*, 2nd ed. (1938; Buenos Aires: Kraft, 1939), 62; and Adolfo Korn Villafañe, *Los derechos proletarios: ensayo novecentista* (La Plata [Argentina], 1922), 30. Later scholars who have focused on Krausism's impact on Yrigoyen include Arturo Roig, *Los krausistas argentinos*, 65–66; Félix Luna, *Yrigoyen* (Buenos Aires: Edi-

torial Sudamericana, 2005), 58–59; O. Álvarez Guerrero, *El Radicalismo y la ética social: Yrigoyen y el krausisimo* (Buenos Aires: Leviatan, 1986); O. Carlos Stoetzer, *Karl Christian Friedrich Krause and His Influence in the Hispanic World* (Köln: Böhlau, 1998), esp. 360–87; Rodríguez, *Irigoyen*, esp. 37–41; and various essays in Hugo E. Biagini, *Orígenes de la democracia argentina: El trasfondo krausista* (Buenos Aires: Editorial Legasa, 1989).

10. On the influence of Krausism in Argentine universities, see Roig, *Los krausistas Argentinos*, 25, 35; and Stoetzer, *Karl Christian Friedrich Krause*, 328.

11. Oyhanarte, *El hombre*, 21; Korn Villafañe, *Los derechos proletarios*, 30. Translations of several of Guillaume Tiberghien's works were published in Spain between 1872 and 1875, and then made their way to Latin America. According to Charles Hale, these works were popular among young Krausists, because they presented Krause's ideas in a clear and accessible manner. Charles Hale, *The Transformation of Liberalism in Late Nineteenth-Century Mexico* (Princeton, NJ: Princeton University Press, 1989), 175.

12. See Hugo E. Biagini's 1989 compilation of essays *Orígenes de la democracia argentina*.

13. This is particularly true of Joaquín Castellanos, a prominent Radical politician from Salta, who came to despise Yrigoyen but who seems to have drunk deeply from the well of Krausism.

14. Hipólito Yrigoyen, first letter to Pedro C. Molina, September 1909. In Marcelo Padoan, *Jesús, el templo y los viles mercaderes: un examen de la discursividad yrigoyenista* Colección "la Ideología Argentina" (Bernal, Buenos Aires: Universidad Nacional de Quilmes Ediciones, 2002), 76.

15. Horacio Oyhanarte, *El hombre*, 84.

16. "La Unión Radical al pueblo de la república," manifesto of the UCR, February 4, 1905, in Rodríguez, *Irigoyen*, 117. According to Rodríguez (27), the document was drawn up by Vicente Gallo and Adolfo Moutier, but its concepts were those of Yrigoyen. For more on the idea of national personality in both Krausism and Radicalism, see Roig, *Los krausistas argentinos*, 75–77.

17. See, for example, Yrigoyen, "Cuarto escrito ante la Suprema Corte Nacional" August 24, 1931. Quoted in Rodríguez, *Irigoyen*, 54. See also Yrigoyen, telegram to Elipidio Gonzalez, November 7, 1915, in Hipólito Yrigoyen, *Discursos, escritos y polémicos del Dr. Hipólito Yrigoyen, 1878–1922*, compiled by Jorge Guillermo Fovie (Buenos Aires: T. Palumbo, 1923), 38.

18. Hipólito Yrigoyen, first letter to Pedro C. Molina, September 1909, in Padoan, *Jesús*, 79.

19. Hipólito Yrigoyen. *Mi vida y mi doctrina*, ed. Hebe Clementi (Buenos Aires: Editoria Leviatan, 1981), 126.

20. Bianco was a prominent Radical jurist, who as a young man was one of the original signers of the UCR's 1892 Declaration of Principles. According to Persello, he became an "irreconcilable enemy of Yrigoyen (*El Partido Radical*, 144). Whether or not this is true is unclear—he clearly supported Yrigoyen in the 1928 elections.

21. José Bianco, *La doctrina radical* (Buenos Aires: Talleres Gráficos de L. J. Rosso, 1927), 354.

22. Alberto Etkin, *Bosquejo de la historia y doctrina de la UCR* (Buenos Aires: El Ateneo, 1928), 317.

23. *La Época*, "Hipólito Yrigoyen," November 25, 1926, 1. First published in the daily *Los Principios* (C. de Uruguay, Entre Rios, n.d.).

24. *La Época*, "Yrigoyen, Presidente," repr., November 14, 1926, 1.

25. *La Época*, "¡Yrigoyen, Presidente!," November 2. 1926, 1. First published in *El Heraldo* (Concordía), n.d.

26. Yrigoyen, *Mi vida*, 67, 92.

27. See also Yrigoyen's claim that "Providence sets the destinies of peoples and men" and that it "projects a ray of light [along] our paths." "Manifiesto posterior a la Revolución, 13 de Mayo, 1905," in Rodríguez, *Irigoyen*, 127.

28. Joaquín Castellanos, speech in Congress, in his *Acción y pensamiento* (Buenos Aires: J. A. Pellegrini, 1917), 245.

29. Antonio Herrero, *Hipólito Yrigoyen, maestro de democracia* (La Plata: Olivieri y Dominguez, 1927), 159.

30. Hipólito Yrigoyen, letter to Pedro C. Molina, 1909, in Rodríguez, *Irigoyen*, 129. In his usual cryptic and overblown language, Yrigoyen continues by proclaiming that, when this schema is fully realized, the nations of the world will "congregate [in order to discern] the sacred contribution each had made in the infinite work of human civilization."

31. On this point see Luna, *Yrigoyen*, 166. The quotation is Luna's.

32. Yrigoyen, *Mi vida*, 116.

33. The delegation included Argentina's minister of the exterior, Honorio Pueyrredón; Marcelo T. Alvear (then ambassador to France); and diplomat Fernándo Pérez. The more seasoned Alvear and Pérez were particularly resistant to Yrigoyen's demands, leaving it to Pueyrredón to carry them out.

34. Telegram to Marcelo T. Alvear, December 30, 1920, in Padoan, *Jesús*, 99–100.

35. Alberto Etkin, *Bosquejo*, 307–8.

36. Adolfo Korn Villafañe, foreword to Antonio Herrero, and Raúl F. Oyhanarte, *El puntero argentino: exégesis de dos oraciones cívicas del diputado nacional Dr. Raúl F. Oyhanarte* (La Plata [Argentina]: Editorial Almafuerte, 1929), 19–20. Note: although catalogued as being coauthored by Herrero and

Oyhanarte, this work contains only two speeches by Oyhanarte, along with extensive "exegeses" by Herrero that have little to do with the speeches and instead provide Herrero with the opportunity to expound on his own views.

37. In Herrero's words, "Las razas están formadas por grandes corrientes de fuerza spiritual, cada una de las cuales corresponde a un sistema de cristalización de la personalidad humana," in Herrero and Oyhanarte, *El puntero*, 31.

38. Herrero and Oyhanarte, *El puntero*, 31.

39. Herrero and Oyhanarte, *El puntero*, 33.

40. Herrero and Oyhanarte, *El puntero*, 89.

41. *La Época*, "Conmemoración del 12 de octubre," October 13, 1926, 1.

42. *La Época*, "Telegramas enviados al Dr. Hipólito Yrigoyen con motivo de la celebración del "Día de la Raza," October 15, 1926, 1.

43. Yrigoyen, *Mi vida*, 106.

44. Yrigoyen, first Letter to Pedro Molina, in Rodríguez, *Irigoyen*, 132.

45. Yrigoyen, *Mi vida*, 131.

46. "Declaración de principios sancionada por la Convención Nacional del 17 de noviembre de 1892." Quoted in O. Álvarez Guerrero, *El Radicalismo y la ética social: Yrigoyen y el krausisimo* (Buenos Aires: Leviatan, 1986), 110. The wording of this document is of interest. The Spanish original uses the word *reparación*, which, to my knowledge, is the first time that this term appears in a UCR document. Here, however, I have translated it simply as "repair," since in this context it seems to mean simply to mend something broken. Later, however, *reparación* took on a larger, more mystical meaning.

47. Letter to Pedro Molina, 1906, in Rodríguez, *Irigoyen*, 130.

48. Telegram to the Juventud del Partido Nacionalista del Uruguay, 1912, in Irigoyen, *Discursos*, 34.

49. Rodriguez, *Irigoyen*, 133.

50. Alonso, *Between Revolution*, 109.

51. Bianco, *La doctrina radical*, 89.

52. Joaquín Castellanos, discourse in Congress, *Diario de Sesiones* 3 (July 24, 1914), 290.

53. Castellanos, discourse in Congress, 290.

54. In the words of Radical politician Vicente Gallo, the UCR represented a "superior, more idealistic concept of civic life" that was a "necessary and fecund reaction" against the "positivist materialism" of the regime. Vicente Gallo, "Aspectos y ensenanzas de una obra," *Revista Argentina de Ciencias Políticas* 10 (July 1915): 330.

55. Antonio Sagarna, "Concepto del Radicalismo Argentino," *Revista Argentina de Ciencias Políticas* 10 (July 1915): 352.

56. Yrigoyen, first letter to Pedro Molina, in Rodríguez, *Irigoyen*, 139. See also Roig, *Los krausistas argentinas*, 210–11, who notes that Argentine Radicals always demonstrated an "elevated and permanent interest in national culture."

57. Korn Villafañe, *Los derechos proletarios*, 24–25.

58. Castellanos, Speech in Congress, in *Acción y pensamiento*, 245.

59. Claudio Pozuelo, "El radicalismo Argentino: origen y finalidad," *Revista Argentina de Ciencias Políticas* 10 (July 1915): 378.

60. Castellanos, *Acción y pensamiento*, 78, 98–99.

61. Yrigoyen, *Mi vida*, 131.

62. Castellanos, *Acción y pensamiento*, 98. Elsewhere he notes, "We Radicals understand the best and most positive form to serve humanity is to form a great nation, with a superior race." See "Programa evolutivo," *Acción y pensamiento*, 107. The idea of Radicals as defenders of a putative Argentine race continued well into the late twentieth century. In his 1985 preface to Yrigoyen's *Mi vida* (25), Radical stalwart Hebe Clemente noted approvingly that the UCR's notion of moral reparation has both an institutional *and* a racial component.

63. Oyhanarte, *El hombre*, 237.

64. Herrero, *El puntero*, 36.

65. Enrique Pérez Colman, *Discursos programas de los candidatos radicales triunfantes en las elecciones del 4 de Junio de 1922* (Paraná [Entre Rios Argentina]: Junta Gobierno de la U. C. Radical de Entre Rios, 1922), 22, 23. (Colman had just won election to the vice-governorship of Entre Rios.)

66. As he proclaimed in a 1921 message to Congress, "I well know that I have come to fulfill a destiny . . . the reintegration of the nationality upon its fundamental bases." Reproduced in Irigoyen, *Discursos*, 90. Ellipses in orginal.

67. Yrigoyen, "Manifiesto posterior a la Revolución—13 de mayo, 1905," in Rodríguez, *Irigoyen*, 121.

68. The manifesto was produced by the executive council of the party's national committee on October 5, 1910. Reproduced partially in Luna, *Yrigoyen*, 187.

69. Yrigoyen, *Mi vida*, 137.

70. Campaign pamphlet for Radical Arturo Goyeneche, signed by the president of the UCR committee (illegible), January 27, 1923, 1, 2, Biblioteca Nacional, Buenos Aires.

71. Oyhanarte, *El hombre*, 153.

72. From Castellanos, *Acción y pensamiento*, 78. For an account of Castellanos's opposition to Yrigoyen, see Persello, *El partido*, 37–38.

73. Yrigoyen, "Manifiesto posterior a la Revolución—13 de mayo, 1905." Quoted in Rodríguez, *Irigoyen*, 125.

74. Yrigoyen, *Mi vida*, 137, 138.

75. Etkin, *Bosquejo*, 238.

76. Oyhanarte, *El hombre*, 159. As Tulio Halperin has noted, it was precisely this stance that so confounded (and incensed) the Radicals' political opponents (*Vida y muerte*, 198). Paula Alonso is even more critical, arguing that the Radicals' refusal to grant legitimacy to their political opponents had long-term consequences. This tendency, she believes, spread from the Radicals to other political forces of the period, becoming "one of the most distinctive features of Argentine political life" (*Between Revolution*, 213).

### CHAPTER 5.   Defining the Essence of *Argentinidad*

1. As Diego Armus has noted, debates over the future of the Argentine race, whether conceptualized in ethno-cultural or biological terms, invariably ignored nonwhites, except for those moments when native peoples were described as a race on the verge of extinction. See "Desirable and Undesirable Migrants. Disease, Eugenics, and Discourses in Modern Buenos Aires," *Journal of Iberian and Latin American Studies* 25, no. 1 (2019): 59, doi.org/10.1080/1470 1847.2019.1579492.

2. On Romantic nationalism and the issue of linguistic contamination, see David Martyn, "Borrowed Fatherland: Nationalism and Language Purism in Fichte's Addresses to the German Nation," *Germanic Review* 72, no. 4 (1997): 303–15.

3. Manuel Gálvez, *El diario de Gabriel Quiroga: Opiniones sobre la vida argentina* (Buenos Aires: Arnoldo Moën, 1910), 67. Thus it was no wonder that Gálvez expressed his satisfaction that the vast majority of Argentina's newcomers came from Italy and Spain. See *El solar de la raza: obra premiada por el gobierno de la República Argentina* (1913; Madrid: Editorial "Saturnino Calleja," 1920), 58–59.

4. Rojas discusses his notion of the gaucho as prototype of the Argentine race in various writings, most directly in his *La literatura argentina: Ensayo filosófico sobre la evolución de la cultura en el Plata*, vol. 8 of *Obras*. On the changing images of the Argentine gaucho, see Richard Slatta, *Gauchos and the Vanishing Frontier* (Lincoln: University of Nebraska Press, 1992). This elite celebration of the gaucho was very different from the phenomenon of popular criollismo— that is, the popular literature and dramas focusing on the "gaucho malo"—and was consumed largely by the immigrant working class. Elite reaction to popular criollismo will be examined in a later section of this chapter.

5. Lugones, "El hijo de la pampa," in Leopolo Lugones, *El payador y antología de poesía y prosa* (Caracas: Biblioteca Ayacucho, 1979), 51. This lecture appeared in *La Nación* on May 9, 1913.

6. This argument is outlined in his final lecture at the Odeón, entitled "The Lineage of Hercules." As will be developed in chapter 6, Lugones's hostility toward Catholicism and his emphasis on the Latin rather than Spanish character of the Argentine people placed him at odds with other right-wing nationalist figures who became active in the late 1920s and early 1930s.

7. Lugones, *El payador*, 51.

8. The English term *first generation* is ambiguous and has been variously defined either as immigrants who undergo formal naturalization or as the children of immigrants. I am using this term in the second sense.

9. Salvador Debenedetti, "Sobre la formación de una raza argentina," *Revista de Filosofía*, yr. 1, 2nd sem. (1915): 416–17.

10. Juan Más y Pi, "El arte en la Argentina," *Renacimiento* 2, no. 6 (January 1911): 307.

11. These were "La raza argentina," *Atlántida* 8, no. 22 (1912): 37–40; and "Alma argentina," *Atlántida* 8, no. 24 (1912): 340–44.

12. Tello, "Alma argentina," 340.

13. Tello, "La raza argentina," 37.

14. Tello, "La raza argentina," 39.

15. Tello, "Alma argentina," 340.

16. Maglione's political affiliations and background are difficult to pin down. Certainly, his ideas about the creole past and his disdain for the new nationalist currents suggest a liberal mindset. However, it is also the case that, during the early 1930s, Maglione served as head of the Departamento Nacional del Trabajo under the right-wing Uriburu regime. On this point see Mirta Lobato, "Historia de las instituciones laborales en Argentina: una asignatura pendiente," *Revista de Trabajo* 3, no. 4 (January–November, 2007): 150.

17. These were "El espíritu nacional y el cosmopolitanismo," *Renacimiento*, yr. 1, vol. 2, no. 5 (October 1909): 191–96; and *Renacimiento*, yr. 1, vol. 2, no. 6 (November 1909): 320–29. Part 2 of the article (no. 6) was published under the inverted title "Cosmopolitanismo y espíritu nacional."

18. Maglione, "Cosmopolitismo y espíritu nacional," 329.

19. Maglione, "Cosmopolitismo y espíritu nacional," 320.

20. Maglione, "Cosmopolitismo y espíritu nacional," 326.

21. The quoted material comes from the degree itself. I have consulted a copy reprinted as "El decreto inmortal instituyendo el Día de la Raza," in *La Época*, October 11, 1927, 1.

22. Hipólito Irigoyen, *Mi vida y mi doctrina*, ed. Hebe Clementi (Buenos Aires: Editoria Leviatan, 1981), 116.

23. Matthew Karush, "Workers, Citizens and the Argentine Nation: Party Politics and the Working Class in Rosario, 1912–3," *Journal of Latin American Studies* 31, no. 3 (October 1999): 596–97.

24. Karush, "Workers," 607.

25. Karush, "Workers," 598.

26. Oyhanarte, *El hombre: Hipólito Irigoyen, apostol de la democracia* (1916; Buenos Aires: Editorial Claridad, 1945), 178.

27. Oyhanarte, *El hombre*, 229. My ellipses.

28. An essential text on the language debate is Alfredo V. E. Rubione, ed., *En torno al criollismo: Ernesto Quesada, "El criollismo en la literatura argentina" y otros textos: estudio crítico y compilación* (Buenos Aires: Centro Editor de América Latina, 1983), which includes reprints of some of the most important texts related to the debate.

29. Luciano Abeille, *Idioma nacional de los argentinos* (Paris: Librairie Emile Bouillon, 1900), 2. The copy I have consulted is located in the Ricardo Rojas Museum, which contains his personal library. My ellipses.

30. Abeille, *Idioma*, 5.

31. Abeille, *Idioma*, 35. This section is underlined in Rojas's copy.

32. Abeille, *Idioma*, 37. This is underlined in Rojas's copy.

33. Abeille, *Idioma*, 424.

34. Abeille, *Idioma*, 424.

35. The term itself came from a theatrical character named "Cocoliche," who was written into a production of the criollista play *Juan Moreira*. The character, which became wildly popular, was a humorous parody of working-class Italian immigrants, who attempted to assimilate into Argentine culture by adopting gaucho customs and dress and became a staple of criollista literature and theater. The classic treatment of the criollista phenomenon is Adolfo Prieto's *El discurso criollista en la formación de la argentina moderna* (Buenos Aires: Editorial Sudamericana, 1988). For a specific reference to origins of the term cocoliche, see p. 66.

36. Quoted in Alfredo V. E. Rubione, "Estudio Preliminar," in *En torno al criollismo: Ernesto Quesada, "El criollismo en la literatura argentina" y otros textos: estudio crítico y compilación*, ed. Alfredo V. E. Rubione (Buenos Aires: Centro Editor de América Latina, 1983), 38. The quotation comes from Cané's 1900 essay "La cuestión del idioma," in *Prosa ligera* (Buenos Aires: La Cultura Argentina, 1919), 61–70.

37. Rubione, "Estudio preliminar," 38.

38. Ernesto Quesada, "El criollismo," *Estudios*, yr. 1, vol. 3 (June–July 1902): 283.

39. Quesada, "El criollismo," 319.

40. Quesada, "El criollismo," 452–53.

41. Miguel Cané, "Carta al Dr. Ernesto Quesada," in *En torno al criollismo: Ernesto Quesada, "El criollismo en la literatura argentina" y otros textos: estudio*

*crítico y compilación*, ed. Alfredo V. E. Rubione (Buenos Aires: Centro Editor de América Latina, 1983), 232. This letter originally appeared in the supplement to *La Nación*, October 11, 1902.

42. Estrada, "Carta," 239. This letter first appeared in *El Tiempo*, October 21, 1902.

43. Paul Groussac, "A propósito de americanismos," *Anales (de la Biblioteca Nacional Argentina)* 1 (1900), 412. Quoted in Arturo Costa Álvarez, *Nuestra Lengua* (Buenos Aires: Sociedad Editorial Argentina, 1922), 123.

44. Carlos Olivera, "El idioma nacional de los argentinos," in *En torno al criollismo: Ernesto Quesada, "El criollismo en la literatura argentina" y otros textos: estudio crítico y compilación*, ed. Alfredo V. E. Rubione (Buenos Aires: Centro Editor de América Latina, 1983), 63. This article appeared originally in *Tribuna*, Buenos Aires, August 7, 1900. Interestingly, *Tribuna*'s editors took pains to distance themselves from Olivera's article (editorial note reproduced in Rubione, *En torno al criollismo*, 62).

45. Olivera, "El idioma nacional," 64.

46. Olivera, "El idioma nacional," 65.

47. Carlos Pellegrini, letter to Luciano Abeille, in *En torno al criollismo: Ernesto Quesada, "El criollismo en la literatura argentina" y otros textos: estudio crítico y compilación*, ed. Alfredo V. E. Rubione (Buenos Aires: Centro Editor de América Latina, 1983), 250. The letter first appeared in *El País*, October 27, 1902. Abeille's letter of request to Pellegrini, also reproduced in Rubione (248–50), appeared in *El País* the previous day (October 26, 1902).

48. Pellegrini, letter to Luciano Abeille, 250.

49. Francisco Soto y Calvo, "De la falta de carácter en la literatura argentina," in *En torno al criollismo: Ernesto Quesada, "El criollismo en la literatura argentina" y otros textos: estudio crítico y compilación*, ed. Alfredo V. E. Rubione (Buenos Aires: Centro Editor de América Latina, 1983), 263. First published in *Estudios*, tomo 2, vol. 4 (1903).

50. Soto y Calvo, "De la falta," 266, 273.

51. Soto y Calvo, "De la falta," 276.

52. Here he is referring specifically to the ancient language "Lacio," which he saw as key to the creation of Latin peoples. Miguel de Toro y Gómez, "Nuestra lengua: Vínculo espiritual de la raza," *Verbum*, yr. 12, no. 46 (October 1918), 29.

53. Toro y Gómez, "Nuestra lengua," 30.

54. On this point, see Costa Álvarez, *Nuestra lengua*, 133.

55. Gálvez, *El solar de la raza*, 22.

56. Manuel Gálvez, response to *Crítica* opinion survey, "¿Llegarémos a tener un idioma propio?," *Crítica*, June 20, 1927.

57. José P. Barros, "La intoxicación del idioma y la terapéutica indicada," in *Séptimo Congreso Nacionalista de la LPA* (Buenos Aires: Imp. A Baiocco, 1926), 78. In his address, Barros notes that he was not an official member of the Liga Patriótica Argentina.

58. Barros, "La intoxicación del idioma," 78, 82.

59. Barros, "La intoxicación del idioma," 78, 83.

60. Barros, "La intoxicación del idioma," 82–83.

61. José Antonio Saldías, response to *Crítica* opinion survey, "¿Llegarémos a tener un idioma propio?," *Crítica*, June 12, 1927.

62. Last Reason, response to *Crítica* opinion survey, "¿Llegarémos a tener un idioma propio?," *Crítica*, June 16, 1927.

63. Leopoldo Lugones, *Didáctica* (Buenos Aires: Otero y Cía, 1910), 394–95.

64. Lugones, *Didáctica*, 247.

65. Given its publication date and the fact that Rojas had clearly read Abeille's work with great attention, it may be that he (Abeille) played an important role in shaping Rojas's Romantic understanding of nationality. This may be true even if Rojas vehemently disagreed with the Frenchman's view of Argentina's future language.

66. Ricardo Rojas, *La literatura argentina: ensayo filosófico sobre la evolución de la cultura en el Plata*, vol. 9 of *Obras de Ricardo Rojas*, 2nd ed. (Buenos Aires: Librería "La Facultad," de J. Roldán, 1924), 867–68.

67. Ricardo Rojas, "La literatura argentina," *Nosotros*, yr. 7, no. 50 (June 1913): 341. This article is the published version of a lecture given by Rojas at the Faculty of Philosophy and Letters (UBA) on the occasion of the inauguration of the Professorship of Argentine Literature.

68. Ricardo Rojas, *Eurindia*, vol. 5 of *Obras de Ricardo Rojas*, 2nd ed. (Buenos Aires: Librería la Facultad, 1924), 49.

69. Rojas, *La literatura argentina*, vol. 9 of *Obras*, 857–58.

70. Ricardo Rojas, *Alocución dirigido a los bachilleres del Colegio Nacional de Buenos Aires*, pamphlet, August 12, 1928, 13, self-published, n.d., Archives of Museo Ricardo Rojas, Buenos Aires.

71. Ricardo Rojas, *Alocución*, 16–17.

## PART TWO.   Introduction

1. The single most important exception was the case of Leopoldo Lugones, who will discussed extensively in the next chapter.

2. It should be noted, as Jorge Nállim has demonstrated, that even many political liberals began to question traditional liberal economic policies in the

aftermath of the 1930 world-economic crash. See chapter 4 of *Transformations and Crisis of Liberalism in Argentina, 1930–1955*, Pitt Latin American Series (Pittsburgh: University of Pittsburgh Press, 2012).

## CHAPTER 6.   The Rise of the Nationalist Right and the Ideal of the Catholic Nation

1. Manuel Gálvez, *Entre la novela y la historia*, vol. 3 of *Recuerdos de la vida literaria* (Buenos Aires: Librería Hachette, 1962), 23–24. According to Gálvez, Carulla was the first to write "in an anti-demoliberal sense" (23).

2. The phrase is David Rock's. See chapter 3 of *Authoritarian Argentina: The Nationalist Movement, Its History, and Its Impact* (Berkeley: University of California Press, 1993).

3. Juan Emiliano Carulla, "Programa para un diario nacionalista," in *Problemas de la cultura: defensa de occidente y otros temas* (Buenos Aires: El Ateneo, Librería Científica y Literaria, 1927), 81–82.

4. Carulla, "Programa para un diario," 82.

5. Rodolfo and Julio Irazusta, "Nuestro programa," *La Nueva República*, December 1, 1927, 1.

6. Eduardo González Calleja, "El hispanismo autoritario español y el movimiento nacionalista argentino: balance de medio siglo de relaciones políticas e intelectuales (1898–1946)," *Hispania* 67, no. 226 (May–August 2007): 607.

7. Rock, *Authoritarian Argentina*, 11; González Calleja, "El hispanismo," 608.

8. González Calleja, "El hispanismo," 609–14.

9. Juan E. Carulla, *Al filo del medio siglo* (Buenos Aires: Editorial Huemul, 1964), 201–2.

10. The question of just how much Maurras shaped the thinking of his Argentine admirers will be considered below.

11. On the positivist roots of Maurras's thought, see Michael Sutton, *Nationalism, Positivism and Catholicism: The Politics of Charles Maurras and French Catholics, 1890–1914* (Cambridge: Cambridge University Press, 1982).

12. Carmen Callil, "Action Man," *New Statesman*, April 9, 2001.

13. In Carulla's words, "[Latin] America's past is called Spain, is called Europe, is called Rome, is called Christianity." See "Defensa de Occidente," in Juan Emiliano Carulla, *Problemas de la cultura: defensa de occidente y otros temas* (Buenos Aires: El Ateneo, Librería Científica y Literaria, 1927), 19.

14. Carulla, "Defensa de occidente," 20, 21.

15. Rodolfo Irazusta, "La Política: La democracia no está en la constitución," *La Nueva República*, April 28, 1928, 1.

16. "Política: La conferencia de la Habana," *La Nueva República*, February 15, 1928. The editorial went on to decry the intervention of the United States in Nicaragua because the United States did not belong to the "comunidad americana."

17. According to Michael Sutton, Maurras's identification of Protestantism with individualism was borrowed from Comte. See *Nationalism, Positivism and Catholicism*, 57. Rodolfo Irazusta agreed with Maurras's analysis, arguing that the French Revolution was in essence a Protestant revolution inspired by the "Calvinist Rousseau." See "La política: La democracia no está en la constitución," *La Nueva República*, May 5, 1928.

18. Julio Irazusta, ed., *El pensamiento político nacionalista: antología* (Buenos Aires: Obligado Editora, 1975), 1:53.

19. Sutton, *Nationalism, Positivism and Catholicism*, 58–59.

20. Ernesto Palacio, "Nacionalismo y democracia," *La Nueva República*, May 5, 1928.

21. Palacio, "Nacionalismo y democracia."

22. Callil, "Action Man," n.p.

23. Rodolfo Irazusta, "La política: El orden del 53," *La Nueva República*, September 27, 1930.

24. Rodolfo and Julio Irazusta, "Nuestro programa."

25. Given these striking similarities, it is no wonder that historian Tulio Halperin Donghi has observed that much of Ernesto Palacio's writing could have easily come from the pen of Ricardo Rojas, despite Palacio's disdain for the older man. See *La Argentina y la tormenta del mundo: ideas y ideologías entre 1930 y 1945* (Buenos Aires: Siglo Veintiuno Editores Argentina, 2003), 208.

26. Still, the contributors to *LNR* were sensitive to criticisms about the foreign sources of their ideas, criticisms that they themselves would later level at other right-wing nationalists. Also problematic was Maurras's personal agnosticism and the fact that the Vatican ultimately condemned Maurras's group *L'Action Francaise*. Thus Julio Irazusta took pains to make clear his belief that Maurras did not provide a "universal recipe for all nations to follow." See Julio Irazusta, "Maurras," in his *Actores y espectadores* (Buenos Aires: Sur, 1937), 144. Quoted in Enrique Zuleta Álvarez, *El nacionalismo argentino*, vol. 1 (Buenos Aires: Ediciones La Bastilla, 1975), 351.

27. Fernando Devoto, *Nacionalismo, fascismo y tradicionalismo en la Argentina moderna: una historia* (Buenos Aires: Siglo Veintiuno de Argentina, 2002), 179.

28. See, for example, "Programa de gobierno de la nueva república," *La Nueva República*, October 20, 1928.

29. On this point see Devoto, *Nacionalismo, fascismo y tradicionalismo*, 179–81.

30. Julio Irazusta, "La forma mixta de gobierno," *La Nueva República* January 31, 1928.

31. Rodolfo Irazusta, "La política: La democracia no está en la constitución," *La Nueva República*, April 28, 1928.

32. This novel interpretation of the Argentine constitution was coupled with a defense of the famed Generation of 1837, and especially of the document's principal author, Juan B. Alberdi. According to Rodolfo Irazusta, the widely held assumption that the 1853 Constitution was a literal copy of the US Constitution was false and overlooked the originality of Alberdi's thought. Alberdi, he argued, had simply used "the technique" of the North American framers, as a kind of "literary clothing" in which to dress the already-established institutions of the country. See Rodolfo Irazusta, "La campaña presidencial," *La Nueva República*, January 15, 1928.

33. Chap. 1, sec. 2 of the 1853 Constitution stated that the federal government supported or sustained the Roman Catholic religion, while sec. 14 of the same chapter established freedom of religion.

34. Rodolfo Irazusta, "La politica: La democracia no está en la constitución," *La Nueva República*, May 5, 1928.

35. Continuing, he noted, "The Argentine State is Catholic by its origins and its Constitution. Democracy is by its very nature anti-Catholic. Democracy, then, is incompatible with Argentina's [political] institutions." See "La politica: La democracia no está en la constitución," *La Nueva República*, May 5, 1928. (Note that Irazusta wrote several editorials on this topic that had this same title.)

36. *La Nueva República*, "Programa de gobierno de La Nueva República," October 20, 1928.

37. Uriburu and Carulla's ties went back to 1925, when the general became one of the few paying subscribers to Carulla's short-lived nationalist publication *La Voz Nacional*. For useful background on Uriburu, see Marvin Goldwert, "The Rise of Modern Militarism in Argentina," *Hispanic American Historical Review* 48, no. 2 (May 1968): 198.

38. Goldwert, "Rise of Modern Militarism," 195.

39. Carulla, *Al filo*, 247.

40. For an account, see Carulla, *Al filo*, 250–52.

41. For background on the formation of the Liga Republicana, see María Inés Tato, *Viento de fronda: liberalismo, conservadurismo y democracia en la*

*Argentina, 1911–1932* (Buenos Aires: Siglo Veintiuno Editores Argentina, 2004), 173–76.

42. According to the Liga's manifesto, Yrigoyen's promotion of labor strife and its "stimulation" of the masses' "instinctive tendency toward disorder" had put constitutionalism in jeopardy. See Julio Irazusta, "Bases y program de acción de la Liga Republicana," in *El pensamiento político nacionalista*, 2:25, 26.

43. The most important study of the rising influence of the Catholic Church on nationalist thought during this period remains Loris Zanatta's *Del estado liberal a la nación católica: iglesia y ejército en los orígenes del peronismo, 1930–1943* (Buenos Aires: Universidad Nacional de Quilmes, 1996). Because Zanatta is particularly concerned with the church's efforts to propagate the identification of *argentinidad* with Catholicism among both civilians and within the military, his work is especially useful for my purposes.

44. For a discussion of the debates surrounding Law 1420, see Carlos Floria, "El clima ideológico de la querella escolar," in *La Argentina del ochenta al centenario*, ed. Gustavo Ferrari and Ezequiel Gallo (Buenos Aires: Editorial Sudamericana, 1980), 851–69.

45. Zanatta, *Del estado liberal*, 27.

46. My account of the early twentieth-century Catholic renaissance draws extensively from Enrique Zuleta Álvarez, *El nacionalismo argentino*, vol. 1 (Buenos Aires: Ediciones La Bastilla, 1975), 180–91.

47. For a basic history of the Cursos, see Raúl Rivero de Olazábal, *Por una cultura católica: El compromiso de una generación argentina* (Buenos Aires: Editorial Claretiana, 1986). On *Convivio* in particular, see 107–23.

48. Alberto Spektorowski, *The Origins of Argentina's Revolution of the Right* (Notre Dame, IN: University of Notre Dame Press, 2003), 114.

49. Zanatta, *Del estado liberal*, 45.

50. Zanatta, *Del estado liberal*, 45. Among the young nationalists who passed through the institution's classrooms during the 1930s were Federico and Carlos Ibarguren (Jr.), Ernesto Palacio, Marcelo Sánchez Sorondo, Juan Carlos Goyeneche, José María de Estrada, Mario Mendioroz, Mario Amadeo, Máximo Etchecopar, Hugo de Achával, and Héctor Llambías. Federico Ibarguren, *Orígenes del nacionalismo argentino* (Buenos Aires: Editorial Celcius, 1969), 215.

51. Daniel Lvovich, *Nacionalismo y antisemitismo en la Argentina* (Buenos Aires: Javier Vergara, Grupo Zeta, 2003), 375.

52. Directed by one of the young Turks, Atilio Dell'Oro, its editorial page was in the hands of Tomás Cullen, a member of the older generation. See Fernando Devoto, *Nacionalismo, fascismo y tradicionalismo*, 208.

53. For an account of the purging of the Martin Fierristas, see Devoto, *Nacionalismo, fascismo y tradicionalismo*, 214–15.

54. According to Devoto, between March 1928 and August 1929, Palacio contributed forty-six articles or commentaries, Casares was second with thirty-two, Pico had twenty-four, Carulla contributed ten, and each of the Irazusta brothers contributed two. See *Nacionalismo, fascismo y tradicionalismo*, 217n156.

55. Ramiro de Maetzu's writings in the magazine *Acción Española*, which were published in book form in his 1934 *Defensa de la hispanidad*, were instrumental in popularizing the notion of *hispanidad* among Argentine Catholics of the period.

56. Zanatta, *Del estado liberal*, 80, 35.

57. Franceschi's article was a direct response to Acción Argentina, a liberal, pro-Allied organization that sought to defend democracy in Argentina and abroad, and in doing so proclaimed democratic principles to be "the very essence of our nationality." See "Totalitarianismo, liberalismo, catolicismo," *Criterio* 13, no. 662 (November 7, 1940): 226.

58. Gabriel Riesco, "El eje diamantino de nuestro ser," *El Pueblo*, October 12, 1941. My ellipses.

59. Luis Barrantes Molina, "Los delitos contra la nacionalidad," *El Pueblo*, July 27, 1941.

60. Julio Meinvielle, *Concepción católica de la economía* (Buenos Aires: Curso de Cultura Católica, 1936), 17–23.

61. Zanatta, *Del estado liberal*, 38–39.

62. One conflict stemmed from the LNR group's open admiration for Maurras. The other arose when Ernesto Palacio published a letter in *Criterio* criticizing the views of its editor and denouncing democracy. For an account of these controversies, see Devoto, *Nacionalismo, fascismo y tradicionalismo*, 226–32.

63. Rock, *Authoritarian Argentina*, 71.

64. Leopoldo Lugones, "Acción ante la doble amenaza," in *Antología de la prosa* (Buenos Aires: Ediciones Centurión, 1949), 372.

65. Devoto, *Nacionalismo, fascismo y tradicionalismo*, 141.

66. Devoto, *Nacionalismo, fascismo y tradicionalismo*, 142.

67. Lugones, "El discurso de Ayacucho," in *La patria fuerte* (Buenos Aires: Taller Gráfico de L. Bernard, 1930), 17.

68. Both quotations are from Lugones, "El discurso," 18.

69. The term *índole* appears repeatedly in Lugones's 1930 publications, and seems to be a substitute for the term *raza*, which was the favored term in his 1913 conferences on the poem "Martín Fierro."

70. Indeed Lugones argued that this form of government was "the most genuine and characteristic" creation of the Anglo-Saxon world. *La grande argentina* (1930; Buenos Aires: Editorial Huemul, 1962), 189.

71. Lugones, *La grande argentina*, 189.

72. Lugones, *La grande argentina*, 189.

73. Echoing the Romantic argument that nations must stay true to their essence and historical mission, Lugones believed that only through a rediscovery of itself could Argentina become a great nation (*La grande argentina*, 25).

74. In contrast to his fellow right-wing nationalists, who saw Argentina and the rest of the Spanish American world as New World branches of the Spanish trunk, Lugones dismissed those who referred to Spain as the "madre patria" as "chorus leaders of the race and other spewers of Hispanofilia nonsense" (*La grande argentina*, 178).

75. Halperin Donghi, *La Argentina y la tormenta*, 24.

76. Devoto, *Nacionalismo, fascismo y tradicionalismo*, 235.

77. Goldwert, "Rise of Modern Militarism," 201.

78. Devoto, *Nacionalismo, fascismo y tradicionalismo*, 250.

79. See José Uriburu, Manifiesto (October 1, 1930), in Tulio Halperin Donghi, *La República imposible* (Buenos Aires: Ariel, 2004), 341, appendix.

80. On this point, see Halperin Donghi, *La Argentina y la tormenta*, 24; and Marcus Klein, "The Legión Cívica and the Radicalization of Argentine Nacionalismo during the Década Infame," *Estudios Interdisciplinarios de América Latina y el Caribe* 13 no. 2 (July–December 2002), www7.tau.ac.il/ojs/index.php/eial/article/view/875/977.

81. Halperin Donghi, *La República imposible*, 29.

82. Zanatta, *Del estado liberal*, 51.

83. Gustavo Juan Franceschi, *El Pueblo*, October 12, 1930. Quoted in Zanatta, *Del estado liberal*, 55.

84. Zanatta, *Del estado liberal*, 55. The phrase is Zanatta's.

85. Gustavo J. Franceschi, "Nacionalismo," *Criterio* 6, no. 290 (September 21, 1933): 56.

86. Rodolfo Irazusta, "La política: El orden del 53," *La Nueva República*, September 27, 1930.

87. This is a reference to the nation's most elite social club. Letter from Rodolfo Irazusta to Julio Irazusta, October 1, 1930, in Julio Irazusta, *Pensamiento político nacionalista*, 2:111–12.

88. Rodolfo Irazusta, "La política: Los principios contra la nación," *La Nueva República*, November 8, 1930.

89. This is detailed in Julio Irazusta, *El pensamiento político nacionalista*, 2:148–51.

90. "Acción Republicana: Preámbulo y programa, July 9, 1931," in Julio Irazusta, *El pensamiento político nacionalista*, 2:171. This manifesto, which appeared in the *LNR*, was signed by the following: Angelino Zorraquín, Arturo Ameghino, Carlos Obligado, Leopoldo Lugones, Rodolfo Irazusta, Ernesto

Palacio, Justo Pallarés Aceba, César Pico, Santiago Lugones, Lisando Galíndez, José Mauricio Acevedo, Mario Lassaga, Jorge Attwel de Veyga, Castelfort Lugones, Julio Irazusta, Lisardo Zía, Oscar Allaría Amézaga, Pablo Buglioni, Juan Carlos de Abelleyra, and Horacio Boneo Pico.

91. Rodolfo Irazusta, "La filiación histórica," *La Nueva República*, October 29, 1931.

92. Rodolfo Irazusta, "La filiación histórica."

93. The LNR members were virtually alone in their reassessment of Radicalism. Other prominent nationalists, such as Lugones, remained convinced that Radicalism was evil.

94. Rodolfo Irazusta, "La profesión del candidato," *La Nueva República*, October 20, 1931.

95. Rodolfo Irazusta, "Notas políticas: La ley Sáenz Peña y la revolución," *La Nueva República*, October 26, 1931, in Julio Irazusta, *El pensamiento político nacionalista*, 3:137.

96. Rodolfo Irazusta, "Notas políticas: La voluntad del soberano," *La Nueva República*, November 5, 1931, in Julio Irazusta, *El pensamiento político nacionalista*, 3:205.

97. Ernesto Palacio, "Notas políticas," *La Nueva República*, October 29, 1931, in Julio Irazusta, *El pensamiento político nacionalista*, 3:147.

98. Rodolfo Irazusta, "Filiación histórica," *La Nueva República*, October 29, 1931.

99. It should be stressed that the LNR group's more sympathetic view of Radicalism had its limits and was based on its highly self-serving assumption that the Argentine masses had an inherent desire to follow a strong personalistic leader that only the nationalists could provide in the post-Yrigoyen era.

100. Even though Justo enjoyed the strong support of the conservative oligarchy, most members of the LNR group supported his candidacy.

101. In the words of Tulio Halperin Donghi, who has dubbed this period that of the "impossible republic," Argentina's governing class was "obligated to systematically violate the principles they invoked to legitimate themselves." See *La Argentina y la tormenta*, 14.

102. On this point, see Halperin Donghi, *La república imposible*, 19.

103. The Partido Democrático Nacional was a coalition of traditional conservatives, the Independent Socialists, and the anti-Personalist Radicals.

104. Additional evidence of the public's continued prodemocracy sentiment was its widespread support for the Republican cause during the Spanish Civil War (1936–39). For more discussion, see Mark Falcoff, "Argentina," in *The Spanish Civil War, 1936–39: Hemispheric Perspectives*, ed. Mark Falcoff and Frederick Pike (Lincoln: University of Nebraska Press, 1982), 291–347.

105. Julio Meinvielle, *¿Que saldrá de la España que sangra?* (Buenos Aires: T. G. San Pablo, 1937), 34. Quoted in Lvovich, *Nacionalismo y antisemitismo*, 413.

106. Ibarguren, *Origenes del nacionalismo argentino*, 364.

107. Federico Ibarguren, "La misión histórica de España," *Criterio* (December 17, 1936), in Ibarguren, *Origenes del nacionalismo argentino*, 365, 374.

108. Much of the debate over this question has centered on different definitions of fascism. Those who have argued against the idea of Argentine fascism include David Rock, *Authoritarian Argentina*; Marysa Navarro Gerrassi, *Los nacionalistas* (Buenos Aires: J. Alvarez, 1968); Ronald Newton, *"The 'Nazi Menace' in Argentina, 1931–47* (Stanford, CA: Stanford University Press, 1992); and Mario Nascimbene and Mauricio Isaac Neuman, "El nacionalismo católico, el fascismo y la inmigración en la Argentina (1927–1943): una aproximación teórica," *Estudios Interdisciplinarios de America Latina y el Caribe* 4, no. 1 (January–June), 1993, https://www7.tau.ac.il/ojs/index.php/eial/article/view/1251/1279. Scholars who believe that Argentina's right-wing nationalists did indeed represent an Argentine version of fascism include Sandra McGee Deutsche, *Las Derechas: The Extreme Right in Argentina, Brazil, and Chile, 1890–1939* (Stanford, CA: Stanford University Press, 1999); Spektorowski, *Origins*; Cristián Buchrucker, *Nacionalismo y peronismo: La Argentina en la crisis ideológica del mundo (1927–1955)* (Buenos Aires: Editorial Sudamericana, 1987); Federico Finchelstein, *Transatlantic Fascism: Ideology, Violence, and the Sacred in Argentina and Italy, 1919–1945* (Durham, NC: Duke University Press, 2010); and Finchelstein, *Fascismo, litugia e imaginario. El mito del general Uriburu y la Argentina nacionalista* (Buenos Aires: Fondo de Cultura Económica, 2002). For an overview of the debate, see Deutsch, *Las Derechas*, 244–47.

109. Finchelstein, *Transatlantic Fascism*, 29–30.

110. Finchelstein, *Transatlantic Fascism*, 35, 108, 157.

111. On this concept, see especially chapter 4 of Finchelstein's *Transatlantic Fascism*.

112. Among those who most openly identified with fascism, at least at one point in their lives, were Manuel Gálvez, Enrique Osés, César Pico, Juan P. Ramos, Carlos Ibarguren, Nimio de Anquín, Julio Meinvielle, and Virgilio Filippo. It is worth noting that these last two were priests.

113. Spektorowski, *Origins*, 115.

114. It should be noted that Gálvez's flirtation with fascism was relatively brief.

115. José María Pemán, "Pasemos a la escucha," *Sol y Luna* 4 (1940): 91. Quoted in and translated by Finchelstein, *Transatlantic Fascism*, 117. Bracketed material is in Finchelstein.

116. For a more complete list, see Christian Buchrucker's helpful chart in his *Nacionalismo y peronismo*, 116–17. For estimates of the numbers for the

affiliates of the Legión and the AJN, see Michael Goebel, "A Movement from Left to Right in Argentine Nationalism? The Alianza Libertadora Nacionalista and Tacuara as Stages of Militancy," *Bulletin of Latin American Research* 26, no. 3 (2007): 359. Also useful is Deutsch, *Las Derechas*, 200–207.

117. In August 1933, for example, the Uriburist group Liga Cívica Argentina agreed to join with the Milicia Cívica Nacionalista and the Legión de Mayo to form the Guardia Argentina under the leadership of Leopoldo Lugones. This umbrella entity proved to be short-lived, as was Afirmación de una Nueva Argentina (ADUNA), a group established by Uriburu confidante Juan P. Ramos. For more on these efforts, see Spektorowski, *Origins*, 154–55.

118. For an example of right-wing nationalists criticizing Argentine fascists for adopting "exotic" ideologies, see Deutsch, *Las Derechas*, 207. See also Rodolfo Irazusta's attack on "filo-fascists" for their pro-oligarchic and "antidemocratic attitudes," in "Los filo-fascistas malmanejan la tópica creada por el nacionalismo," *Nuevo Orden* 2, no. 58 (August 29, 1941): 1–2. Quoted in Zuleta, *El nacionalismo argentino*, 369.

119. "Carta pastoral del Episcopado Argentino. 30 de mayo de 1936," *Revista Eclesiática del Arzobispada de Buenos Aires y Sucedáneos* (July 1936), 433–39. Quoted in Zanatta, *Del estado liberal*, 189. Even among those who identified themselves as fascists there was conflict. By the mid-1930s, Juan Carulla, who had once been a core member of the LNR group, openly advocated fascism. But in contrast to such nationalists as Enrique Osés, who argued that fascism would have to be imposed by another military coup, Carulla placed his faith in politicians, such as Manuel Fresco, governor of Buenos Aires Province, who sought to bring about fascist-style changes while observing democratic forms.

120. Despite such actions, some staunch nationalists remained hostile to Uriburu's successor. Some, such as Roberto de Laferrère, conspired repeatedly with Uriburista military officers to unseat Justo. For more on the relationship between nationalists and conservatives during the 1930s, see María Inés Tato, "Alianzas estratégicas o confluencias? Conservadores y nacionalistas en la Argentina de los años treinta," *Cuadernos del CLAEH* 28, no. 91 (2005): 126.

121. On these crackdowns, which made bitter enemies of Radicals, see Halperin Donghi, *La república imposible*, 107.

122. Zanatta, *Del estado liberal*, 109. At the Congress, Justo appeared whenever possible, even delivering a fervent public oration, in which he affirmed his own personal faith.

123. The pact was named after its two chief negotiators, Argentine vice president Julio Roca (Jr.) and Walter Runciman, head of the British Board of Trade.

124. During the world depression, Great Britain stepped away from its traditional free trade policies and declared its intention of granting preferential treatment to imports from its dominions.

125. During the 1920s, for instance, cultural nationalist Ricardo Rojas and Liga Patriótica founder Manuel Carlés had sounded alarms about the growing influence of foreign capital in Argentina (Deutsche, *Las Derechas*, 100–101). Similarly, elite economist Alejandro Bunge had warned Argentines about the country's excessive reliance on the agro-export model and had urged the state to foster export diversity and industrialization. See Juan Carlos Korol and Hilda Sábato, "Incomplete Industrialization: An Argentine Obsession," *Latin American Research Review* 25, no. 1 (1990): 8. Perhaps the most persistent voice calling for economic independence in the pre-1930 period was Radical politician Manuel Ortíz Pereyra (1883–1941), who in his books *La tercera emancipación* (1926) and *Por nuestra redención cultural y económica* (1928) linked Argentina's lack of economic independence with the elite's penchant for ignoring local realities. The ideas of Ortíz Pereyra will be examined in chapter 7.

126. Julio Irazusta, *El pensamiento político nacionalista*, 3:120.

127. Julio Irazusta, "Sobre el capital extranjero," *La Nueva República*, October 22, 1931.

128. Julio Irazusta, *El pensamiento político nacionalista*, 3:121.

129. Rodolfo and Julio Irazusta, *La Argentina y el imperialismo británico: Los eslabones de una cadena. 1806–1833* (Buenos Aires: Editorial Tor, 1934), 133.

130. R. and J. Irazusta, *La argentina*, 149.

131. R. and J. Irazusta, *La argentina*, 149.

132. R. and J. Irazusta, *La argentina*, 167.

133. R. and J. Irazusta, *La argentina*, 166.

134. R. and J. Irazusta, *La argentina*, 167.

135. R. and J. Irazusta, *La argentina*, 168.

136. R. and J. Irazusta, *La argentina*, 102.

137. The literature on Argentine historical revisionism is extensive. Some useful treatments are Tulio Halperin Donghi, *El revisionismo histórico argentino: Colección mínima* (Buenos Aires: Siglo Veintiuno Editores, 1970); Tulio Halperin Donghi, *El revisionismo histórico argentina como visión decadentista de la historia nacional* (Buenos Aires: Siglo XXI Editores, 2006); and Diana Quattrocchi-Woisson, *Los males de la memoria: Historia y política en la Argentina* (Buenos Aires: Emecé Editores, 1998).

138. Quattrocchi-Woisson, *Los males*, 119.

139. On the importance and reception of the Irazustas' book, see Halperin Donghi, *La Argentina y la tormenta*, 80–88; Spektorowski, *Origins*, 127; and Quattrocchi-Woisson, *Los males*, 119–22.

140. Halperin Donghi, *La Argentina y la tormenta*, 85–86.

141. See Julio Irazusta's comments in his *El pensamiento político naciona-lista*, 2:60.

142. Doll, "Grandeza," 43. The review appeared originally in *Claridad*, yr. 13, no. 277, 1934, and was reprinted as "Grandeza y miseria de la oligarquía argentina: la realidad nacional sin cartabones extranjeros," in Ramón Doll, *Liberalismo en la literatura y la política* (Buenos Aires: Editorial Claridad, 1936).

143. Doll, "Grandeza," 42.

144. Doll, "Grandeza," 48.

145. Doll, "Grandeza," 49.

146. Doll, "Grandeza," 43.

147. Doll, "Grandeza," 47.

148. Rojas, as noted in chapter 3, borrowed this concept from the Generation of 1898.

149. On this point see Spektorowski, *Origins*, 106.

150. During the early 1940s, these two strands of right-wing nationalism produced competing journals. The Irazusta brothers, Doll, and Palacio formed the core contributors to the nationalist magazine *Nuevo Orden*, while Federico Ibarguren, Alberto Escurra Medrano, Ricardo Font Escurra, Héctor Llambías, and H. Sáenz y Quesada worked together on its rival, *Nueva Política*.

151. Federico Ibarguren, "La dictadura tradicionalista," *El Pampero*, October 4, 1940.

152. Ernesto Palacio, *La historia falsificada, con una introducción de Leonardo Castellani* (Buenos Aires: Editorial Difusión, 1939), 59.

153. Palacio, *La historia falsificada*, 71.

154. Palacio, *La historia falsificada*, 63.

155. Federico Ibarguren, "La dictadura tradicionalista."

156. Alberto Ezcurra Medrano, *Catholicismo y nacionalismo* (Buenos Aires: ADSUM, 1939), 64.

157. Sandra McGee Deutsch also makes the case that, despite the many divisions within the nationalist right, their similarities far outweighed their differences. In her words, the "importance lies in the whole, rather than in individual groups" (*Las Derechas*, 207).

CHAPTER 7.   Anti-imperialism, FORJA, and the Defense of the
True Argentina

1. Mark Falcoff has divided the membership of FORJA into militants and partisans. Militants, who numbered three hundred, were required to be members of the Unión Cívica Radical (UCR). Partisans, who attended meet-

ings and helped with organizational tasks, numbered about three thousand. FORJA was strongest in the province of Buenos Aires, but it had small groups in almost every national province. For information on these numbers, as well as for the organizational structure of FORJA, see Mark Falcoff, "Argentine Nationalism on the Eve of Perón: The Force of Radical Orientation of Young Argentina and Its Rivals, 1935–45" (PhD diss., Princeton University, 1970), 99–103.

2. Although Yrigoyen reconstituted the UCR's National Committee in 1904, he convened it only once more, in 1906. Similarly, he refused to convene a national convention for the party that would allow input from delegates from across the country, a modern political practice the UCR had pioneered under Alem. See Félix Luna, *Yrigoyen* (Buenos Aires: Editorial Sudamericana, 2005), 177.

3. David Rock, *Politics in Argentina, 1890–1930: The Rise and Fall of Radicalism*, Cambridge Latin American studies 19 (Cambridge: Cambridge University Press, 1975), 112.

4. The rabidly anti-Yrigoyenist newspaper *La Fronda*, for example, praised Alvear for serving as the president of all Argentines rather than behaving as though non-Radicals were enemies. Argentina, the newspaper proclaimed, was finally returning to "normalcy and civilization" after six long years of "barbarism." "Aspectos del mensaje," *La Fronda*, May 11, 1923. Quoted in María Inés Tato, *Viento de fronda: liberalismo, conservadurismo y democracia en la Argentina, 1911–1932* (Buenos Aires: Siglo Veintiuno Editores Argentina, 2004), 129. See also Luna, *Yrigoyen*, 350–52. Most outrageous to personalists was Alvear's 1923 appointment of Vicente Gallo to head the Ministry of the Interior. Gallo was one of the ringleaders of the party's anti-Yrigoyen faction.

5. The candidates were Leopoldo Melo and Vicente Gallo for president and vice president, respectively.

6. Of 319 electoral votes, Yrigoyen received 245, with Melo receiving 71. Carlos Alberto Giacobone and Gallo Edit Rosalía, *Radicalismo bonaerense: la ingeniería política de Hipólito Yrigoyen, 1891–1931* (Buenos Aires: Corregidor, 1999), 276.

7. Ana Virginia Persello, *El partido Radical: gobierno y oposición, 1916–1943* (Buenos Aires: Siglo Veintiuno Editores Argentina, 2004), 131–32.

8. Lacking direction at the national level, several provincial leaders began reunification efforts, and by early 1931, most UCR leaders had agreed on such a strategy. See Persello, *El partido*, 137.

9. This was despite the fact that Alvear and the Buenos Aires–based leadership had no knowledge of the uprising. See Persello, *El partido*, 139–40. It should be noted that, as a result of prohibiting Alvear's candidacy, the UCR

leadership decided to abstain from the upcoming electoral process, a policy that remained in place until 1935. Internal debate over the abstentionist policy was intense. Among the most avid advocates of abstaining from participating in elections was Ricardo Rojas, who penned the party's manifesto stating the reasons for this decision (140).

10. Manuel Ortiz Pereyra, *La tercera emancipación: Actualidad económica y social de la República Argentina* (Buenos Aires: J. Lajouane, 1926). Quoted in Norberto Galasso, *Testimonio del precursor de FORJA: Manuel Ortiz Pereira [sic]* (Buenos Aires: Centro Editor de America Latina, 1981), 68, 69. Page numbers refer to the Galasso book.

11. Manuel Ortiz Pereyra, *Por nuestra redención cultural y económica (Apuntes de crítica social argentina)* (Buenos Aires: Talleres Casa Jacobo Peuser, Ltda., 1928), 39, 37.

12. On Pereya's influence on Barcos, see Julio R. Barcos, *Por el pan del pueblo* (Buenos Aires: Librería "Renacimiento," 1933), 25–38.

13. It should be noted that many formerly pro-Alvarista Radicals were also displeased by Alvear's efforts at reconciliation. Several important anti-personalists, such as José Camilo Crotto, Juan B. Castro, Federico Cantoni, and Rogelio Araya, let it be known that they would not participate in the newly reorganized UCR if Alvear refused to purge it of Yrigoyen supporters. See Persello, *El partido*, 139. For more on the internal dissidents, see Miguel Ángel Scenna, *F.O.R.J.A.; una aventura argentina (de Yrigoyen a Perón)* (Buenos Aires: Ediciones La Bastilla, 1972), 50–51.

14. Barcos, *Por el pan*, 9. Barcos went so far as to argue that "imperialist capitalists" had conspired behind the scenes to mastermind Yrigoyen's overthrow. On this point, see Barcos, *Por el pan*, 22.

15. Barcos, *Por el pan*, 10.

16. Barcos, *Por el pan*, 60, 60–61.

17. Barcos, *Por el pan*, 197.

18. Barcos, *Por el pan*, 198.

19. Barcos, *Por el pan*, 199.

20. Barcos, *Por el pan*, 200. For other essentialist statements in this work, see 26, 52, 63.

21. Barcos, *Por el pan*, 185.

22. Barcos, *Por el pan*, 99.

23. Barcos, *Por el pan*, 125.

24. Barcos, *Por el pan*, 125.

25. Barcos, *Por el pan*, 63.

26. Barcos, *Por el pan*, 62.

27. The name came from the small town of Paso de los Libres, where much of the action took place and where several deaths occurred. This town was later immortalized by Jauretche in a poem of the same name he wrote and published just a few months after the events.

28. The key spokespersons for the abstentionists were Ricardo Rojas and Adolfo Güemes. Also included in this group were Carlos Sánchez, Pedro Duhalde, Emir Mercader, Juan O'Farrell, Atilio Cattáneo, Guillermo Watson, Francisco Albarracín, and of course Jauretche. See Persello, *El partido*, 156–58.

29. Published as "Vocación revolucionaria del radicalismo," *Cuadernos de F.O.R.J.A*, nos. 10–12 (November 1939), 45. The document in *Cuadernos* is dated December 1934.

30. The term *vendepatria* appeared in both the 1934 and 1939 versions. Note that there was a slight difference in the two versions, with the original using the term *los vendepatria* (see Scenna, *F.O.R.J.A.*, 77); *vendepatrias* was the term used in the 1939 version, reproduced in *Cuadernos de F.O.R.J.A.* ("Vocación revolucionaria," 45).

31. Although the original list of participants in this first meeting has been lost, Scenna has pieced together what appears to be the most complete list. See *F.O.R.J.A.*, 98–99.

32. Scenna, whose history of FORJA is one of the most exhaustive, attributes the phrase to Yrigoyen. Mark Falcoff, however, rejects this claim ("Argentine Nationalism," 75–76).

33. Once Yrigoyen was released from prison, Jauretche became a regular visitor and was in the former president's home when the elderly man died. Such was Jauretche's stature within the personalist branch of the party that he remained at the corpse's side during the public viewing.

34. Little has been written about this oppositional current within the main body of Radicalism, or about their views of FORJA. For an introduction to this topic, see Susana Brauner Rodgers's "El nacionalismo yrigoyenista (1930–1943)," *Estudios Interdisciplinarios de América Latina y el Caribe* 1, no. 2 (July–December, 1990), http://eial.tau.ac.il/index.php/eial/issue/view/92.

35. Scenna, *F.O.R.J.A.*, 179.

36. This explanation comes from Norberto Galasso, *Jauretche y su época* (Buenos Aires: Peña Lillo, 1985), 339.

37. For example, in *Cuadernos de F.O.R.J.A.*, the organization's most important publication, Scalabrini Ortiz contributed roughly half of the page count. Most of his writings focused on British imperialism and included lengthy articles, such as "Política británica en el Río de la Plata," "Historia del Ferrocarril Central Córdoba," "Historia del primer emprésito argentino," and

"Petróleo e imperialismo" (this last was coauthored with Luis Dellepiane). In 1940, he reworked many of these writings and published them in two separate volumes titled *Política británica en el Río de la Plata* and *Historia del los ferro-carriles argentinos*.

38. Arturo Jauretche, *FORJA y la década infame: Con un apéndice de manifiestos, declaraciones y textos volantes* (Buenos Aires: Ed. Coyoacán, 1962), 40–41.

39. Background information on Scalabrini Ortiz comes from Mark Falcoff, "Raúl Scalabrini Ortiz: The Making of an Argentine Nationalist," *Hispanic American Historical Review* 52, no. 1 (February 1972): 74–101; and Alejandro Cattaruzza and Fernando D. Rodríguez's preface to Raúl Scalabrini Ortiz, *El hombre que está solo y espera: una biblia porteña* (Buenos Aires: Editorial Biblos, 2005).

40. In Spanish, *esperar* can be translated as either "to wait" or "to hope." Scalabrini left its meaning deliberately ambiguous.

41. Scalabrini Ortiz, *El hombre*, 39.

42. It is difficult to determine just how many editions of the book have been published. Relying on data from WorldCat, which includes only those editions that have made their way into US libraries, *El hombre* has gone through at least eighteen editions, eight of which appeared during Scalabrini Ortiz's lifetime. Because no study has been done on the size of the various printings, it's impossible to gauge actual sales of the book. Of interest, however, is the fact that the work went through four printings between 1971 and 1976.

43. Writing about the rebellion in 1934, Scalabrini said nothing about its Radical character, instead describing it as a conflict that had "on the one side the entire nation . . . and on the other, its English and North American exploiters along with their local representatives." Raúl Scalabrini Ortiz, "La creación de una realidad," *Gaceta de Buenos Aires*, November 3, 1934. Quoted in Halperin Donghi, *Argentina y la tormenta del mundo: Ideas y ideologías entre 1930 y 1945* (Buenos Aires: Siglo Veintiuno Editores Argentina, 2003), 63. On the anti-imperialist thrust of the manifesto, see also Falcoff, "Raúl Scalabrini Ortiz," 83–84.

44. The two articles Scalabrini contributed were republished in *Living Age* (New York), in August and September 1934, respectively, under the titles "Argentina's Tragedy" and "Who Owns Argentina?" These are discussed in Falcoff, "Raúl Scalabrini Ortiz," 84–86.

45. Raúl Scalabrini Ortiz, "Who Owns Argentina?," *Living Age* (New York), September 1934, 28. Quoted in Falcoff, "Raúl Scalabrini Ortiz," 85.

46. Falcoff, "Raúl Scalabrini Ortiz," 84.

47. Halperin, *Argentina y la tormenta*, 66.

48. *Cipayo*, a term employed by Jauretche and popularized by the nationalist left, was the name for Hindu soldiers who allied with the British to defend the colonial empire.

49. Jauretche was particularly active in promoting historical revisionism. It should be noted, however, that his revisionism focused on attacking the liberal elite rather than glorifying Rosas. See, for example, his comments on Rosas in Arturo Jauretche, *Política nacional y revisionismo histórico*, vol 7 of *Obras completas*, ed. Norberto D'Atri (Buenos Aires: Corridor, 2006), 78.

50. On the "devouring" of Palacio's book by Forjistas, see Scenna, *F.O.R.J.A.*, 380.

51. Raúl Scalabrini Ortiz, "Nuestra historia," *FORJANDO* (Rojas, Province of Buenos Aires), yr. 1, no. 3 (September 30, 1940): 6.

52. As noted, Jauretche was an early promoter of revisionism and of the notion that the British helped distort Argentines' understanding of their past. His most thorough treatment of this theme came later, which can be found in his already cited 1959 work, *Política nacional y revisionismo histórico*.

53. "Vocación revolucionaria del radicalismo." Republished under the same title in *Cuadernos de F.O.R.J.A.*, nos. 10–12 (November 1939): 44–45. I have consulted the 1934 version.

54. "Vocación revolucionaria del radicalismo," 45.

55. Titled "F.O.R.J.A.: Al Pueblo de la República," it was published both as a pamphlet and in *Señales*, September 4, 1935, a weekly review, whose principal collaborators were Scalabrini and Jauretche. It was republished in *Cuadernos de F.O.R.J.A*, yr. 2, nos. 10–12 (November 1939): 17–43. I have consulted this version. The quoted material is from 43. Significantly, the cover of the pamphlet boasts the name "Unión Cívica Radical." Although unsigned, its length (when it was reprinted in *Cuadernos* in 1939, it was over twenty-five double-columned pages) and its dozens of sections dealing with a variety of matters suggest that it was produced by multiple authors, including, according to Scenna, Juan Luís Alvardo, Juan Mola Terán, Arturo Jauretche, Luis Dellepiane, Homero Manzione, Jorge de Río, and Oscar Correa and Raúl Scalabrini Ortiz (Scenna, *F.O.R.J.A*, 110).

56. "Al Pueblo de La Republica," Manifesto of F.O.R.J.A., September 2, 1935, in *Cuadernos de F.O.R.J.A*, yr. 2, nos. 10–12 (November 1939): 42.

57. Atilio García Mellid, "Alem, Yrigoyen y Perón: símbolos de las muchedumbres argentinas," *Hechos e Ideas*, yr. 9, no. 54 (September 1948): 288.

58. "Vocación revolucionaria del radicalismo," 44.

59. "Vocación revolucionaria del radicalismo," 45.

60. "Vocación revolucionaria del radicalismo," 44.

61. "El sentido de Yrigoyen," *F.O.R.J.A.: Boletín de la Fuerza de Orienta-ción Radical de la Joven Argentina* (Buenos Aires), November 26, 1936, 3.

62. Amable Gutiérrez Diez, "Repudiamos el Frente Popular," *F.O.R.J.A*, no. 1 (September 14, 1936). Quoted in Scenna, *F.O.R.J.A.*, 206.

63. Gabriel del Mazo, "Yrigoyen," *FORJANDO* (Rojas, Buenos Aires Province), yr. 1, no. 2 (August 27, 1940): 2.

64. "Vocación revolucionaria del radicalismo," 45.

65. Gabriel del Mazo, "Yrigoyen," *Cuadernos de F.O.R.J.A.*, yr. 1, no. 2 (July 3, 1936): 4.

66. "La voluntad de F.O.R.J.A." (1935), in *F.O.R.J.A.: El destino es un ca-mello ciego*, ed. Oscar Sbarra Mitre (Buenos Aires: Quinqué Editores, 2005), 30.

67. Gabriel del Mazo, "La Reforma Universitaria, una conciencia de emancipación en desarrollo," in *Reforma universitaria y cultural nacional* (Bue-nos Aires: n.p., 1947), 57. This speech was delivered in Córdoba on June 15, 1938.

68. Gabriel del Mazo, "Meditación en el día de la raza," in *Reforma uni-versitaria*, 73. This speech was delivered at the Universidad Nacional de la Plata on October 12, 1940.

69. "Declaración de FORJA," August 16, 1941, in Norberto Galasso, *Jauretche y su época* (Buenos Aires: Peña Lillo Editor, 1985), 496.

70. Atilio García Mellid, "La posición de América," FORJANDO (Rojas, Buenos Aires Province), yr. 2, no. 11 (January 1942): 5. This article was reprinted from the magazine *Itinerario de América*, of which García Mellid served as director.

71. Although all right-wing nationalists agreed that Argentine nationality was inextricably tied to its Spanish origins and to the Catholic faith, there were some differences in how they viewed Argentina's relationship with the former colonial power. As Diana Quattrocchi-Woisson has pointed out, individuals, such as Julio Irazusta, criticized other members of the nationalist right for seeming to lament the fact that Argentina had achieved independence from Spain, a position he strongly rejected. See *Los males*, 216.

72. See Arturo Jauretche, *FORJA y la década infame: Con un apéndice de manifiestos, declaraciones y textos volantes* (Buenos Aires: Editorial Coyoacán, 1962), 15n2, for an example of Jauretche's somewhat grudging praise for the right's contribution to the revalorization of the "Hispanic-American roots of Argentina" and his description of its contribution to historical revisionism.

73. "Forja y su concepto sobre la neutralidad radical: Con ninguno de los imperialismos en lucha," May 1941. Quoted from fragments of this manifesto that are reproduced in Scenna, *F.O.R.J.A.*, 419–20.

74. Quoted in Scenna, *F.O.R.J.A.*, 421.

75. Beatriz Sarlo, *Una modernidad periférica: Buenos Aires 1920 y 1930* (Buenos Aires: Nueva Visión, 1988), 216.

76. Here my observations are similar to those of Beatriz Sarlo, who notes Scalabrini relies on an interpretive model that is "at the same time, organicistic and mechanistic" (*Una modernidad*, 240).

77. As will be discussed below, Scalabrini Ortiz believed this intersection in downtown Buenos Aires to be the spiritual epicenter of *argentinidad*.

78. Scalabrini Ortiz, *El hombre*, 62.

79. Scalabrini Ortiz, *El hombre*, 62.

80. Both José Hernández Arregui and Nicola Miller argued that Ricardo Rojas was an important influence on Scalabrini Ortiz. See Hernández Arregui, *La formación de la conciencia nacional, 1930–1960* (Buenos Aires: Editorial Plus Ultra, 1973), 332; and Miller, *In the Shadow of the State: Intellectuals and the Quest for National Identity in Twentieth-Century Spanish America* (London: Verso, 1999), 198.

81. Scalabrini Ortiz, *El hombre*, 41.

82. Scalabrini Ortiz, *El hombre*, 53.

83. Scalabrini Ortiz, *El hombre*, 58.

84. Scalabrini Ortiz, *El hombre*, 39.

85. Scalabrini Ortiz, *El hombre*, 39.

86. Scalabrini Ortiz, *El hombre*, 39.

87. Scalabrini Ortiz, *El hombre*, 66.

88. Scalabrini Ortiz, *El hombre*, 109.

89. Scalabrini Ortiz, *El hombre*, 85. The direct English translation of *pálpito* is "hunch" or "premonition."

90. Scalabrini Ortiz, *El hombre*, 90. The wording *ha impedido* was changed to *procuró impedir* in later editions.

91. Scalabrini Ortiz, *El hombre*, 51.

92. Scalabrini Ortiz, *El hombre*, 51.

93. Scalabrini Ortiz, *El hombre*, 50.

94. Scalabrini Ortiz, *El hombre*, 87.

95. Scalabrini Ortiz, *El hombre*, 86.

96. Scalabrini Ortiz, *El hombre*, 87.

97. But perhaps nothing reflects Scalabrini Ortiz's continuing preoccupation with the archetype limned in *El hombre* than his now famous reaction to the popular, pro-Perón demonstration of October 17, 1945. Describing this spectacle, Scalabrini Ortiz proclaimed, "That which I had dreamed of and intuited during [so] many years was present there, corporal, tense, multifaceted,

but together in a single spirit. There were the men who were alone, and were waiting/hoping for their work of vindication to begin again. The spirit of the land was present as I never believed I would see it." See Scalabrini Ortiz, "Los enemigos del pueblo argentino." This speech, which will be examined in chapter 8, was delivered on July 3, 1948, at the Instituto "Hipólito Yrigoyen," Mercedes, Buenos Aires Province, first published in 1948 by the institute, and reprinted in Scalabrini Ortiz, *Yrigoyen y Perón* (Buenos Aires: Plus Ultra, 1972 ), 9–30.

98. Miller, *In the Shadow*, 199.

99. Jauretche, *FORJA y la década*, 17.

100. *Argentinidad* (Buenos Aires), "Este periódico . . .," October 1938, 4. In Argentina, the term *gringo* generally refers to an Italian immigrant.

101. Arturo Jauretche, *FORJA y la década infame: Con un apéndice de manifiestos, declaraciones y textos volantes* (Buenos Aires: Editorial Coyoacán, 1962), 102–7.

102. The details of the 1943 military coup, and the events leading up to it, will be discussed in the next chapter.

103. Organización Universitario de F.O.R.J.A., "La falsa opción," 103.

104. Organización Universitario de F.O.R.J.A., "La falsa opción," 103.

105. Luis Peralta Ramos, "Del tronco español, pero americanos," *AHORA*, December 1944. Quoted in Falcoff, "Argentine Nationalism," 298.

106. Jauretche, *FORJA y la década*, 15n2.

107. Jauretche, *FORJA y la década*, 17.

108. Arturo Jauretche, speech delivered after June 1943 coup: mimeo, papers of Darío Alessandro, Biblioteca del Congreso Nacional, Argentina, 11. In his words, it was absurd *"pretender restaurar lo argentino en base al origen de la sangre; aquí, donde somos el producto de todas las cruzas. Este no significa eluidir el probema que crea las minorías inadaptables, idiomáticas, de sangre y de confesión. Todas ellas tendrán que fundirse en lo argentino o desparecer, sobre la base de una creación cultural propia que cerrará el paso a toda consttucción [sic] extraña."*

109. Arturo Jauretche, letter to José Benjamín Ábalos. Quoted in Scenna, *F.O.R.J.A.*, 518. Italics in the original. The idea of the submerged or hidden Argentina would continue to be a central theme in Jauretche's writings. In his 1962 account of the FORJA years, for example, he wrote of the decision to split FORJA from its Radical roots, arguing that Argentina's political parties, including the UCR, had become hollow shells. The masses, or the "submerged Argentina," would return to the political arena only when they had new leaders, who would defend their interests. Jauretche, *FORJA y la década*, 37, note.

110. Jauretche, *FORJA y la década*, 17.

111. "Argentina-America-Europa," *FORJANDO* (Rojas, Province of Buenos Aires), yr. 2, no. 11 (January 1942), 5. This article first appeared in the FORJA publication *Argentinidad*, no. 2 (December 1938).

112. Scenna, *F.O.R.J.A.*, 646. Even earlier, Scalabrini Ortiz had publicly criticized the jurors of the Municipal Prize in Literature for failing to give its 1934 award to the Irazustas for *La argentina y el imperialism británico.* On this point, see Arregui, *La formación*, 338.

113. Jauretche, *Forja y la década*, 43.

114. Jauretche, *Forja y la década*, 103.

115. Jauretche, *Forja y la década*, 43.

116. The manifesto "Al Pueblo de la República" originally appeared in *Señales*, September 4, 1935. The edition I consulted was the one republished in *Cuadernos de F.O.R.J.A.*, yr. 2, nos. 10–12, November 1939, 17–43. Although the manifesto is unsigned, its length suggests that it was produced by multiple authors. According to Scenna (*F.O.R.J.A.*, 110), it was jointly written by Juan Luis Alvardo, Juan Mola Terán, Arturo Jauretche, Luis Dellepiane, Homero Manzi, Jorge de Río, and Oscar Correa and Raúl Scalabrini Ortiz. Although most of the manifesto was devoted to the issue of economic imperialism, it contains several positive references to the constitution that are of interest. It complained, for example, about a recent speech by Argentine general Fassola Castaña, who openly praised Italy's Mussolini. Such actions, it warned, were completely contrary to the ideals of Argentina's "founding fathers" (el patriciado argentino)—that is, the liberal authors of the constitution—and were aimed at "getting the public accustomed to arbitrary military interventions and governments that intervene and govern at the margins of the constitution and its laws." Similarly, the manifesto lambasted the current government for its de facto "abolition of the civil rights guaranteed by the constitution." All quotations from *Cuadernos*, 34.

117. Certainly not all Radicals, Forjistas or otherwise, proved reluctant to toss aside the constitution. Recall, for example, that one of Radicalism's first anti-imperialist voices, Julio Barcos, had lamented that the state established by the 1853 document had served the "right hand" of international capitalism.

118. Scenna, *F.O.R.J.A.*, 384.

119. Scenna, *F.O.R.J.A.*, 384–85.

120. This fear was intensified by Justo's first choice for the vice presidential slot: Miguel Angel Cárcano of Córdoba. Because Cárcano had earlier expressed reservations about the use of fraud in provincial elections, conservatives deemed him an unacceptable candidate. After negotiations with provincial elites, Justo finally named Ramón S. Castillo, a deeply conservative Catholic

from Catamarca. For a discussion, see Halperin Donghi, *La república imposible*, 236–37.

121.  Halperin Donghi, *La república imposible*, 247.

122.  For example, *Cuadernos de F.O.R.J.A*, no. 9 was devoted entirely to Dellepiane's proneutrality essay "Conducta argentina ante la crisis de Europa." I have been unable to consult this issue, but I surmise that its publication date was probably October 1939.

123.  Scenna, *F.O.R.J.A.*, 456.

124.  Published in late 1939 and lasting only forty-one issues, *Reconquista*'s primary purpose was to champion the cause of continuing Argentine neutrality in the war. Although it was not an official F.O.R.J.A. publication, most of the articles were penned by Scalabrini and Jauretche. See Mark Falcoff, "Raúl Scalabrini Ortiz," 95–96.

125.  Falcoff has argued that *Reconquista* did not receive German funds, maintaining that (1) it never engaged in pro-Axis propaganda and (2) it was too short-lived, suggesting that it had no steady source of funding. Perhaps most significant, however, was the fact that documents seized from the German Foreign Office after the war mention several Argentine dailies that at one time or another received German subsidies. *Reconquista* was not among them. See Falcoff, "Argentine Nationalism," 334.

126.  Scenna, *F.O.R.J.A.*, 328–34.

127.  This account of these events comes from Mark Falcoff, who drew from a personal interview he conducted with Jauretche on May 4, 1968, and from a copy of Dellepiane's letter, which he gained access to through the graces of historian Roberto Etchepareborda. See Falcoff, "Argentine Nationalism," 334–38. Significantly, in his general history of the UCR, written decades later, Gabriel del Mazo devoted only a few pages to FORJA. He described it as having entered a "definitive crisis" in 1940, which was caused by an "internal tendency" that separated it from the UCR. The organization's main accomplishment, he claimed, was that during a five-year period it had a great influence on the Radical masses and helped renovate Radical doctrine. See *El radicalismo: ensayo sobre su historia y doctrina* (Buenos Aires: Ediciones Gure, 1957), 23.

128.  "Democracia en peligro," *FORJANDO* (Rojas, Province of Buenos Aires), yr. 1, no. 2 (August 27, 1940): 5. See also Arturo Jauretche, "Opinión pública y democracia," *FORJANDO* (Rojas, Buenos Aires Province), yr. 2, no. 10 (November 1941): 2.

129.  Scalabrini Ortiz's speech was published as "La Argentina, base y arma de abastecimiento inglés," in *Cuadernos de F.O.R.J.A*, yr. 1, no. 1 (May 25, 1936): 20.

130. "Una nueva traición del electoralismo," *FORJANDO* (Rojas, Buenos Aires Province), yr. 1, no. 3 (September 30, 1940): 5.

131. Jauretche, *Política nacional*, 81.

132. Raúl Scalabrini Ortiz, *Política británica en el Río de la Plata* (Buenos Aires: Editorial Reconquista, 1940), 16.

133. Atilio García Mellid, "La abstención electoral y el comicio de Buenos Aires, *FORJANDO* (Rojas, Buenos Aires Province), yr. 2, no. 11 (January 1942): 1.

134. Raúl Scalabrini Ortiz. Quoted in René Orzi, *Jauretche y Scalabrini Ortiz* (Buenos Aires: Peña Lillo, 1985), 55. The complete citation for the original source is not provided, but it appears to come from one of Scalabrini Ortiz's editorials in his newspaper *Reconquista* (1939).

135. "Nacionalismo y democracia," *FORJANDO* (Rojas, Buenos Aires Province), yr. 2, no. 10 (November 1941): 1.

136. Jauretche, *FORJA y la década*, 18.

137. Arturo Jauretche, *Argentinidad* (March 1939). Also quoted in Scenna, *F.O.R.J.A.*, 406. The original title of the article is not provided.

138. Jauretche, "Opinión pública y democracia," 5.

139. Atilio García Mellid, "Alem, Yrigoyen y Perón: símbolos de las muchedumbres argentinas," *Hechos e Ideas*, yr. 9, no. 54 (September 1948): 297.

140. García Mellid, "Alem," 300.

141. García Mellid, "Alem," 297, 300.

142. García Mellid, "Alem," 299.

143. García Mellid, "Alem," 302.


CHAPTER 8.    Essentialism in the Era of Perón

1. Historians differ over the exact meaning of these initials. Military historian Robert Potash, who argues that they stand for Grupo de Oficiales Unidos, is probably reliable. See *The Army & Politics in Argentina*, vol. 5, *1928–1945: Yrigoyen to Perón* (Stanford, CA: Stanford University Press, 1969), 185.

2. "Situación interna," n.d., ca. May 1943, in Robert Potash, *Perón y el G.O.U.: los documentos de una logia secreta* (Buenos Aires: Editorial Sudamericana, 1984), 200.

3. The phrase is the title of a book by nationalist Marcelo Sánchez Sorondo, *La revolución que anunciamos* (Buenos Aires: Ediciones Nueva Política, 1945).

4. *Cabildo*, "La revolución triunfante," June 5, 1943, 4.

5. Loris Zanatta, *Perón y el mito de la nación católica: Iglesia y Ejército en los orígenes del peronismo (1943–1946)* (Buenos Aires: Editorial Sudamericana, 1999), 26.

6. Gustavo J. Franceschi, "Consideraciones sobre la revolución," *Criterio*, yr. 16, no. 789 (June 17, 1943): 149–53, in *Textos y documentos: El autoritarismo y los argentinos: la hora de la espada, 1924–1946*, ed. Alicia García and Ricardo E. Rodríguez Molas, Biblioteca Política Argentina (Buenos Aires: Centro Editor de América Latina, 1988), 219–20.

7. Cristián Buchrucker, *Nacionalismo y peronismo: La Argentina en la crisis ideológica del mundo (1927–1955)* (Buenos Aires: Editorial Sudamericana, 1987), 280.

8. Pedro Pablo Ramírez, "Carta del Excmo. Sr. Presidente de la Nación Pedro Pablo Ramírez al director del *Criterio*, monseñor Gustavo J. Franceschi," June 22, 1943, in García and Rodríguez Molas, *Textos y documentos*, 225–26. First published in *Criterio*, yr. 16, no. 800 (July 1, 1943).

9. Pedro Pablo Ramírez, "Discurso en la cena de camaradería de las Fuerzas Armadas," July 7, 1943, in García and Rodríguez Molas, *Textos y documentos*, 228. First published in *Ejército y Armada* (July 1943): 15–21.

10. G.O.U., internal document, in *El G.O.U.: los documentos de una logia secreta*, ed. Robert Potash (Buenos Aires: Editorial Sudamericana, 1984), 101–3.

11. Pedro Pablo Ramírez, excerpt from radio address, October 12, 1943, in "Habla el Presidente," *El Pampero*, October 13, 1943, 5.

12. The decree (11.609, October 13, 1943) made a slight exception for indigenous peoples but still required that native names be restricted to those "indigenous sounds or words that have been incorporated into the national language." Quoted in Romina Silvia Zamborain, "El derecho al nombre indígena en la legislación argentina" (unpublished manuscript), www.linguasur.org.ar/panel/archivos/92b6f44c23218cfa4615840d293b59f4PONENCIA2006.pdf.

13. Zanatta, *Perón y el mito*, 106.

14. Buchrucker, *Nacionalismo y peronismo*, 281.

15. *Cabildo*, "Por decreto del ejecutivo, ha sido creado el Instituto Nacional de la Tradición," December 22, 1943, 6.

16. Jauretche first received news of the coup in the early hours of June 4, while he was at the Edelweis restaurant in central Buenos Aires. By chance, at the same restaurant, he met the Irazusta brothers, who—unaware of the coup in progress—proposed to Jauretche that he join them in another military conspiracy. See Norberto Galasso, *Jauretche y su época: De Yrigoyen a Perón, 1901–1955* (Buenos Aires: Peña Lillo Editor, 1985), 531.

17. Missing from the crowd was Scalabrini Ortiz, who some months earlier had distanced himself from FORJA, although he had continued his friendship with Jauretche.

18. Miguel Angel Scenna, *F.O.R.J.A.: una aventura argentina (de Yrigoyen a Perón)* (Buenos Aires: Ediciones La Bastilla, 1972), 544.

19. Arturo Jauretche, "Declaración de FORJA," June 4, 1943. Quoted in Galasso, *Jauretche y su época*, 532.

20. Untitled Forjista pamphlet, July 1943. Quoted in Galasso, *Jauretche y su época*, 540. The word *radicalism* is not capitalized in the original.

21. Galasso, *Jauretche y su época*, 541–42.

22. On Perón's interest in FORJA's publications, see Buchrucker, *Nacionalismo y peronismo*, 308. Perón continued to read Forjista publications, even while serving as a military attaché in Italy from 1938 to 1940. Galasso, *Jauretche y su época*, 501.

23. This meeting took place roughly a month after the June 4 coup. Jauretche relayed this information to Miguel Ángel Scenna and was uncertain about the exact date of the meeting. On this point see Galasso, *Jauretche y su época*, 544.

24. Undated interview with Jauretche by Miguel Ángel Scenna. Related in Galasso, *Jauretche y su época*, 544–47.

25. On this episode, see Galasso, *Jauretche y su época*, 567–70, 583.

26. For a discussion, see Richard Walter, "The Right and the Peronists, 1943–55," in *The Argentine Right: Its History and Intellectual Origins, 1910 to the Present*, ed. Sandra McGee Deutsch and Ronald H. Dolkart (Wilmington, DE: SR Books, 1993), 108.

27. For an account of that day and its symbolic meanings, see Daniel James, "October 17th and 18th, 1945: Mass Protest, Peronism and the Argentine Working Class," *Journal of Social History* 21, no. 3 (Spring 1988): 441–60.

28. Also helping was US ambassador Spruille Braden's clumsy attempt to sway the electorate by tarring Perón as a fascist, an effort that backfired.

29. Published in *La Época*, October 17, 1945. See Galasso, *Jauretche y su época*, 614.

30. Galasso, *Juaretche y su época*, 617.

31. "Disolución de F.O.R.J.A," December 15, 1945, in Arturo Jauretche, *F.O.R.J.A. y la década infame: Con un apéndice de manifiestos, declaraciones y textos volantes* (Buenos Aires: Ed. Coyoacán, 1962), 118.

32. Raúl Scalabrini Ortiz, *Yrigoyen y Perón* (Buenos Aires: Plus Ultra, 1972), 26. The quotation comes from a speech titled "Los enemigos del pueblo argentino," which was delivered on July 3, 1948, at the Instituto "Hipólito Yrigoyen" of Mercedes, Province of Buenos Aires. It was first published by the institute in 1948.

33. Scalabrini Ortiz, *Yrigoyen y Perón*, 27.

34. Scalabrini Ortiz, *Yrigoyen y Perón*, 28.

35. Atilio García Mellid, "Dimensión spiritual de la Revolución," *Hechos e Ideas*, yr. 9, nos. 56–57 (November–December 1948): 49, 50.

36. Atilio García Mellid, "Alem, Yrigoyen y Perón: Símbolos de las muchedumbres argentinas," *Hechos e Ideas*, yr. 9, no. 54 (September 1948): 288.

37. García Mellid, "Alem, Yrigoyen y Perón," 300, 302.

38. Raúl Scalabrini Ortiz, "Identidad de la línea histórica de Yrigoyen y Perón," *Hechos e Ideas*, yr. 9, no. 54 (September 1948): 324.

39. "Radicalismo y Peronismo se identifican en sus proyecciones históricas," *Hechos e Ideas*, yr. 7, no. 47 (February 1948): 378.

40. Useful overviews of the relationship between the nationalist right and Perón include Richard Walter, "The Right and the Peronists, 1943–1955," in Deutsch and Dolkart, *The Argentine Right*, 99–118, and Elena Piñeiro, *La tradición nacionalista ante el peronismo: Itinerario de una esperanza a una desilusión* (Buenos Aires: A–Z Editoria, 1997).

41. Zanatta, *Perón y el mito*, 145.

42. Quoted in Buchrucker, *Nacionalismo y peronismo*, 296.

43. Eduardo Elena, "Peronism in 'Good Taste': Culture and Consumption in the Magazine *Argentina*," in *The New Cultural History of Peronism: Power and Identity in Mid-Twentieth-Century Argentina*, ed. Matthew Karush and Oscar Chamosa (Durham, NC: Duke University Press, 2010), 209–37.

44. See, for example, Ernesto Palacio, "Lugones Vivo," *Sexto Continente*, no. 2 (August–September 1949): 16–21; Alberto Ezcurra Medrano, "El Caso Rosas," *Sexto Continente*, nos. 3–4 (October–November 1949): 51–57.

45. The history of the ALN is complex. For a brief account of its transformations, see Michael Goebel, "A Movement from Right to Left in Argentine Nationalism? The Alianza Libertadora Nacionalista and Tacuara as Stages of Militancy," *Bulletin of Latin American Research* 26, no. 3 (2007): 359. Also useful is Juan Besoky, "El nacionalismo populista de derecha en Argentina: La Alianza Libertadora Nacionalista, 1937–1975," *Mediações* (Brazil) 19, no. 1 (2014): 61–83.

46. The size of the ALN is highly uncertain. For an account of the different estimates, see Goebel, "Movement," 359n2, 359n3.

47. Walter, "Right and the Peronists," 110. During the 1946 general elections, the ALN ran its own slate of candidates rather than support the Peronist slate. All failed miserably at the ballot box. Eventually, when Queraltó was ousted in 1953, the ALN came under complete Peronist control.

48. As noted, both Sánchez Sorondo and Llambías were awarded university posts. Ernesto Palacio became president of the National Commission of Culture, and Vicente Sierra received the top post at the Instituto de Investigaciones Históricas of the University of Buenos Aires. Jauretche, who was tapped

to head the Provincial Bank of Buenos Aires, was one of the few nationalists to receive a position outside of the cultural realm.

49. Diana Quattrocchi-Woisson, *Los males de la memoria: Historia y política en la Argentina*, 2nd ed. (Buenos Aires: Emecé Editores, 1995), 287, 289.

50. Juan D. Perón, "Mensaje del Excelentísimo Señor Presidente de la Nación Juan Perón en el Acto del Juramento al Asumir la Primera Magistratura, el 4 de junio de 1946," in *Pensamiento político del general de brigada Juan Perón: directivas del presidente de la nación* (Buenos Aires: Subsecretaría de Informaciones, 1946), 13–27. Quotes from 14–15.

51. Juan D. Perón, "La cultura," sec. 4 of "Problemas políticos, sociales y económicos de la República Argentina," *Hechos e Ideas*, yr. 7, no. 5 (May 1948): 415–16.

52. "Juicios del Presidente Perón sobre la enseñanza y nueva ley universitaria," *Hechos e Ideas*, yr. 7, no. 46 (January 1948): 348.

53. Michael Goebel, *Argentina's Partisan Past: Nationalism and the Politics of History*, Liverpool Latin American Studies, new ser. 11 (Liverpool: Liverpool University Press, 2011), 82.

54. Juan Perón, "Doctrinas nacionales," in Juan Perón, *Descartes: Política y estrategia*, first published in *Democracia*, May 15, 1952, www.labaldrich.com .ar/wp-content/uploads/2013/03/Pol%C3%ADtica-y-Estrategia-Descartes -Per%C3%B3n.pdf.

55. Juan Perón, "Doctrinas nacionales." For more discussion of Perón's "Third Way," see Buchrucker, *Nacionalismo y peronismo*, 331–35; and Donald Hodges, *Argentina's "Dirty War": An Intellectual Biography* (Austin: University of Texas Press, 1991), 55–56.

56. The precise source of this quotation is unclear. According to the Internet resource *Obras completas de General Domingo Perón: El General Perón le habla a los trabajadores*, Cuadernillos de Formación Político-Syndical, no. 1 (Argentina: Unión de Personal Civil de la Nación), www.upcndigital.org/files /publicaciones/CDN/cuadernillos_de_Peron-1.pdf, Perón uttered these words in a speech celebrating the first anniversary of the Secretaria of Trabajo y Provisión on November 24, 1944. The quotation also appears (inserted into a different, untitled essay) in Juan Perón, *Selección de sus escritos, conferencias y discursos* (Buenos Aires: Ediciones Síntesis, 1973), 128.

57. Juan Perón, "Mensaje leído ante el Honorable Congreso de la Nación el 26 de junio de 1946," in Argentina, *Pensamiento político*, 31. In the version I have consulted, the italics are in the original. As numerous scholars have noted, Perón seemed unwilling to dispense entirely with the liberal past and shared none of the nationalists' obsession with vindicating Rosas. See Quattrocchi-Woisson, *Los males*, 225; and Colin Winston, "Between Rosas and Sarmiento:

Notes on Nationalism in Peronist Thought," *Americas* 39, no. 3 (January 1983): 305–32. His nationalist supporters, of course, had no such qualms. Ernesto Palacio, for example, praised the constitutional reform project by dismissing the 1853 document as having been written by men who were "completely disconnected from the race" and who had nothing but contempt for the "Spanish bloodline (estirpe española) and the . . . reality of the country." See "¿Se trata de elaborar, al fin, una Constitución para los argentinos?," *Hechos e Ideas*, yr. 9, no. 54 (September 1948): 280, 281. My ellipses.

58. On this point see Rock, *Argentina, 1516–1987*, 289.

59. Juan Perón, *El modelo argentino para el proyecto nacional* (Buenos Aires: Cid Editor, 1981), 25. Quoted in Roberto Surra, *Peronismo y cultura* (Buenos Aires: Corregidor, 2003), 38.

60. The obligatory teaching of Catholic education in public schools became law in 1947, although Perón allowed students of other faiths to substitute a course in morality.

61. Juan Perón, "Conferencia en la Academia Argentina de Letras para honrar Cervantes en el cuarto centenario de su nacimiento," October 9, 1947. This speech was published repeatedly during the 1940s. The Peronist newspaper *La Época* covered the speech the day after it was delivered, in an article with the somewhat disconcerting title "Cervantes, los descamisados, y Perón," *La Época*, October 13, 1947, 1. In that same year, it was published in booklet form in Juan D. Perón, *Discurso del presidente de la Nación Argentina, pronunciado en la Academia Argentina de Letras con motivo del día de La Raza y como homenaje en memoria de don Miguel Cervantes Saavedra en el cuarto centenario de su nacimiento* (1947); and in *Hechos e Ideas*, yr. 7, no. 4 (October 1947), 67–83, under the title "El homenaje a Cervantes y el Día de la Raza." In 1948, the Peronist newspaper *La Época* reprinted excerpts from the address under the title "Como define el Gral, Perón la esencia y contenido de nuestra herencia español," *La Época*, October 12, 1948, 12. I have consulted the booklet version.

62. Perón, *Discurso del presidente*, 9, 6, 7.

63. The occasion was the public awarding of a honorary doctorate to Perón by "the Argentine Universities." See Perón, "Juicios del Presidente Perón," 343.

64. Perón, "Juicios del Presidente Perón," 351.

65. Perón, "Juicios del Presidente Perón," 351.

66. Perón, Juan, *Plan quinquenal de gobierno del presidente Perón, 1947–1951* (Buenos Aires: Editorial Primicias, 1946), 61.

67. For a discussion of these restrictive policies, see Leonardo Senkman, "Etnicidad e inmigración durante el primer peronismo," *Estudios Interdisciplinarios de América Latina y el Caribe* 3, no. 2 (June 1, 1992), http://eial.tau.ac.il/index.php/eial/article/view/1258; and Miguel Alberto Galante, "La construc-

ción de políticas migratorias en tiempos de transición y consolidación del primer peronismo: del nacionalismo racista a la planificación económico-social y la promoción de la inmigración," *Ciclos en la Historia, la Economía y la Sociedad* 15, no. 30 (2005): 247–72, http://bibliotecadigital.econ.uba.ar/download/ciclos/ciclos_v15_n30_09.pdf.

68. Perón, *Plan Quinquenal*, 28. Italics in the original.

69. Perón, *Plan Quinquenal*, 28.

70. On this point, see Goebel, *Argentina's Partisan Past*, 82. As Goebel notes, until Perón's decree, Hernández's birthday, a holiday known as the Day of Tradition, had been celebrated only in the province of Buenos Aires.

71. Carlos Astrada, "Surge el hombre argentino con fisonomía propia," in *Argentina en marcha*, Comisión Nacional de Cooperación Intelectual and Homero M. Guglielmini, vol. 1 (Buenos Aires: Comisión Nacional de Cooperación Intelectual, 1947), 21. This was an official publication of the National Commision of Intellectual Cooperation. Astrada also lauded the gauchos in his work *Martín Fierro y el hombre argentino* (Buenos Aires: Ediciones Cruz del Sur, 1948).

72. Astrada, "Surge el hombre argentino," 35, 38. The term *roca viva* was the metaphor used by Miguel de Unamuno to characterize the eternal or living essence of the Spanish people.

73. On Peronist criollismo's challenge to the notion of a white Argentina, see Oscar Chamosa, "Criollo and Peronist: The Argentine Folklore Movement during the First Peronism, 1943–1955," in Karush and Chamosa, *New Cultural History*, 123–25. For descriptions of folklore festivals during the Peronist years, see 127–34.

74. Perón, "Mensaje del Excelentísimo," 26.

75. Perón, *Plan Quinquenal*, 28.

76. In 1935, the number of internal migrants to Buenos Aires was approximately 400,000 and by 1947, it had risen to 1.5 million. See Natalia Milanesio, "Peronistas and *Cabecitas:* Stereotypes and Anxieties at the Peak of Social Change," in Karush and Chamosa, *New Cultural History*, 53.

77. The Organización Israelita Argentina was established in 1947 by a group of pro-Peronist Argentine Jews. It vied with the much larger DAIA (Delegación de Asociaciones Israelitas Argentinas), which served as an umbrella group for Argentina's traditional Jewish organizations.

78. Juan Perón, Speech given in the headquarters of the Organización Israelita Argentina, August 20, 1948. Quoted in Buchrucker, *Nacionalismo y peronism*, 355.

79. Raanan Rein, "Melting the Pot? Peronism, Jewish Argentines, and the Struggle for Diversity," in *Making Citizens in Argentina*, ed. Benjamin Bryce and David M. K. Sheinin (Pittsburgh: University of Pittsburgh Press, 2017), 102.

80. Rein, "Melting the Pot," 115.

81. "Papá Noel y Santa Claus son personajes ajenos a nuestra fe," *La Época*, January 6, 1949, 3.

82. This is the title of his already-cited 1991 work *Perón y el mito de la nación católica: Iglesia y ejército en los orígenes del peronismo (1943–1946).*

83. Quoted in Carlos Altamirano, "La hora de las masas," *Istor*, yr. 6, no. 25 (Summer 2006): 26–27. The quote is taken from a speech that was given by Perón before the constitutional convention in January 1949 and reprinted in *La Nación.*

84. Juan Perón, "Discurso del General Juan Perón ante los delegados del Congreso General Constituyente del Partido Peronista," December 1, 1947. Available at http://www.elhistoriador.com.ar/documentos/ascenso_y_auge _del_peronismo/doctrina_peronista.php.

85. Juan D. Perón, message to the Legislative Assembly, May 1, 1950. Quoted in Silvia Sigal and Eliseo Verón, *Perón o muerte: los fundamentos discursivos del fenómeno peronista* (Buenos Aires: Editorial Legasa, 1986), 69.

86. On this last point, see Rock, *Authoritarian Argentina*, 177. For a good introduction to Peronist cultural policies and the promotion of the cult of the personality, see Mariano Ben Plotkin, *Mañana es San Perón: A Cultural History of Peron's Argentina* (Wilmington, DE: Scholarly Resources, 2002).

87. Rock, *Authoritarian Argentina*, 174.


CHAPTER 9.    Resistance and Revisionism

1. Juan Luís Besoky, "La derecha peronista: Prácticas políticas y representaciones (1943–76)" (PhD diss., Universidad Nacional de La Plata, 2016), 110, http://sedici.unlp.edu.ar/bitstream/handle/10915/55209/Documento _completo__.pdf?sequence=3&isAllowed=y.

2. It is important to note that not all left-wing members of the Peronist Resistance came to embrace Marxism.

3. Michael Goebel, "A Movement from Right to Left in Argentine Nationalism? The Alianza Libertadora Nacionalista and Tacuara as Stages of Militancy," *Bulletin of Latin American Research* 26, no. 3 (2007): 369.

4. Rock, *Authoritarian Argentina: The Nationalist Movement, Its History, and Its Impact* (Berkeley: University of California Press, 1993), 214–16.

5. See for example, Juan García Elorrio, "Octubre," *Cristianismo y Revolución* 10 (October 1968): 1–2. The simultaneous glorification and identification of Peronism and Che were constant themes.

6. On the fate of the nationalist right under Perón, see Juan Manuel Padrón, *¡Ni yanquis, ni marxistas! nacionalistas: nacionalismo, militancia y violencia*

*política: el caso del Movimiento Nacionalista Tacuara en la Argentina, 1955–1966*
(La Plata, Argentina: Editorial de la Universidad Nacional de General Sar-
miento, 2017), Libro digital, PDF, https://archive.org/details/Nacionalismo
MilitanciaYViolenciaPoltica.

7. Mario Amadeo became Lonardi's minister of foreign relations, Atilio
Dell'Oro Maini became minister of education, and Juan Carlos Goyeneche was
appointed as his press secretary. All were prominent nationalists, who had once
served in Perón's government before souring on the populist leader. Other nationalists who received posts in the Lonardi government included former Peronist lawyer Luis B. Cerruti Costa, General Juan José Urganga, César Bunge,
and General Justo León Bengoa. These last two had served in Perón's government but had resigned when Perón broke with the church. See Paul Lewis,
"The Right and Military Rule, 1955–1983," in *The Argentine Right: Its History
and Intellectual Origins, 1910 to the Present*, ed. Sandra McGee Deutsch and
Ronald H. Dolkart (Wilmington, DE: SR Books, 1993), 151–52.

8. *Gorilismo* was a term that came into use in 1955 to denote an anti-
Peronist. Hence, a gorila was someone who opposed Perón.

9. The 1853 Constitution was not officially reinstituted until 1957, when
the military government convened a constitutional assembly to legalize Aramburu's abrogation of the 1949 Constitution and to bring the older document
up to date.

10. Nationalists were especially harsh critics of economy minister Raúl
Prebisch, whom they erroneously accused of advocating laissez-faire economic
policies. Prebisch, as is well known, was in fact a strong proponent of state-
assisted industrialization. Through his work with CEPAL (Economic Commission of Latin America), he developed some of the concepts that would lead
to dependency theory. For a discussion of the misperception of Prebisch in Argentina, see Kathryn Sikkink, "The Influence of Raúl Prebisch on Economic
Policy-Making in Argentina, 1950–1962," *Latin American Research Review* 23,
no. 2 (1988): 91–114.

11. María Valeria Galván, "Militancia nacionalista en la era posperonista:
las organizaciones Tacuara y sus vínculos con el peronismo," *Nuevo Mundo/
Mundos Nuevos* [online], Questions du temps présent, mis en ligne (May 24,
2013), http://journals.openedition.org/nuevomundo/65364; DOI: 10.4000
/nuevomundo.65364. For a more in-depth analysis of *Azul y Blanco* and its importance for the nationalist right during this period, see also María Valeria
Galván, "El nacionalismo de derecha ante la cuestión peronista: la perspectiva
del grupo Azul y Blanco/2nd República (1956–63)," *Prohistoria*, no. 18 (2013),
www.academia.edu/7243185/El_nacionalismo_de_derecha_ante_la_cuesti
%C3%B3n_peronista_laperspectiva_del_grupo_Azul_y_Blanco_2da_Rep%
C3%BAblica_1956–1963.

12. Leonard Senkman "The Right and Civilian Regimes," in Deutsch and Dolkart, *Argentine Right*, 124.

13. Significant contributors included Mario Amadeo (who along with Sánchez Sorondo was one of the leading right-wing nationalists of the period), Ricardo Curutchet (who later founded the magazine *Cabildo*), Juan Pablo Oliver, Bonifacio Lastra, Juan Carlos Goyeneche, Raúl Puigbó, and Alberto Tedín. Also appearing in its pages were occasional articles by older nationalists, such as Máximo Etchecopar, Julio Irazusta, Federico Ibarguren, Ramón Doll, and Roberto de Laferrère. In considering the degree to which *Azul y Blanco* represented right-wing nationalist opinion during this period, it should be noted that in mid-1958, a group led by Amadeo broke with Sánchez Sorondo over a dispute concerning whether or not the nationalists should form a new political party or ally themselves with an existing party. (Amadeo favored the latter course and quarreled bitterly with Sánchez Sorondo.) But as had occurred during previous decades, this splintering of the nationalist right was over strategy rather than fundamentals. Thus despite their differences, Amadeo and Sánchez Sorondo continued to agree on the key assumptions that had always undergirded Argentine right-wing nationalist thought. For more details on the Sánchez Sorondo-Amadeo split, see Luis Fernando Beraza, *Nacionalistas: la trayectoria política de un grupo polémico, 1927–1983* (Buenos Aires: Cántaro, 2005), 102–3.

14. Criticizing this pledge, an editorial lamented that such a move would only continue the errors of the traditional liberal elite. This elite, according to a 1957 editorial, had foisted onto the Argentine people "dead 'phrases' and 'formulas'" based on "bourgeois" models of liberal democracy. See "¿Un nacionalismo marxista?," *Azul y Blanco*, October 1, 1957, 2.

15. For criticism of the decision not to reinstate religious education, see "Los 'Católicos' del gobierno," *Azul y Blanco*, January 9, 1957, 3. For criticism of economic policy, see "El gobierno termina de contradecir al Presidente," *Azul y Blanco*, January 2, 1957, 1.

16. Mario Amadeo, "Ante la reforma constitucional," *Azul y Blanco*, February 6, 1957, 3. As María Valeria Galván has noted, Amadeo was the first right-wing nationalist intellectual to highlight the positive aspects of the Peronist experience for Argentina, which he did in his 1956 book *Ayer, hoy y mañana*. See "Militancia nacionalista," n.p.

17. Domingo Mercante, "Declaraciones del Coronel Mercante," *Azul y Blanco*, July 16, 1957, 2. Mercante had been part of Perón's innermost circle and had served as the president of the assembly that produced the 1949 Constitution.

18. Amadeo, "Ante la Reforma Constitucional," 3. See also, "Manifiesto de nuestro partido," *Azul y Blanco*, July 2, 1957, 1.

19. Editorial, *Azul y Blanco*, July 31, 1957, 5.

20. Arturo Frondizi, *Industria argentina y desarrollo nacional* (Buenos Aires: Ediciones Qué, 1957), 19–20.

21. On the importance of Catholicism, see "El país dijo basta: La revolución nacional reanuda su camino y tiene que recuperar dos años perdidos," *Azul y Blanco*, February 26, 1958, 1. See also Leonardo Castellani, "Sobre las elecciones," *Azul y Blanco*, February 26, 1958, 3, in which the nationalist priest expressed his gratitude to God for Frondizi's victory. On Frondizi's victory as the triumph of the "Real Country," see "La voluntad nacional superó el fraude," *Azul y Blanco*, February 26, 1958, 1.

22. "El Caso Frondizi," *Azul y Blanco*, March 18, 1958, 1. Emphasis in the original.

23. "La universidad contra el programa nacional," *Azul y Blanco*, April 15, 1958, 1.

24. Argentines, one editorial intoned, were a people who were inherently "personalistic," in that they responded to—and indeed demanded—a strong, charismatic leader. See "Hemos tocado el fondo," *Azul y Blanco*, June 2, 1958, 1.

25. All quotations are from "La inmigración: problema fundamental de la nacionalidad," *Azul y Blanco*, October 28, 1958, 2.

26. Francisco P. Olmedo, "La inmigración, la Universidad y la FUBA," *Azul y Blanco*, November 11, 1958, 2. Criticisms of Frondizi's economic policies also rested on essentialist assumptions. The president, according to his right-wing nationalist critics, had sold out the country's resources to foreign interests and submitted Argentina to the Anglo-US form of "super capitalism" ("La única solución: Iglesia-F.F.A.A. y Pueblo Unidos," *Azul y Blanco*, November 3, 1959, 3). Another contributor argued that Catholicism had also served as a protective barrier against the foreign exploitation. Thus, this writer concluded, the best way for foreigners to "dominate Argentina and to transform it into a submissive factory" was to "take away its soul, its tradition: Catholicism and the Hispanic-Creole tradition" ("¿Universidad Católica?," *Azul y Blanco*, September 21, 1959, 3).

27. On the issue of sensualism, see Nimio de Anquín, "La crisis del patriotismo," *Azul y Blanco*, May 5, 1959, 9. On the idolatry of money, see Máximo Etchecopar, "De la democracia política a la democracia social," *Azul y Blanco*, March 27, 1957, 5.

28. Federico Ibarguren, "Para un examen de conciencia nacional," *Azul y Blanco*, December 2, 1958, 3.

29. There was a direct line, Marcelo Sánchez Sorondo affirmed, that ran though "capitalism, masonry and communism." See "Pueblo, Iglesia y Fuerzas Armadas," *Azul y Blanco*, June 23, 1959, 3.

30. Right-wing nationalists continued to despise the British and believed the spread of masonry in Argentina was part of a British plot. On this point, see "Origen británico de la masonería," *Azul y Blanco*, March 24, 1959, 3; "La corona Británica y la masonría," *Azul y Blanco*, March 31, 1959, 3; and Patricio Maguire, "Los ingleses y la expansión de la masonería argentina," *Azul y Blanco*, May 12, 1959, 1.

31. "La voluntad nacional superó el fraude," *Azul y Blanco*, February 26, 1958), 1 (my ellipses). On the "país legal-país real" dichotomy in *Azul y Blanco*, see Galván, "El nacionalismo de derecha."

32. "Un libro de historia para Mr. Nixon," *Azul y Blanco*, June 17, 1958, 3.

33. See for example, "El caso Frondizi," *Azul y Blanco*, 1.

34. Máximo Etchecopar, "La clase necesaria," *Azul y Blanco*, April 10, 1957, 3.

35. Rodolfo Irazusta, "Permanencia del régimen," *Azul y Blanco*, May 5, 1959, 6.

36. Ramón Doll, "El funesto error del peronismo," *Azul y Blanco*, May 5, 1959, 5. Sánchez Sorondo also stressed the importance of the popular classes in any nationalist program. Like Irazusta, he believed the Argentine masses possessed an "intuition" or "vital instinct" that "always alerted them to the enemies of the political and spiritual community to which they belonged." See "Pueblo, Iglesia y Fuerzas Armadas," *Azul y Blanco*, June 23, 1959, 3.

37. "Tacuara" had also been the name of a magazine published by the UNES in the 1940s. Thus the name chosen for this new organization signaled its identification with both the nineteenth-century Federalist past and the earlier nationalist group.

38. De Mahieu's influence came around 1960, and his emphasis on communitarism had a strong impact on Alberto Ezcurra, one of Tacuara's founding members and its director from 1957 to 1964.

39. Padrón, *¡Ni yanquis, ni marxistas!*, 122.

40. Galván, "Militancia nacionalista."

41. Movimiento Nacionalista Tacuara, "Programa Básico Revolucionario del Movimiento Nacionalista Tacuara" (1957), www.cedema.org/ver.php?id =7163.

42. The identification of *argentinidad* with ancestry was also made clear in 1960, when a group broke away from Tacuara to form the even more right-wing Guardia Restauradora Nacionalista (GRN). According to Michael Goebel, the group stipulated that members be able to trace their roots in Argentina over at least five generations (*Argentina's Partisan Past*, 132–33).

43. As María Valeria Galván has noted, the Tacuaristas described the Argentine state as "entreguista." See "El nacionalismo de derecha," n.p.

44. Rogelio García Lupo, "Diálogo con los jovenes fascistas," in *La rebelión de los generales* (Buenos Aires: Vegara, 2014), 86. This article first appeared in *Marcha* 16, no. 2 (1962).

45. Alberto Ezcurra Medrano, "Los 'jovenes rebeldes'," *Tacuara: Vocero de la revolución nacionalista* (September 1961): 3.

46. Movimiento Nacionalista Tacuara, "Programa Básico Revolucionario del Movimiento Nacionalista Tacuara" (1957), www.cedema.org/ver.php?id =7163.

47. Richard Gillespie, *Soldiers of Perón: Argentina's Montoneros* (Oxford: Clarendon Press, 1982), 49.

48. Padrón, *¡Ni yanquis!*, 107.

49. Padrón, *¡Ni yanquis!*, 203.

50. Movimiento Nacionalista Tacuara, "Programa Básico Revolucionario del Movimiento Nacionalista Tacuara" (1957), www.cedema.org/ver.php?id =7163.

51. "Carta a un joven militar argentino," from "Un militante de Tacuara" (1963), pamphlet, http://eltopoblindado.com/nacionalismo-derecha/decada -1960-nacionalismo-derecha/tacuara/carta-a-un-joven-militar-argentino/. Ta-cuara's admiration for Nasser has been treated by various scholars. See for ex-ample, Padrón, *¡Ni yanquis!*, 137; and Besoky, "La derecha peronista" (diss.), 128–35.

52. Michael Goebel describes Tacuara as having developed a "cult of vi-olence" ("Movement," 363).

53. On the importance of masculine images for right-wing nationalists of this period, including Tacuara, see María Valeria Galván, "Los hombres del imaginario nacionalista: Representaciones de la masculinidad en publicaciones periódicas nacionalistas de derecha argentinas durante la larga década del sesenta (1959–1969)," *História* (São Paulo) 31, no. 2 (July–December 2012): 277–309, www.scielo.br/pdf/his/v31n2/13.pdf.

54. Interview with Jorge Savino (2007), by Juan Manuel Padrón, in *¡Ni yanquis!*, 216.

55. Testimony of Andrés Castillo, militant in the Peronist Youth (JP), then member of the MNA, then member of the Montoneros, in Oscár Anzo-rena, *JP: historia de la Juventud Peronista (1955/1988)* (Buenos Aires: Ediciones del Cordón, 1989), 96. Quoted in Padrón, *¡Ni yanquis!*, 174.

56. Galván, "Militancia nacionalista," n.p.

57. Galván, "El nacionalismo de derecha," n.p.

58. Galván, "El nacionalismo de derecha," n.p. There were, however, divi-sions within this group. The most reactionary members, such as Ricardo Curutchet, remained intransigent, while Sánchez Sorondo and Mario Amadeo

were affiliated with FREJULI. On this point, see Besoky, "La derecha peronista" (diss.), 140.

59. Aramburu's efforts to rid the labor movement of Peronism proved unsuccessful, and by 1957 most of the unions were dominated by Peronists. That year witnessed the establishment of the pro-Peronist "62 Organizations," a block of unions that gained control of the Confederación General del Trabajo and served as the principal political arm of the Peronist Resistance. Other individuals identified with the "blanda" tendency were a handful of "neo-Peronist" political parties, whose leaders also took an accommodationist stance. For a discussion, see Lucas Lanusse, *Montoneros: El mito de sus 12 fundadores* (Buenos Aires: Zeta, 2010), 48–49.

60. Historian Daniel James's description of Vandor and his significance is both succinct and comprehensive. In his words, "Vandor came to personify—especially for his opponents within the Peronist movement—the transformation of the movement and its unions from a position of outright antagonism to the post-1955 status quo to one of acceptance of the need to compromise with it and find a space within its boundaries. *Vandorismo* came to be synonymous, on both a political and union level, with negotiation, pragmatism, and the acceptance of the realities of the *realpolitik* which governed Argentina after 1955. On the political plane, *vandorismo* implied the use of the political power and representativeness which the unions derived from their position as the dominant force within Peronism, and from being the only fully legal part of the movement, in order to negotiate and bargain with the other 'factors of power.'" See *Resistance and Integration: Peronism and the Working Class, 1946–1976* (New York: Cambridge University Press, 1988), 162.

61. On Perón's encouragement of violence, see Samuel Amaral, "El avión negro: retórica y práctica de la violencia," in *Perón del exilio al poder*, ed. Samuel Amaral and Mariano Ben Plotkin (Buenos Aires: Cántaro, 1993), 69–94.

62. It is tempting to conflate the duras with the left and the blanda-dominated labor movement with the right, especially given that, by the late 1960s, several groups within the Peronist right had joined forces with elements of the Peronist labor movement. However, as Juan A. Bozza has demonstrated, there were sectors of the labor movement that challenged Vandorismo and adopted a revolutionary stance. See "El peronismo revolucionario: corrientes y experiencias en al radicalización sindical (1958/68)," *Cuestiones de Sociología* 3 (2006): 88–116.

63. For an account of these events, see Besoky, "La derecha peronista" (diss.), 95.

64. Padrón, *¡Ni yanquis!*, 90, https://archive.org/details/Nacionalismo MilitanciaYViolenciaPoltica.

65. According to Julio César Melón, the desire to "do something" to resist the new status quo prompted many younger Peronists to turn to the ALN, which helped train these younger militants in violent tactics. See "La resistencia peronista, alcances y significados," *Anuario del IEHS* (Tandil) 8 (1993): 228.

66. Goebel, *Argentina's Partisan Past*, 125. One of Olmos's most important efforts to rally the Peronist faithful was his call for a demonstration in honor of a group of military men who were executed after a failed coup attempt against Aramburu. This demonstration, which became known as the "March of Silence," became an important annual ritual for the Peronists. *Palabra Argentina* also helped Perón communicate with his followers. In the elections to establish a constitutional convention to replace the 1949 Constitution, for example, Olmos's publication conveyed Perón's directive to submit blank ballots. See María Arias and Raúl Garcia Heras, "Carisma disperso y rebelión: los partidos neoperonistas," in Amaral and Plotkin, *Perón del exilio*, 98.

67. Aritz Recalde, "José María Rosa, nuestra contemporáneo," *Cuaderno de Trabajo*, no. 7 de Centro de Estudios Juan José Hernández Arregui (October 2014), http://hernandezarregui.blogspot.com/2018/05/biografias-del-pensa miento-nacional.html.

68. As a Peronist representative in Congress, Cooke often used his position to strongly defend revisionism. For a discussion, see Diana Quattrocchi-Woisson, *Los males de la memoria: Historia y política en la Argentina* (Buenos Aires: Emecé Editories, 1998), 252–53.

69. In 1959, when Perón refused to back him up in a dispute with labor leaders, Cooke's radicalism would cost him his role as leader of the resistance.

70. Samuel Amaral, "En las raíces ideológicas de Montoneros: John William Cooke lee a Gramsci," *Temas de historia argentina y americana*, no. 17 (2010): 15–51, http://bibliotecadigital.uca.edu.ar/repositorio/revistas/raices -ideologicas-de-montoneros.pdf.

71. On this movement, see Cesar Tcach, "Sabattinismo: identidad radical y oposición disruptiva," *Desarrollo Económico* 28, no. 110 (July–September 1988): 183–208.

72. Martín Gerlo, "Marxismo y cuestión nacional: aportes de Hernández Arregui al pensamiento de izquierda," *Jornadas de Sociología*, Facultad de Ciencias Sociales, Universidad de Buenos Aires, XI (2015), n.p., www.aacademica .org/000-061/593.

73. Argentina's Communist and Socialist Parties had been implacable foes of Perón from the beginning, scorning him either as a fascist or as an old-styled caudillo manipulating the masses. Accordingly, during the 1950s, both parties joined with the mainstream liberal groups in the opposition coalition known as the Unión Democrática. After Perón's ouster, however, the continued attach-

ment of the working class to the deposed leader prompted many members of the traditional left to reassess Peronism's significance. At the heart of this collective soul-searching was the stubborn fact that, after decades of organizing, neither the Communist nor Socialist Party had been able to win the loyalty of the Argentine masses, something that Perón had accomplished in a few short years. Even more importantly, he had successfully transformed them into a potent political force. The workers' unwavering loyalty to the ousted president convinced many members of the traditional left that they had been wrong to see Peronism as an artificial movement destined to fade quickly. Instead, like the Peronists themselves, these intellectuals came to associate the Peronist masses with the "real country" and to accuse their former colleagues on the left of elitism. On the left's rethinking of Peronism, see Goebel, *Argentina's Partisan Past*, 94–95; and Pablo Ponza, "Los intelectuales críticos y la transformación social en Argentina (1955–1973)" (PhD diss., Universidad de Barcelona, 2007), 111. For a more personal discussion of the shift, see Oscár Terán's *Nuestros años sesentas. la formación de la nueva izquierda intelectual en la Argentina, 1956–1966* (Buenos Aires: Puntosur, 1991).

74.  Scalabrini Ortiz, who died in 1959, briefly took over the editorship in 1958. For a history of the magazine, see Ana Jaramilla's prologue to Raúl Scalabrini Ortiz and Arturo Jauretche, eds., *Forjando una nación: Scalabrini Ortiz y Jauretche en la revista Qué sucedió en siete días* (Buenos Aires: Ediciones de la Universidad Nacional de Lanús, 2007), 11–21. This two-volume work contains reprints of all of Jauretche and Scalabrini Ortiz's contributions to the magazine. As Goebel has noted, besides Jauretche's and Scalabrini Ortiz's, *Qué*'s contributors also included such individuals as Raúl Puigbó, from the nationalist right, and Eduardo Astesano, from the nationalist left. Goebel also notes the frequency with which *Qué* treated historical themes informed by revisionist thinking and advertised revisionist books (*Argentina's Partisan Past*, 128).

75.  María Arias and Raúl García Heras, "Carisma disperso y rebelión," in Amaral and Plotkin, *Peron del exilio*, 98.

76.  Omar Acha, who has both unearthed the emergence of this first JP and insightfully analyzed why its history has been largely erased, has colorfully characterized this first JP as the Cinderella of the Peronist movement. Describing the first JP as marginalized and ignored, he notes that the group nonetheless had to take care of all the mundane chores of the Peronist "household." See *Los muchachos peronistas: Orígenes olvidados de la Juventud Peronista (1945–1955)* (Buenos Aires: Planeta, 2011), 85–86.

77.  Acha, *Los muchachos peronistas*, 216.

78.  The JP's respect for the *abuelos*, to use Jorge Rulli's term, was striking and sharply contrasted with its dismissive attitude toward the generation that filled the ranks of the Peronist bureaucracy in the late 1940s and early 1950s.

As will be noted below, after 1955, a favorite gathering place for the Peronist Resistance was the intersection of Corrientes Avenue and Esmeralda Street, where, according to Rulli, the "very young or very old" mingled. Quoted in Acha, *Los muchachos peronistas*, 219.

79. Within a few years, of course, the desire for Perón's return would no longer unite the movement, as sectors of the Vandorist branch of the labor movement became unenthusiastic about the former leader's return and sought instead to establish "Peronism without Perón."

80. Goebel, *Argentina's Partisan Past*, 93.

81. Padrón, *¡Ni yanquis!*, 90, esp. note 56. To be sure, Cooke did observe in a letter to Perón that, while he admired Kelly, he believed the members of the ALN had a "special mentality," and it was "useless to mix ourselves" with other people in the organization. With Kelly in control, Cooke assured Perón, the ALN would be able to carry out useful acts of sabotage and play an important role at a later moment. See Cooke to Perón, April 11, 1957, in *Correspondencia Perón-Cooke: Obras completas*, ed. John William Cooke and Eduardo Luis Duhalde (Buenos Aires: Colihue, 2007), 82.

82. See chapter 4 of Daniel Gutman, *Tacuara: historia de la primera guerrilla urbana argentina* (Buenos Aires: Sudamérica), Digital Edition.

83. Laura Ehrlich, "Los espacios de sociabilidad en la estructuración de la Juventud Peronista post '55 en la ciudad de Buenos Aires," *Apuntes de Investigación del CECYP*, yr. 16, no. 21 (2012): 157–75, https://unq.academia.edu /LauraEhrlich.

84. Goebel, *Argentina's Partisan Past*, 113.

85. Besoky, "Las derechas peronistas" (diss.), 142.

86. Special bulletin of the magazine *Alianza* (June 1964). Quoted in Goebel, "Movement," 361.

87. Padrón provides a useful chart of these splits and spinoffs in *¡Ni yanquis!*, 154.

88. Within a year, disagreements over tactics led *this* group to split, so that there emerged a MNRT Baxter and an MNRT Ossorio. See Padrón, *¡Ni yanquis!*, 186.

89. The MNRT very quickly established a reputation for revolutionary violence. According to police reports, between January 1963 and March 1964, Baxter's group launched over fifty attacks on commercial establishments and military depositories, with the aim of gathering funds and weapons for an armed insurrection. See Padrón, *¡Ni yanquis!*, 189.

90. These included Jorge Cataldo, Rubén Rodríguez, Jorge Caffatti, Carlos Arbelos, Alfredo Roca, Horacio Rossi, Amílcar Fidanza, Norberto Espina, and Tomislav Rivaric. See Goebel, "Movement," 368n9.

91. In Juan Besoky's words, "un joven con inclinaciones políticas podía verse tentado de ingresar a diferentes organizaciones, pasar de una a otra o recorrer diverso cículos dentro de un abanico diverso." See "La derecha peronista en perspectiva," *Nuevo Mundo/Mundos Nuevos* (May 24, 2013), https://journals.openedition.org/nuevomundo/65374.

92. On the right-wing Catholic backgrounds of the Montoneros and other Peronist activists, see Goebel, *Argentina's Partisan Past*, 159–60.

93. Federico Finchelstein provides information on Abal Medina's participation in the GRN in *The Ideological Origins of the Dirty War: Fascism, Populism, and Dictatorship in Twentieth Century Argentina* (New York: Oxford University Press, 2014), 111. For more background, especially on Abal Medina and his brother Juan Manuel Abal Medina, see Luis Fernándo Beraza, *Nacionalistas: la trayectoria política de un grupo polémico, 1927–1983* (Buenos Aires: Cántaro, 2005), chap. 7.

94. See chapter 8 of Miguel Bonasso, *Lo que no dije en "Recuerdo de la muerte"* (Buenos Aires: Sudamericana, 2014), Kindle.

95. The Comando de Organización was one of the right-wing Peronist groups that opened fire on the Montoneros during the infamous confrontation at Ezeiza airport, when Perón returned to Argentina in 1973. During the brief presidency of Héctor Cámpora, Kennedy worked in the Ministry of Social Welfare under José López Rega. She was one of five individuals in charge of planning the public event at Ezeiza. See "Falleció Norma Kennedy, una histórica dirigente de la llamada resistencia peronista," *Clarín*, June 24, 2017. See also Goebel, "Movement," 368.

96. Besoky, "La derecha peronista" (diss.), 111; Michael Goebel, "Movement," 372.

97. Humberto Cucchetti, "¿Derechas peronistas? Organizaciones militantes entre nacionalismo, cruzada anti-montoneros y profesionalización política," *Nouveaux mondes nouveaux—Nuevo Mundo/Mundos Nuevos* (June 1, 2013), n.p., http://journals.openedition.org/nuevomundo/65363. Cucchetti's analysis bears similarities to that of Laura Ehrlich, who in her already-mentioned work on "spaces of sociability" ("Los espacios") argues these shared spaces, where young militants interacted and formed relationships, contributed to the ideological fluidity of the period.

98. Quattrocchi-Woisson, *Los males*, 318.

99. Quoted in Quattrocchi-Woisson, *Los males*, 223.

100. For a discussion of the abruptness of this change, see Mariano Plotkin's analysis of the first two editions of Perón's book, which appeared in 1956 and 1957, as *La fuerza de el derecho de béstias* "La 'ideología' de Perón: Continui-

dades y rupturas," in *Perón del exilio al poder*, ed. Samuel Amaral and Mariano Ben Plotkin (Buenos Aires: Cántaro, 1993), 53–54.

101. Plotkin, "La 'ideología'," 53. Michael Goebel has also noted the pressure on the exiled Perón to embrace historical revisionism, describing this conversion as "more forced than desired." See "La prensa peronista como medio de difusión del revisionismo historico bajo la Revolución Libertadora," *Prohistoria*, yr. 8, no. 8 (Spring 2004): 260.

102. On this point, see Juan Besoky (citing unpublished work by Laura Ehrlich), "Las derechas peronistas" (diss.), 26; and Tulio Halperin Donghi, *El revisionismo histórico argentino como visión decadentista de la historia nacional* (Buenos Aires: Siglo XXI Editores Argentina, 2005), 34.

103. Goebel, "La prensa peronista," 262.

104. Plotkin, "La 'ideología'," 50.

105. Jauretche's 1966 *El medio pelo en la sociedad argentina* went through nine printings in a single year; his 1967 *La yapa* went through five printings in a single year. On Jauretche during the 1960s, see Pablo Ponza, "Los intelectuales críticos y la transformación social en la Argentina (1955–1973): Historia intelectual, discursos políticos y conceptualizaciones de la violencia en la Argentina de los años sesenta-setenta" (PhD diss., Universidad de Barcelona, 2007), 123. http://www.tdx.cat/bitstream/handle/10803/710/PP_TESIS.pdf?sequence=1. Indeed, as historian Fernando Devoto has observed, it was only in the 1960s that Jauretche "finally found the audience he had so eagerly sought [since] the 1930s." See "Reflexiones en torno de la izquierda nacional y la historiografía argentina," in *La historiografía académica y la historiografía militante en Argentina y Uruguay*, ed. Fernando Devoto and Nora Pagano (Buenos Aires: Editorial Biblos, 2004), 120.

106. Arturo Jauretche, *Política nacional y revisionismo histórico*, ed. Norberto D'Atri, vol. 7 of *Obras completas de Arturo Jauretche* (Buenos Aires: Corregidor, 2006), 81.

107. Jauretche, *Política nacional*, 16–17.

108. Jauretche, *Política nacional*, 18.

109. Jauretche, *Política nacional*, 16.

110. Atilio García Mellid, *Proceso al liberalismo argentino* (Buenos Aires: Ediciones Theoría, 1957), 10.

111. These figures are conservative and reflect only those editions that can be located in US libraries. Undoubtedly there are editions that never made their way into US depositories.

112. On the importance of this gathering place, see Jorge Rulli's comments in Omar Acha, *Los muchachos peronistas: Orígenes olvidados de la Juventud*

*Peronista (1945–1955)* (Buenos Aires: Planeta, 2011), 219. Also highlighting the writer's continued prestige was the establishment of the Raúl Scalabrini Ortiz Essay Grand Prize in 1973 (*Gran Premio de Ensayo Raúl Scalabrini Ortiz*) by the University of Buenos Aires Press (EUDEBA). Offering a substantial cash award of twenty thousand pesos, the contest solicited essays analyzing "forms of economic [and] cultural dependency." A notice for the contest can be found on the inside front cover of *Militancia*, yr. 1, no. 6 (July 19, 1973). It reappears in two subsequent issues. Among the judges were key intellectuals of the Peronist Resistance of the 1950s, including Rodofo Puiggrós, Juan José Hernández Arregui, and José María Rosa.

113. As occurred with Jauretche, these years also witnessed Hernández Arregui's high-water mark. He quickly followed his 1960 *La formación de la conciencia nacional* and *¿Qué es el ser nacional? la conciencia histórica iberoamericana* (1963) with *Nacionalismo y liberación* (1969) and *Socialismo y peronismo* (1972), all of which rapidly went through multiple editions. Perón himself acknowledged the significance of Hernández Arregui's work. Writing from Madrid in December 1969, and addressing Hernández Arregui as "Mi querido amigo," the exiled former president praised the writer for inspiring Latin American youth in the struggle against neocolonialism. See Perón to Hernández Arregui, December 10, 1969, repr. *Peronismo y Socialismo*, yr. 1, no. 1 (September 1973): 31–32.

114. Juan José Hernández Arregui, *La formación de la conciencia nacional, 1930–1960* (Buenos Aires: Editorial Plus Ultra, 1973), 24–25.

115. On the significance of *¿Que es el ser nacional?* for the youth of the 1960s, see Terán, *Nuestros años sesentas*, 64.

116. J. J. Hernández Arregui, *¿Qué es el ser nacional? La conciencia histórica iberoamericana* (Buenos Aires: Plus Ultra, 1973), 27, 179.

117. See, for example, Fermín Chávez's prologue to the 1971 edition of Rojas's *La restauración nacionalista*. According to Chávez, despite Rojas's unfortunate liberal tendencies, his 1909 work was "incredibly current in it fundamental postulates." See Chávez, "Proemio a la tercera edición" to Ricardo Rojas, *La restauración nacionalista* (Buenos Aires: A. Peña Lillo, 1971), 10.

118. Hernández Arregui, *¿Qué es el ser nacional?*, 179.

119. Hernández Arregui, *¿Qué es el ser nacional?*, 201.

120. Hernández Aregui, *¿Qué es el ser nacional?*, 201.

121. Jorge Abelardo Ramos, *Revolución y contrarrevolución en la argentina* (Buenos Aires: Senado de la Nación, 2006), 62.

122. Abelardo Ramos, *Revolución y contrarrevolución*, 110.

123. Abelardo Ramos, *Revolución y contrarrevolución*, 148. On the left-wing revisionists' attitudes toward Rosas, see Michael Goebel, *Argentina's Partisan Past*, 112.

124. Jorge Abelardo Ramos, *Revolución y contrarrevolución*, 145.

125. José María Rosa, *Estudios revisionistas* (Buenos Aires: Editoria Sudestada, 1967), 22–23.

126. Fermín Chávez, *Civilización y barbarie en la historia de la cultura argentina* (Buenos Aires: Ediciones Theoría, 1974), 69.

127. Chávez, *Civilización*, 13.

128. Chávez, *Civilización*, 101.

129. Accordingly, Chávez believed that the duty of his generation was to demand "a severe and clean explication of *el ser nacional.*" See *Civilización*, 17.

130. Chávez, *Civilización*, 11, 101, 106. In making this criticism of the liberal elite's belief in the need for patriotic education, he singles out early twentieth-century educational reformer José María Ramos Mejía.

131. Chávez, *Civilización*, 109.

132. Borrowing a phrase from Father Franciso Castañeda, Chávez affirmed that "because of Castille, we are a people" (*Por Castilla somos gente*). See *Civilización*, 21.

133. Chávez, *Civilización*, 112. Chávez is quoting Saúl Taborda but does not identify the source.

134. Chávez, *Civilización*, 113. Again, Chávez is quoting Saúl Taborda without identifying the source.

135. Fermín Chávez, "La Argentina es deformada cuando termina el caudillaje," interview by Jorge B. Rivera, *Revista Crisis*, May 1975. https://www.elhistoriador.com.ar/fermin-chavez-2/.


CHAPTER 10.    From Revisionism to Revolution and Repression

1. This is not to say that all youth were against the regime. Indeed, Perón enjoyed substantial support among working-class and lower middle-class adolescents, as well as among certain nationalist youth groups, such as the Alianza Libertadora Nacionalista (ALN) and the Unión Nacionalista de Estudiantes Secundarios (UNES). For a discussion of youth support for Perón, as well as anti-Peronism among this same age cohort, see Omar Acha, *Los muchachos peronistas: Orígenes olvidados de la Juventud Peronista, 1945–1955* (Buenos Aires: Planeta, 2011), 42–47.

2. Juan A. Bozza, "Combates y conjuras: Notas sobre las hipótesis conspirativas y antisemitas en la historigrafía revisionista," in *Mitos, altares y fantasmas: aspectos ideológicos en la historia del nacionalismo argentino*, Serie Estudios/Investigaciones 12 (La Plata, Argentina: Universidad Nacional de La Plata, Facultad de Humanidades y Ciencias de la Educación, 1992), 69.

3. Tulio Halperin Donghi, *El revisionismo histórico argentino*. Colección mínima 38 (Buenos Aires: Siglo Veintiuno Editories, 1971), 43.

4. Other guerrilla groups emerging from the traditional left were the much smaller Communist Vanguard and the Revolutionary Communist Party.

5. Daniel Lutzky, "Una visión de la sociedad," in *La nueva izquierda argentina, 1960–1980: Política y violencia*, ed. Claudia Hilb and Daniel Lutzky (Buenos Aires: Centro Editor de América Latina, 1984), 40.

6. Lutzky, "Una visión," 43.

7. Claudia Hilb, "Nueva izquierda, política, democracia," in *La nueva izquierda argentina, 1960–1980: Política y violencia*, ed. Claudia Hilb and Daniel Lutzky (Buenos Aires: Centro Editor de América Latina, 1984), 33.

8. Quoted in Ceferino Reato, *Disposición final: la confesión de Videla sobre los desaparecidos* (Buenos Aires: Editorial Sudamericana, 2012), 145. Reato notes that this distinction was shared by other military leaders.

9. Tulio Halperin Donghi, "Argentina's Unmastered Past," *Latin American Research Review* 23, no. 2 (1988): 19.

10. Movimiento Nacional Peronista, *Nacionalismo o guerra civil*, pamphlet (La Plata, Argentina: Centro de Cultura Nacional "José Hernández," 1967 [?]), www.ruinasdigitales.com/documentos-montoneros/.

11. Given the document's reference to certain political events, this seems accurate.

12. *Nacionalismo o guerra civil*, 1.

13. *Nacionalismo o guerra civil*, 7.

14. *Nacionalismo o guerra civil*, 1, 9. I have followed the pamphlet's capitalization.

15. *Nacionalismo o guerra civil*, 1.

16. According to Perdía, by linking nineteenth-century montonero/Federalist forces to twentieth-century Peronism, historical revisionism had been instrumental in luring young people from non-Peronist homes into the Peronist fold. Roberto Cirilo Perdía, *La otra historia: Testimonio de un jefe montonero* (Argentina: Grupo Agora, 1997), 60.

17. Raúl Cuestas published an extensive anthology of excerpts from nationalist works that influenced the Montoneros. Among the authors represented are Raúl Scalabrini Ortiz, John William Cooke, Rodolfo Puiggrós, Juan José Hernández Arregui, and Arturo Jauretche. Cuestas also includes unsigned FORJA publications. Raúl Cuestas, *Montoneros y el pensamiento nacional, popular y revolucionario: 1810–1982* (Neuquén, Argentina: Editorial de la Universidad Nacional del Comahue, 2011).

18. "Hablan los Montoneros," *Cristianismo y Revolución*, no. 26 (November–December 1970): 11.

19. Mario Firmenich, *La historia es un arma*, 1981. Quoted in Cuestas, *Montoneros y el pensamiento*, 128.

20. Quoted in "El compañero Presidente Cámpora y la lucha de liberación," *Militancia* 1, no. 1 (June 14, 1973): 19.

21. "Las armas de la independencia hoy están apuntadas hacia el Pueblo," *Cristianismo y Revolución*, no. 30 (September 1971): 13.

22. "Hablan los Montoneros," *Cristianismo y Revolución*, no. 26 (November–December 1970), 11. Italics in original. On this point, see also Oscár Terán, "Rasgos de la cultura intelectual argentina, 1956–66" (Working Paper 2, Latin American Studies Center, University of Maryland, College Park, 1991), 22, www.lasc.umd.edu/publications/papers.php.

23. Ignacio Vélez Suarez, "Montoneros, los grupos originarios," *Revista Lucha Armada*, yr. 1, no. 2 (2005), 12, www.cedema.org/ver.php?id=3392.

24. Carlos Arbelos, "El exilio de un muchacho peronista," interview by Roberto Bardini, September 18, 2006, https://bambupress.wordpress.com/2006/09/17/el-exilio-de-un-muchacho-peronista/.

25. "Plan de movilización cultural en la provincial de Buenos Aires," *Militancia*, yr. 1, no. 8 (August 2, 1973): 23.

26. "Juan Moreira: cine para la liberación y la liberación para el cine," *Militancia*, yr. 1, no. 2 (June 21, 1973): 21.

27. Perdía, *La otra historia*, 155.

28. The Montoneros especially stressed the "antipatria," or *cipayo*, nature of the Argentine military. See, for example, "Los militares cipayos," *Evita Montonera*, yr. 1, no. 10 (December 1975): 5–6; and the description in a photo caption of Generals Videla and Viola as "Generals of the antipatria," *Evita Montonera*, yr. 1, no. 9 (November 1975): 17.

29. *Militancia*, yr. 1, no. 5 (July 12, 1973): back cover.

30. Mario Eduardo Firmenich. Quoted in Montoneros, "Bases para la Alianza Constituyente de una Nueva Argentina," www.elortiba.org/old/doc mon.html. First published in *Vencer*, Mexico, 1982.

31. Juan Luís Besoky, "La derecha peronista: Prácticas políticas y representaciones (1943–1976)" (PhD diss., Universidad Nacional de la Plata, 2016), 21.

32. A recent series of studies by Juan Besoky, Humberto Cucchetti, María Valeria Galván, Juan Manuel Padrón, Juan Iván Ladeuix, and Laura Ehrlich has begun to fill this gap. Besoky's 2016 dissertation, cited above, provides an up-to-date bibliography. Also useful is Humberto Cucchetti's essay "¿Derechas peronistas? Organizaciones militantes entre nacionalismo, cruzada antimontoneros y profesionalización política," *Nuevo Mundo/Mundos Nuevos* (June 1, 2013), http://journals.openedition.org/nuevomundo/65363.

33. According to Juan M. Padrón, who conducted a series of interviews with activists who filled leadership roles in various right-wing Peronist organizations, his informants continued to refer to themselves as "orthodox" (ortodoxo) rather than right-wing Peronists (derecha peronista). Juan Manuel Padrón, ¡*Ni yanquis, ni marxistas! nacionalistas: nacionalismo, militancia y violencia política: el caso del Movimiento Nacionalista Tacuara en la Argentina, 1955–1966* (La Plata, Argentina: Editorial de la Universidad Nacional de General Sarmiento, 2017), 36, https://archive.org/details/NacionalismoMilitanciaY ViolenciaPoltica. Similarly, Besoky has noted how members of the Peronist right used the terms *loyal* or *orthodox* to describe themselves, while referring to the Peronist left as "traitors, infiltradors, and heterodox." See "La derecha peronista" [diss.], 22.

34. Interview with Pedro Eladio Vázquez, *Retorno*, no. 64 (September 1965). Quoted in Besoky, "La derecha peronista" (diss.), 156.

35. Besoky, "La derecha peronista" (diss.), 154.

36. Quoted in Federico Finchelstein, *The Ideological Origins of the Dirty War: Fascism, Populism, and Dictatorship in Twentieth Century Argentina* (New York: Oxford University Press, 2014), 106.

37. Raúl Jassén, *Patria Barbarie*, no. 2 (1964). Quoted in Besoky, "La derecha peronista" (diss.), 183.

38. Juan Ladeuix, "El General frente a la Sinarquía: El discurso de Carlos Disandro in la formación de la Concentración Nacionalista Universitaria y su impacto en el peronismo" (XI Jornadas Interescuelas/Departamentos de Historia, Universidad de Tucumán, 2007), 15, www.aacademica.org/000-108/581.

39. Plotkin, "La 'ideología' de Perón: Continuidades y rupturas," in *Perón del exilio al poder*, ed. Samuel Amaral and Mariano Ben Plotkin (Buenos Aires: Cántaro, 1993), 55. For a discussion of Perón's own understanding of socialism, see 55–59.

40. María José Moyano, *Argentina's Lost Patrol: Armed Struggle, 1969–1979* (New Haven, CT: Yale University Press, 1995), 176n59.

41. On Perón's relationship with Disandro, see Ladeuix, "El General," 8. On Perón's praise for Cornejo Linares's *El nuevo orden sionista en la Argentina*, see Juan Besoky, "Los muchachos peronistas antijudíos: A propósito del antisemitismo en el movimiento peronista," *Trabajos y Comunicaciones*, no. 47 (2018): 13, https://doi.org/10.24215/23468971e057.

42. According to Mariana Pozzoni, this was the first time the term *Tendencia Revolucionaria* was used. By the time this term entered circulation, the Tendencia represented the overwhelming majority of Peronist youth organizations, including the Montoneros, the Fuerzas Armadas Revolucionarias, the Peronismo de Base, and the Fuerzas Armadas Revolucionarias. Those who re-

jected armed struggle at this point included Comando de Organización and Guardia de Hierro, groups that would later be considered part of the Peronist right. See Pozzoni, "La Tendencia Revolucionaria del peronismo en la apertura política, Provincia de Buenos Aires, 1971–1974," *Estudios Sociales*, 1st sem. (2009): 176. As Pozzoni notes (177), between 1972 and 1974, the Tendencia became increasingly identified with the Montoneros, as that organization absorbed several smaller organizations.

43. Besoky, "Las derechas peronistas" (diss.), 194–211.

44. On the parceling out of posts between different sectors of the movement, see Paul Lewis, *Guerrillas and Generals: The "Dirty War" in Argentina* (Westport, CT: Praeger, 2002), 84–85.

45. Besoky, "Las derechas peronistas" (diss.), 195.

46. Hernán Merele, "'El germen genera sus propios anticuerpos': La 'depuración' interna peronista y el proceso represivo entre 1973–1976," *Anuario*, no. 29 (2017): 164, www.anuariodehistoria.unr.edu.ar/ojs/index.php/Anuario /issue/view/14.

47. Merele, "El germen," 165.

48. Merele, "El germen," 165.

49. Juan D. Perón, "Orden Reservada del 1° de octubre de 1973," www .lagazeta.com.ar/orden_reservada.htm.

50. Lewis, *Guerrillas and Generals*, 91.

51. Julieta Rostica, "Apuntes 'Triple A': Argentina 1973–76," *Desafíos* 23, no. 2 (December 2011): 35–36.

52. Juan Besoky, "La revista El Caudillo de la Tercera Posición: Órgano de expresión de la extrema derecha," *Conflicto Social*, yr. 3, no. 3 (June 2010).

53. "La patria peronista es la patria federal," *El Caudillo*, yr. 1 (November 16, 1973): n.p.

54. "La patria peronista," n.p.

55. "¡Peronista en pie de guerra!," *El Caudillo*, yr. 2, no. 18 (March 14, 1974): n.p.

56. All quotations in this paragraph are from "Ética Justicialista," *El Caudillo*, yr. 1, no. 6 (December 21, 1973). No citation is provided for the quotations from Perón; I have preserved the capitalization that appeared in *El Caudillo*. It is unclear whether the original quotation had the same capitalization.

57. "¡Las Cabecitas Negras!," *El Caudillo*, yr. 1, no. 6 (December 21, 1973): n.p.

58. "¡Oíme, milico!," *El Caudillo*, yr. 2, no. 8 (January 4, 1974): n.p.

59. "Por los Caudillos federales hacia la liberación nacional," *El Caudillo*, yr. 1 (November 16, 1973): n.p.

60. Felipe Romeo, "La tendencia se acabó: el que manda es Perón," *El Caudillo*, yr. 2, no. 10 (January 18, 1974): n.p.

61. "¡Oime! Barbudo!," *El Caudillo*, yr. 1, no. 2 (November 23, 1973): n.p. "Bluyins" (also spelled "blue-jeens" elsewhere) seem to have been a key preoccupation of *El Caudillo*. The publication's solid funding allowed for lavish photographic spreads that often featured young people lounging around wearing the bell-bottomed blue jeans of the era.

62. "Hoy: La guerrilla," *El Caudillo*, yr. 2, no. 14 (February 15, 1974): n.p.

63. "Doctrina: estado peronista, cultura y comunicación," *El Caudillo*, yr. 2, no. 54 (November 26, 1974): n.p.

64. *Cité Catholique* was founded in 1946 by Jean Ousset, former secretary of Charles Maurras. See Elena Scirica, "Ciudad Cathólica-*Verbo*: Discurso, redes y relaciones en pos de una apuesta [contra] revolucionaria," [2006?], http://historiapolitica.com/datos/biblioteca/scirica_levant.pdf/.

65. "Carta de un sacerdote a un militar," *Verbo*, no. 4 (August 1959): 26–30. Quoted in Scirica, "Ciudad Cathólica-*Verbo.*"

66. *Verbo*, no. 9 (January–February 1960): 36–60. Quoted in Scirica, "Ciudad Cathólica-*Verbo.*" This article also reveals that Cuidad Católica's ambitions spread further to include the public sector and those individuals with experience in the state bureaucracy.

67. Donald Hodges, *Argentina's "Dirty War": An Intellectual Biography* (Austin: University of Texas Press, 1991), 167. Scholar Mark Osiel concurs with this assessment. On his view of the importance of both Genta and Meinvielle, see "Constructing Subversion in Argentina's Dirty War," *Representations*, no. 75 (Summer 2001): 129–30.

68. See, for example, Julio Meinvielle, *El comunismo en la revolución anticristiana* (Buenos Aires: Ediciones Theoría, 1961).

69. Fortunato Mallimaci, Humberto Cucchetti, and Luis Donatello, "Caminos sinuosos: nacionalismo y catolicismo en la Argentina contemporánea," in *El altar y el trono: Ensayos sobre el catolicismo político latinoamericano*, ed. Francisco Colom and Angel Rivero (Barcelona: Antrophos/Unibiblos, 2006), 178.

70. On Genta's ties with air force chaplain Eliseo Melchiori and his classes within the Escuela de Aviación Militar of the air force, see Luis Fernando Beraza, *Nacionalistas: la trayectoria política de un grupo polémico, 1927–1983* (Buenos Aires: Cántaro, 2005), 141.

71. It should be noted that this instructional manual proved controversial. Although approved by the air force and distributed to cadets, the booklet provoked such an outcry from the liberal press that the air force halted its production and even collected copies it had already distributed. See Jordán Bruno Genta, *Guerra contrarevolucionaria* (Buenos Aires: Editorial Nuevo Orden, 1963), 9.

72. Genta, *Guerra contrarevolucionaria*, 29–32, 228.

73. Genta, *Guerra contrarevolucionaria*, 42.

74. Genta, *Guerra contrarevolucionaria*, 233, 249.

75. Genta, *Guerra contrarevolucionaria*, 137.

76. Genta, *Guerra contrarevolucionaria*, 249. Italics in original

77. The Cursillos de Cristiandad was an apostolic movement with Spanish roots. The Argentine branch, founded in 1950, was conceived as a cultural movement directly connected with the nationalism inspired by Julio Meinvielle's 1932 *Concepción católica de la política*. See Arturo Claudio Laguado Duca, "Onganía y el nacionalismo military en Argentina," *Universitas Humanistica* [Bogotá], no. 62 (July–December 2006): 254. See also Rock, *Authoritarian Argentina: The Nationalist Movement, Its History, and Its Impact* (Berkeley: University of California Press, 1993), 209, 283n25.

78. The Ateneo members appointed to the Onganía cabinet were Nicanor Costa Méndez, who became foreign minister, and Mario Díaz Colodrero, who took charge of the Ministry of the Interior. Ateneo founder Mario Amadeo received the ambassadorship to Brazil. For a more extensive list of Ateneo members who participated in the Onganía administration, see Paul Lewis, "The Right and Military Rule, 1955–1983," in *The Argentine Right: Its History and Intellectual Origins, 1910 to the Present*, ed. Sandra McGee Deutsch and Ronald H. Dolkart (Wilmington, DE: SR Books, 1993), 163–64. For a list of individuals with close ties to Ciudad Católica, see Elena Scirica, "Visión religiosa y acción política. El caso de Ciudad Católica-Verbo en la Argentina de los años sesenta," en: PROHAL MONOGRÁFICO, *Revista del Programa de Historia de América Latina*, vol. 2, Primera Sección: *Vitral Monográfico Nro. 2*, Instituto Ravignani, Facultad de Filosofía y Letras, Universidad de Buenos Aires, 2010, 47–48, www.filo.uba.ar/contenidos/investigacion/institutos/ravignani/prohal/Vitral_Mono_N2/dossier/dossierhere2.html.

79. Rock, *Authoritarian Argentina*, 200–201.

80. According to Liliana De Riz, liberal sectors within the military were greatly upset by Borda's appointment because of his prior activism within Peronism and his well-known belief that "political pluralism should be replaced with the participation of the organized community and a strong state." See *Historia argentina: la política en suspenso, 1966/1976* (Buenos Aires: Paidós, 2000), 56.

81. The plan called for a system in which different interest groups and social sectors would be represented through a new array of advisory councils. See Lewis, "Right and Military Rule," 168.

82. De Riz, *Historia argentina*, 44–50.

83. On the effort to make religious education mandatory, see De Riz, *Historia argentina*, 52. On the effort to reform the high school curriculum to reflect nationalist views, see Goebel, *Argentina's Partisan Past*, 148.

84. On film censorship, see Goebel, *Argentina's Partisan Past*, 147. On the harassment of couples and women wearing pants and miniskirts, see De Riz, *Historia argentina*, 53.

85. For a useful treatment of the liberal faction of the military, see Donald Hodges, *Argentina's "Dirty War": An Intellectual Biography* (Austin: University of Texas Press, 1991), 146–48. For the divisions between liberals and nationalist factions, see Lewis, "Right and Military Rule," 148–49. The other important division was between the Colorados and the Azules (Reds and Blues), with members of the Colorado faction usually placing themselves within the liberal camp and the Azules associated with more nationalist tendencies. The liberal/ Colorado and nationalist/Azules division, however, did not always coincide. Because the Colorados were more adamantly anti-Peronist, they also attracted nationalists both within and outside the military. See Rock, *Authoritarian Argentina*, 223.

86. It should be noted that, within the liberal faction, there was some softening toward Perón approaching the end of the 1960s and early 1970s. This was especially the case with Generals Aramburu and Lanusse.

87. Paul Lewis, *Guerrillas and Generals*, 142.

88. Within the military, the right-liberals often dismissed the nationalists' thought as "medieval," while nationalist officers believed the right-liberals were cosmopolitan, antinational, and in bed with the imperialists. On this point, see Lewis, "Right and Military Rule," 148.

89. The 1976 coup capped off a chaotic six-year period that began with the overthrow of Onganía in 1970 by his own commander-in-chief of the army, General Alejandro Lanusse. For a useful overview of this period, see David Rock, *Argentina 1516–1987: From Spanish Colonization to the Falklands War* (Berkeley: University of California Press, 1985), esp. chap. 8; and Donald Hodges, *Argentina, 1943–1987* (Albuquerque: University of New Mexico Press, 1988). A good introduction to these years in Spanish is De Riz, *Historia Argentina*.

90. Moyano, *Argentina's Lost Patrol*, 84.

91. See Pablo Calvo, "Una duda histórica: no se sabe cuántos son los desaparecidos," *Clarín*, October 5, 2003, http://edant.clarin.com/diario/2003 /10/06/p-00801.htm.

92. On these and other forms of torture, see Argentina, *Nunca Más: The Report of the Argentine National Commission on the Disappeared; with an Introduction by Ronald Dworkin*, Comisión Nacional Sobre la Desaparición de Per-

sonas, 1st American ed. (New York: Farrar, Straus, and Giroux, 1986). On the rectoscope, see 72.

93. Rock, *Authoritarian Argentina*, 194.

94. James Scorer, "From *la guerra sucia* to 'A Gentleman's Fight': War, Disappearance and Nation in the 1976–1983 Argentine Dictatorship," *Bulletin of Latin American Research* 27, no.1 (2008): 50–53. See also Fabiana Alonso, who has also stressed the links between the Catholic nationalism of the 1930s and the dictatorship, arguing that the idea of Argentina as a Hispanic, Catholic nation was a central tenet of the 1976 regime. See "Nacionalismo y catolicismo en la educación pública santafesiana (1976–1983)," *Prohistoria*, yr. 11, no. 11 (Spring 2007): 111, www.scielo.org.ar/pdf/prohist/v11/v11a06.pdf.

95. Rock, *Authoritarian Argentina*, 227.

96. The victims were General Jorge Cáceres Monié and his wife, Beatriz Sasiain. Jáuregui was selected to organize the official ceremony honoring the deceased general. Jáuregui's words appeared in *La Opinión*, December 5, 1975. Quoted in Beraza, *Nacionalistas*, 333.

97. Jorge Rafael Videla, Emilio Eduardo Massera, and Orlando Ramón Agosti, "Proceso de reorganización nacional," Buenos Aires, March 24, 1976. Rprt. *Presidencias y golpes militares del siglo XX* (Buenos Aires: Centro Editor de America Latina, 1986), 108. It should be noted here that the use of the term *el ser nacional* by the liberals within the junta can be misleading. As will be discussed below, like the term *Western Civilization, el ser nacional* could mean different things to liberals and Catholic nationalist military men.

98. Law 21.325, promulgated June 9, 1976. The text of this law, as well as a complete list of the targeted organizations, can be found at www.lafogata .org/proyecto2/instrucciones.htm.

99. "Carta abierta de Rodolfo Walsh a la junta militar," March 24, 1977. This letter appears on scores of websites and was recently published by the Ministry of Justice as an educational booklet, along with commentary and student questions. Interestingly, the military's role as the defender of *el ser nacional* also figured in the junta's legal defense during the 1985 human rights trials. In the words of Jaime Prats Cardona, defense attorney for junta member Admiral Emilio Massera, the military was the most important "support and guarantee of all that gives essence to *el ser nacional*, which is not only a geographic entity, but also a bundle of historical, ethical, and spiritual values that define [the nation] and confer upon it its [unique] personality within the concert of pueblos." See Prats Cardona's statements in "El alegato" (of Emilio Eduardo Massera), October 2–3, 1985, in *El libro de El Diario del Juicio*, Argentina, Cámara Nacional de Apelaciones en lo Criminal y Correccional de la Capital Federal (Buenos Aires: Editorial Perfil, 1985), 352.

100. Information on the coup attempt comes from Beraza, *Nacionalistas*, 333.

101. "Editorial," *Cabildo*, yr. 1, no. 1 (May 1973): 1.

102. "Editorial," *Cabildo*, yr. 1, no. 2 (June 1973): 3.

103. "El destino de las Fuerzas Armadas Argentinas," *Cabildo*, yr. 1, no. 1 (May 1973): 10. On the Catholic basis of *argentinidad*, see Federico Ibarguren, "Trigo y cizaña en nuestra historia," *Cabildo*, yr. 1, no. 5 (September 1973): 12; and Federico Ibarguren, "La tradición hispanocatólica peligra," *Cabildo*, yr. 1, no. 7 (November 1973): 19.

104. *Cabildo*, yr. 2, no. 20 (December 1974). Caps in original.

105. Beraza, *Nacionalistas*, 338.

106. See, for example, an open letter to Massera from Walter Beveraggi Allende published in *Cabildo*, yr. 2, no. 21 (January 1975), 17. Massera had invited Beveraggi Allende, a prominent nationalist and president of the Confederación Nacionalista Argentina, to give a lecture at the Escuela de Guerra Naval. See also Goebel, *Argentina's Partisan Past*, 185. Of the three members of the junta, Massera was the only one to participate directly in the "search-and-destroy operations" and to engage in torture of the suspected subversives. On this point, see Lewis, *Guerrillas and Generals*, 153. One of the most intriguing and troubling revelations about Massera was the discovery that, in 1978, he conducted secret talks in Paris with the exiled leaders of the Montoneros, including Firmenich. Rumors about his relationship with Firmenich, and about Firmenich's motives, have swirled for decades. For a brief treatment of the Massera/Montonera connection, and of the murder of Elena Holmberg, the Argentine diplomat who learned about the secret Paris meetings, see Martin Edwin Andersen, *Dossier Secreto: Argentina's Desaparecidos and the Myth of the "Dirty War"* (Boulder: Westview Press, 1993), 279, 283.

107. Quoted in Reato, *Disposición Final*, 157.

108. On the impact of the National Security Doctrine within the Argentine military, see Hodges, *Argentina's "Dirty War,"* 133–41; and David Pion-Berlin, "The National Security Doctrine, Military Threat Perception, and the 'Dirty War' in Argentina," *Comparative Political Studies* 21, no. 3 (October 1988): 382–407. An exhaustive Spanish-language treatment is Daniel Frontalini and María Cristina Caiati, *El mito de la "Guerra Sucia"* (Buenos Aires: Ed. CELS, 1984), esp. chap. 1. It is important to note that the Argentine military's willingness to use torture owed more to French influences. As numerous authors have noted, it was French counterinsurgency methods (developed during the French-Algerian war and disseminated through the Superior War College of Paris) that had the most direct impact on the Argentines, including the actual forms of torture. See, for example, Reato, *Disposición final*, esp. chap. 3.

109. Or, in the words of Donald Hodges, "Violations of human rights were justified on the pretext of defending them." See *Argentina's "Dirty War,"* 125.

110. On this point, see Lewis, *Guerrillas and Generals,* 119–20.

111. Jorge Rafael Videla, interview by Ceferino Reato, in Reato, *Disposición final,* 16.

112. For an illuminating analysis on these differing interpretations, see chap. 6 of Hodges, *Argentina's "Dirty War."*

113. In Videla's words, "Argentina belongs to the West and we recognize the leadership role of the United States" (*Clarín,* May 3, 1980). Quoted in Frontalini and Caiati, *El mito,* 18.

114. When these measures failed to tame inflation, make the economy more competitive, and grow GDP, the regime veered from one set of policies to another. The overall effect was the destruction of much of domestic industry, the gutting of the middle class, and the increased immiseration of the poor. By 1981, the economy was in shambles. The result was a nationalist nightmare, as Argentina became mired in debt and more of its faltering economy fell under foreign control. For useful discussions of the regime's economic policies and their impact, see Rock, *Argentina, 1516–1987,* 368–74; and Juan Carlos Torre and Liliana De Riz, "Argentina since 1946," in *Argentina since Independence,* ed. Leslie Bethell (Cambridge: Cambridge University Press, 1993), 330–38.

115. Well-known scholars Juan Carlos Torre and Liliana De Riz, for example, have argued that during this period "the ideas of liberal-conservatism" predominated within the military. See "Argentina since 1946," 330.

116. Mark Osiel, "Constructing Subversion in Argentina's Dirty War," *Representations,* no. 75 (Summer 2001), 121. Osiel's conclusions are based on extensive interviews with former members of the military who actively participated in the repression. Paula Canelo's detailed examination of the changing cabinet appointments during the first five years of the regime provides additional supporting evidence of this division of labor. See "Las 'dos almas' del Proceso: Nacionalistas y liberales durante la última dictadura military argentina (1976–1981)," *Páginas: Revista Digital de la Escuela de Historia,* yr. 1, no. 1 (2008): 69–85.

117. Because of the clandestine nature of the guerrilla enterprise, information on the age and occupations of the participants is difficult to piece together. Moyano has concluded that the vast majority of the guerrillas had founded or joined their organizations while in their late teens or twenties. In his estimate, students formed the single largest component of these organizations. See *Argentina's Lost Patrol,* 110–12.

118. Andersen, *Dossier Secreto,* 196.

119. This figure comes from Osiel, "Constructing Subversion," 138.

120. Andersen, *Dossier Secreto*, 196.

121. Ministerio de Cultura y Educación, *Subversión en el ámbito educativo (Conozcamos a nuestro enemigo)*, prologue by Minister of Culture and Education Juan José Catalán, Decree 1728, June 14, 1977, www.bnm.me.gov.ar/giga1/normas/11997.pdf.

122. Ministerio de Cultura y Educación, *Subversión*, 3, 59.

123. Ministerio de Cultura y Educación, *Subversion*, 59.

124. Resolution 2, Consejo Federal de Educación, San Miguel de Tucumán, September 16, 1976. Quoted in Ministerio de Cultura y Educación, Resolution 1614, expte. 48.470/80, September 8, 1980, http://repositorio.educacion.gov.ar/dspace/handle/123456789/85442?show=full.

125. Ovidio J. A. Solari, "Texto del discurso del Ministro de Educación de la Provincia de Buenos Aires, General Ovidio J. A. Solari, pronunciado en la escuela Num 2 de Carmen de Patagones" (March 7, 1977), 1, Biblioteca Nacional de Maestros, Argentina, www.bnm.me.gov.ar/giga1/documentos/EL 002872.pdf. Capitalization in original.

126. Luciano B. Menéndez, *La Opinión*, May 13, 1977. Quoted in Equipo de Educación del Comité de Solidaridad con el Pueblo Argentino, "La política educative de la junta military en Argentina," *Cuadernos Políticos* (Mexico), no. 17 (July–September, 1978): 102–13. www.cuadernospoliticos.unam.mx/cuadernos/contenido/CP.17/17.9.InformeArgentina.pdf.

127. Equipo de Educación del Comité de Solidaridad, "La política educativa," n.p.

128. Admiral Emilio Massera, speech at the Universidad del Salvador (Buenos Aires), published in *La Opinión*, February 7, 1978. Here quoted in Equipo de Educación del Comité de Solidaridad, "La política educativa," n.p. On Massera as the junta's "grand orator," see Marguerite Feitlowitz, *A Lexicon of Terror: Argentina and the Legacies of Torture* (New York: Oxford University Press, 1998), 19.

129. On this point, see Andersen, *Dossier Secreto*, 196.

130. Quoted in Andersen, *Dossier Secreto*, 195. The translation is Andersen's.

131. Equipo de Educación del Comité de Solidaridad, "La política educativa," n.p.

132. Andersen, *Dossier Secreto*, 203.

133. María José Moyano, "The Dirty War in Argentina: Was It a War and How Dirty Was It?," in *Staatliche und parastaatliche Gewalt in Lateinamerika*, ed. Hans Werner Tobler and Peter Waldmann (Frankfurt: Vervuert Verlag, 1991), 69.

134. This term is used by Canelo, in "Las 'dos almas'," 74; and Reato, in *Disposición final*, 62.

135. Osiel, "Constructing Subversion," 129–30.

136. Zone II included the provinces of Formosa, Chaco, Santa Fe, Misiones, Corrientes, and Santa Fe. Bessone was in charge of this zone only until September 1976, when he was selected to head the newly established Ministry of Planning.

137. Lewis, *Guerrillas and Generals*, 147. This list comes from Canelo, "Las 'dos almas.'"

138. Moyano, *Lost Patrol*, 85.

139. For Bessone on the autonomy of the zone commanders, see Reato, *Disposición Final*, 65. Reato himself likened the zone commanders to "feudal lords" (62).

140. Jorge Rafael Videla. Quoted in Reatos, *Disposición final*, 62–63.

141. In the months before the coup, for example, Videla had made it clear that "as many persons must die in Argentina as are necessary to guarantee the country's security" (*Clarín*, October 24, 1975). Quoted in Frontalini and Caiati, *El mito*, 25. Decades later, Videla would be more specific, confiding that he and his coconspirators had calculated that "seven or eight thousand people" would be killed. See Reato, *Disposición final*, 27.

142. Osiel, "Constructing Subversion," 121. According to Moyano, approximately 98 percent of the killing took place during the first three years of the dictatorship. See *Argentina's Lost Patrol*, 84.

143. Quoted in Lewis, *Guerrillas and Generals*, 147.

144. Quoted in Lewis, *Guerrillas and Generals*, 143. Originally quoted in Raúl Veiga, *Las organizaciones de derechos humano* (Buenos Aires: Centro Editor de América Latina, 1985), 43.

145. Antonius C. G. M. Robben, "Combat Motivation, Fear and Terror in Twentieth-Century Argentinian Warfare," *Journal of Contemporary History* 41, no. 2 (April 2006): 361.

146. Acdel Edgardo Vilas, "Reflexiones sobre la guerra subversive," *Revista de la Escuela Superior de Guerra* 54, no. 427 (1976), 10. Quoted in Robben, "Combat Motivation," 361. The translation is Robben's, although I have altered spellings to reflect US usage. On the use of religious fervor to motivate the troops, see also Argentina, *Nunca más*, 68–69.

147. Argentina, *Nunca más*, 69.

148. Mark Falcoff, "The Timerman Case," *Commentary*, July 1981): 22. For more on this point, see "The Timerman Case," 15–28. On the use of religion to motivate the troops, see also the section on anti-Semitism, in "The Repression," in part 1 of Argentina, *Nunca más*.

149. This was the so-called Plan Andina. The details in this paragraph on the treatment of Jewish prisoners come from Argentina, *Nunca más*, 67–72.

## CONCLUSION

1. For a recent discussion of the problem of teleology in Argentine history, see Michael Goebel, "Some Historical Observations on the Relationship between Nationalism and Political Violence in Argentina," in *Political Violence and the Construction of National Identity in Latin America*, ed. Will Fowler and Peter Lambert (New York: Palgrave Macmillan, 2006), 207–25.

2. Indeed, in the regions of Latin America, especially those most threatened by the United States, the notion of intrinsic differences between "Latin" and "Anglo-" Americans dates back to the mid-nineteenth century. On this point, see Aims McGuinness, "Searching for 'Latin America': Race and Sovereignty in the Americas in the 1850s," in *Race and Nation in Modern Latin America*, ed. Nancy Appelbaum, Anne S. Macpherson, and Karin Alejandra Rosemblatt (Chapel Hill: University of North Carolina Press, 2003), 87–107. Michel Gobat extends this argument by pointing to the impact of the pan–Latin American reaction to US president Franklin Pierce's 1856 recognition of filibusterer William Walker's claims on Nicaragua. See "The Invention of Latin America: A Transnational History of Anti-Imperialism, Democracy and Race," *American Historica Review* 118, no. 5 (December 2013), 1345–75.

3. For an overview of the impact of Krausism throughout Hispanic America, see O. Carlos Stoetzer, *Karl Christian Friedrich Krause and His Influence in the Hispanic World* (Cologne: Böhlau, 1998).

4. Several US scholars also followed this path, most notably Howard Wiarda in *The Soul of Latin America: The Cultural and Political Tradition* and Glen C. Dealy in *The Public Man: An Interpretation of Latin American and Other Catholic Countries*.

5. See McGuinness, "Searching for 'Latin America'"; and Gobat, "Invention of Latin America."

6. Liah Greenfeld, *Nationalism: Five Roads to Modernity* (Cambridge, MA: Harvard University Press, 1992), 16.

7. Greenfeld, *Nationalism*, 15–16.

8. Greenfeld, *Nationalism*, 258.

9. For her analysis of how a sense of collective ressentiment worked in Russia and how it helped produce an ethnic form of nationalism that celebrated the superior virtues of the "Russian soul," see *Nationalism*, 253–58.

10. Jorge Nállim, *Transformations*, 189.

11. Goebel, *Argentina's Partisan Past*, 15.

12. Despite the different political leanings of their authors, these works have long been seen by literary scholars as forming a kind of holy trinity of 1930s essays seeking to plumb the depths of the so-called *ser nacional*. See, for example, José Morales-Saravia, "El discurso argentinista en los años treinta: Scalabrini Ortiz, Martínez Estrada, Mallea" (PhD diss., Free University of Berlin, 1986).

13. Eduardo Mallea, *Historia de una pasión argentina* (Buenos Aires: Editorial Sudamericana, 1986), 17.

14. Mallea, *Historia*, 198. For a fuller discussion of Mallea's vision and Argentine liberalism, see Leonardo Senkman, "Nacionalismo e inmigración: la cuestión étnica en las elites liberales e intelectuales argentinas: 1919–1940," *Estudios Interdisciplinarios de America Latina y el Caribe* 1, no. 1 (January–June 1990), www.tau.ac.il/eial/I_1/Senkman.htm.

15. Ezequiel Martínez Estrada, *X-ray of the Pampa* (Austin: University of Texas Press, 1971), 44–45. It should be noted that, in other ways, Martínez Estrada resembled the liberals he criticized. In contrast to the nationalists, who celebrated the authentic, hidden Argentina, this author argued that the original national personality was actually barbaric and should be erased. This could be accomplished, he believed, by courageously accepting the "profound reality" of the nation's underlying barbarity, which would "cause it to dissipate and to allow [Argentines] to live united in health" (399).

16. Carlos Altamirano, "Algunas notas sobre nuestra cultura," *Punto de Vista* 6, no. 18 (August 1983): 8; Hilda Sábato, "Pluralismo y nación," *Punto de Vista* 7, no. 34 (July–September, 1989), 2; Luis Alberto Romero, "Apogeo y crisis de la Argentina vital," *Revista de las Américas*, no. 1 (Spring 2003): 99, 100, 101.

17. Raúl Alfonsín, "Mensaje presidencial del doctor Raúl Alfonsín a la Honorable Asamblea Legislativa," Buenos Aires, May 1, 1987, www.alfonsin .org/mensaje-presidencial-del-doctor-raul-alfonsin-a-la-honorable-asamblea -legislativa-3/.

18. Raúl Alfonsín, "Discurso de Asunción del Dr. Raúl Alfonsín como Presidente de la Nación ante la Asamblea Legislativa," December 10, 1983, in *Raúl Alfonsín por Raúl Afonsín: Discursos presidenciales ante la Asamblea Legislativa*, ed. Horacio Garcete and Nathalie Goldwaser Yanelvich (Buenos Aires: Facultad de Derecho, Universidad de Buenos Aires, 2018), 44.

19. Shirley Christian, "Argentine Army, after Half-Century as the Power, Finds Itself under Siege," *New York Times*, June 7, 1987. www.nytimes.com /1987/06/07/world/argentine-army-after-half-century-as-the-power-finds -itself-under-siege.html?pagewanted=all&src=pm.

20. Mohamed Alí Seineldín, from an interview partially reproduced in "Con la cruz y la espada: Murió de ex Coronel Carapintada Mohamed Alí Seineldín," *Página* 12, September 3, 2009, www.pagina12.com.ar/diario /elpais/1-131094-2009-09-03.html.

21. From *El Bimestre Político y Económico*, December 10, 1983. Quoted in Rock, *Authoritarian Argentina*, 233. Translation and ellipses are Rock's.

22. "Democracia, responsibilidad y esperanza." Document produced by the Argentine Episcopado at the 48th Plenary Assembly in San Miguel, April 13, 1984, and published on the website of the Pastoral Social of the Archdiocese of Buenos Aires, www.pastoralsocialbue.org.ar/documento/democracia -responsabilidad-y-esperanz.

23. The facts of these cases remain shrouded in mystery. Both investigations were deeply flawed and, in the case of the AMIA attack, led to the indictment of the overseeing judge, Juan José Galeano, on the charge of attempting to pay a witness to implicate a member of the Buenos Aires Provincial Police. For a discussion, see Karen Ann Faulk, *In the Wake of Neoliberalism: Citizenship and Human Rights in Argentina* (Stanford, CA: Stanford University Press, 2013), 69–70.

24. Goebel, *Argentina's Partisan Past*, 203.

25. Faulk, *In the Wake*, 90.

26. Faulk, *In the Wake*, 98.

27. Argentine Constitution, Article 75, section 17.

28. Constitution of the City of Buenos Aires. Quoted in Faulk, *In the Wake*, 99.

29. For the City of Buenos Aires, see www.buenosaires.gob.ar/areas /registrocivil/nombres/busqueda/buscador_nombres.php?nombre=Peter&sexo =ambos&Buscar_bt=Buscar&buscar=1. The provincial list can be found at www.gob.gba.gov.ar/registro/nombres/.

30. Faulk, *In the Wake*, 100.

31. Paulina Alberto and Eduardo Elena, introduction to *Rethinking Race in Modern Argentina* (New York: Cambridge University Press, 2016), 10.

32. Goebel, *Argentina's Partisan Past*, 216.

33. Goebel, *Argentina's Partisan Past*, 217. During her presidency, Fernández de Kirchner established both a think tank called the Instituto de Estrategia y Desarrollo Arturo Jauretche Avellaneda and a new university named in Jauretche's honor (Universidad Nacional Arturo Jauretche).

# BIBLIOGRAPHY

## SERIALS CONSULTED (ALL BUENOS AIRES)

*Anales (de la Biblioteca Nacional Argentina)*
*Atlántida*
*Azul y Blanco*
*Boletín de la Institución Libre de Enseñanza*
*Boletín Mensual del Museo Social Argentino*
*Cabildo* (daily newspaper, founded 1942)
*Cabildo* (monthly magazine, founded 1973)
*Cristianismo y Revolución*
*Criterio*
*Crítica*
*Cuaderno Colegio Novecentista*
*Cuadernos de F.O.R.J.A.*
*El Caudillo*
*El Monitor de la Educación Común*
*El Pampero*
*Estudios*
*Evita Montonero*
*F.O.R.J.A. Boletín de la Fuerza de Orientación Radical de la Joven Argentina*
FORJANDO
*Hechos e Ideas*
*Ideas* (1903)
*Ideas* (1918)
*La Época*
*La Nueva República*
*La Vanguardia*
*Leoplan*
*Militancia*

*Nosotros*
*Renacimiento*
*Revista Argentina de Ciencias Políticas*
*Revista de Filosofía*
*Revista de la Universidad de Buenos Aires*, 2nd series
*Sagitario*
*Sexto Continente*
*Síntesis*
*Verbum*


## PRIMARY SOURCES

Abeille, Luciano. *Idioma nacional de los argentinos*. Paris: Librairie Emile Bouillon, 1900.

———. [1902]. Letter to Carlos Pellegrini. In *En torno al criollismo: Ernesto Quesada, "El criollismo en la literatura argentina" y otros textos: estudio crítico y compilación*, edited by Alfredo V. E. Rubione and Ernesto Quesada, 248–50. Buenos Aires: Centro Editor de América Latina, 1983.

Alberdi, Juan Bautista. [1852]. *Argentina, 1852: bases y puntos de partida para la organización política de la República Argentina*. Barcelona: Linkgua Ediciones, 2007.

———. [1837]. "Doble harmonía entre el objeto de esta institución." In *Antecedentes de la Asociación de Mayo, 1837–1937: homenaje del honorable Consejo Deliberante de la Ciudad de Buenos Aires en su fundación*, 39–46. Buenos Aires: Consejo Deliberante, 1939.

———. [1837]. *Fragmento preliminar al estudio del derecho*. Buenos Aires: Ciudad Argentina, 1998.

———. [1837]. "Páginas explicativas." In *Argentina, 1852: bases y puntos de partida para la organización política de la República Argentina*, 21–29. Barcelona: Linkgua Ediciones, 2007.

Alfonsín, Raúl. "Discurso de Asunción del Dr. Raúl Alfonsín como Presidente de la Nación ante la Asamblea Legislativa." December 10, 1983. In *Raúl Alfonsín por Raúl Alfonsín. Discursos presidenciales ante la Asamblea Legislativa*, edited by Horacio Garcete and Nathalie Goldwaser Yanelvich, 25–93. Buenos Aires: Facultad de Derecho, Universidad de Buenos Aires, 2018.

Álvarez, Juan. "La escuela argentina y el nacionalismo." *Revista Argentina de Ciencias Políticas* 12 (1916): 334–42.

Amadeo, Mario. "Ante la reforma constitucional." *Azul y Blanco*, February 6, 1957.

Anquín, Nimio de. "La crisis del patriotismo." *Azul y Blanco*, May 5, 1959.

Aparicio, Francisco de. "El arte nacional en 1918." *Cuaderno Colegio Novecentista*, yr. 3, no. 7 (January 1919).

Arbelos, Carlos. "El exilio de un muchacha peronista." Interview with Carlos Arbelos. By Roberto Bardini. September 18, 2006. https://bambupress .wordpress.com/2006/09/17/el-exilio-de-un-muchacho-peronista/.

Argentina. *Tercer Censo Nacional, Levantado el 1° de junio de 1914, Etc.* Buenos Aires: Oficina del Censo, 1916.

Argentine Episcopado. "Democracia, responsibilidad y esperanza." Document produced by the Argentine Episcopado, at the 48th Plenary Assembly in San Miguel, April 13, 1984. www.pastoralsocialbue.org.ar/documento /democracia-responsabilidad-y-esperanza.

Astrada, Carlos. "La deshumanización del occidente." *Sagitario* 1, no. 2 (July–August 1925): 193–209.

———. *Martín Fierro y el hombre argentino.* Buenos Aires: Ediciones Cruz del Sur, 1948.

———. "Surge el hombre argentino con fisonomía propia." In *Argentina en marcha*, edited by Comisión Nacional de Cooperación Intelectual and Homero M. Guglielmini, 15–58. Vol. 1. Buenos Aires: Comisión Nacional de Cooperación Intelectual, 1947.

Ayarragaray, Lucas. "Política inmigratoria." In Liga Patriótica Argentina, *Noveno Congreso Nacionalista*, 469–79. Buenos Aires: Imp. P. Ventriglia, 1928.

Azcárate, D. Gumersindo de. "Educación y enseñanza según Costa." *Boletín de la Institución Libre de Enseñanza* 44, no. 720 (March 31, 1920): 65–71. https://babel.hathitrust.org/cgi/pt?id=uc1.b2877074&view=1up&seq=78.

Barcos, Julio R. *Por el pan del pueblo.* Buenos Aires: Librería "Renacimiento," 1933.

Barrantes Molina, Luis. "Los delitos contra la nacionalidad." *El Pueblo*, July 27, 1941.

Barros, José P. "La intoxicación del idioma y la terapéutica indicada." In Séptima Congreso Nacionalista de La Liga Patriótica Argentina: Sesiones del 22, 23, yr. 24 de Mayo, May 1926, 77–89. N.p.: Buenos Aires, 1926.

Becher, Emilio. "La ciudad." *La Nación*, April 26, 1906.

———. [1906]. "La tradición y el patriotismo." In *Diálogo de las sombras y otras páginas*, 219–25. Buenos Aires: Facultad de Filosofiá y Letras, Instituto de literatura Argentina, 1938.

Beveraggi Allende, Walter. Letter to Massera. *Cabildo* (magazine), 2, no. 21 (January 1975): 17.

Bianco, José. *La doctrina radical.* Buenos Aires: Talleres Gráficos de L. J. Rosso, 1927.

Bonasso, Miguel. *Diario de un clandestino*. Buenos Aires: Planeta, 2000.

Bunge, Augusto. *El ideal argentino y el socialismo*. Buenos Aires: Libreria La Vanguardia, 1918.

Bunge, Carlos Octavio. [1903]. *Nuestra América*. 2nd ed. Buenos Aires: Coni Hermanos, 1905.

Calandrelli, A. "Cultura y nacionalismo." *Revista de la Universidad de Buenos Aires*. 2nd epoch, sec. 2, nos. 1–2 (1925): 261–68.

Cané, Miguel. [1902]. "Carta al Dr. Ernesto Quesada." In *En torno al criollismo: Ernesto Quesada, "El criollismo en la literatura argentina" y otros textos; estudio crítico y compilación*, edited by Alfredo V. E. Rubione, 231–39. Buenos Aires: Centro Editor de América Latina, 1983.

———. "La cuestión del idioma." In *Prosa ligera*. Buenos Aires: La Cultura Argentina, 1919.

Carlés, Manuel. *Definition of the Argentine Patriotic League (A Guide to Social Welfare)*. Buenos Aires, 1922. English translation of Manuel Carlés, *Definición de la Liga Patriótica (Guía del buen sentido social)*. Pamphlet. 1920.

———. "Interview with Dr. Carlés." *Buenos Aires Herald*, May 2, 1919.

———. "Opening Address, 9th Congress of the Liga Patriótica Argentina, May 1928." In Liga Patriótica Argentina, *Noveno Congreso Nacionalista*, 69–104. Biblioteca De La Liga Patriótica Argentina. Buenos Aires: Imp. P. Ventriglia, 1928.

Carulla, Juan Emiliano. *Al filo del medio siglo*. Buenos Aires: Editorial Huemul, 1964.

———. "Defensa de occidente." In *Problemas de la cultura: defensa de occidente y otros temas*, 13–21. Buenos Aires: El Ateneo, Librería Científica y Literaria, 1927.

———. "Programa para un diario nacionalista." In *Problemas de la cultura: defensa de occidente y otros temas*, 81–82. Buenos Aires: El Ateneo, Librería Científica y Literaria, 1927.

Casabal, Adolfo. "Algo sobre el carácter nacional." *Estudios* 4, yr. 2 (n.d., ca. 1902/ 1903): 429–49.

Castellani, Leonardo. "Sobre las elecciones." *Azul y Blanco*, February 26, 1958.

Castellanos, Joaquín. *Acción y pensamiento*. Buenos Aires: J. A. Pellegrini, 1917.

———. Discourse in Congress. *Diario de Sesiones* 3 (July 24, 1914): 286–91.

———. Speech in Congress. In *Acción y pensamiento*. Buenos Aires: J. A. Pellegrini, 1917.

Chávez, Fermín. *Civilización y barbarie en la historia de la cultura argentina*. Buenos Aires: Ediciones Theoría, 1974.

———. "La Argentina es deformada cuando termina el caudillaje." Interview by Jorge B. Rivera. *Revista Crisis* (May 1975). www.elhistoriador.com.ar /fermin-chavez-2/.

————. "Proemio a la tercera edición." In *La restauración nacionalista*, by Ricardo Rojas, 7–10. Buenos Aires: A. Peña Lillo, 1971.

*Clarín*, "Falleció Norma Kennedy: una histórica dirigente de la llamada resistencia peronista." June 24, 2017.

Cooke, John William. Letter to Juan Perón, April 11, 1957. In *Correspondencia Perón-Cooke: obras completas*, edited by John William Cooke and Eduardo Luis Duhalde, 68–86. Buenos Aires: Colihue, 2007.

Costa Álvarez, Arturo. *Nuestra lengua*. Buenos Aires: Sociedad Editorial Argentina, 1922.

Debenedetti, Salvador. "Sobre la formación de una raza argentina." *Revista de Filosofía*, yr. 1, 2nd sem. (1915): 415–22.

Dickmann, Adolfo. *Nacionalismo y socialismo: el socialismo y el principio de nacionalidad. Los argentinos naturalizados en la política*. Buenos Aires: Talleres gráficos Porter hnos, 1933.

Doll, Ramón. "El funesto error del peronismo." *Azul y Blanco*, May 5, 1959.

————. "Grandeza y miseria de la oligarquía argentina: la realidad nacional sin cartabones extranjeros." In *Liberalismo en la literatura y la política*. Buenos Aires: Editorial Claridad,1936.

Echeverría, Esteban. [1846]. *Dogma socialista y otras páginas políticas*. Barcelona: Red Ediciones S.L., 2011. E-book.

"El alegato, October 23, 1985," in *El libro de El Diario del Juicio*, 348–69. Argentina. Cámara Nacional de Apelaciones en lo Criminal y Correccional de la Capital Federal. Buenos Aires: Editorial Perfil, 1985.

Equipo de Educación del Comité de Solidaridad con el Pueblo Argentino. "La política educative de la junta military en Argentina." *Cuadernos Políticos* (Mexico), no. 17 (July–September, 1978): 102–13. www.cuadernospoliticos .unam.mx/cuadernos/contenido/CP.17/17.9.InformeArgentina.pdf.

Estrada, Carlos. [1902]. "Carta al Dr. Ernesto Quesada." In *En torno al criollismo: Ernesto Quesada, "El criollismo en la literatura argentina" y otros textos: estudio crítico y compilación*, edited by Alfredo V. E. Rubione, 239–42. Buenos Aires: Centro Editor de América Latina, 1983.

Etchecopar, Máximo. "De la democracia política a la democracia social." *Azul y Blanco*, March 27, 1957.

————. "La clase necesaria." *Azul y Blanco*, April 10, 1957.

Etkin, Alberto. *Bosquejo de la historia y doctrina de la UCR*. Buenos Aires: El Ateneo, 1928.

Ezcurra Medrano, Alberto. *Catholicismo y nacionalismo*. Buenos Aires: ADSUM, 1939.

————. "El caso Rosas." *Sexto Continente*, nos. 3–4 (October–November, 1949): 51–57.

———. "Los 'jovenes rebeldes.'" *Tacuara: Vocero de la Revolución Nacionalista* (September 1961): 3.

Franceschi, Gustavo J. "Consideraciones sobre la revolución." *Criterio*, yr. 16, no. 789 (June 17, 1943): 149–53. In *Textos y documentos: el autoritarismo y los argentinos: la hora de la espada, 1924–1946*, edited by Alicia García and Ricardo E. Rodríguez Molas, 209–20. Biblioteca Política Argentina. Buenos Aires: Centro Editor de América Latina, 1988.

———. "Nacionalismo." *Criterio* 6, no. 290 (September 21, 1933): 53–56.

———. "Totalitarianismo, liberalismo, catolicismo." *Criterio* 13, no. 662 (November 7, 1940): 221–27.

Frondizi, Arturo. *Industria argentina y desarrollo nacional.* Buenos Aires: Ediciones Qué, 1957.

Galarce, A. "Las escuelas de truantes." In *Noveno Congreso Nacionalista*, Liga Patriótica Argentina, 261–92. Buenos Aires: Imp. P. Ventriglia, 1928.

Gallo, Vicente. "Aspectos y ensenanzas de una obra." *Revista Argentina de Ciencias Políticas* 10 (July 1915): 329–36.

Gálvez, Manuel. [1961]. *Amigos y maestros de mi juventud.* Vol. 1 of *Recuerdos de la vida literaria.* 4 vols. Buenos Aires: Hachette, 1961.

———. *El diario de Gabriel Quiroga: opiniones sobre la vida argentina.* Buenos Aires: Arnoldo Moën, 1910.

———. *El mal metafísico: (vida romántica) novela.* Buenos Aires: Sociedad Cooperativa "Nosotros," 1916.

———. [1961]. *Entre la novela y la historia.* Vol. 3 of *Recuerdos de la vida literaria.* 4 vols. Buenos Aires: Librería Hachette, 1962.

———. "Los himnos a la nueva energía." *El Monitor de la Educación Común*, yr. 30, vol. 39 (1911): 73.

———. Response to "¿Llegarémos a tener un idioma propio?" Survey. *Crítica*, June 20, 1927.

———. *Vida de Hipólito Yrigoyen, El hombre de misterio.* 2nd ed. Buenos Aires: Kraft, 1939. First published 1938.

Ganivet, Ángel. *Cartas finlandesas.* Granada: Impr. de el Defensor de Granada, 1906.

———. [1896]. *Idearium español: el porvenir de España.* Edited by E. Inman Fox. Madrid: Espasa-Calpe, 1999.

García Elorrio, Juan. "Octubre." *Cristianismo y Revolución* 10 (October 1968 ): 1–2.

García Lupo, Rogelio. "Diálogo con los jovenes fascistas." In *La rebelión de los generales*, 81–87. Buenos Aires: Vegara, 2014.

García Mellid, Atilio. "Alem, Yrigoyen y Perón: símbolos de las muchedumbres argentinas." *Hechos e Ideas*, yr. 9, no 54 (September 1948): 283–310.

————. "Dimensión spiritual de la Revolución." *Hechos e Ideas*, yr. 9, nos. 56–57 (November–December 1948): 43–53.

————. "La abstención electoral y el comicio de Buenos Aires. *FORJANDO* (Rojas, Buenos Aires Province), yr. 2, no. 11 (January 1942): 1.

————. "La posición de América." *FORJANDO* (Rojas, Buenos Aires Province), yr. 2, no. 11 (January 1942): 5.

————. *Proceso al liberalismo argentino*. Buenos Aires: Ediciones Theoría, 1957.

Gerchunoff, Alberto. "La obra de Payró." *Nosotros*, yr. 6, vol. 7, no. 36 (January 1912): 19–25.

Giner de los Ríos, Francisco D. *Estudios de literatura y arte*. Madrid: Suarez, 1876.

————. "Poesía erudita y poesía vulgar." In *Estudios literarios*, 161–70. Madrid, 1866.

————. "Problemas urgentes de nuestra educación nacional." *Boletín de la Institución Libre de Enseñanza*, yr. 26, no. 509 (August 31, 1902): 225–28. http://prensahistorica.mcu.es/es/publicaciones/numeros_por_mes.cmd ?anyo=1902&idPublicacion=1000225.

Gorriti, Juan Ignacio, and Valentín Gómez. "Discursos de Juan Ignacio Gorriti y Valentín Gómez en el debate relativo a la creación y organización del Ejército Nacional, iniciado en la sesión del 3 de mayo de 1825." In *Ciudades, provincias, estados: orígenes de la Nación Argentina, 1800–1846*, edited by José Carlos Chiaramonte, 518–26. Argentina: Compañia Editora Espasa Calpe Argentina/Ariel, 1997.

G.O.U. Internal document of the GOU. In *El G.O.U.: los documentos de una logia secreta*, edited by Robert Potash, 101–3. Buenos Aires: Editorial Sudamericana, 1984.

Hernández Arregui, Juan José. [1960]. *La formación de la conciencia nacional, 1930–1960*. Buenos Aires: Editorial Plus Ultra, 1973.

————. [1963]. *¿Qué es el ser nacional? La conciencia histórica iberoamericana*. Buenos Aires: Plus Ultra, 1973.

Herrero, Antonio. *Hipólito Yrigoyen, maestro de democracia*. La Plata: Olivieri y Dominguez, 1927.

Herrero, Antonio, and Raúl F. Oyhanarte. *El puntero argentino: exégesis de dos oraciones cívicas del diputado nacional Dr. Raúl F. Oyhanarte*. La Plata, Argentina: Editorial Almafuerte, 1929.

Ibarguren, Federico. "La dictadura tradicionalista." *El Pampero*, October 4, 1940.

————. "La tradición hispanocatólica peligra." *Cabildo* (magazine), 1, no. 7 (November 1973): 19.

————. *Origenes del nacionalismo argentino*. Buenos Aires: Editorial Celcius, 1969.

———. "Para un examen de conciencia naciona." *Azul y Blanco*, December 2, 1958.

———. "Trigo y cizaña en nuestra historia." *Cabildo* (magazine), 1, no. 5 (September 1973): 12–13.

Ingenieros, José. "La formación de una raza argentina." *Revista de Filosofía* 1, 2nd sem. (1915): 464–83.

Irazusta, Julio. *Actores y espectadores*. Buenos Aires: Sur, 1937.

———. "Bases y programa de acción de la Liga Republicana." In *El pensamiento político nacionalista: antología*, 25–28. Vol. 2. Buenos Aires: Obligado Editora, 1975.

———, ed. *El Pensamiento político nacionalista: antología*. 3 vols. Buenos Aires: Obligado Editora, 1975.

———. "La forma mixta de gobierno." *La Nueva República*, January 31, 1928.

———. "Sobre el capital extranjero." *La Nueva República*, October 22, 1931.

Irazusta, Rodolfo. "La campaña presidencial." *La Nueva República*, January 15, 1928.

———. "La filiación histórica." *La Nueva República*, October 29, 1931.

———. "La política: el orden del 53." *La Nueva República*, September 27, 1930.

———. "La política: la democracia no está en la constitución." *La Nueva República*, April 28, 1928.

———. "La política: La democracia no está en la constitución." *La Nueva República*, May 5, 1928.

———. "La política: los principios contra la nación." *La Nueva República*, November 8, 1930.

———. "La profesión del candidato." *La Nueva República*, October 20, 1931.

———. [1931]. "Notas políticas: la ley Sáenz Peña y la revolución." In *El Pensamiento político nacionalista: antología*, edited by Julio Irazusta, 136–37. Vol. 3. Buenos Aires: Obligado Editora, 1975.

———. "Permanencia del régimen." *Azul y Blanco*, May 5, 1959.

Irazusta, Rodolfo, and Julio Irazusta. *La Argentina y el imperialismo británico: Los eslabones de una cadena, 1806–1833*. Buenos Aires: Editorial Tor, 1934.

———. "Nuestro programa." *La Nueva República*, December 1, 1927.

Jauretche, Arturo. *FORJA y la década infame: con un apéndice de manifiestos, declaraciones y textos volantes*. Buenos Aires: Editorial Coyoacán, 1962.

———. "Opinión pública y democracia." *FORJANDO* (Rojas, Buenos Aires Province), yr. 2, no. 10 (November 1941): 2, 5.

———. *Política nacional y revisionismo histórico*. Vol. 7 of *Obras completas de Arturo Jauretche*. Buenos Aires: Corregidor, 2006.

———. Speech delivered in the aftermath of the June 4, 1943, coup. 36 pp. Papers of Darío Alessandro. Biblioteca del Congreso Nacional, Argentina. Mimeo.

Justo, Juan B. "1 de Mayo de 1918." In *Internacionalismo y patria*, 155–58. Buenos Aires: Vanguardia, 1933.

———. *La Vanguardia*, December 9, 1918.

Korn Villafañe, Adolfo. *Los derechos proletarios: ensayo novecentista*. La Plata, Argentina: n.p., 1922.

Krause, Karl Christian Friedrich, and Julián Sanz del Río. *Ideal de la humanidad para la vida*. Madrid: Imprenta de F. Martínez García, 1871.

Last Reason [pseud.]. Response to "¿llegarémos a tener un idioma propio?" Survey. *Crítica*, June 16, 1927.

Lestard, Gastón. "El sentimiento de la nacionalidad y la selección inmigratoria." In Liga Patriótica Argentina. *Noveno Congreso Nacionalista*, 463–68. Biblioteca de La Liga Patriótica Argentina. Buenos Aires: Imp. P. Ventriglia, 1928.

Liga Patriótica Argentina. *Humanitismo práctico*. Buenos Aires: Comisión de Propaganda, 1921.

Lugones, Leopoldo. [1923]. "Acción ante la doble amenaza." In *Antología de la prosa*, 365–75. Buenos Aires: Ediciones Centurión, 1949.

———. *Didáctica*. Buenos Aires: Otero y Cía, 1910.

———. [1924]. "El discurso de Ayacucho." In *La patria fuerte*, 14–25. Buenos Aires: Taller Gráfico de L. Bernard, 1930.

———. [1920]. *La grande argentina*, Buenos Aires: Editorial Huemul, 1962.

Maetzu, Ramiro de. *Defensa de la hispanidad*. Galiciana: Biblioteca Digital de Galicia, 1934. http://biblioteca.galiciana.gal/es/consulta/registro.cmd ?id=378201.

Maguire, Patricio. "Los ingleses y la expansión de la masonería argentina." *Azul y Blanco*, May 12, 1959.

Mallea, Eduardo. [1937]. *Historia de una pasión argentina*. Buenos Aires: Editorial Sudamericana, 1986.

Martín, Gaspar. "La raza como ideal: posibilidad y necesidad de su concreción." *Verbum* 12, no. 46 (October 1918): 47–51.

Martínez Estrada, Ezequiel. [1933]. *X-ray of the Pampa*. Austin: University of Texas Press, 1971.

Más y Pi, Juan. "El arte en la Argentina." *Renacimiento*, yr. 2, no. 6 (January 1911): 307–14.

Mazo, Gabriel del. El radicalismo: ensayo sobre su historia y doctrina. Buenos Aires: Ediciones Gure, 1957.

———"La Reforma Universitaria, una conciencia de emancipación en desarrollo." Speech delivered in Córdoba, June 15, 1938. In *Reforma universitaria y cultura nacional*, 40–64. Buenos Aires: n.p., 1947.

———. "Meditación en el día de la raza." In *Reforma universitaria y cultura nacional*, 68–77. Buenos Aires: n.p., 1947.

————. "Yrigoyen." *Cuadernos de F.O.R.J.A*, yr. 1, no. 2 (July 3, 1936): 4–6.

————. "Yrigoyen." *FORJANDO* (Rojas, Buenos Aires Province), yr. 1, no. 2 (August 27, 1940): 2.

Meinvielle, Julio. *Concepción católica de la economía*. Buenos Aires: Curso de Cultura Católica, 1936.

————. *El comunismo en la revolución anticristiana*. Buenos Aires: Ediciones Theoría, 1961.

Mercante, Domingo. "Declaraciones del Coronel Mercante." *Azul y Blanco*, July 16, 1957.

Ministerio de Cultura y Educación, Argentina. Resolution 1614, expte. 48.470/80. September 8, 1980. http://repositorio.educacion.gov.ar/dspace /handle/123456789/85442?show=full.

————. *Subversion en el ámbito educativo (Conozcamos a nuestro enemigo)*. Prologue by Minister of Culture and Education Juan José Catalán. Decree 1728, June 14, 1977. www.bnm.me.gov.ar/giga1/normas/11997.pdf.

Montoneros. "Bases para la Alianza Constituyente de una Nueva Argentina." First published *Vencer* (Mexico), 1982. www.elortiba.org/old/docmon.html.

Movimiento Nacional Peronista, *Nacionalismo o guerra civil*. Pamphlet. La Plata, Argentina: Centro de Cultura Nacional "José Hernández" [1967?]. www.ruinasdigitales.com/documentos-montoneros/.

Movimiento Nacionalista Tacuara. "Programa básico revolucionario del Movimiento Nacionalista Tacuara." 1957. http://www.cedema.org/ver.php ?id=7163.

Olivera, Carlos. [1900]. "El idioma nacional de los argentines." In *En torno al criollismo: Ernesto Quesada, "El criollismo en la literatura argentina" y otros textos: estudio crítico y compilación*, edited by Alfredo V. E. Rubione, 62–66. Buenos Aires: Centro Editor de América Latina, 1983.

Olmedo, Francisco P. "La inmigración, la Universidad y la FUBA." *Azul y Blanco*, November 11, 1958.

Organización Universitario de F.O.R.J.A. "La falsa opción de los dos colonialismos." In *FORJA y la década infame: con un apéndice de manifiestos, declaraciones y textos volantes*, by Arturo Jauretche, 102–7. Buenos Aires: Editorial Coyoacán, 1962.

Ortíz, Raymundo. "La inmigración." In *Séptimo Congreso Nacionalista de la LPA*, 195–96. Buenos Aires: Imp. A Baiocco, 1926.

Ortíz Pereyra, Manuel. *La tercera emancipación: actualidad económica y social de la República Argentina*. Buenos Aires: J. Lajouane, 1926.

————. *Por nuestra redención cultural y económica (Apuntes de crítica social argentina)*. Buenos Aires: Talleres Casa Jacobo Peuser, Ltda., 1928.

Orzi, Rene. *Jauretche y Scalabrini Ortiz*. Buenos Aires: Peña Lillo, 1985.

Oyhanarte, Horacio B. *El hombre: Hipólito Irigoyen, apostol de la democracia*. Buenos Aires: Editorial Claridad, 1945. First published 1916.

Palacio, Ernesto. *La historia falsificada, con una introducción de Leonardo Castellani*. Buenos Aires: Editorial Difusión, 1939.

———. "Lugones vivo." *Sexto Continente*, no. 2 (August–September 1949): 16–21.

———. "Nacionalismo y democracia." *La Nueva República*, May 5, 1928.

———. [1931]. "Notas políticas." In *El pensamiento político nacionalista: antología*, edited by Julio Irazusta, 145–48. Vol. 3. Buenos Aires: Obligado Editora, 1975.

———. "Se trata de elaborar, al fin, una constitución para los argentinos?" *Hechos e Ideas*, yr. 9, no. 54 (September 1948): 280–82.

Palacios, Esteban. "El ambiente migratorio." In *Séptimo Congreso Nacionalista de la LPA*, 151–54. Buenos Aires: Imp. A Baiocco, 1926.

Pellegrini, Carlos. [1902]. Letter to Luciano Abeille. In *En torno al criollismo: Ernesto Quesada, "El criollismo en la literatura argentina" y otros textos: estudio crítico y compilación*, edited by Alfredo V. E. Rubione, 250. Buenos Aires: Centro Editor de América Latina, 1983.

Perdía, Roberto Cirilo. *La otra historia: Testimonio de un jefe montonero*. Argentina: Grupo Agora, 1997.

Pérez Colman, Enrique. *Discursos programas de los candidatos radicales triunfantes en las elecciones del 4 de Junio de 1922*. Paraná, Argentina: Junta Gobierno de la U.C. Radical de Entre Rios, 1922.

Perón, Juan D. "Cervantes, los descamisados, y Perón." *La Época*, October 13, 1947.

———. "Como define el Gral. Perón la esencia y contenido de nuestra herencia español." *La Época*, October 12, 1948.

———. *Discurso del Presidente de la Nación Argentina, pronunciado en la Academia de Letras con motivo del día de la raza, y como homenaje en memoria de don Miguel de Cervantes Saavedra en el cuarto centenario de su nacimiento*. Buenos Aires: n.p., 1947.

———. "Doctrinas Nacionales." In *Descartes: Política y estrategia*. www.labaldrich.com.ar/wp-content/uploads/2013/03/Pol%C3%ADtica-y-Estrategia-Descartes-Per%C3%B3n.pdf. First published May 15, 1952.

———. "El homenaje a Cervantes y el Día de la Raza." *Hechos e Ideas*, yr. 7, no. 4 (October 1947): 67–83.

———. "En la celebración del primer aniversario de la Secretaria de Trabajo." In *Obras completas del General Domingo Perón*, 28–31. Cuadernillos de Formación Político-Syndical 1. Argentina: Unión de Personal Civil de la Nación. www.upcndigital.org/files/publicaciones/CDN/cuadernillos_de_Peron-1.pdf.

———. "Juicios del Presidente Perón sobre la enseñanza y nueva ley universitaria." *Hechos e Ideas*, yr. 7, no. 46 (January 1948): 343–48.

———. *La comunidad organizada y el estado justicialista*. Cartilla Doctrinaria 2. Buenos Aires: Presidencia de la Nación, Secretaria de Prensa y Difusión, 1974.

———. "La cultura." Sec. 4 of "Problemas políticos, sociales y económicos de la República Argentina." *Hechos e Ideas*, yr. 7, no. 50 (May 1948): 395–430.

———. Letter to Juan José Hernández Arregui, December 10, 1969. Repr. *Peronismo y Socialismo* 1, no. 1 (September 1973): 31–32.

———. "Mensaje del excelentísimo señor presidente de la nación general de brigada D. Juan Perón en el acto del juramento al asumir la primera magistratura, en el Congreso de la Nación, el 4 de junio de 1946." In *Pensamiento político del general de brigada Juan Perón: directivas del presidente de la nación*, 13–27. Buenos Aires: Subsecretaría de Informaciones, 1946.

———. "Mensaje leído ante el Honorable Congreso de la Nación el 26 de junio de 1946." In *Pensamiento político del general de brigada Juan Perón: directivas del presidente de la nación*, 29–59. Buenos Aires: Subsecretaría de Informaciones, 1946.

———. "Orden Reservada del 1° de octubre de 1973." www.lagazeta.com.ar/orden_reservada.htm.

———. *Plan quinquenal de gobierno del presidente Perón, 1947–1951*. Buenos Aires: Editorial Primicias, 1946.

———. *Selección de sus escritos, conferencias y discursos*. Buenos Aires: Ediciones Sintesis, 1973.

Pozuelo, Claudio. "El radicalismo argentino: origen y finalidad." *Revista Argentina de Ciencias Políticas* 10 (July 1915): 377–85.

Propst, Juan. Editor's note. *Verbum* 12, no. 45 (October 1918): 5.

Quesada, Ernesto. "El criollismo." *Estudios*, yr. 1, vol. 3 (June–July 1902): 251–453.

———"El día de la raza y su significado in Hispano-América." *Verbum* 12, no. 46 (October 1918): 7–20.

Ramírez, Pedro Pablo. "Carta del Excmo. Sr. Presidente de la Nación Pedro Pablo Ramírez al director del *Criterio*, monseñor Gustavo J. Franceschi." In *Textos y documentos: el autoritarismo y los argentinos. la hora de la espada, 1924–1946*, edited by Alicia García and Ricardo E. Rodríguez Molas, 225–26. Buenos Aires: Centro Editor de América Latina, 1988.

———. [1943]. "Discurso en la cena de camaradería de las Fuerzas Armadas." In *Textos y documentos: el autoritarismo y los argentinos. la hora de la espada, 1924–1946*, edited by Alicia García and Ricardo E. Rodríguez Molas, 227–34. Buenos Aires: Centro Editor de América Latina, 1988.

———. "Habla el Presidente." *El Pampero*, October 13, 1943, 5.

Ramos, Jorge Abelardo. [1957]. *Revolución y contrarrevolución en la argentina.* Buenos Aires: Senado de la Nación, 2006.

Ramos Mejía, José María. [1899]. *Las multitudes argentinas.* Edited by José María Bolaño. Biblioteca Universal de Sociología. Buenos Aires: Guillermo Kraft, 1952.

Riesco, Gabriel. "El eje diamantino de nuestro ser." *El Pueblo*, October 12, 1941.

Rodó, José Enrique. [1900]. *Ariel.* Translated by Margaret Peden. Austin: University of Texas Press, 1988.

Rohde, Jorge. "Apuntes." *Cuaderno Colegio Novecentista*, yr. 1, vol. 1, no. 3 (December 1917): 131–40.

Rojas, Ricardo. *Alocución dirigido a los bachilleres del Colegio Nacional de Buenos Aires*, August 12, 1928. Pamphlet. Archives of Museo Ricardo Rojas, Buenos Aires. Self-published, n.d.

———. "Dante y la gente latina." *La Nación*, June 15, 1921.

———. *Eurindia.* Vol. 5 of *Obras de Ricardo Rojas.* 2nd ed. Buenos Aires: Librería la Facultad, 1924.

———. Interview. By Silvano. *Atlántida*, November 15, 1923, n.p.

———. "La demonstración a R. Rojas." *Nosotros*, yr. 2, vol. 3, nos. 13–14 (August–September 1908): 124–27.

———. "La literatura argentina." *Nosotros*, yr. 7, no. 50 (June 1913): 337–64.

———. *La literatura argentina: ensayo filosófico sobre la evolución de la cultura en el Plata.* Vols. 8–9, *Obras de Ricardo Rojas,* 2nd ed. Buenos Aires: Librería "La Facultad," de J. Roldán [ca. 1924].

———. [1909]. *La restauración nacionalista.* 3rd ed. Buenos Aires: A. Peña Lillo, 1971.

———. Letter to Miguel de Unamuno, November 17, 1904. Repr. García Blanco, "Ricardo Rojas y Unamuno." *Revista de la Universidad de Buenos Aires* 3, no. 3 (July–September 1958): 403–56.

———. "Letras españoles." *Ideas*, yr. 2, vol. 3, no. 10 (February 1904): 162–80.

———. Postcard to Miguel de Unamuno, March 2, 1908. In Manuel García Blanco, "Ricardo Rojas y Unamuno." *Revista de la Universidad de Buenos Aires* 3, no. 3 (July–September 1958): 403–56.

———. *Retablo español.* Buenos Aires: Editorial Losada, 1938.

———. "Ricardo Rojas, maestro y discípulo de sí mismo." *Leoplan* (July 4, 1945): 19.

———. *Silabario de la decoración americana.* Buenos Aires: Editorial Losada, 1930.

Romeo, Felipe. "La tendencia se acabó: él que manda es Perón." *El Caudillo* 2, no. 10 (January 18, 1974): n.p.

Rosa, José María. *Estudios revisionistas*. Buenos Aires: Editoria Sudestada, 1967.

Rubione, Alfredo V. E. "Estudio Preliminar." In *En torno al criollismo: Ernesto Quesada, "El criollismo en la literatura argentina" y otros textos: estudio crítico y compilación*, edited by Alfredo V. E. Rubione, 9–42. Buenos Aires: Centro Editor de América Latina, 1983.

Rubione, Alfredo V. E., ed. *En torno al criollismo: Ernesto Quesada, "El criollismo en la literatura argentina" y otros textos: estudio crítico y compilación*. Buenos Aires: Centro Editor de América Latina, 1983.

Ruíz, J. Martínez [Azorín]. *El alma castellana: 1600–1800*. Madrid: Librería internacional, 1900. https://babel.hathitrust.org/cgi/pt?id=txu.05917302432 5649&view=1up&seq=153.

———. [1929]. "La España de un pintor." In *Tiempos y cosas*, by J. Martínez Ruíz [Azorín], 143–45. Spain: Salvat, 1970.

———. [1902]. *La voluntad*. Edited by Inman Fox. Madrid: Castalia, 1972.

———. [1913]. *Los valores literarios*. Madrid: Rafael Caro Raggio, 1921.

Sagarna, Antonio. "Concepto del radicalismo argentino." *Revista Argentina de Ciencias Políticas* 10 (July 1915): 348–66.

Saítta, Sylvia. "Entre la cultura y la política: Los escritores de izquierda." In *Nueva historia argentina*. Vol. 7, *Crisis económica, avance del estado e incertidumbre política (1930–1943)*, edited by Alejandro Cattaruzza and Juan Suriano, 383–428. Buenos Aires: Ed. Sudamericana, 2001.

Saldías, José Antonio. Response to "¿Llegarémos a tener un idioma propio?" Survey. *Crítica*, June 12, 1927.

Sánchez Sorondo, Marcelo. *La revolución que anunciamos*. Buenos Aires: Ediciones Nueva Política, 1945.

———. "Pueblo, Iglesia y Fuerzas Armadas." *Azul y Blanco*, June 23, 1959.

Sarmiento, Domingo F. *Conflicto y armonías de las razas en América: Tomo Primero*. 8th ed. Buenos Aires: Impr. de D. Tuñez, 1883.

———. "Espíritu y condiciones de la historia en América" (Memoria leída el 11 de Octubre de 1858, en el Ateneo del Plata). In *Obras de D. F. Sarmiento*. Vol. 21, edited by Augusto Belin Sarmiento, 99–115. Buenos Aires: n.p., 1899.

———. [1845]. *Facundo*. Buenos Aires: Editorial Losada, 1963.

———. [1881]. "La Nostalgia en América." In *Obras completas*. Vol. 36, *La Condición del Extranjero en América*, 73–78. Buenos Aires: Libraría "La Faculdad" de Juan Roldan, 1900.

Scalabrini Ortiz, Raúl. [1931]. *El hombre que está solo y espera: una biblia porteña*. Buenos Aires: Editorial Biblos, 2005.

———. "Identidad de la línea histórica de Yrigoyen y Perón. *Hechos e Ideas*, yr. 9, no. 54 (September 1948): 314–24.

————. "LA ARGENTINA, base y arma de abastecimiento inglés." *Cuadernos de F.O.R.J.A.*, yr. 1, no. 1 (May 25, 1936).

————. "Los enemigos del pueblo argentino." Speech delivered July 3, 1948, at the Instituto "Hipólito Yrigoyen," Mercedes, Buenos Aires Province. In *Yrigoyen y Perón*, 9–30. Buenos Aires: Plus Ultra, 1972.

————. "Nuestra historia." *FORJANDO* (Rojas, Province of Buenos Aires), yr. 1, no. 3 (September 30, 1940).

————. *Política británica en el Río de la Plata.* Buenos Aires: Editorial Reconquista, 1940.

————. *Yrigoyen y Perón.* Buenos Aires: Plus Ultra, 1972.

Solari, Ovidio J. A. "Texto del discurso del Ministro de Educación de la Provincia de Buenos Aires, General Ovidio J.A. Solari, pronunciado en la escuela Num 2 de Carmen de Patagones." March 7, 1977. Biblioteca Nacional de Maestros, Argentina. www.bnm.me.gov.ar/giga1/documentos/EL002872.pdf.

Sonego, Victor Mariano. *Las dos argentinas: para una lectura crítica de nuestra historia.* Buenos Aires: Edebe Editorial Don Bosco Argentina, 1999.

Soto y Calvo, Francisco. [1903]. "De la falta de carácter en la literatura argentina." In *En torno al criollismo: Ernesto Quesada, "El criollismo en la literatura argentina" y otros textos: estudio crítico y compilación,* edited by Alfredo V. E. Rubione, 261–76. Buenos Aires: Centro Editor de América Latina, 1983.

Stach, Francisco. "La defensa social y la inmigración." *Boletín Mensual del Museo Social Argentino* 5, nos. 55–56 (July–August 1916): 360–89.

Suárez, José León, *La Liga Patriótica.* Pamphlet. Buenos Aires, 1919.

Tello, Wenceslao. "Alma argentina." *Atlántida* 8, no. 24 (1912): 340–44.

————. "La raza argentina." *Atlántida* 8, no. 22 (1912): 37–40.

Tiberghien, Guillaume, A. García Moreno, Nicolás Salmerón y Alonso, Urbano González Serrano, and Federico Escámez Centeno. *Ensayo teórico é histórico sobre la generación de los conocimientos humanos.* Madrid: Nueva Biblioteca Universal, 1875.

Toro y Gómez, Miguel de. "Nuestra lengua: Vínculo espiritual de la raza." *Verbum,* yr. 12, no. 46 (October 1918): 25–40.

Ugarte, Manuel. *El porvenir de la América Latina: la raza; la integridad territorial y moral; la organización interior.* Valencia: Sempere, 1911.

Unamuno, Miguel de. "Excursión." In vol. 1 of *Obras completas,* edited by Manuel García Blanco, 281–86. Madrid: Escelicer, 1966.

————. [1895]. *En torno al casticismo.* Edited by Enrique Rull Fernández. Madrid: Alianza Editorial, 2000.

Uriburu, José. Manifiesto (October 1, 1930). In appendix to Tulio Halperin Donghi, *La república imposible,* 340–41. Ariel Historia. Buenos Aires: Ariel, 2004.

Videla, Jorge Rafael, Emilio Eduardo Massera, and Orlando Ramón Agosti. "Proceso de reorganización nacional." In *Presidencias y golpes militares del siglo XX*. Buenos Aires: Centro Editor de America Latina, 1986, 107–9.

Walsh, Rodolfo. "Carta abierta de Rodolfo Walsh a la junta militar." March 24, 1977. www.educ.ar/recursos/129063/carta-abierta-de-rodolfo-walsh-a-la-junta-militar.

———. *Discursos, escritos y polémicas del Dr. Hipólito Yrigoyen, 1878–1922*. Edited by Jorge Guillermo Fovie. Buenos Aires: T. Palumbo, 1923.

———. Letter to Pedro C. Molina, September 1909. In *Jesús, el templo y los viles mercaderes: un examen de la discursividad yrigoyenista*, by Marcelo Padoan, 75–86. Colección "la Ideología Argentina." Buenos Aires: Universidad Nacional de Quilmes Ediciones, 2002.

———. [1909]. Letter to Pedro Molina. In *Irigoyen; su revolución política y social: La Unión Cívica Radical*, edited by Carlos J. Rodríguez, 127–30. Buenos Aires: Librería y editorial "La Facultad," Bernabé y cía, 1943.

———. "Mensaje al Congreso." October 15, 1921. http://constitucionweb.blogspot.com/2012/06/mensaje-al-congreso-del-presidente-h.html.

———. *Mi vida y mi doctrina*. Edited by Hebe Clementi. Buenos Aires: Editoria Leviatan, 1981. Written in 1923; first published in 1957.

## UNSIGNED SOURCES

"Al Pueblo de la Republica." Manifesto of F.O.R.J.A. September 2, 1935. In *Cuadernos de F.O.R.J.A*, yr. 2, nos. 10–12 (November 1939): 17–43.

"Argentina-America-Europa," *FORJANDO* (Rojas, Province of Buenos Aires), yr. 2, no. 11 (January 1942): 5.

*Argentinidad* (Buenos Aires). "Este periódico. . . . ." October 1938, 4.

*Azul y Blanco*. Editorial. July 31, 1957.

*Azul y Blanco*. "El Caso Frondizi," March 18, 1958.

*Azul y Blanco*. "El gobierno termina de contradecir al presidente." January 2, 1957.

*Azul y Blanco*. "El orden necesario a la prosperidad del país." May 12, 1959.

*Azul y Blanco*. "El país dijo basta: la revolución nacional reanuda su camino y tiene que recuperar dos años perdidos." February 26, 1958.

*Azul y Blanco*. "Hemos tocado el fondo." June 2, 1958.

*Azul y Blanco*. "La corona británica y la masonería." March 31, 1959.

*Azul y Blanco*. "La inmigración: problema fundamental de la nacionalidad." October 28, 1958.

*Azul y Blanco*. "La única solución: Iglesia-F.F.A.A. y Pueblo unidos." November 3, 1959.

*Azul y Blanco*. "La universidad contra el programa nacional." April 15, 1958.

*Azul y Blanco*. "La voluntad nacional superó el fraude." February 26, 1958.

*Azul y Blanco*. "Los 'católicos' del gobierno." January 9, 1957.

*Azul y Blanco*. "Manifiesto de nuestro partido." July 2, 1957.

*Azul y Blanco*. "Origen británico de la masonería." March 24, 1959.

*Azul y Blanco*. "¿Universidad católica?" September 21, 1959.

*Azul y Blanco*. "Un libro de historia para Mr. Nixon." June 17, 1958.

*Azul y Blanco*. "¿Un nacionalismo marxista?" October 1, 1957.

*Cabildo* (newspaper). "La revolución triunfante." June 5, 1943.

*Cabildo* (newspaper). "Por decreto del ejecutivo, ha sido creado el Instituto Nacional de la Tradición." December 22, 1943.

*Cabildo* (magazine). Editorial. Vol. 1, no. 1 (May 1973): 1.

*Cabildo* (magazine). Editorial. Vol. 1, no. 2 (June 1973): 3.

*Cabildo* (magazine). "El destino de las Fuerzas Armadas Argentinas." Vol. 1, no. 1 (May 1973): 10.

"Carta a un joven militar argentino." From "Un militante de Tacuara" (1963). Pamphlet. http://eltopoblindado.com/nacionalismo-derecha/decada-1960 -nacionalismo-derecha/tacuara/carta-a-un-joven-militar-argentino/.

"Democracia en peligro." *FORJANDO* (Rojas, Province of Buenos Aires), yr. 1, no. 2 (August 27, 1940): 5.

"Día de la raza." *Ideas*, yr. 1, no. 1 (October 1918): 2.

"Disolución de F.O.R.J.A." In *F.O.R.J.A. y la década infame: con un apéndice de manifiestos, declaraciones y textos volantes*, edited by Arturo Jauretche, 118. Buenos Aires: Ed. Coyoacán, 1962.

*El Caudillo*. "Doctrina: estado peronista, cultura y comunicación." Vol. 2, no. 54 (November 26, 1974): n.p.

*El Caudillo*. "Ética justicialista." Vol. 1, no. 6 (December 21, 1973): n.p.

*El Caudillo*. "Hoy: la guerrilla." Vol. 2, no. 14 (February 15, 1974): n.p.

*El Caudillo*. "La patria peronista es la patria federal." Yr. 1 (November 16, 1973): n.p.

*El Caudillo*. "¡Las cabecitas negras!" Vol. 1, no. 6 (December 21, 1973): n.p.

*El Caudillo*. "¡Oime! Barbudo!" Vol. 1, no. 2 (November 23, 1973): n.p.

*El Caudillo*. "¡Oime! Milico!" Vol. 2, no. 8 (January 4, 1974): n.p.

*El Caudillo*. "¡Peronista en pie de guerra!" Vol. 2, no. 18 (March 14, 1974): n.p.

*El Caudillo*. "Por los caudillos federales hacia la liberación nacional." Vol. 1 (November 16, 1973): n.p.

"El redactor de la Asamblea de 1813." In *Pensamiento político de la emancipación*, compiled by José Luis Romero and Luis Alberto Romero, 309. Caracas: Biblioteca Ayacucho, 1977.

"El sentido de Yrigoyen." *F.O.R.J.A.: Boletín de la Fuerza de Orientación Radical de la Joven Argentina* (Buenos Aires) (November 26, 1936), 3.

"Hablan los Montoneros." *Cristianismo y Revolución*, no. 26 (November–December 1970): 11–14.

"Juan Moreira: cine para la liberación y la liberación para el cine." *Militancia*, yr. 1, no. 2 (June 21, 1973): 21.

*La Época*. "Conmemoración del 12 de octubre." October 13, 1926.

———. "El decreto inmortal instituyendo el día de la raza." October 11, 1927.

———. "Hipólito Yrigoyen." November 25, 1926.

———. "Papá Noel y Santa Claus son personajes ajenos a nuestra fe." January 6, 1949.

———. "Telegramas enviados al Dr. Hipólito Yrigoyen con motivo de la celebración del 'Día de la Raza.'" October 15, 1926.

———. "¡Yrigoyen, Presidente!" November 2. 1926. First published *El Heraldo*. Concordía, n.d.

———. "Yrigoyen, Presidente." Repr. November 14, 1926.

"La nueva dirección." *Síntesis* 1, no. 8 (December 1927): 133–34.

*La Nueva República*. "Política: la conferencia de la Habana." February 15, 1928.

———. "Programa de gobierno de la nueva república." October 20, 1928.

"Las armas de la independencia hoy están apuntadas hacia el Pueblo." *Cristianismo y Revolución*, no. 30 (September 1971): 13.

"Los militares cipayos." *Evita Montonera*, yr. 1, no. 10 (December 1975): 5–6.

"Nacionalismo y democracia." *FORJANDO* (Rojas, Buenos Aires Province), yr. 2, no. 10 (November 1941), 1.

Plan de movilización cultural en la provincial de Buenos Aires." *Militancia*, yr. 1, no. 8 (August 2, 1973): 23.

"Radicalismo y Peronismo se identifican en sus proyecciones históricas." *Hechos e Ideas*, yr. 7, no. 47 (February 1948): 371–86.

"Reglamiento de la división de poderes sancionado por la Junta conservadora, September 30–October 29, 1811." In *Ciudades, provincias, estados: orígenes de la Nación Argentina, 1800–1846*, compiled by José Carlos Chiaramonte, 349–53. Biblioteca Del Pensamiento Argentino 1. Argentina: Compañia Editora Espasa Calpe Argentina/Ariel, 1997.

"Una nueva traición del electoralismo." *FORJANDO* (Rojas, Buenos Aires Province), yr. 1, no. 3 (September 30, 1940): 5.

"Vocación revolucionaria del radicalismo." *Cuadernos de F.O.R.J.A*, nos. 10–12 (November 1939): 44–45.

## SECONDARY SOURCES

Acha, Omar. *Los muchachos peronistas: orígenes olvidados de la Juventud Peronista (1945–1955)*. Buenos Aires: Planeta, 2011.

Adelman, Jeremy. "Between Order and Liberty: Juan Bautista Alberdi and the Intellectual Origins of Argentine Constitutionalism." *Latin American Research Review* 42, no. 2 (June 2007): 86–110.

———. *Republic of Capital: Buenos Aires and the Legal Transformation of the Atlantic World.* Stanford, CA: Stanford University Press, 1999.

Alberto, Paulina, and Eduardo Elena. "The Shades of the Nation." Introduction to *Rethinking Race in Modern Argentina*, edited by Paulina Alberto and Eduardo Elena, 1–22. New York: Cambridge University Press, 2016.

Alonso, Fabiana. "Nacionalismo y catolicismo en la educación pública santafesiana (1976–1983)." *Prohistoria*, yr. 11, no. 11 (Spring 2007): 108–23. www.scielo.org.ar/pdf/prohist/v11/v11a06.pdf.

Alonso, Paula. *Between Revolution and the Ballot Box: The Origins of the Argentine Radical Party in the 1890s.* Cambridge: Cambridge University Press, 2000.

Altamirano, Carlos. "Algunas notas sobre nuestra cultura," *Punto de Vista* 6, no. 18 (August 1983): 6–10.

———. *Bajo el signo de las masas (1943–1973).* Vol. 6 of *Biblioteca del Pensamiento Argentino.* Buenos Aires: Ariel Historia, 2001.

———. "La hora de las masas." *Istor*, yr. 6, no. 25 (Summer 2006): 6–29.

———. "Las dos Argentinas." In *Peronismo y cultura de izquierda*, 27–38. Colección Temas sociales 4. Buenos Aires: Temas Grupo Ed., 2001.

———. *Peronismo y cultura de izquierda.* Buenos Aires: Temas Grupo Editoriales, 2001.

Altamirano, Carlos, and Beatriz Sarlo. "La Argentina del centenario: Campo intelectual, vida literaria y temas ideológicos." In *Ensayos Argentinos: de Sarmiento a la vanguardia*, 69–106. Buenos Aires: Centro Editor de América Latina, 1983.

Álvarez Guerrero, O. *El Radicalismo y la ética social: Yrigoyen y el krausismo.* Buenos Aires: Leviatan, 1986.

Amaral, Samuel. "El avión negro: retórica y práctica de la violencia." In *Perón del exilio al poder*, edited by Samuel Amaral and Mariano Ben Plotkin, 69–94. Buenos Aires: Cántaro, 1993.

———. "En las raíces ideológicas de Montoneros: John William Cooke lee a Gramsci." *Temas de Historia Argentina y Americana*, no. 17 (2010): 15–51. http://bibliotecadigital.uca.edu.ar/repositorio/revistas/raices-ideologicas-de-montoneros.pdf.

Andersen, Martin Edwin. *Dossier Secreto: Argentina's Desaparecidos and the Myth of the "Dirty War."* Boulder: Westview Press, 1993.

Anderson, Benedict. *Imagined Communities: Reflections on the Origin and Spread of Nationalism.* Rev. ed. London: Verso, 2006.

Anzorena, Oscár. *JP: historia de la Juventud Peronista (1955/1988)*. Buenos Aires: Ediciones del Cordón, 1989.

Argentina. *Nunca Más: The Report of the Argentine National Commission on the Disappeared; With an Introduction by Ronald Dworkin*. Comisión Nacional Sobre la Desaparición de Personas. 1st American ed. New York: Farrar, Straus, and Giroux, 1986.

Arias, María, and Raúl Garcia Heras. "Carisma disperso y rebelión: los partidos neoperonistas." In *Perón del exilio al poder*, edited by Samuel Amaral and Mariano Ben Plotkin, 95–125. Buenos Aires: Cántaro, 1993.

Armus, Diego. "Desirable and Undesirable Migrants. Disease, Eugenics, and Discourses in Modern Buenos Aires." *Journal of Iberian and Latin American Studies* 25, no. 1 (2019): 57–79. doi.org/10.1080/14701847.2019.1579492.

Bagú, Sergio. "Estrateficación social y estructura nacional del conocimiento en la Argentina, 1880–1930." *Revista de la Universidad Nacional de Córdoba* 2, nos. 1–2 (March–June 1962): 14–29.

Barbero, María Inés, and Fernando Devoto. *Los nacionalistas (1910–1932)*. Buenos Aires: Centro Editor de América Latina, 1983.

Baubök, Rainer. "Cultural Citizenship, Minority Rights and Self-Government." In *Citizenship Today: Global Perspectives and Practices*, edited by T. A. Aleinikoff and Douglas Klusmeyer, 319–48. Washington, DC: Carnegie Endowment for International Peace, 2001.

Beraza, Luis Fernando. *Nacionalistas: la trayectoria política de un grupo polémico, 1927–1983*. Buenos Aires: Cántaro, 2005.

Bertoni, Lilia Ana. *Patriotas, cosmopolitas y nacionalistas: la construcción de la nacionalidad argentina a fines del siglo XIX*. Buenos Aires: Fondo de cultura económica, 2001.

Besoky, Juan Luís. "El nacionalismo populista de derecha en Argentina: La Alianza Libertadora Nacionalista, 1937–1975." *Mediações* (Brazil) 19, no. 1 (2014): 61–83.

———. "La derecha peronista en perspectiva." *Nuevo Mundo/Mundos Nuevos* (May 24, 2013). https://journals.openedition.org/nuevomundo/65374.

———. "La derecha peronista: Prácticas políticas y representaciones (1943–76)." PhD diss., Universidad Nacional de La Plata, 2016. http://sedici.unlp.edu.ar/bitstream/handle/10915/55209/Documento_completo__.pdf?sequence=3&isAllowed=yBesoky.

———. "La revista El Caudillo de la Tercera Posición: órgano de expresión de la extrema derecha." *Conflicto Social* 3, no. 3 (June 2010).

———. "Los muchachos peronistas antijudíos: a propósito del antisemitismo en el movimiento peronista." *Trabajos y Comunicaciones* 47, 1–29. https://doi.org/10.24215/23468971e057.

Biagini, Hugo, ed. *El movimiento positivista argentino*. Buenos Aires: Editorial de Belgrano, 1985.

———. *Orígenes de la democracia argentina: el trasfondo krausista*. Buenos Aires: Editorial Legasa, 1989.

Blakkisrud, Helge. "Blurring the Boundary between Civic and Ethnic: The Kremlin's New Approach to National Identity under Putin's Third Term." In *The New Russian Nationalism: Imperialism, Ethnicity and Authoritarianism 2000–2015*, edited by Helge Blakkisrud and Pål Kolstø, 249–74. Edinburgh: Edinburgh University Press, 2016. www.jstor.org/stable/10.3366/j.ctt1bh2kk5.16.

Bonasso, Miguel. *Lo que no dije en "Recuerdo de la muerte."* Buenos Aires: Sudamericana, 2014. Kindle.

Botana, Natalio, and Ezequiel Gallo. *De la República posible a la República verdadera (1880–1910)*. Buenos Aires: Espasa Calpe, 1997.

Bozza, Juan A. "Combates y conjuras: notas sobre las hipótesis conspirativas y antisemitas en la historigrafía revisionista." In *Mitos, altares y fantasmas: aspectos ideológicos en la historia del nacionalismo argentino*, 63–75. Serie Estudios/Investigaciones 12. La Plata, Argentina: Universidad Nacional de La Plata, Facultad de Humanidades y Ciencias de la Educación, 1992.

———. "El peronismo revolucionario: corrientes y experiencias en al radicalización sindical (1958/68)." *Cuestiones de Sociología* 3 (2006): 88–116.

Brauner Rodgers, Susana. "El nacionalismo yrigoyenista (1930–1943)." *Estudios Interdisciplinarios de América Latina y el Caribe* 1, no. 2 (July–December, 1990). http://www.tau.ac.il/eial/I_2/rodgers.htm.

Buchrucker, Cristián. *Nacionalismo y peronismo: La Argentina en la crisis ideológica del mundo (1927–1955)*. Buenos Aires: Editorial Sudamericana, 1987.

Calhoun, Craig. *Nations Matter: Culture, History, and the Cosmopolitan Dream*. London: Routledge, 2007.

Callil, Carmen. "Action Man." *New Statesman*, April 9, 2001.

Calvo, Pablo. "Una duda histórica: no se sabe cuántos son los desaparecidos." *Clarín*, October 5, 2003. http://edant.clarin.com/diario/2003/10/06/p-00801.htm.

Canclini, Néstor García. *Imagined Globalization*. Durham, NC: Duke University Press, 2014.

Canelo, Paula. "Las 'dos almas' del Proceso; nacionalistas y liberales durante la última dictadura military argentina (1976–1981)." *Páginas: Revista Digital de la Escuela de Historia* 1, no. 1 (2008): 69–85.

Capoccia, Giovanni, and R. Daniel Kelemen. "The Study of Critical Junctures: Theory, Narrative, and Counterfactuals in Historical Institutionalism." *World Politics* 59, no. 3 (April 2007): 341–69.

Cárdenas, Eduardo José, and Carlos Manuel Payá. *El primer nacionalismo argentino en Manuel Gálvez y Ricardo Rojas.* Buenos Aires: A. Peña Lillo, 1978.

Cattaruzza, Alejandro, and Fernando D. Rodríguez. Preface to *El hombre que está solo y espera: una biblia porteña,* by Raúl Scalabrini Ortiz. Buenos Aires: Editorial Biblos, 2005.

Chamosa, Oscar. "Criollo and Peronist: The Argentine Folklore Movement during the First Peronism, 1943–1955." In *The New Cultural History of Peronism: Power and Identity in Mid-twentieth-Century Argentina,* edited by Matthew Karush and Oscar Chamosa, 114–42. Durham, NC: Duke University Press, 2010.

———. "People as Landscape: The Presentation of the C*riollo* Interior in Early Tourist Literature in Argentina, 1920–1930." In *Rethinking Race in Modern Argentina,* edited by Paulina Alberto and Eduardo Elena, 53–72. New York: Cambridge University Press, 2016.

Chasteen, John, and Sarah Chambers, eds. *Beyond Imagined Communities: Reading and Writing the Nation in Nineteenth-Century Latin America.* Baltimore: Johns Hopkins University Press, 2003.

Chiaramonte, José Carlos, ed. *Ciudades, provincias, estados: orígenes de la Nación Argentina, 1800–1846.* Argentina: Compañia Editora Espasa Calpe Argentina/Ariel, 1997.

———. "Formas de identidad en la región de la Plata luego de 1810." *Boletín del Instituto de Historia Argentina y Americana "Dr. E. Ravignani,"* 3rd ser., sem. 1, no. 1 (1989): 71–92.

Christian, Shirley. "Argentine Army, after Half-Century as the Power, Finds Itself under Siege." *New York Times,* June 7, 1987. www.nytimes.com /1987/06/07/world/argentine-army-after-half-century-as-the-power -finds-itself-under-siege.html?pagewanted=all&src=pm.

Ciria, Alberto. "Elite Culture and Popular Culture in Argentina, 1930–1955," *Interamerican Review of Bibliography* 37, no. 4 (1987): 501–16 .

Conforti, Yitzhak. "Between Ethnic and Civic: The Realistic Utopia of Zionism." *Israel Affairs* 17, no. 4 (2011): 563–82. https://doi.org/10.1080/135371 21.2011.603521.

Cornblit, Oscár, Ezequiel Gallo, and Alfredo O'Connell. "La generación del 80 y su proyecto: antecedentes y consequencias." In *Argentina, sociedad de masas,* edited by Torcuato S. Di Tella, Gino Germani, and Jorge Graciarena, 18–58. Buenos Aires: Editorial Universitaria de Buenos Aires, 1966.

Cortés Conde, Roberto. "The Growth of the Argentine Economy, c. 1870–1914." In *Argentina since Independence,* edited by Leslie Bethell, 47–77. Cambridge: Cambridge University Press, 1993.

Cucchetti, Humberto. "¿Derechas peronistas? Organizaciones militantes entre nacionalismo, cruzada anti-Montoneros y profesionalización política." *Nuevo Mundo/Mundos Nuevos* (June 1, 2013). http://journals.openedition.org/nuevomundo/65363.

Cuestas, Raúl. *Montoneros y el pensamiento nacional, popular y revolucionario: 1810–1982.* Neuquén, Argentina: Editorial de la Universidad Nacional del Comahue, 2011.

David, Paul. "Clio and the Economics of QWERTY." *American Economic Review* 75, no. 2 (1985): 332–37. www.jstor.org/stable/1805621.

Dealy, Glen Caudill. *The Public Man: An Interpretation of Latin American and Other Catholic Countries.* Amherst: University of Massachusetts Press, 1977.

De la Fuente, Ariel. *Children of Facundo: Caudillo and Gaucho Insurgency during the Argentine State-Formation Process (La Rioja, 1853–1870).* Durham, NC: Duke University Press, 2000.

DeLaney, Jeane. "Imagining *El Ser Argentino*: Cultural Nationalism and Romantic Concepts of Nationhood in Early Twentieth-Century Argentina." *Journal of Latin American Studies* 34, no. 3 (2002): 625–58. www.jstor.org/stable/3875463?seq=1#page_scan_tab_contents.

De Riz, Liliana. *Historia argentina: la política en suspenso; 1966/1976.* Buenos Aires: Paidós, 2000.

Deutsch, Sandra McGee. "The Argentine Right and the Jews, 1919–1933." *Journal of Latin American Studies* 18, no. 1 (1986): 113–34.

———. *Counterrevolution in Argentina, 1900–1932: The Argentine Patriotic League.* Lincoln: University of Nebraska Press, 1986.

———. "Insecure Whiteness: Jews between Civilization and Barbarism, 1880–1940s." In *Rethinking Race in Modern Argentina*, edited by Paulina Alberto and Eduardo Elena, 25–52. New York: Cambridge University Press, 2016.

———. *Las Derechas: The Extreme Right in Argentina, Brazil, and Chile, 1890–1939.* Stanford, CA: Stanford University Press. 1999.

Deutsch, Sandra McGee, and Ronald H. Dolkart. *The Argentine Right: Its History and Intellectual Origins, 1910 to the Present.* Wilmington, DE: Scholarly Resources, 1993.

Devoto, Fernando J. *Nacionalismo, fascismo y tradicionalismo en la Argentina moderna: Una historia.* Buenos Aires: Siglo Veintiuno de Argentina, 2002.

———. "Reflexiones en torno de la izquierda nacional y la historiografía argentina." In *La historiografía académica y la historiografía militante en Argentina y Uruguay*, edited by Fernando Devoto and Nora Pagano, 102–31. Buenos Aires: Editorial Biblos, 2004.

Di Tella, Torcuato. "El impacto inmigratorio sobre el sistema político argentino." *Estudios Migratorios Latinoamericanos* 4, no. 2 (August 1989).

Doyle, Don, and Marco Antonio Pamplona. "Americanizing the Conversation on Nationalism." In *Nationalism in the New World*, edited by Don Doyle and Marco Antonio Pamplona, 1–15. Athens: University of Georgia Press, 2006.

Dürnhöfer, Eduardo. "Trascendencia de la filosofía de la revolución francesa en la Revolución de Mayo." In *Imagen y recepción de la revolución francesa en la Argentina*, edited by Noemí Goldman, 69–99. Buenos Aires: Grupo Ed. Latinoamericano, 1990.

Ehrlich, Laura. "Los espacios de sociabilidad en la estructuración de la Juventud Peronista post '55 en la ciudad de Buenos Aires." *Apuntes de Investigación del CECYP*, yr. 16, no. 21 (2012): 157–75. https://unq.academia.edu /LauraEhrlich.

———. "Nacionalismo y arquetipo heróico en la juventud peronista a comienzos de la década del '60." *Anuario* IEHS 28 (2013): 37–57.

Elena, Eduardo. "Argentina in Black and White: Race, Peronism, and the Color of Politics, 1940s to the Present." In *Rethinking Race in Modern Argentina*, edited by Paulina Alberto and Eduardo Elena, 184–209. New York: Cambridge University Press, 2016.

———. "Nation, Race and Latin Americanism in Argentina: The Life and Times of Manuel Ugarte, 1900s–1960s." In *Making Citizens in Argentina*, edited by Benjamin Bryce and David Sheinin, 62–82. Pittsburgh: University of Pittsburgh Press, 2017.

———. "Peronism in 'Good Taste': Culture and Consumption in the Magazine *Argentina*." In *The New Cultural History of Peronism: Power and Identity in Mid-twentieth-Century Argentina*, edited by Matthew Karush and Oscar Chamosa, 209–37. Durham, NC: Duke University Press, 2010.

Escudé, Carlos. *El fracaso del proyecto argentino: educación e ideología*. Buenos Aires: Instituto Torcuato Di Tella, 1990.

Falcoff, Mark. "Argentina." In *The Spanish Civil War, 1936–39: Hemispheric Perspectives*, edited by Mark Falcoff and Frederick Pike, 291–347. Lincoln: University of Nebraska Press, 1982.

———. "Argentine Nationalism on the Eve of Perón: The Force of Radical Orientation of Young Argentina and Its Rivals, 1935–45." PhD diss., Princeton University, 1970.

———. "Raúl Scalabrini Ortiz: The Making of an Argentine Nationalist." *Hispanic American Historical Review* 52, no. 1 (February, 1972): 74–101.

———. "The Timerman Case." *Commentary*, July 1981, 15–28.

Faulk, Karen Ann. *In the Wake of Neoliberalism: Citizenship and Human Rights in Argentina*. Stanford, CA: Stanford University Press, 2013.

Feitlowitz, Marguerite. *A Lexicon of Terror: Argentina and the Legacies of Torture*. New York: Oxford University Press, 1998.

Finchelstein, Federico. *Fascismo, litugia e imaginario. El mito del general Uriburu y la Argentina nacionalista*. Buenos Aires: Fondo de Cultura Económica, 2002.

———. *The Ideological Origins of the Dirty War: Fascism, Populism, and Dictatorship in Twentieth Century Argentina*. New York: Oxford University Press, 2014.

———. *Transatlantic Fascism: Ideology, Violence, and the Sacred in Argentina and Italy, 1919–1945*. Durham, NC: Duke University Press, 2010.

Floria, Carlos. "El clima ideológico de la querella escolar." In *La Argentina del ochenta al centenario*, edited by Gustavo Ferrari and Ezequiel Gallo, 851–69. Buenos Aires: Editorial Sudamericana, 1980.

Fox, Inman. *La invención de España: nacionalismo liberal e identidad nacional*. Madrid: Cátedra, 1997.

Frontalini, David, and María Cristina Caiati. *El mito de la "Guerra Sucia."* Buenos Aires: Ed. CELS, 1984.

Galante, Miguel Alberto. "La construcción de políticas migratorias en tiempos de transición y consolidación del primer peronismo: del nacionalismo racista a la planificación económico-social y la promoción de la inmigración." *Ciclos en la Historia, la Economía y la Sociedad* 15, no. 30 (2005): 247–72. http://bibliotecadigital.econ.uba.ar/download/ciclos/ciclos_v15 _n30_09.pdf.

Galasso, Norberto. *Jauretche y su época*. Buenos Aires: Peña Lillo Editor, 1985.

———. *Testimonio del precursor de FORJA: Manuel Ortiz Pereira*. Buenos Aires: Centro Editor de América Latina, 1981.

Gallo, Ezequiel. "Society and Politics, 1880–1916." In *Argentina since Independence*, edited by Leslie Bethell, 79–112. Cambridge: Cambridge University Press, 1993.

Galván, María Valeria. "El nacionalismo de derecha ante la cuestión peronista: la perspectiva del grupo Azul y Blanco/2nd República (1956–63)." *Prohistoria*, no. 18 (2013). www.academia.edu/7243185/El_nacionalismo_de _derecha_ante_la_cuesti%C3%B3n_peronista_laperspectiva_del_grupo _Azul_y_Blanco_2da_Rep%C3%BAblica_1956-1963.

———. "Los hombres del imaginario nacionalista: representaciones de la masculinidad en publicaciones periódicas nacionalistas de derecha argentinas durante la larga década del sesenta (1959–1969)." *História* (São Paulo) 31, no. 2 (July–December 2012): 277–309. www.scielo.br/pdf/his/v31n2/13.pdf.

———. "Militancia nacionalista en la era posperonista: las organizaciones Tacuara y sus vínculos con el peronismo." *Nuevo Mundo Mundos Nuevos* (May 24, 2013). http://journals.openedition.org/nuevomundo/65364 ;DOI: 10.4000/nuevomundo.65364.

Gandolfo, Romolo. "Inmigrantes y política en Argentina: La Revolución de 1890 y la campaña en favor de la naturalización automática de residentes extranjeras." *Estudios Migratorios Latinoamericanos* 6, no. 17 (1991): 23–55.

Genta, Jordán Bruno. *Guerra contrarevolucionaria.* Buenos Aires: Editorial Nuevo Orden, 1963.

Gerlo, Martín. "Marxismo y cuestión nacional: aportes de Hernández Arregui al pensamiento de izquierda." *Jornadas de Sociología* 11 (2015). https://www .academia.edu/37676459/Marxismo_y_cuesti%C3%B3n_nacional _aportes_de_Hern%C3%A1ndez_Arregui_al_pensamiento_de _izquierda.

Gerrassi, Marysa Navarro. *Los nacionalistas.* Buenos Aires: J. Alvarez, 1968.

Gerstle, Gary. *American Crucible: Race and Nation in the Twentieth Century.* Princeton, NJ: Princeton University Press, 2001.

Giacobone, Carlos Alberto, and Gallo Edit Rosalía. *Radicalismo bonaerense: la ingeniería política de Hipólito Yrigoyen, 1891–1931.* Buenos Aires: Corregidor, 1999.

Gil Cremades, Juan José. *Krausistas y liberales.* Madrid: Seminarios y Ediciones Castilla, S. A., 1975.

Gillespie, Richard. *Soldiers of Perón: Argentina's Montoneros.* Oxford: Clarendon Press, 1982.

Glauert, Earl T. "Ricardo Rojas and the Emergence of Argentine Cultural Nationalism." *Hispanic American Historical Review* 43, no. 3 (August 1963): 1–13.

Gobat, Michel. "The Invention of Latin America: A Transnational History of Anti-Imperialism, Democracy and Race." *American Historical Review* 118, no. 5 (December 2013): 1345–75.

Goebel, Michael. *Argentina's Partisan Past: Nationalism and the Politics of History.* Liverpool Latin American Studies. New ser. 11. Liverpool: Liverpool University Press, 2011.

———. "La prensa peronista como medio de difusión del revisionismo historico bajo la Revolucion Libertadora." *Prohistoria* yr. 8, no. 8 (Spring 2004): 251–65.

———. "A Movement from Right to Left in Argentine Nationalism? The Alianza Libertadora Nacionalista and Tacuara as Stages of Militancy." *Bulletin of Latin American Research* 26, no. 3 (2007): 356–77.

———. "Some Historical Observations on the Relationship between Nationalism and Political Violence in Argentina." In *Political Violence and the Construction of National Identity in Latin America*, edited by Will Fowler and Peter Lambert, 207–25. New York: Palgrave Macmillan, 2006.

Goldwert, Marvin. "The Rise of Modern Militarism in Argentina." *Hispanic American Historical Review* 48, no. 2 (May 1968): 189–205.

Gómez Molleda, Dolores. *Los reformadores de la españa contemporanea*. Madrid: C.S.I.C., 1966.

González Calleja, Eduardo. "El hispanismo autoritario español y el movimiento nacionalista argentino: balance de medio siglo de relaciones políticas e intelectuales (1898–1946)." *Hispania* (May–August 2007): 599–642.

Gramuglio, María Teresa, and Beatriz Sarlo. "José Hernández." In *Historia de la literatura argentina*. Vol. 2. Buenos Aires: Centro Editor de América Latina, 1980, 1–23.

Greenfeld, Liah. *Nationalism: Five Roads to Modernity*. Cambridge, MA: Harvard University Press, 1992.

Gutman, Daniel. *Tacuara: historia de la primera guerrilla urbana argentina*. Buenos Aires: Sudamérica. Digital Edition.

Hale, Charles. "Political and Social Ideas in Latin America, 1870–1930." In *The Cambridge History of Latin America*, edited by Leslie Bethell, 367–442. Vol. 4. New York: Cambridge University Press, 1986.

———. *The Transformation of Liberalism in Late Nineteenth-Century Mexico*. Princeton, NJ: Princeton University Press, 1989.

Halperin Donghi, Tulio. "Argentina: Liberalism in a Country Born Liberal." In *Guiding the Invisible Hand: Economic Liberalism and the State in Latin American History*, edited by Joseph Love and Nils Jacobsen, 99–116. New York: Praeger, 1988.

———. "Argentina's Unmastered Past." *Latin American Research Review* 23, no. 2 (1988): 3–24.

———. "Argentine Counterpoint: Rise of the Nation, Rise of the State." In *Beyond Imagined Communities: Reading and Writing the Nation in Nineteenth-Century Latin America*, edited by Sara Castro-Klarén and John Charles Chasteen, 33–52. Washington, DC: Woodrow Wilson Center Press, 2003.

———. *El revisionismo histórico argentino*. Colección mínima 38. Buenos Aires: Siglo Veintiuno Editores, 1971.

———. *El revisionismo histórico argentino como visión decadentista de la historia nacional*. Buenos Aires: Siglo XXI, 2005.

———. *La Argentina en la tormenta del mundo: ideas y ideologías entre 1930 y 1945*. Buenos Aires: Siglo Veintiuno Editores Argentina, 2003.

———. *La república imposible*. Buenos Aires: Ariel, 2004.

———. "¿Para que la inmigración? Ideología y política inmigratoria y aceleración del proceso modernizador: el caso argentino (1810–1914)." *Jahrbuch für Geschichte von Staat, Wirtschaft und Gesellschaft Lateinamerikas* 13, no. 1 (1976): 437–89.

————. *Politics, Economics and Society in Argentina in the Revolutionary Period.* Translated by Richard Southern. Cambridge: Cambridge University Press, 1975.

————. *Tradición política española e ideología revolucionaria de Mayo.* Buenos Aires: Centro Editor de América Latina, 1985.

————. "Un término de comparación: liberalismo y nacionalismo en el Río de la Plata." In *Los intelectuales y el poder en México. Intellectuals and power in Mexico: memorias de la VI Conferencia de Historiadores Mexicanos y Estadounidenses; Papers Presented at the VI Conference of Mexican and United States Historians,* edited by Roderic Ai Camp, Charles Adams Hale, and Josefina Zoraida Vázquez, 103–20. México: El Colegio de México, 1991.

————. *Vida y muerte de la República verdadera (1910–1930).* Vol. 4 of *Biblioteca del pensamiento argentino.* Buenos Aires: Ariel, 2000.

Hanson, Allan. "The Making of the Maori: Cultural Invention and Its Logic." *American Anthropologist* 91, no. 4 (1989): 890–902.

Hersfeld, Michael. "Essentialism." In *The Routledge Encyclopedia of Social and Cultural Anthropology,* edited by Alan Bernard and Jonathan Spencer, 288–90. London: Routledge, 2010.

Hilb, Claudia, and Daniel Lutzky. *La nueva izquierda Argentina, 1960–1980: política y violencia.* Buenos Aires: Centro Editor de América Latina, 1984.

————. "Nueva izquierda, política, democracia." In *La nueva izquierda argentina, 1960–1980: política y violencia,* 29–38. Buenos Aires: Centro Editor de América Latina, 1984.

Hobsbawm, Eric. "Nationalism and Nationality in Latin America." In *Pour une histoire economicque et social internationale: mélanges offerts à Paul Bairoch,* edited by Bouda Etemad, Jean Baton, and Thomas David, 313–26. Geneva: Editions Passé Présent, 1995.

————. *Nations and Nationalism since 1780: Programme, Myth, Reality.* The Wiles Lectures. Cambridge: Cambridge University Press, 1990.

Hodges, Donald. *Argentina, 1943–1987.* Albuquerque: University of New Mexico Press, 1988.

————. *Argentina's "Dirty War": An Intellectual Biography.* Austin: University of Texas Press, 1991.

Iturrieta, Aníbal. "El primer nacionalismo argentino." In *El pensamiento político argentino contemporáneo,* edited by A. Iturrieta, 17–43. Buenos Aires: Grupo Editor Latinoamericano, 1994.

James, Daniel. "October 17th and 18th, 1945: Mass Protest, Peronism and the Argentine Working Class." *Journal of Social History* 21, no. 3 (Spring 1988): 441–60.

————. *Resistance and Integration: Peronism and the Working Class, 1946–1976.* New York: Cambridge University Press, 1988.

Jaramilla, Ana. Prologue to *Forjando una nación: Scalabrini Ortiz y Jauretche en la revista Qué sucedió en siete días*, by Raúl Scalabrini Ortiz and Arturo Jauretche, 11–21. Buenos Aires: Ediciones de la Universidad Nacional de Lanús, 2007.

Jaskulowski, Krzysztof. "Western (Civic) 'versus' Eastern (Ethnic) Nationalism: The Origins and Critique of the Dichotomy." *Polish Sociological Review*, no. 171 (2010): 289–303. www.jstor.org/stable/41275158.

Jongh Rossel, Elena M. de. *El krausismo y la generación de 1898*. Valencia: Albatros Hispanófila, 1985.

Karush, Matthew. "Workers, Citizens and the Argentine Nation: Party Politics and the Working Class in Rosario, 1912–3." *Journal of Latin American Studies* 31, no. 3 (October 1999): 589–616.

Klein, Marcus. "The Legión Cívica and the Radicalization of Argentine Nacionalismo during the Década Infame." *Estudios Interdisciplinarios de América Latina y el Caribe* 13, no. 2 (July–December 2002). www7.tau.ac .il/ojs/index.php/eial/article/view/875/977.

Kohn, Hans. *The Idea of Nationalism: A Study in Its Origins and Background*. New York: Macmillan, 1944.

Koopmans, Ruud, and Paul Statham. "Ethnic and Civic Conceptions of Nationhood and the Differential Success of the Extreme Right in Germany and Italy." In *How Social Movements Matter: Social Movements, Protest and Contention*, edited by Giugni Marco, Doug McAdam, and Charles Tilly, 225–52. Minneapolis: University of Minnesota Press, 1999.

Korol, Juan Carlos, and Hilda Sábato. "Incomplete Industrialization: An Argentine Obsession." *Latin American Research Review* 25, no. 1 (1990): 7–30.

Ladeuix, Juan. "El General frente a la Sinarquía: el discurso de Carlos Disandro in la formación de la Concentración Nacionalista Universitaria y su impacto en el peronismo. XI Jornadas Interescuelas/Departamentos de Historia, Universidad de Tucumán, 2007, 1–21. www.aacademica.org/000 -108/581.

Lafleur, Hector René, Sergio D. Provenzano, and Fernando Alonso. *Las revistas literarias argentinas, 1893–1967*. Buenos Aires: Centro Editor de América Latina, 1968.

Laguado Duca, Arturo Claudio. "Onganía y el nacionalismo military en Argentina." *Universitas Humanistica* (Bogotá), no. 62 (July–December 2006): 239–59.

Lambert, Peter. "Myth, Manipulation, and Violence: Relationships between National Identity and Political Violence." In *Political Violence and the Construction of National Identity in Latin America*, edited by Peter Lambert and Will Fowler, 19–35. New York: Palgrave Macmillan, 2006.

Landi, Oscár. *Reconstrucciones: las nuevas formas de la cultura política.* Buenos Aires: Punto Sur, 1988.

Lanusse, Lucas. *Montoneros: el mito de sus 12 fundadores.* Buenos Aires: Zeta, 2010.

Lecours, André. "Ethnic and Civic Nationalism: Towards a New Dimension." *Space and Polity* 4, no. 2 (2000): 153–65.

Lepsius, M. Rainer. "The Nation and Nationalism in Germany." *Social Research* 52, no. 1 (Summer 1985): 43–64.

Lewis, Paul. *Guerrillas and Generals: The "Dirty War" in Argentina.* Westport, CT: Praeger, 2002.

———. "The Right and Military Rule, 1955–1983." In *The Argentine Right: Its History and Intellectual Origins, 1910 to the Present,* edited by Sandra McGee Deutsch and Ronald H. Dolkart, 147–80. Wilmington, DE: Scholarly Resources, 1993.

Lobato, Mirta. "Historia de las instituciones laborales en Argentina: una asignatura pendiente," *Revista de Trabajo* 3, no. 4 (January–November 2007): 145–54.

López-Morillas, Juan. *The Krausist Movement and Ideological Change in Spain, 1854–74.* New York: Cambridge University Press, 1981.

Lugones, Leopoldo. *El payador y antología de poesía y prosa.* Caracas: Biblioteca Ayacucho, 1979.

Luna, Felix. *Yrigoyen.* Buenos Aires: Editorial Sudamericana, 2005.

Lutzky, Daniel. "Una visión de la sociedad." In *La nueva izquierda argentina, 1960–1980: Política y violencia,* edited by Claudia Hilb and Daniel Lutzky, 39–45. Buenos Aires: Centro Editor de América Latina, 1984.

Lvovich, Daniel. *Nacionalismo y antisemitismo en la Argentina.* Buenos Aires: Javier Vergara, Grupo Zeta, 2003.

Lynch, John. *Argentine Dictator: Juan Manuel De Rosas, 1829–1852.* Oxford: Clarendon Press, 1981.

Mahoney, James. "Path Dependence in Historical Sociology." *Theory and Society* 29, no. 4 (August 2000): 507–48.

Mainer, José Carlos. "Tres lecturas de los clásicos españoles (Unamuno, Azorín y Machado)." *Mélanges de la Casa de Velázquez* 31–32 (1995): 171–92. www .persee.fr/web/revues/home/prescript/article/casa_0076-230x_1995 _num_31_2_2743.

Mallimaci, Fortunato, Humberto Cucchetti, and Luis Donatello. "Caminos sinuosos: nacionalismo y catolicismo en la Argentina contemporánea." In *El altar y el trono. Ensayos sobre el catolicismo político latinoamericano,* edited by Francisco Colom and Angel Rivero, 155–90. Barcelona, Antrophos /Unibiblos, 2006.

Martyn, David. "Borrowed Fatherland: Nationalism and Language Purism in Fichte's Addresses to the German Nation." *Germanic Review* 72, no. 4 (1997): 303–15.

McGuinness, Aims. "Searching for 'Latin America': Race and Sovereignty in the Americas in the 1850s." In *Race and Nation in Modern Latin America*, edited by Nancy Appelbaum, Anne S. Macpherson, and Karin Alejandra Rosemblatt, 87–107. Chapel Hill: University of North Carolina Press, 2003.

Mejía, Sergio. "Las historias de Bartolomé Mitre: operación nacionalista al gusto de los argentinos." *Historia Crítica*, no. 33 (January–June 2007): 98–121.

Melón, Julio Cesár. "La resistencia peronista, alcances y significados." *Anuario del IEHS* (Tandil) 8 (1993): 215–46. http://anuarioiehs.unicen.edu.ar/Files /1993/011%20-%20La%20resistencia%20peronista,%20alcances%20y%20 significados..pdf.

Merele, Hernán. "'El germen genera sus propios anticuerpos': la 'depuración' interna peronista y el proceso represivo entre 1973–1976." *Anuario*, no. 29 (2017): 161–81. www.anuariodehistoria.unr.edu.ar/ojs/index.php/Anuario /issue/view/14.

Milanesio, Natalia. "Peronistas and *Cabecitas*: Stereotypes and Anxieties at the Peak of Social Change." In *The New Cultural History of Peronism: Power and Identity in Mid-twentieth-Century Argentina*, edited by Matthew Karush and Oscar Chamosa, 53–84. Durham, NC: Duke University Press, 2010.

Miller, Nicola. *In the Shadow of the State: Intellectuals and the Quest for National Identity in Twentieth-Century Spanish America.* London: Verso, 1999.

Mitre, Jorge Carlos. "La inmigración en la Argentina y la identidad nacional." *Historia* 7, no. 26 (June–August 1987): 43–58.

Morales-Saravia, José. "El discurso argentinista en los años treinta: Scalabrini Ortiz, Martínez Estrada, Mallea." PhD diss., Free University of Berlin, 1986.

Moyano, María José. *Argentina's Lost Patrol: Armed Struggle, 1969–1979.* New Haven, CT: Yale University Press, 1995.

———. "The Dirty War in Argentina: Was It a War and How Dirty Was It?" In *Staatliche und parastaatliche Gewalt in Lateinamerika*, edited by Hans Werner Tobler and Peter Waldmann, 45–73. Frankfurt: Vervuert Verlag, 1991.

Myers, Jorge. "Language, History and Politics in Argentine Identity, 1840–1880." In *Nationalism in the New World*, edited by Don Doyle and Marco Antonio Pamplona, 117–42. Athens: University of Georgia Press, 2006.

———. "La revolución en las ideas: la generación romántica de 1837 en la cultura y en la política argentinas." In *Revolución, república, confederación (1806–1853)*, edited by Noemí Goldman, 382–443. Buenos Aires: Editorial Sudamericana, 1998.

———. *Orden y virtud: el discurso republicano en el régimen rosista.* Buenos Aires: Universidad Nacional de Quilmes, 1995.

———. "Representations of the Nation: Language, History and Politics in the Elaboration of an Argentine Identity." Paper presented at the Conference on Nationalism in the New World, Vanderbilt University, Nashville, TN, October 2003.

Nállim, Jorge. *Transformations and Crisis of Liberalism in Argentina, 1930–1955.* Pitt Latin American Series. Pittsburgh: University of Pittsburgh Press, 2012.

Nascimbene, Mario, and Mauricio Isaac Neuman. "El nacionalismo católico, el fascismo y la inmigración en la Argentina (1927–1943): una aproximación teórica." *Estudios Interdisciplinarios de América Latina y el Caribe* 4, no. 1 (January–June 1993). www7.tau.ac.il/ojs/index.php/eial/article/view/1251/1279.

Neiberg, Federico. "Ciencias sociales y mitologías nacionales: la constitución de la sociología en la Argentina y la invención del peronismo." *Desarrollo Económico* 34, no. 136 (January–March 1995): 533–56.

Newton, Ronald. *The 'Nazi Menace' in Argentina, 1931–47.* Stanford, CA: Stanford University Press, 1992.

Osiel, Mark. "Constructing Subversion in Argentina's Dirty War." *Representations*, no. 75 (Summer 2001): 129–30.

Padoan, Marcelo. *Jesús, el templo y los viles mercaderes: un examen de la discursividad yrigoyenista*; Colección "la Ideología Argentina." Bernal, Buenos Aires: Universidad Nacional de Quilmes Ediciones, 2002.

Padrón, Juan Manuel. *¡Ni yanquis, ni marxistas! nacionalistas: nacionalismo, militancia y violencia política: el caso del Movimiento Nacionalista Tacuara en la Argentina, 1955–1966.* La Plata, Argentina: Editorial de la Universidad Nacional de General Sarmiento, 2017. Libro Digital, PDF. https://archive.org/details/NacionalismoMilitanciaYViolenciaPoltica.

Palti, Elías José. El momento romántico: nación, historia y lenguajes políticos en la argentina del siglo XIX. Buenos Aires: Eudeba, 2009.

———. "Historicism as an *Idea* and as a *Language*." *History and Theory* 44 (October 2005): 431–40.

Pedroso, Manuel. "En el cincuentinario de la Institución Libre de Enseñanza." *Boletín de la Institución Libre de Enseñanza* 51, no. 802 (January 31, 1927): 27–30. http://prensahistorica.mcu.es/es/publicaciones/numeros_por_mes.cmd?anyo=1927&idPublicacion=1000225.

Perosio, Graciela, and Nannina Rivarola. "Ricardo Rojas: primer profesor de literature argentina." In *Historia de la literatura argentina*. Vol. 3, *Las primeras décadas del siglo*, 217–40. Buenos Aires: Centro Ed. de América Latina, 1981.

Persello, Ana Virginia. *El partido radical: gobierno y oposición, 1916–1943*. Buenos Aires: Siglo Veintiuno Editores Argentina, 2004.

Pike, Frederick. *Hispanismo, 1898–1936: Spanish Conservatives and Liberals and Their Relations with Spanish America*. Notre Dame, IN: University of Notre Dame Press, 1971.

Piñeiro, Elena. *La tradición nacionalista ante el peronismo: itinerario de una esperanza a una desilusión*. Buenos Aires: A-Z Editora, 1997.

Pion-Berlin, David. "The National Security Doctrine, Military Threat Perception, and the 'Dirty War' in Argentina." *Comparative Political Studies* 21, no. 3 (October 1988): 382–407.

Plotkin, Mariano Ben. "La 'ideología' de Perón: continuidades y rupturas." In *Perón del exilio al poder*, edited by Samuel Amaral and Mariano Ben Plotkin. Buenos Aires: Cántaro, 1993.

———. *Mañana es San Perón: A Cultural History of Peron's Argentina*. Wilmington, DE: Scholarly Resources, 2002.

Ponza, Pablo. "Los intelectuales críticos y la transformación social en Argentina (1955–1973): Historia intelectual, discursos políticos y conceptualizaciones de la violencia en la Argentina de los años sesenta-setenta." PhD diss., Universidad de Barcelona, 2007. www.tdx.cat/bitstream/handle /10803/710/PP_TESIS.pdf?sequence=1.

Potash, Robert. *The Army & Politics in Argentina*. Vol. 1, *1928–1945: Yrigoyen to Perón*. Stanford, CA: Stanford University Press, 1969.

Pozzoni, Mariana. "La Tendencia Revolucionaria del peronismo en la apertura política, Provincia de Buenos Aires, 1971–1974." *Estudios Sociales*, 1st sem. (2009): 173–202.

Quattrocchi-Woisson, Diana. *Los males de la memoria: historia y política en la Argentina*. 2nd ed. Buenos Aires: Emecé Editores, 1998.

Quijada, Mónica. "¿'Hijos de los barcos' o diversidad invisibilizada? La articulación de la población indígena en la construcción nacional argentina (siglo XIX)." *HMex* 53, no. 2 (2003): 469–510.

———. "Imaginando la homogeneidad: la alquimía de la tierra." In *Homogeneidad y nación: con un estudio de caso: Argentina, siglos XIX y XX*, edited by Mónica Quijada, Carmen Bertrand, and Arnd Schneider, 179–217. Madrid: CSIC, 2000.

———. "Latinos y anglosajones: el 98 en el fin de siglo sudamericano." *Hispania: Revista Española de Historia* 57, no. 2 (1997): 589–609.

————. *Manuel Gálvez: 60 años de pensamiento nacionalista.* Buenos Aires: Centro Editor de America Latina, 1985.

Ramsden, H. *The 1898 Movement in Spain: Towards a Reinterpretation with Special Reference to En Torno Al Casticismo and Idearium Español.* Manchester, UK: Manchester University Press, 1974.

————. "The Spanish 'Generation of 1898': The History of a Concept." *Bulletin of the John Rylands University Library,* issue 56 (1973–74): 463–91.

Real de Azúa, Carlos. "'Ariel,' libro porteño." In *Historia visible e historia esotérica,* 157–73. Montevideo: ARCA Editorial, 1975.

————. *Historia visible e historia esotérica: Personajes y claves del debate latinoamericano.* Montevideo: Arca, 1975.

Reato, Ceferino. *Disposición final: la confesión de Videla sobre los desaparecidos.* Buenos Aires: Editorial Sudamericana, 2012.

Recalde, Aritz. "José María Rosa, nuestro contemporáneo." Cuaderno de Trabajo no. 7 de Centro de Estudios Juan José Hernández Arregui (October 2014). http://hernandezarregui.blogspot.com/2018/05/biografias-del-pensamiento-nacional.html.

Rein, Raanan. "Entre el peronismo y el nacionalismo de extrema derecha: Jauretche, los argentinos-judios y la acusación de doble leadtad." In *Pensar a Jauretche,* edited by Gustavo Maragoni, 215–38. Buenos Aires: UNIPE, 2015.

————. "Melting the Pot? Peronism, Jewish Argentines, and the Struggle for Diversity." In *Making Citizens in Argentina,* edited by Benjamin Bryce and David M. K. Sheinin, 102–18. Pittsburgh: University of Pittsburgh Press, 2017.

Rivera, Jorge. "La forja del escritor professional (1900–1930)." In *Historia de la literatura argentina.* Vol. 3, *Las primeras décadas del siglo,* 337–84. Buenos Aires: Centro Ed. de América Latina, 1986.

Rivero de Olazábal, Raúl. *Por una cultura católica: el compromiso de una generación argentina.* Buenos Aires: Editorial Claretiana, 1986.

Robben, Antonius C. G. M. "Combat Motivation, Fear and Terror in Twentieth-Century Argentinian Warfare." *Journal of Contemporary History* 41, no. 2 (April 2006): 357–77.

Rock, David. "Antecedents of the Argentine Right." In *The Argentine Right: Its History and Intellectual Origins, 1910 to the Present,* edited by Sandra McGee Deutsch and Ronald Dolkart, 1–34. Wilmington, DE: Scholarly Resources, 1993.

————. *Argentina, 1516–1982: From Spanish Colonization to the Falklands War.* Berkeley: University of California Press, 1985.

————. *Authoritarian Argentina: The Nationalist Movement, Its History, and Its Impact.* Berkeley: University of California Press, 1993.

———. "Intellectual Precursors of Conservative Nationalism in Argentina." *Hispanic American Historical Review* 67, no. 2 (1987): 271–300.

———. *Politics in Argentina, 1890–1930: The Rise and Fall of Radicalism.* Cambridge: Cambridge University Press, 1975.

Rodríguez, Carlos J. *Irigoyen; su revolución política y social: la Unión Cívica Radical.* Buenos Aires: Librería y editorial "La Facultad," Bernabé y cía, 1943.

Roig, Arturo Andrés. *Los krausistas argentinos.* Puebla: José M. Cajica Jr, 1969.

Romero, José Luis. "Las ideologias de la cultura nacional." In *La ideologías de la cultura nacional y otros ensayos,* 75–85. Buenos Aires: Centro Editor de América Latina, 1982.

Romero, Luis Alberto. "Apogeo y crisis de la Argentina vital." *Revista de las Américas,* no. 1 (Spring 2003): 85–109.

Rostica, Julieta. "Apuntes 'Triple A': Argentina 1973–76." *Desafíos* 23, no. 2 (December 2011): 21–51.

Sábato, Hilda. "Citizenship, Political Participation and the Formation of the Public Sphere in Buenos Aires, 1850s–1880s." *Past and Present,* no. 136 (August 1992): 139–63.

———. "Pluralismo y nación." *Punto de Vista* 7, no. 34 (July–September, 1989): 2–5.

Saito, Hiro. "Reiterated Commemoration: Hiroshima as National Trauma." *Sociological Theory* 24, no. 4 (December 2009): 353–76.

Sarlo, Beatriz. *La pasión y la excepción.* Buenos Aires: Siglo Veintiuno Editores Argentina, 2003.

———. *Una modernidad periférica: Buenos Aires 1920 y 1930.* Buenos Aires: Nueva Visión, 1988.

Sbarra Mitre, Oscár. *F.O.R.J.A.: El destino es un camello ciego.* Buenos Aires: Quinqué Editores, 2005.

Scenna, Miguel Ángel. *F.O.R.J.A.: una aventura argentina (de Yrigoyen a Perón).* Buenos Aires: Ediciones La Bastilla, 1972.

Scirica, Elena. "Ciudad Cathólica-*Verbo*: Discurso, redes y relaciones en pos de una apuesta [contra] revolucionaria." [2006?] http://historiapolitica.com /datos/biblioteca/scirica_levant.pdf.

———. "Visión religiosa y acción política: El caso de Ciudad Católica-Verbo en la Argentina de los años sesenta," en PROHAL MONOGRÁFICO, *Revista del Programa de Historia de América Latina.* Vol. 2, Primera Sección: *Vitral Monográfico Nro. 2.* Instituto Ravignani, Facultad de Filosofía y Letras, Universidad de Buenos Aires, 2010. www.filo.uba.ar/contenidos /investigacion/institutos/ravignani/prohal/Vitral_Mono_N2/dossier /dossierhere2.html.

Scorer, James. "From *la guerra sucia* to 'A Gentleman's Fight': War, Disappearance and Nation in the 1976–1983 Argentine Dictatorship." *Bulletin of Latin American Research* 27, no. 1 (2008): 43–60.

Sebreli, Juan José. *Los deseos imaginarios del peronismo: ensayos críticos.* Buenos Aires: Editorial Legasa, 1983.

Segato, Rita Laura. "Identidades políticas/Alteridades históricas: una crítica a las certezas del pluralismo global." In *La nación y sus otros: raza, etnicidad y diversidad religiosa en tiempos de políticas de la identidad*, 37–69. Ciudad Autónoma de Buenos Aires: Prometeo Libros, 2007.

Senkman, Leonardo. "Etnicidad e inmigración durante el primer peronismo." *Estudios Interdisciplinarios de América Latina y el Caribe* 3, no. 2 (June 1, 1992). http://eial.tau.ac.il/index.php/eial/article/view/1258.

———. "Nacionalismo e inmigración: La cuestión étnica en las elites liberales e intelectuales Argentinas: 1919–1940." *Estudios Interdisciplinarios de America Latin y el Caribe* 1, no.1 (January–June 1990). www.tau.ac.il/eial /I_1/Senkman.htm.

———. "The Right and Civilian Regimes." In *The Argentine Right: Its History and Intellectual Origins, 1910 to the Present*, edited by Sandra McGee Deutsch and Ronald Dolkart, 119–45. Wilmington, DE: Scholarly Resources, 1993.

Shulman, Stephen. "The Contours of Civic and Ethnic National Identification in Ukraine." *Europe-Asia Studies* 56, no. 1 (2004): 35–56. www.jstor.org /stable/4147437.

Shumway, Nicolas. *The Invention of Argentina.* Berkeley: University of California Press, 1991.

Sigal, Silvia, and Eliseo Verón. *Perón o muerte: los fundamentos discursivos del fenómeno peronista.* Buenos Aires: Editorial Legasa, 1986.

Sikkink, Kathryn. "The Influence of Raúl Prebisch on Economic Policy-Making in Argentina, 1950–1962." *Latin American Research Review* 23, no. 2 (1988): 91–114.

Singer, Brian. "Cultural versus Contractual Nations: Rethinking Their Opposition." *History and Theory* 35, no. 3 (October 1996): 309–37.

Slatta, Richard. *Gauchos and the Vanishing Frontier.* Lincoln: University of Nebraska Press, 1992.

Smith, Anthony. *Nationalism and Modernism.* London: Routledge, 1998.

Spalding, Hobart. "Education in Argentina, 1890–1914: The Limits of Oligarchical Reform." *Journal of Interdisciplinary History* 3, no. 1 (Summer 1972): 31–61.

Spektorowski, Alberto. *The Origins of Argentina's Revolution of the Right* (Notre Dame, IN: University of Notre Dame Press, 2003.

Stoetzer, O. Carlos. *Karl Christian Friedrich Krause and His Influence in the Hispanic World.* Cologne: Böhlau, 1998.

Suny, Ronald Grigor, and Michael D. Kennedy. *Intellectuals and the Articulation of the Nation.* Ann Arbor: University of Michigan Press, 2001.

Surra, Roberto. *Peronismo y cultura.* Buenos Aires: Corregidor, 2003.

Sutton, Michael. *Nationalism, Positivism and Catholicism: The Politics of Charles Maurras and French Catholics, 1890–1914.* Cambridge: Cambridge University Press, 1982.

Tato, María Inés. "Alianzas estratégicas o confluencias? Conservadores y nacionalistas en la Argentina de los años treinta." *Cuadernos del CLAEH* 28, no. 91 (2005): 119–35.

———. *Viento de fronda: liberalismo, conservadurismo y democracia en la Argentina, 1911–1932.* Buenos Aires: Siglo Veintiuno Editores Argentina, 2004.

Taylor, Lucy. *Citizenship, Participation and Democracy: Changing Dynamics in Chile and Argentina.* New York: St. Martin's Press, 1998.

Tcach, Cesar. "Sabattinismo: identidad radical y oposición disruptiva." *Desarrollo Económico* 28, no. 110 (July –September 1988): 183–208.

Terán, Oscár. *Nuestros años sesentas: la formación de la nueva izquierda intelectual en la Argentina 1956–1966.* Buenos Aires: Puntosur, 1991.

———. "Rasgos de la cultura intelectual argentina, 1956–66." Working Paper 2, Latin American Studies Center, University of Maryland, College Park, 1991. www.lasc.umd.edu/publications/papers.php.

———. *Vida intelectual en el Buenos Aires fin-de-siglo (1880–1910): Derivas de la "cultura científica".* Buenos Aires: Fondo de Cultura Económica de Argentina, 2000.

Torre, Juan Carlos, and Liliana De Riz. "Argentina since 1946." In *Argentina since Independence*, edited by Leslie Bethell, 243–363. Cambridge: Cambridge University Press, 1993.

Tortti, María Cristina, Mauricio Chama, Adrián Celentano, and Horacio Robles. *La nueva izquierda argentina (1955–1976): socialismo, peronismo y revolución.* Rosario, Colombia: Colección Universidad, 2014.

Vallejos de Llobet, Patricia. "El léxico de la revolución francesa en el proceso de estandarización lingüistica del español bonarense." In *Imagen y recepción de la revolución francesa en la Argentina*, edited by Noemí Goldman, 79–99. Buenos Aires: Grupo Ed. Latinoamericano, 1990.

Van Young, Eric. "Revolution and Imagined Communities in Mexico, 1810–1821." In *Nationalism in the New World*, edited by Don Doyle and Marco Antonio Pamplona, 184–207. Athens: University of Georgia Press, 2006.

Vazeilles, José. "Positivismo, política e ideología: El caso de Carlos Octavio Bunge." *Punto de Vista*, no. 6 (June 1979): 19–27.

Vélez Suarez, Ignacio. "Montoneros, los grupos originarios." *Revista Lucha Armada*, yr. 1, no. 2 (2005): 4–25. www.cedema.org/ver.php?id=3392.

Verdury, Katherine "Whither 'Nation and Nationalism'?" *Daedalus* (Summer 1993): 37–46.

Vezzetti, Hugo. *Sobre la violencia revolucionaria: memorias y olvidos*. Buenos Aires: Siglo Veintiuno, 2009.

Vogel, Hans. "New Citizens for a New Nation: Naturalization in Early Independent Argentina." *Hispanic American Historical Review* 71, no. 1 (February 1991): 107–13.

Walter, Richard. "The Right and the Peronists, 1943–55." In *The Argentine Right: Its History and Intellectual Origins, 1910 to the Present*, edited by Sandra McGee Deutsch and Ronald H. Dolkart, 99–118. Wilmington, DE: Scholarly Resources, 1993.

Warren, Kay, and Jean E. Jackson. "Introduction to *Indigenous Movements, Self-Representation, and the State in Latin America*, edited by Kay Warren and Jean E. Jackson, 1–45. Austin: University of Texas Press. 2002.

Wiarda, Howard J. *The Soul of Latin America: The Cultural and Political Tradition*. New Haven, CT: Yale University Press, 2001.

Winston, Colin. "Between Rosas and Sarmiento: Notes on Nationalism in Peronist Thought." *Americas* 39, no. 3 (January 1983): 305–32.

Yack, Bernard. "The Myth of the Civic Nation." In *Theorizing Nationalism*, edited by Ronald Beiner, 103–18. Albany: State University of New York Press, 1999.

Yalcintas, Altug. "Historical Small Events and the Eclipse of *Utopia*: Perspectives on Path Dependence in Human Thought." *Culture, Theory, and Critique* 47, no. 1 (2006): 53–70.

Zamborain, Romina Silvia. "El derecho al nombre indígena en la legislación argentina." Unpublished manuscript. www.linguasur.com.ar/panel /archivos/92b6f44c23218cfa4615840d293b59f4PONENCIA2006.pdf.

Zanatta, Loris. *Del estado liberal a la nación católica: iglesia y ejército en los orígenes del peronismo, 1930–1943*. Buenos Aires: Universidad Nacional de Quilmes, 1996.

———. *Perón y el mito de la nación católica: Iglesia y Ejército en los orígenes del peronismo (1943–1946)*. Buenos Aires: Editorial Sudamericana, 1999.

Zimmermann, Eduardo. "Racial Ideas and Social Reform: Argentina, 1890–1916." *Hispanic American Historical Review* 72, no. 1 (February 1992): 23–46. www.jstor.org/stable/2515946?seq=1#page_scan_tab_contents.

Zubrzycki, Geneviève. "'We, the Polish Nation': Ethnic and Civic Visions of Nationhood in Post-Communist Constitutional Debates." *Theory and Society* 30, no. 5 (2001): 629–68. www.jstor.org/stable/658104.

Zuleta Álvarez, Enrique. *El nacionalismo argentino*. Vol. 1. Buenos Aires: Ediciones La Bastilla, 1975.

# INDEX

Carlés, Manuel, 59, 61, 146. *See also* Liga
    Patriótica Argentina
Carulla, Juan E., 135–37, 140–41. See
    also *La Nueva República*
Castellanos, Joaquín, 102, 107–9, 165
Catholic Church
    ideal of Catholic nation, 144–45, 149
    military connections, 144–45, 149
    and Perón, 210–11
    rise of right-wing nationalism,
        141–45
    *See also* Cursos de Cultura Católica
Chamosa, Oscar, 207, 293n14
Chávez, Fermín, 227, 239–40
Ciudad Católica, 262
Constitution of 1853, 45
    as integral to national identity, 197,
        282, 285
    and nationalist left, 167, 185–86,
        188–89, 289
    and nationalist right, 139–40, 146–47,
        217, 259, 263–64, 268
    *See also* Alberdi, Juan Bautista;
        Barcos, Julio; FORJA; *La Nueva
        República*; Lugones, Leopoldo
Cooke, John William, 228, 230
Cornejo Linares, Juan, 251–52
coup of 1930, 148–49
    and nationalist right, 141, 148, 150
    See also *La Nueva República*
coup of 1943, 193–94
    and nationalist left, 196
    and nationalist right, 193–95
    *See also* GOU; Ramírez, Pedro Pablo
coup of 1955, 211
    and nationalist left, 228–30
    and nationalist right, 215–16
coup of 1966, 264
    and nationalist right, 264–65
    *See also* Onganía, Juan Carlos
coup of 1976, 266–67
    and nationalist right, 268

*See also* Dirty War; Massera, Emilio;
    Videla, Jorge Rafael
criollismo, 120–22
*Criterio*, 143–44
*Cuaderno Colegio Novecentista*, 71–72,
    321n11
Cuban Revolution
    and nationalist right, 224–25
    and Peronist left, 228, 244, 250–51
Cuban-Spanish-American War, 79
    impact on Latin American identity,
        79–81, 323n18
    See also *hispanismo*
Cucchetti, Huberto, 233–34, 383n32
cultural nationalism, 10, 325n36
    affinities with Radicalism, 100–109
    intellectual influences on, 81–82
    and Romanticism, 62–69
    *See also* Argentine race; Gálvez,
        Manuel; Rojas, Ricardo
Cursos de Cultura Cathólica, 143, 145,
    195

Day of the Race, 70, 104–5, 117, 258,
    195. *See also* Yrigoyen, Hipólito
De Riz, Liliana, 387n80
Debenedetti, Salvador, 116
Dellepiane, Luis, 169, 187–88
democracy
    as contrary to national character, 22,
        132, 146–47, 220, 222
    as imperialist tool, 158, 168, 188, 260,
        272
    *See also* Constitution of 1853;
        liberalism
Deutsch, Sandra McGee, 4, 11, 314n12
Dickmann, Enrique, 74–75
Dirty War, 3
    and anti-Semitism, 266, 272, 275
    and nationalist myths, 266
Disandro, Carlos Alberto, 252–53
Doll, Ramón, 160–61, 195

Halperin Donghi, Tulio, 243, 245,
302n64, 335n76, 349n3
Herder, Johann Gottfried von, 82, 84,
325n36
Hernández Arregui, Juan José, 228,
237–38
Herrero, Antonio, 102–4, 108
Hilb, Claudia, 245
*hispanismo*, 66, 68. *See also* Gálvez,
Manuel; Krausism; Quesada,
Ernesto
historical revisionism
during 1930s, 160–63, 172
and Perón, 201, 235
post-1955, 234–40, 243
Hobsbawm, Eric, 10, 301n57

Ibarguren, Federico, 195, 262
immigration, 10, 50–52
and shifts in identity, 10, 13, 31
Instituto de Investigaciones Históricas
Juan Manuel de Rosas. *See* Rosas
Institute for Historical Research
Irazusta, Julio
critique of Roca-Runciman pact,
158–61
and *La Nueva República*, 134–38
Irazusta, Rodolfo
critique of Roca-Runciman pact,
158–61
and *La Nueva República*, 134–38,
150–52
Irigoyen, Hipólito. *See* Yrigoyen,
Hipólito

Jauretche, Arturo
and FORJA, 168–71, 186–90
and historical revisionism, 172, 236
and nationalist right, 172, 183, 185
and Peronist Resistance, 229
rejection of pluralism, 24, 304n69
relationship with Perón, 197

Justicialista Party. *See* Peronism
Justo, Agustín, 148, 152, 156–57
Justo, Juan B., 73
Juventud Peronista, 229–30, 254–55

Karush, Matthew, 118
Kennedy, Michael, 21
Kennedy, Norma, 233
Kirchner, Cristina Fernández de, 1, 289
Krause, Karl Christian Friedrich, 82–83
Krausism, 29–30
and *hispanismo*, 86
in Spain, 82–89
teleological visions of history, 85–88
*See also* Generation of 1898; Yrigoyen,
Hipólito

*La Nueva Republica*, 134–36
and Charles Maurras, 136–39
and Constitution of 1853, 139–41,
150–51, 342n32
and coup of 1930, 135, 148
and Yrigoyen, 140, 151–52, 346n99
language
nineteenth-century debates, 57–58
twentieth-century debates, 119–27
liberalism
as alien to *el ser nacional*, 20, 35,
131–32, 158, 220, 237, 243
as imperialist tool, 20, 131–32, 149,
157–59, 222
in nineteenth century, 6, 39, 49, 305n2
weakness of, 2, 281–84
*See also* Constitution of 1853; historical revisionism; Nállim, Jorge
liberation theology, 17, 214
Liga Patriótica Argentina, 59–62, 125
Lonardi, Eduardo, 211, 215–16
López Rega, José, 255, 257
Lugones, Leopoldo
criticism of Constitution of 1853,
146–48

JEANE DELANEY
teaches Latin American history and
Latin American studies at St. Olaf College.

www.ingramcontent.com/pod-product-compliance
Lightning Source LLC
Chambersburg PA
CBHW050622280326
41932CB00015B/2496